Merriam-Webster's easy learning Complete Spanish

Merriam-Webster, Incorporated
Springfield, Massachusetts, USA

DEVELOPED IN ASSOCIATION WITH Collins

HarperCollins Publishers
Westerhill Road
Bishopbriggs
Glasgow
G64 2QT
Great Britain

First Edition 2011

Reprint 10 9 8 7 6 5 4 3 2 1 0

ISBN 978-0-87779-562-9

www.collinslanguage.com

Typeset by Davidson Pre-Press, Glasgow, UK

Printed in the USA by RR Donnelley

Acknowledgements
We would like to thank those authors and publishers who kindly gave permission for copyright material to be used in the Collins Word Web. We would also like to thank Times Newspapers Ltd for providing valuable data.

SERIES EDITOR
Rob Scriven

MANAGING EDITOR
Gaëlle Amiot-Cadey

PROJECT MANAGER
John Whitlam

CONTRIBUTORS
Beatriz Jarman
Steve Spencer
John Whitlam

Contents

Foreword for language teachers

Merriam-Webster's Easy Learning Complete Spanish is designed to be used with both young and adult learners, as a group reference book to complement your course book during classes, or as a recommended text for self-study and homework/coursework.

The text is intended for learners from beginner to intermediate and advanced levels, and therefore its content and vocabulary have been matched to the needs of students at each level.

The approach aims to develop knowledge and understanding of grammar and to improve the ability of learners to apply it by:

- defining parts of speech at the start of each major section, with examples in English to clarify concepts
- minimizing the use of grammar terminology and providing clear explanations of terms within the text and in the **Glossary**
- illustrating points with examples (and their translations) based on topics and contexts which are relevant to beginner and intermediate course content

The text helps your students develop positive attitudes to grammar learning by:

- giving clear, easy-to-follow explanations
- prioritizing content according to relevant specifications for learner levels
- sequencing points to reflect course content, e.g. verb tenses
- highlighting useful **Tips** to deal with common difficulties
- summarizing **Key points** at the end of sections to consolidate learning

In addition to fostering success and building a thorough foundation in Spanish grammar, the optional **Grammar Extra** sections will encourage and challenge your learners to further their studies to higher and advanced levels.

The blue pages in the middle section of the book contain **Verb Tables** and a **Verb Index** which students can use as a reference in their work.

Finally, the **Vocabulary** section in the last part of the book provides thematic vocabulary lists which can either be used for self-study or as an additional teaching resource.

Introduction for students

Whether you are starting to learn Spanish for the very first time, brushing up on topics you have learned in class, or studying to improve your mastery of the language, *Merriam-Webster's Easy Learning Complete Spanish* is here to help. This easy-to-use guide takes you through all the basics you will need to speak and understand modern, everyday Spanish.

Newcomers can sometimes struggle with the technical terms they come across when they start to explore the grammar of a new language. This book explains how to come to grips with all the parts of speech you will need to know, using simple, jargon-free language.

The text is divided into sections, each dealing with a particular area of grammar. Each section can be studied individually, as numerous cross-references in the text guide you to relevant points in other sections of the book for further information.

Every major section begins with an explanation of the area of grammar covered in the pages that follow. For quick reference, these definitions are also collected together on pages viii–xii in a glossary of essential grammar terms.

What is a verb?
A **verb** is a 'doing' word which describes what someone or something does, what someone or something is, or what happens to them. For example: *be*, *sing*, *live*.

Each grammar point in the text is followed by simple examples of real Spanish, complete with English translations, thus helping you to understand the rules. Underlining has been used in examples throughout the text to highlight the grammatical point being explained.

➤ In orders and instructions telling someone TO DO something, the pronoun is attached to the end of the verb to form one word.

Ayúdame.	Help me.
Acompáñanos.	Come with us.

In Spanish, as with any foreign language, there are certain pitfalls which have to be avoided. **Tips** and **Information** notes throughout the text are useful reminders of the things that often trip learners up.

Tip

Don't forget to use personal **a** before indefinite pronouns referring to people when they are the object of a verb.

¿Viste a alguien? Did you see anybody?

No vi a nadie. I didn't see anybody.

Key points sum up all the important facts about a particular area of grammar, saving you time when you are reviewing and helping you focus on the main grammatical points.

Key points

- ✔ Like other adjectives, Spanish indefinite adjectives (such as **otro** and **todo**) must agree with what they describe.
- ✔ They go before the noun to which they relate.

If you think you would like to continue your Spanish studies at a higher level, check out the **Grammar Extra** sections. These are intended for advanced students who are interested in knowing a little more about the structures they will come across as they widen their exposure to the language.

Grammar Extra!

por is often combined with other Spanish prepositions and words, usually to show movement.

Saltó por encima de la mesa. She jumped over the table.

Nadamos por debajo del puente. We swam under the bridge.

Pasaron por delante de la iglesia. They went past the church.

The blue pages in the middle of the book contain **Verb Tables**, where 120 important Spanish verbs (both regular and irregular) are fully conjugated. Examples show you how to use these verbs in a sentence. You can look up any common verb in the **Verb Index** on pages 464–468 to find a cross-reference to a model verb.

Finally, the **Vocabulary** section at the end of the book is divided into 50 topics, followed by a list of supplementary vocabulary.

Glossary of grammar terms

ABSTRACT NOUN a word used to refer to a quality, idea, feeling or experience, rather than a physical object. For example: *size, reason, happiness*. Compare with **concrete noun**.

ACTIVE a form of the verb that is used when the subject of the verb is the person or thing doing the action. For example: *They sold a lot of books*. Compare with **passive**.

ADJECTIVE a 'describing' word that tells you more about a person or thing, such as their appearance, color, size or other qualities. For example: *pretty, interesting, big*.

ADVERB a word usually used with verbs, adjectives or other adverbs that gives more information about when, where, how or in what circumstances something happens or to what degree something is true. For example: *quickly, happily, now, extremely, very*.

AGREE (with) in the case of adjectives and pronouns, to have the correct word ending or form according to whether what is referred to is masculine, feminine, singular or plural; in the case of verbs, to have the form that goes with the person or thing carrying out the action.

APOSTROPHE S an ending ('s) added to a noun to show who or what someone or something belongs to. For example: *Danielle's dog, the doctor's wife, the book's cover*.

ARTICLE a word such as *the*, *a* and *an*, which is used in front of a noun. See also **definite article**, **indefinite article**.

AUXILIARY VERB a verb such as *be*, *have* or *do* used with a main verb to form tenses and questions.

BASE FORM the form of the verb without any endings added to it. For example: *walk, have, be, go*.

CARDINAL NUMBER a number used in counting. For example: *one, seven, ninety*. Compare with **ordinal number**.

CLAUSE a group of words containing a verb.

COMPARATIVE an adjective or adverb with *-er* on the end of it or *more* or *less* in front of it that is used to compare people, things or actions. For example: *slower, less important, more carefully*.

COMPOUND NOUN a word for a living being, thing or an idea, which is made up of two or more words. For example: *old-fashioned, railroad station*.

CONCRETE NOUN a word that refers to an object you can touch with your hand, rather than to a quality or an idea. For example: *ball, map, apples*. Compare with **abstract noun**.

CONDITIONAL a verb form used to talk about things that would happen or would be true under certain conditions. For example: *I <u>would help</u> you if I could*. It is also used to say what you would like or need. For example: *<u>Could</u> I <u>have</u> the check, please?*

CONJUGATE to give a verb different endings according to whether you are referring to *I*, *you*, *they* and so on, and according to whether you are referring to the present, past or future. For example: *I have, she had, they will have*.

CONJUGATION a group of verbs that have the same endings as each other or change according to the same pattern.

CONJUNCTION a word such as *and*, *because* or *but* that links two words or phrases of a similar type or two parts of a sentence. For example: *Diane* <u>*and*</u> *I have been friends for years; I left* <u>*because*</u> *I was bored*.

CONSONANT a letter that isn't a vowel. For example: *b, f, m, s, v*. Compare with **vowel**.

CONTINUOUS TENSE a verb tense formed using *to be* and the *-ing* form of the main verb. For example: *They're swimming* (present continuous); *He was eating* (past continuous).

DEFINITE ARTICLE the word *the*. Compare with **indefinite article**.

DEMONSTRATIVE ADJECTIVE a word such as *this*, *that*, *these* or *those* used with a noun to refer to particular people or things. For example: <u>*this*</u> *woman*, <u>*that*</u> *dog*.

DEMONSTRATIVE PRONOUN a word such as *this*, *that*, *these* or *those* used instead of a noun to point out people or things. For example: <u>*That*</u> *looks fun*.

DIRECT OBJECT a noun or pronoun used with verbs to show who or what is acted on by the verb. For example, in *He wrote a letter* and *He wrote me a letter*, *letter* is the direct object. Compare **indirect object**.

DIRECT OBJECT PRONOUN a word such as *me, him, us* and *them* which is used instead of a noun to stand in for the person or thing directly affected by the action expressed by the verb. Compare with **indirect object pronoun**.

ENDING a form added to a verb (for example, *go* → *go*<u>*es*</u>) and to adjectives, nouns and pronouns depending on whether they refer to masculine, feminine, singular or plural things or persons.

EXCLAMATION a word, phrase or sentence that you use to show you are surprised, shocked, angry and so on. For example: *Wow!; How dare you!; What a surprise!*

FEMININE a form of noun, pronoun or adjective that is used to refer to a living being, thing or an idea that is not classed as masculine.

FUTURE a verb tense used to talk about something that will happen or will be true.

GENDER the masculine or feminine category to which a noun, pronoun, or adjective belongs.

GERUND a verb form in English ending in *-ing*. For example: *eating*, *sleeping*.

IMPERATIVE the form of a verb used when giving orders and instructions. For example: *Shut the door!; Sit down!; Don't go!; Let's eat*.

IMPERFECT one of the verb tenses used to talk about the past, especially in descriptions, and to say what was happening or used to happen. For example: *He was tall and thin; We were living in Mexico at the time; I used to walk to school*. Compare to **preterite**.

IMPERSONAL VERB a verb whose subject is *it*, but where the *it* does not refer to any specific thing. For example: *It's raining; It's 10 o'clock*.

INDEFINITE ADJECTIVE one of a small group of adjectives used to talk about people or things in a general way, without saying who or what they are. For example: *several, all, every*.

INDEFINITE ARTICLE the words *a* and *an*. Compare with **definite article**.

INDICATIVE ordinary verb forms that aren't subjunctive, such as the present, preterite or future. Compare with **subjunctive**.

INDEFINITE PRONOUN a small group of pronouns such as *everything*, *nobody* and *something*, which are used to refer to people or things in a general way, without saying exactly who or what they are.

INDIRECT OBJECT a noun or pronoun used with verbs to show who benefits or is harmed by an action. For example, in *I gave the carrot to the rabbit*, *the rabbit* is the indirect object and *the carrot* is the direct object. Compare with **direct object**.

INDIRECT OBJECT PRONOUN a pronoun used with verbs to show who benefits or is harmed by an action. For example, in *I gave him the carrot* and *I gave it to him*, *him* is the indirect object and the *carrot* and *it* are the direct objects. Compare with **direct object pronoun**.

INDIRECT QUESTION a question that is embedded in another question or instruction such as *Can you tell me what time it is?; Tell me why you did it*. Also used for reported speech such as *He asked me why I did it*.

INDIRECT SPEECH the words you use to report what someone has said when you aren't using their actual words. For example: *He said that he was going out*. Also called **reported speech**.

INFINITIVE a form of the verb that hasn't any endings added to it and doesn't relate to any particular tense. In English the infinitive is usually shown with *to*, as in *to speak, to eat*.

INTERROGATIVE ADJECTIVE a question word used with a noun. For example: *What instruments do you play?; Which shoes do you like?*

INTERROGATIVE PRONOUN a word such as *who, whose, whom, what* or *which* when it is used instead of a noun to ask questions. For example: *What's that?; Who's coming?*

INTRANSITIVE VERB a type of verb that does not take a direct object. For example: *to sleep, to rise, to swim*. Compare with **transitive verb**.

INVARIABLE used to describe a form which does not change.

IRREGULAR VERB a verb whose forms do not follow a general pattern. Compare with **regular verb**.

MASCULINE a form of noun, pronoun or adjective that is used to refer to a living being, thing or idea that is not classed as feminine.

NEGATIVE a question or statement which contains a word such as *not, never* or *nothing*, and is used to say that something is not happening, is not true or is absent. For example: *I never eat meat; Don't you love me?* Compare with **positive**.

NOUN a 'naming' word for a living being, thing or an idea. For example: *woman, desk, happiness, Andrew*.

NOUN GROUP, NOUN PHRASE a word or group of words that acts as the subject or object of a verb, or as the object of a preposition. For example: *my older sister; the man next door; that big house on the corner*.

NUMBER used to say how many things you are referring to or where something comes in a sequence. See also **ordinal number** and **cardinal number**. Also the condition of being singular or plural.

OBJECT a noun or pronoun that refers to a person or thing that is affected by the action described by the verb. Compare with **direct object**, **indirect object** and **subject**.

OBJECT PRONOUN one of the set of pronouns including *me, him* and *them*, which are used instead of the noun as the object of a verb or preposition. Compare with **subject pronoun**.

ORDINAL NUMBER a number used to indicate where something comes in an order or sequence. For example: *first, fifth, sixteenth*. Compare with **cardinal number**.

PART OF SPEECH a word class. For example: *noun*, *verb*, *adjective*, *preposition*, *pronoun*.

PASSIVE a form of the verb that is used when the subject of the verb is the person or thing that is affected by the action. For example: *A lot of books were sold*.

PAST PARTICIPLE a verb form which is used to form perfect and pluperfect tenses and passives. For example: *watched*, *swum*. Some past participles are also used as adjectives. For example: *a broken watch*.

PAST PERFECT see **pluperfect**.

PERFECT a verb form which is used to talk about what has or hasn't happened. For example: *I've broken my glasses; We haven't spoken about it*.

PERSON one of the three classes: the first person (*I*, *we*), the second person (*you* singular and *you* plural), and the third person (*he*, *she*, *it* and *they*).

PERSONAL PRONOUN one of the group of words including *I*, *you* and *they* which are used to refer to you, the people you are talking to, or the people or things you are talking about.

PLUPERFECT one of the verb tenses used to describe something that had happened or had been true at a point in the past. For example: *I had forgotten to finish my homework*. Also called **past perfect**.

PLURAL the form of a word which is used to refer to more than one person or thing. Compare with **singular**.

POSITIVE a positive sentence or instruction is one that does not contain a negative word such as *not*. Compare with **negative**.

POSSESSIVE ADJECTIVE a word such as *my*, *your*, *his*, *her*, *its*, *our* or *their*, used with a noun to show who it belongs to.

POSSESSIVE PRONOUN a word such as *mine*, *yours*, *hers*, *his*, *ours* or *theirs*, used instead of a noun to show who something belongs to.

PREPOSITION a word such as *at*, *for*, *with*, *into* or *from*, which is usually followed by a noun, pronoun or, in English, a word ending in *-ing*. Prepositions show how people and things relate to the rest of the sentence. For example: *She's at home; a tool for cutting grass; It's from David*.

PRESENT a verb form used to talk about what is true at the moment, what happens regularly, and what is happening now. For example: *I'm a student; I travel to college by train; I'm studying languages*.

PRESENT PARTICIPLE a verb form in English ending in *-ing*. For example: *eating*, *sleeping*.

PRETERITE a Spanish verb form used to talk about actions that were completed in the past. It often corresponds to the ordinary past tense in English. For example: *I bought a new bike; Mary went to the store on Friday; I typed two reports yesterday*.

PRONOUN a word which you use instead of a noun, when you do not need or want to name someone or something directly. For example: *it*, *you*, *none*.

PROPER NOUN the name of a person, place, organization or thing. Proper nouns are always written with a capital letter. For example: *Kevin*, *Boston*, *Europe*, *Newsweek*.

QUESTION WORD a word such as *why*, *where*, *who*, *which* or *how*, that is used to ask a question.

RADICAL-CHANGING VERBS in Spanish, verbs which change their stem or root in certain tenses and for certain persons.

REFLEXIVE PRONOUN a word ending in *-self* or *-selves*, such as *myself* or *themselves*, which refers back to the subject. For example: *He hurt himself; Take care of yourself.*

REFLEXIVE VERB a verb where the subject and object are the same, and where the action 'reflects back' on the subject. A reflexive verb is used with a reflexive pronoun such as *myself, yourself* or *herself*. For example: *I washed myself; He cut himself.*

REGULAR VERB a verb whose forms follow a general pattern or the normal rules. Compare with **irregular verb**.

RELATIVE PRONOUN a word such as *that, who* or *which*, when it is used to link two parts of a sentence together.

REPORTED SPEECH see **indirect speech**.

SENTENCE a group of words which usually has a verb and a subject. In writing, a sentence begins with a capital letter and ends with a period, question mark or exclamation point.

SIMPLE TENSE a verb tense in which the verb form is made up of one word, rather than being formed from *to have* and a past participle or *to be* and an *-ing* form. For example: *She plays tennis; He wrote a book.*

SINGULAR the form of a word which is used to refer to one person or thing. Compare with **plural**.

STEM the main part of a verb to which endings are added.

SUBJECT a noun or pronoun that refers to the person or thing doing the action or being in the state described by the verb. For example: *My cat doesn't drink milk*. Compare with **object**.

SUBJECT PRONOUN a word such as *I, he, she* and *they* which carries out the action described by the verb. Pronouns stand in for nouns when it is clear who is being talked about. For example: *My brother isn't here at the moment. He'll be back in an hour.* Compare with **object pronoun**.

SUBJUNCTIVE a verb form used in certain circumstances to indicate some sort of feeling, or to show doubt about whether something will happen or whether something is true. It is only used occasionally in modern English. For example: *If I were you, I wouldn't bother; So be it.*

SUPERLATIVE an adjective or adverb with *-est* on the end of it or *most* or *least* in front of it that is used to compare people, things or actions. For example: *thinnest, most quickly, least interesting*.

SYLLABLE consonant+vowel units that make up the sounds of a word. For example: *ca-the-dral (3 syllables), im-po-ssi-ble (4 syllables).*

TENSE the form of a verb which shows whether you are referring to the past, present or future.

TRANSITIVE VERB a type of verb that takes a direct object. For example: *to spend, to raise, to waste*. Compare with **intransitive verb**.

VERB a 'doing' word which describes what someone or something does, is, or what happens to them. For example: *be, sing, live.*

VOWEL one of the letters *a, e, i, o* or *u*. Compare with **consonant**.

Nouns

What is a noun?
A **noun** is a 'naming' word for a living being, thing or idea. For example: *woman*, *desk*, *happiness*, *Andrew*.

Using nouns

➤ In Spanish, all nouns are either masculine or feminine. This is called their gender. Even words for things have a gender.

➤ Whenever you are using a noun, you need to know whether it is masculine or feminine as this affects the form of other words used with it, such as:

- adjectives that describe it
- articles (such as **el** or **una**) that go before it

⇨ *For more information on* **Articles** *and* **Adjectives**, *see pages 10 and 19.*

➤ You can find information about gender by looking the word up in a dictionary. When you come across a new noun, always learn the word for *the* or *a* that goes with it to help you remember its gender.

- **el** or **un** before a noun usually tells you it is masculine
- **la** or **una** before a noun tells you it is feminine

➤ We refer to something as singular when we are talking about just one of them, and as plural when we are talking about more than one. The singular is the form of the noun you will usually find when you look a noun up in the dictionary. As in English, nouns in Spanish change their form in the plural.

➤ Adjectives, articles and pronouns are also affected by whether a noun is singular or plural.

Tip
Remember that you have to use the right word for *the*, *a* and so on according to the gender of the Spanish noun.

Gender

1 Nouns referring to people

➤ Most nouns referring to men and boys are masculine.

el hombre	the man
el rey	the king

➤ Most nouns referring to women and girls are feminine.

la mujer	the woman
la reina	the queen

➤ When the same word is used to refer to either men/boys or women/girls, its gender usually changes depending on the sex of the person it refers to.

el estudiante	the (male) student
la estudiante	the (female) student
el artista	the (male) artist
la artista	the (female) artist

Grammar Extra!

Some words for people have only one possible gender, whether they refer to a male or a female.

la persona	the (male *or* female) person
la víctima	the (male *or* female) victim

➤ In English, we can sometimes make a word masculine or feminine by changing the ending, for example, *policeman* and *policewoman* or *prince* and *princess*. In Spanish, very often the ending of a noun changes depending on whether it refers to a man or a woman.

el americano	the American (*male*)
la americana	the American (*female*)
el empleado	the employee (*male*)
la empleada	the employee (*female*)
el anfitrión	the host
la anfitriona	the hostess

For further explanation of grammatical terms, please see pages viii-xii.

> *Tip*
> Note that a noun ending in **-o** is usually masculine and a noun ending in **-a** is usually feminine.

⇨ *For more information on* ***Masculine and feminine forms of words****, see page* 5.

2 Nouns referring to animals

➤ In English we can choose between words like *bull* or *cow*, depending on the sex of the animal. In Spanish too there are sometimes separate words for male and female animals.

el toro	the bull
la vaca	the cow

➤ Sometimes, the same word with different endings is used for male and female animals.

el perro	the (male) dog
la perra	the (female) dog, bitch
el gato	the (male) cat
la gata	the (female) cat

> *Tip*
> When you do not know or care what sex the animal is, you can usually use the masculine form as a general word.

➤ Words for other animals don't change according to the sex of the animal. In these instances, you only need to learn the Spanish word with its gender, which always remains the same.

el sapo	the toad
el hámster	the hamster
la ardilla	the squirrel
la tortuga	the turtle

3 Nouns referring to things

➤ In English, we call all things – for example, *table, car, book, apple* – 'it'. In Spanish, however, things are either masculine or feminine. As things don't divide into sexes the way humans and animals do, there are no physical clues to help you determine their gender in Spanish. Try to learn the gender as you learn the word.

➤ There are lots of rules to help you. Certain endings are usually found on masculine nouns, while other endings are usually found on feminine nouns.

Nouns

➤ The following ending is usually found on masculine nouns.

Masculine ending	Examples
-o	**el libro** the book **el periódico** the newspaper EXCEPTIONS: **la mano** the hand **la foto** the photo **la moto** the motorcycle

➤ The following types of word are also masculine.

- the names of the days of the week and the months of the year

  Te veo el lunes. — I'll see you on Monday.

- the names of languages

  el inglés — English
  el español — Spanish
  El japonés es difícil. — Japanese is difficult.

- the names of rivers, mountains and seas

  el Amazonas — the Amazon
  el Everest — Everest
  el Atlántico — the Atlantic

➤ The following endings are usually found on feminine nouns.

Feminine ending	Examples
-a	**la casa** the house **la cara** the face EXCEPTIONS: **el día** the day **el mapa** the map **el planeta** the planet **el tranvía** the streetcar, and many words ending in **-ma** (**el problema** the problem, **el programa** the program, **el sistema** the system, **el clima** the climate)
-ción -sión	**la lección** the lesson **la estación** the station; the season **la expresión** the expression
-dad -tad -tud	**la ciudad** the city **la libertad** freedom **la multitud** the crowd

For further explanation of grammatical terms, please see pages viii-xii.

Grammar Extra!

Some words have different meanings depending on whether they are masculine or feminine.

Masculine	Meaning	Feminine	Meaning
el capital	the capital (meaning *money*)	**la capital**	the capital (meaning *city*)
el frente	the front	**la frente**	the forehead
el policía	the police officer (*male*)	**la policía**	the police (force); the police officer (*female*)
el guía	the guide (*man*)	**la guía**	the guidebook; the guide (*woman*)

Invirtieron mucho capital. They invested a lot of capital.
Viven en la capital. They live in the capital.

4 Masculine and feminine forms of words

➤ Like English, Spanish sometimes has very different words for males and females.

el hombre the man
la mujer the woman

el rey the king
la reina the queen

➤ Many Spanish words can be used to talk about men or women simply by changing the ending. For example, if the word for the male ends in **-o**, you can almost always make it feminine by changing the **-o** to **-a**.

el amigo the (male) friend
la amiga the (female) friend

el hermano the brother
la hermana the sister

el empleado the (male) employee
la empleada the (female) employee

el viudo the widower
la viuda the widow

i Note that some words referring to people end in **-a** in the masculine as well as in the feminine. Only the article (**el** or **la**, **un** or **una**) can tell you what is the gender of the noun.

el dentista the (male) dentist
la dentista the (female) dentist

el deportista the sportsman
la deportista the sportswoman

➤ Many masculine nouns ending in a consonant (any letter other than a vowel) become feminine by adding an **-a**.

el español	the Spanish man
la española	the Spanish woman
el profesor	the (male) teacher
la profesora	the (female) teacher

Tip

If the last vowel of the masculine word has an accent, this is dropped in the feminine form.

un inglés	an Englishman
una inglesa	an Englishwoman
un león	a lion
una leona	a lioness

⇨ *For more information about* ***Spelling*** *and* ***Stress****, see pages 198 and 202.*

Key points

✔ The ending of a Spanish word often helps you determine its gender: for instance, if a word ends in **-o**, it is probably masculine; if it ends in **-a**, it is probably feminine.

✔ These endings generally mean that the noun is feminine: **-ción**, **-sión**, **-dad**, **-tad**, **-tud**.

✔ Days of the week and months of the year are masculine. So are languages, mountains and seas.

✔ You can change the ending of some nouns from **-o** to **-a** to make a masculine noun feminine.

Forming plurals

1 Plurals ending in -s and -es

➤ In English we usually make nouns plural by adding an -*s* to the end (*garden* → *gardens*; *house* → *houses*), although we do have some nouns which are irregular and do not follow this pattern (*mouse* → *mice*; *child* → *children*).

> *Tip*
>
> Remember that you have to use **los** (for masculine nouns) or **las** (for feminine nouns) with plural nouns in Spanish. Any adjective that goes with the noun also has to agree with it, as does any pronoun that replaces it.
>
> ➪ *For more information on* ***Articles***, ***Adjectives*** *and* ***Pronouns***, *see pages 10, 19 and 41.*

➤ To form the plural in Spanish, add **-s** to most nouns ending in a vowel (*a*, *e*, *i*, *o* or *u*) which doesn't have an accent.

el libro	the book
los libros	the books
el hombre	the man
los hombres	the men
la profesora	the (female) teacher
las profesoras	the (female) teachers

➤ Add **-es** to singular nouns ending in a consonant (any letter other than a vowel).

el profesor	the (male) teacher
los profesores	the (all male or male and female) teachers
la ciudad	the town/city
las ciudades	the towns/cities

ℹ Note that some foreign words (that is, words which have come from another language, such as English) ending in a consonant just add **-s**.

el coñac	the brandy
los coñacs	the brandies
el mail	the email
los mails	the emails

➤ Words ending in **-s** which have an unstressed final vowel do not change in the plural.

el paraguas	the umbrella
los paraguas	the umbrellas
el lunes	(on) Monday
los lunes	(on) Mondays

➪ *For more information on* ***Stress****, see page 202.*

➤ Some singular nouns ending in an accented vowel add **-es** in the plural while other very common ones add **-s**.

el rubí	the ruby
los rubíes	the rubies
el café	the coffee/the café
los cafés	the coffees/the cafés
el sofá	the sofa
los sofás	the sofas

Grammar Extra!

When nouns are made up of two separate words, they are called compound nouns, for example, **el abrelatas** (meaning *the can-opener*) and **el hombre rana** (meaning *the deep sea diver*). Some of these nouns don't change in the plural, for example, **los abrelatas**, while others do, for example, **los hombres rana**. It is always best to check in a dictionary to see what the plural is.

---

2 Spelling changes with plurals ending in -es

➤ Singular nouns which end in an accented vowel and either **-n** or **-s** drop the accent in the plural.

la canción	the song
las canciones	the songs
el francés	the Frenchman
los franceses	the French

➤ Singular nouns of more than one syllable which end in **-en** and don't already have an accent, add one in the plural.

el examen	the exam
los exámenes	the exams
el origen	the origin
los orígenes	the origins

➤ Singular nouns ending in **-z** change to **-ces** in the plural.

la luz	the light
las lu<u>ces</u>	the lights
la vez	the times
las ve<u>ces</u>	the times

➪ *For further information on **Spelling** and **Stress**, see pages 198 and 202.*

3 Plural versus singular

➤ A few words relating to clothing that are plural in English can be singular in Spanish.

<u>un</u> calzoncillo	(a pair of) underpants
<u>un</u> pantalón	(a pair of) pants
<u>un</u> short	(a pair of) shorts

➤ A few common words behave differently in Spanish from the way they behave in English.

un mueble	a piece of furniture
unos muebles	some furniture
una noticia	a piece of news
unas noticias	some news
un consejo	a piece of advice
unos consejos	some advice

Key points

- ✔ Add **-s** to form the plural of a noun ending in an unaccented vowel.
- ✔ Add **-es** to form the plural of most nouns ending in a consonant.
- ✔ Drop the accent when adding plural **-es** to nouns ending in an accented vowel + **-n** or **-s**.
- ✔ Add an accent when adding plural **-es** to words of more than one syllable ending in **-en**.
- ✔ Change **-z** to **-ces** when forming the plural of words like **luz**.
- ✔ A few common words are plural in English but not in Spanish.

Articles

What is an article?
In English, an **article** is one of the words *the*, *a*, and *an* which is given in front of a noun.

Different types of article

➤ There are two types of article:

- the <u>definite</u> article: *the* in English. This is used to identify a particular thing or person.

  I'm going to <u>the</u> supermarket.
  That's <u>the</u> woman I was talking to.

- the <u>indefinite</u> article: *a* or *an* in English, whose plural is *some* or *any* (or no word at all). This is used to refer to something unspecific, or that you do not really know about.

  Is there <u>a</u> supermarket near here?
  I need <u>a</u> day off.

For further explanation of grammatical terms, please see pages viii-xii.

The definite article: el, la, los and las

1 The basic rules

- In English, there is only <u>one</u> definite article: *the*. In Spanish, you have to choose between <u>four</u> definite articles: **el**, **la**, **los** and **las**. Which one you choose depends on the noun which follows.
- In Spanish, all nouns (including words for things) are either masculine or feminine – this is called their <u>gender</u>. And, just as in English, they can also be either singular or plural. You must bear this in mind when deciding which Spanish word to use for *the*.

⇨ *For more information on **Nouns**, see page 1.*

- **el** is used before <u>masculine singular nouns</u>.

<u>el</u> hombre	the man
<u>el</u> periódico	the newspaper

- **la** is used before <u>feminine singular nouns</u>.

<u>la</u> mujer	the woman
<u>la</u> revista	the magazine

> *Tip*
>
> To help you produce correct Spanish, always learn the <u>article</u> or the <u>gender</u> together with the noun when learning words.

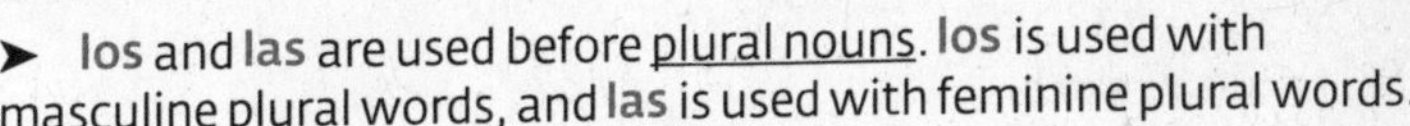

- **los** and **las** are used before <u>plural nouns</u>. **los** is used with masculine plural words, and **las** is used with feminine plural words.

<u>los</u> hombres	the men
<u>las</u> mujeres	the women
<u>los</u> periódicos	the newspapers
<u>las</u> revistas	the magazines

ℹ Note that you use **el** instead of **la** immediately before a feminine singular word beginning with **a** or **ha** when the stress falls on the beginning of the word. This is because **la** sounds wrong before the '*a*' sound, and the use of **el** does not affect the feminine gender of the noun. <u>BUT</u> if you add an adjective in front of the noun, you use **la** instead, since the two 'a' sounds do not come next to each other.

<u>el</u> agua limpia	the clean water
<u>el</u> hacha	the ax
<u>la</u> misma agua	the same water
<u>la</u> mejor hacha	the best ax

2 a and de with the definite article

➤ If **a** is followed by **el**, the two words become **al**.

al cine	to the movies
al empleado	to the employee
al hospital	to the hospital
Vio al mesero.	He saw the waiter.

➤ If **de** is followed by **el**, the two words become **del**.

del departamento	of/from the apartment
del autor	of/from the author
del presidente	of/from the president

3 Using the definite article

➤ **el**, **la**, **los** and **las** are often used in Spanish in the same way as *the* is used in English. However, there are some cases where the article is used in Spanish but not in English.

➤ The definite article IS used in Spanish:

- when talking about people, animals and things in a general way

Me encantan los animales.	I love animals.
Están subiendo los precios.	Prices are going up.
No me gusta el café.	I don't like coffee.
El chocolate engorda.	Chocolate is fattening.

- when talking about abstract qualities, for example, *time, hope, darkness, violence*

El tiempo es oro.	Time is money.
Admiro la sinceridad en la gente.	I admire honesty in people.

ℹ Note that the definite article is NOT used in certain set phrases consisting of **tener** and a noun or after certain prepositions.

tener hambre	to be hungry	(*literally: to have hunger*)
sin duda	no doubt	(*literally: without doubt*)
con cuidado	carefully	(*literally: with care*)

⇨ *For more information on* **Prepositions**, *see page 180.*

- when talking about colors

El azul es mi color favorito.	Blue is my favorite color.

- when talking about parts of the body – you do not use *my, your, his* and so on as you would in English

Tiene los ojos verdes.	He has green eyes.
No puedo mover las piernas.	I can't move my legs.

Note that possession is often shown by a personal pronoun in Spanish.

Me duele la rodilla.	My knee hurts.
Lávate las manos.	Wash your hands.

For more information on ***Personal pronouns****, see page* 42.

- when using someone's title – for example, *Doctor, Mr.* – but talking ABOUT someone rather than to them.

El doctor Vidal no está.	Dr. Vidal isn't here.
El señor Pelayo vive aquí.	Mr. Pelayo lives here.

- when talking about institutions, such as school or church

en el colegio	at school
en la universidad	at college
en la iglesia	at church
en la cárcel	in prison

- when talking about meals, games or sports

La cena es a las nueve.	Dinner is at nine o'clock.
Me gusta el tenis.	I like tennis.
No me gusta el ajedrez.	I don't like chess.

- when talking about days of the week and dates, where we use the preposition *on* in English

Te veo el lunes.	I'll see you on Monday.
Los domingos vamos al cine.	We go to the movies on Sundays.
Nací el 17 de marzo.	I was born on March 17.

- when talking about the time

Es la una.	It's one o'clock.
Son las tres.	It's three o'clock.
Son las cuatro y media.	It's half past four.

- when talking about prices and rates

  Cuestan dos dólares la docena. They cost two dollars a dozen.

  Cobra 200 pesos la hora. He charges 200 pesos an hour.

Key points

✔ Before masculine singular nouns → use **el**.

✔ Before feminine singular nouns → use **la**.

✔ Before feminine singular nouns starting with stressed **a** or **ha** → use **el**.

✔ Before masculine plural nouns → use **los**.

✔ Before feminine plural nouns → use **las**.

✔ **a + el → al**

✔ **de + el → del**

✔ There are some important cases when you would use a definite article in Spanish when you wouldn't in English. For example, when talking about:
- things in a general way
- abstract qualities
- colors
- parts of the body
- someone with a title in front of their name
- institutions
- meals, games or sports
- the time, days of the week and dates (*using the preposition on in English*)
- prices and rates

For further explanation of grammatical terms, please see pages viii-xii.

The indefinite article: un, una, unos and unas

1 The basic rules

- In English, the indefinite article is *a*, which changes to *an* when it comes before a vowel or a vowel sound (for example, *an apple*). In the plural, we use *some* or *any*.
- In Spanish, you have to choose between four indefinite articles: **un**, **una**, **unos** and **unas**. Which one you choose depends on the noun that follows.
- In Spanish, all nouns (including words for things) are either masculine or feminine – this is called their gender. And, just as in English, they can also be either singular or plural. You must bear this in mind when deciding which Spanish word to use for *a*.

➪ *For more information on* **Nouns**, *see page 1.*

- **un** is used before masculine singular nouns.

un hombre	a man
un periódico	a newspaper

- **una** is used before feminine singular nouns.

una mujer	a woman
una revista	a magazine

- **unos** is used before masculine plural nouns.

unos hombres	some men
unos periódicos	some newspapers

- **unas** is used before feminine plural nouns.

unas mujeres	some women
unas revistas	some magazines

i Note that you use **un** instead of **una** immediately before a feminine singular word beginning with **a** or **ha** when the stress falls on the beginning of the word. This is because **una** sounds wrong before the '*a*' sound.

un ave	a bird
un hada	a fairy

2 Using the indefinite article

- The indefinite article is often used in Spanish in the same way as it is in English. However, there are some cases where the article is not used in Spanish but is in English, and vice versa.

➤ The indefinite article is NOT used in Spanish:

- when you say what someone's job is

Es profesor.	He's a teacher.
Mi madre es enfermera.	My mother is a nurse.

- after **tener**, **buscar**, or **llevar (puesto)** when you are only likely *to have*, *be looking for* or *be wearing* one of the items in question

No tengo celular.	I don't have a cell phone.
¿Llevaba sombrero?	Was he wearing a hat?

[i] Note that when you use an adjective to describe the noun, you DO use an article in Spanish too.

Es un excelente médico.	He's an excellent doctor.
Tiene una novia peruana.	He has a Peruvian girlfriend.
Llevaba un sombrero de paja.	He was wearing a straw hat.

➤ The indefinite article is NOT used in Spanish with the words **otro**, **cierto**, **cien**, **mil**, **sin**, and **qué**.

otro libro	another book
cierta calle	a certain street
cien soldados	a hundred soldiers
mil años	a thousand years
sin casa	without a house
¡Qué sorpresa!	What a surprise!

Key points

✔ Before masculine singular nouns → use **un**.
✔ Before feminine singular nouns → use **una**.
✔ Before feminine singular nouns starting with stressed **a** or **ha** → use **un**.
✔ Before masculine plural nouns → use **unos**.
✔ Before feminine plural nouns → use **unas**.
✔ You do not use an indefinite article in Spanish for saying what someone's job is.
✔ You do not use an indefinite article in Spanish with the words **otro**, **cierto**, **cien**, **mil**, **sin**, and **qué**.

For further explanation of grammatical terms, please see pages viii-xii.

The article lo

➤ Unlike the other Spanish articles, and articles in English, **lo** is NOT used with a noun.

➤ **lo** can be used with a masculine singular adjective or past participle (the **-ado** and **-ido** forms of regular verbs) to form a noun.

Lo único que no me gusta ...	The only thing I don't like ...
Eso es lo importante.	That's the important thing.
Lo bueno es que ...	The good thing is that ...
Sentimos mucho lo ocurrido.	We are very sorry about what happened.

➪ *For more information on the **Past participle**, see page 118.*

➤ **lo** is also used in a number of very common phrases:

- **a lo mejor** — maybe, perhaps
  A lo mejor no lo sabe. — Maybe he doesn't know.
- **por lo menos** — at least
  Hubo por lo menos cincuenta heridos. — At least fifty people were injured.
- **por lo general** — generally
  Por lo general me acuesto temprano. — I generally go to bed early.

➤ **lo** can also be used with **que** to make **lo que** (meaning *what*).

Vi lo que pasó.	I saw what happened.
Lo que más me gusta es nadar.	What I like best is swimming.

Grammar Extra!

lo can be used with **de** followed by a noun phrase to refer back to something the speaker and listener both know about.

Lo de tu hermano me preocupa mucho.	I'm very worried about that business with your brother.
Lo de ayer es mejor que lo olvides.	It would be best to forget what happened yesterday.

lo can be used with an adjective followed by **que** to emphasize how big/small/beautiful and so on something is or was. The adjective must agree with the noun it describes.

No sabíamos lo antigua que era la casa.	We didn't know how old the house was.
No te imaginas lo simpáticos que son.	You can't imagine how nice they are.

lo can also be used in a similar way with an adverb followed by **que**.

Sé lo mucho que te gusta la música.	I know how much you like music.

Key points

- ✔ **lo** is classed as an article in Spanish, but is not used with nouns.
- ✔ You can use **lo** with a masculine adjective or past participle to form a noun.
- ✔ You also use **lo** in a number of common phrases.
- ✔ **lo que** can be used to mean *what* in English.

Adjectives

What is an adjective?
An **adjective** is a 'describing' word that tells you more about a person or thing, such as their appearance, color, size or other qualities. For example: *pretty*, *blue*, *big*.

Using adjectives

➤ Adjectives are words like *smart*, *expensive* and *good* that tell you more about a noun (a living being, thing or idea). They can also tell you more about a pronoun, such as *he* or *they*. Adjectives are sometimes called 'describing words'. They can be used right next to a noun they are describing, or can be separated from the noun by a verb like *be*, *look*, *feel* and so on.

a smart girl
an expensive car
a good idea

⇨ *For more information on* ***Nouns*** *and* ***Pronouns****, see pages 1 and 41.*

➤ In English, the only time an adjective changes its form is when you are making a comparison.

She's smarter than her brother.
That's the best idea you've ever had!

➤ In Spanish, however, most adjectives agree with what they are describing. This means that their endings change depending on whether the person or thing you are referring to is masculine or feminine, singular or plural.

un hombre alto	a tall man
una mujer alta	a tall woman
unos hombres altos	some tall men
unas mujeres altas	some tall women

➤ In English, adjectives come BEFORE the noun they describe, but in Spanish you usually put them AFTER it.

una casa blanca a white house

⇨ *For more information on* ***Word order with adjectives****, see page 24.*

Making adjectives agree

1 Forming feminine adjectives

➤ The form of the adjective shown in dictionaries is generally the masculine singular form. This means that you need to know how to change its form to make it agree with the person or thing it is describing.

➤ Adjectives ending in **-o** in the masculine change to **-a** for the feminine.

Mi padre es mexicano.	My father is Mexican.
Mi madre es mexicana.	My mother is Mexican.

➤ Adjectives ending in any vowel other than **-o** (that is: *a*, *e*, *i* or *u*) or ending in a vowel with an accent on it do NOT change for the feminine.

el vestido verde	the green dress
la blusa verde	the green blouse
un pantalón caqui	some khaki pants
una camisa caqui	a khaki shirt
un médico iraquí	an Iraqi doctor
una familia iraquí	an Iraqi family

➤ Adjectives ending in a consonant (any letter other than a vowel) do NOT change for the feminine except in the following cases:

- Adjectives of nationality or place ending in a consonant add **-a** for the feminine. If there is an accent on the final vowel in the masculine, they lose this in the feminine.

un periódico inglés	an English newspaper
una revista inglesa	an English magazine
el equipo francés	the French team
la cocina francesa	French cooking
el vino español	Spanish wine
la lengua española	the Spanish language

i Note that these adjectives do not start with a capital letter in Spanish.

- Adjectives ending in **-or** in the masculine usually change to **-ora** for the feminine.

un niño encantador	a charming little boy
una niña encantadora	a charming little girl

For further explanation of grammatical terms, please see pages viii-xii.

i Note that a few adjectives ending in **-or** used in comparisons – such as **mejor** (meaning *better* or *best*), **peor** (meaning *worse* or *worst*), **mayor** (meaning *older* or *bigger*), **superior** (meaning *upper* or *top*), **inferior** (meaning *lower* or *inferior*) as well as **exterior** (meaning *outside* or *foreign*) and **posterior** (meaning *rear*) do not change in the feminine.

- Adjectives ending in **-án**, **-ón** and **-ín** in the masculine change to **-ana**, **-ona** and **-ina** (without an accent) in the feminine.

un gesto burlón	a mocking gesture
una sonrisa burlona	a mocking smile
un hombre parlanchín	a talkative man
una mujer parlanchina	a talkative woman

➤ Adjectives ending in a consonant which do not fall into the above categories do NOT change in the feminine.

un muchacho joven	a young boy
una muchacha joven	a young girl
un final feliz	a happy ending
una infancia feliz	a happy childhood

2 Forming plural adjectives

➤ Adjectives ending in an unaccented vowel (*a*, *e*, *i*, *o* or *u*) in the singular add **-s** in the plural.

el último tren	the last train
los últimos trenes	the last trains
una casa vieja	an old house
unas casas viejas	some old houses
una chica muy habladora	a very talkative girl
unas chicas muy habladoras	some very talkative girls
una pintora francesa	a French (woman) painter
unas pintoras francesas	some French (women) painters
una mesa verde	a green table
unas mesas verdes	some green tables

➤ Adjectives ending in a consonant in the masculine or feminine singular add **-es** in the plural. If there is an accent on the FINAL syllable in the singular, they lose it in the plural.

un chico muy hablador	a very talkative boy
unos chicos muy habladores	some very talkative boys
un pintor francés	a French painter
unos pintores franceses	some French painters

un examen fácil	an easy exam
unos exámenes fáciles	some easy exams
la tendencia actual	the current trend
las tendencias actuales	the current trends

➤ **-z** at the end of a singular adjective changes to **-ces** in the plural.

un día feliz	a happy day
unos días felices	happy days

Tip

When an adjective describes a mixture of both masculine and feminine nouns, use the masculine plural form of the adjective.

El pan y la fruta son baratos.	Bread and fruit are cheap.

Grammar Extra!

Adjectives ending in an accented vowel in the singular add **-es** in the plural.

un médico iraní	an Iranian doctor
unos médicos iraníes	some Iranian doctors

3 Invariable adjectives

➤ A small number of adjectives do not change in the feminine or plural. They are called invariable because their form NEVER changes, no matter what they are describing. These adjectives are often made up of more than one word – for example **azul marino** (meaning *navy blue*) – or come from the names of things – for example **naranja** (meaning *orange*).

las chaquetas azul marino	navy-blue jackets
los vestidos naranja	orange dresses

4 Short forms for adjectives

➤ The following adjectives drop the final **-o** before a masculine singular noun.

bueno	→	**buen**	→	**un buen libro**	a good book
malo	→	**mal**	→	**mal tiempo**	bad weather
alguno	→	**algún**	→	**algún libro**	some book
ninguno	→	**ningún**	→	**ningún hombre**	no man
uno	→	**un**	→	**un día**	one day

For further explanation of grammatical terms, please see pages viii-xii.

primero →	**primer** →	**el primer hijo**	the first child
tercero →	**tercer** →	**el tercer hijo**	the third child

ℹ Note that the adjectives **alguno** and **ninguno** add accents when they are shortened to become **algún** and **ningún**.

➤ **grande** (meaning *big* or *great*) is shortened to **gran** before a singular noun.

un gran actor	a great actor
una gran sorpresa	a big surprise

➤ **ciento** (meaning *a hundred*) changes to **cien** before all plural nouns as well as before **mil** (meaning *thousand*) and **millones** (meaning *millions*).

cien años	a hundred years
cien millones	a hundred million
cien mil euros	a hundred thousand euros

ℹ Note that you use the form **ciento** before other numbers.

ciento tres	one hundred and three

⇨ *For more information on* **Numbers**, *see page 208.*

Grammar Extra!

➤ **cualquiera** drops the final **a** before any noun.

cualquier día	any day
a cualquier hora	any time

Key points

✔ Most Spanish adjectives change their form according to whether the person or thing they are describing is masculine or feminine, singular or plural.
✔ In Spanish, adjectives usually go after the noun they describe.
✔ Don't forget to make adjectives agree with the person or thing they describe – they change for the feminine and plural forms:
un hombre americano
una mujer americana
unos hombres americanos
unas mujeres americanas
✔ Some adjectives never change their form.
✔ Some adjectives drop the final **-o** before a masculine singular noun.
✔ **grande** and **ciento** also change before certain nouns.

Word order with adjectives

➤ When adjectives are used right beside the noun they are describing, they go BEFORE it in English. Spanish adjectives usually go AFTER the noun.

una corbata azul	a blue tie
una palabra española	a Spanish word
la página siguiente	the following page
la hora exacta	the precise time

➤ When you have two or more adjectives after the noun, you use **y** (meaning *and*) between the last two.

un hombre alto y delgado	a tall, thin man

➤ A number of types of Spanish adjectives go BEFORE the noun:

- demonstrative adjectives
  este sombrero — this hat
- possessive adjectives (**mi**, **tu**, **su** and so on)
  mi padre — my father
- numbers
  tres días — three days
- interrogative adjectives
  ¿qué hombre? — which man?
- indefinite adjectives
  cada día — every day
- shortened adjectives
  mal tiempo — bad weather

For further explanation of grammatical terms, please see pages viii-xii.

➤ Some adjectives can go both BEFORE and AFTER the noun, but their meaning changes depending on where they go.

Adjective	Before Noun	Examples	After Noun	Examples
antiguo	former	**un antiguo colega** a former colleague	old, ancient	**la historia antigua** ancient history
diferente	various	**diferentes idiomas** various languages	different	**personas diferentes** different people
grande	great	**un gran pintor** a great painter	big	**una casa grande** a big house
medio	half	**medio melón** half a melon	average	**el ingreso medio** the average income
mismo	same	**la misma respuesta** the same answer	self, very, precisely	**yo mismo** myself **eso mismo** precisely that
nuevo	new (= *taking the place of an old one*)	**mi nuevo profesor** my new teacher	(brand) new (= *recently made, built, etc.*)	**una bicicleta nueva** a (brand) new bike
pobre	poor (= *wretched*)	**esa pobre mujer** that poor woman	poor (= *not rich*)	**un país pobre** a poor country
viejo	old (= *long-standing*)	**un viejo amigo** an old friend	old (= *aged*)	**esas toallas viejas** those old towels

Key points

✔ Most Spanish adjectives go after the noun.

✔ Certain types of adjectives go before the noun.

✔ Some adjectives can go before or after the noun – the meaning changes according to the position in the sentence.

Comparatives and superlatives of adjectives

1 Making comparisons using comparative adjectives

What is a comparative adjective?
A **comparative adjective** in English is one with *-er* on the end of it or *more* or *less* in front of it, which is used to compare people or things. For example: *shorter*, *less important*, *more beautiful*.

➤ In Spanish, to say something is *cheaper*, *more expensive* and so on, you use **más** (meaning *more*) before the adjective.

Esta bicicleta es más barata.	This bicycle is cheaper.
La verde es más cara.	The green one is more expensive.

➤ To say something is *less expensive*, *less beautiful* and so on, you use **menos** (meaning *less*) before the adjective.

La azul es menos cara.	The blue one is less expensive.

➤ To introduce the person or thing you are making the comparison with, use **que** (meaning *than*).

Es más alto que yo/mi hermano.	He's taller than me/my brother.
La otra bicicleta es más cara que esta.	The other bicycle is more expensive than this one.
Esta bicicleta es menos cara que la otra.	This bicycle is less expensive than the other one.

Grammar Extra!

When *than* in English is followed by a verbal construction, use **de lo que** rather than **que** alone.

Está más cansada de lo que parece.	She is more tired than she seems.

---

2 Making comparisons using superlative adjectives

What is a superlative adjective?
A **superlative adjective** in English is one with *-est* on the end of it or *most* or *least* in front of it, which is used to compare people or things. For example: *thinnest*, *most beautiful*, *least interesting*.

For further explanation of grammatical terms, please see pages viii-xii.

➤ In Spanish, to say something is *the cheapest*, *the most expensive* and so on, you use **el/la/los/las** (+ noun) + **más** + adjective.

el caballo más viejo	the oldest horse
la casa más antigua	the oldest house
los hoteles más baratos	the cheapest hotels
las manzanas más caras	the most expensive apples
¿Quién es el más alto?	Who's the tallest?

➤ To say something is *the least expensive*, *the least intelligent* and so on, you use **el/la/los/las** (+ noun) + **menos** + adjective.

el hombre menos simpático	the least likeable man
la niña menos habladora	the least talkative girl
los temas menos interesantes	the least interesting topics
el problema menos urgente	the least urgent problem
¿Quién es el menos trabajador?	Who's the least hardworking?

Tip

In phrases like *the most popular girl in the school* and *the tallest man in the world*, you use **de** to translate *in*.

el hombre más alto del mundo — the tallest man in the world

3 Irregular comparatives and superlatives

➤ Just as English has some irregular comparative and superlative forms – *better* instead of '*more good*', and *worst* instead of '*most bad*' – Spanish also has a few irregular forms.

Adjective	Meaning	Comparative	Meaning	Superlative	Meaning
bueno	good	**mejor**	better	**el mejor**	the best
malo	bad	**peor**	worse	**el peor**	the worst
grande	big	**mayor**	older	**el mayor**	the oldest
pequeño, chico	small	**menor**	younger	**el menor**	the youngest

El tuyo es mejor que el mío.	Yours is better than mine.
Es el mejor de todos.	It's the best of them all.
Hoy me siento peor.	I feel worse today.
la peor alumna de la clase	the worst student in the class

i Note that **mejor**, **peor**, **mayor** and **menor** don't change their endings in the feminine. In the plural, they become **mejores**, **peores**, **mayores** and **menores**. Don't forget to use **el**, **la**, **los** or **las** as appropriate, depending on whether the person or thing described is masculine or feminine, singular or plural.

Tip

más grande and **más pequeño/más chico** are used mainly to talk about the actual size of something.

Este plato es <u>más grande</u> que aquel.	This plate is bigger than that one.
Mi casa es <u>más pequeña/ más chica</u> que la tuya.	My house is smaller than yours.

mayor and **menor** are used mainly to talk about age.

mis hermanos <u>mayores</u>	my older brothers
la hija <u>menor</u>	the youngest daughter

4 Other ways of making comparisons

➤ To say *as ... as* (for example, *as pretty as*, *not as pretty as*) you use **tan ... como** in Spanish.

Pedro es <u>tan</u> alto <u>como</u> Miguel.	Pedro is as tall as Miguel.
No es <u>tan</u> atractiva <u>como</u> su madre.	She isn't as attractive as her mother.
No es <u>tan</u> grande <u>como</u> yo creía.	It isn't as big as I thought.

Grammar Extra!

In some expressions, you use **tanto** with a noun rather than **tan** with an adjective. This is because in Spanish you would use a noun where in English we would use an adjective.

Pablo tiene <u>tanto</u> miedo <u>como</u> yo.	Pablo is as frightened as I am.
Yo no tengo <u>tanta</u> hambre <u>como</u> tú.	I'm not as hungry as you are.

➤ To make an adjective stronger, you can use **muy** (meaning *very*).

Este libro es <u>muy</u> interesante.	This book is very interesting.

For further explanation of grammatical terms, please see pages viii-xii.

Grammar Extra!

For even more emphasis, you can attach **-ísimo** (meaning *really* or *extremely*) to the end of an adjective. Drop the final vowel if the adjective already ends in one. For example, **delgado** (meaning *thin*) becomes **delgadísimo** (meaning *really thin*).

Se compró un traje carísimo.	He bought himself a really expensive suit.
Es delgadísima.	She's extremely thin.

If you attach **-ísimo**, you need to drop any other accent. For example, **fácil** (meaning *easy*) becomes **facilísimo** (meaning *extremely easy*) and **rápido** (meaning *fast*) becomes **rapidísimo** (meaning *extremely fast*).

Es facilísimo de hacer.	It's really easy to make.
Iban rapidísimo.	They were going extremely fast.

When the adjective ends in **-co**, **-go** or **-z**, spelling changes are required to keep the same sound. For example, **rico** (meaning *rich*) becomes **riquísimo** (meaning *extremely rich*) and **feroz** (meaning *fierce*) becomes **ferocísimo** (meaning *extremely fierce*).

Se hizo riquísimo.	He became extremely rich.
un tigre ferocísimo	an extremely fierce tiger

➪ *For more information on* ***Spelling*** *and* ***Stress****, see pages 198 and 202.*

Key points

✔ Comparative adjectives in Spanish are formed by:
- **más** + adjective + **que**
- **menos** + adjective + **que**

✔ Superlative adjectives in Spanish are formed by:
- **el/la/los/las** + **más** + adjective
- **el/la/los/las** + **menos** + adjective

✔ There are a few irregular comparative and superlative forms in Spanish.

✔ You can use **tan ... como** to say *as ... as*.

✔ To make an adjective stronger, use **muy**.

Demonstrative adjectives

What is a demonstrative adjective?
In English, a **demonstrative adjective** is a word such as *this, that, these* or *those* which is used with a noun to point out a particular thing or person. For example, *this woman*, *that dog*.

1 Using demonstrative adjectives

➤ Just as in English, Spanish demonstrative adjectives go BEFORE the noun. Like other adjectives in Spanish, they have to change for the feminine and plural forms.

	Masculine	Feminine	Meaning
Singular	este ese aquel	esta esa aquella	this that (*close by*) that (*further away*)
Plural	estos esos aquellos	estas esas aquellas	these those (*close by*) those (*further away*)

➤ Use **este/esta/estos/estas** (meaning *this/these)* to talk about things and people that are near you.

Este bolígrafo no escribe. This pen isn't working.
Traje estos libros. I brought these books.

➤ Use **ese/esa/esos/esas** and **aquel/aquella/aquellos/aquellas** (meaning *that/those)* to talk about things that are further away.

Esa revista es muy mala. That magazine is very bad.
¿Conoces a esos señores? Do you know those men?
No le gusta aquella muñeca. She doesn't like that doll.
¿Ves aquellos árboles? Do you see those trees (over there)?

2 ese or aquel?

➤ In English we use *that* and *those* to talk about anything that is not near by, but in Spanish you need to be a bit more precise.

For further explanation of grammatical terms, please see pages viii-xii.

➤ Use **ese/esa/esos/esas**:

- to talk about things and people that are nearer to the person you are talking to than to you.

ese libro que estás leyendo	that book you are reading
¿Cuánto te costó esa falda?	How much did that skirt cost you?

- to talk about things and people that aren't very far away.

No me gustan esos cuadros.	I don't like those pictures.

➤ Use **aquel/aquella/aquellos/aquellas** to talk about things that are further away from you and the person you are speaking to.

Me gusta más aquella mesa.	I prefer that table (over there).

Grammar Extra!

You should use **ese/esa/esos/esas** when you are referring back to something which has already been mentioned in the conversation.

¿1999? No me acuerdo de dónde pasamos las vacaciones ese año.	1999? I can't remember where we went on vacation that year.

You should use **aquel/aquella/aquellos/aquellas** when you refer to something for the first time in the conversation.

aquellas vacaciones que pasamos en Francia	that vacation we had in France

---

Key points

- ✔ this + noun = **este/esta** + noun
- ✔ these + noun = **estos/estas** + noun
- ✔ that + noun = **ese/esa** + noun (*when the object is not far away from you or the person you're talking to*)
- ✔ that + noun = **aquel/aquella** + noun (*when the object is more distant*)
- ✔ those + noun = **esos/esas** + noun (*when the objects are not far away from you or the person you're talking to*)
- ✔ those + noun = **aquellos/aquellas** + noun (*when the objects are more distant*)

Interrogative adjectives

What is an interrogative adjective?
An **interrogative adjective** is a question word or expression used with a noun, such as *which*, *what*, *how much* and *how many*. For example: *Which shirt are you going to wear?*; *How much time do we have?*

➤ In Spanish the interrogative adjectives are **qué** (meaning *which* or *what*) and **cuánto/cuánta/cuántos/cuántas** (meaning *how much/how many*). Note that, like all other question words in Spanish, **qué** and **cuánto** have accents on them.

➤ **¿qué?** (meaning *what?* or *which?*) doesn't change for the feminine and plural forms.

¿Qué clase de diccionario necesitas?	What kind of dictionary do you need?
¿Qué instrumentos tocas?	Which instruments do you play?
¿Qué ofertas has recibido?	What offers have you received?
¿Qué libro te gusta más?	Which book do you like best?

➤ **¿cuánto?** means the same as *how much?* in English. It changes to **¿cuánta?** in the feminine form.

¿Cuánto dinero te queda?	How much money do you have left?
¿Cuánta fruta compraste?	How much fruit did you buy?

i Note that with **gente** (meaning *people*), which is a feminine singular noun, **cuánta** must be used.

¿Cuánta gente vino?	How many people came?

➤ **¿cuántos?** means the same as *how many?* in English. It changes to **¿cuántas?** in the feminine plural.

¿Cuántos primos tienes?	How many cousins do you have?
¿Cuántas personas van a venir?	How many people are coming?

Tip
Don't forget to add the opening, upside-down question mark in Spanish questions.

For further explanation of grammatical terms, please see pages viii-xii.

Grammar Extra!

In English we can say, *Tell me what time it is*, *He asked me how much sugar there was* and *I don't know which dress to choose* to express doubt, report a question, or ask a question in a roundabout or indirect way. In Spanish you can use **qué** and **cuánto/cuánta/cuántos/cuántas** in the same way.

Dime qué hora es.	Tell me what time it is.
Me preguntó cuánto dinero tenía.	He asked me how much money I had.
No sé qué vestido ponerme.	I don't know which dress to wear.
No sé a qué hora llegó.	I don't know what time she arrived.
Dime cuántas postales quieres.	Tell me how many postcards you'd like.

Adjectives used in exclamations

➤ In Spanish **¡qué...!** is often used where, in English, we might say *What a ...!*

¡Qué lástima!	What a pity!
¡Qué sorpresa!	What a surprise!

Tip

Don't forget to add the opening, upside-down exclamation point in Spanish exclamations.

Grammar Extra!

¡qué...! combines with **más** or **tan** and an adjective in Spanish to mean *What (a)...!* in English.

¡Qué hombre más insoportable!	What an intolerable man!
¡Qué tiempo más horrible!	What terrible weather!
¡Qué gente tan simpática!	What nice people!

In Spanish **cuánto/cuánta/cuántos/cuántas** can be used to mean *What a lot of ...!* in English.

¡Cuánto dinero!	What a lot of money!
¡Cuánta gente!	What a lot of people!
¡Cuántos CDs!	What a lot of CDs!
¡Cuánto tiempo!	What a long time!

For further explanation of grammatical terms, please see pages viii-xii.

Possessive adjectives (1)

What is a possessive adjective?
In English a **possessive adjective** is one of the words *my, your, his, her, its, our* or *their* used with a noun to show that one person or thing belongs to another.

➤ Like other adjectives in Spanish, possessive adjectives change for the plural and sometimes for the feminine forms.

Singular		Plural		Meaning
masculine	**feminine**	**masculine**	**feminine**	
mi	mi	mis	mis	my
tu	tu	tus	tus	your (*belonging to someone you address as* tú)
su	su	sus	sus	his; her; its; your (*belonging to someone you address as* usted)
nuestro	nuestra	nuestros	nuestras	our
vuestro*	vuestra*	vuestros*	vuestras*	your (*belonging to people you address as* vosotros/vosotras)
su	su	sus	sus	their; your (*belonging to people you address as* ustedes)

➪ * *These forms are not normally used in Latin America, where the pronoun* ustedes *is used instead of* vosotros. *For more information on* ***Ways of saying 'you' in Spanish****, see page 44.*

¿Dónde está tu hermana?	Where's your sister?
José perdió sus llaves.	José lost his keys.
¿Dónde están nuestros pasaportes?	Where are our passports?
¿Por qué no traen a sus hijos?	Why don't you bring your children?
Mis tíos van a vender su casa.	My uncle and aunt are going to sell their house.

Tip

Possessive adjectives agree with what they describe NOT with the person who owns that thing.

Pablo trajo su diccionario.	Pablo brought his dictionary.
Pablo trajo sus diccionarios.	Pablo brought his dictionaries.

Note that possessive adjectives aren't normally used with parts of the body. You usually use the definite article instead.

Tiene los ojos verdes.	He has green eyes.
No puedo mover las piernas.	I can't move my legs.

⇨ *For more information on **Articles**, see page 10.*

Tip

As **su** and **sus** can mean *his*, *her*, *its*, *your* or *their*, it can sometimes be a bit confusing. When you need to avoid confusion, you can use the Spanish equivalent of *of him* and so on.

su casa	→	**la casa de él**	his house (*literally: the house of him*)
sus amigos	→	**los amigos de usted**	your friends (*literally: the friends of you*)
sus padres	→	**los padres de ellos**	their parents (*literally: the parents of them*)
su abrigo	→	**el abrigo de ella**	her coat (*literally: the coat of her*)

⇨ *For more information on **Personal pronouns**, see page 42.*

Key points

✔ The Spanish possessive adjectives are:
- **mi/tu/su/nuestro/vuestro** (in Spain)/**su** with a masculine singular noun
- **mi/tu/su/nuestra/vuestra** (in Spain)/**su** with a feminine singular noun
- **mis/tus/sus/nuestros/vuestros** (in Spain)/**sus** with a masculine plural noun
- **mis/tus/sus/nuestras/vuestras** (in Spain)/**sus** with a feminine plural noun

✔ Possessive adjectives come before the noun they refer to. They agree with what they describe, rather than with the person who owns that thing.

✔ Possessive adjectives are not usually used with parts of the body. Use **el/la/los** or **las** as appropriate instead.

✔ To avoid confusion, it is sometimes clearer to use **el coche de él/ella/ellas/ellos/usted** and so on rather than **su coche**.

Possessive adjectives (2)

➤ In Spanish, there is a second set of possessive adjectives, which mean *(of) mine*, *(of) yours* and so on. Like other adjectives in Spanish, they change in the feminine and plural forms.

Singular		Plural		Meaning
masculine	**feminine**	**masculine**	**feminine**	
mío	mía	míos	mías	mine/of mine
tuyo	tuya	tuyos	tuyas	yours/of yours (*belonging to* **tú**)
suyo	suya	suyos	suyas	his/of his; hers/of hers; of its; yours/of yours (*belonging to* **usted**)
nuestro	nuestra	nuestros	nuestras	ours/of ours
vuestro*	vuestra*	vuestros*	vuestras*	yours/of yours (*belonging to* **vosotros/as**)
suyo	suya	suyos	suyas	theirs/of theirs; yours/ of yours (*belonging to* **ustedes**)

➪ * *These forms are not normally used in Latin America, where the pronoun* **ustedes** *is used instead of* **vosotros**. *For more information on* ***Ways of saying 'you' in Spanish****,* *see page 44*.

un amigo <u>mío</u>	a (male) friend of mine, one of my (male) friends
una revista <u>tuya</u>	a magazine of yours, one of your magazines
una tía <u>suya</u>	an aunt of his/hers/theirs/yours, one of his/her/their/your aunts
unas amigas <u>nuestras</u>	some (female) friends of ours, some of our friends
¿De quién es esta bufanda? – Es <u>mía</u>.	Whose scarf is this? – It's mine.

ℹ Note that unlike the other possessive adjectives, these adjectives go <u>AFTER</u> the noun they describe.

un primo <u>mío</u>	a (male) cousin of mine, one of my cousins

Tip

Possessive adjectives agree with what they describe NOT with the person who owns that thing.

Estos guantes son míos. These gloves are mine.

Grammar Extra!

mío/mía and so on are also used in exclamations and when addressing someone. In this case they mean the same as *my* in English.

¡Dios mío! My God!
amor mío my love, (my) darling
Muy señor mío Dear Sir (*in very formal letters*)

For further explanation of grammatical terms, please see pages viii-xii.

Indefinite adjectives

> **What is an indefinite adjective?**
> An **indefinite adjective** is one of a small group of adjectives used to talk about people or things in a general way without saying exactly who or what they are. For example: *several*, *all*, *every*.

➤ In English, indefinite adjectives do not change, but in Spanish most indefinite adjectives change for the feminine and plural forms.

Singular		**Plural**		**Meaning**
masculine	**feminine**	**masculine**	**feminine**	
algún	alguna	algunos	algunas	some; any
cada	cada			each; every
mismo	misma	mismos	mismas	same
mucho	mucha	muchos	muchas	a lot of, much, many
otro	otra	otros	otras	another; other
poco	poca	pocos	pocas	little; few
tanto	tanta	tantos	tantas	so much; so many
todo	toda	todos	todas	all; every
		varios	varias	several

algún día	some day
algunas personas	some people
el mismo día	the same day
las mismas películas	the same movies
otro tren	another train
otra manzana	another apple
poca agua	(a) little water
pocos amigos	few friends

ℹ Note that you can never use **otro** (meaning *other* or *another*) with **un** or **una**.

¿Me das otra manzana?	Will you give me another apple?
¿Tienes otro suéter?	Do you have another sweater?

Tip

Some and *any* are usually not translated before nouns that you can't count, like bread, butter, water.

Hay pan en la mesa.	There's some bread on the table.
¿Quieres café?	Would you like some coffee?
¿Hay leche?	Is there any milk?
No hay mantequilla.	There isn't any butter.

➤ **todo/toda/todos/todas** (meaning *all* or *every*) can be followed by:

- a definite article (**el**, **la**, **los**, **las**)

  Bailaron toda la noche. — They danced all night.
  Vengo todos los días. — I come every day.

- a demonstrative adjective (**este**, **ese**, **aquel** and so on)

  Planché toda esta ropa. — I ironed all these clothes.

- a possessive adjective (**mi**, **tu**, **su** and so on)

  Voy a invitar a todos mis amigos. — I'm going to invite all my friends.

- a place name

  Lo sabe todo Bogotá. — All of Bogotá knows it.

⇨ *For more information on* ***Articles, Demonstrative adjectives*** *and* ***Possessive adjectives****, see pages 10, 30 and 35.*

➤ As in English, Spanish indefinite adjectives come BEFORE the noun they describe.

las mismas películas — the same movies

Key points

✔ Like other adjectives, Spanish indefinite adjectives (such as **otro** and **todo**) must agree with what they describe.

✔ They go before the noun to which they relate.

Pronouns

What is a pronoun?
A **pronoun** is a word you use instead of a noun, when you do not need or want to name someone or something directly. For example: *it*, *you*, *none*.

➤ There are several different types of pronoun:

- Personal pronouns such as *I*, *you*, *he*, *her* and *they*, which are used to refer to you, the person you are talking to, or other people and things. They can be either subject pronouns (*I*, *you*, *he* and so on) or object pronouns (*him*, *her*, *them*, and so on).
- Possessive pronouns like *mine* and *yours*, which show who someone or something belongs to.
- Indefinite pronouns like *someone* or *nothing*, which refer to people or things in a general way without saying exactly who or what they are.
- Relative pronouns like *who*, *which* or *that*, which link two parts of a sentence together.
- Interrogative pronouns like *who*, *what* or *which*, which are used in questions.
- Demonstrative pronouns like *this* or *those*, which point things or people out.
- Reflexive pronouns, a type of object pronoun that forms part of Spanish reflexive verbs like **levantarse** (meaning *to get up* or *to stand up*) or **llamarse** (meaning *to be called*).

⇨ *For more information on* **Reflexive verbs**, *see page* 92.

➤ Pronouns often stand in for a noun to save repeating it.

I finished my homework and gave it to my teacher.

Do you remember Jack? I saw him this past weekend.

➤ Word order with personal pronouns is usually different in Spanish and English.

Personal pronouns: subject

What is a subject pronoun?
A **subject pronoun** is a word such as *I*, *he*, *she* and *they*, that carries out the action expressed by the verb. Pronouns stand in for nouns when it is clear who or what is being talked about. For example: *My brother isn't here at the moment. He'll be back in an hour.*

1 Using subject pronouns

➤ Here are the Spanish subject pronouns:

Singular	Meaning	Plural	Meaning
yo	I	**nosotros** (*masculine*)/ **nosotras** (*feminine*)	we
tú	you	**vosotros** (*masculine*)/ **vosotras** (*feminine*)*	you
él	he	**ellos** (*masculine*)	they
ella	she	**ellas** (*feminine*)	they
usted (**Vd.**)	you	**ustedes** (**Vds.**)	you

Vosotros and vosotras are not normally used in Latin America, where* **ustedes *is used instead. For more information on* ***Ways of saying 'you' in Spanish****,* *see page 44.*

Note that there is an accent on **tú** (*you*) and **él** (*he*) so that they are not confused with **tu** (*your*) and **el** (*the*).

Tip
The abbreviations **Vd.** and **Vds.** are often used instead of **usted** and **ustedes**.

➤ In English, we use subject pronouns all the time – *I walk, you eat, they are going*. In Spanish, you don't need them if the verb endings and context make it clear who the subject is. For example **hablo español** can only mean *I speak Spanish* since the **-o** ending on the verb is only used with *I*. Similarly, **hablamos francés** can only mean *we speak French* since the **-amos** ending is only used with *we*. So the subject pronouns are not needed in these examples.

Tengo un hermano.	I have a brother.
Tenemos dos perros.	We have two dogs.

➤ Spanish subject pronouns are normally only used:

- for emphasis

¿Y tú qué piensas?	What do you think about it?
Ellos sí que llegaron tarde.	They really did arrive late.

- for contrast or clarity

Yo estudio español pero él estudia francés.	I study Spanish but he studies French.
Él llamó pero ella no.	He called but she didn't.

- after **ser** (meaning *to be*)

Soy yo.	It's me.
¿Eres tú?	Is that you?

- in comparisons after **que** and **como**

Enrique es más alto que yo.	Enrique is taller than I am *or* than me.
Antonio no es tan alto como tú.	Antonio isn't as tall as you (are).

➪ *For more information on **Making comparisons**, see page 26.*

- on their own without a verb

¿Quién dijo eso? – Él.	Who said that? – He did.
¿Quién quiere venir? – Yo.	Who wants to come? – I do.

- after certain prepositions

Es para ella.	It's for her.

➪ *For more information on **Pronouns after prepositions**, see page 54.*

[i] Note that *it* used as the subject, and *they* referring to things, are NEVER translated into Spanish.

¿Qué es? – Es una sorpresa.	What is it? – It's a surprise.
¿Qué son? – Son abrelatas.	What are they? – They are can openers.

2 Ways of saying '*you*' in Spanish

- In English, we have only one way of saying *you*. In Spanish, there are several words to choose from. The word you use depends on:
  - whether you are talking to one person or more than one person
  - whether you are talking to a friend or family member, or someone else.
- If you are talking to one person you know well, such as a friend, a young person or a relative, use **tú**.
- If you are talking to one person you do not know so well, such as your teacher, your boss or a stranger, use the polite form **usted**.
- If you are talking to more than one person you know well, use **ustedes** in Latin America. Use **vosotros** (or **vosotras**, if you are talking to women only) in Spain.
- Use **ustedes** everywhere if you are talking to more than one person you do not know so well.

> *Tip*
>
> Remember that adjectives describing **tú** and **usted** should be feminine if you're talking to a woman or girl, while adjectives describing **ustedes** should be feminine plural if you're talking to women or girls only.

3 Using the plural subject pronouns

- When you are talking about males only, use **nosotros**, **vosotros** (in Spain only) or **ellos**.

Nosotros no somos italianos.	We are not Italian.

- When you are talking about females only, use **nosotras**, **vosotras** (in Spain only) or **ellas**.

Hablé con mis hermanas.	I spoke to my sisters.
Ellas estaban de acuerdo conmigo.	They agreed with me.

- When you are talking about both males and females, use **nosotros**, **vosotros** (in Spain) or **ellos**.

Martín y Raquel no llegaron hasta la medianoche.	Martín and Raquel didn't arrive till midnight.
Ellos sí que llegaron tarde.	They really did arrive late.

For further explanation of grammatical terms, please see pages viii-xii.

Key points

✔ The Spanish subject pronouns are: **yo**, **tú**, **él**, **ella**, **usted** in the singular, and **nosotros/nosotras**, **vosotros/vosotras** (in Spain only), **ellos/ellas**, **ustedes** in the plural.

✔ Don't use the subject pronouns with verbs except for emphasis or clarity.

✔ Make sure you choose the correct form of the verb.

✔ Do use the subject pronouns:
- after **ser** (meaning *to be*)
- in comparisons after **que** and **como**
- in one-word answers to questions.

✔ Choose the word for *you* carefully. Remember to think about how many people you are talking to and your relationship with them when deciding between **tú**, **usted** and **ustedes** (or **vosotros/vosotras** in Spain only).

✔ *It* as the subject of the verb, and *they* when it refers to things are NOT translated in Spanish.

✔ Use masculine plural forms (**nosotros**, **vosotros** (in Spain only), **ellos**) for groups made up of men and women.

✔ Remember to make any adjectives describing the subject agree.

Personal pronouns: direct object

What is a direct object pronoun?
A **direct object pronoun** is a word such as *me*, *him*, *us* and *them*, which is used instead of the noun to stand in for the person or thing most directly affected by the action expressed by the verb.

1 Using direct object pronouns

➤ Direct object pronouns stand in for nouns when it is clear who or what is being talked about, and save having to repeat the noun.

I've lost my glasses. Have you seen <u>them</u>?
'Have you met Jo?' – 'Yes, I really like <u>her</u>!'

➤ Here are the Spanish direct object pronouns:

Singular	Meaning	Plural	Meaning
me	me	**nos**	us
te	you (*relating to* **tú**)	**los** **las** **os***	you (*relating to* **ustedes** *when there are males in the group*) you (*relating to* **ustedes** *when there are no males in the group*) you (*relating to* **vosotros/vosotras**)
lo	him it (*masculine*) you (*relating to* **usted** *– masculine*)	**los**	them (*relating to* **ellos**)
la	her it (*feminine*) you (*relating to* **usted** *– feminine*)	**las**	them (*relating to* **ellas**)

**Not normally used in Latin America.*

<u>Te</u> quiero. — I love you.
No <u>los</u> toques. — Don't touch them.

i Note that you cannot use the Spanish direct object pronouns on their own without a verb or after a preposition such as **a** or **de**.

⇨ *For more information on* **Pronouns after prepositions**, *see page* 54.

2 Word order with direct object pronouns

➤ The direct object pronoun usually comes BEFORE the verb.

¿Las ves?	Can you see them?
¿No me oyen?	Can't you hear me?
Tu hija no nos conoce.	Your daughter doesn't know us.
¿Lo has visto?	Have you seen it?

➤ In orders and instructions telling someone TO DO something, the pronoun is attached to the end of the verb to form one word.

Ayúdame.	Help me.
Acompáñanos.	Come with us.

[i] Note that you will often need to add a written accent to preserve the spoken stress when attaching pronouns to the end of verbs.

⇨ *For more information on **Stress**, see page 202.*

➤ In orders and instructions telling someone NOT TO DO something, the pronoun is NOT attached to the end of the verb.

No los toques.	Don't touch them.

➤ If the pronoun is the object of an infinitive (the *to* form of the verb) or a gerund (the *-ing* form of the verb), you always attach the pronoun to the end of the verb to form one word, unless the infinitive or gerund follows another verb. Again, you may have to add a written accent to preserve the stress.

Se fue después de arreglarlo.	He left after fixing it.
Practicándolo, aprenderás.	You'll learn by practicing it.

⇨ *For more information on **Verbs** and **Gerunds**, see pages 69 and 128.*

➤ Where an infinitive or gerund follows another verb, you can put the pronoun either at the end of the infinitive or gerund, or before the other verb.

Vienen a vernos *or* **Nos vienen a ver.**	They are coming to see us.
Está comiéndolo *or* **Lo está comiendo.**	He's eating it.

⇨ *For further information on the **Order of object pronouns**, see page 52.*

3 Special use of lo

➤ **lo** is sometimes used to refer back to an idea or information that has already been introduced. The word *it* is often missed out in English.

¿Va a venir María? – No lo sé.	Is María coming? – I don't know.
Ya habían comido pero no nos lo dijeron.	They had already eaten, but they didn't tell us.

Key points

- ✔ The Spanish direct object pronouns are: **me**, **te**, **lo**, **la** in the singular, and **nos**, **os** (in Spain only), **los**, **las** in the plural.
- ✔ The object pronoun usually comes before the verb.
- ✔ Object pronouns are attached to the end of infinitives, gerunds or verbs instructing someone to do something.
- ✔ If an infinitive or gerund follows another verb, you can choose whether to attach the object pronoun to the end of the infinitive or gerund or to put it before the first verb.
- ✔ **lo** is sometimes used to refer back to an idea or information that has already been introduced.

For further explanation of grammatical terms, please see pages viii-xii.

Personal pronouns: indirect object

What is an indirect object pronoun?
An **indirect object pronoun** is used instead of a noun to show the person or thing an action is intended to benefit or harm, for example, *me* in *He gave me a book.; Can you get me a towel?; He wrote to me.*

1 Using indirect object pronouns

➤ It is important to understand the difference between direct and indirect object pronouns in English, as they can have different forms in Spanish.

➤ You can usually test whether an object is a direct object or an indirect one by asking questions about the action using *what* and *who*:

- an indirect object answers the question *who ... to?* or *who ... for?*, equally *what ... to?* or *what ... for?*

  He gave me a book. → *Who did he give the book to?* → me (=*indirect object pronoun*)
  Can you get me a towel? → *Who can you get a towel for?* → me (=*indirect object pronoun*)

  We got some paint for it. → *What did you get the paint for?* → it (=*indirect object pronoun*)

- if something answers the question *what* or *who*, then it is the direct object and NOT the indirect object.

  He gave me a book. → *What did he give me?* → a book (=*direct object*)
  I saw Mandy. → *Who did you see?* → Mandy (=*direct object*)
  We got some paint for it. → *What did you get?* → some paint (=*direct object*)

i Note that a verb won't necessarily have both a direct and an indirect object.

➤ Here are the Spanish indirect object pronouns:

Singular	Meaning	Plural	Meaning
me	me, to me, for me	**nos**	us, to us, for us
te	you, to you, for you (*relating to* **tú**)	**les** **os***	you, to you, for you (*relating to* **ustedes**) you, to you, for you (*relating to* **vosotros/vosotras**)
le	him, to him, for him, her, to her, for her, it, to it, for it, you, to you, for you (*relating to* **usted**)	**les**	them, to them, for them, you, to you, for you (*relating to* **ustedes**)

**Not normally used in Latin America.*

➤ The pronouns shown in the table are used instead of using the prepositions **a** or **para** with a noun.

Mandó una carta a todos los socios. She sent a letter to all the members. → **Les mandó una carta.** She sent them a letter.

Compra un regalo para tu hermana. Buy your sister a present. → **Cómprale un regalo.** Buy her a present.

➤ Some Spanish verbs like **mirar** (meaning *to look at*), **esperar** (meaning *to wait for*) and **buscar** (meaning *to look for*) take a direct object, because the Spanish construction is different from the English.

Grammar Extra!

You should usually use direct object pronouns rather than indirect object pronouns when replacing the personal **a** + noun.

Vi a Teresa. → La vi. I saw Teresa. → I saw her.

⇨ *For more information on* **Personal a**, *see page 184.*

2 Word order with indirect object pronouns

➤ The indirect object pronoun usually comes BEFORE the verb.

Sofía le escribió. Sofía wrote to him.
¿Le escribió Sofía? Did Sofía write to him?

Carlos no nos habla. Carlos doesn't speak to us.
¿Qué te pedían? What were they asking you for?

➤ In orders and instructions telling someone TO DO something, the pronoun is attached to the end of the verb to form one word.

Contéstame.	Answer me.
Dime la respuesta.	Tell me the answer.

[i] Note that you will often need to add a written accent to preserve the spoken stress.

➪ *For more information on **Stress**, see page 202.*

➤ In orders and instructions telling someone NOT TO DO something, the pronoun is NOT attached to the end of the verb.

No me digas la respuesta.	Don't tell me the answer.

➤ If the pronoun is the object of an infinitive (the *to* form of the verb) or a gerund (the *-ing* form of the verb), you always attach the pronoun to the end of the verb to form one word, unless the infinitive or gerund follows another verb. Again, you may have to add a written accent to preserve the stress.

Darle tu dirección no fue muy prudente.	It wasn't very smart to give him your address.
Gritándole así lo vas a asustar.	You'll frighten him by shouting at him like that.

➤ Where an infinitive or gerund follows another verb, you can put the pronoun either at the end of the infinitive or gerund, or before the other verb.

Quiero decirte algo. *or* **Te quiero decir algo.**	I want to tell you something.
Estoy escribiéndole. *or* **Le estoy escribiendo.**	I am writing to him/her.

➪ *For further information on the **Order of object pronouns**, see page 52.*

Key points

- ✔ The Spanish indirect object pronouns are: **me**, **te**, **le** in the singular, and **nos**, **os** (in Spain only), **les** in the plural.
- ✔ They can replace the prepositions **a** or **para** (meaning *to* or *for*) + noun.
- ✔ Like the direct object pronoun, the indirect object pronoun usually comes before the verb.
- ✔ Object pronouns are attached to the end of infinitives, gerunds or verbs instructing someone to do something.
- ✔ If an infinitive or gerund follows another verb, you can choose whether to attach the object pronoun to the end of the infinitive or gerund or to put it before the first verb.

Order of object pronouns

➤ Two object pronouns are often used together in the same sentence (for example: *he gave me them* or *he gave them to me*). In Spanish, you should always put the indirect object pronoun BEFORE the direct object pronoun.

Indirect		**Direct**
me	BEFORE	**lo**
te		**la**
nos		**los**
os (*in Spain only*)		**las**

Ana nos lo mandará mañana.	Ana will send it to us tomorrow.
¿Te los mostró mi hermana?	Did my sister show them to you?
No me lo digas.	Don't tell me (that).
No quiere prestárnosla.	He won't lend it to us.

➤ You have to use **se** instead of **le** (*to him, to her, to you*) and **les** (*to them, to you*) before the object pronouns **lo**, **la**, **los**, or **las**.

Se lo di ayer.	I gave it to him/her/you/them yesterday.
Se las enviaré.	I'll send them to him/her/you/them.

Key points

✔ When combining two object pronouns, put the indirect object pronoun before the direct object pronoun.

✔ Use **se** as the indirect object pronoun rather than **le** or **les** when there is more than one object pronoun.

Further information on object pronouns

- The object pronoun **le** can mean *(to) him*, *(to) her* and *(to) you*; **les** can mean *(to) them* and *(to) you*, and **se** can mean all of these things, which could lead to some confusion.

- To make it clear which one is meant, **a él** (meaning *to him*), **a ella** (meaning *to her*), **a usted** (meaning *to you*) and so on can be added to the phrase.

A ella le escriben mucho.	They write to her often.
Se lo van a mandar pronto a ellos.	They will be sending it to them soon.

- When a noun object comes before the verb, the corresponding object pronoun must be used too.

  A tu hermano lo conozco bien. I know your brother well.
  (*literally: Your brother I know him well.*)
  A María la vemos algunas veces. We sometimes see María.
  (*literally: María we see her sometimes.*)

- Indirect object pronouns are often used in constructions with the definite article and parts of the body or items of clothing to show who they belong to. In English, we use a possessive adjective.

La chaqueta le quedaba grande.	His jacket was too big for him.
Me dio la mano.	He held my hand/shook my hand.

➪ *For more information on **The definite article** and **Possessive adjectives**, see pages 11, 35 and 37.*

- Indirect object pronouns can also be used in certain common phrases which use reflexive verbs.

Se me perdieron las llaves.	I lost my keys.

➪ *For more information on **Reflexive verbs**, see page 92.*

ⓘ Note that in Spain, you will often hear **le** and **les** used instead of **lo** and **los** as direct object pronouns when referring to men and boys.

Pronouns after prepositions

➤ In English, we use *me*, *you*, *him* and so on after a preposition (for example: *he came toward me*; *it's for you*; *books by him*). In Spanish, there is a special set of pronouns which are used after prepositions.

➤ In Spanish, the pronouns used after a preposition are the same as the subject pronouns, except for the forms **mí** (meaning *me*), **ti** (meaning *you*), and **sí** (meaning *himself, herself, yourself, themselves, yourselves*).

Singular	Meaning	Plural	Meaning
mí	me	**nosotros**	us (*masculine*)
ti	you	**nosotras**	us (*feminine*)
él	him	**vosotros***	you (*masculine*)
ella	her	**vosotras***	you (*feminine*)
usted (Vd.)	you	**ellos**	them (*masculine*)
sí	himself herself yourself	**ellas**	them (*feminine*)
		ustedes (Vds.)	you
		sí	themselves yourselves

Not normally used in Latin America, where* **ustedes *is used instead.*

Pienso en ti.	I think about you.
¿Son para mí?	Are they for me?
No he sabido nada de él.	I haven't heard from him.
Es para ella.	It's for her.
Venían hacia nosotros.	They were coming toward us.
Volvió sin ellos.	He came back without them.
Volaban sobre ustedes.	They were flying above you.

[i] Note that **mí**, **sí** and **él** each have an accent, to distinguish them from **mi** (meaning *my*) , **si** (meaning *if*), and **el** (meaning *the*), but **ti** does not have an accent.

➤ These pronouns are often used for emphasis.

¿A ti no te escriben?	Don't they write to you?
Me lo manda a mí, no a ti.	She's sending it to me, not to you.

➤ **con** (meaning *with*) is combined with **mí**, **ti** and **sí** to form:

- **conmigo** with me

  Ven conmigo. Come with me.

- **contigo** with you
  Me gusta estar contigo. I like being with you.
- **consigo** with himself/herself/yourself/themselves/yourselves
  Lo trajeron consigo. They brought it with them.

➤ **entre**, **hasta**, **salvo**, **menos** and **según** are always used with the subject pronouns (**yo** and **tú**), rather than with the object pronouns (**mí** and **ti**).

- **entre** between, among
  entre tú y yo between you and me
- **hasta** even, including
  Hasta yo puedo hacerlo. Even I can do it.
- **menos** except
  todos menos yo everybody except me
- **salvo** except
  todos salvo yo everyone except me
- **según** according to
  según tú according to you

⇨ *For more information on **Subject pronouns**, see page 42.*

Key points

✔ Most prepositions are followed by the forms: **mí**, **ti**, **sí** and so on.

✔ **entre**, **hasta**, **menos**, **salvo** and **según** are followed by the subject pronouns **yo** and **tú**.

✔ **con** is combined with **mí**, **ti** and **sí** to form **conmigo**, **contigo** and **consigo**.

Possessive pronouns

What is a possessive pronoun?
A **possessive pronoun** is one of the words *mine*, *yours*, *hers*, *his*, *ours* or *theirs*, which are used instead of a noun to show that one person or thing belongs to another. For example: *Ask Carole if this pen is hers.*; *Mine's the blue one.*

➤ Here are the Spanish possessive pronouns:

Masculine singular	Feminine singular	Masculine plural	Feminine plural	Meaning
el mío	la mía	los míos	las mías	mine
el tuyo	la tuya	los tuyos	las tuyas	yours (*belonging to* tú)
el suyo	la suya	los suyos	las suyas	his; hers; its; yours (*belonging to* usted)
el nuestro	la nuestra	los nuestros	las nuestras	ours
el vuestro*	la vuestra*	los vuestros*	las vuestras*	yours (*belonging to* vosotros/vosotras)
el suyo	la suya	los suyos	las suyas	theirs; yours (*belonging to* ustedes)

Not normally used in Latin America, where* **el suyo, **la suya**, *etc. are used instead. For more information on* ***Ways of saying 'you' in Spanish***, *see page 44.*

Pregúntale a Cristina si este abrigo es el suyo.	Ask Cristina if this coat is hers.
¿Qué equipo ganó, el suyo o el nuestro?	Which team won – theirs or ours?
Mi perro es más joven que el tuyo.	My dog is younger than yours.
Daniel pensó que esos libros eran los suyos.	Daniel thought those books were his.
Si no tienes lápices, te prestaré los míos.	If you haven't got any pencils, I'll lend you mine.
Nuestros productos compiten con los suyos.	Our products compete with yours.

> *Tip*
> In Spanish, possessive pronouns agree with what they describe, NOT with the person who owns that thing. For example, **el suyo** can mean *his*, *hers*, *yours* or *theirs*, but can only be used to replace a masculine singular noun.

[i] Note that the prepositions **a** and **de** combine with the article **el** to form **al** and **del**. For example: **a + el mío** becomes **al mío**, and **de + el mío** becomes **del mío**.

Prefiero tu barrio al mío.	I prefer your neighborhood to mine.
Su vestido se parece al tuyo.	Her dress is similar to yours.
Mi abrigo estaba al lado del suyo.	My coat was next to hers/his/yours.
El colegio de Lupe está cerca del nuestro.	Lupe's school is near ours.

➤ Instead of **el suyo/la suya/los suyos/las suyas**, it is sometimes clearer to say **el/la/los/las de usted**, **el/la/los/las de ustedes**, **el/la/los/las de ellos** and so on. You choose between **el/la/los/las** to agree with the noun that is being referred to.

mi casa y la de ustedes	my house and yours

➤ **el/la/los/las de** can also be used with a name or other noun that is referring to somebody.

El dibujo de Juan no está mal pero yo prefiero el de Ana.	Juan's drawing is not bad, but I prefer Ana's.
Nuestro jardín no es tan grande como el de los vecinos.	Our yard isn't as big as the neighbors'.

Key points

✔ The Spanish possessive pronouns are **el mío**, **el tuyo**, **el suyo**, **el nuestro**, **el vuestro** (in Spain only) and **el suyo** when they stand in for a masculine noun. If they stand in for a feminine or a plural noun, their forms change accordingly.

✔ In Spanish, the pronoun you choose has to agree with the noun it replaces and not with the person who owns that thing.

✔ **el/la/los/las de** are used with a noun or pronoun to mean the *one(s) belonging to ...*

Indefinite pronouns

What is an indefinite pronoun?
An **indefinite pronoun** is one of a small group of pronouns, such as *everything*, *nobody* and *something*, which are used to refer to people or things in a general way, without saying exactly who or what they are.

➤ Here are the most common Spanish indefinite pronouns:

- **algo** something, anything

  Tengo algo para ti. — I have something for you.
  ¿Viste algo? — Did you see anything?

- **alguien** somebody, anybody

  Alguien me lo dijo. — Somebody told me.
  ¿Viste a alguien? — Did you see anybody?

Tip

Don't forget to use the personal **a** before indefinite pronouns that refer to people when they are used as the object of a verb.

¿Viste a alguien? — Did you see anybody?
No vi a nadie. — I didn't see anybody.

➪ *For more information on **Personal** a, see page 184.*

- **alguno/alguna/algunos/algunas** some, a few

  Algunos de los niños ya saben leer. — Some of the children can already read.

- **cada uno/una** each (one), everybody

  Le dio una manzana a cada uno. — She gave each one an apple.
  Cada uno pidió lo que quiso. — Everybody ordered what they wanted.

- **cualquiera** anybody; any

  Cualquiera puede hacerlo. — Anybody can do it.
  Cualquiera de las explicaciones vale. — Any of the explanations is valid.

- **mucho/mucha/muchos/muchas** much; many

  Muchas de las casas no tenían jardín. — Many of the houses didn't have a yard.

- **nada** nothing, anything

  ¿Qué tienes en la mano? – Nada. What do you have in your hand? – Nothing.

  No dijo nada. He didn't say anything.

- **nadie** nobody, anybody

  Nadie nos vio. Nobody saw us.

  No quiere ver a nadie. He doesn't want to see anybody.

Tip

Don't forget to use the personal **a** before indefinite pronouns that refer to people when they are used as the object of a verb.

¿Viste a alguien? Did you see anybody?

No vi a nadie. I didn't see anybody.

➪ *For more information on **Personal** a, see page 184.*

- **ninguno/ninguna** none, any

  ¿Cuántas tienes? – Ninguna. How many do you have? – None.

  No me queda ninguno. I haven't any left *or* I have none left.

- **otro/otra/otros/otras** another one; others

  No me gusta este modelo. ¿Tienes otro? I don't like this model. Do you have another?

ℹ Note that you can never put **un** or **una** before **otro** or **otra**.

- **poco/poca/pocos/pocas** little; few

  sólo unos pocos only a few

- **tanto/tanta/tantos/tantas** so much; so many

  ¿Se oía mucho ruido? – No tanto. Was there a lot of noise? – Not so much.

- **todo/toda/todos/todas** all; everything

  Lo estropeó todo. He spoiled everything.

  Todo va bien. It's all going well.

- **uno … el otro/una … la otra** (the) one … the other

  Uno dijo que sí y el otro que no. One said yes while the other said no.

- **unos … los otros/unas … las otras** some … the others

  Unos son de oro, los otros de plata. Some are gold, the others silver.

- **varios/varias** several

Varios de ellos me gustan mucho.	I like several of them very much.

Tip

Don't forget to make those pronouns that have feminine and plural forms agree with the noun they refer to.

Toma esta goma, yo tengo otra.	Take his eraser, I have another one.

Note that **algo**, **alguien** and **alguno** can NEVER be used after a negative such as **no**. Instead you must use the appropriate negative pronouns, **nada**, **nadie**, **ninguno**.

No veo a nadie.	I can't see anybody.
No tengo nada que hacer.	I don't have anything to do.

➤ You use **nada**, **nadie** and **ninguno** on their own, without **no**, to answer questions.

¿Qué pasa? – Nada.	What's happening? – Nothing.
¿Quién llamó? – Nadie.	Who called? – Nobody.
¿Cuántos quedan? – Ninguno.	How many are left? – None.

➤ You also use **nada**, **nadie** and **ninguno** on their own, without **no**, when they come before a verb.

Nada lo asusta.	Nothing frightens him.
Nadie dijo nada.	Nobody said anything.
Ninguno de mis amigos quiso venir.	None of my friends wanted to come.

➪ *For more information on* **Negatives**, *see page 159.*

Key points

✔ Where indefinite pronouns have alternative endings, they must agree with the noun they refer to.

✔ *Anything* is usually translated by **algo** in questions and by **nada** in sentences containing **no**.

✔ *Anybody* is usually translated by **alguien** in questions and by **nadie** in sentences containing **no**.

✔ When **nada**, **nadie** or **ninguno** come after the verb, remember to put **no** before it. When they come before the verb, don't use **no**.

Relative pronouns

What is a relative pronoun?
In English, a **relative pronoun** is a word such as *who*, *which* or *that* (and the more formal *whom*) which can be used to introduce information that makes it clear which person or thing is being talked about. For example: *The man who has just come in is Ann's boyfriend.*; *The vase that you broke was quite valuable.*
Relative pronouns can also introduce additional information about someone or something. For example: *Peter, who is a brilliant painter, wants to study art.*; *Jane's house, which was built in 1890, needs a lot of repairs.*

1 Relative pronouns referring to people

➤ In English, we use the relative pronouns *who*, *whom* and *that* to talk about people. In Spanish, **que** is used.

el hombre que vino ayer	the man who came yesterday
Mi hermano, que tiene veinte años, es mecánico.	My brother, who is twenty, is a mechanic.
el hombre que vi en la calle	the man (that) I saw in the street

Tip
In English, we often leave out the relative pronouns *who*, *whom* and *that*. For example, we can say both *the friends that I see most*, or *the friends I see most*.
In Spanish, you can NEVER leave out **que** in this way.

➤ When the relative pronoun is used with a preposition, use **el/la/los/las que** or **quien/quienes** which must agree with the noun it replaces; **el que** changes for the feminine and plural forms, **quien** changes only in the plural.

➤ Here are the Spanish relative pronouns referring to people that are used after a preposition:

	Masculine	Feminine	Meaning
Singular	**el que** **quien**	**la que** **quien**	who, that, whom
Plural	**los que** **quienes**	**las que** **quienes**	who, that, whom

las mujeres con <u>las que</u> *or* **con <u>quienes</u> estaba hablando**	the women (that) she was talking to
La chica de <u>la que</u> *or* **de <u>quien</u> te hablé llega mañana.**	The girl (that) I told you about is arriving tomorrow.
los niños de <u>los que</u> *or* **de <u>quienes</u> te ocupas**	the children (that) you take care of

i Note that when **de** is used with **el que**, they combine to become **del que**. When **a** is used with **el que**, they combine to become **al que**.

el hombre <u>del que</u> te hablé	the man I told you about
Vive con un hombre <u>al que</u> adora.	She lives with a man she adores.

> *Tip*
>
> In English, we often put prepositions at the end of the sentence (for example: *the man she was talking to*). In Spanish, you can <u>never</u> put a preposition at the end of a sentence.
>
> | | |
> |---|---|
> | **el hombre <u>con el que</u>** *or* **<u>con quien</u> estaba hablando** | the man she was talking to |
>
> ⇨ *For more information on* ***Prepositions****, see page 180.*

2 Relative pronouns referring to things

➤ In English, we use the relative pronouns *which* and *that* to talk about things. In Spanish, **que** is used.

la novela <u>que</u> ganó el premio	the novel <u>that</u> *or* <u>which</u> won the prize
el CD <u>que</u> compré	the CD (<u>that</u> *or* <u>which</u>) I bought

> *Tip*
>
> In English, we often leave out the relative pronouns *which* and *that*. For example, we can say both *the house <u>which</u> we want to buy*, or *the house we want to buy*.
>
> In Spanish, you can <u>NEVER</u> leave out **que** in this way.

➤ When the relative pronoun is used with a preposition, use **el/la/los/las que**, which must agree with the noun it replaces. Here are the Spanish relative pronouns referring to things that are used after a preposition:

	Masculine	Feminine	Meaning
Singular	el que	la que	which, that
Plural	los que	las que	which, that

la iglesia a la que siempre va	the church (that *or* which) she always goes to
los temas de los que habla	the subjects he talks about

[i] Note that when **de** is used with **el que**, they combine to become **del que**. When **a** is used with **el que**, they combine to become **al que**.

el programa del que te hablé	the program I told you about
el banco al que fuiste	the bank you went to

➤ The neuter form **lo que** is used when referring to the whole of the previous part of the sentence.

No había nadie, lo que me pareció raro.	There was nobody there, which I thought was strange.

⇨ *For more information on lo que, see page 17.*

Tip

In English, we often put prepositions at the end of the sentence (for example: *the church she always goes to*). In Spanish, you can never put a preposition at the end of a sentence.

la iglesia a la que siempre va	the church she always goes to
la película de la que te hablaba	the movie I was telling you about

Grammar Extra!

In English, we can use *whose* to show possession (for example: *the woman whose son is ill*). In Spanish, you use **cuyo/cuya/cuyos/cuyas**; **cuyo** is actually an adjective and must agree with the noun it describes NOT with the person who owns that thing.

La mujer, cuyo nombre era Antonia, estaba jubilada.	The woman, whose name was Antonia, was retired.
el señor en cuya casa me alojé	the gentleman whose house I stayed in

In your reading, you may come across the forms **el cual/la cual/los cuales/las cuales**, which are a more formal alternative to **el que/la que/los que/las que** after a preposition.

las mujeres con las cuales estaba hablando	the women (that *or* who) she was talking to
la ventana desde la cual nos observaban	the window from which they were watching us

In other cases, where the pronoun does not immediately follow the person or thing it refers to, **el cual/la cual/los cuales/las cuales** are also useful to make it clear who you are talking about.

El padre de Elena, el cual tiene mucho dinero, es ...	Elena's father, who has a lot of money, is ...

3 Other uses of el que, la que, los que, las que

➤ You can use **el que**, **la que**, **los que**, **las que** to mean *the one(s) (who/which)* or *those who*.

Esa película es la que quiero ver.	That movie is the one I want to see.
los que quieren irse	those who want to leave

Key points

- ✔ **que** can refer to both people and things in Spanish.
- ✔ In English we often leave out the relative pronouns *who*, *which* and *that*, but in Spanish you can never leave out **que**.
- ✔ After a preposition you use **el que/la que/los que/las que** or **quien/quienes** if you are referring to people; you use **el que/la que/los que/las que** if you are referring to things. **el que** and **quien** must agree with the nouns they replace.
- ✔ **a + el que → al que**
  de + el que → del que
- ✔ In Spanish, never put the preposition at the end of a sentence.
- ✔ **el que/la que/los que** and **las que** are also used to mean *the one(s) who/which* or *those who*.

Interrogative pronouns

What is an interrogative pronoun?
In English, an **interrogative pronoun** is one of the words *who*, *which*, *whose*, *whom*, and *what* when they are used without a noun to ask questions.

➤ These are the interrogative pronouns in Spanish:

Singular	Plural	Meaning
¿qué?	¿qué?	what?
¿cuál?	¿cuáles?	which? which one(s)?; what?
¿quién?	¿quiénes?	who? (*as subject or after a preposition*)
¿cuánto?/¿cuánta?	¿cuántos?/¿cuántas?	how much? how many?

[i] Note that, in Spanish, question words have an accent on them.

1 ¿qué?

➤ ¿qué? is the equivalent of *what?* in English.

¿Qué están haciendo? — What are they doing?
¿Qué dices? — What are you saying?
¿Para qué lo quieres? — What do you want it for?

➤ You can use **¿por qué?** in the same way as *why?* in English.

¿Por qué no vienes? — Why don't you come?

2 ¿cuál?, ¿cuáles?

➤ ¿cuál? and **¿cuáles?** are usually the equivalent of *which?* in English and are used when there is a choice between two or more things.

¿Cuál de estos vestidos te gusta más? — Which of these dresses do you like best?
¿Cuáles quieres? — Which (ones) do you want?

[i] Note that you don't use **cuál** before a noun; use **qué** instead.

¿Qué libro es más interesante? — Which book is more interesting?

⇨ *For more information on **Interrogative adjectives**, see page 32.*

3 qué es or cuál es?

➤ You should only use **¿qué es …?** (meaning *what is…?*) and **¿qué son …?** (meaning *what are…?*) when you are asking someone to define, explain or classify something.

¿Qué es esto?	What is this?
¿Qué son los genes?	What are genes?

➤ Use **¿cuál es …?** and **¿cuáles son …?** (also meaning *what is …?* and *what are …?*) when you want someone to specify a particular detail, number, name and so on.

¿Cuál es la capital de Venezuela?	What is the capital of Venezuela?
¿Cuál es tu consejo?	What's your advice?

4 ¿quién?

➤ **¿quién?** and **¿quiénes?** are the equivalent of *who?* in English when it is the subject of the verb or when used with a preposition.

¿Quién ganó la carrera?	Who won the race?
¿Con quiénes los viste?	Who did you see them with?
¿A quién se lo diste?	Who did you give it to?

➤ **¿a quién?** and **¿a quiénes?** are the equivalent of *who(m)?* when it is the object of the verb.

¿A quién viste?	Who did you see? *or* Whom did you see?
¿A quiénes ayudaste?	Who did you help? *or* Whom did you help?

➤ **¿de quién?** and **¿de quiénes?** are the equivalent of *whose?* in English.

¿De quién es este libro?	Whose is this book? *or* Whose book is this?
¿De quiénes son estos coches?	Whose are these cars? *or* Whose cars are these?

5 ¿cuánto?, ¿cuántos?

➤ **¿cuánto?** (*masculine*) and **¿cuánta?** (*feminine*) are the equivalent of *how much?* in English. **¿cuántos?** (*masculine plural*) and **¿cuántas?** (*feminine plural*) are the equivalent of *how many?*

¿Cuánto es?	How much is it?
¿Cuántos tienes?	How many do you have?

For further explanation of grammatical terms, please see pages viii-xii.

Demonstrative pronouns

What is a demonstrative pronoun?
In English, a **demonstrative pronoun** is one of the words *this*, *that*, *these*, and *those* used instead of a noun to point people or things out. For example: *That looks fun*.

1 Using demonstrative pronouns

➤ These are the demonstrative pronouns in Spanish:

	Masculine	Feminine	Neuter	Meaning
Singular	**este** **ese** **aquel**	**esta** **esa** **aquella**	**esto** **eso** **aquello**	this, this one that, that one (*nearby*) that, that one (*further away*)
Plural	**estos** **esos** **aquellos**	**estas** **esas** **aquellas**		these, these ones those, those ones (*nearby*) those, those ones (*further away*)

ℹ Note that the masculine and feminine forms of demonstrative pronouns used to be spelled with an accent on the first 'e', to distinguish them from demonstrative adjectives. The accented forms **éste**, **ésos**, **aquéllas**, etc. are still used by many people but the accent is only necessary in the rare cases when the sentence might otherwise be misunderstood.

➤ In Spanish, demonstrative pronouns have to agree with the noun that they are replacing.

¿Qué abrigo te gusta más? – Este. — Which coat do you like best? – This one.

Estos libros son míos y esos son tuyos. — These books are mine and those are yours.

Esas sandalias son de cuero pero aquellos no. — Those sandals are made of leather but those over there aren't.

2 ¿ese or aquel?

➤ In English we use *that* and *those* to talk about anything that is not nearby. In Spanish, you need to be a bit more precise.

➤ Use **ese/esa** and so on to indicate things and people that are nearer to the person you're talking to than to you.

Me gusta más ese que tienes en la mano. — I prefer the one you have in your hand.

➤ Use **ese/esa** and so on to indicate things and people that aren't very far away.

Si no apetece este restaurante podemos ir a ese de enfrente.	If you don't like this restaurant, we can go to that one opposite.

➤ Use **aquel/aquella** and so on to talk about things that are further away.

Mi casa es aquella al fondo de la calle.	My house is that one at the end of the street.

➤ The neuter forms (**esto**, **eso**, **aquello**) are used to talk about an object you don't recognize or about an idea or statement.

¿Qué es eso que llevas en la mano?	What's that you have in your hand?
No puedo creer que esto me esté pasando a mí.	I can't believe this is really happening to me.
Aquello sí que me gustó.	I really did like that.

ℹ Note that the neuter forms of demonstrative pronouns NEVER have an accent.

Key points

✔ In Spanish, demonstrative pronouns agree with the noun they are replacing.

✔ In Spanish you have to choose the correct pronoun to emphasize the difference between something that is near to you and something that is further away:
- **este/esta/estos** and **estas** (meaning *this/these*) are used to indicate things and people that are very close.
- **ese/esa/esos** and **esas** (meaning *that/those*) are used to indicate things and people that are near the person you are talking to or that aren't too far away.
- **aquel/aquella/aquellos/aquellas** (meaning *that/those*) are used to indicate things and people that are further away.

✔ The neuter pronouns (**esto**, **eso** and **aquello**) are used to talk about things you don't recognize or to refer to statements or ideas. They never have an accent.

Verbs

What is a verb?
A **verb** is a 'doing' word which describes what someone or something does, what someone or something is, or what happens to them. For example: *be*, *sing*, *live*.

Overview of verbs

➤ Verbs are frequently used with a noun, with somebody's name or, particularly in English, with a pronoun such as *I*, *you* or *she*. They can relate to the present, the past and the future; this is called their tense.

➪ *For more information on* **Nouns** *and* **Pronouns**, *see pages 1 and 41.*

➤ Verbs are either:

- **regular**; their forms follow the normal rules
- **irregular**; their forms do not follow the normal rules

➤ Almost all verbs have a form called the infinitive. This is a base form of the verb (for example, *walk*, *see*, *hear*) that hasn't had any endings attached to it and doesn't relate to any particular tense. In English, the infinitive is usually shown with *to*, as in *to speak*, *to eat*, *to live*.

➤ In Spanish, the infinitive is always made up of just one word (never two, as in *to speak* in English) and ends in **-ar**, **-er** or **-ir**. For example: **hablar** (meaning *to speak*), **comer** (meaning *to eat*) and **vivir** (meaning *to live*). All Spanish verbs belong to one of these three types, which are called conjugations. We will look at each of these three conjugations in turn on the next few pages.

➤ Regular English verbs have other forms apart from the infinitive: a form ending in *-s* (*walks*), a form ending in *-ing* (*walking*), and a form ending in *-ed* (*walked*).

➤ Spanish verbs have many more forms than this, which are made up of endings attached to a stem. The stem of a verb can usually be worked out from the infinitive.

➤ Spanish verb endings change depending on who or what is doing the action and on when the action takes place. In fact, the ending is very often the only thing that shows you <u>who</u> is doing the action, as the Spanish equivalents of *I*, *you*, *he* and so on (**yo**, **tú**, **él** and so on) are not used very much. So, both **hablo** on its own and **yo hablo** mean *I speak*. Sometimes there is a name or a noun in the sentence to make it clear who is doing the action.

<u>José</u> habla español.	<u>José</u> speaks Spanish.
<u>El profesor</u> habla español.	<u>The teacher</u> speaks Spanish.

➪ *For more information on* ***Subject pronouns****, see page 42.*

➤ Spanish verb forms also change depending on whether you are talking about the present, past or future, so **(yo) habl<u>aré</u>** means *I will speak* while **(yo) habl<u>é</u>** means *I spoke*.

➤ Some verbs in Spanish do not follow the usual patterns. These <u>irregular verbs</u> include some very common and important verbs like **ir** (meaning *to go*), **ser** and **estar** (meaning *to be*) and **hacer** (meaning *to do* or *to make*). Other verbs are only slightly irregular, changing their stems in certain tenses.

➪ *For* ***Verb Tables****, see the middle section of this book.*

Key points

✔ Spanish verbs have different forms depending on who or what is doing the action and on the tense.

✔ Spanish verb forms are made up of a stem and an ending. The stem is usually based on the infinitive of the verb. The ending depends on who or what is doing the action and on when the action takes place.

✔ Regular verbs follow the standard patterns for **-ar**, **-er** and **-ir** verbs. Irregular verbs do not.

The present tenses

> **What are the present tenses?**
> The **present tenses** are the verb forms that are used to talk about what is true at the moment, what happens regularly and what is happening now. For example: *I'm a student*; *I travel to college by train*; *I'm studying languages*.

➤ In English, there are two tenses you can use to talk about the present:

- the present simple tense

  I live here.
  They get up early.

- the present continuous tense

  He is eating an apple.
  You aren't working very hard.

➤ In Spanish, there is also a present simple and a present continuous tense. As in English, the present simple in Spanish is used to talk about:

- things that are generally true

  En invierno hace frío. It's cold in winter.

- things that are true at the moment

  Carlos no come carne. Carlos doesn't eat meat.

- things that happen at intervals

  A menudo vamos al cine. We often go to the movies.

➤ The present continuous tense in Spanish is used to talk about things that are happening right now or at the time of writing:

  Marta está viendo las noticias. Marta is watching the news.

➤ However, there are times where the use of the present tenses in the two languages is not exactly the same.

⇨ *For more information on the use of the* ***Present tenses****, see pages 79 and 85.*

The present simple tense

1 Forming the present simple tense of regular -ar verbs

➤ If the infinitive of the Spanish verb ends in **-ar**, it means that the verb belongs to the first conjugation. For example: **hablar**, **lavar**, **llamar**.

➤ To know which form of the verb to use in Spanish, you need to determine what the stem of the verb is and then attach the correct ending. The stem of regular **-ar** verbs in the present simple tense is formed by taking the infinitive and chopping off **-ar**.

Infinitive	Stem (without -ar)
hablar (*to speak*)	**habl-**
lavar (*to wash*)	**lav-**

➤ Now that you know how to find the stem of a verb you can attach the correct ending. The one you choose will depend on who or what is doing the action.

Note that as the ending generally makes it clear who is doing the action, you usually don't need to add a subject pronoun, such as **yo** (meaning *I*) or **tú** (meaning *you*), as well.

For more information on ***Subject pronouns****, see page 42.*

➤ Here are the present simple endings for regular **-ar** verbs:

Present simple endings	Present simple of hablar	Meaning: *to speak*
-o	(yo) habl<u>o</u>	I speak
-as	(tú) habl<u>as</u>	you speak
-a	(él/ella) habl<u>a</u>	he/she/it speaks
	(usted) habl<u>a</u>	you speak
-amos	(nosotros/nosotras) habl<u>amos</u>	we speak
-áis*	(vosotros/vosotras) habl<u>áis</u>*	you speak
-an	(ellos/ellas) habl<u>an</u> (ustedes) habl<u>an</u>	they speak you speak

*only used in Spain

➤ You use the **él/ella** (*third person singular*) form of the verb with nouns and with people's names when you are just talking about one person, animal or thing.

Lydia habl<u>a</u> inglés. Lydia speaks English.
Mi profesor me ayud<u>a</u> mucho. My teacher helps me a lot.

➤ You use the **ellos/ellas** (*third person plural*) form of the verb with nouns and with people's names when you are talking about more than one person, animal or thing.

Lydia y Carlos hablan inglés.	Lydia and Carlos speak English.
Mis profesores me ayudan mucho.	My teachers help me a lot.

ℹ Note that even though you use the **él/ella** and **ellos/ellas** forms of the verb to talk about things in Spanish, you should never include the pronouns **él**, **ella**, **ellos** or **ellas** themselves in the sentence when referring to things.

Funciona bien.	It works well.
Funcionan bien.	They work well.

➪ *For more information on* ***Ways of saying 'you' in Spanish****, see page 44.*

Key points

✔ Verbs ending in **-ar** belong to the first conjugation. Regular **-ar** verbs form their present tense stem by losing the **-ar**.

✔ The present tense endings for regular **-ar** verbs are: **-o**, **-as**, **-a**, **-amos**, **-áis** (in Spain), **-an**.

✔ You usually don't need to use a pronoun in Spanish as the ending of the verb makes it clear who or what is doing the action.

2 Forming the present simple tense of regular -er verbs

➤ If the infinitive of the Spanish verb ends in **-er**, it means that the verb belongs to the second conjugation. For example, **comer**, **depender**.

➤ The stem of regular **-er** verbs in the present simple tense is formed by taking the infinitive and chopping off **-er**.

Infinitive	**Stem** (without **-er**)
comer (*to eat*)	**com-**
depender (*to depend*)	**depend-**

➤ Now attach the correct ending, depending on who or what is doing the action.

ℹ Note that as the ending generally makes it clear who is doing the action, you usually don't need to add a subject pronoun, such as **yo** (meaning *I*) or **tú** (meaning *you*), as well.

➪ *For more information on* ***Subject pronouns****, see page 42.*

➤ Here are the present simple endings for regular **-er** verbs:

Present simple endings	**Present simple of** comer	**Meaning:** ***to eat***
-o	(yo) como	I eat
-es	(tú) comes	you eat
-e	(él/ella) come	he/she/it eats
	(usted) come	you eat
-emos	(nosotros/nosotras) comemos	we eat
-éis*	(vosotros/vosotras) coméis*	you eat
-en	(ellos/ellas) comen	they eat
	(ustedes) comen	you eat

*only used in Spain

➤ You use the **él/ella** (*third person singular*) form of the verb with nouns and with people's names when you are just talking about one person, animal or thing.

Juan come demasiado. Juan eats too much.
Mi padre me debe 150 pesos. My father owes me 150 pesos.

➤ You use the **ellos/ellas** (*third person plural*) form of the verb with nouns and with people's names when you are talking about more than one person, animal or thing.

Juan y Pedro comen demasiado. Juan and Pedro eat too much.
Mis padres me deben 150 pesos. My parents owe me 150 pesos.

[i] Note that even though you use the **él/ella** and **ellos/ellas** forms of the verb to talk about things in Spanish, you should never include the pronouns **él**, **ella**, **ellos** or **ellas** themselves in the sentence when referring to things.

Vale mucho dinero. It's worth a lot of money.

⇨ *For more information on* ***Ways of saying 'you' in Spanish****, see page 44.*

Key points

✔ Verbs ending in **-er** belong to the second conjugation. Regular **-er** verbs form their present tense stem by losing the **-er**.

✔ The present tense endings for regular **-er** verbs are: **-o**, **-es**, **-e**, **-emos**, **-éis** (in Spain), **-en**.

✔ You usually don't need to use a pronoun in Spanish as the ending of the verb makes it clear who or what is doing the action.

For further explanation of grammatical terms, please see pages viii-xii.

3 Forming the present simple tense of regular -ir verbs

➤ If the infinitive of the Spanish verb ends in **-ir**, it means that the verb belongs to the third conjugation. For example: **vivir**, **recibir**.

➤ The stem of regular **-ir** verbs in the present simple tense is formed by taking the infinitive and chopping off **-ir**.

Infinitive	**Stem** (without -ir)
vivir (*to live*)	viv-
recibir (*to receive, to get*)	recib-

➤ Now attach the correct ending depending on who or what is doing the action.

ℹ Note that as the ending generally makes it clear who is doing the action, you usually don't need to add a subject pronoun, such as **yo** (meaning *I*) or **tú** (meaning *you*), as well.

➪ *For more information on* ***Subject pronouns****, see page 42.*

➤ Here are the present simple endings for regular **-ir** verbs:

Present simple endings	**Present simple of** vivir	**Meaning:** ***to live***
-o	(yo) viv<u>o</u>	I live
-es	(tú) viv<u>es</u>	you live
-e	(él/ella) viv<u>e</u>	he/she/it lives
	(usted) viv<u>e</u>	you live
-imos	(nosotros/nosotras) viv<u>imos</u>	we live
-ís*	(vosotros/vosotras) viv<u>ís</u>*	you live
-en	(ellos/ellas) viv<u>en</u>	they live
	(ustedes) viv<u>en</u>	you live

*only used in Spain

➤ You use the **él/ella** (*third person singular*) form of the verb with nouns and with people's names when you are just talking about one person, animal or thing.

Javier viv<u>e</u> en Palenque. Javier lives in Palenque.
Mi padre recib<u>e</u> muchas cartas. My father gets a lot of letters.

➤ You use the **ellos/ellas** (*third person plural*) form of the verb with nouns and with people's names, when you are talking about more than one person, animal or thing.

Javier y Antonia viv<u>en</u> en Palenque. Javier and Antonia live in Palenque.

Mis padres reciben muchas cartas. My parents get a lot of letters.

Note that even though you use the **él/ella** and **ellos/ellas** forms of the verb to talk about things in Spanish, you should never include the pronouns **él**, **ella**, **ellos** or **ellas** themselves in the sentence when referring to things.

Ocurre muy a menudo. It happens very often.

For more information on ***Ways of saying 'you' in Spanish****, see page 44.*

Key points

- ✔ Verbs ending in **-ir** belong to the third conjugation. Regular **-ir** verbs form their present tense stem by losing the **-ir**.
- ✔ The present tense endings for regular **-ir** verbs are: **- o**, **-es**, **-e**, **-imos**, **-ís** (in Spain), **-en**.
- ✔ You usually don't need to use a pronoun in Spanish as the ending of the verb makes it clear who or what is doing the action.

4 Forming the present simple tense of less regular verbs

- ➤ Many Spanish verbs do not follow the regular patterns shown previously. There are lots of verbs that change their stem in the present tense when the stress is on the stem. This means that all forms are affected in the present simple APART FROM the **nosotros** and **vosotros** forms. Such verbs are often called radical-changing verbs, meaning root-changing verbs.
- ➤ For example, some verbs containing an **-o** in the stem change it to **-ue** in the present simple for all forms APART FROM the **nosotros/nosotras** and **vosotros/vosotras** forms.

	encontrar *to find*	**recordar** *to remember*	**poder** *to be able*	**dormir** *to sleep*
(yo)	**encuentro**	**recuerdo**	**puedo**	**duermo**
(tú)	**encuentras**	**recuerdas**	**puedes**	**duermes**
(él/ella/usted)	**encuentra**	**recuerda**	**puede**	**duerme**
(nosotros/as)	**encontramos**	**recordamos**	**podemos**	**dormimos**
(vosotros/as)*	**encontráis***	**recordáis***	**podéis***	**dormís***
(ellos/ellas/ustedes)	**encuentran**	**recuerdan**	**pueden**	**duerme**

*only used in Spain

➤ Other verbs containing an **-e** in the stem change it to **-ie** for all forms APART FROM the **nosotros/nosotras** and **vosotros/vosotras** forms.

	cerrar *to close, to shut*	pensar *to think*	entender *to understand*	perder *to lose*	preferir *to prefer*
(yo)	cierro	pienso	entiendo	pierdo	prefiero
(tú)	cierras	piensas	entiendes	pierdes	prefieres
(él/ella/usted)	cierra	piensa	entiende	pierde	prefiere
(nosotros/as)	cerramos	pensamos	entendemos	perdemos	preferimos
(vosotros/as)*	cerráis*	pensáis*	entendéis*	perdéis*	preferís*
(ellos/ellas/ustedes)	cierran	piensan	entienden	pierden	prefieren

*only used in Spain

➤ A few **-ir** verbs containing **-e** in the stem change this to **-i** in the present simple for all forms APART FROM the **nosotros/nosotras** and **vosotros/vosotras** forms.

	pedir *to ask (for)*	servir *to serve*
(yo)	pido	sirvo
(tú)	pides	sirves
(él/ella/usted)	pide	sirve
(nosotros/as)	pedimos	servimos
(vosotros/as)*	pedís*	servís*
(ellos/ellas/ustedes)	piden	sirven

*only used in Spain

➤ If you are not sure whether a Spanish verb belongs to this group of radical-changing verbs, you can look up the **Verb Tables** in the middle section of this book.

➪ *For more information on **Spelling**, see page 198.*

5 Forming the present simple tense of common irregular verbs

➤ There are many other verbs that do not follow the standard patterns in Spanish. These include some very common and important verbs such as **tener** (meaning *to have*), **hacer** (meaning *to do* or *to make*) and **ir** (meaning *to go*). These verbs are shown in full on the next page.

➤ Here are the present simple tense endings for **tener**:

	tener	**Meaning:** ***to have***
(yo)	tengo	I have
(tú)	tienes	you have
(él/ella/usted)	tiene	he/she/it has, you have
(nosotros/nosotras)	tenemos	we have
(vosotros/vosotras)*	tenéis*	you have
(ellos/ellas/ustedes)	tienen	they have, you have

*only used in Spain

Tengo dos hermanas.	I have two sisters.
No tengo dinero.	I don't have any money.
¿Cuántas clases tienes hoy?	How many classes do you have today?
Tiene el pelo largo.	He has long hair.

➤ Here are the present simple tense endings for **hacer**:

	hacer	**Meaning:** ***to do, to make***
(yo)	hago	I do, I make
(tú)	haces	you do, you make
(él/ella/usted)	hace	he/she/it does, he/she/it makes, you do, you make
(nosotros/nosotras)	hacemos	we do, we make
(vosotros/vosotras)*	hacéis*	you do, you make
(ellos/ellas/ustedes)	hacen	they do, they make, you do, you make

*only used in Spain

Hago la cena todos los días.	I make dinner every day.
No hago mucho deporte.	I don't play a lot of sports.
¿Qué haces?	What are you doing?
¿Qué hace tu padre?	What does your father do?

For further explanation of grammatical terms, please see pages viii-xii.

➤ Here are the present simple tense endings for **ir**:

	ir	**Meaning:** ***to go***
(yo)	voy	I go
(tú)	vas	you go
(él/ella/usted)	va	he/she/it goes, you go
(nosotros/nosotras)	vamos	we go
(vosotros/vosotras)*	vais*	you go
(ellos/ellas/ustedes)	van	they go, you go

*only used in Spain

Voy a Miami. — I'm going to Miami.
¿Adónde vas? — Where are you going?
No va al colegio. — He doesn't go to school.
Nunca van al teatro. — They never go to the theater.

➪ *For other irregular verbs in the present simple tense, see* ***Verb Tables*** *in the middle section of this book.*

6 How to use the present simple tense in Spanish

➤ The present simple tense is often used in Spanish in the same way as it is in English, although there are some differences.

➤ As in English, you use the Spanish present simple to talk about:

- things that are generally true

  En verano hace calor. — It's hot in summer.

- things that are true now

  Viven en Guatemala. — They live in Guatemala.

- things that happen all the time or at certain intervals or that you do as a habit

  Marta usa lentes. — Marta wears glasses.
  Mi tío viaja mucho. — My uncle travels a lot.

- things that you are planning to do

  El domingo jugamos en León. — We're playing in León on Sunday.
  Mañana voy a Puebla. — I am going to Puebla tomorrow.

➤ There are some instances when you would use the present simple in Spanish, but you wouldn't use it in English:

- to talk about current projects and activities that may not actually be going on right at this very minute

¿**Llueve**?	Is it raining?

- when you use certain time expressions in Spanish, especially **desde** (meaning *since*), **desde hace** (meaning *for*) and **hace ... que** (meaning *for*) to talk about activities and states that started in the past and are still going on now

Jaime estudia inglés desde hace dos años.	Jaime has been learning English for two years.
Daniel trabaja aquí desde 1999.	Daniel has worked here since 1999.
Hace tres años que vivo en California.	I've been living in California for three years.
Hace años que no la veo.	I haven't seen her for years.

⇨ *For more information on the use of tenses with* **desde**, *see page* 191.

ser and estar

➤ In Spanish there are two irregular verbs, **ser** and **estar**, that both mean *to be*, although they are used very differently. In the present simple tense, they follow the patterns shown below.

Pronoun	ser	estar	Meaning: *to be*
(yo)	soy	estoy	I am
(tú)	eres	estás	you are
(él/ella/usted)	es	está	he/she/it is, you are
(nosotros/nosotras)	somos	estamos	we are
(vosotros/vosotras)*	sois*	estáis*	you are
(elllos/ellas/ustedes)	son	están	they/you are

*only used in Spain

➤ **ser** is used:

- with an adjective when talking about a characteristic or fairly permanent quality (for example: shape, size, height, color, material, nationality).

  Mi hermano es alto. — My brother is tall.
  María es inteligente. — María is intelligent.
  Es americana. — She's American.
  Es muy bonita. — She's very pretty.
  Es rojo. — It's red.
  Es de algodón. — It's made of cotton.
  Sus padres son italianos. — His parents are Italian.
  Es joven/viejo. — He's young/old.
  Son muy ricos/pobres. — They're very rich/poor.

- followed by a noun or pronoun that tells you what someone or something is

  Miguel es abogado. — Miguel is a lawyer.
  Soy yo, Enrique. — It's me, Enrique.
  Madrid es la capital de España. — Madrid is the capital of Spain.

- to say that something belongs to someone

  La casa es de mis padres. — The house belongs to my parents.
  Es mío. — It's mine.

- to talk about where someone or something comes from

  Yo soy de Santa Clara. — I'm from Santa Clara.
  Mi esposa es de La Habana. — My wife is from Havana.

- to say what time it is or what the date is

Son las tres y media.	It's half past three.
Mañana es sábado.	Tomorrow is Saturday.

- in calculations

Tres y dos son cinco.	Three and two are five.
¿Cuánto es? – Son veinte dólares.	How much is it? It's twenty dollars.

- when followed by an infinitive

Lo importante es decir la verdad.	The important thing is to tell the truth.

⇨ *For more information on the **Infinitive**, see page 146.*

- to describe actions using the passive (for example *they are made, it is sold*)

Son pintados a mano.	They are hand painted.

- to talk about where an event is taking place

La boda será en Madrid.	The wedding will be in Madrid.

⇨ *For more information on the **Passive**, see page 125.*

➤ **estar** is used:

- to talk about where someone or something (other than an event) is

Estoy en casa.	I'm at home.
¿Dónde está la estación?	Where's the station?

- with an adjective when there has been a change in the condition of someone or something or to suggest that there is something unexpected about them

El café está frío.	The coffee's cold.
¡Qué elegante estás con ese vestido!	How elegant you look in that dress!

⇨ *For more information on **Adjectives**, see page 19.*

- with a past participle used as an adjective, to describe the state that something is in

Las tiendas están cerradas.	The stores are closed.
No está terminado.	It isn't finished.
Está roto.	It's broken.

⇨ *For more information on **Past participles**, see page 118.*

- when talking about someone's health

¿Cómo están?	How are you?
Estamos todos bien.	We're all well.

- to form continuous tenses such as the present continuous tense

Está comiendo.	He's eating.
Estamos aprendiendo mucho.	We are learning a great deal.

➪ *For more information on the **Present continuous**, see page 85.*

➤ Both **ser** and **estar** can be used with certain adjectives, but the meaning changes depending on which is used.

➤ Use **ser** to talk about permanent qualities.

Es muy viejo.	He's very old.
Juan es alto y delgado.	Juan is tall and slim.
Viajar es cansado.	Traveling is tiring.
La química es aburrida.	Chemistry is boring.

➤ Use **estar** to talk about temporary states or qualities.

Está muy viejo.	He's not young any more./ He's aged a lot.
¡Estás muy delgada!	You're looking very thin!/ You've lost a lot of weight!
Hoy estoy cansado.	I'm tired today.
Estoy aburrido.	I'm bored.

➤ **ser** is used with adjectives such as **importante** (meaning *important*) and **imposible** (meaning *impossible*) when the subject is *it* in English.

Es muy interesante.	It's very interesting.
Es imposible.	It's impossible.
Es fácil.	It's easy.

➤ **ser** is used in certain set phrases.

Es igual *or* **Es lo mismo.**	It's all the same.
Es para ti.	It's for you.

➤ **estar** is also used in some set phrases.

- **estar de pie** — to be standing
  Juan está de pie. — Juan is standing.
- **estar de vacaciones** — to be on vacation
  Mi jefe está de vacaciones. — My boss is on vacation.
- **estar de viaje** — to be on a trip
  Mi padre está de viaje. — My father's on a trip.

- **estar de moda** — to be in fashion
  El negro está de moda. — Black is in fashion.
- **estar claro** — to be obvious
  Está claro que no entiendes. — It's obvious that you don't understand.

Grammar Extra!

Both **ser** and **estar** can be used with past participles.

Use **ser** and the past participle in passive constructions to describe an action.

Son pintados a mano. — They are hand painted.

Use **estar** and the past participle to describe a state.

Está terminado. — It's finished.

➪ *For more information on **Past participles**, see page 118.*

Key points

- ✔ **ser** and **estar** both mean *to be* in English, but are used very differently.
- ✔ **ser** and **estar** are irregular verbs. You have to learn them.
- ✔ Use **ser** with adjectives describing permanent qualities or characteristics; with nouns or pronouns telling you who or what somebody or something is; with time and dates; and to form the passive.
- ✔ Use **estar** to talk about location and health; with adjectives describing a change of state; and with past participles used as adjectives to describe states.
- ✔ **estar** is also used to form present continuous tenses.
- ✔ **ser** and **estar** can sometimes be used with the same adjectives, but the meaning changes depending on which verb is used.
- ✔ **ser** and **estar** are both used in a number of set phrases.

The present continuous tense

➤ In Spanish, the present continuous tense is used to talk about something that is happening at this very moment.

➤ The Spanish present continuous tense is formed from the present tense of **estar** and the gerund of the verb. The gerund is the form of the verb that ends in **-ando** (for **-ar** verbs) or **-iendo** (for **-er** and **-ir** verbs) and is the same as the *-ing* form of the verb in English (for example, *walking*, *swimming*).

Estoy trabajando — I'm working.
No estamos discutiendo. — We aren't arguing.
¿Estás escuchando? — Are you listening?

➪ *For more information on estar and the **Gerund**, see pages 80 and 128.*

➤ To form the gerund of an **-ar** verb, drop the **-ar** ending of the infinitive and attach **-ando:**

Infinitive	Meaning	Stem (without -ar)	Gerund	Meaning
hablar	to speak	**habl-**	**hablando**	speaking
trabajar	to work	**trabaj-**	**trabajando**	working

➤ To form the gerund of an **-er** or **-ir** verb, drop the **-er** or **-ir** ending of the infinitive and attach **-iendo**:

Infinitive	Meaning	Stem (without -er/-ir)	Gerund	Meaning
comer	to eat	**com-**	**comiendo**	eating
escribir	to write	**escrib-**	**escribiendo**	writing

Tip

Only use the present continuous to talk about things that are in the middle of happening right now. Use the present simple tense instead to talk about activities that are current, but which may not be happening at this minute.

Mariá trabaja en el hospital. — Mariá works at the hospital.

➪ *For more information on the **Present simple tense**, see page 72.*

Key points

✔ Only use the present continuous in Spanish for actions that are happening right now.

✔ To form the present continuous tense in Spanish, take the present tense of **estar** and add the gerund of the main verb.

The imperative

What is the imperative?
An **imperative** is a form of the verb used when giving orders and instructions. For example: *Sit down!; Don't go!; Let's start!*

1 Using the imperative

➤ In Spanish, the form of the imperative that you use for giving instructions depends on:

- whether you are telling someone to do something or not to do something
- whether you are talking to one person or to more than one person
- whether you are on familiar or more formal terms with the person or people

➤ These imperative forms correspond to the familiar **tú** (and **vosotros/vosotras** in Spain), to the more formal **usted** and to **ustedes**, although you don't actually say these pronouns when giving instructions.

➪ *For more information on **Ways of saying 'you' in Spanish**, see page 44.*

➤ There is also a form of the imperative that corresponds to *let's* in English.

2 Forming the imperative: instructions not to do something

➤ In orders that tell you NOT to do something and that have **no** in front of them in Spanish, the imperative forms for **tú**, **usted**, **nosotros/nosotras**, **vosotros/vosotras** and **ustedes** are all taken from a verb form called the present subjunctive. It's easy to remember because the endings for **-ar** and **-er** verbs are the opposite of what they are in the ordinary present tense.

➪ *For more information on the **Present tense** and the **Subjunctive**, see pages 71 and 134.*

➤ In regular **-ar** verbs, you drop the **-as**, **-a**, **-amos**, **-áis** and **-an** endings of the present tense and replace them with: **-es**, **-e**, **-emos**, **-éis** and **-en**.

-ar verb	trabajar	to work
tú form	¡no trabajes!	Don't work!
usted form	¡no trabaje!	Don't work!
nosotros/as form	¡no trabajemos!	Let's not work!
vosotros/as form*	¡no trabajéis!*	Don't work!
ustedes form	¡no trabajen!	Don't work!

*only used in Spain

➤ In regular **-er** verbs, you drop the **-es**, **-e**, **-emos**, **-éis** and **-en** endings of the present tense and replace them with **-as**, **-a**, **-amos**, **-áis** and **-an**.

-er **verb**	comer	**to eat**
tú **form** usted **form** nosotros/as **form** vosotros/as **form*** ustedes **form**	¡no comas! ¡no coma! ¡no comamos! ¡no comáis!* ¡no coman!	Don't eat! Don't eat! Let's not eat! Don't eat! Don't eat!

*only used in Spain

➤ In regular **-ir** verbs, you drop the **-es**, **-e**, **-imos**, **-ís** and **-en** endings of the present tense and replace them with **-as**, **-a**, **-amos**, **-áis** and **-an**.

-ir **verb**	decidir	**to decide**
tú **form** usted **form** nosotros/as **form** vosotros/as **form*** ustedes **form**	¡no decidas! ¡no decida! ¡no decidamos! ¡no decidáis!* ¡no decidan!	Don't decide! Don't decide! Let's not decide! Don't decide! Don't decide!

*only used in Spain

➤ A number of irregular verbs also have irregular imperative forms. These are shown in the table below.

	dar **to give**	decir **to say**	estar **to be**	hacer **to do/make**	ir **to go**
tú **form**	¡no des! don't give!	¡no digas! don't say!	¡no estés! don't be!	¡no hagas! don't do/make!	¡no vayas! don't go!
usted **form**	¡no dé! don't give!	¡no diga! don't say!	¡no esté! don't be!	¡no haga! don't do/make!	¡no vaya! don't go!
nosotros **form**	¡no demos! let's not give!	¡no digamos! let's not say!	¡no estemos! let's not be!	¡no hagamos! let's not do/make!	¡no vayamos! let's not go!
vosotros **form***	¡no deis!* don't give!	¡no digáis!* don't say!	¡no estéis!* don't be!	¡no hagáis!* don't do/make!	¡no vayáis!* don't go!
ustedes **form**	¡no den! don't give!	¡no digan! don't say!	¡no estén! don't be!	¡no hagan! don't do/make!	¡no vayan! don't go!
	poner **to put**	salir **to leave**	ser **to be**	tener **to have**	venir **to come**
tú **form**	¡no pongas! don't put!	¡no salgas! don't leave!	¡no seas! don't be!	¡no tengas! don't have!	¡no vengas! don't come!
usted **form**	¡no ponga! don't put!	¡no salga! don't leave!	¡no sea! don't be!	¡no tenga! don't have!	¡no venga! don't come!
nosotros **form**	¡no pongamos! let's not put!	¡no salgamos! let's not leave!	¡no seamos! let's not be!	¡no tengamos! let's not have!	¡no vengamos! let's not come!
vosotros **form***	¡no pongáis!* don't put!	¡no salgáis!* don't leave!	¡no seáis!* don't be!	¡no tengáis!* don't have!	¡no vengáis!* don't come!
ustedes **form**	¡no pongan! don't put!	¡no salgan! don't leave!	¡no sean! don't be!	¡no tengan! don't have!	¡no vengan! don't come!

*only used in Spain

ℹ Note that, for instructions NOT TO DO something, some of these irregular forms will be more predictable if you take the **yo** form of the present tense, drop the **-o** and attach the endings to this instead.

digo *I say* → negative imperative stem → **dig-**
hago *I do* → negative imperative stem → **hag-**
pongo *I put* → negative imperative stem → **pong-**
salgo *I leave* → negative imperative stem → **salg-**
tengo *I have* → negative imperative stem → **teng-**
vengo *I come* → negative imperative stem → **veng-**

3 Forming the imperative: instructions to do something

➤ In instructions telling you TO DO something, the forms for **usted**, **nosotros** and **ustedes** are exactly the same as they are in negative instructions (instructions telling you not to do something) except that there isn't a **no**.

	trabajar to work	**comer to eat**	**decidir to decide**
usted form	**¡Trabaje!**	**¡Coma!**	**¡Decida!**
nosotros/as form	**¡Trabajemos!**	**¡Comamos!**	**¡Decidamos!**
ustedes form	**¡Trabajen!**	**¡Coman!**	**¡Decidan!**

➤ In positive instructions (instructions telling you to do something), there are special forms of the imperative for **tú** and **vosotros/vosotras**.

➤ The **tú** form of the imperative is the same as the **tú** form of the ordinary present simple tense, but without the final **-s**.

trabajar → **¡Trabaja!**
to work — Work!
comer → **¡Come!**
to eat — Eat!
decidir → **¡Decide!**
to decide — Decide!

⇨ *For more information on the* ***Present simple tense****, see page 72.*

➤ The **vosotros/vosotras** form of the imperative, only used in Spain, is the same as the infinitive, except that you drop the final **-r** and attach **-d** instead.

trabajar → **Trabajad!**
to work — Work!
comer → **Comed!**
to eat — Eat!
decidir → **Decidid!**
to decide — Decide!

➤ In Spanish, there are a number of imperative forms that are irregular. The irregular imperative forms for **usted**, **nosotros/nosotras** and **ustedes** are the same as the irregular negative imperative forms without the **no**. The **tú** and **vosotros/vosotras** forms are different again.

	dar to give	**decir** to say	**estar** to be	**hacer** to do/make	**ir** to go
tú **form**	**¡da!** give!	**¡di!** say!	**¡está!** be!	**¡haz!** do/make!	**¡ve!** go!
usted **form**	**¡dé!** give!	**¡diga!** say!	**¡esté!** be!	**¡haga!** do/make!	**¡vaya!** go!
nosotros/as **form**	**¡demos!** let's give!	**¡digamos!** let's say!	**¡estemos!** let's be!	**¡hagamos!** let's do/make!	**¡vamos!** let's go!
vosotros/as **form***	**¡dad!*** give!	**¡decid!*** say!	**¡estad!*** be!	**¡haced!*** do/make!	**¡id!*** go!
ustedes **form**	**¡den!** give!	**¡digan!** say!	**¡estén!** be!	**¡hagan!** do/make!	**¡vayan!** go!
	poner to put	**salir** to leave	**ser** to be	**tener** to have	**venir** to come
tú **form**	**¡pon!** put!	**¡sal!** leave!	**¡sé!** be!	**¡ten!** have!	**¡ven!** come!
usted **form**	**¡ponga!** put!	**¡salga!** leave!	**¡sea!** be!	**¡tenga!** have!	**¡venga!** come!
nosotros/as **form**	**¡pongamos!** let's put!	**¡salgamos!** let's leave!	**¡seamos!** let's be!	**¡tengamos!** let's have!	**¡vengamos!** let's come!
vosotros/as* **form**	**¡poned!*** put!	**¡salid!*** leave!	**¡sed!*** be!	**¡tened!*** have!	**¡venid!*** come!
ustedes **form**	**¡pongan!** put!	**¡salgan!** leave!	**¡sean!** be!	**¡tengan!** have!	**¡vengan!** come!

*only used in Spain

[i] Note that, in instructions TO DO something, the **nosotros/as** form for **ir** is **vamos**; in instructions NOT TO DO something, it is **no vayamos**.

4 Position of object pronouns

➤ An object pronoun is a word that is used instead of a noun as the object of a sentence, like **me** (meaning *me* or *to me*), **la** (meaning *her/it*) or **les** (meaning *to them/to you*). In orders and instructions, the position of these object pronouns in the sentence changes depending on whether you are telling someone TO DO something or NOT TO DO something.

⇨ *For more information on **Object pronouns**, see page 46.*

- If you are telling someone NOT TO DO something, the object pronouns go BEFORE the verb.

¡No me lo mandes!	Don't send it to me!
¡No me molestes!	Don't disturb me!
¡No los castigue!	Don't punish them!
¡No se la devolvamos!	Let's not give it back to him/her/them!

- If you are telling someone TO DO something, the object pronouns are attached to the END of the verb. An accent is usually added to make sure that the stress in the imperative verb stays the same.

¡Explícamelo!	Explain it to me!
¡Perdóneme!	Excuse me!
¡Dígame!	Tell me!
¡Esperémosla!	Let's wait for her/it!

[i] Note that when there are two object pronouns, the indirect object pronoun always goes before the direct object pronoun.

⇨ *For more information on **Stress**, see page 202.*

5 Other ways of giving instructions

- For directions in instruction manuals, recipes and so on, the infinitive form is often used instead of the imperative.

Ver página 9.	See page 9.

- **vamos a** with the infinitive is often used to mean *let's*.

Vamos a ver.	Let's see.
Vamos a empezar.	Let's start.

Key points

- ✔ In Spanish, in instructions not to do something, the endings are taken from the present subjunctive. They are the same as the corresponding endings for **-ar** and **-er** verbs in the ordinary present tense, except that the **-e** endings are attached to the **-ar** verbs and the **-a** endings are attached to the **-er** and **-ir** verbs.
- ✔ For **-ar** verbs, the forms are: **no hables** (**tú** form); **no hable** (**usted** form); **no hablemos** (**nosotros/as** form); **no habléis** (**vosotros/as** form)*; **no hablen** (**ustedes** form).
- ✔ For **-er** verbs, the forms are: **no comas** (**tú** form); **no coma** (**usted** form); **no comamos** (**nosotros/as** form); **no comáis** (**vosotros/as** form)*; **no coman** (**ustedes** form).
- ✔ For **-ir** verbs, the forms are: **no decidas** (**tú** form); **no decida** (**usted** form); **no decidamos** (**nosotros/as** form); **no decidáis** (**vosotros/as** form)*; **no decidan** (**ustedes** form).
- ✔ In instructions to do something, the forms for **usted**, **nosotros/as** and **ustedes** are the same as they are in instructions not to do something.
- ✔ The forms for **tú** and **vosotros/as*** are different:
  - the **tú** form is the same as the corresponding form in the ordinary present tense, but without the final **-s**: **trabaja**; **come**; **decide**
  - the **vosotros/as** form* is the same as the infinitive but with a final **-d** instead of the **-r**: **trabajad**; **comed**; **decidid**
- ✔ A number of verbs have irregular imperative forms.
- ✔ The object pronouns in imperatives go before the verb when telling someone not to do something; they are attached to the end of the verb when telling someone to do something.

*only used in Spain

Reflexive verbs

What is a reflexive verb?
A **reflexive verb** is one where the subject and object are the same, and where the action 'reflects back' on the subject. It is used with a reflexive pronoun such as *myself*, *yourself* and *herself* in English. For example: *I washed myself.*; *He cut himself.*

1 Using reflexive verbs in Spanish

➤ In Spanish, reflexive verbs are not only used to describe things you do to yourself, as they are in English. They often describe actions that involve a change of some sort, for example, going to bed, sitting down, getting angry, and so on, as well as other types of actions. The infinitive form of a reflexive verb has **se** attached to the end of it (for example: **secarse**, which means *to get dry* or *to dry oneself*). This is the way reflexive verbs are shown in dictionaries. **se** is called a reflexive pronoun.

Some of the most common reflexive verbs in Spanish are listed here.

acostarse	to go to bed
afeitarse	to shave
bañarse	to take a bath, to take a shower, to have a swim
dormirse	to go to sleep, to fall asleep
enojarse	to get angry
lavarse	to wash (yourself)
levantarse	to get up, to stand up
llamarse	to be called
secarse	to dry, to get dry, to dry yourself
sentarse	to sit down
vestirse	to get dressed

Siempre nos acostamos temprano.	We always go to bed early.
¿Por qué no te afeitas?	Why don't you shave?
Mi marido se baña por la mañana.	My husband takes a bath in the morning.
¡Duérmete!	Go to sleep!
No te enojes conmigo.	Don't be angry with me.
Mi hermano no se lava.	My brother doesn't wash.
Me levanto a las siete.	I get up at seven o'clock.
¿Cómo te llamas?	What's your name?
¡Siéntense!	Sit down!
Me visto en el baño.	I get dressed in the bathroom.

For further explanation of grammatical terms, please see pages viii-xii.

i Note that **se**, **me** and so on are very rarely translated into English as *himself*, *myself* and so on.

➤ Many Spanish verbs can be used both as reflexive verbs and as ordinary verbs (without the reflexive pronoun). When they are used as ordinary verbs, the person or thing doing the action is not the same as the person or thing receiving the action, so the meaning is different.

Me lavo.	I wash (myself).
Lavo la ropa a mano.	I wash the clothes by hand.
Me llamo Antonio.	I'm called Antonio./ My name is Antonio.
¡Llama a la policía!	Call the police!
Me acuesto a las 11.	I go to bed at 11 o'clock.
Acuesta a Sarita.	Put Sarita to bed.

Grammar Extra!

With some verbs there is a small but important difference in meaning between the reflexive and non-reflexive forms.

Duermo.	I sleep.
Me duermo.	I go to sleep, I fall asleep.
Miguel va al cine todos los sábados.	Miguel goes to the movies every Saturday.
Miguel se va mañana.	Miguel's leaving tomorrow.

2 Forming the present tense of reflexive verbs

➤ When you use a reflexive verb in Spanish, the reflexive pronoun that goes with it varies according to the subject of the verb. The table on the next page shows you which reflexive pronoun to use.

Subject of the verb	Reflexive pronoun to use
(yo)	me
(tú)	te
(él) (ella) (uno) (usted) any singular noun	se
(nosotros/nosotras)	nos
(vosotros/vosotras)*	os*
(ellos) (ellas) (ustedes) Any plural noun or combination or singular or plural nouns joined with y	se

*only used in Spain

(Yo) me levanto temprano.	I get up early.
Pancho todavía no se afeita.	Pancho doesn't shave yet.
(Nosotros) nos vamos mañana.	We are leaving tomorrow.
Ana y Pedro se acuestan a las once.	Ana and Pedro go to bed at eleven.

➤ The present tense forms of a reflexive verb work exactly the same way as an ordinary verb, except that the reflexive pronoun is used as well.

⇨ *For more information on the* ***Present tense****, see page 71.*

➤ The following table shows the reflexive verb **levantarse** in full.

Reflexive forms of levantarse	Meaning
(yo) me levanto	I get up
(tú) te levantas	you get up
(él) se levanta (ella) se levanta (uno) se levanta se levanta (usted) se levanta	he gets up she gets up one gets up it gets up you get up
(nosotros/nosotras) nos levantamos	we get up
(vosotros/vosotras) os levantáis*	you get up
(ellos) se levantan (ellas) se levantan (ustedes) se levantan	they get up they get up you get up

*only used in Spain

➤ Some reflexive verbs, such as **acostarse**, are irregular. Some of these irregular verbs are shown in the **Verb tables** in the middle section of this book.

3 Position of reflexive pronouns

➤ In ordinary tenses such as the present simple, the reflexive pronoun goes BEFORE the verb.

Me acuesto temprano. — I go to bed early.
¿Cómo se llama usted? — What's your name?

➪ *For more information on the **Present simple tense**, see page 72.*

➤ When telling someone NOT TO DO something, you also put the reflexive pronoun BEFORE the verb.

No te levantes. — Don't get up.
¡No se vayan todavía! — Don't go yet!

➤ When telling someone TO DO something, you attach the reflexive pronoun onto the end of the verb.

¡Siéntense! — Sit down!
¡Cállate! — Be quiet!

➪ *For more information on the **Imperative**, see page 86.*

Tip

When attaching reflexive pronouns to the end of the imperative, you drop the final **-s** of the **nosotros** form and the final **-d** of the **vosotros** form, before the pronoun.

¡Vámonos!	Let's go!
¡Sentaos! (*Spain only*)	Sit down!

➤ You always attach the reflexive pronoun onto the end of infinitives and gerunds (the **-ando** or **-iendo** forms of the verb) unless the infinitive or gerund follows another verb.

Hay que relajarse de vez en cuando.	You have to relax from time to time.
Acostándose temprano, se descansa mejor.	You feel more rested if you go to bed early.

➤ Where the infinitive or gerund follows another verb, you can either attach the reflexive pronoun to the end of the infinitive or gerund or put it before the other verb.

Quiero bañarme *or* **Me quiero bañar.**	I want to take a bath.
Tienes que vestirte *or* **Te tienes que vestir.**	You must get dressed.
Está vistiéndose *or* **Se está vistiendo.**	She's getting dressed.
¿Estás durmiéndote? *or* **¿Te estás durmiendo?**	Are you falling asleep?

⇨ *For more information on* ***Gerunds****, see page 128.*

ℹ When attaching pronouns to the ends of verb forms, note that you will often have to add a written accent to preserve the stress.

⇨ *For more information on* ***Stress****, see page 202.*

4 Using reflexive verbs with parts of the body and clothes

➤ In Spanish, you often talk about actions to do with your body or your clothing using a reflexive verb.

Se está secando el pelo.	She's drying her hair.
Nos lavamos los dientes.	We brush our teeth.
Se está poniendo el abrigo.	He's putting on his coat.

Note that in Spanish you do not use a possessive adjective such as *my* and *her* when talking about parts of the body. You use **el**, **la**, **los** and **las** with a reflexive verb instead.

Me estoy lavando las manos.	I'm washing my hands.

For more information on **Articles**, *see page* 10.

5 Other uses of the pronoun se

- In English, we often use a passive construction (for example: *goods are transported all over the world, most of our tea is imported from India and China*). In Spanish, this construction is not used very often. Instead, a construction with **se** is used.

Aquí se vende café.	Coffee is sold here.
Aquí se venden muchos libros.	Lots of books are sold here.
Se habla inglés.	English is spoken here.
En Suiza se hablan tres idiomas.	Three languages are spoken in Switzerland.

Note that the verb has to be singular or plural depending on whether the subject is singular or plural.

For more information on the **Passive**, *see page* 125.

- **se** is also used in impersonal expressions. In this case, it often corresponds to *you* in English.

No se puede entrar.	You can't go in.
No se permite.	It isn't allowed.
¿Cómo se dice "siesta" en inglés?	How do you say "siesta" in English?
¿Cómo se escribe "Tarragona"?	How do you spell "Tarragona"?

For more information on **Impersonal verbs**, *see page* 132.

6 Other uses of the pronoun se, nos and os

- **se**, **nos** and **os** (in Spain only), are all also used to mean *each other* and *one another*.

Nos escribimos.	We write to one another.
Nos queremos.	We love each other.
Rachel y Julie se odian.	Rachel and Julie hate each other.
No se conocen.	They don't know each other.

Key points

- ✔ A reflexive verb is made up of a reflexive pronoun and a verb.
- ✔ The reflexive pronouns are: **me**, **te**, **se**, **nos**, **os** (in Spain only), **se**.
- ✔ The reflexive pronoun goes before the verb, except when you are telling someone to do something and with infinitives and gerunds.

For further explanation of grammatical terms, please see pages viii-xii.

The future tense

What is the future tense?
The **future** tense is a verb tense used to talk about something that will happen or will be true in the future. For example: *He'll be here soon; I'll give you a call; What will you do?; It will be sunny tomorrow*.

1 Ways of talking about the future

➤ In Spanish, just as in English, you can often use the present tense to refer to something that is going to happen in the future.

La película empieza a las nueve. The movie starts at nine o'clock.
Mañana voy a Madrid. I am going to Madrid tomorrow.

➤ In English, we often use *going to* with an infinitive to talk about the immediate future or our future plans. In Spanish, you can use the present tense of **ir** followed by **a** and an infinitive.

Va a perder el tren. He's going to miss the train.
Va a llevar una media hora. It's going to take half an hour.
Voy a hacerlo mañana. I'm going to do it tomorrow.

2 Forming the future tense

➤ In English, we can form the future tense by putting *will* or its contracted form *'ll* before the verb. In Spanish, you have to change the verb endings. So, just as **hablo** means *I speak*, **hablaré** means *I will speak* or *I shall speak*.

➤ To form the future tense of regular **-ar**, **-er** and **-ir** verbs, attach the following endings to the infinitive of the verb: **-é**, **-ás**, **-á**, **-emos**, **-éis**, **-án**.

➤ The following table shows the future tense of three regular verbs: **hablar** (meaning *to speak*), **comer** (meaning *to eat*) and **vivir** (meaning *to live*).

(yo)	hablaré	comeré	viviré	I'll speak/eat/live
(tú)	hablarás	comerás	vivirás	you'll speak/eat/live
(él) (ella) (usted)	hablará	comerá	vivirá	he'll speak/eat/live she'll speak/eat/live it'll speak/eat/live you'll speak/eat/live
(nosotros/nosotras)	hablaremos	comeremos	viviremos	we'll speak/eat/live
(vosotros/vosotras)*	hablaréis*	comeréis*	viviréis*	you'll speak/eat/live
(ellos/ellas/ustedes)	hablarán	comerán	vivirán	they'll/you'll speak/eat/live

*only used in Spain

Hablaré con ella. I'll speak to her.
Comeremos en casa de José. We'll eat at José's.
No volverá. He won't come back.
¿Lo entenderá? Will she understand it?

[i] Note that in the future tense only the **nosotros/nosotras** form doesn't have an accent.

Tip

Remember that Spanish has no direct equivalent of the word *will* in verb forms like *will rain* or *will look* and so on. Instead, you change the Spanish verb ending to form the future tense.

Grammar Extra!

In English, we sometimes use *will* with the meaning of *be willing to* rather than simply to express the future, for example, *Will you wait for me a moment?* In Spanish you don't use the future tense to say this; you use the present tense or the verb **querer** (meaning *to want*) instead.

¿Me esperas un momento, por favor? Will you wait a moment for me,please?
¿Te quieres callar? Will you shut up?

3 Verbs with irregular stems in the future tense

➤ There are a few verbs that DO NOT use their infinitives as the stem for the future tense. Here are some of the most common.

Verb	Stem	(yo)	(tú)	(él) (ella) (usted)	(nosotros) (nosotras)	(vosotros)* (vosotras)*	(ellos) (ellas) (ustedes)
decir to say	dir-	diré	dirás	dirá	diremos	diréis*	dirán
haber to have	habr-	habré	habrás	habrá	habremos	habréis*	habrán
hacer to do/make	har-	haré	harás	hará	haremos	haréis*	harán
poder to be able to	podr-	podré	podrás	podrá	podremos	podréis*	podrán
poner to put	pondr-	pondré	pondrás	pondrá	pondremos	pondréis*	pondrán
querer to want	querr-	querré	querrás	querrá	querremos	querréis*	querrán

Verb	Stem	(yo)	(tú)	(él) (ella) (usted)	(nosotros) (nosotras)	(vosotros)* (vosotras)*	(ellos) (ellas) (ustedes)
saber to know	sabr-	sabré	sabrás	sabrá	sabremos	sabréis*	sabrán
salir to leave	saldr-	saldré	saldrás	saldrá	saldremos	saldréis*	saldrán
tener to have	tendr-	tendré	tendrás	tendrá	tendremos	tendréis*	tendrán
venir to come	vendr-	vendré	vendrás	vendrá	vendremos	vendréis*	vendrán

*only used in Spain

Lo haré mañana. I'll do it tomorrow.
No podremos hacerlo. We won't be able to do it.
Lo pondré aquí. I'll put it here.
Saldrán por la mañana. They'll leave in the morning.
¿A qué hora vendrás? What time will you come?

[i] Note that the verb **haber** is only used when forming other tenses, such as the perfect tense, and in the expression **hay** (meaning *there is* or *there are*).

⇨ *For more information on the **Perfect tense** and on **hay**, see pages 118 and 133.*

4 Reflexive verbs in the future tense

➤ The future tense of reflexive verbs is formed in just the same way as for ordinary verbs, except that you have to remember to include the reflexive pronoun (**me**, **te**, **se**, **nos**, **os**, **se**).

Me levantaré temprano. I'll get up early.

Key points

✔ In Spanish, you can use the present tense to talk about something that will happen or be true, just as in English.

✔ You can use **ir a** with an infinitive to talk about things that will happen in the immediate future.

✔ In Spanish, there is no direct equivalent of the word *will* in verb forms like *will rain* and *will look*. Instead, you must change the verb endings.

✔ To form the future tense, attach the endings **-é**, **-ás**, **á**, **-emos**, **-éis** (in Spain), **-án** to the infinitive.

✔ Some verbs have irregular stems in the future tense. It is worth learning these.

The conditional

What is the conditional?
The **conditional** is a verb form used to talk about things that would happen or that would be true under certain conditions. For example: I *would help you if I could*.
It is also used to say what you would like or need. For example: *Could you help me, please?*

1 Using the conditional

➤ In English, you can often recognize a conditional by the word *would* or its contracted form *'d*.

I would be sad if you left.
If you asked him, he'd help you.

➤ You use the conditional for:

- saying what you would like to do

  Me gustaría conocerlo. — I'd like to meet him.

- making suggestions

  Podrías quedarte en su casa. — You could stay at their house.

- giving advice

  Deberías hacer más ejercicio. — You should exercise more.

- saying what you would do

  Te dije que te ayudaría. — I said I would help you.

Tip
There is no direct Spanish translation of *would* in verb forms like *would be*, *would like*, *would help* and so on. Instead, you change the Spanish verb ending.

2 Forming the conditional

➤ To form the conditional of regular **-ar**, **-er**, and **-ir** verbs, attach the following endings to the infinitive of the verb: **-ía**, **-ías**, **-ía**, **-íamos**, **-íais**, **-ían**.

For further explanation of grammatical terms, please see pages viii-xii.

➤ The following table shows the conditional tense of three regular verbs: **hablar** (meaning *to speak*), **comer** (meaning *to eat*) and **vivir** (meaning *to live*).

(yo)	**hablaría**	**comería**	**viviría**	I would speak/eat/live
(tú)	**hablarías**	**comerías**	**vivirías**	you would speak/eat/live
(él) **(ella)** **(usted)**	**hablaría**	**comería**	**viviría**	he would speak/eat/live she would speak/eat/live it would speak/eat/live you would speak/eat/live
(nosotros/nosotras)	**hablaríamos**	**comeríamos**	**viviríamos**	we would speak/eat/live
(vosotros/vosotras)*	**hablaríais***	**comeríais***	**viviríais***	you would speak/eat/live
(ellos/ellas) **(ustedes)**	**hablarían**	**comerían**	**vivirían**	they would speak/eat/live you would speak/eat/live

*only used in Spain

Me gustaría ir a China.	I'd like to go to China.
Dije que hablaría con ella.	I said that I would speak to her.
Debería llamar a mis padres.	I should call my parents.

Tip

Don't forget to put an accent on the í in the conditional.

ℹ Note that the endings in the conditional tense are identical to those of the imperfect tense for **-er** and **-ir** verbs. The difference is that they are attached to a different stem.

⇨ *For more information on the* ***Imperfect tense****, see page* 112.

3 Verbs with irregular stems in the conditional

➤ To form the conditional of irregular verbs, use the same stem as for the future tense, then attach the usual endings for the conditional. The same verbs that are irregular in the future tense are irregular in the conditional.

Verb	Stem	(yo)	(tú)	(él) (ella) (usted)	(nosotros) (nosotras)	(vosotros)* (vosotras)*	(ellos) (ellas) (ustedes)
decir to say	dir-	diría	dirías	diría	diríamos	diríais*	dirían
haber to have	habr-	habría	habrías	habría	habríamos	habríais*	habrían
hacer to do/ make	har-	haría	harías	haría	haríamos	haríais*	harían
poder to be able to	podr-	podría	podrías	podría	podríamos	podríais*	podrían
poner to put	pondr-	pondría	pondrías	pondría	pondríamos	pondríais*	pondrían
querer to want	querr-	querría	querrías	querría	querríamos	querríais*	querrían
saber to know	sabr-	sabría	sabrías	sabría	sabríamos	sabríais*	sabrían
salir to leave	saldr-	saldría	saldrías	saldría	saldríamos	saldríais*	saldrían
tener to have	tendr-	tendría	tendrías	tendría	tendríamos	tendríais*	tendrían
venir to come	vendr-	vendría	vendrías	vendría	vendríamos	vendríais*	vendrían

*only used in Spain

⇨ *For more information on the* **Future tense**, *see page 99.*

¿Qué harías tú en mi lugar? — What would you do if you were me?
¿Podrías ayudarme? — Could you help me?
Yo lo pondría aquí. — I would put it here.

ℹ Note that the verb **haber** is only used when forming other tenses, such as the perfect tense, and in the expression **hay** (meaning *there is/there are*).

⇨ *For more information on the* **Perfect tense** *and on* **hay**, *see pages 118 and 133.*

4 Reflexive verbs in the conditional

➤ The conditional of reflexive verbs is formed in the same way as it is for ordinary verbs, except that you have to remember to include the reflexive pronoun (**me**, **te**, **se**, **nos**, **os**, **se**).

Le dije que <u>me levantaría</u> temprano.	I told him I would get up early.

Key points

✔ In Spanish, there is no direct equivalent of the word *would* in verb forms like *would go* and *would look* and so on. Instead, you change the verb ending.

✔ To form the conditional tense, attach the endings **-ía**, **ías**, **-ía**, **-íamos**, **-íais** (in Spain), **-ían** to the infinitive. The conditional uses the same stem as the future.

✔ Some verbs have irregular stems which are used for both the conditional and the future. It is worth learning these.

The preterite

What is the preterite?
The Spanish **preterite** is a form of the verb that is used to talk about actions that were completed in the past. It often corresponds to the simple past in English, as in *I bought a new bike; Mary went shopping on Friday; I typed two reports yesterday.*

1 Using the preterite

➤ In English, we use the simple past tense to talk about actions:

- that were completed at a certain point in the past
  I bought a dress yesterday.
- that were part of a series of events
  I got up, got dressed and made breakfast.
- that went on for a certain amount of time
  The war lasted for three years.

➤ In English, we also use the simple past tense to describe actions that occurred frequently (*Our parents took us swimming during our vacations*), and to describe settings (*It was a dark and stormy night*).

➤ In Spanish, the preterite is the most common tense for talking about the past. You use the preterite for actions:

- that were completed at a certain point in the past

Ayer compré un vestido.	I bought a dress yesterday.

- that were part of a series of events

Me levanté, me vestí y preparé el desayuno.	I got up, got dressed and made breakfast.

- that went on for a certain amount of time

La guerra duró tres años.	The war lasted three years.

➤ However, you use the imperfect tense for actions that happened frequently (where, in English, you could use *used to*) and for descriptions of settings.

➪ *For more information on the* **Imperfect tense**, *see page* 112.

2 Forming the preterite of regular verbs

➤ To form the preterite of any regular **-ar** verb, you drop the **-ar** ending to form the stem and attach the endings: **-é**, **-aste**, **-ó**, **-amos**, **-asteis**, **-aron**.

➤ To form the preterite of any regular **-er** or **-ir** verb, you also drop the **-er** or **-ir** ending to form the stem and attach the endings: **-í**, **-iste**, **-ió**, **-imos**, **-isteis**, **-ieron**.

➤ The following table shows the preterite of three regular verbs: **hablar** (meaning *to speak*), **comer** (meaning *to eat*) and **vivir** (meaning *to live*).

(yo)	**habl<u>é</u>**	**com<u>í</u>**	**viv<u>í</u>**	I spoke/ate/lived
(tú)	**habl<u>aste</u>**	**com<u>iste</u>**	**viv<u>iste</u>**	you spoke/ate/lived
(él) (ella) (usted)	**habl<u>ó</u>**	**com<u>ió</u>**	**viv<u>ió</u>**	he spoke/ate/lived she spoke/ate/lived it spoke/ate/lived you spoke/ate/lived
(nosotros/nosotras)	**habl<u>amos</u>**	**com<u>imos</u>**	**viv<u>imos</u>**	we spoke/ate/lived
(vosotros/vosotras)*	**habl<u>asteis</u>***	**com<u>isteis</u>***	**viv<u>isteis</u>***	you spoke/ate/lived
(ellos/ellas) (ustedes)	**habl<u>aron</u>**	**com<u>ieron</u>**	**viv<u>ieron</u>**	they spoke/ate/lived you spoke/ate/lived

*only used in Spain

<u>Bailé</u> con mi hermana.	I danced with my sister.
No <u>hablé</u> con ella.	I didn't speak to her.
<u>Cenamos</u> en un restaurante.	We had dinner in a restaurant.
¿<u>Cerraste la</u> ventana?	Did you close the window?

ℹ Note that Spanish has no direct translation of *did* or *didn't* in questions or negative sentences. You simply use a past tense and make it a question by making your voice go up at the end or changing the word order; you make it negative by adding **no**.

⇨ *For more information on* **Questions** *and* **Negatives**, *see pages 162 and 159.*

> *Tip*
>
> Remember the accents on the **yo** and **él/ella/usted** forms of regular verbs in the preterite. Only an accent shows the difference, for example, between **hablo** *I speak* and **habló** *he spoke*.

3 Irregular verbs in the preterite

➤ A number of verbs have very irregular forms in the preterite. The table shows some of the most common.

Verb	(yo)	(tú)	(él) (ella) (usted)	(nosotros) (nosotras)	(vosotros)* (vosotras)*	(ellos) (ellas) (ustedes)
andar to walk	anduve	anduviste	anduvo	anduvimos	anduvisteis*	anduvieron
conducir to drive	conduje	condujiste	condujo	condujimos	condujisteis*	condujeron
dar to give	di	diste	dio	dimos	disteis*	dieron
decir to say	dije	dijiste	dijo	dijimos	dijisteis*	dijeron
estar to be	estuve	estuviste	estuvo	estuvimos	estuvisteis*	estuvieron
hacer to do, to make	hice	hiciste	hizo	hicimos	hicisteis*	hicieron
ir to go	fui	fuiste	fue	fuimos	fuisteis*	fueron
poder to be able to	pude	pudiste	pudo	pudimos	pudisteis*	pudieron
poner to put	puse	pusiste	puso	pusimos	pusisteis*	pusieron
querer to want	quise	quisiste	quiso	quisimos	quisisteis*	quisieron
saber to know	supe	supiste	supo	supimos	supisteis*	supieron
ser to be	fui	fuiste	fue	fuimos	fuisteis*	fueron
tener to have	tuve	tuviste	tuvo	tuvimos	tuvisteis*	tuvieron
traer to bring	traje	trajiste	trajo	trajimos	trajisteis*	trajeron
venir to come	vine	viniste	vino	vinimos	vinisteis*	vinieron
ver to see	vi	viste	vio	vimos	visteis*	vieron

*only used in Spain

ⓘ Note that **hizo** (the **él/ella/usted** form of **hacer**) is spelled with a **z**.

⇨ *For more information on **Spelling**, see page 198.*

<u>Fue</u> a Madrid.	He went to Madrid.
Te <u>vi</u> en el parque.	I saw you in the park.
No <u>vinieron</u>.	They didn't come.
¿Qué <u>hizo</u>?	What did she do?
Se lo <u>di</u> a Teresa.	I gave it to Teresa.
<u>Fue</u> en 2007.	It was in 2007.

Tip

The preterite forms of **ser** (meaning *to be*) are the same as the preterite forms of **ir** (meaning *to go*).

➤ Some other verbs are regular <u>EXCEPT FOR</u> the **él/ella/usted** and **ellos/ellas/ustedes** forms (*third persons singular and plural*). In these forms the stem vowel changes.

Verb	(yo)	(tú)	(él) (ella) (usted)	(nosotros) (nosotras)	(vosotros)* (vosotras)*	(ellos) (ellas) (ustedes)
dormir to sleep	**dormí**	**dormiste**	**d<u>u</u>rmió**	**dormimos**	**dormisteis***	**d<u>u</u>rmieron**
morir to die	**morí**	**moriste**	**m<u>u</u>rió**	**morimos**	**moristeis***	**m<u>u</u>rieron**
pedir to ask for	**pedí**	**pediste**	**p<u>i</u>dió**	**pedimos**	**pedisteis***	**p<u>i</u>dieron**
reír to laugh	**reí**	**reíste**	**r<u>i</u>o**	**reímos**	**reísteis***	**r<u>i</u>eron**
seguir to follow	**seguí**	**seguiste**	**s<u>i</u>guió**	**seguimos**	**seguisteis***	**s<u>i</u>guieron**
sentir to feel	**sentí**	**sentiste**	**s<u>i</u>ntió**	**sentimos**	**sentisteis***	**s<u>i</u>ntieron**

*only used in Spain

Antonio <u>durmió</u> diez horas.	Antonio slept for ten hours.
<u>Murió</u> en 1066.	He died in 1066.
<u>Pidió</u> fajitas.	He ordered fajitas.
¿Los <u>siguió</u>?	Did she follow them?
<u>Sintió</u> un dolor en la pierna.	He felt a pain in his leg.
Nos <u>reímos</u> mucho.	We laughed a lot.
Juan no se <u>rio</u>.	Juan didn't laugh.

➤ **caer** (meaning *to fall*) and **leer** (meaning *to read*) have an accent in all persons apart from the **ellos/ellas/ustedes** form (*third person plural*). In addition, the vowel changes to **y** in the **él/ella/usted** and **ellos/ellas/ustedes** forms (*third persons singular and plural*).

Verb	(yo)	(tú)	(él) (ella) (usted)	(nosotros) (nosotras)	(vosotros)* (vosotras)*	(ellos) (ellas) (ustedes)
caer to fall	caí	caíste	cayó	caímos	caísteis*	cayeron
construir to build	construí	construiste	construyó	construimos	construisteis*	construyeron
leer to read	leí	leíste	leyó	leímos	leísteis*	leyeron

*only used in Spain

i Note that **construir** also changes to **y** in the **él/ella/usted** and **ellos/ellas/ustedes** forms (*third persons singular and plural*), but only has accents in the **yo** and **él/ella/usted** forms.

Se cayó por la ventana.	He fell out of the window.
Ayer leí un artículo muy interesante.	I read a very interesting article yesterday.
Construyeron una nueva autopista.	They built a new highway.

4 Other spelling changes in the preterite

➤ Spanish verbs that end in **-zar**, **-gar** and **-car** in the infinitive change the **z** to **c**, the **g** to **gu** and the **c** to **qu** in the **yo** form (*first person singular*).

Verb	(yo)	(tú)	(él) (ella) (usted)	(nosotros) (nosotras)	(vosotros)* (vosotras)*	(ellos) (ellas) (ustedes)
cruzar to cross	crucé	cruzaste	cruzó	cruzamos	cruzasteis*	cruzaron
empezar to begin	empecé	empezaste	empezó	empezamos	empezasteis*	empezaron
pagar to pay for	pagué	pagaste	pagó	pagamos	pagasteis*	pagaron
sacar to take out	saqué	sacaste	sacó	sacamos	sacasteis*	sacaron

*only used in Spain

Crucé el río.	I crossed the river.
Empecé a hacer mis deberes.	I began doing my homework.
No pagué la cuenta.	I didn't pay the bill.
Saqué las llaves del bolsillo.	I took my keys out of my pocket.

i Note that the change from **g** to **gu** and **c** to **qu** before **e** is to keep the sound hard.

➪ *For more information on **Spelling**, see page 198.*

5 Reflexive verbs in the preterite

➤ The preterite of reflexive verbs is formed the same way as for ordinary verbs, except that you have to remember to include the reflexive pronoun (**me**, **te**, **se**, **nos**, **os**, **se**).

Me levanté a las siete.	I got up at seven.

Key points

- ✔ The preterite is the most common way to talk about the past in Spanish.
- ✔ To form the preterite of regular **-ar** verbs, drop the **-ar** ending and attach the endings: **-é**, **-aste**, **-ó**, **-amos**, **-asteis** (in Spain), **-aron**.
- ✔ To form the preterite of regular **-er** and **-ir** verbs, drop the **-er** and **-ir** endings and attach the endings: **-í**, **-iste**, **-ió**, **-imos**, **-isteis** (in Spain), **-ieron**.
- ✔ There are a number of verbs which are irregular in the preterite. These forms have to be learned.
- ✔ With some verbs, the accents and spelling change in certain forms.

The imperfect tense

What is the imperfect tense?
The **imperfect tense** is one of the verb tenses used to talk about the past, especially in descriptions, and to say what was happening or used to happen. For example: *It was sunny at the weekend; We were living in Spain at the time; I used to walk to school.*

1 Using the imperfect tense

➤ In Spanish, the imperfect tense is used:

- to describe what things were like and how people felt in the past

Hacía calor.	It was hot.
No teníamos agua.	We didn't have any water.
Teníamos sed.	We were thirsty.

- to say what used to happen or what you used to do regularly in the past

Llamaba a su madre todos los días.	He used to call his mother every day.

- to describe what was happening or what the situation was when something else took place

Volvía del trabajo cuando la vi.	I was on my way back from work when I saw her.
Me caí cuando cruzaba la calle.	I fell down when I was crossing the street.

Grammar Extra!

Sometimes, instead of the ordinary imperfect tense being used to describe what was happening at a given moment in the past when something else occurred and interrupted it, the continuous form is used. This is made up of the imperfect tense of **estar** (**estaba**, **estabas** and so on), followed by the **-ando/-iendo** form of the main verb. The other verb – the one that relates the event that occurred – is in the preterite.

Inés miraba la televisión *or* **Inés estaba mirando la televisión cuando sonó el teléfono.**	Inés was watching television when the telephone rang.

➪ *For further information on the* **Preterite**, *see page 106.*

2 Forming the imperfect tense

➤ To form the imperfect of any regular **-ar** verb, you drop the **-ar** ending of the infinitive to form the stem and attach the endings: **-aba**, **-abas**, **-aba**, **-ábamos**, **-abais**, **-aban**.

➤ The following table shows the imperfect tense of one regular **-ar** verb: **hablar** (meaning *to speak*).

(yo)	**habl<u>aba</u>**	I spoke I was speaking I used to speak
(tú)	**habl<u>abas</u>**	you spoke you were speaking you used to speak
(él/ella/usted)	**habl<u>aba</u>**	he/she/it/you spoke he/she/it was speaking, you were speaking he/she/it/you used to speak
(nosotros/nosotras)	**habl<u>ábamos</u>**	we spoke we were speaking we used to speak
(vosotros/vosotras)*	**habl<u>abais</u>***	you spoke you were speaking you used to speak
(ellos/ellas/ustedes)	**habl<u>aban</u>**	they/you spoke they/you were speaking they/you used to speak

*only used in Spain

[i] Note that in the imperfect tense of **-ar** verbs, the only accent is on the **nosotros/nosotras** form

Hablaba francés e italiano.	He spoke French and Italian.
Jugaba al tenis cuando era joven.	He used to play tennis when he was young.
Notamos que olía a gas.	We noticed there was a smell of gas.

➤ To form the imperfect of any regular **-er** or **-ir** verb, you drop the **-er** or **-ir** ending of the infinitive to form the stem and attach the endings: **-ía**, **-ías**, **-ía**, **-íamos**, **-íais**, **-ían**.

➤ The following table shows the imperfect of two regular verbs: **comer** (meaning *to eat*) and **vivir** (meaning *to live*).

(yo)	com<u>ía</u>	viv<u>ía</u>	I ate/lived I was eating/living I used to eat/live
(tú)	com<u>ías</u>	viv<u>ías</u>	you ate/lived you were eating/living you used to eat/live
(él/ella/usted)	com<u>ía</u>	viv<u>ía</u>	he/she/it/you ate/lived he/she/it was eating/living, you were eating/living he/she/it was eating/living, you were eating/living
(nosotros/nosotras)	com<u>íamos</u>	viv<u>íamos</u>	we ate/lived we were eating/living we used to eat/live
(vosotros/vosotras)*	com<u>íais</u>*	viv<u>íais</u>*	you ate/lived you were eating/living you used to eat/live
(ellos/ellas/ustedes)	com<u>ían</u>	viv<u>ían</u>	they/you ate/lived they/you were eating/living they/you used to eat/live

*only used in Spain

ℹ Note that in the imperfect tense of **-er** and **-ir** verbs, there's an accent on all the endings.

A veces, <u>comíamos</u> en casa de Pepe.	We sometimes used to eat at Pepe's.
<u>Vivía</u> con sus suegros.	He was living with his in-laws.
Cuando llegó el médico, ya se <u>sentían</u> mejor.	They were already feeling better when the doctor arrived.

Tip

The imperfect endings for **-er** and **-ir** verbs are the same as the endings used to form the conditional for all verbs. The difference is that, in the conditional, the endings are attached to the future stem.

➪ *For more information on the **Conditional**, see page 102.*

3 Irregular verbs in the imperfect tense

➤ **ser**, **ir** and **ver** are irregular in the imperfect tense.

	ser	**Meaning:** to be
(yo)	era	I was
(tú)	eras	you were
(él/ella/usted)	era	he/she/it was, you were
(nosotros/nosotras)	éramos	we were
(vosotros/vosotras)*	erais*	you were
(ellos/ellas/ustedes)	eran	they were/you were

*only used in Spain

Era un muchacho muy simpático. He was a very nice boy.
Mi madre era profesora. My mother was *or* used to be a teacher.

	ir	**Meaning:** to go
(yo)	iba	I went/used to go/was going
(tú)	ibas	you went/used to go/were going
(él/ella/usted)	iba	he/she/it went/used to go/was going, you went/used to go/were going
(nosotros/nosotras)	íbamos	we went/used to go/were going
(vosotros/vosotras)*	ibais*	you went/used to go/were going
(ellos/ellas/ustedes)	iban	they/you went/used to go/were going

*only used in Spain

Iba a verla todos los días. He would go *or* used to go and see her every day.
¿Adónde iban? Where were they going?

	ver	**Meaning:** to see/to watch
(yo)	veía	I saw/used to see I watched/used to watch/was watching
(tú)	veías	you saw/used to see you watched/used to watch/were watching
(él/ella/usted)	veía	he/she/it saw/used to see he/she/it watched/used to watch/ was watching you saw/used to see you watched/used to watch/were watching
(nosotros/nosotras)	veíamos	we saw/used to see we watched/used to watch/were watching
(vosotros/vosotras)*	veíais*	you saw/used to see you watched/used to watch/were watching
(ellos/ellas/ustedes)	veían	they/you saw/used to see they/you watched/used to watch/ were watching

*only used in Spain

Lo veíamos a menudo. — We saw him *or* used to see him often.

Veía cada vez menos. — He could see less and less.

4 Reflexive verbs in the imperfect tense

➤ The imperfect of reflexive verbs is formed the same way as for ordinary verbs, except that you have to remember to include the reflexive pronoun (**me**, **te**, **se**, **nos**, **os**, **se**).

Antes se levantaba temprano. — He used to get up early.

Grammar Extra!

In Spanish, you also use the imperfect tense with certain time expressions, in particular with **desde** (meaning *since*), **desde hacía** (meaning *for*) and **hacía ... que** (meaning *for*) to talk about activities and states that had started previously and were still going on at a particular point in the past:

Estaba enfermo desde 2000.	He had been ill since 2000.
Lo conocía desde hacía tres meses.	She had known him for three months.
Hacía mucho tiempo que salían juntos.	They had been dating for a long time.
Hacía dos años que vivíamos en Nueva York.	We had been living in New York for two years.

Compare the use of **desde**, **desde hacía** and **hacía ... que** with the imperfect with that of **desde**, **desde hace**, and **hace ... que** with the present.

➪ *For more information on the use of tenses with* **desde**, *see page 191.*

Key points

- ✔ To form the imperfect tense of **-ar** verbs, drop the **-ar** ending and attach the endings: **-aba**, **-abas**, **-aba**, **-ábamos**, **-abais** (in Spain), **-aban**.
- ✔ To form the imperfect tense of **-er** and **-ir** verbs, drop the **-er** and **-ir** endings and attach the endings: **-ía**, **-ías**, **-ía**, **-íamos**, **-íais** (in Spain), **-ían**.
- ✔ **ser**, **ir** and **ver** are irregular in the imperfect.

The perfect tense

What is the perfect tense?
The **perfect** tense is a verb form used to talk about what has or hasn't happened. For example: *I've broken my glasses; We haven't spoken about it*.

1 Using the perfect tense

➤ In English, we use the perfect tense (*have*, *has* or their contracted forms *'ve* and *'s* followed by a past participle such as *spoken*, *eaten*, *lived*, *been*) to talk about what has or hasn't happened today, this week, this year or in our lives up to now.

➤ The Spanish perfect tense is used in a similar way.

He terminado el libro.	I've finished the book.
Nunca ha estado en Bolivia.	He's never been to Bolivia.
Ha vendido su caballo.	She has sold her horse.
Todavía no hemos comprado una impresora.	We still haven't bought a printer.
Ya se han ido.	They've already left.

Grammar Extra!

In some Latin American countries, the preterite is often used instead of the perfect tense in colloquial language. This is also true in English. So you may hear **¿Ya comiste?** (Did you eat yet?) instead of **¿Ya has comido?** (Have you eaten yet?), **Ya vi esa película.** (I already saw that movie.) instead of **Ya he visto esa película.** (I've already seen that movie.), etc.

2 Forming the perfect tense

➤ As in English, the perfect tense in Spanish has two parts to it. These are:

- the present tense of the verb **haber** (meaning *to have*)
- a part of the main verb called the past participle.

3 Forming the past participle

➤ To form the past participle of regular **-ar** verbs, drop the **-ar** ending of the infinitive and attach **-ado**.

hablar (*to speak*) → **hablado** (*spoken*)

➤ To form the past participle of regular **-er** or **-ir** verbs, drop the **-er** or **-ir** ending of the infinitive and attach **-ido**.

comer (*to eat*) → **comido** (*eaten*)
vivir (*to live*) → **vivido** (*lived*)

For further explanation of grammatical terms, please see pages viii-xii.

4 The perfect tense of some regular verbs

➤ The following table shows how you can combine the present tense of **haber** with the past participle of any verb to form the perfect tense. In this case, the past participles are taken from the following regular verbs: **hablar** (meaning *to speak*); **trabajar** (meaning *to work*); **comer** (meaning *to eat*); **vender** (meaning *to sell*); **vivir** (meaning *to live*); **decidir** (meaning *to decide*).

	Present of haber	Past participle	Meaning
(yo)	he	hablado	I have spoken
(tú)	has	trabajado	you have worked
(él/ella/usted)	ha	comido	he/she/it has eaten, you have eaten
(nosotros/nosotras)	hemos	vendido	we have sold
(vosotros/vosotras)*	habéis*	vivido	you have lived
(ellos/ellas/ustedes)	han	decidido	they/you have decided

*only used in Spain

Has trabajado mucho. — You've worked hard.
No he comido nada. — I haven't eaten anything.

Note that you should not confuse **haber** with **tener**. Even though they both mean *to have*, **haber** is only used for forming tenses and in certain impersonal expressions such as **hay** and **había** meaning *there is, there are, there was, there were*, and so on.

*For further information on **Impersonal verbs**, see page 132.*

5 Verbs with irregular past participles

➤ Some past participles are irregular. There aren't too many, so try to learn them.

abrir (*to open*) → **abierto** (*opened*)
cubrir (*to cover*) → **cubierto** (*covered*)
decir (*to say*) → **dicho** (*said*)
escribir (*to write*) → **escrito** (*written*)
freír (*to fry*) → **frito** (*fried*)
hacer (*to do, to make*) → **hecho** (*done, made*)
morir (*to die*) → **muerto** (*died*)
oír (*to hear*) → **oído** (*heard*)
poner (*to put*) → **puesto** (*put*)

romper (*to break*)	→	**roto** (*broken*)
ver (*to see*)	→	**visto** (*seen*)
volver (*to return*)	→	**vuelto** (*returned*)

He abierto una cuenta en el banco.	I've opened a bank account.
No ha dicho nada.	He hasn't said anything.
Ha escrito muchas novelas.	He has written many novels.
Han muerto tres personas.	Three people have died.
¿Dónde has puesto mis zapatos?	Where have you put my shoes?
Carlos ha roto el espejo.	Carlos has broken the mirror.
Jamás he visto una cosa parecida.	I've never seen anything like it.
¿Ha vuelto Ana?	Has Ana come back?

Tip

he/has/ha and so on must NEVER be separated from the past participle. Any object pronouns go before the form of **haber** being used, and NOT between the form of **haber** and the past participle.

No lo he visto.	I haven't seen it.
¿Lo has hecho ya?	Have you done it yet?

6 Reflexive verbs in the perfect tense

➤ The perfect tense of reflexive verbs is formed in the same way as it is for ordinary verbs. The reflexive pronouns (**me**, **te**, **se**, **nos**, **os**, **se**) come before **he**, **has**, **ha**, and so on. The table on the next page shows the perfect tense of **levantarse** in full.

(Subject pronoun)	Reflexive pronoun	Present tense of haber	Past Participle	Meaning
(yo)	me	he	levantado	I have gotten up
(tú)	te	has	levantado	you have gotten up
(él) (ella) (uno) (usted)	se	ha	levantado	he has gotten up she has gotten up one has gotten up it has gotten up you have gotten up
(nosotros) (nosotras)	nos	hemos	levantado	we have gotten up we have gotten up
(vosotros)* (vosotras)*	os*	habéis*	levantado	you have gotten up you have gotten up
(ellos) (ellas) (ustedes)	se	han	levantado	they have gotten up they have gotten up you have gotten up

*only used in Spain

Grammar Extra!

Don't use the perfect tense with **desde**, **desde hace** and **hace ... que** when talking about how long something has been going on for. Use the present tense instead.

Está enfermo desde julio.	He has been ill since July.
Trabaja conmigo desde hace tres meses.	She's been working with me for three months.
Hace mucho tiempo que salen juntos.	They have been dating for a long time.

For more information on the ***Present tense****, see page 72.*

➤ In European Spanish you CAN use the perfect tense in the negative with **desde** and **desde hace**.

No lo he visto desde hace mucho tiempo.	I haven't seen him for a long time.

Key points

✔ The Spanish perfect tense is formed using the present tense of **haber** and a past participle.

✔ In Spanish, the perfect tense is used in very much the same way as it is in English. In some Latin American countries, the preterite is often used instead of the perfect tense in colloquial language.

✔ The past participle of regular **-ar** verbs ends in **-ado**, and the past participle of regular **-er** and **-ir** verbs ends in **-ido**.

✔ Make sure you know the following irregular past participle forms: **abierto**, **cubierto**, **dicho**, **escrito**, **frito**, **hecho**, **muerto**, **oído**, **puesto**, **roto**, **visto**, **vuelto**.

The pluperfect or past perfect tense

What is the pluperfect tense?
The **pluperfect** is a verb tense that is used to talk about what had happened or had been true at a point in the past. For example: *I'd seen the movie twice before*.

1 Using the pluperfect tense

➤ When talking about the past, we sometimes refer to things that had happened previously. To do this in English, we often use *had* followed by a past participle such as *seen*, *eaten*, *lived* or *been*. This tense is known as the pluperfect or past perfect tense.

➤ The Spanish pluperfect tense is used and formed in a similar way.

Ya habíamos comido cuando llegó.	We'd already eaten when he arrived.
Nunca lo había visto antes.	I'd never seen him before.

2 Forming the pluperfect tense

➤ Like the perfect tense, the pluperfect tense in Spanish has two parts to it:
- the imperfect tense of the verb **haber** (meaning *to have*)
- the past participle.

⇨ *For more information on the* ***Imperfect tense*** *and* ***Past participles****, see pages 112 and 118.*

➤ The table below shows how you can combine the imperfect tense of **haber** with the past participle of any verb to form the pluperfect tense. Here, the past participles are taken from the following regular verbs: **hablar** (meaning *to speak*); **trabajar** (meaning *to work*); **comer** (meaning *to eat*); **vender** (meaning *to sell*); **vivir** (meaning *to live*); **decidir** (meaning *to decide*).

(Subject pronoun)	Imperfect of haber	Past Participle	Meaning
(yo)	había	hablado	I had spoken
(tú)	habías	trabajado	you had worked
(él/ella/usted)	había	comido	he/she/it/you had eaten
(nosotros/nosotras)	habíamos	vendido	we had sold
(vosotros/vosotras)*	habíais*	vivido*	you had lived
(ellos/ellas/ustedes)	habían	decidido	they/you had decided

*only used in Spain

No <u>había trabajado</u> antes. He hadn't worked before.
<u>Había vendido</u> su caballo. She had sold her horse.

➤ Remember that some very common verbs have irregular past participles.

abrir (*to open*) → **abierto** (*opened*)
cubrir (*to cover*) → **cubierto** (*covered*)
decir (*to say*) → **dicho** (*said*)
escribir (*to write*) → **escrito** (*written*)
freír (*to fry*) → **frito** (*fried*)
hacer (*to do, to make*) → **hecho** (*done, made*)
morir (*to die*) → **muerto** (*died*)
oír (*to hear*) → **oído** (*heard*)
poner (*to put*) → **puesto** (*put*)
romper (*to break*) → **roto** (*broken*)
ver (*to see*) → **visto** (*seen*)
volver (*to return*) → **vuelto** (*returned*)

No <u>había dicho</u> nada. He hadn't said anything.
Tres personas <u>habían muerto</u>. Three people had died.

Tip

había/habías/habían and so on must <u>NEVER</u> be separated from the past participle. Any object pronouns go before the form of **haber** being used, and <u>NOT</u> between the form of **haber** and the past participle.

No lo había visto. I hadn't seen it.

3 Reflexive verbs in the pluperfect tense

➤ The pluperfect tense of reflexive verbs is formed in the same way as it is for ordinary verbs. The reflexive pronouns (**me**, **te**, **se**, **nos**, **os**, **se**) come before **había**, **habías**, **había**, and so on. The table on the next page shows the pluperfect tense of **levantarse** in full.

(Subject pronoun)	Reflexive pronoun	Imperfect tense of haber	Past Participle	Meaning
(yo)	me	había	levantado	I had gotten up
(tú)	te	habías	levantado	you had gotten up
(él) (ella) (uno) (usted)	se	había	levantado	he had gotten up she had gotten up one had gotten up it had gotten up you had gotten up
(nosotros) (nosotras)	nos	habíamos	levantado	we had gotten up we had gotten up
(vosotros)* (vosotras)	os*	habíais*	levantado	you had gotten up you had gotten up
(ellos) (ellas) (ustedes)	se	habían	levantado	they had gotten up they had gotten up you had gotten up

*only used in Spain

Grammar Extra!

Don't use the pluperfect with **desde**, **desde hacía** and **hacía ... que** when talking about how long something had been going on. Use the imperfect instead.

Estaba enfermo desde 2000.	He had been ill since 2000.
Trabajaba conmigo desde hacía tres meses.	He had been working with me for three months.
Hacía mucho tiempo que salían juntos.	They had been dating for a long time.

➪ *For more information on the **Imperfect tense**, see page 112.*

Key points

- ✔ The Spanish pluperfect tense is formed using the imperfect tense of **haber** and a past particple.
- ✔ In Spanish, the pluperfect tense is used in very much the same way as it is in English.
- ✔ The past participle of regular **-ar** verbs ends in **-ado**, while that of regular **-er** and **-ir** verbs ends in **-ido**.
- ✔ Make sure you know the irregular forms: **abierto**, **cubierto**, **dicho**, **escrito**, **frito**, **hecho**, **muerto**, **oído**, **puesto**, **roto**, **visto**, **vuelto**.

The passive

What is the passive?
The **passive** is a verb form that is used when the subject of the verb is the person or thing that is affected by the action. For example: *Mary is liked by everyone; Two children were hurt in an accident; The house was sold.*

1 Using the passive

➤ Verbs can be either active or passive.

➤ In a normal or active sentence, the subject of the verb is the person or thing doing the action described by the verb. The object of the verb is the person or thing that the verb most directly affects.

They (*subject*) received (*active verb*) many letters of complaint (*object*).
Someone (*subject*) hit (*active verb*) me (*object*).

➤ So long as the verb has an object, in English, as in Spanish, you can turn an active sentence around to make it a passive sentence by using *to be* followed by a past participle. In this case the person or thing directly affected by the action becomes the subject of the verb.

Many letters of complaint (*subject*) were received (*passive verb*).
I (*subject*) was hit (*passive verb*).

➤ In English, to show who or what is responsible for the action in a passive construction, you use *by*.

I (*subject*) was hit (*passive verb*) by someone.

➤ You use the passive rather than the active when you want to focus attention on the person or thing affected by the action rather than the person or thing that carries it out.

The man was arrested.

➤ You can also use the passive when you don't know who is responsible for the action.

Several buses were vandalized.

2 Forming the passive

➤ In English, we use the verb *to be* with a past participle (*was painted, were seen, are made*) to form the passive. In Spanish, the passive is formed in exactly the same way, using the verb **ser** (meaning *to be*) and a past participle. When you say who the action is or was done by, you use the preposition **por** (meaning *by*).

⇨ *For more information on the **Past participle**, see page 118.*

Es respetada <u>por</u> todos.	She is respected by everybody.
El cuadro fue pintado <u>por</u> uno de sus discípulos.	The picture was painted by one of his pupils.
Estas casas fueron construidas en 1956.	These houses were built in 1956.
El problema ya ha sido solucionado.	The problem has already been solved.
La película no había sido estrenada.	The movie hadn't been premiered.
El nuevo edificio va a ser inaugurado <u>por</u> el presidente.	The new building is going to be opened by the president.

[i] Note that the ending of the past participle agrees with the subject of the verb **ser** in exactly the same way as an adjective would.

⇨ *For more information on* ***Adjectives****, see page* 19.

➤ Here is the preterite of the **-ar** verb **enviar** (meaning *to send*) in its passive form.

(Subject pronoun)	Preterite of ser	Past Participle	Meaning
(yo)	fui	enviado (masculine) enviada (feminine)	I was sent
(tú)	fuiste	enviado (masculine) enviada (feminine)	you were sent
(él) (ella) (usted)	fue	enviado enviada enviado (masculine) enviada (feminine)	he was sent she was sent you were sent
(nosotros) (nosotras)	fuimos fuimos	enviados enviadas	we were sent we were sent
(vosotros)* (vosotras)*	fuisteis*	enviados enviadas	you were sent you were sent
(ellos) (ellas) (ustedes)	fueron	enviados enviadas enviados (masculine) enviadas (feminine)	they were sent they were sent you were sent you were sent

*only used in Spain

➤ You can form other tenses in the passive by changing the tense of the verb **ser**.

Future:	**Serán enviados.**	They will be sent.
Perfect:	**Eran enviados.**	They were/used to be sent.

➤ Irregular past participles are the same as they are in the perfect tense.

⇨ *For more information on **Irregular past participles**, see page 119.*

3 Avoiding the passive

➤ Passives are not as common in Spanish as they are in English. Spanish native speakers usually prefer to avoid using the passive by:

- using the active construction instead of the passive

La policía interrogó al sospechoso.	The suspect was interrogated by the police.
Su madre le regaló un libro.	He was given a book by his mother.

- using an active verb in the third person plural

Ya han solucionado el problema.	The problem has already been solved.

- using a passive or impersonal construction with the pronoun **se** (as long as you don't need to say who the action is done by). Note the the verb is in the third person (singular or plural, depending on the subject).

En Brasil se habla portugués.	Portuguese is spoken in Brazil.
La casa se construyó en 1956.	The house was built in 1956.
Todos los libros se vendieron.	All the books were sold.
No se había estrenado la película.	The movie hadn't been premiered.
Se cree que va a morir.	It is thought he will die.

⇨ *For more information on **passive and impersonal** constructions with **se**, see pages 97 and 135.*

Tip

Active verbs often have both a direct object and an indirect object.
He gave me (*indirect object*) a book (*direct object*).
In English, both of these objects can be made the subject of a passive verb. For example: *I was given a book.* or *A book was given to me.*
In Spanish, an indirect object can NEVER become the subject of a passive verb.

Key points

- ✔ The passive is formed using **ser** + past participle, sometimes followed by **por** (meaning *by*).
- ✔ The past participle must agree with the subject of **ser**.
- ✔ Passive constructions are not as common as they are in English. You can often avoid the passive by using the third person plural of the active verb or by using a construction with the pronoun **se**.

The gerund

What is a gerund?
The **gerund** is a verb form ending in *-ing* which is used to form verb tenses and which in English may also be used as an adjective and a noun. For example: *What are you doing?; the setting sun; Swimming is easy!*

1 Using the gerund

➤ In Spanish, the gerund is a form of the verb that usually ends in **-ando** or **-iendo** and is used to form continuous tenses.

Estoy trabajando.	I'm working.
Estamos comiendo.	We are eating.

➤ It is used with **estar** to form continuous tenses such as:

- the present continuous

Está planchando su camisa.	He's ironing his shirt.
Estoy escribiendo una carta.	I'm writing a letter.

⇨ *For more information on the* **Present continuous**, *see page 85.*

- the imperfect continuous

Estaba arreglando el carro.	She was fixing the car.
Estaban esperándonos.	They were waiting for us.

ℹ Note that, in Spanish, continuous tenses should only be used to describe actions that are or were happening at the precise moment to which you are referring.

Grammar Extra!

In continuous tenses, another verb, such as **ir** or **venir**, is sometimes used with a gerund instead of **estar**. These verbs emphasize the gradualness or the slowness of the process.

Iba aprendiendo poco a poco.	He was learning little by little.
Eso es lo que vengo diciendo desde el principio.	That's what I've been saying all along.

➤ The gerund is also used after certain other verbs:

- **seguir haciendo algo** and **continuar haciendo algo** are both used with the meaning of *to go on doing something* or *to continue doing something*.

Siguió cantando *or* **Continuó cantando.**	He went on singing *or* He continued singing.
Siguieron leyendo *or* **Continuaron leyendo.**	They went on reading *or* They continued reading.

- **llevar** with a time expression followed by the gerund is used to talk about how long someone has been doing something:

Lleva dos años estudiando inglés.	He's been studying English for two years.
Llevo una hora esperando aquí.	I've been waiting here for an hour.

[i] Note that the present tense of **llevar** followed by a gerund means the same as the English *have/has been + -ing*.

➤ **pasar(se)** with a time expression followed by the gerund is used to talk about how long you've spent doing something.

Pasé *or* **Me pasé el fin de semana estudiando.**	I spent the weekend studying.
Pasamos *or* **Nos pasamos el día leyendo.**	We spent the day reading.

➤ Verbs expressing movement, such as **salir** (meaning *to come out* or *to go out*), **entrar** (meaning *to come in* or *to go in*), and **irse** (meaning *to leave*) are sometimes followed by a gerund such as **corriendo** (meaning *running*) or **cojeando** (meaning *limping*). In such cases, the English equivalent of **salir corriendo**, **entrar corriendo** or **irse cojeando**, would be *to run out*, *to run in* or *to limp off*.

Salió corriendo.	He ran out.
Se fue cojeando.	He limped off.

Tip

To talk about physical position, use a past participle not a gerund.

Estaba acostado en el sofá.	He was lying on the sofa.
Estaba sentada.	She was sitting down.
Lo encontré tendido en el suelo.	I found him lying on the floor.
La escalera estaba apoyada contra la pared.	The ladder was leaning against the wall.

➪ *For more information on the* ***Past participles****, see page 118.*

➤ You will also come across the gerund used in other ways. For example:

Los vimos jugando al fútbol.	We saw them playing football.
Estudiando, aprobarás.	If you study, you'll pass.

2 Forming the gerund of regular verbs

➤ To form the gerund of regular **-ar** verbs, drop the **-ar** ending of the infinitive to form the stem, and attach **-ando.**

Infinitive	Stem	Gerund
hablar	habl-	hablando
trabajar	trabaj-	trabajando

➤ To form the gerund of regular **-er** and **-ir** verbs, drop the **-er** and **-ir** ending of the infinitive to form the stem, and attach **-iendo.**

Infinitive	Stem	Gerund
comer	com-	comiendo
vivir	viv-	viviendo

3 The gerund of irregular verbs

➤ Some verbs have an irregular gerund form. You have to learn these.

Infinitives	Meaning	Gerund	Meaning
decir	to say	diciendo	saying
dormir	to sleep	durmiendo	sleeping
freír	to fry	friendo	frying
morir	to die	muriendo	dying
pedir	to ask for	pidiendo	asking for
poder	to be able to	pudiendo	being able to
reír	to laugh	riendo	laughing
seguir	to follow	siguiendo	following
sentir	to feel	sintiendo	feeling
venir	to come	viniendo	coming
vestir	to dress	vistiendo	dressing

➤ In the next group of verbs there is a **y** rather than the normal **i**.

Infinitives	Meaning	Gerund	Meaning
caer	to fall	cayendo	falling
creer	to believe	creyendo	believing
leer	to read	leyendo	reading
oír	to hear	oyendo	hearing
traer	to bring	trayendo	bringing
ir	to go	yendo	going

Tip

In English, we often use *-ing* forms as adjectives (for example: *running water, shining eyes, the following day*). In Spanish, you cannot use the **-ando** and **-iendo** forms like this.

Instead, there are sometimes corresponding forms ending in **-ante** and **-iente** that can be used as adjectives.

agua corriente	running water
ojos brillantes	shining eyes
Al día siguiente, visitamos Cozumel.	The following day we visited Cozumel.

Similarly, in English, we often use the *-ing* forms as nouns. In Spanish you have to use the infinitive instead.

Fumar es malo para la salud.	Smoking is bad for you.

4 Position of pronouns with the gerund

➤ Object pronouns and reflexive pronouns are usually attached to the end of the gerund, although often, in continuous tenses, you can also put them before **estar**.

Estoy hablándote *or* **Te estoy hablando.**	I'm talking to you.
Está vistiéndose *or* **Se está vistiendo.**	He's getting dressed.
Estaban mostrándoselo *or* **Se lo estaban mostrando.**	They were showing it to him/her/them/you.

i Note that, when attaching pronouns to the end of a gerund, you will always have to add an accent to keep the stress in the same place.

➪ *For more information on* **Stress**, *see page 202.*

Key points

- ✔ Use the gerund in continuous tenses with **estar** as well as after **seguir** and **continuar**.
- ✔ Gerunds for **-ar** verbs attach **-ando** to the stem of the verb.
- ✔ Gerunds for **-er** and **-ir** verbs usually attach **-iendo** to the stem of the verb.
- ✔ **-ando** and **-iendo** gerunds cannot be used as adjectives or nouns.
- ✔ You can attach pronouns to the end of the gerund, or sometimes put them before the previous verb.

Impersonal verbs

What is an impersonal verb?
An **impersonal verb** is a verb whose subject is *it*, but this '*it*' does not refer to any specific thing. For example: *It's going to rain; It's nine o'clock*.

1 Verbs that are always used impersonally

➤ There are some verbs, such as **llover** (meaning *to rain*) and **nevar** (meaning *to snow*), that are only used in the '*it*' form, the infinitive, and as a gerund (the *-ing* form of the verb). These are called impersonal verbs because there is no person, animal or thing performing the action.

Llueve.	It's raining.
Está lloviendo.	It's raining.
Va a llover.	It's going to rain.
Nieva.	It's snowing.
Está nevando.	It's snowing.
Nevaba.	It was snowing.
Estaba nevando.	It was snowing.
Mañana va a nevar.	It's going to snow tomorrow.

2 Verbs that are sometimes used impersonally

➤ There are also several other very common verbs that are sometimes used as impersonal verbs, for example **hacer**, **haber** and **ser**.

➤ **hacer** is used in a number of impersonal expressions relating to the weather:

Hace frío/calor.	It's cold/hot.
Ayer hacía mucho frío/calor.	It was very cold/hot yesterday.
Hace sol/viento.	It's sunny/windy.
Va a hacer sol/viento.	It's going to be sunny/windy.
Hace un tiempo horrible.	It's a horrible day./The weather's horrible.

➤ **hacer** is also used in combination with **que** and **desde** in impersonal time expressions, to talk about how long something has been going on or how long it has been since something happened.

Hace seis meses que vivo aquí. *or* **Vivo aquí desde hace seis meses.**	I've been living here for six months.
Hace tres años que estudio español *or* **Estudio español desde hace tres años.**	I've been studying Spanish for three years.

For further explanation of grammatical terms, please see pages viii-xii.

Hace mucho tiempo que no la veo *or* **No la veo desde hace mucho tiempo.**	I haven't seen her for ages *or* It's been ages since I saw her.
Hace varias semanas que no voy por allí *or* **No voy por allí desde hace varias semanas.**	I haven't been there for several weeks *or* It's been several weeks since I went there.

ℹ Note in the above examples the use of the present simple in Spanish where in English we'd use the perfect tense or the past tense.

➤ **hacer** is also used impersonally in the expression **(me/te/le) hace falta**, which means *it is necessary* (*for me/you/him*).

Si hace falta, voy.	I'll go if necessary.
No hace falta llamar.	We/You/I don't need to call.
Me hace falta otro vaso más.	I need another glass.
No hace falta ser un experto.	You don't need to be an expert.
No hacía falta.	It wasn't necessary.

ℹ Note that not all impersonal expressions in Spanish are translated into English using impersonal expressions.

➤ **haber** too can be used impersonally with the meaning *there is/there are, there was/there were, there will be*, and so on. It has the special form **hay** in the present. For the other tenses, you take the third person singular (the '*it*' form) of **haber** in the appropriate tense.

Hay un cine cerca de aquí.	There's a movie theater near here.
Hay dos supermercados.	There are two supermarkets.
No hay bares.	There are no bars.
Había mucho ruido.	There was a lot of noise.
Había muchos perros.	There were a lot of dogs.
Hubo un accidente.	There was an accident.
Hubo varios problemas.	There were several problems.
¿Habrá tiempo?	Will there be time?
¿Habrá suficientes sillas?	Will there be enough chairs?

ℹ Note that you should ALWAYS use the singular form (never the plural), no matter how many things there are.

➤ **haber** is used in the construction **hay que** with an infinitive to talk about actions that need to be taken.

Hay que trabajar más.	We/You need to work harder.
Hay que ser respetuoso.	You/We/One must be respectful.
Habrá que decírselo.	We'll/You'll have to tell him.

➤ **ser** can be used in certain impersonal constructions with adjectives, for example:

- **es/era/fue** + adjective + infinitive

Es importante ahorrar dinero.	It's important to save money.
Fue ridículo hacer eso.	It was ridiculous to do that.
Sería mejor esperar.	It would be better to wait.

- **es/era/fue** + adjective + **que** + verb

Es cierto que tengo problemas.	It's true that I have problems.
Es verdad que trabaja mucho.	It's true that he works hard.

ⓘ Note that when they are used in the negative (**no es cierto que...**; **no es verdad que...**), these expressions have to be followed by the subjunctive.

⇨ *For more information on the* ***Subjunctive****, see page 136.*

Grammar Extra!

When impersonal expressions that don't state facts are followed by **que** (meaning *that*) and a verb, this verb must be in the subjunctive.

For this reason, the following non-factual impersonal expressions are all followed by the subjunctive:

• **Es posible que...**	It's possible that... / ...might...
Es posible que ganen.	They might win.
• **Es imposible que...**	It's impossible that... / ...can't possibly...
Es imposible que lo sepan.	They can't possibly know.
• **Es necesario que...**	It's necessary that... / ...need to...
No es necesario que vengas.	You don't need to come.
• **Es mejor que...**	It's better to/if...
Es mejor que no se entere.	It's better if he doesn't find out.

⇨ *For more information on the* ***Subjunctive****, see page 136.*

➤ **ser** is also used impersonally with **de día** and **de noche** to say whether it's day or night.

Era de noche cuando llegamos.	It was night when we arrived.
Todavía es de día allí.	It's still day there.

⇨ *For other time expressions with* ***ser****, see page 82.*

➤ **basta con** is used impersonally:

- with a following infinitive to mean *it's enough to/all you need do is*

Basta con llamar para reservar una mesa.	All you need to do is to call to reserve a table.

Basta con dar una vuelta por la ciudad para...	You only need to take a walk around the city to ...

- with a noun or pronoun to mean *all you need is* or *all it takes is*

Basta con un error para que se enoje.	All it takes is one mistake to make him angry.

➤ **(me) parece que** is used to give opinions.

Parece que va a llover.	It looks as if it's going to rain.
Me parece que estás equivocado.	I think that you are wrong.

i Note that when **(me) parece que** is used in the negative, the following verb has to be in the subjunctive.

⇨ *For more information on the **Subjunctive**, see page 136.*

➤ **vale la pena** is used to talk about what's worth doing.

Vale la pena.	It's worth it.
No vale la pena.	It's not worth it.
Vale la pena hacer el esfuerzo.	It's worth making the effort.
No vale la pena gastar tanto dinero.	It's not worth spending so much money.

Grammar Extra!

se is often used in impersonal expressions, especially with the verbs **creer**, **decir**, **poder**, and **tratar**. In such cases it often corresponds to *it*, *one* or *you* in English.

• **Se cree que...**	It is thought *or* People think that...
Se cree que es un mito.	It is thought to be a myth.
• **Se dice que...**	It is said *or* People say that...
Se dice que es rico.	He is said to be rich.
• **Se puede...**	One can.../People can.../You can...
Aquí se puede estacionar.	One can park here.
• **Se trata de...**	It's a question of.../It's about...
No se trata de dinero.	It isn't a question of money.
Se trata de resolverlo.	We must solve it.

⇨ *For more information on contructions with se, see page 97.*

Key points

- ✔ Impersonal verbs and expressions can only be used in the *'it'* form, the infinitive and the gerund.
- ✔ Impersonal expressions relating to the weather are very common.
- ✔ Although in English we use *there is* or *there are* depending on the number of people or things that there are, in Spanish **hay**, **había**, **hubo** and so on should be used in the singular form only.
- ✔ Some very common ordinary verbs are also used as impersonal verbs.

The subjunctive

What is the subjunctive?
The **subjunctive** is a verb form that is used in certain circumstances especially when expressing some sort of feeling or when there is doubt about whether something will happen or whether something is true. It is only used occasionally in modern English. For example: *If I were you, ...; So be it.; I wish you were here.*

1 Using the subjunctive

➤ Although you may not know it, you will already be familiar with many of the forms of the present subjunctive, as it is used when giving orders and instructions not to do something as well as in the **usted**, **ustedes** and **nosotros** forms of instructions to do something.

➪ *For more information on* ***Imperatives***, *see page 86.*

➤ In Spanish, the subjunctive is used after certain verbs and conjunctions when two parts of a sentence have different subjects.

Yo tengo miedo de que le ocurra algo.	I'm afraid something may (*subjunctive*) happen to him.

(The subject of the first part of the sentence is *I*; the subject of the second part of the sentence is *something*.).

➤ In English, in a sentence like *We want him/José to be happy*, we use an infinitive (*to be*) for the second verb even though *want* and *be happy* have different subjects (*we* and *him/José*).

➤ In Spanish, you cannot do this. You have to use the subjunctive for the second verb.

Queremos que nuestros hijos sean felices.	We want our children to be happy. (*Literally*: We want that our children be (*subjunctive*) happy.)
Queremos que (tú) seas feliz.	We want you to be happy. (*Literally*: We want that you be (*subjunctive*) happy.)

➤ You CAN use an infinitive for the second verb in Spanish when the subject of both verbs is the same.

Queremos ser felices.	We want to be happy.

2 Recognizing the subjunctive

➤ The subjunctive has several tenses, the main ones being the present subjunctive and the imperfect subjunctive. The tense used for the subjunctive verb depends on the tense of the previous verb.

➪ *For more information on **Tenses with the subjunctive**, see page 141.*

➤ In sentences containing two verbs with different subjects, you will find that the second verb is in the subjunctive when the first verb:

- expresses a wish

  Quiero que vengan. — I want them to come.
  Prefiero que te quedes. — I'd rather you stayed.
  Deseamos que tengan éxito. — We want them to be successful.

- expresses an emotion

  Siento mucho que no puedas venir. — I'm very sorry that you can't come.
  Espero que venga. — I hope he comes.
  Me sorprende que no esté aquí. — I'm surprised that he isn't here.
  Me alegro de que te gusten. — I'm pleased that you like them.

➤ If the subject of both verbs is the same, an infinitive is used as the second verb instead of a subjunctive.

➤ Compare the following examples. In the examples on the left, both the verb expressing the wish or emotion and the second verb have the same subject, so the second verb is an infinitive. In the examples on the right, each verb has a different subject, so the second verb is in the subjunctive.

Infinitive construction	Subjunctive construction
Quiero estudiar. I want to study.	**Quiero que José estudie.** I want José to study.
Elena quiere irse. Elena wants to leave.	**Elena quiere que me vaya.** Elena wants me to leave.
Siento no poder venir. I'm sorry I can't come.	**Siento que no puedas venir.** I'm sorry that you can't come.
Me alegro de poder ayudar. I'm pleased to be able to help.	**Me alegro de que puedas ayudar.** I'm pleased you can help.

➤ You will also come across the verb + **que** + subjunctive construction (often with a personal object such as **me**, **te** and so on) when the first verb is one you use to ask or advise somebody to do something.

  Solo te pido que tengas cuidado. — I'm only asking you to be careful.
  Te aconsejo que no llegues tarde. — I'd advise you not to be late.

➤ You will also come across the subjunctive in the following cases:

- after verbs expressing doubt or uncertainty, and verbs saying what you think about something that are used with **no**

Dudo que tenga tiempo.	I doubt I'll have time.
No creo que venga.	I don't think she'll come.
No pienso que esté bien.	I don't think it's right.

- in impersonal constructions that show a need to do something

¿Hace falta que vaya Jaime?	Does Jaime need to go?
No es necesario que vengas.	You don't need to come.

- in impersonal constructions that do not express facts

Es posible que tengan razón.	They may be right.

⇨ *For more information on* ***Impersonal verbs****, see page 132.*

Grammar Extra!

Use the indicative (that is, any verb form that isn't subjunctive) after impersonal expressions that state facts provided they are NOT in the negative.

Es verdad que es interesante.	It's true that it's interesting.
Es cierto que me gusta el café.	It's true I like coffee.
Parece que se va a ir.	It seems that he's going to go.

➤ The subjunctive is used after **que** to express wishes.

¡Que lo pases bien!	Have a good time!
¡Que te diviertas!	Have fun!

➤ The subjunctive is also used after certain conjunctions linking two parts of a sentence which each have different subjects.

• **antes de que**	before
¿Quieres decirle algo antes de que se vaya?	Do you want to say anything to him before he goes?
• **para que**	so that
Es para que te acuerdes de mí.	It's so that you'll remember me.
• **sin que**	without
Salimos sin que nos vieran.	We left without them seeing us.

⇨ *For more information on* ***Conjunctions****, see page 194.*

Tip

Use **para**, **sin** and **antes de** with the infinitive when the subject of both verbs is the same.

Fue en taxi para no llegar tarde.	He went by taxi so that he wouldn't be late.
Pedro se fue sin esperarnos.	Pedro left without waiting for us.
Cenamos antes de ir al teatro.	We had dinner before we went to the theater.

3 Forming the present subjunctive

➤ To form the present subjunctive of most verbs, drop the **-o** ending of the **yo** form of the present simple, and attach a fixed set of endings.

➤ For **-ar** verbs, the endings are: **-e**, **-es**, **-e**, **-emos**, **-éis** (in Spain), **-en**.

➤ For both **-er** and **-ir** verbs, the endings are: **-a**, **-as**, **-a**, **-amos**, **-áis** (in Spain), **-an**.

➤ The following table shows the present subjunctive of three regular verbs: **hablar** (meaning *to speak*), **comer** (meaning *to eat*) and **vivir** (meaning *to live*).

Infinitive	(yo)	(tú)	(él) (ella) (usted)	(nosotros) (nosotras)	(vosotros)* (vosotras)*	(ellos) (ellas) (ustedes)
hablar to speak	**hable**	**hables**	**hable**	**hablemos**	**habléis***	**hablen**
comer to eat	**coma**	**comas**	**coma**	**comamos**	**comáis***	**coman**
vivir to live	**viva**	**vivas**	**viva**	**vivamos**	**viváis***	**vivan**

*only used in Spain

Quiero que comas algo.	I want you to eat something.
Me sorprende que no hable inglés.	I'm surprised he doesn't speak English.
No es verdad que trabajen aquí.	It isn't true that they work here.

➤ Some verbs have very irregular **yo** forms in the ordinary present tense and these irregular forms are reflected in the stem for the present subjunctive.

Infinitive	(yo)	(tú)	(él) (ella) (usted)	(nosotros) (nosotras)	(vosotros)* (vosotras)*	(ellos) (ellas) (ustedes)
decir to say	diga	digas	diga	digamos	digáis*	digan
hacer to do/make	haga	hagas	haga	hagamos	hagáis*	hagan
poner to put	ponga	pongas	ponga	pongamos	pongáis*	pongan
salir to leave	salga	salgas	salga	salgamos	salgáis*	salgan
tener to have	tenga	tengas	tenga	tengamos	tengáis*	tengan
venir to come	venga	vengas	venga	vengamos	vengáis*	vengan

*only used in Spain – note that this verb form has an accent.

Voy a limpiar la casa antes de que vengan. I'm going to clean the house before they come.

Tip

The present subjunctive endings are the opposite of what you'd expect, as **-ar** verbs have endings starting with **-e**, and **-er** and **-ir** verbs have endings starting with **-a**.

4 Forming the present subjunctive of irregular verbs

➤ The following verbs have irregular subjunctive forms:

Infinitive	(yo)	(tú)	(él) (ella) (usted)	(nosotros) (nosotras)	(vosotros)* (vosotras)*	(ellos) (ellas) (ustedes)
dar to give	dé	des	dé	demos	deis*	den
estar to be	esté	estés	esté	estemos	estéis*	estén
haber to have	haya	hayas	haya	hayamos	hayáis*	hayan
ir to go	vaya	vayas	vaya	vayamos	vayáis*	vayan
saber to know	sepa	sepas	sepa	sepamos	sepáis*	sepan
ser to be	sea	seas	sea	seamos	seáis*	sean

*only used in Spain

No quiero que te vayas. I don't want you to go.
Dudo que esté aquí. I doubt if it's here.
No piensan que sea él. They don't think it's him.
Es posible que haya problemas. There may be problems.

For further explanation of grammatical terms, please see pages viii-xii.

➤ Verbs that change their stems (radical-changing verbs) in the ordinary present usually change them in the same way in the present subjunctive.

☞ *For more information on **radical-changing verbs**, see page 76.*

Infinitive	(yo)	(tú)	(él) (ella) (usted)	(nosotros) (nosotras)	(vosotros)* (vosotras)*	(ellos) (ellas) (ustedes)
pensar to think	piense	pienses	piense	pensemos	penséis*	piensen
entender to understand	entienda	entiendas	entienda	entendamos	entendáis*	entiendan
poder to be able	pueda	puedas	pueda	podamos	podáis*	puedan
querer to want	quiera	quieras	quiera	queramos	queráis*	quieran
volver to return	vuelva	vuelvas	vuelva	volvamos	volváis*	vuelvan

*only used in Spain

No hace falta que vuelvas. There's no need for you to come back.
Es para que lo entiendas. It's so you'll understand.
Me alegro de que puedas venir. I'm pleased you can come.

➤ Sometimes the stem of the **nosotros** and **vosotros** forms isn't the same as it is in the ordinary present tense.

Infinitive	(yo)	(tú)	(él) (ella) (usted)	(nosotros) (nosotras)	(vosotros)* (vosotras)*	(ellos) (ellas) (ustedes)
dormir to sleep	duerma	duermas	duerma	durmamos	durmáis*	duerman
morir to die	muera	mueras	muera	muramos	muráis*	mueran
pedir to ask for	pida	pidas	pida	pidamos	pidáis*	pidan
seguir to follow	siga	sigas	siga	sigamos	sigáis*	sigan
sentir to feel	sienta	sientas	sienta	sintamos	sintáis*	sientan

*only used in Spain

No quieren que sigamos cantando. They don't want us to go on singing.

5 Tenses with the subjunctive

➤ If the verb in the first part of the sentence is in the present, future or imperative, the second verb will usually be in the present subjunctive.

Quiero (*present*) **que lo hagas** (*present subjunctive*).
I want you to do it.

Lo pondré (*future*) **en el closet para que no lo vea** (*present subjunctive*).
I'll put it in the closet so she won't see it.

Ven (*imperative*) **cuando quieras** (*present subjunctive*).
Come whenever you want.

➤ If the verb in the first part of the sentence is in the conditional or a past tense, the second verb will usually be in the imperfect subjunctive.

Me gustaría *(conditional)* **que llegaras** *(imperfect subjunctive)* **temprano.** I'd like you to arrive early.

Les pedí *(preterite)* **que me esperaran** *(imperfect subjunctive)*. I asked them to wait for me.

6 Indicative or subjunctive?

➤ Many expressions are followed by the indicative (the ordinary form of the verb) when they state facts, and by the subjunctive when they refer to possible or intended future events and outcomes.

➤ Certain conjunctions relating to time such as **cuando** (meaning *when*), **hasta que** (meaning *until*), **en cuanto** (meaning *as soon as*) and **mientras** (meaning *while*) are used with the indicative when the action has happened or when talking about what happens regularly.

¿Qué dijo cuando te vio? What did he say when he saw you?

Siempre lo veo cuando voy a San Francisco. I always see him when I go to San Francisco.

Me quedé allí hasta que volvió Antonio. I stayed there until Antonio came back.

➤ The same conjunctions are followed by the subjunctive when talking about a future time.

Dale recuerdos cuando lo veas. Give him my regards when you see him.

Lo veré cuando vaya a San Francisco. I'll see him when I go to San Francisco.

¿Por qué no te quedas aquí hasta que vuelva Antonio? Why don't you stay here until Antonio comes back?

Grammar Extra!

aunque is used with the indicative (the ordinary verb forms) when it means *although* or *even though*. In this case, the second part of the sentence is stating a fact.

Me gusta el francés, aunque prefiero el alemán. I like French, although I prefer German.

Aunque estaba cansada, seguí trabajando. Although I was tired, I continued working.

aunque is used with the subjunctive when it means *even if*. Here, the second part of the sentence is not a fact.

Tienes que seguir aunque estés cansada. You have to go on, even if you are tired.

For further explanation of grammatical terms, please see pages viii-xii.

7 Forming the imperfect subjunctive

➤ For all verbs, there are two imperfect subjunctive forms that are exactly the same in meaning.

➤ The stem for both imperfect subjunctive forms is the same: you drop the **-aron** or **-ieron** ending of the **ellos** form of the preterite and attach a fixed set of endings to what is left.

⇨ *For more information on the **Preterite**, see page 106.*

➤ For **-ar** verbs, the endings are: **-ara**, **-aras**, **-ara**, **-áramos**, **-arais** (in Spain), **-aran** *or* **-ase**, **-ases**, **-ase**, **-ásemos**, **-aseis** (in Spain), **-asen**. The first form is more common.

➤ For **-er** and **-ir** verbs, the endings are: **-iera**, **-ieras**, **-iera**, **-iéramos**, **-ierais** (in Spain), **-ieran** *or* **-iese**, **-ieses**, **-iese**, **-iésemos**, **-ieseis** (in Spain), **-iesen**. The first form is more common.

➤ The following table shows the imperfect subjunctive of three regular verbs: **hablar** (meaning *to speak*), **comer** (meaning *to eat*) and **vivir** (meaning *to live*).

Infinitive	(yo)	(tú)	(él) (ella) (usted)	(nosotros) (nosotras)	(vosotros)* (vosotras)*	(ellos) (ellas) (ustedes)
hablar *to speak*	hablara	hablaras	hablara	habláramos	hablarais*	hablaran
	hablase	hablases	hablase	hablásemos	hablaseis*	hablasen
comer *to eat*	comiera	comieras	comiera	comiéramos	comierais*	comieran
	comiese	comieses	comiese	comiésemos	comieseis*	comiesen
vivir *to live*	viviera	vivieras	viviera	viviéramos	vivierais*	vivieran
	viviese	vivieses	viviese	viviésemos	vivieseis*	viviesen

*only used in Spain

➤ Many verbs have irregular preterite forms which are reflected in the stem for the imperfect subjunctive. For example:

Infinitive	(yo)	(tú)	(él) (ella) (usted)	(nosotros) (nosotras)	(vosotros)* (vosotras)*	(ellos) (ellas) (ustedes)
dar to give	diera	dieras	diera	diéramos	dierais*	dieran
	diese	dieses	diese	diésemos	dieseis*	diesen
estar to be	estuviera	estuvieras	estuviera	estuviéramos	estuvierais*	estuvieran
	estuviese	estuvieses	estuviese	estuviésemos	estuvieseis*	estuviesen
hacer to do/ make	hiciera	hicieras	hiciera	hiciéramos	hicierais*	hicieran
	hiciese	hicieses	hiciese	hiciésemos	hicieseis*	hiciesen
poner to put	pusiera	pusieras	pusiera	pusiéramos	pusierais*	pusieran
	pusiese	pusieses	pusiese	pusiésemos	pusieseis*	pusiesen
tener to have	tuviera	tuvieras	tuviera	tuviéramos	tuvierais*	tuvieran
	tuviese	tuvieses	tuviese	tuviésemos	tuvieseis*	tuviesen
ser to be	fuera	fueras	fuera	fuéramos	fuerais*	fueran
	fuese	fueses	fuese	fuésemos	fueseis*	fuesen
venir to come	viniera	vinieras	viniera	viniéramos	vinierais*	vinieran
	viniese	vinieses	viniese	viniésemos	vinieseis*	viniesen

*only used in Spain

8 Forming the imperfect subjunctive of some irregular -ir verbs

➤ In some irregular **-ir** verbs – the ones that don't have an **i** in the **ellos** form of the preterite – **-era**, **-eras**, **-era**, **-éramos**, **-erais**, **-eran** *or* **-ese**, **-eses**, **-ese**, **-ésemos**, **-eseis**, **-esen** are added to the preterite stem instead of **-iera** and **-iese** and so on.

⇨ *For more information on the **Preterite**, see page 106.*

Infinitive	(yo)	(tú)	(él) (ella) (usted)	(nosotros) (nosotras)	(vosotros)* (vosotras)*	(ellos) (ellas) (ustedes)
decir to say	dijera	dijeras	dijera	dijéramos	dijerais*	dijeran
	dijese	dijeses	dijese	dijésemos	dijeseis*	dijesen
ir to go	fuera	fueras	fuera	fuéramos	fuerais*	fueran
	fuese	fueses	fuese	fuésemos	fueseis*	fuesen

*only used in Spain

ℹ Note that the imperfect subjunctive forms of **ir** and **ser** are identical.

Teníamos miedo de que se fuera. We were afraid he might leave.
No podíamos creer que fuera él. We couldn't believe it was him.

9 Present indicative or imperfect subjunctive after si

➤ Like some other conjunctions, **si** (meaning *if*) is sometimes followed by the ordinary present tense (the present indicative) and sometimes by the imperfect subjunctive.

➤ **si** is followed by the present indicative when talking about likely possibilities.

Si quieres, te acompaño.	If you like, I'll come with you. *(and you might want me to come with you)*
Si venden periódicos, compra uno.	If they sell newspapers, get one. *(and they might sell newspapers)*

➤ **si** is followed by the imperfect subjunctive when talking about unlikely or impossible conditions.

Si tuviera más dinero, me lo compraría.	If I had more money, I'd buy it. *(but I haven't got more money)*
Si yo fuera tú, lo compraría.	If I were you, I'd buy it. *(but I'm not you)*

Tip

You probably need the imperfect subjunctive in Spanish after **si** if the English sentence has *would* in it.

Key points

✔ After certain verbs you have to use a subjunctive in Spanish when there is a different subject in the two parts of a sentence.

✔ A subjunctive is also found after impersonal expressions, as well as after certain conjunctions.

✔ The subjunctive can be avoided if the subject of both verbs is the same. An infinitive is normally used instead.

✔ The endings of the present subjunctive in regular **-ar** verbs are: **-e**, **-es**, **-e**, **-emos**, **-éis** (in Spain), **-en**.

✔ The endings of the present subjunctive in regular **-er** and **-ir** verbs are: **-a**, **-as**, **-a**, **-amos**, **-áis** (in Spain), **-an**.

✔ The endings of the imperfect subjunctive in regular **-ar** verbs are: **-ara**, **-aras**, **-ara**, **-áramos**, **-arais** (in Spain), **-aran**, or **-ase**, **-ases**, **-ase**, **-ásemos**, **-aseis** (in Spain), **-asen**.

✔ The endings of the imperfect subjunctive in regular **-er** and **-ir** verbs are: **-iera**, **-ieras**, **-iera**, **-iéramos**, **-ierais** (in Spain), **-ieran** or **-iese**, **-ieses**, **-iese**, **-iésemos**, **-ieseis** (in Spain), **-iesen**.

✔ Some verbs have irregular subjunctive forms.

The Infinitive

What is the infinitive?
The **infinitive** is a form of the verb that hasn't had any endings added to it and doesn't relate to any particular tense. In English, the infinitive is usually shown with *to*, as in *to speak*, *to eat*, *to live*.

1 Using the infinitive

➤ In English, the infinitive is usually thought of as being made up of two words (for example: *to speak*). In Spanish, the infinitive consists of one word and is the verb form that ends in **-ar**, **-er** or **-ir** (for example: **hablar**, **comer**, **vivir**).

➤ When you look up a verb in the dictionary, you will find that information is usually listed under the infinitive form.

➤ In Spanish, the infinitive is often used in the following ways:

- after a preposition such as **antes de** (meaning *before*), **después de** (meaning *after*)

Después de comer, fuimos al club.	After eating, we went to the club.
Salió sin hacer ruido.	She went out without making a noise.
Siempre leo antes de acostarme.	I always read before going to bed.

i Note that in English we always use the *-ing* form of the verb after a preposition (for example: *before going*). In Spanish, you have to use the infinitive form after a preposition.

- in set phrases, particularly after adjectives or nouns

Estoy encantada de poder ayudarte.	I'm delighted to be able to help you.
Está contento de vivir aquí.	He's happy living here.
Tengo ganas de salir.	I feel like going out.
No hace falta comprar leche.	We/You don't need to buy any milk.
Me dio mucha alegría verla.	I was very pleased to see her.
Me da miedo ir sola.	I'm scared of going on my own.

- after another verb, sometimes as the object of it

Tengo que llamar a casa.	I have to call home.
Prefiero esquiar.	I prefer skiing.
Me gusta escuchar música.	I like listening to music.
Nos encanta nadar.	We love swimming.
Odio esperar.	I hate waiting.

i Note that, after verbs expressing like and dislike, the Spanish infinitive often corresponds to the *-ing* form in English.

- in instructions that are aimed at the general public – for example in cook books or on signs

Cocer a fuego lento.	Cook on a low heat.
Prohibido sacar fotos.	No photography.

- as a noun, where in English we would use the *-ing* form of the verb

Lo importante es intentarlo.	Trying is the important thing.

> *Tip*
>
> Be especially careful when translating the English *-ing* form. It is often translated by the infinitive in Spanish.

2 Linking two verbs together

➤ There are three ways that verbs can be linked together when the second verb is an infinitive:

- with no linking word in between

¿Quieres venir?	Do you want to come?
Necesito hablar contigo.	I need to talk to you.

- with a preposition:

ir a hacer algo	to be going to do something
aprender a hacer algo	to learn to do something
dejar de hacer algo	to stop doing something
Voy a comprarme un celular.	I'm going to buy a cell phone.
Aprendimos a esquiar.	We learned to ski.
Quiere dejar de fumar.	He wants to stop smoking.

i Note that you have to learn the preposition required for each verb.

- in set structures

tener que hacer algo	to have to do something
Tengo que salir.	I've got to go out.
Tendrías que comer más.	You should eat more.
Tuvo que devolver el dinero.	He had to pay back the money.

3 Verbs followed by the infinitive with no preposition

➤ Some Spanish verbs and groups of verbs can be followed by an infinitive with no preposition:

- **poder** (meaning *to be able to, can, may*), **saber** (meaning *to know how to, can*), **querer** (meaning *to want*) and **deber** (meaning *to have to, must*)

No puede venir.	He can't come.
¿Sabes esquiar?	Can you ski?
Quiere estudiar medicina.	He wants to study medicine.
Debes hacerlo.	You must do it.

- verbs like **gustar** and **encantar**, where the infinitive is the subject of the verb

Me gusta estudiar.	I like studying.
Nos encanta bailar.	We love dancing.

- verbs that relate to seeing or hearing, such as **ver** (meaning *to see*) and **oír** (meaning *to hear*)

Nos ha visto llegar.	He saw us arrive.
Te oí cantar.	I heard you singing.

- the verbs **hacer** (meaning *to make*) and **dejar** (meaning *to let*)

¡No me hagas reír!	Don't make me laugh!
Mis padres no me dejan salir por la noche.	My parents don't let me go out at night.

- the following common verbs

decidir	to decide
desear	to wish, want
esperar	to hope
evitar	to avoid
necesitar	to need
odiar	to hate
olvidar	to forget
pensar	to think
preferir	to prefer
recordar	to remember
sentir	to regret

Decidieron comprarse una casa.	They decided to buy a house.
No desea tener más hijos.	She doesn't want to have any more children.
Espero poder ir.	I hope to be able to go.

For further explanation of grammatical terms, please see pages viii-xii.

<u>Evita gastar</u> demasiado dinero.	Avoid spending too much money.
<u>Necesito salir</u> un momento.	I need to go out for a moment.
<u>Olvidó dejar</u> su dirección.	She forgot to leave her address.
<u>Pienso hacer</u> enchiladas.	I'm thinking of making enchiladas.
<u>Siento molestarte</u>.	I'm sorry to bother you.

➤ Some of these verbs combine with infinitives to make set phrases with a special meaning:

- **querer decir** — to mean
  ¿Qué <u>quiere decir</u> eso? — What does that mean?
- **dejar caer** — to drop
  <u>Dejó caer</u> la bandeja. — She dropped the tray.

4 <u>Verbs followed by the preposition a and the infinitive</u>

➤ The following verbs are the most common ones that can be followed by **a** and the infinitive:

- verbs relating to movement such as **ir** (meaning *to go*) and **venir** (meaning *to come*)

Se va <u>a</u> comprar un caballo.	He's going to buy a horse.
Viene <u>a</u> vernos.	He's coming to see us.

- the following common verbs

aprender <u>a</u> hacer algo	to learn to do something
comenzar <u>a</u> hacer algo	to begin to do something
decidirse <u>a</u> hacer algo	to decide to do something
empezar <u>a</u> hacer algo	to begin to do something
llegar <u>a</u> hacer algo	to manage to do something
llegar <u>a</u> ser algo	to become something
probar <u>a</u> hacer algo	to try to do something
volver <u>a</u> hacer algo	to do something again
Me gustaría aprender <u>a</u> nadar.	I'd like to learn to swim.
No llegó <u>a</u> terminar la carrera.	He didn't manage to finish college.
Llegó <u>a</u> ser presidente.	He became president.
No vuelvas <u>a</u> hacerlo nunca más.	Don't ever do it again.

➤ The following verbs can be followed by **a** + a person's name or by **a** + a noun or pronoun referring to a person, and by **a** + infinitive. In the case of **a** + a person's name or **a** + a noun, this can also be placed after the **a** + infinitive.

ayudar <u>a</u> alguien <u>a</u> hacer algo	to help someone to do something
enseñar <u>a</u> alguien <u>a</u> hacer algo	to teach someone to do something
invitar <u>a</u> alguien <u>a</u> hacer algo	to invite someone to do something

Ayuda a mamá a poner la mesa.	Help Mom set the table.
¿Por qué no le enseñas a nadar a tu hermano?	Why don't you teach your brother to swim?
Los invité a cenar en casa.	I invited them over for dinner.

5 Verbs followed by the preposition de and the infinitive

➤ The following verbs are the most common ones that can be followed by **de** and the infinitive:

aburrirse de hacer algo	to get bored with doing something
acabar de hacer algo	to have just done something
acordarse de haber hecho/de hacer algo	to remember doing/to do something
alegrarse de hacer algo	to be glad to do something
dejar de hacer algo	to stop doing something
tener ganas de hacer algo	to feel like doing something
tratar de hacer algo	to try to do something

Me aburrí de jugar a las cartas.	I got bored with playing cards.
Acabo de comprar un celular.	I just bought a cell phone.
Acababan de llegar cuando...	They had just arrived when...
Me alegro de verte.	I'm glad to see you.
¿Quieres dejar de hablar?	Will you stop talking?
Tengo ganas de ir al cine.	I feel like going to the movies.

6 Verbs followed by the preposition con and the infinitive

➤ The following verbs are the most common ones that can be followed by **con** and the infinitive:

amenazar con hacer algo	to threaten to do someting
soñar con hacer algo	to dream of doing something

Amenazó con denunciarlos.	He threatened to report them.
Sueño con hacer un crucero.	I dream of going on a cruise.

7 Verbs followed by the preposition en and the infinitive

➤ The verb **quedar** is the most common one that can be followed by **en** and the infinitive:

quedar en hacer algo	to agree to do something
Habíamos quedado en encontrarnos a las ocho.	We had agreed to meet at eight.

For further explanation of grammatical terms, please see pages viii-xii.

Key points

- ✔ Infinitives are found after prepositions, set phrases and in instructions to the general public.
- ✔ They can also function as the subject or object of a verb, when the infinitive corresponds to the *-ing* form in English.
- ✔ Many Spanish verbs can be followed by another verb in the infinitive.
- ✔ Two verbs may be linked by nothing at all, or by **a**, **de** or another preposition.
- ✔ In Spanish, the construction does not always match the English. It's best to learn these constructions when you learn a new verb.

Prepositions after verbs

➤ In English, there are some phrases which are made up of verbs and prepositions (for example: *to accuse somebody of something*, *to look forward to something* and *to rely on something*).

➤ In Spanish, there are also lots of set phrases made up of verbs and prepositions. Often the prepositions in Spanish are not the same as they are in English, so you will need to learn them. Listed below are phrases using verbs and some common Spanish prepositions.

➪ *For more information on verbs used with a preposition and the infinitive, see page* 149.

1 Verbs followed by a

➤ **a** is often the equivalent of the English word *to* when it is used with an indirect object after verbs like **enviar** (meaning *to send*), **dar** (meaning *to give*) and **decir** (meaning *to say*).

darle algo a alguien	to give something to someone
decirle algo a alguien	to say something to someone
enviarle algo a alguien	to send something to someone
escribirle algo a alguien	to write something to someone
mostrarle algo a alguien	to show something to someone

➪ *For more information on* **Indirect objects**, *see page* 49.

Tip

There is an important difference between Spanish and English with this type of verb. In English, you can say either *I gave the keys to Susan* or *I gave Susan the keys*, leaving out the *to*.
You can NEVER leave out **a** in Spanish in this way: *Le di las llaves a Susan*.

➤ Here are some verbs using **a** in Spanish that have a different construction in English.

asistir a algo	to attend something, to be at something
dirigirse a (un lugar)	to head for (a place)
dirigirse a alguien	to address somebody
llegar a (un lugar)	to arrive at (a place)
oler a algo	to smell of something
parecerse a alguien/algo	to look like somebody/something

subir(se) a un tren/un coche	to get on a train/into a car
subir(se) a un árbol	to climb a tree
tenerle miedo a alguien	to be afraid of somebody
Este perfume huele a jazmín.	This perfume smells of jasmine.
Se parece a tu hermana.	She looks like your sister.
Nunca le tuvieron miedo a su padre.	They were never afraid of their father.

➪ *For verbs such as **gustar**, **encantar** and **faltar**, see **Verbal idioms** on page 156.*

2 Verbs followed by de

➤ Here are some verbs using **de** in Spanish that have a different construction in English:

acordarse de algo/alguien	to remember something/ somebody
alegrarse de algo	to be glad about something
bajarse de un tren/un coche	to get off a train/out of a car
darse cuenta de algo	to realize something
depender de algo/alguien	to depend on something/ somebody
despedirse de alguien	to say goodbye to somebody
preocuparse de (*or* **por**) **algo/alguien**	to worry about something/ somebody
quejarse de algo	to complain about something
reírse de algo/alguien	to laugh at something/somebody
salir de (un cuarto/un edificio)	to leave (a room/a building)
tener ganas de algo	to want something, to feel like something
trabajar de (mecánico/ secretario)	to work as (a mechanic/ secretary)
tratarse de algo/alguien	to be a question of something/ to be about somebody
Nos acordamos muy bien de aquellas vacaciones.	We remember that vacation very well.
Se bajó del tren.	He got off the train.
No depende de mí.	It doesn't depend on me.
No te rías de ella.	Don't laugh at her.

3 Verbs followed by con

➤ Here are some verbs using **con** in Spanish that have a different construction in English:

contar con alguien/algo	to rely on somebody/something
encontrarse con alguien	to meet somebody (*by chance*)
enojarse con alguien	to get annoyed with somebody
hablar con alguien	to talk to somebody
soñar con alguien/algo	to dream about somebody/something
Cuento contigo.	I'm relying on you.
Me encontré con ella al salir del banco.	I met her as I was leaving the bank.
¿Puedo hablar con usted un momento?	May I talk to you for a moment?

4 Verbs followed by en

➤ Here are some verbs using **en** in Spanish that have a different construction in English:

entrar en (un edificio/un cuarto)	to enter, go into (a building/a room)
pensar en algo/alguien	to think about *or* of something/somebody
No quiero pensar en eso.	I don't want to think about that.

5 Verbs followed by por

➤ Here are some verbs using **por** in Spanish that have a different construction in English:

interesarse por algo/alguien	to take an interest in something/somebody; to ask about something/somebody
preguntar por alguien	to ask for/about somebody
preocuparse por (*or* de) algo/alguien	to worry about something/somebody
Se interesó por la marcha del proyecto.	He asked about the progress of the project.
Se preocupa mucho por su apariencia.	He worries a lot about his appearance.

For further explanation of grammatical terms, please see pages viii-xii.

6 Verbs taking a direct object in Spanish but not in English

➤ In English there are a few verbs that are followed by *at*, *for* or *to* which, in Spanish, are not followed by any preposition other than the personal **a**.

➪ *For more information on **Personal** a, see page 184.*

mirar algo/a alguien	to look at something/somebody
escuchar algo/a alguien	to listen to something/somebody
buscar algo/a alguien	to look for something/somebody
pedir algo	to ask for something
esperar algo/a alguien	to wait for something/somebody
pagar algo	to pay for something
Mira esta foto.	Look at this photo.
Me gusta escuchar música.	I like listening to music.
Estoy buscando los lentes.	I'm looking for my glasses.
Pidió una taza de té.	He asked for a cup of tea.
Estamos esperando el tren.	We're waiting for the train.
Ya pagué el recibo del teléfono.	I've already paid the phone bill.
Estoy buscando a mi hermano.	I'm looking for my brother.

Key points

✔ The prepositions used with Spanish verbs are often very different from those used in English, so make sure you learn common expressions involving Spanish prepositions.

✔ In Spanish, the most common prepositions used with verbs are **a**, **de**, **con**, **en** and **por**.

✔ Some Spanish verbs are not followed by a preposition, but are used with a preposition in English.

Verbal Idioms

1 Present tense of gustar

➤ You will probably already have come across the phrase **me gusta...** meaning *I like...* . Actually, **gustar** literally means *to please*. If you remember this, you will be able to use **gustar** much more easily.

Me gusta el chocolate.	I like chocolate. (*literally: chocolate pleases me*)
Me gustan los animales.	I like animals. (*literally: animals please me*)
Nos gusta el tenis.	We like tennis. (*literally: tennis pleases us*)
Nos gustan todos los deportes.	We like all sports. (*literally: all sports please us*)

➤ Even though **chocolate**, **animales**, and so on, come after **gustar**, they are the subject of the verb (the person or thing performing the action) and, therefore, the endings of **gustar** change to agree with them.

➤ When the thing that you like is singular, you use **gusta** (*third person singular*), and when the thing that you like is plural, you use **gustan** (*third person plural*).

Le gusta Colombia.	He/She likes Colombia. (*literally: Colombia pleases him/her*)
Le gustan los colombianos.	He/She likes Colombians. (*literally: Colombians please him/her*)

i Note that **me**, **te**, **le**, **nos**, **os** and **les**, which are used with **gustar**, are indirect object pronouns.

⇨ *For more information on* **Indirect object pronouns**, *see page* 49.

2 Other tenses of gustar

➤ You can also use **gustar** in other tenses.

Les gustó la fiesta.	They liked the party.
Les gustaron los fuegos artificiales.	They liked the fireworks.
Te va a gustar la película.	You'll like the movie.
Te van a gustar las fotos.	You'll like the photos.

➤ You can also use **más** with **gustar** to say what you prefer.

A mí me gusta más el rojo.	I prefer the red one. (*literally: the red one pleases me more*)
A mí me gustan más los rojos.	I prefer the red ones. (*literally: the red ones please me more*)

3 Other verbs like gustar

➤ There are several other verbs which behave in the same way as **gustar**:

- **encantar**

Me encanta el jazz.	I love jazz.
Me encantan los animales.	I love animals.

- **faltar**

Le faltaba un botón.	He had a button missing.
Le faltaban tres dientes.	He had three teeth missing.

- **quedar**

No les queda nada.	They have nothing left.
Sólo nos quedan dos capítulos.	We only have two chapters left.

- **doler**

Le dolía la cabeza.	His head hurt.
Le dolían las muelas.	His teeth hurt.

- **interesar**

Le interesó la oferta.	He was interested in the offer.
Siempre me interesaron estos temas.	I've always been interested in these issues.

- **importar**

No me importa el dinero.	Money doesn't matter to me.
Me importan mucho mis estudios.	My studies matter to me a lot.

- **hacer falta**

Nos hace falta una computadora.	We need a computer.
Nos hacen falta libros.	We need books.

Grammar Extra!

All of the examples above are in the third persons singular and plural as these are by far the most common. However, it is also possible to use these verbs in other forms.

Creo que le gustas.	I think he likes you. (*literally: I think you please him*)

---

4 Verbal idioms used with another verb

➤ In English, you can say *I like playing chess*, *we love swimming* and so on. In Spanish, you can also use another verb with most of the verbs similar to **gustar**. However, in Spanish, the verb form you use for the second verb is the infinitive.

Le gusta jugar tenis.	He/She likes playing tennis.
No me gusta bailar.	I don't like dancing.
Nos encanta cocinar.	We love cooking.
No me importa tener que esperar.	I don't mind having to wait.

⇨ *For more information on the* ***Infinitive****, see page 146.*

Key points

- ✔ In Spanish, there are a number of common verbs which are used in the opposite way to English, for example, **gustar**, **encantar**, **hacer falta**, and so on. With all of these verbs, the object of the English verb is the subject of the Spanish verb.
- ✔ The endings of these verbs change according to whether the thing liked or needed and so on is singular or plural.
- ✔ All of these verbs can be followed by another verb in the infinitive.

Negatives

What is a negative?
A **negative** question or statement is one which contains a word such as *not*, *never* or *nothing* and is used to say that something is not happening, is not true or is absent.

1 no

➤ In English, we often make sentences negative by adding *don't*, *doesn't* or *didn't* before the verb. In Spanish you simply add **no** before the main verb.

Affirmative			Negative	
Trabaja.	He works.	→	**No trabaja.**	He doesn't work.
Comen.	They eat.	→	**No comen.**	They don't eat.
Salió.	She went out.	→	**No salió.**	She didn't go out.
Lo sabía.	I knew (it).	→	**No lo sabía.**	I didn't know (it).
Sabe nadar.	He can swim.	→	**No sabe nadar.**	He can't swim.

Tip
don't, *doesn't* and *didn't* do not have an equivalent in Spanish. You just add **no** to form the negative.

➤ When there is a subject (the person doing the action) in the sentence, put **no** between the subject and the verb.

Juan no vive aquí. Juan doesn't live here.
Mi hermana no lee mucho. My sister doesn't read much.
Mis padres no llamaron. My parents didn't call.
Él no lo entenderá. He won't understand.

ℹ Note that the Spanish word **no** also means *no* in answer to a question.

➤ Where the subject is only shown by the verb ending, **no** goes before the verb.

No tenemos tiempo. We don't have time.
Todavía no ha llegado. He hasn't arrived yet.
No habíamos comido. We hadn't eaten.
No va a llevar mucho tiempo. It won't take long.

➤ If there are any object pronouns (for example: **me**, **te**, **lo**, **los**, **le** and so on) before the verb, **no** goes BEFORE them.

No la vi. I didn't see her.
No me gusta el beisbol. I don't like baseball.

➤ In phrases consisting only of *not* and another word, such as *not now* or *not me*, the Spanish **no** usually goes AFTER the other word.

Ahora no.	Not now.
Yo no.	Not me.
Todavía no.	Not yet.

➤ Some phrases have a special construction in Spanish.

Espero que sí.	I hope so.	→	**Espero que no.**	I hope not.
Creo que sí.	I think so.	→	**Creo que no.**	I don't think so.

2 Other negative words

➤ In Spanish, you can form negatives using pairs and groups of words, as you can in English.

- **no … nunca** never *or* not … ever
  No la veo nunca. — I never see her *or* I don't ever see her.
- **no … jamás** never *or* not … ever
  No la veo jamás. — I never ever see her *or* I don't ever see her.
- **no … nada** nothing *or* not … anything
  No dijo nada. — He said nothing *or* He didn't say anything.
- **no … nadie** nobody *or* not … anybody
  No hablaron con nadie. — They spoke to nobody *or* They didn't speak to anybody.
- **no … tampoco** not … either
  Yo no la vi. – Yo tampoco. — I didn't see her. – Neither did I *or* I didn't either *or* Nor did I.
  A él no le gusta el café y a mí tampoco. — He doesn't like coffee and neither do I.
- **no … ni … ni** neither … nor
  No vinieron ni Carlos ni Ana. — Neither Carlos nor Ana came.
- **no … más** no longer *or* not .. any more
  No te veré más. — I won't see you any more.
- **no … ningún/ninguna** + *noun* no *or* not … any
  No tiene ningún interés en ir. — She has no interest in going.

➤ In answers to questions or before a verb, most of these negative words can also be used without **no**.

¿Qué compraste? – Nada.	What did you buy? – Nothing.
¿Quién llamó? – Nadie.	Who called? – No one.
Nunca la veo.	I never see her.
Nadie nos ayudó.	No one helped us.
Ni Pedro ni Pablo fuman.	Neither Pedro nor Pablo smokes.

➤ Sometimes negative expressions combine with each other.

Nunca hacen nada.	They never do anything.
Nunca viene nadie.	No one ever comes.
No lo haré nunca más.	I'll never do it again.

3 Word order with negatives

➤ In English you can put words like *never* and *ever* between *have/has/had* and the past participle, for example, *We have never been to Argentina*. In Spanish, you should NEVER separate **he**, **has**, **ha**, **había** and so on from the past participle of the verb.

Nunca hemos estado en Argentina.	We have never been to Argentina.
Nunca había visto nada así.	I had never seen anything like this.
Ninguno de nosotros había esquiado nunca.	None of us had ever skied.

⇨ *For more information on **Past participles**, see page 118.*

Key points

✔ The Spanish word **no** is equivalent to both *no* and *not* in English.

✔ You can make sentences negative by putting **no** before the verb (and before any object pronouns that are in front of the verb).

✔ Other negative words also exist, such as **nunca**, **nadie** and **nada**. Use them in combination with **no**, with the verb sandwiched in between. Most of them also work on their own, in answers to questions or before a verb.

✔ Never insert negative words, or anything else, between **he**, **has**, **ha**, **había** and so on and the past participle.

Questions

What is a question?
A **question** is a sentence which is used to ask someone about something and which often has the verb in front of the subject. Questions often include a question word such as *why*, *when*, *where*, *who*, *which* or *how*.

Asking questions in Spanish

In Spanish, there are three main ways of asking questions:

- by making your voice go up at the end of the sentence
- by changing normal word order
- by using a question word

Tip

Don't forget the opening question mark in written Spanish. It goes at the beginning of the question or of the question part of a sentence.

¿No quieres tomar algo?	Wouldn't you like something to eat or drink?
Eres cubano, ¿no?	You're Cuban, aren't you?

1 Asking a question by making your voice go up

➤ If you are expecting a *yes* or *no* answer, there is a very simple way of asking a question. You keep the word order exactly as it would be in a normal sentence but you turn it into a question by making your voice go up at the end.

¿Hablas español?	Do you speak Spanish?
¿Es profesor?	Is he a teacher?
¿Hay leche?	Is there any milk?
¿Te gusta la música?	Do you like music?

➤ When the subject (the person or thing doing the action) of the verb is a noun, pronoun or name, it can be placed before the verb, as in an ordinary sentence. The difference is that you turn the statement into a question by making your voice go up at the end.

¿Tu hermana compró pan?	Did your sister buy any bread?
¿Tú lo hiciste?	Did you do it?
¿Tu padre te vio?	Did your father see you?
¿Paula va a venir?	Is Paula coming?

For further explanation of grammatical terms, please see pages viii-xii.

2 Asking a question by changing word order

➤ When the subject of the verb is specified, another common way of asking questions is to change the word order so that the verb comes BEFORE the subject instead of after it.

¿Lo hiciste tú?	Did you do it?
¿Te vio tu padre?	Did your father see you?
¿Va a venir Paula?	Is Paula coming?

ℹ Note that the position of object pronouns is not affected.

⇨ *For more information on* ***Word order with object pronouns****, see pages 47, 50 and 52.*

Grammar Extra!

If the verb has an object, such as *any bread* in *Did your sister buy any bread?*, the subject comes AFTER the object, provided the object is short.

¿Compró pan tu hermana?	Did your sister buy any bread?
¿Trajo la cámara tu novio?	Did your boyfriend bring the camera?

If the object is made up of several words, the subject goes BEFORE it.

Se compraron tus padres aquella casa de que me hablaste?	Did your parents buy that house you told me about?

When there is an adverbial phrase after the verb (*to the party*, *in Lima*) , the subject can go BEFORE OR AFTER the adverbial phrase, depending on the emphasis of the question.

¿Viene a la fiesta Andrés? *or* **¿Viene Andrés a la fiesta?**	Is Andrés coming to the party?

3 Asking a question by using a question word

➤ Question words are words like *when*, *what*, *who*, *which*, *where* and *how* that are used to ask for information. In Spanish, ALL question words have an accent on them.

¿adónde?	where ... to?
¿cómo?	how?
¿cuál/cuáles?	which?
¿cuándo?	when?
¿cuánto/cuánta?	how much?
¿cuántos/cuántas?	how many?
¿dónde?	where?
¿para qué?	what for?
¿por qué?	why?
¿qué?	what?, which?
¿quién?	who?

Tip

Be careful not to mix up **por qué** (meaning *why*) with **porque** (meaning *because*).

¿Cuándo se fue?	When did he go?
¿Qué te pasa?	What's the matter?
¿Qué vestido te vas a poner?	Which dress are you going to wear?
¿Cuál de los dos quieres?	Which do you want?
¿Cuánto café quieres?	How much coffee do you want?
¿Cuánto tiempo hace que esperas?	How long have you been waiting?

For more information on question words, see ***Interrogative adjectives*** *on page 32 and* ***Interrogative pronouns*** *on page 65.*

➤ When a question starts with a question word that isn't the subject of the verb, the subject noun or pronoun (if expressed) goes AFTER the verb.

¿De qué color es la alfombra?	What color's the rug?
¿A qué hora empieza el concierto?	What time does the concert start?
¿Dónde están tus pantalones?	Where are your pants?
¿Adónde iba tu padre?	Where was your father going?
¿Cómo están tus padres?	How are your parents?
¿Cuándo volverán los inspectores?	When will the inspectors come back?

4 Which question word to use?

➤ **qué** or **cuál** or **cuáles** can be used to mean *which*:

- always use **qué** before a noun

¿Qué vestido te vas a poner?	Which dress are you going to wear?

- otherwise use **cuál** (*singular*) or **cuáles** (*plural*)

¿Cuál quieres?	Which (one) do you want?
¿Cuáles quieres?	Which (ones) do you want?

➤ **quién** or **quiénes** can be used to mean *who*:

- use **quién** when asking about one person

¿Quién ganó?	Who won?

- use **quiénes** when asking about more than one person

¿Quiénes estaban?	Who was there?

i Note that you need to put the personal **a** before **quién** and **quiénes** when they act as objects.

¿A quién viste?	Who did you see?

⇨ *For more information on* ***Personal a****, see page 184.*

➤ **de quién** and **de quiénes** are used to mean *whose*:

- use **de quién** when there is likely to be one owner

¿De quién es este abrigo?	Whose coat is this?

- use **de quiénes** when there is likely to be more than one owner

¿De quiénes son estos abrigos?	Whose coats are these?

i Note that, in Spanish, the structure is the equivalent of *Whose is this coat?/Whose are these coats?* Don't try putting **¿de quién?** or **¿de quiénes?** immediately before a noun.

➤ **qué**, **cómo**, **cuál** and **cuáles** can all be used to mean *what* although **qué** is the most common translation:

- use **cómo** not **qué** when asking someone to repeat something that you didn't hear properly

¿Cómo?	What (did you say)?

- use **¿cuál es ... ?** and **¿cuáles son ... ?** to mean *what is ... ?* and *what/are ... ?* when you aren't asking for a definition

¿Cuál es la capital de Francia?	What's the capital of France?
¿Cuál es su número de teléfono?	What's his telephone number?

- use **¿qué es ... ?** and **¿qué son ... ?** to mean *what is ... ?* and *what are ... ?* when you are asking for a definition

¿Qué son los genes?	What are genes?

- always use **qué** to mean *what* before another noun

¿Qué hora es?	What time is it?
¿Qué materias estudias?	What subjects are you studying?

Tip

You can finish an English question (or sentence) with a preposition such as *about*, for example, *Who did you write to? What are you talking about?*. In Spanish, you can NEVER end a question or sentence with a preposition.

¿Con quién hablaste?	Who did you speak to?

Grammar Extra!

All the questions we have looked at so far have been straight questions, otherwise known as direct questions. However, sometimes instead of asking directly (for example: *Where is it?* or *Why did you do it?*), we ask the question in a more roundabout way (for example: *Can you tell me where it is?* or *Please tell me why you did it*). These are called indirect questions.

In English indirect questions we say *where it is* instead of *where is it* and *why you did it* instead of *why did you do it*. In Spanish, however, you still put the subject AFTER the verb.

¿Sabes adónde iba tu papá?	Do you know where your dad was going?
¿Puedes decirme para qué sirven los diccionarios?	Can you tell me what dictionaries are for?

In Spanish, the subject also goes AFTER the verb when you report a question in indirect speech.

Quería saber adónde iba mi papá.	He wanted to know where my dad was going.

i Note that, in Spanish, you still put accents on question words even when they are in indirect and reported questions or when they come after expressions of uncertainty:

No sé qué hacer.	I don't know what to do.
No sabemos por qué se fue.	We don't know why he left.

5 Negative questions

➤ When you want to make a negative question, put **no** before the verb in the same way that you do in statements (non-questions).

¿No vienes?	Aren't you coming?
¿No lo viste?	Didn't you see it?

➤ You can also use **o no** at the end of a question in the same way that we can ask *or not* in English.

¿Vienes o no?	Are you coming or not?
¿Lo quieres o no?	Do you want it or not?

6 Short questions

➤ In English we sometimes check whether our facts and beliefs are correct by putting *isn't it?*, *don't they?*, *are they?* and so on at the end of a comment. In Spanish, you can add **¿no?** or **¿verdad?** in the same way.

Hace calor, ¿no?	It's hot, isn't it?
Te gusta, ¿no?	You like it, don't you?

For further explanation of grammatical terms, please see pages viii-xii.

No te vas a olvidar, ¿<u>no</u>?	You won't forget, <u>will you</u>?
No vino, ¿<u>verdad</u>?	He didn't come, <u>did he</u>?

7 Answering questions

➤ To answer a question which requires a *yes* or *no* answer, just use **sí** or **no**.

¿Te gusta? – Sí/No.	Do you like it? – Yes, I do/No, I don't.
¿Está aquí? – Sí/No.	Is he here? – Yes he is/No, he isn't.
¿Tienes prisa? – Sí/No.	Are you in a hurry? – Yes, I am/ No, I'm not.
No te acordaste, ¿verdad? – Sí/No.	You didn't remember, did you? – Yes, I did/No, I didn't.

➤ You can also often answer **sí** or **no** followed by the verb in question.

¿Tienes celular? – Sí, tengo.	Do you have a cell phone? – Yes, I do.
¿Vas a la fiesta? – No, no voy.	Are you going to the party? – No, I'm not.

Key points

✔ In Spanish, you ask a question by making your voice go up at the end of the sentence, by changing normal word order, and by using question words.

✔ Question words always have an accent on them.

✔ To make a negative question, add **no** before the verb.

✔ You can add **¿no?** or **¿verdad?** to check whether your facts or beliefs are correct.

Adverbs

What is an adverb?
An **adverb** is a word usually used with verbs, adjectives or other adverbs that gives more information about when, how, where, or in what circumstances something happens, or to what degree something is true. For example: *quickly, happily, now, extremely, very*.

How adverbs are used

➤ In general, adverbs are used together with verbs, adjectives and other adverbs (for example: *act quickly; smile cheerfully; rather long; a lot happier; really slowly; very well*).

➤ Adverbs can also relate to the whole sentence. In this case they often tell you what the speaker is thinking or feeling.

Fortunately, Jan had already left.

How adverbs are formed

1 The basic rules

➤ In English, adverbs that tell you how something happened are often formed by adding *-ly* to an adjective (for example: *sweet → sweetly*). In Spanish, you form this kind of adverb by attaching **-mente** to the feminine singular form of the adjective.

Masculine adjective	Feminine adjective	Adverb	Meaning
lento	lenta	lentamente	slowly
normal	normal	normalmente	normally

Habla muy lentamente. He speaks very slowly.
¡Hazlo inmediatamente! Do it immediately!
Normalmente llego a las nueve. I normally arrive at nine o'clock.

ℹ Note that, in Spanish, adverbs NEVER change their endings to agree with anything.

Tip
You don't have to worry about adding or removing accents on the adjective when you attach **-mente**; they stay as they are.

fácil easy → **fácilmente** easily

For further explanation of grammatical terms, please see pages viii-xii.

Grammar Extra!

When there are two or more adverbs joined by a conjunction such as **y** (meaning *and*) or **pero** (meaning *but*), omit the **-mente** ending on all but the last adverb.

Lo hicieron lenta pero eficazmente.	They did it slowly, but efficiently.

Use the form **recién**, rather than **recientemente** (meaning *recently*), before a past participle (the form of the verb ending in **-ado** and **-ido** in regular verbs).

El comedor está recién pintado.	The dining room has just been painted.

➪ *For more information on **Past participles**, see page 118.*

In Spanish, adverbs ending in **-mente** are not as common as adverbs ending in *-ly* in English. For this reason, you will come across other ways of expressing an adverb in Spanish (for example: **con** used with a noun or **de manera** used with an adjective).

Maneja con cuidado.	Drive carefully.
Todos estos cambios ocurren de manera natural.	All these changes happen naturally.

2 Irregular adverbs

➤ The adverb that comes from **bueno** (meaning *good*) is **bien** (meaning *well*). The adverb that comes from **malo** (meaning *bad*) is **mal** (meaning *badly*).

Habla bien el español.	He speaks Spanish well.
Está muy mal escrito.	It's very badly written.

➤ Additionally, there are some other adverbs in Spanish which are exactly the same as the related masculine singular adjective:

- **alto** (adjective: *high*, *loud*; adverb: *high*, *loudly*)

El avión volaba alto sobre las montañas.	The plane flew high over the mountains.
Pepe habla muy alto.	Pepe talks very loudly.

- **bajo** (adjective: *low, quiet*; adverb: *low, quietly*)

El avión volaba muy bajo.	The plane was flying very low.
¡Habla bajo!	Speak quietly.

- **barato** (adjective: *cheap, inexpensive*; adverb: *cheaply, inexpensively*)

Aquí se come muy barato.	You can eat really inexpensively here.

- **claro** (adjective: *clear*; adverb: *clearly*)

Lo oí muy claro.	I heard it very clearly.

- **derecho** (adjective: *right*, *straight*; adverb: *straight*)

Vino derecho hacia mí.	He came straight towards me.

- **fuerte** (adjective: *loud*, *hard*; adverb: *loudly*, *hard*)

  Habla muy fuerte. — He talks very loudly.

  No lo golpees tan fuerte. — Don't hit it so hard.

- **rápido** (adjective: *fast*, *quick*; adverb: *fast*, *quickly*)

  Manejas demasiado rápido. — You drive too fast.

  Lo hice tan rápido como pude. — I did it as quickly as I could.

[i] Note that, when used as adverbs, these words do NOT agree with anything.

➪ *For more information on words that can be both adjectives and adverbs, see page 177.*

Grammar Extra!

Sometimes an adjective is used in Spanish where in English we would use an adverb.

Esperaban impacientes. — They were waiting impatiently.

Vivieron muy felices. — They lived very happily.

[i] Note that these Spanish adjectives describe the person or thing being talked about and, therefore, MUST agree with them.

Equally, you can often use an adverb or an adverbial expression.

Esperaban impacientemente *or* **con impaciencia.** — They were waiting impatiently.

Key points

- ✔ To form adverbs in Spanish that tell you how something happens, you can usually attach **-mente** to the feminine singular adjective.
- ✔ Adverbs don't agree with anything.
- ✔ Some Spanish adverbs are irregular, just as they are in English.
- ✔ Some Spanish adverbs are identical in form to their corresponding adjectives; when used as adverbs, they never agree with anything.

Comparatives and superlatives of adverbs

1 Comparative adverbs

What is a comparative adverb?
A **comparative adverb** is one which, in English, has *-er* on the end of it or *more* or *less* in front of it. For example: *earlier*, *later*, *more/less often*.

➤ Adverbs can be used to make comparisons in Spanish, just as they can in English. The comparative of adverbs (*more often*, *more efficiently*, *faster*) is formed by using the same phrases as for adjectives:

- **más ... (que)** — more ... (than)
  más rápido (que) — faster (than), more quickly (than)
  Corre más rápido que tú. — He runs faster than you do.
- **menos ... (que)** — less ... (than)
  menos rápido (que) — less fast (than), less quickly (than)
  Lo hizo menos rápido que tú. — He did it less fast than you.

2 Superlative adverbs

What is a superlative adverb?
A **superlative adverb** is one which, in English, has *-est* on the end of it or *most* or *least* in front of it. For example: *soonest*, *most/least often*.

➤ In Spanish, the superlative of adverbs (*the most often*, *the most efficiently*, *the fastest*) is formed in the same way as is the comparative, using **más** and **menos**. In this case they mean *the most* and *the least*.

María es la que corre más rápido. — María is the one who runs (the) fastest.
la chica que sabe más — the girl who knows (the) most
la chica que sabe menos — the girl who knows (the) least
El que llegó menos tarde fue Miguel. — Miguel was the one who arrived least late.

ℹ Note that, even though comparative and superlative adverbs are usually identical in Spanish, you can tell which is which from the rest of the sentence.

3 Irregular comparative and superlative adverbs

➤ Some common Spanish adverbs have irregular comparatives and superlatives.

Adverb	Meaning	Comparative	Meaning	Superlative	Meaning
bien	well	**mejor**	better	**mejor**	(the) best
mal	badly	**peor**	worse	**peor**	(the) worst
mucho	a lot	**más**	more	**más**	(the) most
poco	little	**menos**	less	**menos**	(the) least

La conozco mejor que tú. — I know her better than you do.
¿Quién lo hace mejor? — Who does it (the) best?
Ahora salgo más/menos. — I go out more/less these days.

Tip

When saying *more than*, *less than* or *fewer than* followed by a number, use **más** and **menos de** rather than **más** and **menos que**.

más/menos de veinte cajas — more/fewer than twenty boxes

Note that, in Spanish, in phrases like *it's the least one can expect* or *it's the least I can do*, where the adverb is qualified by further information, you have to put **lo** before the adverb.

Es lo menos que se puede esperar. — It's the least one can expect.

4 Other ways of making comparisons

➤ In Spanish, there are other ways of making comparisons:

- **tanto como** as much as

  No lee tanto como tú. — He doesn't read as much as you.

- **tan ... como** as ... as

  Vine tan pronto como pude. — I came as fast as I could.

Key points

✔ **más** + adverb (+ **que**) = *more* + adverb + (*than*)
✔ **menos** + adverb (+ **que**) = *less* + adverb + (*than*)
✔ **más** + adverb = (*the*) *most* + adverb
✔ **menos** + adverb = (*the*) *least* + adverb
✔ There are a few irregular comparative and superlative adverbs.
✔ There are other ways of making comparisons in Spanish: **tanto como, tan ... como**.

For further explanation of grammatical terms, please see pages viii-xii.

Common adverbs

1 One-word adverbs not ending in -mente

➤ There are some common adverbs that do not end in **-mente**, most of which give more information about when or where something happens or to what degree something is true.

- **abajo** down, below, downstairs
  Ponlo aquí abajo. Put it down here.
  el departamento de abajo the apartment below
  Abajo están los dormitorios. The bedrooms are downstairs.
- **adelante** forward
  Dio un paso adelante. He stepped forward.
  Siéntate más adelante. Sit further forward.
- **adentro** inside, indoors
  Me llevó adentro. He took me inside/indoors.
- **afuera** outside, outdoors
  Vayamos afuera. Let's go outside.
- **ahí** there
  ¡Ahí están! There they are!
- **ahora** now
  ¿Adónde vamos ahora? Where are we going now?
- **allá** there
  allá arriba up there
- **allí** there
  Allí está. There it is.
- **anoche** last night
  Anoche llovió. It rained last night.
- **anteanoche** *or* **antenoche** the night before last
  Llegaron anteanoche. They arrived the night before last.
- **anteayer** *or* **antier** the day before yesterday
  Anteayer hubo tormenta. There was a storm the day before yesterday.
- **antes** before, beforehand
  Llámalos antes. Call them beforehand.
- **apenas** hardly
  Apenas podía levantarse. He could hardly stand up.

- **aquí** here
  Aquí está el informe. Here's the report.
- **arriba** up, above, upstairs
  Ponlo aquí arriba. Put it up here.
  el departamento de arriba the apartment above
  Arriba están los dormitorios. The bedrooms are upstairs.
- **atrás** (at the/in the) back
  Dio un paso atrás. He stepped back.
  Siéntate más atrás. Sit further back.
- **aun** even
  Aun sentado me duele la pierna. Even when I'm sitting down, my leg hurts.
- **aún** still, yet
  ¿Aún te duele? Does it still hurt?

> *Tip*
> The following mnemonic (memory jogger) should help you remember when to use **aun** and when to use **aún**:
> Even **aun** doesn't have an accent.
> **aún** still has an accent.
> **aún** hasn't lost its accent yet.

- **ayer** yesterday
  Ayer fue mi cumpleaños. It was my birthday yesterday.
- **casi** almost
  Son casi las cinco. It's almost five o'clock.
- **cerca** near
  El colegio está muy cerca. The school is very near.
- **claro** clearly
  Lo oí muy claro. I heard it very clearly.
- **debajo** underneath
  Miré debajo. I looked underneath.
- **dentro** inside
  ¿Qué hay dentro? What's inside?

- **despacio** slowly

Maneja despacio.	Drive slowly.

- **después** afterwards

Después estábamos muy cansados.	We were very tired afterwards.

- **detrás** behind

Vienen detrás.	They're following behind.

- **enfrente** opposite

la casa de enfrente	the house opposite

- **enseguida** right away, immediately

La ambulancia llegó enseguida.	The ambulance arrived right away.

- **entonces** then

¿Qué hiciste entonces?	What did you do then?

- **hasta** even

Estudia hasta cuando está de vacaciones.	He studies even when he's on vacation.

- **hoy** today

Hoy no tenemos clase.	We don't have any classes today.

- **jamás** never (ever)

Jamás he visto nada parecido.	I've never seen anything like it.

- **lejos** far

¿Está lejos?	Is it far?

- **luego** then, later

Luego nos fuimos a dormir.	Then we went to bed.

- **muy** very

Estoy muy cansada.	I'm very tired.

- **no** no, not

No, no me gusta.	No. I don't like it.

- **nunca** never

No viene nunca.	He never comes.
Nunca nos vienes a ver.	You never come to see us.

- **pronto** soon

Llegarán pronto.	They'll be here soon.

- **quizás** perhaps

Quizás está cansado.	Perhaps he's tired.

i Note that, if referring to the future, you use the present subjunctive after **quizás**.

Quizás venga mañana. — Perhaps he'll come tomorrow.

⇨ *For more information on the **Subjunctive**, see page 136.*

- **sí** yes

  ¿Quieres un café? – Sí, gracias. — Would you like a cup of coffee? – Yes, please.

- **siempre** always

  Siempre dicen lo mismo. — They always say the same thing.

- **solo** only

  Solo hay que apretar este botón. — You only have to press this button.

i Note that **solo** is sometimes spelled **sólo** to distinguish it from the adjective, meaning *alone*. The accent is only necessary if there is a risk that the sentence might be misunderstood.

- **también** also, too

  A mí también me gusta. — I like it too.

- **tampoco** either, neither

  Yo tampoco lo compré. — I didn't buy it either.

  Yo no la vi. – Yo tampoco. — I didn't see her. – Neither did I.

- **tan** as, so

  Vine tan pronto como pude. — I came as fast as I could.

  Hablas tan rápido que no te entiendo. — You speak so fast that I can't understand you.

- **tarde** late

  Se está haciendo tarde. — It's getting late.

- **temprano** early

  Tengo que levantarme temprano. — I've got to get up early.

- **todavía** still, yet, even

  Todavía tengo dos. — I've still got two.

  Todavía no han llegado. — They haven't arrived yet.

  mejor todavía — even better

- **ya** already

  Ya están aquí. — They're already here.

2 Words which are used both as adjectives and adverbs

➤ **bastante**, **demasiado**, **tanto**, **mucho** and **poco** can be used both as adjectives and as adverbs. When they are adjectives, their endings change in the feminine and plural to agree with what they describe. When they are adverbs, the endings don't change.

	Adjective use	Adverb use
bastante enough; quite a lot; quite	**Hay bastantes libros.** There are enough books.	**Ya comiste bastante.** You've had enough to eat. **Son bastante ricos.** They are quite rich.
demasiado too much (*plural*: too many); too	**demasiada mantequilla** too much butter **demasiados libros** too many books	**Comí demasiado.** I ate too much. **Llegamos demasiado tarde.** We arrived too late.
tanto as much (*plural*: as many); as often	**Ahora no bebo tanta leche.** I don't drink as much milk these days. **Tengo tantas cosas que hacer.** I have so many things to do.	**Se preocupa tanto que no puede dormir.** He worries so much that he can't sleep. **Ahora no la veo tanto.** I don't see her so often now.
mucho a lot (of), much (*plural*: many)	**Había mucha gente.** There were a lot of people. **muchas cosas** a lot of things	**¿Lees mucho?** Do you read a lot? **¿Está mucho más lejos?** Is it much further?
poco little, not much, (*plural*: few, not many); not very	**Hay poca leche.** There isn't much milk. **Tiene pocos amigos.** He doesn't have many friends.	**Habla muy poco.** He speaks very little. **Es poco sociable.** He's not very sociable.

Tip

Don't confuse **poco**, which means *little*, *not much* or *not very*, with **un poco**, which means *a little* or *a bit*.

Come poco. — He doesn't eat much.
¿Me das un poco? — Can I have a bit?

➤ **más** and **menos** can also be used both as adjectives and adverbs. However, they NEVER change their endings, even when used as adjectives.

	Adjective use	Adverb use
más more	**No tengo más dinero.** I don't have any more money. **más libros** more books	**Es más inteligente que yo.** He's more intelligent than I am. **No le des más.** Don't give her any more.
menos less; fewer	**menos mantequilla** less butter **Había menos gente que ayer.** There were fewer people than yesterday.	**Estoy menos sorprendida que tú.** I'm less surprised than you are. **Trata de beber menos.** Try and drink less.

3 Adverbs made up of more than one word

➤ Just as in English, some Spanish adverbs are made up of two or more words instead of just one.

a veces	sometimes
a menudo	often
de vez en cuando	from time to time
todo el tiempo	all the time
hoy en día	nowadays

Key points

✔ In Spanish, there are a number of common adverbs which do not end in **-mente**.

✔ **bastante**, **demasiado**, **tanto**, **mucho** and **poco** can be used both as adjectives and as adverbs. Their endings change in the feminine and plural when they are adjectives, but when they are adverbs their endings do not change.

✔ **más** and **menos** can be both adjectives and adverbs – their endings never change.

✔ A number of Spanish adverbs are made up of more than one word.

Position of adverbs

1 Adverbs with verbs

➤ In English, adverbs can appear in various places in a sentence – at the beginning, in the middle or at the end.

I'm never coming back.
See you soon!
Suddenly, the phone rang.
I'd really like to come.

➤ In Spanish, the adverb can either go immediately BEFORE the verb or AFTER it.

Todavía estoy esperando.	I'm still waiting.
Siempre le regalaban flores. *or* **Le regalaban siempre flores.**	They always gave her flowers.

➤ When the adverb goes with a verb in the perfect tense or in the pluperfect, you can NEVER put the adverb between **haber** and the past participle.

Lo han firmado ya. *or* **Ya lo han firmado.**	They have already signed it.
No había estado nunca en Italia. *or* **Nunca había estado en Italia.**	She'd never been to Italy.

⇨ *For more information on the **Perfect tense**, see page 118.*

➤ Adverbs which explain how something is done are normally placed between the verb and its object.

Habla bien inglés.	He speaks English well.
Le quitó cuidadosamente la tapa.	He carefully took the lid off.

2 Adverbs with adjectives and adverbs

➤ The adverb normally goes BEFORE any adjective or adverb it is used with.

un sombrero muy bonito	a very nice hat
hablar demasiado alto	to talk too loudly

Key points

✔ In most cases, adverbs follow the verb.
✔ Adverbs can go before or after verbs.
✔ You can never separate **haber**, **he**, **ha** and so on from the following past participle (the **-ado/-ido** form of regular verbs).
✔ Adverbs generally come just before an adjective or another adverb.

Prepositions

What is a preposition?
A **preposition** is a word such as *at*, *for*, *with*, *into* or *from*, which is usually followed by a noun, pronoun or, in English, a word ending in *-ing*. Prepositions show how people and things relate to the rest of the sentence. For example: *She's <u>at</u> home.*; *a tool <u>for</u> cutting grass*; *It's <u>from</u> David*.

Using prepositions

➤ Prepositions are used in front of nouns and pronouns (such as *people*, *the man*, *me*, *him* and so on), and show the relationship between the noun or pronoun and the rest of the sentence. Although, in English, prepositions can be used before verb forms ending in *-ing*, in Spanish, they're followed by the <u>infinitive</u> – the form of the verb ending in **-ar**, **-er**, or **-ir**.

Le mostré la foto <u>a</u> Pedro.	I showed the photo <u>to</u> Pedro.
Ven <u>con</u> nosotros.	Come <u>with</u> us.
Sirve <u>para</u> limpiar zapatos.	It's <u>for</u> polishing shoes.

➪ *For more information on* ***Nouns***, ***Pronouns*** *and* ***Infinitives***, *see pages 1, 41 and 146.*

➤ Prepositions are also used after certain adjectives and verbs, linking them to the rest of the sentence.

Estoy muy contento <u>con</u> tu trabajo.	I'm very happy <u>with</u> your work.
Estamos hartos <u>de</u> repetirlo.	We're fed up <u>with</u> repeating it.
Anoche soñé con Gustavo.	I dreamed about Gustavo last night.

➤ As in English, Spanish prepositions can be made up of several words instead of just one.

delante de	in front of
antes de	before

➤ In English, we can end a sentence with a preposition such as *for*, *with* or *into*, even though some people think this is not good grammar. You can <u>NEVER</u> end a Spanish sentence with a preposition.

¿<u>Para</u> qué es?	What's it <u>for</u>?
la chica <u>con</u> la que hablaste	the girl you spoke <u>to</u>

For further explanation of grammatical terms, please see pages viii-xii.

Tip

As English speakers, the choice of an appropriate Spanish preposition is not always what we might expect. It is often difficult to identify a single English equivalent for a particular Spanish preposition, since prepositions are used so differently in the two languages. This means that you need to learn how they are used and use a dictionary to look up common phrases involving prepositions (such as *to depend on something* or *dressed in white*) in order to find an equivalent expression in Spanish.

a, de, en, para and por

1 a

> *Tip*
>
> When **a** is followed by **el**, the two words merge to become **al**.

- **a** can mean *to* with places and destinations.

Voy a la fiesta.	I'm going to the party.
Voy al médico.	I'm going to the doctor's.

> *Tip*
>
> **de** is also used with **a** to mean *from ... to ...*
>
> | | |
> |---|---|
> | **de la mañana a la noche** | from morning to night |
> | **de 10 a 12** | from 10 to 12 |

- **a** can mean *to* with indirect objects.

Dale el dinero a María.	Give the money to María.

- **a** can mean *to* after **ir** when talking about what someone is *going to* do.

Voy a verlo mañana.	I'm going to see him tomorrow.

- **a** can mean *at* with times.

a las cinco	at five o'clock
a la una y media	at half past one
a medianoche	at midnight

- **a** can mean *at* with prices and rates.

a dos dólares el kilo	(at) two dollars a kilo
a 100 millas por hora	at 100 miles per hour

- **a** can mean *at* with ages.

a los 18 años	at (the age of) 18

- **a** can mean *at* with places, but generally only after verbs suggesting movement.

Te voy a buscar a la estación.	I'll meet you at the station.
cuando llegó al aeropuerto	when he arrived at the airport

Tip

You can't use **a** to mean *at* when talking about a building, area, or village where someone is at a given moment. Use **en** instead.

Está en casa. He's at home.

➤ **a** can mean *onto*.

Se cayó al suelo. He fell onto the floor.

➤ **a** can mean *into*.

traducir algo al inglés to translate something into English

➤ **a** is also used to talk about distance.

a pocas cuadras de aquí just a few blocks from here

➤ **a** is also used after certain adjectives and verbs.

parecido a esto similar to this

➤ **a** can mean *from* after certain verbs.

Se lo compré a mi hermano. I bought it from my brother.

Les robaba dinero a sus compañeros de clase. He was stealing money from his classmates.

⇨ *For more information on* ***Prepositions after verbs****, see page* 152.

➤ **a** is used in common phrases.

a final/finales/fines de mes	at the end of the month
a veces	at times
a menudo	often
a la puerta	at the door
a mano	by hand, to hand
a caballo	on horseback
a pie	on foot
a tiempo	on time
al sol	in the sun
a la sombra	in the shade

Grammar Extra!

a is often used to talk about the manner in which something is done.

a la inglesa	English style
a paso lento	slowly
poco a poco	little by little

The Spanish equivalent of the English construction *on* with a verb ending in *-ing* is **al** followed by the infinitive.

al levantarse	on getting up
al abrir la puerta	on opening the door

2 Personal a

➤ When the direct object of a verb is a specific person or pet animal, **a** is placed immediately before it.

Querían mucho a sus sobrinas.	They were very fond of their nieces.
Cuido a mi hermanita.	I look after my little sister.

[i] Note that personal **a** is NOT used after the verb **tener**.

Tienen dos hijos.	They have two children.

➪ *For more information on* **Direct objects**, *see page* 46.

3 de

> *Tip*
>
> When **de** is followed by **el**, the two words merge to become **del**.

➤ **de** can mean *from*.

Soy de Mérida.	I'm from Mérida.
un médico de Buenos Aires	a doctor from Buenos Aires

> *Tip*
>
> **de** is also used with **a** to mean *from ... to ...*
>
> | | |
> |---|---|
> | **de la mañana a la noche** | from morning to night |
> | **de 10 a 12** | from 10 to 12 |

➤ **de** can mean *of*.

el presidente de Francia	the president of France
dos litros de leche	two liters of milk

➤ **de** shows who or what something belongs to.

el sombrero de mi padre	my father's hat (*literally: the hat of my father*)
la oficina del presidente	the president's office (*literally: the office of the president*)

➤ **de** can indicate what something is made of, what it contains or what it is used for.

un vestido de seda	a silk dress
una caja de cerillas	a box of matches
una taza de té	a cup of tea *or* a teacup
una silla de cocina	a kitchen chair
un traje de baño	a swimsuit

➤ **de** is used in comparisons when a number is mentioned.

Había más/menos de cien personas.	There were more/fewer than a hundred people.

[i] Note that you do NOT use **que** with **más** or **menos** when there is a number involved.

➤ **de** can mean *in* after superlatives (*the most..., the biggest, the least...*).

la ciudad más/menos contaminada del mundo	the most/least polluted city in the world

⇨ *For more information on* ***Superlative adjectives****, see page 26.*

➤ **de** is used after certain adjectives and verbs.

Es fácil/difícil de entender.	It's easy/difficult to understand.
Es capaz de olvidarse.	He's quite capable of forgetting.

⇨ *For more information on* ***Prepositions after verbs****, see page 152.*

Grammar Extra!

de is often used in descriptions.

la mujer del sombrero verde	the woman in the green hat
un chico de ojos azules	a boy with blue eyes

4 en

➤ **en** can mean *in* with places.

en el campo	in the country
en Uruguay	in Uruguay
en la cama	in bed
con un libro en la mano	with a book in his hand

➤ **en** can mean *at* with places and with certain holidays.

en casa	at home
en el colegio	at school
en el aeropuerto	at the airport
en la parada de autobús	at the bus stop
en Navidad	at Christmastime

➤ **en** can mean *in* with months, years, and seasons, and when saying how long something takes or took.

en marzo	in March
en 2005	in 2005
Nació en invierno.	He was born in winter.
Lo hice en dos días.	I did it in two days.

i Note the following time phrase, which, in English, does not use *in*.

en este/ese *or* **aquel momento**	at this/that moment

> *Tip*
>
> When talking about parts of the day in Spanish, you can use either **en** or **por**:
>
> **en** *or* **por la mañana** in the morning
> **en** *or* **por la tarde** in the afternoon/evening
> **en** *or* **por la noche** at night
>
> In Spain, only **por** is used.

➤ **en** can mean *in* with languages and in common phrases indicating manner.

Está escrito en español.	It's written in Spanish.
en voz baja	in a low voice
en silencio	in silence

➤ **en** can mean *on*.

sentado en una silla	sitting on a chair
Lo dejé en la mesa.	I left it on the table.
Hay dos cuadros en la pared.	There are two pictures on the wall.

➤ **en** can mean *by* with most types of transportation.

en coche	by car
en avión	by plane
en tren	by train

➤ **en** can mean *into*.

No entremos en la casa.	Let's not go into the house.
Metió todo en la caja.	She put everything into the box.

➤ **en** is also used after certain adjectives and verbs.

Es muy buena/mala en geografía.	She is very good/bad at geography.
Fueron los primeros/últimos/ únicos en llegar.	They were the first/last/only ones to arrive.
No pienses en eso.	Don't think about that.

➪ *For more information on* ***Prepositions after verbs****, see page* 152.

5 para

➤ **para** can mean *for* with a person, destination or purpose.

Para mí un jugo de naranja.	An orange juice for me.
Mañana salen para Panamá.	They are leaving for Panamá tomorrow.
¿Para qué lo quieres?	What do you want it for?

ℹ Note that, in Spanish, you cannot end a sentence with a preposition as you can in English.

➤ **para** can mean *for* with time.

Es para mañana.	It's for tomorrow.
una habitación para dos noches	a room for two nights

➤ **para** is also used with an infinitive with the meaning of *(in order) to*.

Lo hace para ganar dinero.	He does it to earn money.
Lo hice para ayudarte.	I did it to help you.

Tip

para mí/él/ella, etc. can be used to mean *in my/his/her etc. opinion*.

<u>Para mí</u>, es estupendo.	<u>In my opinion</u>, it's great.

6 por

➤ **por** can mean *for* when it means *for the benefit of* or *because of*.

Lo hago <u>por</u> ellos.	I'm doing it <u>for</u> them.
<u>por</u> la misma razón	<u>for</u> the same reason

➤ **por** can mean *for* when it means *in exchange for*.

¿Cuánto me darán <u>por</u> este libro?	How much will they give me <u>for</u> this book?
Te lo cambio <u>por</u> este.	I'll swap you <u>for</u> this one.

➤ **por** can mean *by* in passive constructions.

descubierto <u>por</u> unos niños	discovered <u>by</u> some children
odiado por <u>sus</u> enemigos	hated <u>by</u> his enemies

⇨ *For more information on the **Passive**, see page 125.*

➤ **por** can mean *by* with types of transportation when talking about <u>freight</u>.

mandar algo <u>por</u> barco	to send something <u>by</u> ship
<u>por</u> avión	<u>by</u> airmail
<u>por</u> correo aéreo	<u>by</u> airmail

➤ **por** can mean *along*.

Vaya <u>por</u> ese camino.	Go <u>along</u> that path.

➤ **por** can mean *through*.

<u>por</u> el túnel	<u>through</u> the tunnel

➤ **por** can mean *around*.

pasear <u>por</u> el campo	to walk <u>around</u> the countryside

➤ **por** is used to talk vaguely about where something or someone is.

Tiene que estar <u>por</u> aquí.	It's got to be around here somewhere.
Lo busqué <u>por</u> todas partes.	I looked for him everywhere.

➤ **por** (or **en**) is used with parts of the day.

por la mañana	in the morning
por la tarde	in the afternoon/evening
por la noche	at night

➤ **por** is used to talk about rates.

90 millas por hora	90 miles an hour
un cinco por ciento	five per cent

➤ **por** is used in certain phrases which talk about the reason for something.

¿por qué?	why?, for what reason?
por todo eso	because of all that
por lo que dice Mario	judging by what Mario says

➤ **por** is used to talk about how something is done.

llamar por teléfono	to telephone
Lo vi por la tele.	I saw it on TV.

Grammar Extra!

por is often combined with other Spanish prepositions and words, usually to show movement.

Saltó por encima de la mesa.	She jumped over the table.
Nadamos por debajo del puente.	We swam under the bridge.
Pasaron por delante de la iglesia.	They went past the church.

Key points

✔ **a**, **de**, **en**, **para** and **por** are the most frequently used prepositions which you will need to study carefully.

✔ Each of them has several possible meanings, which depend on the context they are used in.

Some other common prepositions

➤ In Spanish, the following prepositions are also frequently used.

- **antes de** before

antes de las 5	before 5 o'clock

ℹ Note that, like many other Spanish prepositions, **antes de** is used before infinitives, whereas in English, we'd use the *-ing* form of the verb.

Antes de abrir el paquete, lea las instrucciones.	Before opening the package, read the instructions.

- **bajo** below, under

un grado bajo cero	one degree below zero
bajo el puente	under the bridge

ℹ Note that **debajo de** is more common than **bajo** when talking about the actual position of something.

debajo de la cama	under the bed

- **con** with

Vino con su amigo.	She came with her friend.

ℹ Note that **con** can be used after certain adjectives as well as in a few very common phrases.

enojado con ellos	angry with them
un café con leche	a (cup of) coffee with milk
un té con limón	a (cup of) lemon tea

- **contra** against

Estaba apoyado contra la pared.	He was leaning against the wall.
El domingo juegan contra Paraguay.	They play against Paraguay on Sunday.

- **debajo de** under

debajo de la cama	under the bed

- **delante de** in front of

Iba delante de nosotros.	He was walking in front of us.

- **desde** from, since

Desde aquí se puede ver.	You can see it from here.
desde otro punto de vista	from a different point of view
desde entonces	from then onwards
desde la una hasta las siete	from one o'clock to seven
desde la fiesta	since the party

Tip

Spanish uses the present tense with **desde** (meaning *since*) and the expressions **desde hace** and **hace ... que** (meaning *for*) to talk about actions that started in the past and are still going on.

Estoy aquí desde las diez.	I've been here since ten o'clock.
Estoy aquí desde hace dos horas. *or* **Hace dos horas que estoy aquí.**	I've been here for two hours.

➪ *For more information on the* ***Present tense*** *and the* ***Perfect tense****, see pages 71 and 118.*

- **después de** after

después del partido	after the game

[i] Note that, like many other Spanish prepositions, **después de** is used before infinitives, whereas in English we'd use the *-ing* form of the verb.

Después de lijarlo, se pinta.	After sanding it down, you paint it.

- **detrás de** behind

Están detrás de la puerta.	They are behind the door.

- **durante** during, for

durante la guerra	during the war
Caminaron durante 3 días.	They walked for 3 days.

- **entre** between, among, amongst

entre 8 y 10	between 8 and 10
Hablaban entre sí.	They were talking amongst themselves.

- **hacia** toward, around

Van hacia ese edificio.	They're heading toward that building.
hacia las tres	at around three (o'clock)
hacia finales de enero	around the end of January

Grammar Extra!

hacia can also combine with some adverbs to show movement in a particular direction.

hacia arriba	upwards
hacia abajo	downwards
hacia adelante	forwards
hacia atrás	backwards

- **hasta** until, as far as, to, up to

hasta el jueves	until Thursday
Caminamos hasta el parque.	We walked as far as the park.
desde la una hasta las tres	from one o'clock to three
Hasta ahora no ha habido quejas.	There have been no complaints up to now.

i Note that there are some very common ways of saying goodbye using **hasta**.

¡Hasta luego!	See you!
¡Hasta mañana!	See you tomorrow!

- **sin** without

sin agua/dinero	without any water/money
sin mi marido	without my husband

Tip

Whereas in English we say *without a doubt*, *without a hat* and so on, in Spanish the indefinite article isn't used after **sin**.

sin duda	without a doubt
sin sombrero	without a hat

➪ *For more information on **Articles**, see page 10.*

i Note that, in Spanish, **sin** is used before infinitives, whereas in English, we would use the *-ing* form of the verb.

Se fue sin decir nada.	He left without saying anything.

- **sobre** on, about

sobre la cama	on the bed
Ponlo sobre la mesa.	Put it on the table.
un libro sobre Shakespeare	a book on *or* about Shakespeare

➤ Spanish prepositions can be made up of more than one word (for example: **antes de, detrás de**). Here are some more common prepositions made up of two or more words:

- **a causa de** because of

No salimos a causa de la lluvia.	We didn't go out because of the rain.

- **al lado de** beside, next to

al lado de su novia	next to his girlfriend

- **cerca de** near, close to

Está cerca de la iglesia.	It's near the church.

- **encima de** on, on top of

Ponlo encima de la mesa.	Put it on the table.

- **por encima de** above, over

Saltó por encima de la mesa.	He jumped over the table.

- **en medio de** in the middle of

Está en medio de la plaza.	It's in the middle of the square.

- **junto a** next to, alongside

junto a la ventana.	next to the window
trabajando junto a su esposa	working alongside his wife

- **junto con** together with

Fue detenido junto con su hijo.	He was arrested together with his son.

- **lejos de** far from

No está lejos de aquí.	It isn't far from here.

Grammar Extra!

In Latin American Spanish, you will often come across **abajo de**, **adelante de**, **adentro de**, **arriba de** and **atrás de** used instead of **debajo de**, **delante de**, **dentro de**, **encima de** and **detrás de** respectively. Although they are used very frequently, especially in the spoken language, they are considered incorrect by some people.

abajo de la cama	under the bed
adelante de papá	in front of Dad
adentro de la caja	inside the box
arriba de la mesa	above the table
atrás de la puerta	behind the door

Conjunctions

What is a conjunction?
A **conjunction** is a word such as *and*, *but*, *or*, *so*, *if* and *because*, that links two words or phrases of a similar type, or two parts of a sentence. For example: *Diane <u>and</u> I have been friends for years. I left <u>because</u> I was bored.*

y, o, pero, porque, que and si

➤ In Spanish, **y**, **o**, **pero**, **porque**, **que** and **si** are the most common conjunctions that you need to know:

- **y** and

  el perro <u>y</u> el gato — the dog <u>and</u> the cat

ℹ Note that you use **e** instead of **y** before words beginning with **i** or **hi** (but not **hie**).

Diana <u>e</u> Isabel — Diana <u>and</u> Isabel
madre <u>e</u> hija — mother <u>and</u> daughter
BUT
árboles <u>y</u> hierba — trees <u>and</u> grass

- **o** or

  papas <u>o</u> arroz — potatoes <u>or</u> rice

ℹ Note that you use **u** instead of **o** before words beginning with **o** or **ho**.

diez <u>u</u> once — ten <u>or</u> eleven
minutos <u>u</u> horas — minutes <u>or</u> hours

ℹ Note that you use **ó** instead of **o** between numerals to avoid confusion with zero.

37 ó 38 — 37 or 38

⇨ *For more information on **Numbers**, see page 208.*

- **pero** but

  Me gustaría ir, <u>pero</u> no puedo. — I'd like to go, <u>but</u> I can't.

ℹ Note that you use **sino** in direct contrasts after a negative.

No es española, <u>sino</u> italiana. — She's not Spanish <u>but</u> Italian.

- **porque** because

  Llamó porque necesita un libro. He called because he needs a book.

Note that you don't use **porque** at the beginning of a sentence; you should use **como** instead.

Como estaba lloviendo, nos quedamos en casa. Because *or* As it was raining, we stayed home.

> *Tip*
> Be careful not to mix up **porque** (meaning *because*) and **por qué** (meaning *why*).

- **que** that

  Dice que me quiere. He says that he loves me.
  Dicen que es millonario. They say that he's a millionaire.
  Sabe que estamos aquí. He knows that we are here.

For more information on **que** *followed by the subjunctive and* **que** *(meaning than) in comparisons, see pages 136 and 26.*

> *Tip*
> In English we can say both *He says he loves me* and *He says that he loves me*, or *She knows you're here* and *She knows that you're here*. In Spanish, you can NEVER omit **que** in the way that you can omit *that* in English.

- **si** if, whether

  Si no estudias, no aprobarás. If you don't study, you won't pass.
  ¿Sabes si tiene novio? Do you know if *or* whether she has a boyfriend?
  Avísenme si no pueden venir. Let me know if you can't come.

For information on **si** *followed by the subjunctive, see page 145.*

> *Tip*
> There is no accent on **si** when it means *if*. Be careful not to confuse **si** (meaning *if*) with **sí** (meaning *yes* or *himself/herself/yourself/themselves/yourselves*).

Some other common conjunctions

➤ Here are some other common Spanish conjunctions:

- **como** as

  Como es domingo, puedes quedarte en la cama. — As it's Sunday, you can stay in bed.

- **cuando** when

  Cuando entré estaba leyendo. — She was reading when I came in.

➪ *For information on* **cuando** *followed by the subjunctive, see page* 142.

- **pues** then, well

  Tengo sueño. – ¡Acuéstate, pues! — I'm tired. – Go to bed then!
  Pues, no lo sabía. — Well, I didn't know.
  Pues, como te iba contando ... — Well, as I was saying ...

- **mientras** while (*referring to time*)

  Lava tú mientras yo seco. — You wash while I dry.
  Canta mientras cocina. — He sings while he cooks.

➪ *For information on* **mientras** *followed by the subjunctive, see page* 142.

- **mientras que** whereas

  Isabel es muy dinámica mientras que Ana es más tranquila. — Isabel is very dynamic whereas Ana is more laid-back.

- **aunque** although, even though

  Me gusta el francés, aunque prefiero el alemán. — I like French although I prefer German.
  Aunque estaba cansada, seguí trabajando. — Although I was tired, I went on working.

Grammar Extra!

aunque is also used to mean *even if*. In this case, it is followed by the subjunctive.

➪ *For more information on the* **Subjunctive**, *see page* 136.

Split conjunctions

In English, we have conjunctions which are made up of two parts (*both ... and*, *neither ... nor*). Spanish also has conjunctions that have more than one part, of which the most common are probably **ni ... ni** (meaning *neither ... nor*) and **o ... o** (meaning *either ... or*):

- **ni ... ni** neither ... nor

Ni Carlos ni Sofía vinieron. *or* **No vinieron ni Carlos ni Sofía.**	Neither Carlos nor Sofía came.

Note that if you're putting **ni ... ni** after the verb, you must put **no** before the verb.

No tengo ni hermanos ni hermanas.	I have neither brothers nor sisters.

- **o ... o** either ... or

Puedes pedir o helado o yogur.	You can order either ice cream or yogurt.

Key points

- ✔ **y, o, pero, porque, que** and **si** are the most common Spanish conjunctions that you need to know.
- ✔ Use **e** rather than **y** before words beginning with **i** or **hi** (but not with **hie**).
- ✔ Use **u** rather than **o** before words beginning with **o** or **ho**.
- ✔ **que** very often means *that*. In English, *that* is often omitted, but **que** can never be omitted in Spanish.
- ✔ Some conjunctions such as **ni ... ni** and **o ... o** consist of two parts.

Spelling

1 Sounds that are spelled differently depending on the letter that follows

➤ In Spanish, certain sounds are spelled differently depending on what letter follows them. For example, the hard [*k*] sound heard in the English word *car* is usually spelled:

- **c** before **a**, **o** and **u**
- **qu** before **e** and **i**

➤ This means that the Spanish word for *singer* is spelled **cantante** (pronounced [*kan-tan-tay*]); the word for *coast* is spelled **costa** (pronounced [*ko-sta*]); and the word for *cure* is spelled **cura** (pronounced [*koo-ra*]).

➤ However, the Spanish word for cheese is spelled **queso** (pronounced [*kay-so*]) and the word for *chemistry* is spelled **química** (pronounced [*kee-mee-ka*]).

ℹ Note that, although the letter **k** is not much used in Spanish, it is found in words relating to *kilos*, *kilometers* and *kilograms* (for example: **un kilo** (meaning *a kilo*); **un kilogramo** (meaning *a kilogram*); **un kilómetro** (meaning *a kilometer*).

➤ Similarly, the [*g*] sound heard in the English word *gone* is spelled:

- **g** before **a**, **o** and **u**
- **gu** before **e** and **i**

➤ This means that the Spanish word for *cat* is spelled **gato** (pronounced [*ga-toh*]); the word for *goal* is spelled **gol** (pronounced [*gol*]); and the word for *worm* is spelled **gusano** (pronounced [*goo-sa-no*]).

➤ However, the Spanish word for *war* is spelled **guerra** (pronounced [*gair-ra*]) and the word for *guitar* is spelled **guitarra** (pronounced [*ghee-tar-ra*]).

For further explanation of grammatical terms, please see pages viii-xii.

2 Letters that are pronounced differently depending on what follows

➤ Certain letters are pronounced differently depending on what follows them. As we have seen, when **c** comes before **a**, **o** or **u**, it is pronounced like a [*k*]. When it comes before **e** or **i**, in Latin American Spanish it is pronounced like the [*s*] in *sing* and in European Spanish it is pronounced like the [*th*] in the English word *pith*.

➤ This means that **casa** (meaning *house*) is pronounced [*ka-sa*], but **centro** (meaning *center*) is pronounced [*sen-tro*] in Latin American Spanish and [*then-tro*] in European Spanish. Similarly, **cita** (meaning *date*) is pronounced [*see-ta*] in Latin American Spanish and [*thee-ta*] in European Spanish.

➤ In the same way, when **g** comes before **a**, **o** or **u**, it is pronounced like the [*g*] in *gone*. When it comes before **e** or **i**, however, it is pronounced like the strong [*h*] sound in the Spanish name *Geraldo* [*He-ral-do*].

➤ This means that **gas** (meaning *gas*) is pronounced [*gas*] but **gente** (meaning *people*) is pronounced [*Hen-tay*]. Similarly, **gimnasio** (meaning *gym*) is pronounced [*Heem-na-see-o*].

3 Spelling changes that are needed in verbs to reflect the pronunciation

➤ Because **c** sounds like [*k*] before **a**, **o** and **u**, and like [*s*] (or [*th*] in European Spanish) before **e** and **i**, you sometimes have to alter the spelling of a verb when adding a particular ending to ensure the word reads as it is pronounced:

- In verbs ending in **-car** (which is pronounced [*kar*]), you have to change the **c** to **qu** before endings starting with an **e** to keep the hard [*k*] pronunciation. So the **yo** form of the preterite tense of **sacar** (meaning *to take out*) is spelled **saqué**. This spelling change affects the preterite and the present subjunctive of verbs ending in **-car**.

- In verbs ending in **-cer** and **-cir** (which are pronounced [*ser*] and [*sir*], or [*ther*] and [*thir*] in European Spanish), you have to change the **c** to **z** before endings starting with **a** or **o** to keep the soft [*s/th*] pronunciation. So while the **yo** form of the preterite tense of **hacer** is spelled **hice**, the **él/ella/usted** form is spelled **hizo**. This spelling change affects the ordinary present tense, as well as the present subjunctive of verbs ending in **-cer** or **-cir**.

➤ Because **g** sounds like the *[g]* of *gone* before **a**, **o** and **u**, and like the *[H]* of *Geraldo* before **e** and **i**, you also sometimes have to alter the spelling of a verb when adding a particular ending to ensure the verb still reads as it is pronounced:

- In verbs ending in **-gar** (which is pronounced *[gar]*), you have to change the **g** to **gu** before endings starting with an **e** or an **i** to keep the hard *[g]* pronunciation. So the **yo** form of the preterite tense of **pagar** (meaning *to pay*) is spelled **pagué**. This spelling change affects the preterite and the present subjunctive of verbs ending in **-gar**.
- In verbs ending in **-ger** and **-gir** (which are pronounced *[Her]* and *[Hir]*), you have to change the **g** to **j** before endings starting with **a** or **o** to keep the soft *[H]* pronunciation. So while the **él/ella/usted** form of the present tense of **escoger** (meaning *to choose*) is spelled **escoge**, the **yo** form is spelled **escojo**. This spelling change affects the ordinary present tense as well as the present subjunctive of verbs ending in **-ger** or **-gir**.

➤ Because **gui** sounds like *[ghee]* in verbs ending in **-guir**, but **gua** and **guo** sound like *[gwa]* and *[gwo]*, you have to drop the **u** before **a** and **o** in verbs ending in **-guir**. So while the **él/ella/usted** form of the present tense of **seguir** (meaning *to follow*) is spelled **sigue**, the **yo** form is spelled **sigo**. This spelling change affects the ordinary present tense as well as the present subjunctive of verbs ending in **-guir**.

➤ Finally, although **z** is always pronounced *[s]* in Latin American Spanish and *[th]* in European Spanish, in verbs ending in **-zar** the **z** spelling is changed to **c** before **e**. So, while the **él/ella/usted** form of the preterite tense of **cruzar** is spelled **cruzó**, the **yo** form is spelled **crucé**. This spelling change affects the preterite and the present subjunctive of verbs ending in **-zar**.

4 Spelling changes that are needed when making nouns and adjectives plural

➤ In the same way that you have to make some spelling changes when modifying the endings of certain verbs, you sometimes have to change the spelling of nouns and adjectives when making them plural.

➤ This affects nouns and adjectives ending in **-z**. When adding the **-es** ending of the plural, you have to change the **z** to **c**.

una vez	once, one time	→	**dos veces**	twice, two times
una luz	a light	→	**unas luces**	some lights
capaz	capable, able (*sing*)	→	**capaces**	capable, able (*pl*)

➤ The following table shows the usual spelling of the various sounds discussed above:

	Usual spelling				
	before a	**before o**	**before u**	**before e**	**before i**
[*k*] sound (as in *cap*)	**ca:** **casa** house	**co:** **cosa** thing	**cu:** **cuna** crib	**que:** **queso** cheese	**qui:** **química** chemistry
[*g*] sound (as in *gap*)	**ga:** **gato** cat	**go:** **gordo** fat	**gu:** **gusto** taste	**gue:** **guerra** war	**gui:** **guitarra** guitar
[*s*] as in *sun** (pronounced [*th*] as in *pith* in European Spanish)	**za:** **zapato** shoe	**zo:** **zorro** fox	**zu:** **zumo** juice	**ce:** **cero** zero	**ci:** **cinta** ribbon
[*H*] sound (as in *Geraldo*)	**ja:** **jardín** garden	**jo:** **joven** young	**ju:** **jugar** to play	**ge:** **gente** people	**gi:** **gimnasio** gym

*[*s*] is also, of course, the pronunciation of the letter **s**, both in Latin American and European Spanish.

ⓘ Note that because **j** is also pronounced [*H*] even when it comes before **e** or **i**, there are quite a number of words that contain **je** or **ji**. For example:

el jefe/la jefa	the boss
el jerez	sherry
el jinete	jockey
la jirafa	giraffe
el ejemplo	the example
dije/dijiste	I said/you said
dejé	I left, I let

Similarly, because **z** is also pronounced [*s*] (or [*th*] in European Spanish) when it comes before **i** or **e**, there are one or two exceptions to the spelling rules described above. For example: **el zigzag** (meaning *zigzag*) and **la zeta** (the name of the letter **z** in Spanish).

Stress

Which syllable to stress

➤ Most words can be broken up into syllables. These are the different groups of sounds that make up a word. They are shown in this section by | and the stressed syllable is underlined.

➤ In Spanish, there are some very simple rules to help you remember which part of the word to stress, and when to use a written accent mark.

➤ In Spanish, words DON'T have a written acute accent if they follow the normal stress rules. If they do not follow the normal stress rules, they DO need an accent.

> *Tip*
> In Spanish, the written accent that shows stress is always an acute accent (´). To remember which way an acute accents slopes try thinking of this saying:
> *It's low on the left, with the height on the right.*

1 Words ending in a vowel or -n or -s

➤ Words ending in a vowel (*a*, *e*, *i*, *o* or *u*) or **-n** or **-s** are normally stressed on the syllable before last. If this is the case, they do NOT have any written accents.

ca|sa house — **ca|sas** houses
pa|la|bra word — **pa|la|bras** words
tar|de afternoon — **tar|des** afternoons
ha|bla he/she speaks — **ha|blan** they speak
co|rre he/she runs — **co|rren** they run

➤ Whenever words ending in a vowel or **-n** or **-s** are NOT stressed on the syllable before last, they have a written accent on the vowel that is stressed.

es|trés stress
ra|tón mouse
pin|té I painted
úl|ti|mo last
llá|ma|los call them

For further explanation of grammatical terms, please see pages viii-xii.

2 Words ending in a consonant other than -n or -s

➤ Words ending in a consonant (a letter that isn't a vowel) other than **-n** or **-s** are normally stressed on the last syllable. If this is the case, they do NOT have an accent.

re|loj	clock, watch
ver|dad	truth
trac|tor	tractor

➤ Whenever words ending in a consonant other than **-n** or **-s** are NOT stressed on the last syllable, they have an accent.

ca|rác|ter	character
di|fí|cil	difficult
cés|ped	lawn

3 Accents on feminine and plural forms

➤ The same syllable is stressed in the plural form of adjectives and nouns as in the singular. To show this, you need to:

- add an accent in the plural in the case of unaccented nouns and adjectives of more than one syllable ending in **-n**

or|den	order	**ór|de|nes**	orders
e|xa|men	exam	**e|xá|me|nes**	exams
BUT: **tren**	train	**tre|nes**	trains

ⓘ Note that in the case of one-syllable words ending in **-n** or **-s**, such as **tren** above, no accent is needed in the plural, since the stress falls naturally on the syllable before last thanks to the plural **-es** ending.

- drop the accent in the plural form of nouns and adjectives ending in **-n** or **-s** which have an accent on the last syllable in the singular

au|to|bús	bus	**au|to|bu|ses**	buses
re|vo|lu|ción	revolution	**re|vo|lu|cio|nes**	revolutions

➤ The feminine forms of nouns or adjectives whose masculine form ends in an accented vowel followed by **-n** or **-s** do NOT have an accent.

un francés	a Frenchman
una francesa	a French woman

Tip

Just because a word has a written accent in the singular does not necessarily mean it has one in the plural, and vice versa.

jo|ven

Ends in n, so the rule is to stress the syllable before last; follows the rule, so no accent needed in the singular

in|glés

Ends in s, so the rule is to stress the syllable before last; breaks the rule, so an accent is needed in singular

jó|ve|nes

Ends in s, so the rule is to stress the syllable before last; breaks rule, so accent is needed in the plural to keep the stress on jo-

in|gle|ses

Ends in s, so the rule is to stress the syllable before last; follows the rule, so no accent needed in the plural to keep the stress on -gle-

4 Which vowel to stress in vowel combinations

- The vowels **i** and **u** are considered to be weak. The vowels **a**, **e** and **o** are considered to be strong.
- When a weak vowel (**i** or **u**) combines with a strong one (**a**, **e** or **o**), they form ONE sound that is part of the SAME syllable. Technically speaking, this is called a diphthong. The strong vowel is emphasized more.

bai|le	dance
cie|rra	he/she/it closes
boi|na	beret
pei|ne	comb
cau|sa	cause

Tip

To remember which are the weak vowels, try thinking of this saying: *U and I are weaklings and always lose out to other vowels!*

- When **i** is combined with **u** or **u** with **i** (the two weak vowels), they form ONE sound within the SAME syllable and there is more emphasis on the second vowel.

ciudad	city, town
fui	I went

➤ When you combine two strong vowels (**a**, **e** or **o**), they form TWO separate sounds and are part of DIFFERENT syllables.

ca|er	to fall
ca|os	chaos
fe|o	ugly

5 Adding accents to some verb forms

➤ When object pronouns are added to the end of certain verb forms, an accent is often required to show that the syllable stressed in the verb form does not change. These verb forms are:

- the gerund, when followed by one or more pronouns

comprando	buying
comprándo(se)lo	buying it (for him/her/them)

- the infinitive, when followed by two pronouns

vender	to sell
vendérselas	to sell them to him/her/them

- imperative forms

compra	buy
cómpralo	buy it
manden	send
mándenselo	send it to him/her/them

➪ *For more information on **Gerunds**, **Infinitives** and the **Imperative**, see pages 128, 146 and 86.*

6 Accents on adjectives and adverbs

➤ Adjectives ending in **-ísimo** always have an accent on the first **-í** of the ending. This means that any other accents are omitted.

caro	→	**carísimo**
expensive		extremely expensive
difícil	→	**dificilísimo**
difficult		extremely difficult

➤ Accents on adjectives are NOT affected when you attach **-mente** to turn them into adverbs.

fácil	→	**fácilmente**
easy		easily

The accent used to show meaning

➤ An accent is often used to distinguish between the written forms of some words which are pronounced the same but have a different meaning or function.

Without an accent		With an accent	
mi	my	**mí**	me
tu	your	**tú**	you
te	you	**té**	tea
si	if	**sí**	yes; himself
el	the	**él**	he
de	of	**dé**	give
solo	alone; by oneself; only	**sólo**	only
mas	but	**más**	more

The accent can also be used to distinguish the demonstrative pronouns, such as **éste** (meaning *this one*), from the corresponding adjective (e.g. **este**, meaning *this*), but this is only necessary in rare cases when there is a risk that the sentence might otherwise be misunderstood.

Mi hermano es médico.	My brother's a doctor.
A mí no me vio.	He didn't see me.
¿Te gusta tu trabajo?	Do you like your job?
¿Tú, qué opinas?	What do you think?
Si no viene, mejor.	If he doesn't come, so much the better.
Sí que lo sabe.	Yes, he does know.
El puerto está cerca.	The harbor's nearby.
Me bebí una cerveza sólo.	I only had one beer.
Me bebí una cerveza solo.	I had a beer on my own.

ℹ Note that nowadays the accent is only used on **sólo** in the sense of *only* where the sentence might otherwise be ambiguous.

➤ An accent is needed on question words in direct and indirect questions as well as after expressions of uncertainty.

¿Cómo estás?	How are you?
Dime cómo estás.	Tell me how you are.
Me preguntó cómo estaba.	He asked me how I was.
¿Con quién viajaste?	Who did you travel with?
¿Dónde encontraste eso?	Where did you find that?
No sé dónde está.	I don't know where it is.

➪ *For more information on **Questions**, see page 162.*

➤ An accent is also needed on exclamation words.

¡Qué asco!	How disgusting!
¡Qué horror!	How awful!
¡Qué raro!	How strange!
¡Cuánta gente!	What a lot of people!

Key points

✔ When deciding whether or not to use a written accent mark on a word, think about how it sounds and what letter it ends in, as there are certain rules that dictate when an accent should be used.

✔ The vowels **i** and **u** are considered to be weak. The vowels **a**, **e** and **o** are considered to be strong. They can combine in a number of ways.

✔ Accents are added to written forms of words which are pronounced the same but have different meanings, for example, **mi/mí**, **tu/tú** and so on.

✔ Adjectives ending in **-ísimo** always have an accent on the first **-í** of the ending, but no accent is added when adverbs are formed by adding **-mente** to adjectives.

✔ Question words used in direct and indirect questions as well as exclamation words always have an acute accent.

Numbers

1	uno (un, una)
2	dos
3	tres
4	cuatro
5	cinco
6	seis
7	siete
8	ocho
9	nueve
10	diez
11	once
12	doce
13	trece
14	catorce
15	quince
16	dieciséis
17	diecisiete
18	dieciocho
19	diecinueve
20	veinte
21	veintiuno (veintiún, veintiuna)
22	veintidós
23	veintitrés
24	veinticuatro
25	veinticinco
26	veintiséis
27	veintisiete
28	veintiocho
29	veintinueve
30	treinta
31	treinta y uno (un, una)
40	cuarenta
41	cuarenta y uno (un, una)
50	cincuenta
52	cincuenta y dos
60	sesenta
65	sesenta y cinco
70	setenta
76	setenta y seis
80	ochenta
87	ochenta y siete
90	noventa
99	noventa y nueve
100	cien (ciento)
101	ciento uno (un, una)
200	doscientos/doscientas
212	doscientos/doscientas doce
300	trescientos/trescientas
400	cuatrocientos/cuatrocientas
500	quinientos/quinientas
600	seiscientos/seiscientas
700	setecientos/setecientas
800	ochocientos/ochocientas
900	novecientos/novecientas
1000	mil
1001	mil (y) uno (un, una)
2000	dos mil
2500	dos mil quinientos/quinientas
1.000.000	un millón (*in English*: 1,000,000)

EJEMPLOS	EXAMPLES
Vive en el número diez.	He lives at number ten.
en la página diecinueve	on page nineteen
un/el diez por ciento	10%
un/el cien por cien(to)	100%

For further explanation of grammatical terms, please see pages viii-xii.

1 uno, un or una?

➤ Use **uno** when counting, unless referring to something or someone feminine.

➤ Use **un** before a masculine noun and **una** before a feminine noun even when the nouns are plural.

un hombre	one man
una mujer	one woman
treinta y un días	thirty-one days
treinta y una noches	thirty-one nights
veintiún años	twenty-one years
veintiuna mujeres	twenty-one women

2 cien or ciento?

➤ Use **cien** before both masculine and feminine nouns as well as before **mil** (meaning *thousand*) and **millones** (meaning *million* in the plural):

cien libros	one hundred books
cien mil hombres	one hundred thousand men
cien millones	one hundred million

➤ Use **ciento** before other numbers.

ciento un perros	one hundred and one dogs
ciento una ovejas	one hundred and one sheep
ciento cincuenta	one hundred and fifty

ℹ Note that you don't translate the *and* in 101, 220 and so on.

➤ Make **doscientos/doscientas**, **trescientos/trescientas**, **quinientos/quinientas** and so on agree with the noun in question.

doscientas veinte personas	two hundred and twenty people
quinientos alumnos	five hundred students

ℹ Note that **setecientos** and **setecientas** have no **i** after the first **s**. Similarly, **novecientos** and **novecientas** have an **o** rather than the **ue** you might expect.

3 Period, comma or space?

➤ A space should be used to separate thousands and millions when writing numbers **of more than four digits** in figures.

42 000 (cuarenta y dos mil)
100 500 (cien mil quinientos/-as)

BUT

2480 (dos mil cuatrocientos ochenta)

➤ However, in many Latin American countries, a comma is often used to separate thousands and millions in figures, just as it is in English.

700,000 (sietecientos mil)	700,000 (seven hundred thousand)
5,000,000 (cinco millones)	5,000,000 (five million)

➤ Many Latin American countries use the decimal point to show decimals, just as we do in English.

0.5 (cero punto cinco)	0.5 (zero point five)
3.4 (tres punto cuatro)	3.4 (three point four)

➤ On the other hand, in Spain and in some South American countries, a period is used to separate thousands and millions and a comma is used to show decimals.

700. 000 (sietecientos mil)	700,000 (seven hundred thousand)
0,5 (cero coma cinco)	0.5 (zero point five)

1st	**primero (1º), primer (1er), primera (1ª)**
2nd	**segundo (2º), segunda (2ª)**
3rd	**tercero (3º), tercer (3er), tercera (3ª)**
4th	**cuarto (4º), cuarta (4ª)**
5th	**quinto (5º), quinta (5ª)**
6th	**sexto (6º), sexta (6ª)**
7th	**séptimo (7º), séptima (7ª)**
8th	**octavo (8º), octava (8ª)**
9th	**noveno (9º), novena (9ª)**
10th	**décimo (10º), décima (10ª)**
100th	**centésimo (100º), centésima (100ª)**
101st	**centésimo primero (101º), centésima primera (101ª)**
1000th	**milésimo (1000º), milésima (1000ª)**

Es la cuarta vez que te lo digo.	This is the fourth time I've told you.
Llegó tercero.	He came in third.

Tip

Shorten **primero** (meaning *first*) to **primer**, and **tercero** (meaning *third*) to **tercer** before a masculine singular noun.

su primer cumpleaños	his first birthday
el tercer premio	the third prize

ⓘ Note that when you are writing these numbers in figures, you must not write *1st*, *2nd*, *3rd* as in English. Use 1º, 1ª, 1er, 2º, 2ª and 3º, 3ª, 3er as required by the noun.

For further explanation of grammatical terms, please see pages viii-xii.

4 primero, segundo, tercero or uno, dos, tres?

➤ Apart from **primero** (meaning *first*) up to **décimo** (meaning *tenth*), as well as **centésimo** (meaning *one hundredth*) and **milésimo** (meaning *one thousandth*), the ordinal numbers tend not to be used very much in Spanish. Cardinal numbers (ordinary numbers) are used instead.

Carlos III (read as: **Carlos tercero**)
Alfonso XIII (read as: **Alfonso trece**)

➪ *For numbers used in dates, see page 213.*

Time and date

LA HORA	THE TIME
¿Qué hora es?	**What time is it?**

To answer this question, you say **Son las dos/las tres/las cuatro**, etc. (It's two/three/four o'clock, etc.) BUT **Es la una** (It's one o'clock).

Es la una.	It's one o'clock.
Es la una y diez.	It's ten after one.
Es la una y cuarto.	It's a quarter after one.
Es la una y veinte.	It's twenty after one.
Es la una y media.	It's one thirty.
Son veinticinco para las dos.*	It's twenty-five to two.
Son cuarto para las dos.*	It's a quarter to two.
Son cinco para las dos.*	It's five to two.
Son las dos.	It's two o'clock.

* This is what you say in most of Latin America. In Spain, people say:

Son las dos menos veinticinco.	It's twenty-five to two.
Son las dos menos cuarto.	It's a quarter to two.
Son las dos menos cinco.	It's five to two.

¿A qué hora?	**At what time?**
a medianoche	at midnight
a mediodía	at midday/noon
a la una (del mediodía)	at one o'clock (in the afternoon)
a las tres (de la tarde)	at three o'clock (in the afternoon)
a las 9:25 *or* **a las nueve (y) veinticinco**	at nine twenty-five
a las 16:50 *or* **a las dieciséis (y) cincuenta**	at 16:50 *or* sixteen fifty

[i] Note that in Spanish, as in English, you can also tell the time using the figures you see on a digital clock or watch or on a 24-hour timetable.

LA FECHA	THE DATE
Los días de la semana	**The days of the week**
lunes	Monday
martes	Tuesday
miércoles	Wednesday
jueves	Thursday

For further explanation of grammatical terms, please see pages viii-xii.

viernes	Friday
sábado	Saturday
domingo	Sunday

¿Cuándo?	**When?**
el lunes	on Monday
los lunes	on Mondays
todos los lunes	every Monday
el martes pasado	last Tuesday
el viernes que viene	next Friday
el sábado que viene no, el otro	a week from Saturday
dentro de tres sábados	two weeks from Saturday

[i] Note that days of the week DON'T have a capital letter in Spanish.

Los meses del año	**Months of the year**
enero	January
febrero	February
marzo	March
abril	April
mayo	May
junio	June
julio	July
agosto	August
septiembre	September
octubre	October
noviembre	November
diciembre	December

¿Cuándo?	**When?**
en febrero	in February
el 1er (primero) *or* **el 1 (uno) de diciembre**	on December 1st
en 1998 (mil novecientos noventa y ocho)	in 1998
el 15 de diciembre de 2003 (dos mil tres)	on December 15th , 2003
el año dos mil	(the year) two thousand

¿Qué día es hoy?	**What day is it today?**
Es martes.	It's Tuesday.
lunes 26 de febrero	Monday, February 26th
domingo 3 de octubre	Sunday, October 3rd

[i] Note that, in Spanish, months of the year DON'T have a capital letter.

Tip

In English we use *first*, *second*, *third* and so on in dates. In Spanish, you use the equivalent of *two*, *three* and so on for all dates except the first of the month: **el 1° (primero) de abril**, **el 2 (dos) de abril**, **el 3 (tres) de abril** etc. (April 1st, 2nd, 3rd etc.). You may also come across **el 1 (uno) de abril**, particularly in European Spanish.

FRASES ÚTILES	USEFUL PHRASES
¿Cuándo?	**When?**
hoy	today
esta mañana	this morning
esta tarde	this afternoon/evening
esta noche	this evening/tonight
¿Con qué frecuencia?	**How often?**
todos los días	every day
cada dos días	every other day
una vez por semana	once a week
dos veces por semana	twice a week
una vez al mes	once a month
¿Cuándo pasó?	**When did it happen?**
en *or* **por la mañana**	in the morning
en *or* **por la tarde**	in the afternoon/evening
en *or* **por la noche**	in the evening/at night
ayer	yesterday
ayer en *or* **por la mañana**	yesterday morning
ayer en *or* **por la tarde**	yesterday afternoon/evening
ayer en *or* **por la noche**	yesterday evening/last night
anoche	last night
anteayer *or* **antier**	the day before yesterday
hace una semana	a week ago
hace quince días	two weeks ago
la semana pasada	last week
el año pasado	last year
¿Cuándo va a pasar?	**When is it going to happen?**
mañana	tomorrow
mañana en *or* **por la mañana**	tomorrow morning
mañana en *or* **por la tarde**	tomorrow afternoon/evening
mañana en *or* **por la noche**	tomorrow evening/night
pasado mañana	the day after tomorrow
dentro de dos días	in two days' time
dentro de una semana	in a week's time
dentro de quince días	in two weeks' time
el mes que viene	next month
el año que viene	next year

For further explanation of grammatical terms, please see pages viii-xii.

Main Index

Verb Tables

Introduction

The **Verb Tables** in the following section contain 120 tables of Spanish verbs (some regular and some irregular) in alphabetical order. Each table shows you the following forms: **Present**, **Present Perfect**, **Preterite**, **Imperfect**, **Future**, **Conditional**, **Present Subjunctive**, **Imperfect Subjunctive**, **Imperative** and the **Past Participle** and **Gerund**. For more information on these tenses and how they are formed you should look at the section on Verbs on pages 69-158.

In order to help you use the verbs shown in the **Verb Tables** correctly, there are also a number of example phrases at the bottom of each page to show the verb as it is used in context.

In Spanish there are both **regular** verbs (their forms follow the normal rules) and **irregular** verbs (their forms do not follow the normal rules). The regular verbs in these tables that you can use as models for other regular verbs are:

hablar (regular **-ar** verb, Verb Table 340-341)
comer (regular **-er** verb, Verb Table 270-271)
vivir (regular **-ir** verb, Verb Table 456-457)

The irregular verbs are shown in full.

The **Verb Index** at the end of this section contains over 1,200 verbs, each of which is cross-referred to one of the verbs given in the **Verb Tables**. The table shows the patterns that the verb listed in the index follows.

abolir (to abolish)

	PRESENT	PRESENT PERFECT
(yo)		he abolido
(tú)		has abolido
(él/ella/usted)		ha abolido
(nosotros/as)	abolimos	hemos abolido
(vosotros/as)	abolís	habéis abolido
(ellos/ellas/ ustedes)		han abolido

Present tense only used in persons shown

	PRETERITE	IMPERFECT
(yo)	abolí	abolía
(tú)	aboliste	abolías
(él/ella/usted)	abolió	abolía
(nosotros/as)	abolimos	abolíamos
(vosotros/as)	abolisteis	abolíais
(ellos/ellas/ ustedes)	abolieron	abolían

GERUND
aboliendo

PAST PARTICIPLE
abolido

EXAMPLE PHRASES

Hay que **abolir** esta ley. This law should be abolished.
Habían abolido la pena de muerte. They had abolished the death penalty.
Abolieron la esclavitud. They abolished slavery.

Remember that subject pronouns are not used very often in Spanish.

abolir

	FUTURE	CONDITIONAL
(yo)	**aboliré**	**aboliría**
(tú)	**abolirás**	**abolirías**
(él/ella/usted)	**abolirá**	**aboliría**
(nosotros/as)	**aboliremos**	**aboliríamos**
(vosotros/as)	**aboliréis**	**aboliríais**
(ellos/ellas/ ustedes)	**abolirán**	**abolirían**

	PRESENT SUBJUNCTIVE	IMPERFECT SUBJUNCTIVE
(yo)	*not used*	**aboliera** *or* **aboliese**
(tú)		**abolieras** *or* **abolieses**
(él/ella/usted)		**aboliera** *or* **aboliese**
(nosotros/as)		**aboliéramos** *or* **aboliésemos**
(vosotros/as)		**abolierais** *or* **abolieseis**
(ellos/ellas/ ustedes)		**abolieran** *or* **aboliesen**

IMPERATIVE

abolid

EXAMPLE PHRASES

Prometieron que **abolirían** la censura. They promised they'd abolish censorship.

Remember that subject pronouns are not used very often in Spanish.

abrir (to open)

	PRESENT	PRESENT PERFECT
(yo)	abro	he abierto
(tú)	abres	has abierto
(él/ella/usted)	abre	ha abierto
(nosotros/as)	abrimos	hemos abierto
(vosotros/as)	abrís	habéis abierto
(ellos/ellas/ ustedes)	abren	han abierto

	PRETERITE	IMPERFECT
(yo)	abrí	abría
(tú)	abriste	abrías
(él/ella/usted)	abrió	abría
(nosotros/as)	abrimos	abríamos
(vosotros/as)	abristeis	abríais
(ellos/ellas/ ustedes)	abrieron	abrían

GERUND
abriendo

PAST PARTICIPLE
abierto

EXAMPLE PHRASES

Hoy **se abre** el periodo de inscripciones. Registration begins today.

Han abierto un nuevo restaurante cerca de aquí. They've opened a new restaurant near here.

¿Quién **abrió** la ventana? Who opened the window?

La llave **abría** el armario. The key opened the closet.

Remember that subject pronouns are not used very often in Spanish.

abrir

	FUTURE	CONDITIONAL
(yo)	**abriré**	**abriría**
(tú)	**abrirás**	**abrirías**
(él/ella/usted)	**abrirá**	**abriría**
(nosotros/as)	**abriremos**	**abriríamos**
(vosotros/as)	**abriréis**	**abriríais**
(ellos/ellas/ ustedes)	**abrirán**	**abrirían**

	PRESENT SUBJUNCTIVE	IMPERFECT SUBJUNCTIVE
(yo)	**abra**	**abriera** *or* **abriese**
(tú)	**abras**	**abrieras** *or* **abrieses**
(él/ella/usted)	**abra**	**abriera** *or* **abriese**
(nosotros/as)	**abramos**	**abriéramos** *or* **abriésemos**
(vosotros/as)	**abráis**	**abrierais** *or* **abrieseis**
(ellos/ellas/ ustedes)	**abran**	**abrieran** *or* **abriesen**

IMPERATIVE

abre / abrid

Use the present subjunctive in all cases other than these tú and vosotros affirmative forms.

EXAMPLE PHRASES

Abrirán todas las puertas de la catedral. They'll open all the doors of the cathedral.

Me dijo que hoy **abrirían** sólo por la tarde. He told me that they'd only be open in the evening today.

No creo que **abran** un nuevo supermercado por aquí. I don't think they'll open a new supermarket here.

No **abras** esa llave. Don't turn on that faucet.

Remember that subject pronouns are not used very often in Spanish.

actuar (to act)

	PRESENT	PRESENT PERFECT
(yo)	**actúo**	**he actuado**
(tú)	**actúas**	**has actuado**
(él/ella/usted)	**actúa**	**ha actuado**
(nosotros/as)	**actuamos**	**hemos actuado**
(vosotros/as)	**actuáis**	**habéis actuado**
(ellos/ellas/ ustedes)	**actúan**	**han actuado**

	PRETERITE	IMPERFECT
(yo)	**actué**	**actuaba**
(tú)	**actuaste**	**actuabas**
(él/ella/usted)	**actuó**	**actuaba**
(nosotros/as)	**actuamos**	**actuábamos**
(vosotros/as)	**actuasteis**	**actuabais**
(ellos/ellas/ ustedes)	**actuaron**	**actuaban**

GERUND
actuando

PAST PARTICIPLE
actuado

EXAMPLE PHRASES

Actúa de una forma muy rara. He's acting very strangely.
Actuó siguiendo un impulso. He acted on impulse.
Ha actuado en varias películas. He has been in several movies.
Actuaba como si no supiera nada. She was behaving as if she didn't know anything about it.

Remember that subject pronouns are not used very often in Spanish.

actuar

	FUTURE	CONDITIONAL
(yo)	**actuaré**	**actuaría**
(tú)	**actuarás**	**actuarías**
(él/ella/usted)	**actuará**	**actuaría**
(nosotros/as)	**actuaremos**	**actuaríamos**
(vosotros/as)	**actuaréis**	**actuaríais**
(ellos/ellas/ ustedes)	**actuarán**	**actuarían**

	PRESENT SUBJUNCTIVE	IMPERFECT SUBJUNCTIVE
(yo)	**actúe**	**actuara** *or* **actuase**
(tú)	**actúes**	**actuaras** *or* **actuases**
(él/ella/usted)	**actúe**	**actuara** *or* **actuase**
(nosotros/as)	**actuemos**	**actuáramos** *or* **actuásemos**
(vosotros/as)	**actuéis**	**actuarais** *or* **actuaseis**
(ellos/ellas/ ustedes)	**actúen**	**actuaran** *or* **actuasen**

IMPERATIVE

actúa / actuad

Use the present subjunctive in all cases other than these tú *and* vosotros *affirmative forms.*

EXAMPLE PHRASES

¿Quién **actuará** en su próxima película? Who will be in his next movie?

Yo nunca **actuaría** así. I'd never behave like that.

Si **actuara** de forma más lógica, sería más fácil atraparlo. It would be easier to catch him if he behaved in a more logical way.

Actúa como mejor te parezca. Do as you think best.

Remember that subject pronouns are not used very often in Spanish.

adquirir (to acquire; to obtain; to purchase)

	PRESENT	PRESENT PERFECT
(yo)	adquiero	he adquirido
(tú)	adquieres	has adquirido
(él/ella/usted)	adquiere	ha adquirido
(nosotros/as)	adquirimos	hemos adquirido
(vosotros/as)	adquirís	habéis adquirido
(ellos/ellas/ustedes)	adquieren	han adquirido

	PRETERITE	IMPERFECT
(yo)	adquirí	adquiría
(tú)	adquiriste	adquirías
(él/ella/usted)	adquirió	adquiría
(nosotros/as)	adquirimos	adquiríamos
(vosotros/as)	adquiristeis	adquiríais
(ellos/ellas/ustedes)	adquirieron	adquirían

GERUND
adquiriendo

PAST PARTICIPLE
adquirido

EXAMPLE PHRASES

Adquiere cada vez mayor importancia. It's becoming more and more important.

Está adquiriendo una reputación que no merece. It's getting a reputation it doesn't deserve.

Han adquirido más acciones. They've purchased more stock.

Con el tiempo **adquirió** madurez. Over the years he gained maturity.

Remember that subject pronouns are not used very often in Spanish.

adquirir

	FUTURE	CONDITIONAL
(yo)	**adquiriré**	**adquiriría**
(tú)	**adquirirás**	**adquirirías**
(él/ella/usted)	**adquirirá**	**adquiriría**
(nosotros/as)	**adquiriremos**	**adquiriríamos**
(vosotros/as)	**adquiriréis**	**adquiriríais**
(ellos/ellas/ ustedes)	**adquirirán**	**adquirirían**

	PRESENT SUBJUNCTIVE	IMPERFECT SUBJUNCTIVE
(yo)	**adquiera**	**adquiriera** *or* **adquiriese**
(tú)	**adquieras**	**adquirieras** *or* **adquirieses**
(él/ella/usted)	**adquiera**	**adquiriera** *or* **adquiriese**
(nosotros/as)	**adquiramos**	**adquiriéramos** *or* **adquiriésemos**
(vosotros/as)	**adquiráis**	**adquirierais** *or* **adquirieseis**
(ellos/ellas/ ustedes)	**adquieran**	**adquirieran** *or* **adquiriesen**

IMPERATIVE

adquiere / adquirid

Use the present subjunctive in all cases other than these tú and vosotros affirmative forms.

EXAMPLE PHRASES

Al final **adquirirán** los derechos de publicación. They will get the publishing rights in the end.

Adquiera o no la nacionalidad, podrá permanecer en el país. She'll be able to stay in the country whether she gets citizenship or not.

Tenía gran interés en que **adquiriera** el cuadro. He was eager that she should purchase the picture.

Remember that subject pronouns are not used very often in Spanish.

advertir (to warn; to notice)

	PRESENT	PRESENT PERFECT
(yo)	**advierto**	**he advertido**
(tú)	**adviertes**	**has advertido**
(él/ella/usted)	**advierte**	**ha advertido**
(nosotros/as)	**advertimos**	**hemos advertido**
(vosotros/as)	**advertís**	**habéis advertido**
(ellos/ellas/ ustedes)	**advierten**	**han advertido**

	PRETERITE	IMPERFECT
(yo)	**advertí**	**advertía**
(tú)	**advertiste**	**advertías**
(él/ella/usted)	**advirtió**	**advertía**
(nosotros/as)	**advertimos**	**advertíamos**
(vosotros/as)	**advertisteis**	**advertíais**
(ellos/ellas/ ustedes)	**advirtieron**	**advertían**

GERUND
advirtiendo

PAST PARTICIPLE
advertido

EXAMPLE PHRASES

Te **advierto** que no va a ser nada fácil. I must warn you that it won't be at all easy.

No **había advertido** nada extraño en su comportamiento. I hadn't noticed anything strange about his behavior.

Ya te **advertí** que no intervinieras. I warned you not to get involved.

Las señales **advertían** del peligro. The signs warned of danger.

Remember that subject pronouns are not used very often in Spanish.

advertir

	FUTURE	CONDITIONAL
(yo)	**advertiré**	**advertiría**
(tú)	**advertirás**	**advertirías**
(él/ella/usted)	**advertirá**	**advertiría**
(nosotros/as)	**advertiremos**	**advertiríamos**
(vosotros/as)	**advertiréis**	**advertiríais**
(ellos/ellas/ ustedes)	**advertirán**	**advertirían**

	PRESENT SUBJUNCTIVE	IMPERFECT SUBJUNCTIVE
(yo)	**advierta**	**advirtiera** *or* **advirtiese**
(tú)	**adviertas**	**advirtieras** *or* **advirtieses**
(él/ella/usted)	**advierta**	**advirtiera** *or* **advirtiese**
(nosotros/as)	**advirtamos**	**advirtiéramos** *or* **advirtiésemos**
(vosotros/as)	**advirtáis**	**advirtierais** *or* **advirtieseis**
(ellos/ellas/ ustedes)	**adviertan**	**advirtieran** *or* **advirtiesen**

IMPERATIVE

advierte / advertid

Use the present subjunctive in all cases other than these tú and vosotros affirmative forms.

EXAMPLE PHRASES

Si **advirtiera** algún cambio, llámenos. If you should notice any change, call us.

Adviértele del riesgo que entraña. Warn him about the risk involved.

Remember that subject pronouns are not used very often in Spanish.

amanecer (to get light; to wake up)

	PRESENT	PRESENT PERFECT
(yo)	amanezco	he amanecido
(tú)	amaneces	has amanecido
(él/ella/usted)	amanece	ha amanecido
(nosotros/as)	amanecemos	hemos amanecido
(vosotros/as)	amanecéis	habéis amanecido
(ellos/ellas/ ustedes)	amanecen	han amanecido

	PRETERITE	IMPERFECT
(yo)	amanecí	amanecía
(tú)	amaneciste	amanecías
(él/ella/usted)	amaneció	amanecía
(nosotros/as)	amanecimos	amanecíamos
(vosotros/as)	amanecisteis	amanecíais
(ellos/ellas/ ustedes)	amanecieron	amanecían

GERUND
amaneciendo

PAST PARTICIPLE
amanecido

EXAMPLE PHRASES

Siempre **amanece** nublado. The day always starts off cloudy.

Estaba amaneciendo. Dawn was breaking.

La ciudad **amaneció** desierta. In the morning, the town was deserted.

Amanecía de un humor de perros. She would wake up in a really bad mood.

Remember that subject pronouns are not used very often in Spanish.

amanecer

	FUTURE	CONDITIONAL
(yo)	amaneceré	amanecería
(tú)	amanecerás	amanecerías
(él/ella/usted)	amanecerá	amanecería
(nosotros/as)	amaneceremos	amaneceríamos
(vosotros/as)	amaneceréis	amaneceríais
(ellos/ellas/ ustedes)	amanecerán	amanecerían

	PRESENT SUBJUNCTIVE	IMPERFECT SUBJUNCTIVE
(yo)	amanezca	amaneciera *or* amaneciese
(tú)	amanezcas	amanecieras *or* amanecieses
(él/ella/usted)	amanezca	amaneciera *or* amaneciese
(nosotros/as)	amanezcamos	amaneciéramos *or* amaneciésemos
(vosotros/as)	amanezcáis	amanecierais *or* amanecieseis
(ellos/ellas/ ustedes)	amanezcan	amanecieran *or* amaneciesen

IMPERATIVE

amanece / amaneced

Use the present subjunctive in all cases other than these tú and vosotros affirmative forms.

EXAMPLE PHRASES

Pronto **amanecerá**. It will soon be daylight.

Saldremos en cuanto **amanezca**. We'll get going as soon as it gets light.

Si **amanecieras** con fiebre, toma una de estas pastillas. If you should wake up with a fever, take one of these pills.

Remember that subject pronouns are not used very often in Spanish.

andar (to be; to work; to ride; to walk)

	PRESENT	PRESENT PERFECT
(yo)	ando	he andado
(tú)	andas	has andado
(él/ella/usted)	anda	ha andado
(nosotros/as)	andamos	hemos andado
(vosotros/as)	andáis	habéis andado
(ellos/ellas/ ustedes)	andan	han andado

	PRETERITE	IMPERFECT
(yo)	anduve	andaba
(tú)	anduviste	andabas
(él/ella/usted)	anduvo	andaba
(nosotros/as)	anduvimos	andábamos
(vosotros/as)	anduvisteis	andabais
(ellos/ellas/ ustedes)	anduvieron	andaban

GERUND
andando

PAST PARTICIPLE
andado

EXAMPLE PHRASES

¿Cómo **andas**? How are you?

La lavadora no **andaba** bien. The washing machine wasn't working properly.

Andaban mal de dinero. They were short of money.

No sabe **andar** en bicicleta. She doesn't know how to ride a bike.

Remember that subject pronouns are not used very often in Spanish.

andar

	FUTURE	CONDITIONAL
(yo)	**andaré**	**andaría**
(tú)	**andarás**	**andarías**
(él/ella/usted)	**andará**	**andaría**
(nosotros/as)	**andaremos**	**andaríamos**
(vosotros/as)	**andaréis**	**andaríais**
(ellos/ellas/ ustedes)	**andarán**	**andarían**

	PRESENT SUBJUNCTIVE	IMPERFECT SUBJUNCTIVE
(yo)	**ande**	**anduviera** *or* **anduviese**
(tú)	**andes**	**anduvieras** *or* **anduvieses**
(él/ella/usted)	**ande**	**anduviera** *or* **anduviese**
(nosotros/as)	**andemos**	**anduviéramos** *or* **anduviésemos**
(vosotros/as)	**andéis**	**anduvierais** *or* **anduvieseis**
(ellos/ellas/ ustedes)	**anden**	**anduvieran** *or* **anduviesen**

IMPERATIVE

anda / andad

Use the present subjunctive in all cases other than these tú and vosotros affirmative forms.

EXAMPLE PHRASES

Andará por los cuarenta. He must be about forty.

Yo **me andaría** con pies de plomo. I'd tread very carefully.

Si **anduvieras** con más cuidado, no te pasarían esas cosas. If you were more careful, this sort of thing wouldn't happen to you.

Remember that subject pronouns are not used very often in Spanish.

apoderarse de (to take control of)

	PRESENT	PRESENT PERFECT
(yo)	me apodero	me he apoderado
(tú)	te apoderas	te has apoderado
(él/ella/usted)	se apodera	se ha apoderado
(nosotros/as)	nos apoderamos	nos hemos apoderado
(vosotros/as)	os apoderáis	os habéis apoderado
(ellos/ellas/ustedes)	se apoderan	se han apoderado

	PRETERITE	IMPERFECT
(yo)	me apoderé	me apoderaba
(tú)	te apoderaste	te apoderabas
(él/ella/usted)	se apoderó	se apoderaba
(nosotros/as)	nos apoderamos	nos apoderábamos
(vosotros/as)	os apoderasteis	os apoderabais
(ellos/ellas/ustedes)	se apoderaron	se apoderaban

GERUND
apoderando

PAST PARTICIPLE
apoderado

EXAMPLE PHRASES

En esas situaciones, el miedo **se apodera** de mí. In situations like that, I find myself gripped by fear.

Poco a poco **se han ido apoderando** de las riquezas del país. Little by little, they've taken control of the country's riches.

Se apoderaron de las joyas y huyeron. They took the jewels and ran off.

Remember that subject pronouns are not used very often in Spanish.

apoderarse de

	FUTURE	CONDITIONAL
(yo)	**me apoderaré**	**me apoderaría**
(tú)	**te apoderarás**	**te apoderarías**
(él/ella/usted)	**se apoderará**	**se apoderaría**
(nosotros/as)	**nos apoderaremos**	**nos apoderaríamos**
(vosotros/as)	**os apoderaréis**	**os apoderaríais**
(ellos/ellas/ ustedes)	**se apoderarán**	**se apoderarían**

	PRESENT SUBJUNCTIVE	IMPERFECT SUBJUNCTIVE
(yo)	**me apodere**	**me apoderara** *or* **apoderase**
(tú)	**te apoderes**	**te apoderaras** *or* **apoderases**
(él/ella/usted)	**se apodere**	**se apoderara** *or* **apoderase**
(nosotros/as)	**nos apoderemos**	**nos apoderáramos** *or* **apoderásemos**
(vosotros/as)	**os apoderéis**	**os apoderarais** *or* **apoderaseis**
(ellos/ellas/ ustedes)	**se apoderen**	**se apoderaran** *or* **apoderasen**

IMPERATIVE

apodérate / apoderaos

Use the present subjunctive in all cases other than these tú and vosotros affirmative forms.

EXAMPLE PHRASES

No dejes que la curiosidad **se apodere** de ti. Don't let curiosity get the better of you.

Remember that subject pronouns are not used very often in Spanish.

aprobar (to pass; to approve of)

	PRESENT	PRESENT PERFECT
(yo)	**apruebo**	**he aprobado**
(tú)	**apruebas**	**has aprobado**
(él/ella/usted)	**aprueba**	**ha aprobado**
(nosotros/as)	**aprobamos**	**hemos aprobado**
(vosotros/as)	**aprobáis**	**habéis aprobado**
(ellos/ellas/ ustedes)	**aprueban**	**han aprobado**

	PRETERITE	IMPERFECT
(yo)	**aprobé**	**aprobaba**
(tú)	**aprobaste**	**aprobabas**
(él/ella/usted)	**aprobó**	**aprobaba**
(nosotros/as)	**aprobamos**	**aprobábamos**
(vosotros/as)	**aprobasteis**	**aprobabais**
(ellos/ellas/ ustedes)	**aprobaron**	**aprobaban**

GERUND
aprobando

PAST PARTICIPLE
aprobado

EXAMPLE PHRASES

No **apruebo** esa conducta. I don't approve of that sort of behavior.
Este año lo **estoy aprobando** todo. So far this year I've passed everything.
Han aprobado una ley antitabaco. They've passed an anti-smoking law.
¿**Aprobaste** el examen? Did you pass the test?
La decisión **fue aprobada** por mayoría. The decision was approved by a majority.

Remember that subject pronouns are not used very often in Spanish.

aprobar

	FUTURE	CONDITIONAL
(yo)	aprobaré	aprobaría
(tú)	aprobarás	aprobarías
(él/ella/usted)	aprobará	aprobaría
(nosotros/as)	aprobaremos	aprobaríamos
(vosotros/as)	aprobaréis	aprobaríais
(ellos/ellas/ ustedes)	aprobarán	aprobarían

	PRESENT SUBJUNCTIVE	IMPERFECT SUBJUNCTIVE
(yo)	apruebe	aprobara *or* aprobase
(tú)	apruebes	aprobaras *or* aprobases
(él/ella/usted)	apruebe	aprobara *or* aprobase
(nosotros/as)	aprobemos	aprobáramos *or* aprobásemos
(vosotros/as)	aprobéis	aprobarais *or* aprobaseis
(ellos/ellas/ ustedes)	aprueben	aprobaran *or* aprobasen

IMPERATIVE

aprueba / aprobad

Use the present subjunctive in all cases other than these tú and vosotros affirmative forms.

Remember that subject pronouns are not used very often in Spanish.

arrancar (to pull up; to start)

	PRESENT	PRESENT PERFECT
(yo)	arranco	he arrancado
(tú)	arrancas	has arrancado
(él/ella/usted)	arranca	ha arrancado
(nosotros/as)	arrancamos	hemos arrancado
(vosotros/as)	arrancáis	habéis arrancado
(ellos/ellas/ ustedes)	arrancan	han arrancado

	PRETERITE	IMPERFECT
(yo)	arranqué	arrancaba
(tú)	arrancaste	arrancabas
(él/ella/usted)	arrancó	arrancaba
(nosotros/as)	arrancamos	arrancábamos
(vosotros/as)	arrancasteis	arrancabais
(ellos/ellas/ ustedes)	arrancaron	arrancaban

GERUND
arrancando

PAST PARTICIPLE
arrancado

EXAMPLE PHRASES

Lo tienes que **arrancar** de raíz. You must pull it up by its roots.
Estaba arrancando malas hierbas. I was pulling up weeds.
El viento **arrancó** varios árboles. Several trees were uprooted in the wind.
La moto no **arranca**. The motorcycle won't start.

Remember that subject pronouns are not used very often in Spanish.

arrancar

	FUTURE	CONDITIONAL
(yo)	**arrancaré**	**arrancaría**
(tú)	**arrancarás**	**arrancarías**
(él/ella/usted)	**arrancará**	**arrancaría**
(nosotros/as)	**arrancaremos**	**arrancaríamos**
(vosotros/as)	**arrancaréis**	**arrancaríais**
(ellos/ellas/ ustedes)	**arrancarán**	**arrancarían**

	PRESENT SUBJUNCTIVE	IMPERFECT SUBJUNCTIVE
(yo)	**arranque**	**arrancara** *or* **arrancase**
(tú)	**arranques**	**arrancaras** *or* **arrancases**
(él/ella/usted)	**arranque**	**arrancara** *or* **arrancase**
(nosotros/as)	**arranquemos**	**arrancáramos** *or* **arrancásemos**
(vosotros/as)	**arranquéis**	**arrancarais** *or* **arrancaseis**
(ellos/ellas/ ustedes)	**arranquen**	**arrancaran** *or* **arrancasen**

IMPERATIVE

arranca / arrancad

Use the present subjunctive in all cases other than these tú and vosotros affirmative forms.

EXAMPLE PHRASES

No **arranques** hojas del cuaderno. Don't tear pages out of the notebook.

Arranca y vámonos. Start the engine and let's get going.

Remember that subject pronouns are not used very often in Spanish.

arrepentirse (to be sorry; to change your mind)

	PRESENT	PRESENT PERFECT
(yo)	**me arrepiento**	**me he arrepentido**
(tú)	**te arrepientes**	**te has arrepentido**
(él/ella/usted)	**se arrepiente**	**se ha arrepentido**
(nosotros/as)	**nos arrepentimos**	**nos hemos arrepentido**
(vosotros/as)	**os arrepentís**	**os habéis arrepentido**
(ellos/ellas/ ustedes)	**se arrepienten**	**se han arrepentido**

	PRETERITE	IMPERFECT
(yo)	**me arrepentí**	**me arrepentía**
(tú)	**te arrepentiste**	**te arrepentías**
(él/ella/usted)	**se arrepintió**	**se arrepentía**
(nosotros/as)	**nos arrepentimos**	**nos arrepentíamos**
(vosotros/as)	**os arrepentisteis**	**os arrepentíais**
(ellos/ellas/ ustedes)	**se arrepintieron**	**se arrepentían**

GERUND
arrepintiéndose, etc

PAST PARTICIPLE
arrepentido

EXAMPLE PHRASES

¡**Te** vas a **arrepentir** de esto! You'll be sorry for this!

No **me arrepiento** de nada. I don't regret anything.

Se arrepintieron y decidieron no vender la casa. They changed their minds and decided not to sell the house.

Arrepintiéndote en serio, seguro que te perdonarán. If you're truly sorry, I'm sure they'll forgive you.

Remember that subject pronouns are not used very often in Spanish.

arrepentirse

	FUTURE	CONDITIONAL
(yo)	me arrepentiré	me arrepentiría
(tú)	te arrepentirás	te arrepentirías
(él/ella/usted)	se arrepentirá	se arrepentiría
(nosotros/as)	nos arrepentiremos	nos arrepentiríamos
(vosotros/as)	os arrepentiréis	os arrepentiríais
(ellos/ellas/ustedes)	se arrepentirán	se arrepentirían

	PRESENT SUBJUNCTIVE	IMPERFECT SUBJUNCTIVE
(yo)	me arrepienta	me arrepintiera *or* arrepintiese
(tú)	te arrepientas	te arrepintieras *or* arrepintieses
(él/ella/usted)	se arrepienta	se arrepintiera *or* arrepintiese
(nosotros/as)	nos arrepintamos	nos arrepintiéramos *or* arrepintiésemos
(vosotros/as)	os arrepintáis	os arrepintierais *or* arrepintieseis
(ellos/ellas/ustedes)	se arrepientan	se arrepintieran *or* arrepintiesen

IMPERATIVE

arrepiéntete / arrepentíos

Use the present subjunctive in all cases other than these tú and vosotros affirmative forms.

EXAMPLE PHRASES

Algún día **se arrepentirá** de no haber estudiado una carrera. One day he'll be sorry he didn't go to college.

No **te arrepientas** nunca de haber dicho la verdad. Don't ever regret having told the truth.

Remember that subject pronouns are not used very often in Spanish.

atravesar (to cross; to go through)

	PRESENT	PRESENT PERFECT
(yo)	atravieso	he atravesado
(tú)	atraviesas	has atravesado
(él/ella/usted)	atraviesa	ha atravesado
(nosotros/as)	atravesamos	hemos atravesado
(vosotros/as)	atravesáis	habéis atravesado
(ellos/ellas/ ustedes)	atraviesan	han atravesado

	PRETERITE	IMPERFECT
(yo)	atravesé	atravesaba
(tú)	atravesaste	atravesabas
(él/ella/usted)	atravesó	atravesaba
(nosotros/as)	atravesamos	atravesábamos
(vosotros/as)	atravesasteis	atravesabais
(ellos/ellas/ ustedes)	atravesaron	atravesaban

GERUND
atravesando

PAST PARTICIPLE
atravesado

EXAMPLE PHRASES

Estamos atravesando un mal momento. We're going through a bad patch.

Atravesamos el río a nado. We swam across the river.

La bala le **atravesó** el cráneo. The bullet went through his skull.

Un camión **se** nos **atravesó** en la carretera. A truck pulled out in front of us on the road.

Remember that subject pronouns are not used very often in Spanish.

atravesar

	FUTURE	CONDITIONAL
(yo)	atravesaré	atravesaría
(tú)	atravesarás	atravesarías
(él/ella/usted)	atravesará	atravesaría
(nosotros/as)	atravesaremos	atravesaríamos
(vosotros/as)	atravesaréis	atravesaríais
(ellos/ellas/ ustedes)	atravesarán	atravesarían

	PRESENT SUBJUNCTIVE	IMPERFECT SUBJUNCTIVE
(yo)	atraviese	atravesara *or* atravesase
(tú)	atravieses	atravesaras *or* atravesases
(él/ella/usted)	atraviese	atravesara *or* atravesase
(nosotros/as)	atravesemos	atravesáramos *or* atravesásemos
(vosotros/as)	atraveséis	atravesarais *or* atravesaseis
(ellos/ellas/ ustedes)	atraviesen	atravesaran *or* atravesasen

IMPERATIVE

atraviesa / atravesad

Use the present subjunctive in all cases other than these tú and vosotros affirmative forms.

EXAMPLE PHRASES

El túnel **atravesará** la montaña. The tunnel will go through the mountain.

Remember that subject pronouns are not used very often in Spanish.

aunar (to join together)

	PRESENT	PRESENT PERFECT
(yo)	**aúno**	**he aunado**
(tú)	**aúnas**	**has aunado**
(él/ella/usted)	**aúna**	**ha aunado**
(nosotros/as)	**aunamos**	**hemos aunado**
(vosotros/as)	**aunáis**	**habéis aunado**
(ellos/ellas/ustedes)	**aúnan**	**han aunado**

	PRETERITE	IMPERFECT
(yo)	**auné**	**aunaba**
(tú)	**aunaste**	**aunabas**
(él/ella/usted)	**aunó**	**aunaba**
(nosotros/as)	**aunamos**	**aunábamos**
(vosotros/as)	**aunasteis**	**aunabais**
(ellos/ellas/ustedes)	**aunaron**	**aunaban**

GERUND
aunando

PAST PARTICIPLE
aunado

EXAMPLE PHRASES

En esta obra **se aúnan** imaginación y técnica. This play combines imagination and technique.
Aunaron esfuerzos. They joined forces.

Remember that subject pronouns are not used very often in Spanish.

aunar

	FUTURE	CONDITIONAL
(yo)	**aunaré**	**aunaría**
(tú)	**aunarás**	**aunarías**
(él/ella/usted)	**aunará**	**aunaría**
(nosotros/as)	**aunaremos**	**aunaríamos**
(vosotros/as)	**aunaréis**	**aunaríais**
(ellos/ellas/ ustedes)	**aunarán**	**aunarían**

	PRESENT SUBJUNCTIVE	IMPERFECT SUBJUNCTIVE
(yo)	**aúne**	**aunara** *or* **aunase**
(tú)	**aúnes**	**aunaras** *or* **aunases**
(él/ella/usted)	**aúne**	**aunara** *or* **aunase**
(nosotros/as)	**aunemos**	**aunáramos** *or* **aunásemos**
(vosotros/as)	**aunéis**	**aunarais** *or* **aunaseis**
(ellos/ellas/ ustedes)	**aúnen**	**aunaran** *or* **aunasen**

IMPERATIVE

aúna / aunad

Use the present subjunctive in all cases other than these tú *and* vosotros *affirmative forms.*

Remember that subject pronouns are not used very often in Spanish.

avergonzar (to shame)

	PRESENT	PRESENT PERFECT
(yo)	avergüenzo	he avergonzado
(tú)	avergüenzas	has avergonzado
(él/ella/usted)	avergüenza	ha avergonzado
(nosotros/as)	avergonzamos	hemos avergonzado
(vosotros/as)	avergonzáis	habéis avergonzado
(ellos/ellas/ ustedes)	avergüenzan	han avergonzado

	PRETERITE	IMPERFECT
(yo)	avergoncé	avergonzaba
(tú)	avergonzaste	avergonzabas
(él/ella/usted)	avergonzó	avergonzaba
(nosotros/as)	avergonzamos	avergonzábamos
(vosotros/as)	avergonzasteis	avergonzabais
(ellos/ellas/ ustedes)	avergonzaron	avergonzaban

GERUND
avergonzando

PAST PARTICIPLE
avergonzado

EXAMPLE PHRASES

Tendrías que **avergonzarte**. You should be ashamed of yourself.
La **avergüenza** no tener dinero. She's ashamed of having no money.
Cuando me lo dijo **me avergoncé**. I was embarrassed when he told me.
Se avergonzaba de su familia. He was ashamed of his family.

Remember that subject pronouns are not used very often in Spanish.

avergonzar

	FUTURE	CONDITIONAL
(yo)	**avergonzaré**	**avergonzaría**
(tú)	**avergonzarás**	**avergonzarías**
(él/ella/usted)	**avergonzará**	**avergonzaría**
(nosotros/as)	**avergonzaremos**	**avergonzaríamos**
(vosotros/as)	**avegonzaréis**	**avergonzaríais**
(ellos/ellas/ ustedes)	**avergonzarán**	**avergonzarían**

	PRESENT SUBJUNCTIVE	IMPERFECT SUBJUNCTIVE
(yo)	**avergüence**	**avergonzara** *or* **avergonzase**
(tú)	**avergüences**	**avergonzaras** *or* **avergonzases**
(él/ella/usted)	**avergüence**	**avergonzara** *or* **avergonzase**
(nosotros/as)	**avergoncemos**	**avergonzáramos** *or* **avergonzásemos**
(vosotros/as)	**avergoncéis**	**avergonzarais** *or* **avergonzaseis**
(ellos/ellas/ ustedes)	**avergüencen**	**avergonzaran** *or* **avergonzasen**

IMPERATIVE

avergüenza / avergonzad

Use the present subjunctive in all cases other than these tú and vosotros affirmative forms.

EXAMPLE PHRASES

Si de verdad **se avergonzaran**, no se comportarían así. They wouldn't behave like that if they were really ashamed.

Remember that subject pronouns are not used very often in Spanish.

averiguar (to find out)

	PRESENT	PRESENT PERFECT
(yo)	**averiguo**	**he averiguado**
(tú)	**averiguas**	**has averiguado**
(él/ella/usted)	**averigua**	**ha averiguado**
(nosotros/as)	**averiguamos**	**hemos averiguado**
(vosotros/as)	**averiguáis**	**habéis averiguado**
(ellos/ellas/ ustedes)	**averiguan**	**han averiguado**

	PRETERITE	IMPERFECT
(yo)	**averigüé**	**averiguaba**
(tú)	**averiguaste**	**averiguabas**
(él/ella/usted)	**averiguó**	**averiguaba**
(nosotros/as)	**averiguamos**	**averiguábamos**
(vosotros/as)	**averiguasteis**	**averiguabais**
(ellos/ellas/ ustedes)	**averiguaron**	**averiguaban**

GERUND
averiguando

PAST PARTICIPLE
averiguado

EXAMPLE PHRASES

Trataron de **averiguar** su paradero. They tried to find out his whereabouts.

Poco a poco **van averiguando** más cosas sobre su vida. They're gradually finding out more about his life.

¿Cómo **averiguaste** dónde vivo? How did you find out where I live?

¿Cuándo lo **averiguaron**? When did they find out?

Remember that subject pronouns are not used very often in Spanish.

averiguar

	FUTURE	CONDITIONAL
(yo)	averiguaré	averiguaría
(tú)	averiguarás	averiguarías
(él/ella/usted)	averiguará	averiguaría
(nosotros/as)	averiguaremos	averiguaríamos
(vosotros/as)	averiguaréis	averiguaríais
(ellos/ellas/ ustedes)	averiguarán	averiguarían

	PRESENT SUBJUNCTIVE	IMPERFECT SUBJUNCTIVE
(yo)	averigüe	averiguara *or* averiguase
(tú)	averigües	averiguaras *or* averiguases
(él/ella/usted)	averigüe	averiguara *or* averiguase
(nosotros/as)	averigüemos	averiguáramos *or* averiguásemos
(vosotros/as)	averigüéis	averiguarais *or* averiguaseis
(ellos/ellas/ ustedes)	averigüen	averiguaran *or* averiguasen

IMPERATIVE

averigua / averiguad

Use the present subjunctive in all cases other than these tú and vosotros affirmative forms.

EXAMPLE PHRASES

Lo **averiguaré** pronto. I'll find out soon.

Dijo que si le dábamos tiempo lo **averiguaría**. She said that she'd find out if we gave her time.

En cuanto lo **averigüe** te lo digo. I'll tell you as soon as I find out.

¡**Averígualo** inmediatamente! Check it out immediately!

Remember that subject pronouns are not used very often in Spanish.

bendecir (to bless)

	PRESENT	PRESENT PERFECT
(yo)	bendigo	he bendecido
(tú)	bendices	has bendecido
(él/ella/usted)	bendice	ha bendecido
(nosotros/as)	bendecimos	hemos bendecido
(vosotros/as)	bendecís	habéis bendecido
(ellos/ellas/ ustedes)	bendicen	han bendecido

	PRETERITE	IMPERFECT
(yo)	bendije	bendecía
(tú)	bendijiste	bendecías
(él/ella/usted)	bendijo	bendecía
(nosotros/as)	bendijimos	bendecíamos
(vosotros/as)	bendijisteis	bendecíais
(ellos/ellas/ ustedes)	bendijeron	bendecían

GERUND
bendiciendo

PAST PARTICIPLE
bendecido

EXAMPLE PHRASES

La vida me **ha bendecido** con unos hijos maravillosos. I've been blessed with wonderful children.
Jesús **bendijo** los panes y los peces. Jesus blessed the loaves and the fishes.
Bendecía el día en que lo conoció. She blessed the day she met him.

Remember that subject pronouns are not used very often in Spanish.

bendecir

	FUTURE	CONDITIONAL
(yo)	bendeciré	bendeciría
(tú)	bendecirás	bendecirías
(él/ella/usted)	bendecirá	bendeciría
(nosotros/as)	bendeciremos	bendeciríamos
(vosotros/as)	bendeciréis	bendeciríais
(ellos/ellas/ ustedes)	bendecirán	bendecirían

	PRESENT SUBJUNCTIVE	IMPERFECT SUBJUNCTIVE
(yo)	bendiga	bendijera *or* bendijese
(tú)	bendigas	bendijeras *or* bendijeses
(él/ella/usted)	bendiga	bendijera *or* bendijese
(nosotros/as)	bendigamos	bendijéramos *or* bendijésemos
(vosotros/as)	bendigáis	bendijerais *or* bendijeseis
(ellos/ellas/ ustedes)	bendigan	bendijeran *or* bendijesen

IMPERATIVE

bendice / bendecid

Use the present subjunctive in all cases other than these tú and vosotros affirmative forms.

EXAMPLE PHRASES

El Papa **bendecirá** a los fieles desde el balcón. The Pope will bless the faithful from the balcony.

Quieren que sea él quien **bendiga** su unión. They want him to marry them.

Pidieron a un sacerdote que **bendijera** su nueva casa. They asked a priest to bless their new house.

Remember that subject pronouns are not used very often in Spanish.

caber (to fit)

	PRESENT	PRESENT PERFECT
(yo)	**quepo**	**he cabido**
(tú)	**cabes**	**has cabido**
(él/ella/usted)	**cabe**	**ha cabido**
(nosotros/as)	**cabemos**	**hemos cabido**
(vosotros/as)	**cabéis**	**habéis cabido**
(ellos/ellas/ ustedes)	**caben**	**han cabido**

	PRETERITE	IMPERFECT
(yo)	**cupe**	**cabía**
(tú)	**cupiste**	**cabías**
(él/ella/usted)	**cupo**	**cabía**
(nosotros/as)	**cupimos**	**cabíamos**
(vosotros/as)	**cupisteis**	**cabíais**
(ellos/ellas/ ustedes)	**cupieron**	**cabían**

GERUND
cabiendo

PAST PARTICIPLE
cabido

EXAMPLE PHRASES

No te preocupes, que va a **caber**. Don't worry, it will fit.
Aquí no **cabe**. There isn't enough room for it here.
Al final **cupo** todo. In the end everything went in.
No le **cupo** la menor duda. She wasn't in any doubt.
No **cabía** en sí de dicha. She was beside herself with joy.

Remember that subject pronouns are not used very often in Spanish.

caber

	FUTURE	CONDITIONAL
(yo)	**cabré**	**cabría**
(tú)	**cabrás**	**cabrías**
(él/ella/usted)	**cabrá**	**cabría**
(nosotros/as)	**cabremos**	**cabríamos**
(vosotros/as)	**cabréis**	**cabríais**
(ellos/ellas/ ustedes)	**cabrán**	**cabrían**

	PRESENT SUBJUNCTIVE	IMPERFECT SUBJUNCTIVE
(yo)	**quepa**	**cupiera** *or* **cupiese**
(tú)	**quepas**	**cupieras** *or* **cupieses**
(él/ella/usted)	**quepa**	**cupiera** *or* **cupiese**
(nosotros/as)	**quepamos**	**cupiéramos** *or* **cupiésemos**
(vosotros/as)	**quepáis**	**cupierais** *or* **cupieseis**
(ellos/ellas/ ustedes)	**quepan**	**cupieran** *or* **cupiesen**

IMPERATIVE

cabe / cabed

Use the present subjunctive in all cases other than these tú and vosotros affirmative forms.

EXAMPLE PHRASES

¿Crees que **cabrá**? Do you think there will be enough room for it?

Cabría cuestionarse si es la mejor solución. We should ask ourselves whether it's the best solution.

Hizo lo imposible para que le **cupiera** la redacción en una página. He did everything he could to fit the essay onto one page.

Remember that subject pronouns are not used very often in Spanish.

caer (to fall)

	PRESENT	PRESENT PERFECT
(yo)	caigo	he caído
(tú)	caes	has caído
(él/ella/usted)	cae	ha caído
(nosotros/as)	caemos	hemos caído
(vosotros/as)	caéis	habéis caído
(ellos/ellas/ ustedes)	caen	han caído

	PRETERITE	IMPERFECT
(yo)	caí	caía
(tú)	caíste	caías
(él/ella/usted)	cayó	caía
(nosotros/as)	caímos	caíamos
(vosotros/as)	caísteis	caíais
(ellos/ellas/ ustedes)	cayeron	caían

GERUND
cayendo

PAST PARTICIPLE
caído

EXAMPLE PHRASES

Su cumpleaños **cae** en viernes. Her birthday falls on a Friday.
Ese edificio **se está cayendo**. That building's falling down.
Se me **cayó** un guante. I dropped one of my gloves.
Me caí por las escaleras. I fell down the stairs.
Me caía muy bien. I really liked him.

Remember that subject pronouns are not used very often in Spanish.

caer

	FUTURE	CONDITIONAL
(yo)	**caeré**	caería
(tú)	**caerás**	caerías
(él/ella/usted)	**caerá**	caería
(nosotros/as)	**caeremos**	caeríamos
(vosotros/as)	**caeréis**	caeríais
(ellos/ellas/ ustedes)	**caerán**	caerían

	PRESENT SUBJUNCTIVE	IMPERFECT SUBJUNCTIVE
(yo)	**caiga**	cayera *or* cayese
(tú)	**caigas**	cayeras *or* cayeses
(él/ella/usted)	**caiga**	cayera *or* cayese
(nosotros/as)	**caigamos**	cayéramos *or* cayésemos
(vosotros/as)	**caigáis**	cayerais *or* cayeseis
(ellos/ellas/ ustedes)	**caigan**	cayeran *or* cayesen

IMPERATIVE

cae / caed

Use the present subjunctive in all cases other than these tú and vosotros affirmative forms.

EXAMPLE PHRASES

Tarde o temprano, **caerá** en manos del enemigo. Sooner or later, it will fall into enemy hands.

Yo **me caería** con esos tacones. I'd fall over if I wore heels like those.

Seguirá adelante **caiga** quien **caiga**. She'll go ahead no matter how many heads have to roll.

No **caigas** tan bajo. Don't stoop so low.

Remember that subject pronouns are not used very often in Spanish.

cambiar (to change)

	PRESENT	PRESENT PERFECT
(yo)	**cambio**	**he cambiado**
(tú)	**cambias**	**has cambiado**
(él/ella/usted)	**cambia**	**ha cambiado**
(nosotros/as)	**cambiamos**	**hemos cambiado**
(vosotros/as)	**cambiáis**	**habéis cambiado**
(ellos/ellas/ ustedes)	**cambian**	**han cambiado**

	PRETERITE	IMPERFECT
(yo)	**cambié**	**cambiaba**
(tú)	**cambiaste**	**cambiabas**
(él/ella/usted)	**cambió**	**cambiaba**
(nosotros/as)	**cambiamos**	**cambiábamos**
(vosotros/as)	**cambiasteis**	**cambiabais**
(ellos/ellas/ ustedes)	**cambiaron**	**cambiaban**

GERUND
cambiando

PAST PARTICIPLE
cambiado

EXAMPLE PHRASES

Necesito **cambiar** de ambiente. I need a change of scenery.
Te **cambio** mi bolígrafo por tu goma. I'll swap my pen for your eraser.
Cambié varias veces de trabajo. I changed jobs several times.
Cambiaban de idea a cada rato. They kept changing their minds.

Remember that subject pronouns are not used very often in Spanish.

cambiar

	FUTURE	CONDITIONAL
(yo)	**cambiaré**	**cambiaría**
(tú)	**cambiarás**	**cambiarías**
(él/ella/usted)	**cambiará**	**cambiaría**
(nosotros/as)	**cambiaremos**	**cambiaríamos**
(vosotros/as)	**cambiaréis**	**cambiaríais**
(ellos/ellas/ ustedes)	**cambiarán**	**cambiarían**

	PRESENT SUBJUNCTIVE	IMPERFECT SUBJUNCTIVE
(yo)	**cambie**	**cambiara** *or* **cambiase**
(tú)	**cambies**	**cambiaras** *or* **cambiases**
(él/ella/usted)	**cambie**	**cambiara** *or* **cambiase**
(nosotros/as)	**cambiemos**	**cambiáramos** *or* **cambiásemos**
(vosotros/as)	**cambiéis**	**cambiarais** *or* **cambiaseis**
(ellos/ellas/ ustedes)	**cambien**	**cambiaran** *or* **cambiasen**

IMPERATIVE

cambia / cambiad

Use the present subjunctive in all cases other than these tú and vosotros affirmative forms.

EXAMPLE PHRASES

Cuando la conozcas, **cambiarás** de idea. You'll change your mind when you meet her.

Si pudiéramos, **nos cambiaríamos** de casa. If we could, we'd move.

No quiero que **cambies**. I don't want you to change.

Cámbiate, que se nos hace tarde. Get changed, it's getting late.

Remember that subject pronouns are not used very often in Spanish.

cazar (to hunt; to shoot)

	PRESENT	PRESENT PERFECT
(yo)	cazo	he cazado
(tú)	cazas	has cazado
(él/ella/usted)	caza	ha cazado
(nosotros/as)	cazamos	hemos cazado
(vosotros/as)	cazáis	habéis cazado
(ellos/ellas/ustedes)	cazan	han cazado

	PRETERITE	IMPERFECT
(yo)	cacé	cazaba
(tú)	cazaste	cazabas
(él/ella/usted)	cazó	cazaba
(nosotros/as)	cazamos	cazábamos
(vosotros/as)	cazasteis	cazabais
(ellos/ellas/ustedes)	cazaron	cazaban

GERUND
cazando

PAST PARTICIPLE
cazado

EXAMPLE PHRASES

Salieron a **cazar** ciervos. They went deer-hunting.

Caza las cosas al vuelo. She's very quick on the uptake.

Los **cacé** robando. I caught them stealing.

Cazaban con lanza. They hunted with spears.

Remember that subject pronouns are not used very often in Spanish.

cazar

	FUTURE	CONDITIONAL
(yo)	**cazaré**	**cazaría**
(tú)	**cazarás**	**cazarías**
(él/ella/usted)	**cazará**	**cazaría**
(nosotros/as)	**cazaremos**	**cazaríamos**
(vosotros/as)	**cazaréis**	**cazaríais**
(ellos/ellas/ ustedes)	**cazarán**	**cazarían**

	PRESENT SUBJUNCTIVE	IMPERFECT SUBJUNCTIVE
(yo)	**cace**	**cazara** *or* **cazase**
(tú)	**caces**	**cazaras** *or* **cazases**
(él/ella/usted)	**cace**	**cazara** *or* **cazase**
(nosotros/as)	**cacemos**	**cazáramos** *or* **cazásemos**
(vosotros/as)	**cacéis**	**cazarais** *or* **cazaseis**
(ellos/ellas/ ustedes)	**cacen**	**cazaran** *or* **cazasen**

IMPERATIVE

caza / cazad

Use the present subjunctive in all cases other than these tú and vosotros affirmative forms.

EXAMPLE PHRASES

¡Quién **cazara** a un millonario! I wish I could land myself a millionaire!

Remember that subject pronouns are not used very often in Spanish.

cerrar (to close; to shut)

	PRESENT	PRESENT PERFECT
(yo)	cierro	he cerrado
(tú)	cierras	has cerrado
(él/ella/usted)	cierra	ha cerrado
(nosotros/as)	cerramos	hemos cerrado
(vosotros/as)	cerráis	habéis cerrado
(ellos/ellas/ ustedes)	cierran	han cerrado

	PRETERITE	IMPERFECT
(yo)	cerré	cerraba
(tú)	cerraste	cerrabas
(él/ella/usted)	cerró	cerraba
(nosotros/as)	cerramos	cerrábamos
(vosotros/as)	cerrasteis	cerrabais
(ellos/ellas/ ustedes)	cerraron	cerraban

GERUND
cerrando

PAST PARTICIPLE
cerrado

EXAMPLE PHRASES

No puedo **cerrar** la maleta. I can't close my suitcase.

No **cierran** al mediodía. They don't close at noon.

Había cerrado la puerta con llave. She'd locked the door.

Cerró el libro. He closed the book.

Se le **cerraban** los ojos. She couldn't keep her eyes open.

Remember that subject pronouns are not used very often in Spanish.

cerrar

	FUTURE	CONDITIONAL
(yo)	**cerraré**	**cerraría**
(tú)	**cerrarás**	**cerrarías**
(él/ella/usted)	**cerrará**	**cerraría**
(nosotros/as)	**cerraremos**	**cerraríamos**
(vosotros/as)	**cerraréis**	**cerraríais**
(ellos/ellas/ ustedes)	**cerrrarán**	**cerrarían**

	PRESENT SUBJUNCTIVE	IMPERFECT SUBJUNCTIVE
(yo)	**cierre**	**cerrara** *or* **cerrase**
(tú)	**cierres**	**cerraras** *or* **cerrases**
(él/ella/usted)	**cierre**	**cerrara** *or* **cerrase**
(nosotros/as)	**cerremos**	**cerráramos** *or* **cerrásemos**
(vosotros/as)	**cerréis**	**cerrarais** *or* **cerraseis**
(ellos/ellas/ ustedes)	**cierren**	**cerraran** *or* **cerrasen**

IMPERATIVE

cierra / cerrad

Use the present subjunctive in all cases other than these **tú** *and* **vosotros** *affirmative forms.*

EXAMPLE PHRASES

No dejes que **se cierre** la puerta de golpe. Don't let the door slam shut.

No **cierres** la ventana. Don't close the window.

Cierra la llave. Turn off the faucet.

Remember that subject pronouns are not used very often in Spanish.

cocer (to boil; to cook)

	PRESENT	PRESENT PERFECT
(yo)	cuezo	he cocido
(tú)	cueces	has cocido
(él/ella/usted)	cuece	ha cocido
(nosotros/as)	cocemos	hemos cocido
(vosotros/as)	cocéis	habéis cocido
(ellos/ellas/ ustedes)	cuecen	han cocido

	PRETERITE	IMPERFECT
(yo)	cocí	cocía
(tú)	cociste	cocías
(él/ella/usted)	coció	cocía
(nosotros/as)	cocimos	cocíamos
(vosotros/as)	cocisteis	cocíais
(ellos/ellas/ ustedes)	cocieron	cocían

GERUND
cociendo

PAST PARTICIPLE
cocido

EXAMPLE PHRASES

El pescado **se cuece** en un momento. Fish takes no time to cook.
Aquí nos **estamos cociendo**. It's boiling in here.
Coció el pan en el horno. He baked the bread in the oven.

Remember that subject pronouns are not used very often in Spanish.

cocer

	FUTURE	CONDITIONAL
(yo)	**coceré**	**cocería**
(tú)	**cocerás**	**cocerías**
(él/ella/usted)	**cocerá**	**cocería**
(nosotros/as)	**coceremos**	**coceríamos**
(vosotros/as)	**coceréis**	**coceríais**
(ellos/ellas/ ustedes)	**cocerán**	**cocerían**

	PRESENT SUBJUNCTIVE	IMPERFECT SUBJUNCTIVE
(yo)	**cueza**	**cociera** *or* **cociese**
(tú)	**cuezas**	**cocieras** *or* **cocieses**
(él/ella/usted)	**cueza**	**cociera** *or* **cociese**
(nosotros/as)	**cozamos**	**cociéramos** *or* **cociésemos**
(vosotros/as)	**cozáis**	**cocierais** *or* **cocieseis**
(ellos/ellas/ ustedes)	**cuezan**	**cocieran** *or* **cociesen**

IMPERATIVE

cuece / coced

Use the present subjunctive in all cases other than these tú and vosotros affirmative forms.

EXAMPLE PHRASES

Te dije que lo **cocieras** tapado. I told you to cook it covered.

No lo **cuezas** demasiado. Don't overcook it.

Cuécelo a fuego lento. Cook it over a low heat.

Remember that subject pronouns are not used very often in Spanish.

colgar (to hang)

	PRESENT	PRESENT PERFECT
(yo)	**cuelgo**	**he colgado**
(tú)	**cuelgas**	**has colgado**
(él/ella/usted)	**cuelga**	**ha colgado**
(nosotros/as)	**colgamos**	**hemos colgado**
(vosotros/as)	**colgáis**	**habéis colgado**
(ellos/ellas/ ustedes)	**cuelgan**	**han colgado**

	PRETERITE	IMPERFECT
(yo)	**colgué**	**colgaba**
(tú)	**colgaste**	**colgabas**
(él/ella/usted)	**colgó**	**colgaba**
(nosotros/as)	**colgamos**	**colgábamos**
(vosotros/as)	**colgasteis**	**colgabais**
(ellos/ellas/ ustedes)	**colgaron**	**colgaban**

GERUND
colgando

PAST PARTICIPLE
colgado

EXAMPLE PHRASES

Hay telarañas **colgando** del techo. There are cobwebs hanging from the ceiling.
Te **colgué** la chaqueta en el clóset. I hung your jacket in the closet.
Me **colgó** el teléfono. He hung up on me.
De la pared **colgaba** un espejo. There was a mirror hanging on the wall.

Remember that subject pronouns are not used very often in Spanish.

colgar

	FUTURE	CONDITIONAL
(yo)	**colgaré**	**colgaría**
(tú)	**colgarás**	**colgarías**
(él/ella/usted)	**colgará**	**colgaría**
(nosotros/as)	**colgaremos**	**colgaríamos**
(vosotros/as)	**colgaréis**	**colgaríais**
(ellos/ellas/ ustedes)	**colgarán**	**colgarían**

	PRESENT SUBJUNCTIVE	IMPERFECT SUBJUNCTIVE
(yo)	**cuelgue**	**colgara** *or* **colgase**
(tú)	**cuelgues**	**colgaras** *or* **colgases**
(él/ella/usted)	**cuelgue**	**colgara** *or* **colgase**
(nosotros/as)	**colguemos**	**colgáramos** *or* **colgásemos**
(vosotros/as)	**colguéis**	**colgarais** *or* **colgaseis**
(ellos/ellas/ ustedes)	**cuelguen**	**colgaran** *or* **colgasen**

IMPERATIVE

cuelga / colgad

Use the present subjunctive in all cases other than these tú and vosotros affirmative forms.

EXAMPLE PHRASES

Colgaremos el cuadro en esa pared. We'll hang the picture on that wall.

No **cuelgue**, por favor. Please don't hang up.

Remember that subject pronouns are not used very often in Spanish.

comer (to eat)

	PRESENT	PRESENT PERFECT
(yo)	como	he comido
(tú)	comes	has comido
(él/ella/usted)	come	ha comido
(nosotros/as)	comemos	hemos comido
(vosotros/as)	coméis	habéis comido
(ellos/ellas/ ustedes)	comen	han comido

	PRETERITE	IMPERFECT
(yo)	comí	comía
(tú)	comiste	comías
(él/ella/usted)	comió	comía
(nosotros/as)	comimos	comíamos
(vosotros/as)	comisteis	comíais
(ellos/ellas/ ustedes)	comieron	comían

GERUND
comiendo

PAST PARTICIPLE
comido

EXAMPLE PHRASES

No **come** carne. He doesn't eat meat.

Se lo **comió** todo. He ate it all.

Comimos en un restaurante. We had lunch in a restaurant.

Siempre **comían** demasiado. They always ate too much.

Remember that subject pronouns are not used very often in Spanish.

comer

	FUTURE	CONDITIONAL
(yo)	**comeré**	**comería**
(tú)	**comerás**	**comerías**
(él/ella/usted)	**comerá**	**comería**
(nosotros/as)	**comeremos**	**comeríamos**
(vosotros/as)	**comeréis**	**comeríais**
(ellos/ellas/ ustedes)	**comerán**	**comerían**

	PRESENT SUBJUNCTIVE	IMPERFECT SUBJUNCTIVE
(yo)	**coma**	**comiera** *or* **comiese**
(tú)	**comas**	**comieras** *or* **comieses**
(él/ella/usted)	**coma**	**comiera** *or* **comiese**
(nosotros/as)	**comamos**	**comiéramos** *or* **comiésemos**
(vosotros/as)	**comáis**	**comierais** *or* **comieseis**
(ellos/ellas/ ustedes)	**coman**	**comieran** *or* **comiesen**

IMPERATIVE

come / comed

Use the present subjunctive in all cases other than these tú and vosotros affirmative forms.

EXAMPLE PHRASES

Me lo **comeré** yo. I'll eat it.

Si no fuera por mí, no **comeríamos**. We wouldn't eat if it weren't for me.

No **comas** tan deprisa. Don't eat so fast.

Remember that subject pronouns are not used very often in Spanish.

conducir (to lead; to drive; to take)

	PRESENT	PRESENT PERFECT
(yo)	**conduzco**	**he conducido**
(tú)	**conduces**	**has conducido**
(él/ella/usted)	**conduce**	**ha conducido**
(nosotros/as)	**conducimos**	**hemos conducido**
(vosotros/as)	**conducís**	**habéis conducido**
(ellos/ellas/ ustedes)	**conducen**	**han conducido**

	PRETERITE	IMPERFECT
(yo)	**conduje**	**conducía**
(tú)	**condujiste**	**conducías**
(él/ella/usted)	**condujo**	**conducía**
(nosotros/as)	**condujimos**	**conducíamos**
(vosotros/as)	**condujisteis**	**conducíais**
(ellos/ellas/ ustedes)	**condujeron**	**conducían**

GERUND
conduciendo

PAST PARTICIPLE
conducido

EXAMPLE PHRASES

Nos **condujo** a su habitación. He took us to his room.

Enojarte no **conduce** a nada. Getting angry doesn't get you anywhere.

La pista nos **condujo** hasta él. The clue led us to him.

Remember that subject pronouns are not used very often in Spanish.

conducir

	FUTURE	CONDITIONAL
(yo)	conduciré	conduciría
(tú)	conducirás	conducirías
(él/ella/usted)	conducirá	conduciría
(nosotros/as)	conduciremos	conduciríamos
(vosotros/as)	conduciréis	conduciríais
(ellos/ellas/ ustedes)	conducirán	conducirían

	PRESENT SUBJUNCTIVE	IMPERFECT SUBJUNCTIVE
(yo)	conduzca	condujera *or* condujese
(tú)	conduzcas	condujeras *or* condujeses
(él/ella/usted)	conduzca	condujera *or* condujese
(nosotros/as)	conduzcamos	condujéramos *or* condujésemos
(vosotros/as)	conduzcáis	condujerais *or* condujeseis
(ellos/ellas/ ustedes)	conduzcan	condujeran *or* condujesen

IMPERATIVE

conduce / conducid

Use the present subjunctive in all cases other than these tú and vosotros affirmative forms.

EXAMPLE PHRASES

Roberto los **conducirá** a su mesa. Roberto will show you to your table.

Remember that subject pronouns are not used very often in Spanish.

conocer (to know; to meet; to recognize)

	PRESENT	PRESENT PERFECT
(yo)	**conozco**	**he conocido**
(tú)	**conoces**	**has conocido**
(él/ella/usted)	**conoce**	**ha conocido**
(nosotros/as)	**conocemos**	**hemos conocido**
(vosotros/as)	**conocéis**	**habéis conocido**
(ellos/ellas/ ustedes)	**conocen**	**han conocido**

	PRETERITE	IMPERFECT
(yo)	**conocí**	**conocía**
(tú)	**conociste**	**conocías**
(él/ella/usted)	**conoció**	**conocía**
(nosotros/as)	**conocimos**	**conocíamos**
(vosotros/as)	**conocisteis**	**conocíais**
(ellos/ellas/ ustedes)	**conocieron**	**conocían**

GERUND
conociendo

PAST PARTICIPLE
conocido

EXAMPLE PHRASES

Conozco un restaurante donde se come bien. I know a restaurant where the food is very good.

La **conocí** en una fiesta. I met her at a party.

Nos conocíamos desde hacía años. We'd known each other for years.

Remember that subject pronouns are not used very often in Spanish.

conocer

	FUTURE	CONDITIONAL
(yo)	conoceré	conocería
(tú)	conocerás	conocerías
(él/ella/usted)	conocerá	conocería
(nosotros/as)	conoceremos	conoceríamos
(vosotros/as)	conoceréis	conoceríais
(ellos/ellas/ ustedes)	conocerán	conocerían

	PRESENT SUBJUNCTIVE	IMPERFECT SUBJUNCTIVE
(yo)	conozca	conociera *or* conociese
(tú)	conozcas	conocieras *or* conocieses
(él/ella/usted)	conozca	conociera *or* conociese
(nosotros/as)	conozcamos	conociéramos *or* conociésemos
(vosotros/as)	conozcáis	conocierais *or* conocieseis
(ellos/ellas/ ustedes)	conozcan	conocieran *or* conociesen

IMPERATIVE

conoce / conoced

Use the present subjunctive in all cases other than these tú and vosotros affirmative forms.

EXAMPLE PHRASES

No sé si la **conocerás** cuando la veas. I don't know if you'll recognize her when you see her.

No quiero que mis padres lo **conozcan**. I don't want my parents to meet him.

Si no la **conociera**, pensaría que lo hizo a propósito. If I didn't know her better, I'd think she had done it on purpose.

Remember that subject pronouns are not used very often in Spanish.

construir (to build)

	PRESENT	PRESENT PERFECT
(yo)	construyo	he construido
(tú)	construyes	has construido
(él/ella/usted)	construye	ha construido
(nosotros/as)	construimos	hemos construido
(vosotros/as)	construís	habéis construido
(ellos/ellas/ ustedes)	construyen	han construido

	PRETERITE	IMPERFECT
(yo)	construí	construía
(tú)	construiste	construías
(él/ella/usted)	construyó	construía
(nosotros/as)	construimos	construíamos
(vosotros/as)	construisteis	construíais
(ellos/ellas/ ustedes)	construyeron	construían

GERUND
construyendo

PAST PARTICIPLE
construido

EXAMPLE PHRASES

Construyen casas de madera. They build wooden houses.

Están construyendo una escuela. They're building a new school.

Construyó la casa él solo. He built the house on his own.

Su empresa **construía** puentes. His company built bridges.

Remember that subject pronouns are not used very often in Spanish.

construir

	FUTURE	CONDITIONAL
(yo)	**construiré**	**construiría**
(tú)	**construirás**	**construirías**
(él/ella/usted)	**construirá**	**construiría**
(nosotros/as)	**construiremos**	**construiríamos**
(vosotros/as)	**construiréis**	**construiríais**
(ellos/ellas/ ustedes)	**construirán**	**construirían**

	PRESENT SUBJUNCTIVE	IMPERFECT SUBJUNCTIVE
(yo)	**construya**	**construyera** *or* **construyese**
(tú)	**construyas**	**construyeras** *or* **construyeses**
(él/ella/usted)	**construya**	**construyera** *or* **construyese**
(nosotros/as)	**construyamos**	**construyéramos** *or* **construyésemos**
(vosotros/as)	**construyáis**	**construyerais** *or* **construyeseis**
(ellos/ellas/ ustedes)	**construyan**	**construyeran** *or* **construyesen**

IMPERATIVE

construye / construid

Use the present subjunctive in all cases other than these tú and vosotros affirmative forms.

EXAMPLE PHRASES

Construirán una nueva autopista. They're going to build a new highway.

Yo **construiría** la oración de otra forma. I'd construct the sentence differently.

Le pedí que lo **construyera** así. I asked him to build it like this.

Remember that subject pronouns are not used very often in Spanish.

contar (to tell; to count)

	PRESENT	PRESENT PERFECT
(yo)	cuento	he contado
(tú)	cuentas	has contado
(él/ella/usted)	cuenta	ha contado
(nosotros/as)	contamos	hemos contado
(vosotros/as)	contáis	habéis contado
(ellos/ellas/ ustedes)	cuentan	han contado

	PRETERITE	IMPERFECT
(yo)	conté	contaba
(tú)	contaste	contabas
(él/ella/usted)	contó	contaba
(nosotros/as)	contamos	contábamos
(vosotros/as)	contasteis	contabais
(ellos/ellas/ ustedes)	contaron	contaban

GERUND
contando

PAST PARTICIPLE
contado

EXAMPLE PHRASES

Sabe **contar** hasta diez. She can count up to ten.

Estoy contando los días. I'm counting the days.

Nos **contó** un secreto. He told us a secret.

Para él sólo **contaba** su carrera. The only thing that mattered to him was his career.

Remember that subject pronouns are not used very often in Spanish.

contar

	FUTURE	CONDITIONAL
(yo)	**contaré**	**contaría**
(tú)	**contarás**	**contarías**
(él/ella/usted)	**contará**	**contaría**
(nosotros/as)	**contaremos**	**contaríamos**
(vosotros/as)	**contaréis**	**contaríais**
(ellos/ellas/ ustedes)	**contarán**	**contarían**

	PRESENT SUBJUNCTIVE	IMPERFECT SUBJUNCTIVE
(yo)	**cuente**	**contara** *or* **contase**
(tú)	**cuentes**	**contaras** *or* **contases**
(él/ella/usted)	**cuente**	**contara** *or* **contase**
(nosotros/as)	**contemos**	**contáramos** *or* **contásemos**
(vosotros/as)	**contéis**	**contarais** *or* **contaseis**
(ellos/ellas/ ustedes)	**cuenten**	**contaran** *or* **contasen**

IMPERATIVE

cuenta / contad

Use the present subjunctive in all cases other than these tú and vosotros affirmative forms.

EXAMPLE PHRASES

Prométeme que no se lo **contarás** a nadie. Promise me you won't tell anyone.

Quiero que me **cuente** exactamente qué pasó. I want you to tell me exactly what happened.

Quería que le **contara** un cuento. She wanted me to tell her a story.

No **cuentes** conmigo. Don't count on me.

Remember that subject pronouns are not used very often in Spanish.

crecer (to grow; to rise)

	PRESENT	PRESENT PERFECT
(yo)	**crezco**	**he crecido**
(tú)	**creces**	**has crecido**
(él/ella/usted)	**crece**	**ha crecido**
(nosotros/as)	**crecemos**	**hemos crecido**
(vosotros/as)	**crecéis**	**habéis crecido**
(ellos/ellas/ustedes)	**crecen**	**han crecido**

	PRETERITE	IMPERFECT
(yo)	**crecí**	**crecía**
(tú)	**creciste**	**crecías**
(él/ella/usted)	**creció**	**crecía**
(nosotros/as)	**crecimos**	**crecíamos**
(vosotros/as)	**crecisteis**	**crecíais**
(ellos/ellas/ustedes)	**crecieron**	**crecían**

GERUND	PAST PARTICIPLE
creciendo	**crecido**

EXAMPLE PHRASES

Esas plantas **crecen** en Chile. Those plants grow in Chile.

¡Cómo **has crecido**! Haven't you grown!

Crecimos juntos. We grew up together.

La ciudad **crecía** a pasos agigantados. The city was growing by leaps and bounds.

Sigue **creciendo** la inflación. Inflation is still rising.

Remember that subject pronouns are not used very often in Spanish.

crecer

	FUTURE	CONDITIONAL
(yo)	creceré	crecería
(tú)	crecerás	crecerías
(él/ella/usted)	crecerá	crecería
(nosotros/as)	creceremos	creceríamos
(vosotros/as)	creceréis	creceríais
(ellos/ellas/ ustedes)	crecerán	crecerían

	PRESENT SUBJUNCTIVE	IMPERFECT SUBJUNCTIVE
(yo)	crezca	creciera *or* creciese
(tú)	crezcas	crecieras *or* crecieses
(él/ella/usted)	crezca	creciera *or* creciese
(nosotros/as)	crezcamos	creciéramos *or* creciésemos
(vosotros/as)	crezcáis	crecierais *or* crecieseis
(ellos/ellas/ ustedes)	crezcan	crecieran *or* creciesen

IMPERATIVE

crece / creced

Use the present subjunctive in all cases other than these tú and vosotros affirmative forms.

EXAMPLE PHRASES

Este año la economía **crecerá** un 2%. The economy will grow by 2% this year.

Crecería mejor en un ambiente húmedo. It would grow better in a humid environment.

Quería que sus hijos **crecieran** en otro ambiente. She wanted her children to grow up in a different environment.

Remember that subject pronouns are not used very often in Spanish.

cruzar (to cross)

	PRESENT	PRESENT PERFECT
(yo)	cruzo	he cruzado
(tú)	cruzas	has cruzado
(él/ella/usted)	cruza	ha cruzado
(nosotros/as)	cruzamos	hemos cruzado
(vosotros/as)	cruzáis	habéis cruzado
(ellos/ellas/ ustedes)	cruzan	han cruzado

	PRETERITE	IMPERFECT
(yo)	crucé	cruzaba
(tú)	cruzaste	cruzabas
(él/ella/usted)	cruzó	cruzaba
(nosotros/as)	cruzamos	cruzábamos
(vosotros/as)	cruzasteis	cruzabais
(ellos/ellas/ ustedes)	cruzaron	cruzaban

GERUND
cruzando

PAST PARTICIPLE
cruzado

EXAMPLE PHRASES

Hace tiempo que no **me cruzo** con él. I haven't seen him for a long time.

La caravana **está cruzando** el desierto. The caravan is crossing the desert.

Cruzaron el puente. They crossed the bridge.

La carretera **cruzaba** el pueblo. The road went through the village.

Remember that subject pronouns are not used very often in Spanish.

cruzar

	FUTURE	CONDITIONAL
(yo)	**cruzaré**	**cruzaría**
(tú)	**cruzarás**	**cruzarías**
(él/ella/usted)	**cruzará**	**cruzaría**
(nosotros/as)	**cruzaremos**	**cruzaríamos**
(vosotros/as)	**cruzaréis**	**cruzaríais**
(ellos/ellas/ ustedes)	**cruzarán**	**cruzarían**

	PRESENT SUBJUNCTIVE	IMPERFECT SUBJUNCTIVE
(yo)	**cruce**	**cruzara** *or* **cruzase**
(tú)	**cruces**	**cruzaras** *or* **cruzases**
(él/ella/usted)	**cruce**	**cruzara** *or* **cruzase**
(nosotros/as)	**crucemos**	**cruzáramos** *or* **cruzásemos**
(vosotros/as)	**crucéis**	**cruzarais** *or* **cruzaseis**
(ellos/ellas/ ustedes)	**crucen**	**cruzaran** *or* **cruzasen**

IMPERATIVE

cruza / cruzad

Use the present subjunctive in all cases other than these tú and vosotros affirmative forms.

EXAMPLE PHRASES

Cruzarán varias especies distintas. They'll cross several different species.

Crucemos los dedos. Let's keep our fingers crossed.

Le dije que **cruzara** con cuidado. I told her to be careful crossing the street.

No **cruces** la calle con el semáforo en rojo. Don't cross the street when the signal's red.

Remember that subject pronouns are not used very often in Spanish.

cubrir (to cover)

	PRESENT	PRESENT PERFECT
(yo)	**cubro**	**he cubierto**
(tú)	**cubres**	**has cubierto**
(él/ella/usted)	**cubre**	**ha cubierto**
(nosotros/as)	**cubrimos**	**hemos cubierto**
(vosotros/as)	**cubrís**	**habéis cubierto**
(ellos/ellas/ ustedes)	**cubren**	**han cubierto**

	PRETERITE	IMPERFECT
(yo)	**cubrí**	**cubría**
(tú)	**cubriste**	**cubrías**
(él/ella/usted)	**cubrió**	**cubría**
(nosotros/as)	**cubrimos**	**cubríamos**
(vosotros/as)	**cubristeis**	**cubríais**
(ellos/ellas/ ustedes)	**cubrieron**	**cubrían**

GERUND
cubriendo

PAST PARTICIPLE
cubierto

EXAMPLE PHRASES

Esto no **cubre** los gastos. This isn't enough to cover expenses.
Lo **cubrieron** con una manta. They covered him with a blanket.
Se cubrió la cara con las manos. She covered her face with her hands.
La nieve **cubría** la montaña. The mountain was covered in snow.

Remember that subject pronouns are not used very often in Spanish.

cubrir

	FUTURE	CONDITIONAL
(yo)	**cubriré**	**cubriría**
(tú)	**cubrirás**	**cubrirías**
(él/ella/usted)	**cubrirá**	**cubriría**
(nosotros/as)	**cubriremos**	**cubriríamos**
(vosotros/as)	**cubriréis**	**cubriríais**
(ellos/ellas/ ustedes)	**cubrirán**	**cubrirían**

	PRESENT SUBJUNCTIVE	IMPERFECT SUBJUNCTIVE
(yo)	**cubra**	**cubriera** *or* **cubriese**
(tú)	**cubras**	**cubrieras** *or* **cubrieses**
(él/ella/usted)	**cubra**	**cubriera** *or* **cubriese**
(nosotros/as)	**cubramos**	**cubriéramos** *or* **cubriésemos**
(vosotros/as)	**cubráis**	**cubrierais** *or* **cubrieseis**
(ellos/ellas/ ustedes)	**cubran**	**cubrieran** *or* **cubriesen**

IMPERATIVE

cubre / cubrid

Use the present subjunctive in all cases other than these tú and vosotros affirmative forms.

EXAMPLE PHRASES

Los corredores **cubrirán** una distancia de 2 km. The runners will cover a distance of 2 km.

¿Quién **cubriría** la vacante? Who'd fill the vacancy?

Quiero que **cubras** la noticia. I want you to cover the story.

Remember that subject pronouns are not used very often in Spanish.

dar (to give)

	PRESENT	PRESENT PERFECT
(yo)	**doy**	**he dado**
(tú)	**das**	**has dado**
(él/ella/usted)	**da**	**ha dado**
(nosotros/as)	**damos**	**hemos dado**
(vosotros/as)	**dais**	**habéis dado**
(ellos/ellas/ ustedes)	**dan**	**han dado**

	PRETERITE	IMPERFECT
(yo)	**di**	**daba**
(tú)	**diste**	**dabas**
(él/ella/usted)	**dio**	**daba**
(nosotros/as)	**dimos**	**dábamos**
(vosotros/as)	**disteis**	**dabais**
(ellos/ellas/ ustedes)	**dieron**	**daban**

GERUND
dando

PAST PARTICIPLE
dado

EXAMPLE PHRASES

Me **da** miedo la oscuridad. I'm afraid of the dark.

Nos **dieron** un par de entradas gratis. They gave us a pair of free tickets.

Mi ventana **daba** al jardín. My window looked out on the garden.

Remember that subject pronouns are not used very often in Spanish.

dar

	FUTURE	CONDITIONAL
(yo)	**daré**	**daría**
(tú)	**darás**	**darías**
(él/ella/usted)	**dará**	**daría**
(nosotros/as)	**daremos**	**daríamos**
(vosotros/as)	**daréis**	**daríais**
(ellos/ellas/ ustedes)	**darán**	**darían**

	PRESENT SUBJUNCTIVE	IMPERFECT SUBJUNCTIVE
(yo)	**dé**	**diera** *or* **diese**
(tú)	**des**	**dieras** *or* **dieses**
(él/ella/usted)	**dé**	**diera** *or* **diese**
(nosotros/as)	**demos**	**diéramos** *or* **diésemos**
(vosotros/as)	**deis**	**dierais** *or* **dieseis**
(ellos/ellas/ ustedes)	**den**	**dieran** *or* **diesen**

IMPERATIVE

da / dad

Use the present subjunctive in all cases other than these tú and vosotros affirmative forms.

EXAMPLE PHRASES

Te **daré** el número de mi celular. I'll give you my cell phone number.

Me **daría** mucha alegría volver a verla. It would be really good to see her again.

Quiero que me lo **des** ahora mismo. I want you to give it to me right now.

Déme 2 kilos. 2 kilos, please.

Remember that subject pronouns are not used very often in Spanish.

decir (to say; to tell)

	PRESENT	PRESENT PERFECT
(yo)	**digo**	**he dicho**
(tú)	**dices**	**has dicho**
(él/ella/usted)	**dice**	**ha dicho**
(nosotros/as)	**decimos**	**hemos dicho**
(vosotros/as)	**decís**	**habéis dicho**
(ellos/ellas/ ustedes)	**dicen**	**han dicho**

	PRETERITE	IMPERFECT
(yo)	**dije**	**decía**
(tú)	**dijiste**	**decías**
(él/ella/usted)	**dijo**	**decía**
(nosotros/as)	**dijimos**	**decíamos**
(vosotros/as)	**dijisteis**	**decíais**
(ellos/ellas/ ustedes)	**dijeron**	**decían**

GERUND
diciendo

PAST PARTICIPLE
dicho

EXAMPLE PHRASES

Pero ¿qué **dices**? What are you saying?

¿Te **dijo** lo de la boda? Did he tell you about the wedding?

Ya me lo había **dicho**. He had already told me.

Siempre nos **decía** que tuviéramos cuidado. She always used to tell us to be careful.

Remember that subject pronouns are not used very often in Spanish.

decir

	FUTURE	CONDITIONAL
(yo)	**diré**	**diría**
(tú)	**dirás**	**dirías**
(él/ella/usted)	**dirá**	**diría**
(nosotros/as)	**diremos**	**diríamos**
(vosotros/as)	**diréis**	**diríais**
(ellos/ellas/ ustedes)	**dirán**	**dirían**

	PRESENT SUBJUNCTIVE	IMPERFECT SUBJUNCTIVE
(yo)	**diga**	**dijera** *or* **dijese**
(tú)	**digas**	**dijeras** *or* **dijeses**
(él/ella/usted)	**diga**	**dijera** *or* **dijese**
(nosotros/as)	**digamos**	**dijéramos** *or* **dijésemos**
(vosotros/as)	**digáis**	**dijerais** *or* **dijeseis**
(ellos/ellas/ ustedes)	**digan**	**dijeran** *or* **dijesen**

IMPERATIVE

di / decid

Use the present subjunctive in all cases other than these tú *and* vosotros *affirmative forms.*

EXAMPLE PHRASES

Yo **diría** que miente. I'd say he's lying.

Si me **dijeras** lo que pasa, a lo mejor podría ayudar. If you told me what was going on, maybe I could help.

No le **digas** que me viste. Don't tell him you saw me.

Remember that subject pronouns are not used very often in Spanish.

despreocuparse (to stop worrying)

	PRESENT	PRESENT PERFECT
(yo)	me despreocupo	me he despreocupado
(tú)	te despreocupas	te has despreocupado
(él/ella/usted)	se despreocupa	se ha despreocupado
(nosotros/as)	nos despreocupamos	nos hemos despreocupado
(vosotros/as)	os despreocupáis	os habéis despreocupado
(ellos/ellas/ustedes)	se despreocupan	se han despreocupado

	PRETERITE	IMPERFECT
(yo)	me despreocupé	me despreocupaba
(tú)	te despreocupaste	te despreocupabas
(él/ella/usted)	se despreocupó	se despreocupaba
(nosotros/as)	nos despreocupamos	nos despreocupábamos
(vosotros/as)	os despreocupasteis	os despreocupabais
(ellos/ellas/ustedes)	se despreocuparon	se despreocupaban

GERUND
despreocupándose, etc

PAST PARTICIPLE
despreocupado

EXAMPLE PHRASES

Deberías **despreocuparte** un poco más de las cosas. You shouldn't worry so much about things.

Se despreocupa de todo. He shows no concern for anything.

Se despreocupó del asunto. He forgot about the matter.

Remember that subject pronouns are not used very often in Spanish.

despreocuparse

	FUTURE	CONDITIONAL
(yo)	me despreocuparé	me despreocuparía
(tú)	te despreocuparás	te despreocuparías
(él/ella/usted)	se despreocupará	se despreocuparía
(nosotros/as)	nos despreocuparemos	nos despreocuparíamos
(vosotros/as)	os despreocuparéis	os despreocuparíais
(ellos/ellas/ ustedes)	se despreocuparán	se despreocuparían

	PRESENT SUBJUNCTIVE	IMPERFECT SUBJUNCTIVE
(yo)	me despreocupe	me despreocupara *or* despreocupase
(tú)	te despreocupes	te despreocuparas *or* despreocupases
(él/ella/usted)	se despreocupe	se despreocupara *or* despreocupase
(nosotros/as)	nos despreocupemos	nos despreocupáramos *or* despreocupásemos
(vosotros/as)	os despreocupéis	os despreocuparais *or* despreocupaseis
(ellos/ellas/ ustedes)	se despreocupen	se despreocuparan *or* despreocupasen

IMPERATIVE

despreocúpate / despreocupaos

Use the present subjunctive in all cases other than these tú and vosotros affirmative forms.

EXAMPLE PHRASES

Yo **me despreocuparía** de él. I wouldn't worry about him.

Despreocúpate de todo. Don't worry about a thing.

Remember that subject pronouns are not used very often in Spanish.

detener (to stop; to arrest)

	PRESENT	PRESENT PERFECT
(yo)	**detengo**	**he detenido**
(tú)	**detienes**	**has detenido**
(él/ella/usted)	**detiene**	**ha detenido**
(nosotros/as)	**detenemos**	**hemos detenido**
(vosotros/as)	**detenéis**	**habéis detenido**
(ellos/ellas/ustedes)	**detienen**	**han detenido**

	PRETERITE	IMPERFECT
(yo)	**detuve**	**detenía**
(tú)	**detuviste**	**detenías**
(él/ella/usted)	**detuvo**	**detenía**
(nosotros/as)	**detuvimos**	**deteníamos**
(vosotros/as)	**detuvisteis**	**deteníais**
(ellos/ellas/ustedes)	**detuvieron**	**detenían**

GERUND
deteniendo

PAST PARTICIPLE
detenido

EXAMPLE PHRASES

Detuvieron a los ladrones. They arrested the thieves.
Nos detuvimos en el semáforo. We stopped at the light.
¡Queda **detenido**! You are under arrest!

Remember that subject pronouns are not used very often in Spanish.

detener

	FUTURE	CONDITIONAL
(yo)	**detendré**	**detendría**
(tú)	**detendrás**	**detendrías**
(él/ella/usted)	**detendrá**	**detendría**
(nosotros/as)	**detendremos**	**detendríamos**
(vosotros/as)	**detendréis**	**detendríais**
(ellos/ellas/ ustedes)	**detendrán**	**detendrían**

	PRESENT SUBJUNCTIVE	IMPERFECT SUBJUNCTIVE
(yo)	**detenga**	**detuviera** *or* **detuviese**
(tú)	**detengas**	**detuvieras** *or* **detuvieses**
(él/ella/usted)	**detenga**	**detuviera** *or* **detuviese**
(nosotros/as)	**detengamos**	**detuviéramos** *or* **detuviésemos**
(vosotros/as)	**detengáis**	**detuvierais** *or* **detuvieseis**
(ellos/ellas/ ustedes)	**detengan**	**detuvieran** *or* **detuviesen**

IMPERATIVE

detén / detened

Use the present subjunctive in all cases other than these tú and vosotros affirmative forms.

EXAMPLE PHRASES

Nada la **detendrá**. Nothing will stop her.

Si **te detuvieras** a pensar, nunca harías nada. If you stopped to think, you'd never do anything.

¡**Deténgase**! Stop!

¡No **te detengas**! Don't stop!

Remember that subject pronouns are not used very often in Spanish.

dirigir (to direct; to run)

	PRESENT	PRESENT PERFECT
(yo)	dirijo	he dirigido
(tú)	diriges	has dirigido
(él/ella/usted)	dirige	ha dirigido
(nosotros/as)	dirigimos	hemos dirigido
(vosotros/as)	dirigís	habéis dirigido
(ellos/ellas/ ustedes)	dirigen	han dirigido

	PRETERITE	IMPERFECT
(yo)	dirigí	dirigía
(tú)	dirigiste	dirigías
(él/ella/usted)	dirigió	dirigía
(nosotros/as)	dirigimos	dirigíamos
(vosotros/as)	dirigisteis	dirigíais
(ellos/ellas/ ustedes)	dirigieron	dirigían

GERUND
dirigiendo

PAST PARTICIPLE
dirigido

EXAMPLE PHRASES

Dirijo esta empresa desde hace dos años. I've been running this company for two years.

Ha dirigido varias películas. She has directed several movies.

No le **dirigió** la palabra. She didn't say a word to him.

Se dirigía a su casa. He was making his way home.

Remember that subject pronouns are not used very often in Spanish.

dirigir

	FUTURE	CONDITIONAL
(yo)	**dirigiré**	**dirigiría**
(tú)	**dirigirás**	**dirigirías**
(él/ella/usted)	**dirigirá**	**dirigiría**
(nosotros/as)	**dirigiremos**	**dirigiríamos**
(vosotros/as)	**dirigiréis**	**dirigiríais**
(ellos/ellas/ ustedes)	**dirigirán**	**dirigirían**

	PRESENT SUBJUNCTIVE	IMPERFECT SUBJUNCTIVE
(yo)	**dirija**	**dirigiera** *or* **dirigiese**
(tú)	**dirijas**	**dirigieras** *or* **dirigieses**
(él/ella/usted)	**dirija**	**dirigiera** *or* **dirigiese**
(nosotros/as)	**dirijamos**	**dirigiéramos** *or* **dirigiésemos**
(vosotros/as)	**dirijáis**	**dirigierais** *or* **dirigieseis**
(ellos/ellas/ ustedes)	**dirijan**	**dirigieran** *or* **dirigiesen**

IMPERATIVE

dirige / dirigid

Use the present subjunctive in all cases other than these tú and vosotros affirmative forms.

EXAMPLE PHRASES

Dirigirá la expedición. He'll be leading the expedition.

Para más información **diríjase** a la página 82. For more information turn to page 82.

Remember that subject pronouns are not used very often in Spanish.

distinguir (to distinguish)

	PRESENT	PRESENT PERFECT
(yo)	**distingo**	**he distinguido**
(tú)	**distingues**	**has distinguido**
(él/ella/usted)	**distingue**	**ha distinguido**
(nosotros/as)	**distinguimos**	**hemos distinguido**
(vosotros/as)	**distinguís**	**habéis distinguido**
(ellos/ellas/ ustedes)	**distinguen**	**han distinguido**

	PRETERITE	IMPERFECT
(yo)	**distinguí**	**distinguía**
(tú)	**distinguiste**	**distinguías**
(él/ella/usted)	**distinguió**	**distinguía**
(nosotros/as)	**distinguimos**	**distinguíamos**
(vosotros/as)	**distinguisteis**	**distinguíais**
(ellos/ellas/ ustedes)	**distinguieron**	**distinguían**

GERUND
distinguiendo

PAST PARTICIPLE
distinguido

EXAMPLE PHRASES

No lo **distingo** del azul. I can't tell the difference between it and the blue one.
Se distinguió por su valentía. He distinguished himself with his bravery.
Se distinguía desde lejos. You could see it from a distance.

Remember that subject pronouns are not used very often in Spanish.

distinguir

	FUTURE	CONDITIONAL
(yo)	**distinguiré**	**distinguiría**
(tú)	**distinguirás**	**distinguirías**
(él/ella/usted)	**distinguirá**	**distinguiría**
(nosotros/as)	**distinguiremos**	**distinguiríamos**
(vosotros/as)	**distinguiréis**	**distinguiríais**
(ellos/ellas/ ustedes)	**distinguirán**	**distinguirían**

	PRESENT SUBJUNCTIVE	IMPERFECT SUBJUNCTIVE
(yo)	**distinga**	**distinguiera** *or* **distinguiese**
(tú)	**distingas**	**distinguieras** *or* **distinguieses**
(él/ella/usted)	**distinga**	**distinguiera** *or* **distinguiese**
(nosotros/as)	**distingamos**	**distinguiéramos** *or* **distinguiésemos**
(vosotros/as)	**distingáis**	**distinguierais** *or* **distinguieseis**
(ellos/ellas/ ustedes)	**distingan**	**distinguieran** *or* **distinguiesen**

IMPERATIVE

distingue / distinguid

Use the present subjunctive in all cases other than these tú and vosotros affirmative forms.

EXAMPLE PHRASES

No los **distinguiría**. I wouldn't be able to tell them apart.

Nos **distinguirá** con su presencia. She will honor us with her presence.

Remember that subject pronouns are not used very often in Spanish.

divertir (to entertain; to amuse)

	PRESENT	PRESENT PERFECT
(yo)	**divierto**	**he divertido**
(tú)	**diviertes**	**has divertido**
(él/ella/usted)	**divierte**	**ha divertido**
(nosotros/as)	**divertimos**	**hemos divertido**
(vosotros/as)	**divertís**	**habéis divertido**
(ellos/ellas/ ustedes)	**divierten**	**han divertido**

	PRETERITE	IMPERFECT
(yo)	**divertí**	**divertía**
(tú)	**divertiste**	**divertías**
(él/ella/usted)	**divirtió**	**divertía**
(nosotros/as)	**divertimos**	**divertíamos**
(vosotros/as)	**divertisteis**	**divertíais**
(ellos/ellas/ ustedes)	**divirtieron**	**divertían**

GERUND
divirtiendo

PAST PARTICIPLE
divertido

EXAMPLE PHRASES

Cantamos sólo para **divertirnos**. We sing just for fun.
Me **divierte** verlos tan serios. It's amusing to see them looking so serious.
¿**Se divirtieron** en la fiesta? Did you enjoy the party?
Nos **divirtió** con sus anécdotas. He entertained us with his stories.
Nos divertíamos mucho jugando en la playa. We were having a great time playing on the beach.

Remember that subject pronouns are not used very often in Spanish.

divertir

	FUTURE	CONDITIONAL
(yo)	**divertiré**	**divertiría**
(tú)	**divertirás**	**divertirías**
(él/ella/usted)	**divertirá**	**divertiría**
(nosotros/as)	**divertiremos**	**divertiríamos**
(vosotros/as)	**divertiréis**	**divertiríais**
(ellos/ellas/ ustedes)	**divertirán**	**divertirían**

	PRESENT SUBJUNCTIVE	IMPERFECT SUBJUNCTIVE
(yo)	**divierta**	**divirtiera** *or* **divirtiese**
(tú)	**diviertas**	**divirtieras** *or* **divirtieses**
(él/ella/usted)	**divierta**	**divirtiera** *or* **divirtiese**
(nosotros/as)	**divirtamos**	**divirtiéramos** *or* **divirtiésemos**
(vosotros/as)	**divirtáis**	**divirtierais** *or* **divirtieseis**
(ellos/ellas/ ustedes)	**diviertan**	**divirtieran** *or* **divirtiesen**

IMPERATIVE

divierte / divertid

Use the present subjunctive in all cases other than these tú and vosotros affirmative forms.

EXAMPLE PHRASES

Si fueras, **te divertirías** mucho. If you went, you'd have a great time.

Hizo lo posible por que **se divirtieran**. He did everything he could to make it fun for them.

¡Que **te diviertas**! Have a good time!

Remember that subject pronouns are not used very often in Spanish.

dormir (to sleep)

	PRESENT	PRESENT PERFECT
(yo)	**duermo**	**he dormido**
(tú)	**duermes**	**has dormido**
(él/ella/usted)	**duerme**	**ha dormido**
(nosotros/as)	**dormimos**	**hemos dormido**
(vosotros/as)	**dormís**	**habéis dormido**
(ellos/ellas/ ustedes)	**duermen**	**han dormido**

	PRETERITE	IMPERFECT
(yo)	**dormí**	**dormía**
(tú)	**dormiste**	**dormías**
(él/ella/usted)	**durmió**	**dormía**
(nosotros/as)	**dormimos**	**dormíamos**
(vosotros/as)	**dormisteis**	**dormíais**
(ellos/ellas/ ustedes)	**durmieron**	**dormían**

GERUND
durmiendo

PAST PARTICIPLE
dormido

EXAMPLE PHRASES

No **duermo** muy bien. I don't sleep very well.
Está durmiendo. She's asleep.
Dormí de un tirón. I slept like a log.
Se me **durmió** la pierna. My leg went to sleep.
Se dormía en clase. She would fall asleep in class.

Remember that subject pronouns are not used very often in Spanish.

dormir

	FUTURE	CONDITIONAL
(yo)	dormiré	dormiría
(tú)	dormirás	dormirías
(él/ella/usted)	dormirá	dormiría
(nosotros/as)	dormiremos	dormiríamos
(vosotros/as)	dormiréis	dormiríais
(ellos/ellas/ ustedes)	dormirán	dormirían

	PRESENT SUBJUNCTIVE	IMPERFECT SUBJUNCTIVE
(yo)	duerma	durmiera *or* durmiese
(tú)	duermas	durmieras *or* durmieses
(él/ella/usted)	duerma	durmiera *or* durmiese
(nosotros/as)	durmamos	durmiéramos *or* durmiésemos
(vosotros/as)	durmáis	durmierais *or* durmieseis
(ellos/ellas/ ustedes)	duerman	durmieran *or* durmiesen

IMPERATIVE

duerme / dormid

Use the present subjunctive in all cases other than these tú and vosotros affirmative forms.

EXAMPLE PHRASES

Si no tomo café, **me dormiré**. I'll fall asleep if I don't have some coffee.

Yo no **dormiría** en esa casa. I wouldn't sleep in that house.

Quiero que **duermas** la siesta. I want you to take a nap.

Si **durmieras** más horas, no estarías tan cansada. You wouldn't be so tired if you got more sleep.

Remember that subject pronouns are not used very often in Spanish.

elegir (to choose; to elect)

	PRESENT	PRESENT PERFECT
(yo)	**elijo**	**he elegido**
(tú)	**eliges**	**has elegido**
(él/ella/usted)	**elige**	**ha elegido**
(nosotros/as)	**elegimos**	**hemos elegido**
(vosotros/as)	**elegís**	**habéis elegido**
(ellos/ellas/ ustedes)	**eligen**	**han elegido**

	PRETERITE	IMPERFECT
(yo)	**elegí**	**elegía**
(tú)	**elegiste**	**elegías**
(él/ella/usted)	**eligió**	**elegía**
(nosotros/as)	**elegimos**	**elegíamos**
(vosotros/as)	**elegisteis**	**elegíais**
(ellos/ellas/ ustedes)	**eligieron**	**elegían**

GERUND
eligiendo

PAST PARTICIPLE
elegido

EXAMPLE PHRASES

Te dan a **elegir** entre dos modelos. You have a choice of two models.

Nosotros no **elegimos** a nuestros padres, ni ellos nos **eligen** a nosotros. We don't choose our parents and they don't choose us either.

Creo que **eligió** bien. I think he made a good choice.

Salió **elegido** presidente. He was elected president.

Remember that subject pronouns are not used very often in Spanish.

elegir

	FUTURE	CONDITIONAL
(yo)	**elegiré**	**elegiría**
(tú)	**elegirás**	**elegirías**
(él/ella/usted)	**elegirá**	**elegiría**
(nosotros/as)	**elegiremos**	**elegiríamos**
(vosotros/as)	**elegiréis**	**elegiríais**
(ellos/ellas/ ustedes)	**elegirán**	**elegirían**

	PRESENT SUBJUNCTIVE	IMPERFECT SUBJUNCTIVE
(yo)	**elija**	**eligiera** *or* **eligiese**
(tú)	**elijas**	**eligieras** *or* **eligieses**
(él/ella/usted)	**elija**	**eligiera** *or* **eligiese**
(nosotros/as)	**elijamos**	**eligiéramos** *or* **eligiésemos**
(vosotros/as)	**elijáis**	**eligierais** *or* **eligieseis**
(ellos/ellas/ ustedes)	**elijan**	**eligieran** *or* **eligiesen**

IMPERATIVE

elige / elegid

Use the present subjunctive in all cases other than these tú and vosotros affirmative forms.

EXAMPLE PHRASES

Yo **elegiría** el más caro. I'd choose the most expensive one.

Elija una carta. Pick a card.

Remember that subject pronouns are not used very often in Spanish.

empezar (to begin; to start)

	PRESENT	PRESENT PERFECT
(yo)	**empiezo**	**he empezado**
(tú)	**empiezas**	**has empezado**
(él/ella/usted)	**empieza**	**ha empezado**
(nosotros/as)	**empezamos**	**hemos empezado**
(vosotros/as)	**empezáis**	**habéis empezado**
(ellos/ellas/ ustedes)	**empiezan**	**han empezado**

	PRETERITE	IMPERFECT
(yo)	**empecé**	**empezaba**
(tú)	**empezaste**	**empezabas**
(él/ella/usted)	**empezó**	**empezaba**
(nosotros/as)	**empezamos**	**empezábamos**
(vosotros/as)	**empezasteis**	**empezabais**
(ellos/ellas/ ustedes)	**empezaron**	**empezaban**

GERUND
empezando

PAST PARTICIPLE
empezado

EXAMPLE PHRASES

Está a punto de **empezar**. It's about to start.

¿Cuándo **empiezas** a trabajar en el sitio nuevo? When do you start work at the new place?

Empezó a nevar. It started snowing.

Las vacaciones **empezaron** el quince. The vacation started on the fifteenth.

Empezaba con *p*. It began with *p*.

Remember that subject pronouns are not used very often in Spanish.

empezar

	FUTURE	CONDITIONAL
(yo)	empezaré	empezaría
(tú)	empezarás	empezarías
(él/ella/usted)	empezará	empezaría
(nosotros/as)	empezaremos	empezaríamos
(vosotros/as)	empezaréis	empezaríais
(ellos/ellas/ ustedes)	empezarán	empezarían

	PRESENT SUBJUNCTIVE	IMPERFECT SUBJUNCTIVE
(yo)	empiece	empezara *or* empezase
(tú)	empieces	empezaras *or* empezases
(él/ella/usted)	empiece	empezara *or* empezase
(nosotros/as)	empecemos	empezáramos *or* empezásemos
(vosotros/as)	empecéis	empezarais *or* empezaseis
(ellos/ellas/ ustedes)	empiecen	empezaran *or* empezasen

IMPERATIVE

empieza / empezad

Use the present subjunctive in all cases other than these tú and vosotros affirmative forms.

EXAMPLE PHRASES

La semana que viene **empezaremos** un curso nuevo. We'll start a new course next week.

Yo **empezaría** desde cero. I'd start from scratch.

Quiero que **empieces** ya. I want you to start now.

Si **empezáramos** ahora, acabaríamos a las diez. If we started now, we'd be finished by ten.

Empieza por aquí. Start here.

Remember that subject pronouns are not used very often in Spanish.

enfrentarse a/con (to face)

	PRESENT	PRESENT PERFECT
(yo)	me enfrento	me he enfrentado
(tú)	te enfrentas	te has enfrentado
(él/ella/usted)	se enfrenta	se ha enfrentado
(nosotros/as)	nos enfrentamos	nos hemos enfrentado
(vosotros/as)	os enfrentáis	os habéis enfrentado
(ellos/ellas/ ustedes)	se enfrentan	se han enfrentado

	PRETERITE	IMPERFECT
(yo)	me enfrenté	me enfrentaba
(tú)	te enfrentaste	te enfrentabas
(él/ella/usted)	se enfrentó	se enfrentaba
(nosotros/as)	nos enfrentamos	nos enfrentábamos
(vosotros/as)	os enfrentasteis	os enfrentabais
(ellos/ellas/ ustedes)	se enfrentaron	se enfrentaban

GERUND
enfrentándose, etc

PAST PARTICIPLE
enfrentado

EXAMPLE PHRASES

Tienes que **enfrentarte** al problema. You have to face up to the problem.
Hoy **se enfrentan** los dos semifinalistas. The two semifinalists meet today.
Padre e hijo **se han enfrentado** varias veces. Father and son have had several confrontations.
Se enfrentaban a un futuro incierto. They faced an uncertain future.

Remember that subject pronouns are not used very often in Spanish.

enfrentarse a/con

	FUTURE	CONDITIONAL
(yo)	me enfrentaré	me enfrentaría
(tú)	te enfrentarás	te enfrentarías
(él/ella/usted)	se enfrentará	se enfrentaría
(nosotros/as)	nos enfrentaremos	nos enfrentaríamos
(vosotros/as)	os enfrentaréis	os enfrentaríais
(ellos/ellas/ ustedes)	se enfrentarán	se enfrentarían

	PRESENT SUBJUNCTIVE	IMPERFECT SUBJUNCTIVE
(yo)	me enfrente	me enfrentara *or* enfrentase
(tú)	te enfrentes	te enfrentaras *or* enfrentases
(él/ella/usted)	se enfrente	se enfrentara *or* enfrentase
(nosotros/as)	nos enfrentemos	nos enfrentáramos *or* enfrentásemos
(vosotros/as)	os enfrentéis	os enfrentarais *or* enfrentaseis
(ellos/ellas/ ustedes)	se enfrenten	se enfrentaran *or* enfrentasen

IMPERATIVE

enfréntate / enfrentaos

Use the present subjunctive in all cases other than these tú and vosotros affirmative forms.

EXAMPLE PHRASES

Los dos equipos **se enfrentarán** mañana. The two teams will play each other tomorrow.

No **te enfrentes** con él. Don't confront him.

Remember that subject pronouns are not used very often in Spanish.

entender (to understand)

	PRESENT	PRESENT PERFECT
(yo)	**entiendo**	**he entendido**
(tú)	**entiendes**	**has entendido**
(él/ella/usted)	**entiende**	**ha entendido**
(nosotros/as)	**entendemos**	**hemos entendido**
(vosotros/as)	**entendéis**	**habéis entendido**
(ellos/ellas/ ustedes)	**entienden**	**han entendido**

	PRETERITE	IMPERFECT
(yo)	**entendí**	**entendía**
(tú)	**entendiste**	**entendías**
(él/ella/usted)	**entendió**	**entendía**
(nosotros/as)	**entendimos**	**entendíamos**
(vosotros/as)	**entendisteis**	**entendíais**
(ellos/ellas/ ustedes)	**entendieron**	**entendían**

GERUND
entendiendo

PAST PARTICIPLE
entendido

EXAMPLE PHRASES

No lo vas a **entender**. You won't understand.

No lo **entiendo**. I don't understand.

Estás entendiéndolo todo al revés. You're getting me all wrong.

¿**Entendiste** lo que dijo? Did you understand what she said?

Mi padre **entendía** mucho de caballos. My father knew a lot about horses.

Remember that subject pronouns are not used very often in Spanish.

entender

	FUTURE	CONDITIONAL
(yo)	**entenderé**	**entendería**
(tú)	**entenderás**	**entenderías**
(él/ella/usted)	**entenderá**	**entendería**
(nosotros/as)	**entenderemos**	**entenderíamos**
(vosotros/as)	**entenderéis**	**entenderíais**
(ellos/ellas/ ustedes)	**entenderán**	**entenderían**

	PRESENT SUBJUNCTIVE	IMPERFECT SUBJUNCTIVE
(yo)	**entienda**	**entendiera** *or* **entendiese**
(tú)	**entiendas**	**entendieras** *or* **entendieses**
(él/ella/usted)	**entienda**	**entendiera** *or* **entendiese**
(nosotros/as)	**entendamos**	**entendiéramos** *or* **entendiésemos**
(vosotros/as)	**entendáis**	**entendierais** *or* **entendieseis**
(ellos/ellas/ ustedes)	**entiendan**	**entendieran** *or* **entendiesen**

IMPERATIVE

entiende / entended

Use the present subjunctive in all cases other than these tú *and* vosotros *affirmative forms.*

EXAMPLE PHRASES

Con el tiempo lo **entenderás**. You'll understand one day.

Yo no lo **entendería** así. I wouldn't interpret it like that.

Si de verdad me **entendieras**, no habrías dicho eso. If you really understood me, you wouldn't have said that.

No me **entiendas** mal. Don't misunderstand me.

Remember that subject pronouns are not used very often in Spanish.

enviar (to send)

	PRESENT	PRESENT PERFECT
(yo)	**envío**	he enviado
(tú)	**envías**	has enviado
(él/ella/usted)	**envía**	ha enviado
(nosotros/as)	**enviamos**	hemos enviado
(vosotros/as)	**enviáis**	habéis enviado
(ellos/ellas/ ustedes)	**envían**	han enviado

	PRETERITE	IMPERFECT
(yo)	**envié**	enviaba
(tú)	enviaste	enviabas
(él/ella/usted)	**envió**	enviaba
(nosotros/as)	enviamos	enviábamos
(vosotros/as)	enviasteis	enviabais
(ellos/ellas/ ustedes)	enviaron	enviaban

GERUND
enviando

PAST PARTICIPLE
enviado

EXAMPLE PHRASES

¿Cómo lo vas a **enviar**? How are you going to send it?
Les **envío** el trabajo por correo electrónico. I send them my work by email.
Ya **está enviando** las invitaciones. She has already started sending out the invitations.
La **han enviado** a Guatemala. They've sent her to Guatemala.
Le **envió** el regalo por correo. He mailed her the present.

Remember that subject pronouns are not used very often in Spanish.

enviar

	FUTURE	CONDITIONAL
(yo)	**enviaré**	**enviaría**
(tú)	**enviarás**	**enviarías**
(él/ella/usted)	**enviará**	**enviaría**
(nosotros/as)	**enviaremos**	**enviaríamos**
(vosotros/as)	**enviaréis**	**enviaríais**
(ellos/ellas/ ustedes)	**enviarán**	**enviarían**

	PRESENT SUBJUNCTIVE	IMPERFECT SUBJUNCTIVE
(yo)	**envíe**	**enviara** *or* **enviase**
(tú)	**envíes**	**enviaras** *or* **enviases**
(él/ella/usted)	**envíe**	**enviara** *or* **enviase**
(nosotros/as)	**enviemos**	**enviáramos** *or* **enviásemos**
(vosotros/as)	**enviéis**	**enviarais** *or* **enviaseis**
(ellos/ellas/ ustedes)	**envíen**	**enviaran** *or* **enviasen**

IMPERATIVE

envía / enviad

Use the present subjunctive in all cases other than these tú and vosotros affirmative forms.

EXAMPLE PHRASES

Nos **enviarán** más información. They'll send us more information.

Yo lo **enviaría** por mensajero. I'd send it by courier.

Necesitamos que lo **envíes** inmediatamente. We need you to send it immediately.

Si lo **enviaras** ahora, llegaría el lunes. If you sent it now it would get there on Monday.

No lo **envíes** sin repasarlo antes. Don't send it in without checking it first.

Envíe sus datos personales. Send in your details.

Remember that subject pronouns are not used very often in Spanish.

equivocarse (to make a mistake; to be wrong)

	PRESENT	PRESENT PERFECT
(yo)	me equivoco	me he equivocado
(tú)	te equivocas	te has equivocado
(él/ella/usted)	se equivoca	se ha equivocado
(nosotros/as)	nos equivocamos	nos hemos equivocado
(vosotros/as)	os equivocáis	os habéis equivocado
(ellos/ellas/ ustedes)	se equivocan	se han equivocado

	PRETERITE	IMPERFECT
(yo)	me equivoqué	me equivocaba
(tú)	te equivocaste	te equivocabas
(él/ella/usted)	se equivocó	se equivocaba
(nosotros/as)	nos equivocamos	nos equivocábamos
(vosotros/as)	os equivocasteis	os equivocabais
(ellos/ellas/ ustedes)	se equivocaron	se equivocaban

GERUND
equivocándose, etc

PAST PARTICIPLE
equivocado

EXAMPLE PHRASES

Si crees que voy a dejarte ir, **te equivocas**. If you think I'm going to let you go, you're mistaken.

Se equivocaron de tren. They took the wrong train.

Siempre **se equivocaba** de calle. He always took the wrong street.

Remember that subject pronouns are not used very often in Spanish.

equivocarse

	FUTURE	CONDITIONAL
(yo)	me equivocaré	me equivocaría
(tú)	te equivocarás	te equivocarías
(él/ella/usted)	se equivocará	se equivocaría
(nosotros/as)	nos equivocaremos	nos equivocaríamos
(vosotros/as)	os equivocaréis	os equivocaríais
(ellos/ellas/ ustedes)	se equivocarán	se equivocarían

	PRESENT SUBJUNCTIVE	IMPERFECT SUBJUNCTIVE
(yo)	me equivoque	me equivocara *or* equivocase
(tú)	te equivoques	te equivocaras *or* equivocases
(él/ella/usted)	se equivoque	se equivocara *or* equivocase
(nosotros/as)	nos equivoquemos	nos equivocáramos *or* equivocásemos
(vosotros/as)	os equivoquéis	os equivocarais *or* equivocaseis
(ellos/ellas/ ustedes)	se equivoquen	se equivocaran *or* equivocasen

IMPERATIVE

equivócate / equivocaos

Use the present subjunctive in all cases other than these tú *and* vosotros *affirmative forms.*

EXAMPLE PHRASES

Sobre todo, no **te equivoques** de hora. Above all, don't get the time wrong.

Si **te equivocaras**, quedarías eliminado del juego. If you made a mistake, you'd be out of the game.

Remember that subject pronouns are not used very often in Spanish.

erguir (to erect)

	PRESENT	PRESENT PERFECT
(yo)	**yergo**	**he erguido**
(tú)	**yergues**	**has erguido**
(él/ella/usted)	**yergue**	**ha erguido**
(nosotros/as)	**erguimos**	**hemos erguido**
(vosotros/as)	**erguís**	**habéis erguido**
(ellos/ellas/ustedes)	**yerguen**	**han erguido**

	PRETERITE	IMPERFECT
(yo)	**erguí**	**erguía**
(tú)	**erguiste**	**erguías**
(él/ella/usted)	**irguió**	**erguía**
(nosotros/as)	**erguimos**	**erguíamos**
(vosotros/as)	**erguisteis**	**erguías**
(ellos/ellas/ustedes)	**irguieron**	**erguían**

GERUND
irguiendo

PAST PARTICIPLE
erguido

EXAMPLE PHRASES

El perro **irguió** las orejas. The dog pricked up its ears.

La montaña **se erguía** majestuosa sobre el valle. The mountain rose majestically above the valley.

Tú mantén siempre la cabeza bien **erguida**. You must always hold your head high.

Remember that subject pronouns are not used very often in Spanish.

erguir

	FUTURE	CONDITIONAL
(yo)	erguiré	erguiría
(tú)	erguirás	erguirías
(él/ella/usted)	erguirá	erguiría
(nosotros/as)	erguiremos	erguiríamos
(vosotros/as)	erguiréis	erguiríais
(ellos/ellas/ ustedes)	erguirán	erguirían

	PRESENT SUBJUNCTIVE	IMPERFECT SUBJUNCTIVE
(yo)	yerga	irguiera *or* irguiese
(tú)	yergas	irguieras *or* irguieses
(él/ella/usted)	yerga	irguiera *or* irguiese
(nosotros/as)	irgamos	irguiéramos *or* irguiésemos
(vosotros/as)	irgáis	irguierais *or* irguieseis
(ellos/ellas/ ustedes)	yergan	irguieran *or* irguiesen

IMPERATIVE

yergue / erguid

Use the present subjunctive in all cases other than these tú and vosotros affirmative forms.

Remember that subject pronouns are not used very often in Spanish.

errar (to err)

	PRESENT	PRESENT PERFECT
(yo)	yerro	he errado
(tú)	yerras	has errado
(él/ella/usted)	yerra	ha errado
(nosotros/as)	erramos	hemos errado
(vosotros/as)	erráis	habéis errado
(ellos/ellas/ ustedes)	yerran	han errado

	PRETERITE	IMPERFECT
(yo)	erré	erraba
(tú)	erraste	errabas
(él/ella/usted)	erró	erraba
(nosotros/as)	erramos	errábamos
(vosotros/as)	errasteis	errabais
(ellos/ellas/ ustedes)	erraron	erraban

GERUND
errando

PAST PARTICIPLE
errado

EXAMPLE PHRASES

Errar es humano. To err is human.

Había errado en su decisión. She had made the wrong decision.

Erró el tiro. He missed.

Remember that subject pronouns are not used very often in Spanish.

errar

	FUTURE	CONDITIONAL
(yo)	erraré	erraría
(tú)	errarás	errarías
(él/ella/usted)	errará	erraría
(nosotros/as)	erraremos	erraríamos
(vosotros/as)	erraréis	erraríais
(ellos/ellas/ ustedes)	errarán	errarían

	PRESENT SUBJUNCTIVE	IMPERFECT SUBJUNCTIVE
(yo)	yerre	errara *or* errase
(tú)	yerres	erraras *or* errases
(él/ella/usted)	yerre	errara *or* errase
(nosotros/as)	erremos	erráramos *or* errásemos
(vosotros/as)	erréis	errarais *or* erraseis
(ellos/ellas/ ustedes)	yerren	erraran *or* errasen

IMPERATIVE

yerra / errad

Use the present subjunctive in all cases other than these tú and vosotros affirmative forms.

Remember that subject pronouns are not used very often in Spanish.

escoger (to choose; to pick)

	PRESENT	PRESENT PERFECT
(yo)	escojo	he escogido
(tú)	escoges	has escogido
(él/ella/usted)	escoge	ha escogido
(nosotros/as)	escogemos	hemos escogido
(vosotros/as)	escogéis	habéis escogido
(ellos/ellas/ ustedes)	escogen	han escogido

	PRETERITE	IMPERFECT
(yo)	escogí	escogía
(tú)	escogiste	escogías
(él/ella/usted)	escogió	escogía
(nosotros/as)	escogimos	escogíamos
(vosotros/as)	escogisteis	escogíais
(ellos/ellas/ ustedes)	escogieron	escogían

GERUND
escogiendo

PAST PARTICIPLE
escogido

EXAMPLE PHRASES

Escogió el más caro. He chose the most expensive one.

Escogía siempre al mismo alumno. She always picked the same student.

Remember that subject pronouns are not used very often in Spanish.

escoger

	FUTURE	CONDITIONAL
(yo)	escogeré	escogería
(tú)	escogerás	escogerías
(él/ella/usted)	escogerá	escogería
(nosotros/as)	escogeremos	escogeríamos
(vosotros/as)	escogeréis	escogeríais
(ellos/ellas/ ustedes)	escogerán	escogerían

	PRESENT SUBJUNCTIVE	IMPERFECT SUBJUNCTIVE
(yo)	escoja	escogiera *or* escogiese
(tú)	escojas	escogieras *or* escogieses
(él/ella/usted)	escoja	escogiera *or* escogiese
(nosotros/as)	escojamos	escogiéramos *or* escogiésemos
(vosotros/as)	escojáis	escogierais *or* escogieseis
(ellos/ellas/ ustedes)	escojan	escogieran *or* escogiesen

IMPERATIVE

escoge / escoged

Use the present subjunctive in all cases other than these tú and vosotros affirmative forms.

EXAMPLE PHRASES

Yo **escogería** el azul. I'd choose the blue one.

Escoja el que más le guste. Pick the one you like best.

Remember that subject pronouns are not used very often in Spanish.

escribir (to write)

	PRESENT	PRESENT PERFECT
(yo)	escribo	he escrito
(tú)	escribes	has escrito
(él/ella/usted)	escribe	ha escrito
(nosotros/as)	escribimos	hemos escrito
(vosotros/as)	escribís	habéis escrito
(ellos/ellas/ ustedes)	escriben	han escrito

	PRETERITE	IMPERFECT
(yo)	escribí	escribía
(tú)	escribiste	escribías
(él/ella/usted)	escribió	escribía
(nosotros/as)	escribimos	escribíamos
(vosotros/as)	escribisteis	escribíais
(ellos/ellas/ ustedes)	escribieron	escribían

GERUND
escribiendo

PAST PARTICIPLE
escrito

EXAMPLE PHRASES

¿Cómo se **escribe** su nombre? How do you spell your name?

¿**Estás escribiendo** la carta? Are you writing the letter?

Eso lo **escribí** yo. I wrote that.

Nos escribimos durante un tiempo. We wrote to each other for a while.

Escribía canciones. She wrote songs.

Remember that subject pronouns are not used very often in Spanish.

escribir

	FUTURE	CONDITIONAL
(yo)	escribiré	escribiría
(tú)	escribirás	escribirías
(él/ella/usted)	escribirá	escribiría
(nosotros/as)	escribiremos	escribiríamos
(vosotros/as)	escribiréis	escribiríais
(ellos/ellas/ ustedes)	escribirán	escribirían

	PRESENT SUBJUNCTIVE	IMPERFECT SUBJUNCTIVE
(yo)	escriba	escribiera *or* escribiese
(tú)	escribas	escribieras *or* escribieses
(él/ella/usted)	escriba	escribiera *or* escribiese
(nosotros/as)	escribamos	escribiéramos *or* escribiésemos
(vosotros/as)	escribáis	escribierais *or* escribieseis
(ellos/ellas/ ustedes)	escriban	escribieran *or* escribiesen

IMPERATIVE

escribe / escribid

Use the present subjunctive in all cases other than these tú and vosotros affirmative forms.

EXAMPLE PHRASES

¿Me **escribirás**? Will you write to me?

Yo lo **escribiría** con mayúscula. I'd write it with a capital letter.

No **escribas** en la mesa. Don't write on the table.

Si de verdad **escribiera** bien, ya le habrían publicado algún libro. If he really was a good writer, he'd have had a book published by now.

Escríbelo en el pizarrón. Write it on the blackboard.

Remember that subject pronouns are not used very often in Spanish.

esforzarse (to make an effort)

	PRESENT	PRESENT PERFECT
(yo)	me esfuerzo	me he esforzado
(tú)	te esfuerzas	te has esforzado
(él/ella/usted)	se esfuerza	se ha esforzado
(nosotros/as)	nos esforzamos	nos hemos esforzado
(vosotros/as)	os esforzáis	os habéis esforzado
(ellos/ellas/ ustedes)	se esfuerzan	se han esforzado

	PRETERITE	IMPERFECT
(yo)	me esforcé	me esforzaba
(tú)	te esforzaste	te esforzabas
(él/ella/usted)	se esforzó	se esforzaba
(nosotros/as)	nos esforzamos	nos esforzábamos
(vosotros/as)	os esforzasteis	os esforzabais
(ellos/ellas/ ustedes)	se esforzaron	se esforzaban

GERUND
esforzándose, etc

PAST PARTICIPLE
esforzado

EXAMPLE PHRASES

Tienes que **esforzarte** si quieres ganar. You have to make an effort if you want to win.

No **te esfuerzas** lo suficiente. You don't make enough effort.

Se esforzó todo lo que pudo por aprobar el examen. He did his best to pass the test.

Me esforzaba por entenderla. I tried hard to understand her.

Remember that subject pronouns are not used very often in Spanish.

esforzarse

	FUTURE	CONDITIONAL
(yo)	me esforzaré	me esforzaría
(tú)	te esforzarás	te esforzarías
(él/ella/usted)	se esforzará	se esforzaría
(nosotros/as)	nos esforzaremos	nos esforzaríamos
(vosotros/as)	os esforzaréis	os esforzaríais
(ellos/ellas/ ustedes)	se esforzarán	se esforzarían

	PRESENT SUBJUNCTIVE	IMPERFECT SUBJUNCTIVE
(yo)	me esfuerce	me esforzara *or* esforzase
(tú)	te esfuerces	te esforzaras *or* esforzases
(él/ella/usted)	se esfuerce	se esforzara *or* esforzase
(nosotros/as)	nos esforcemos	nos esforzáramos *or* esforzásemos
(vosotros/as)	os esforcéis	os esforzarais *or* esforzaseis
(ellos/ellas/ ustedes)	se esfuercen	se esforzaran *or* esforzasen

IMPERATIVE

esfuérzate / esforzaos

Use the present subjunctive in all cases other than these tú and vosotros affirmative forms.

EXAMPLE PHRASES

No **te esfuerces**, no me vas a convencer. Don't bother trying, you're not going to convince me.

Si **te esforzaras** un poco más, lo conseguirías. You'd manage it if you made a little more effort.

Remember that subject pronouns are not used very often in Spanish.

establecer (to establish)

	PRESENT	PRESENT PERFECT
(yo)	**establezco**	**he establecido**
(tú)	**estableces**	**has establecido**
(él/ella/usted)	**establece**	**ha establecido**
(nosotros/as)	**establecemos**	**hemos establecido**
(vosotros/as)	**establecéis**	**habéis establecido**
(ellos/ellas/ustedes)	**establecen**	**han establecido**

	PRETERITE	IMPERFECT
(yo)	**establecí**	**establecía**
(tú)	**estableciste**	**establecías**
(él/ella/usted)	**estableció**	**establecía**
(nosotros/as)	**establecimos**	**establecíamos**
(vosotros/as)	**establecisteis**	**establecíais**
(ellos/ellas/ustedes)	**establecieron**	**establecían**

GERUND
estableciendo

PAST PARTICIPLE
establecido

EXAMPLE PHRASES

Lograron **establecer** contacto con el barco. They managed to make contact with the boat.

La ley **establece** que... The law states that...

Se ha establecido una buena relación entre los dos países. A good relationship has been established between the two countries.

En 1945, la familia **se estableció** en Lima. In 1945, the family settled in Lima.

Remember that subject pronouns are not used very often in Spanish.

establecer

	FUTURE	CONDITIONAL
(yo)	**estableceré**	**establecería**
(tú)	**establecerás**	**establecerías**
(él/ella/usted)	**establecerá**	**establecería**
(nosotros/as)	**estableceremos**	**estableceríamos**
(vosotros/as)	**estableceréis**	**estableceríais**
(ellos/ellas/ ustedes)	**establecerán**	**establecerían**

	PRESENT SUBJUNCTIVE	IMPERFECT SUBJUNCTIVE
(yo)	**establezca**	**estableciera** *or* **estableciese**
(tú)	**establezcas**	**establecieras** *or* **establecieses**
(él/ella/usted)	**establezca**	**estableciera** *or* **estableciese**
(nosotros/as)	**establezcamos**	**estableciéramos** *or* **estableciésemos**
(vosotros/as)	**establezcáis**	**establecierais** *or* **establecieseis**
(ellos/ellas/ ustedes)	**establezcan**	**establecieran** *or* **estableciesen**

IMPERATIVE

establece / estableced

Use the present subjunctive in all cases other than these tú and vosotros affirmative forms.

EXAMPLE PHRASES

El año que viene **se establecerá** por su cuenta. Next year she'll set up on her own.

Remember that subject pronouns are not used very often in Spanish.

estar (to be)

	PRESENT	PRESENT PERFECT
(yo)	estoy	he estado
(tú)	estás	has estado
(él/ella/usted)	está	ha estado
(nosotros/as)	estamos	hemos estado
(vosotros/as)	estáis	habéis estado
(ellos/ellas/ ustedes)	están	han estado

	PRETERITE	IMPERFECT
(yo)	estuve	estaba
(tú)	estuviste	estabas
(él/ella/usted)	estuvo	estaba
(nosotros/as)	estuvimos	estábamos
(vosotros/as)	estuvisteis	estabais
(ellos/ellas/ ustedes)	estuvieron	estaban

GERUND
estando

PAST PARTICIPLE
estado

EXAMPLE PHRASES

Estoy cansado. I'm tired.

¿Cómo **estás**? How are you?

¿No **había estado** nunca en París? He'd never been to Paris?

Estuvimos en casa de mis padres. We were at my parents'.

¿Dónde **estabas**? Where were you?

Remember that subject pronouns are not used very often in Spanish.

estar

	FUTURE	CONDITIONAL
(yo)	**estaré**	**estaría**
(tú)	**estarás**	**estarías**
(él/ella/usted)	**estará**	**estaría**
(nosotros/as)	**estaremos**	**estaríamos**
(vosotros/as)	**estaréis**	**estaríais**
(ellos/ellas/ ustedes)	**estarán**	**estarían**

	PRESENT SUBJUNCTIVE	IMPERFECT SUBJUNCTIVE
(yo)	**esté**	**estuviera** *or* **estuviese**
(tú)	**estés**	**estuvieras** *or* **estuvieses**
(él/ella/usted)	**esté**	**estuviera** *or* **estuviese**
(nosotros/as)	**estemos**	**estuviéramos** *or* **estuviésemos**
(vosotros/as)	**estéis**	**estuvierais** *or* **estuvieseis**
(ellos/ellas/ ustedes)	**estén**	**estuvieran** *or* **estuviesen**

IMPERATIVE

está / estad

Use the present subjunctive in all cases other than these tú and vosotros affirmative forms.

EXAMPLE PHRASES

¿A qué hora **estarás** en casa? What time will you be home?

Dijo que **estaría** aquí a las ocho. She said she'd be here at eight o'clock.

Avísame cuando **estés** lista. Let me know when you're ready.

¡**Estáte** quieto! Keep still!

Si **estuviera** enfermo, habría llamado. If he were sick, he would have called.

Remember that subject pronouns are not used very often in Spanish.

evacuar (to evacuate)

	PRESENT	PRESENT PERFECT
(yo)	evacuo	he evacuado
(tú)	evacuas	has evacuado
(él/ella/usted)	evacua	ha evacuado
(nosotros/as)	evacuamos	hemos evacuado
(vosotros/as)	evacuáis	habéis evacuado
(ellos/ellas/ ustedes)	evacuan	han evacuado

	PRETERITE	IMPERFECT
(yo)	evacué	evacuaba
(tú)	evacuaste	evacuabas
(él/ella/usted)	evacuó	evacuaba
(nosotros/as)	evacuamos	evacuábamos
(vosotros/as)	evacuasteis	evacuabais
(ellos/ellas/ ustedes)	evacuaron	evacuaban

GERUND
evacuando

PAST PARTICIPLE
evacuado

EXAMPLE PHRASES

Van a **evacuar** a los heridos. They're going to evacuate the injured.

Han evacuado la zona. The area has been evacuated.

Remember that subject pronouns are not used very often in Spanish.

evacuar

	FUTURE	CONDITIONAL
(yo)	evacuaré	evacuaría
(tú)	evacuarás	evacuarías
(él/ella/usted)	evacuará	evacuaría
(nosotros/as)	evacuaremos	evacuaríamos
(vosotros/as)	evacuaréis	evacuaríais
(ellos/ellas/ ustedes)	evacuarán	evacuarían

	PRESENT SUBJUNCTIVE	IMPERFECT SUBJUNCTIVE
(yo)	evacue	evacuara *or* evacuase
(tú)	evacues	evacuaras *or* evacuases
(él/ella/usted)	evacue	evacuara *or* evacuase
(nosotros/as)	evacuemos	evacuáramos *or* evacuásemos
(vosotros/as)	evacuéis	evacuarais *or* evacuaseis
(ellos/ellas/ ustedes)	evacuen	evacuaran *or* evacuasen

IMPERATIVE

evacua / evacuad

Use the present subjunctive in all cases other than these tú and vosotros affirmative forms.

EXAMPLE PHRASES

Seguirá existiendo peligro mientras no **evacuen** el edificio. The danger won't be over until the building has been evacuated.

Remember that subject pronouns are not used very often in Spanish.

forzar (to force)

	PRESENT	PRESENT PERFECT
(yo)	**fuerzo**	**he forzado**
(tú)	**fuerzas**	**has forzado**
(él/ella/usted)	**fuerza**	**ha forzado**
(nosotros/as)	**forzamos**	**hemos forzado**
(vosotros/as)	**forzáis**	**habéis forzado**
(ellos/ellas/ ustedes)	**fuerzan**	**han forzado**

	PRETERITE	IMPERFECT
(yo)	**forcé**	**forzaba**
(tú)	**forzaste**	**forzabas**
(él/ella/usted)	**forzó**	**forzaba**
(nosotros/as)	**forzamos**	**forzábamos**
(vosotros/as)	**forzasteis**	**forzabais**
(ellos/ellas/ ustedes)	**forzaron**	**forzaban**

GERUND
forzando

PAST PARTICIPLE
forzado

EXAMPLE PHRASES

Nos **forzaron** a hacerlo. They forced us to do it.

Habían forzado la puerta de entrada. They had forced the front door.

Los **forzaban** a trabajar largas horas. They would force them to work long hours.

Remember that subject pronouns are not used very often in Spanish.

forzar

	FUTURE	CONDITIONAL
(yo)	**forzaré**	**forzaría**
(tú)	**forzarás**	**forzarías**
(él/ella/usted)	**forzará**	**forzaría**
(nosotros/as)	**forzaremos**	**forzaríamos**
(vosotros/as)	**forzaréis**	**forzaríais**
(ellos/ellas/ ustedes)	**forzarán**	**forzarían**

	PRESENT SUBJUNCTIVE	IMPERFECT SUBJUNCTIVE
(yo)	**fuerce**	**forzara** *or* **forzase**
(tú)	**fuerces**	**forzaras** *or* **forzases**
(él/ella/usted)	**fuerce**	**forzara** *or* **forzase**
(nosotros/as)	**forcemos**	**forzáramos** *or* **forzásemos**
(vosotros/as)	**forcéis**	**forzarais** *or* **forzaseis**
(ellos/ellas/ ustedes)	**fuercen**	**forzaran** *or* **forzasen**

IMPERATIVE

fuerza/forzad

Use the present subjunctive in all cases other than these tú and vosotros affirmative forms.

EXAMPLE PHRASES

No te **forzaremos** a ir. We won't force you to go.

No **fuerces** la cerradura. Don't force the lock.

Lo hizo sin que nadie lo **forzara**. He did it without anybody forcing him to.

Remember that subject pronouns are not used very often in Spanish.

freír (to fry)

	PRESENT	PRESENT PERFECT
(yo)	frío	he frito
(tú)	fríes	has frito
(él/ella/usted)	fríe	ha frito
(nosotros/as)	freímos	hemos frito
(vosotros/as)	freís	habéis frito
(ellos/ellas/ ustedes)	fríen	han frito

	PRETERITE	IMPERFECT
(yo)	freí	freía
(tú)	freíste	freías
(él/ella/usted)	frio	freía
(nosotros/as)	freímos	freíamos
(vosotros/as)	freísteis	freíais
(ellos/ellas/ ustedes)	frieron	freían

GERUND
friendo

PAST PARTICIPLE
frito

EXAMPLE PHRASES

No sabe ni **freír** un huevo. He can't even fry an egg.

Había frito el pescado. He had fried the fish.

Se está friendo demasiado por ese lado. It's getting overdone on that side.

Lo **frio** en mantequilla. She fried it in butter.

Nos **freíamos** de calor. We were roasting in the heat.

Remember that subject pronouns are not used very often in Spanish.

freír

	FUTURE	CONDITIONAL
(yo)	**freiré**	**freiría**
(tú)	**freirás**	**freirías**
(él/ella/usted)	**freirá**	**freiría**
(nosotros/as)	**freiremos**	**freiríamos**
(vosotros/as)	**freiréis**	**freiríais**
(ellos/ellas/ ustedes)	**freirán**	**freirían**

	PRESENT SUBJUNCTIVE	IMPERFECT SUBJUNCTIVE
(yo)	**fría**	**friera** *or* **friese**
(tú)	**frías**	**frieras** *or* **frieses**
(él/ella/usted)	**fría**	**friera** *or* **friese**
(nosotros/as)	**friamos**	**friéramos** *or* **friésemos**
(vosotros/as)	**friais**	**frierais** *or* **frieseis**
(ellos/ellas/ ustedes)	**frían**	**frieran** *or* **friesen**

IMPERATIVE

fríe / freíd

Use the present subjunctive in all cases other than these tú and vosotros affirmative forms.

EXAMPLE PHRASES

Fríelo en aceite de oliva. Fry it in olive oil.

Me dijo que **friera** la cebolla. She told me to fry the onion.

Remember that subject pronouns are not used very often in Spanish.

gruñir (to grumble; to growl)

	PRESENT	PRESENT PERFECT
(yo)	**gruño**	**he gruñido**
(tú)	**gruñes**	**has gruñido**
(él/ella/usted)	**gruñe**	**ha gruñido**
(nosotros/as)	**gruñimos**	**hemos gruñido**
(vosotros/as)	**gruñís**	**habéis gruñido**
(ellos/ellas/ ustedes)	**gruñen**	**han gruñido**

	PRETERITE	IMPERFECT
(yo)	**gruñí**	**gruñía**
(tú)	**gruñiste**	**gruñías**
(él/ella/usted)	**gruñó**	**gruñía**
(nosotros/as)	**gruñimos**	**gruñíamos**
(vosotros/as)	**gruñisteis**	**gruñíais**
(ellos/ellas/ ustedes)	**gruñeron**	**gruñían**

GERUND

gruñendo

PAST PARTICIPLE

gruñido

EXAMPLE PHRASES

¿A quién le **gruñe** el perro? Who's the dog growling at?

Siempre **está gruñendo**. He's always grumbling.

El oso nos **gruñía** sin parar. The bear kept growling at us.

Remember that subject pronouns are not used very often in Spanish.

gruñir

	FUTURE	CONDITIONAL
(yo)	**gruñiré**	**gruñiría**
(tú)	**gruñirás**	**gruñirías**
(él/ella/usted)	**gruñirá**	**gruñiría**
(nosotros/as)	**gruñiremos**	**gruñiríamos**
(vosotros/as)	**gruñiréis**	**gruñiríais**
(ellos/ellas/ ustedes)	**gruñirán**	**gruñirían**

	PRESENT SUBJUNCTIVE	IMPERFECT SUBJUNCTIVE
(yo)	**gruña**	**gruñera** *or* **gruñese**
(tú)	**gruñas**	**gruñeras** *or* **gruñeses**
(él/ella/usted)	**gruña**	**gruñera** *or* **gruñese**
(nosotros/as)	**gruñamos**	**gruñéramos** *or* **gruñésemos**
(vosotros/as)	**gruñáis**	**gruñerais** *or* **gruñeseis**
(ellos/ellas/ ustedes)	**gruñan**	**gruñeran** *or* **gruñesen**

IMPERATIVE

gruñe / gruñid

Use the present subjunctive in all cases other than these tú and vosotros affirmative forms.

EXAMPLE PHRASES

¡No **gruñas** tanto! Don't grumble so much.

Remember that subject pronouns are not used very often in Spanish.

guiar (to guide)

	PRESENT	PRESENT PERFECT
(yo)	**guío**	**he guiado**
(tú)	**guías**	**has guiado**
(él/ella/usted)	**guía**	**ha guiado**
(nosotros/as)	**guiamos**	**hemos guiado**
(vosotros/as)	**guiais**	**habéis guiado**
(ellos/ellas/ ustedes)	**guían**	**han guiado**

	PRETERITE	IMPERFECT
(yo)	**guie**	**guiaba**
(tú)	**guiaste**	**guiabas**
(él/ella/usted)	**guio**	**guiaba**
(nosotros/as)	**guiamos**	**guiábamos**
(vosotros/as)	**guiasteis**	**guiabais**
(ellos/ellas/ ustedes)	**guiaron**	**guiaban**

GERUND
guiando

PAST PARTICIPLE
guiado

EXAMPLE PHRASES

Los perros **se guían** por su olfato. Dogs follow their sense of smell.
Me guié por el instinto. I followed my instinct.
Nos guiamos por un mapa que teníamos. We found our way using a map we had.
Siempre me protegía y me **guiaba**. He always protected me and guided me.

Remember that subject pronouns are not used very often in Spanish.

guiar

	FUTURE	CONDITIONAL
(yo)	**guiaré**	**guiaría**
(tú)	**guiarás**	**guiarías**
(él/ella/usted)	**guiará**	**guiaría**
(nosotros/as)	**guiaremos**	**guiaríamos**
(vosotros/as)	**guiaréis**	**guiaríais**
(ellos/ellas/ ustedes)	**guiarán**	**guiarían**

	PRESENT SUBJUNCTIVE	IMPERFECT SUBJUNCTIVE
(yo)	**guíe**	**guiara** *or* **guiase**
(tú)	**guíes**	**guiaras** *or* **guiases**
(él/ella/usted)	**guíe**	**guiara** *or* **guiase**
(nosotros/as)	**guiemos**	**guiáramos** *or* **guiásemos**
(vosotros/as)	**guieis**	**guiarais** *or* **guiaseis**
(ellos/ellas/ ustedes)	**guíen**	**guiaran** *or* **guiasen**

IMPERATIVE

guía / guiad

Use the present subjunctive in all cases other than these tú and vosotros affirmative forms.

EXAMPLE PHRASES

Los **guiaré** hasta allí. I'll take you there.

Guíate por la razón. Use reason as your guide.

Remember that subject pronouns are not used very often in Spanish.

haber (to have – *auxiliary*)

	PRESENT	PRESENT PERFECT
(yo)	**he**	*not used except impersonally*
(tú)	**has**	*See* hay
(él/ella/usted)	**ha**	
(nosotros/as)	**hemos**	
(vosotros/as)	**habéis**	
(ellos/ellas/ ustedes)	**han**	

	PRETERITE	IMPERFECT
(yo)	**hube**	**había**
(tú)	**hubiste**	**habías**
(él/ella/usted)	**hubo**	**había**
(nosotros/as)	**hubimos**	**habíamos**
(vosotros/as)	**hubisteis**	**habíais**
(ellos/ellas/ ustedes)	**hubieron**	**habían**

GERUND

habiendo

PAST PARTICIPLE

habido

EXAMPLE PHRASES

De **haber**lo sabido, **habría** ido. If I'd known, I would have gone.

¿**Has** visto eso? Did you see that?

Eso nunca **había** pasado antes. That had never happened before.

Remember that subject pronouns are not used very often in Spanish.

haber

	FUTURE	CONDITIONAL
(yo)	**habré**	**habría**
(tú)	**habrás**	**habrías**
(él/ella/usted)	**habrá**	**habría**
(nosotros/as)	**habremos**	**habríamos**
(vosotros/as)	**habréis**	**habríais**
(ellos/ellas/ ustedes)	**habrán**	**habrían**

	PRESENT SUBJUNCTIVE	IMPERFECT SUBJUNCTIVE
(yo)	**haya**	**hubiera** *or* **hubiese**
(tú)	**hayas**	**hubieras** *or* **hubieses**
(él/ella/usted)	**haya**	**hubiera** *or* **hubiese**
(nosotros/as)	**hayamos**	**hubiéramos** *or* **hubiésemos**
(vosotros/as)	**hayáis**	**hubierais** *or* **hubieseis**
(ellos/ellas/ ustedes)	**hayan**	**hubieran** *or* **hubiesen**

IMPERATIVE

not used

EXAMPLE PHRASES

Como se **hayan** olvidado, los mato. I'll kill them if they've forgotten.

Si me lo **hubieras** dicho, te lo **habría** traído. I'd have brought it, if you'd told me.

Para esa hora ya **habremos** terminado. We'll have finished by that time.

Lo **habrías** logrado si **hubieras** intentado. You'd have succeeded if you'd tried.

Remember that subject pronouns are not used very often in Spanish.

hablar (to speak; to talk)

	PRESENT	PRESENT PERFECT
(yo)	**hablo**	**he hablado**
(tú)	**hablas**	**has hablado**
(él/ella/usted)	**habla**	**ha hablado**
(nosotros/as)	**hablamos**	**hemos hablado**
(vosotros/as)	**habláis**	**habéis hablado**
(ellos/ellas/ ustedes)	**hablan**	**han hablado**

	PRETERITE	IMPERFECT
(yo)	**hablé**	**hablaba**
(tú)	**hablaste**	**hablabas**
(él/ella/usted)	**habló**	**hablaba**
(nosotros/as)	**hablamos**	**hablábamos**
(vosotros/as)	**hablasteis**	**hablabais**
(ellos/ellas/ ustedes)	**hablaron**	**hablaban**

GERUND
hablando

PAST PARTICIPLE
hablado

EXAMPLE PHRASES

María no **habla** inglés. María doesn't speak English.
No **nos hablamos** desde hace tiempo. We haven't spoken to each other for a long time.
Está hablando por teléfono. He's on the phone.
Hoy **hablé** con mi hermana. I spoke to my sister today.
Hablaba rapidísimo. He spoke really fast.

Remember that subject pronouns are not used very often in Spanish.

hablar

	FUTURE	CONDITIONAL
(yo)	**hablaré**	**hablaría**
(tú)	**hablarás**	**hablarías**
(él/ella/usted)	**hablará**	**hablaría**
(nosotros/as)	**hablaremos**	**hablaríamos**
(vosotros/as)	**hablaréis**	**hablaríais**
(ellos/ellas/ ustedes)	**hablarán**	**hablarían**

	PRESENT SUBJUNCTIVE	IMPERFECT SUBJUNCTIVE
(yo)	**hable**	**hablara** *or* **hablase**
(tú)	**hables**	**hablaras** *or* **hablases**
(él/ella/usted)	**hable**	**hablara** *or* **hablase**
(nosotros/as)	**hablemos**	**habláramos** *or* **hablásemos**
(vosotros/as)	**habléis**	**hablarais** *or* **hablaseis**
(ellos/ellas/ ustedes)	**hablen**	**hablaran** *or* **hablasen**

IMPERATIVE

habla / hablad

Use the present subjunctive in all cases other than these tú and vosotros affirmative forms.

EXAMPLE PHRASES

Luego **hablaremos** de ese tema. We'll talk about that later.

Recuérdame que **hable** con Daniel. Remind me to speak to Daniel.

¿Quieres que **hablemos**? Shall we talk?

Hay que darles una oportunidad para que **hablen**. We need to give them an opportunity to speak.

Remember that subject pronouns are not used very often in Spanish.

hacer (to do; to make)

	PRESENT	PRESENT PERFECT
(yo)	**hago**	**he hecho**
(tú)	**haces**	**has hecho**
(él/ella/usted)	**hace**	**ha hecho**
(nosotros/as)	**hacemos**	**hemos hecho**
(vosotros/as)	**hacéis**	**habéis hecho**
(ellos/ellas/ ustedes)	**hacen**	**han hecho**

	PRETERITE	IMPERFECT
(yo)	**hice**	**hacía**
(tú)	**hiciste**	**hacías**
(él/ella/usted)	**hizo**	**hacía**
(nosotros/as)	**hicimos**	**hacíamos**
(vosotros/as)	**hicisteis**	**hacíais**
(ellos/ellas/ ustedes)	**hicieron**	**hacían**

GERUND
haciendo

PAST PARTICIPLE
hecho

EXAMPLE PHRASES

¿Qué **hace** tu padre? What does your father do?
Están haciendo mucho ruido. They're making a lot of noise.
¿Quién **hizo** eso? Who did that?
Hicieron pintar la fachada del colegio. They had the front of the school painted.
Lo **hacía** para molestarme. He was doing it to annoy me.

Remember that subject pronouns are not used very often in Spanish.

hacer

	FUTURE	CONDITIONAL
(yo)	**haré**	haría
(tú)	**harás**	harías
(él/ella/usted)	**hará**	haría
(nosotros/as)	**haremos**	haríamos
(vosotros/as)	**haréis**	haríais
(ellos/ellas/ ustedes)	**harán**	harían

	PRESENT SUBJUNCTIVE	IMPERFECT SUBJUNCTIVE
(yo)	**haga**	hiciera *or* hiciese
(tú)	**hagas**	hicieras *or* hicieses
(él/ella/usted)	**haga**	hiciera *or* hiciese
(nosotros/as)	**hagamos**	hiciéramos *or* hiciésemos
(vosotros/as)	**hagáis**	hicierais *or* hicieseis
(ellos/ellas/ ustedes)	**hagan**	hicieran *or* hiciesen

IMPERATIVE

haz / haced

Use the present subjunctive in all cases other than these tú and vosotros affirmative forms.

EXAMPLE PHRASES

Lo **haré** yo mismo. I'll do it myself.

Dijiste que lo **harías.** You said you'd do it.

¿Quieres que **haga** las camas? Do you want me to make the beds?

Preferiría que **hiciera** menos calor. I wish it wasn't so hot.

Hazlo como te dije. Do it the way I told you.

Remember that subject pronouns are not used very often in Spanish.

hay (there is; there are)

PRESENT
hay

PRESENT PERFECT
ha habido

PRETERITE
hubo

IMPERFECT
había

GERUND
habiendo

PAST PARTICIPLE
habido

EXAMPLE PHRASES

Esta tarde va a **haber** una manifestación. There's going to be a demonstration this evening.
Hay una iglesia en la esquina. There's a church on the corner.
Ha habido muchos problemas. There have been a lot of problems.
Hubo una guerra. There was a war.
Había mucha gente. There were a lot of people.

Remember that subject pronouns are not used very often in Spanish.

hay

FUTURE
habrá

CONDITIONAL
habría

PRESENT SUBJUNCTIVE
haya

IMPERFECT SUBJUNCTIVE
hubiera *or* hubiese

IMPERATIVE
not used

EXAMPLE PHRASES

Habrá que repasarlo. We'll have to check it.

Habría que limpiarlo. We should clean it.

No creo que **haya** mucha gente en el recital. I don't think there'll be many people at the concert.

Si **hubiera** más espacio, pondría un sofá. I'd have a sofa if there was more room.

Remember that subject pronouns are not used very often in Spanish.

herir (to injure)

	PRESENT	PRESENT PERFECT
(yo)	**hiero**	**he herido**
(tú)	**hieres**	**has herido**
(él/ella/usted)	**hiere**	**ha herido**
(nosotros/as)	**herimos**	**hemos herido**
(vosotros/as)	**herís**	**habéis herido**
(ellos/ellas/ ustedes)	**hieren**	**han herido**

	PRETERITE	IMPERFECT
(yo)	**herí**	**hería**
(tú)	**heriste**	**herías**
(él/ella/usted)	**hirió**	**hería**
(nosotros/as)	**herimos**	**heríamos**
(vosotros/as)	**heristeis**	**heríais**
(ellos/ellas/ ustedes)	**hirieron**	**herían**

GERUND
hiriendo

PAST PARTICIPLE
herido

EXAMPLE PHRASES

Vas a **herir** sus sentimientos. You're going to hurt her feelings.
Me **hiere** que me digas eso. I'm hurt that you should say such a thing.
Lo **hirieron** en el pecho. He was wounded in the chest.
Su actitud la **hería** en lo más hondo. She was deeply hurt by his attitude.

Remember that subject pronouns are not used very often in Spanish.

herir

	FUTURE	CONDITIONAL
(yo)	**heriré**	**heriría**
(tú)	**herirás**	**herirías**
(él/ella/usted)	**herirá**	**heriría**
(nosotros/as)	**heriremos**	**heriríamos**
(vosotros/as)	**heriréis**	**heriríais**
(ellos/ellas/ ustedes)	**herirán**	**herirían**

	PRESENT SUBJUNCTIVE	IMPERFECT SUBJUNCTIVE
(yo)	**hiera**	**hiriera** *or* **hiriese**
(tú)	**hieras**	**hirieras** *or* **hirieses**
(él/ella/usted)	**hiera**	**hiriera** *or* **hiriese**
(nosotros/as)	**hiramos**	**hiriéramos** *or* **hiriésemos**
(vosotros/as)	**hiráis**	**hirierais** *or* **hirieseis**
(ellos/ellas/ ustedes)	**hieran**	**hirieran** *or* **hiriesen**

IMPERATIVE

hiere / herid

Use the present subjunctive in all cases other than these tú *and* vosotros *affirmative forms.*

EXAMPLE PHRASES

Mi madre siempre tenía miedo que nos **hiriéramos**. My mom was always scared we'd hurt ourselves.

Remember that subject pronouns are not used very often in Spanish.

huir (to escape; to run away; to flee)

	PRESENT	PRESENT PERFECT
(yo)	**huyo**	**he huido**
(tú)	**huyes**	**has huido**
(él/ella/usted)	**huye**	**ha huido**
(nosotros/as)	**huimos**	**hemos huido**
(vosotros/as)	**huis**	**habéis huido**
(ellos/ellas/ ustedes)	**huyen**	**han huido**

	PRETERITE	IMPERFECT
(yo)	**hui**	**huía**
(tú)	**huiste**	**huías**
(él/ella/usted)	**huyó**	**huía**
(nosotros/as)	**huimos**	**huíamos**
(vosotros/as)	**huisteis**	**huíais**
(ellos/ellas/ ustedes)	**huyeron**	**huían**

GERUND
huyendo

PAST PARTICIPLE
huido

EXAMPLE PHRASES

Salió **huyendo.** He ran away.

Huyeron del país. They fled the country.

Remember that subject pronouns are not used very often in Spanish.

huir

	FUTURE	CONDITIONAL
(yo)	**huiré**	**huiría**
(tú)	**huirás**	**huirías**
(él/ella/usted)	**huirá**	**huiría**
(nosotros/as)	**huiremos**	**huiríamos**
(vosotros/as)	**huiréis**	**huiríais**
(ellos/ellas/ ustedes)	**huirán**	**huirían**

	PRESENT SUBJUNCTIVE	IMPERFECT SUBJUNCTIVE
(yo)	**huya**	**huyera** *or* **huyese**
(tú)	**huyas**	**huyeras** *or* **huyeses**
(él/ella/usted)	**huya**	**huyera** *or* **huyese**
(nosotros/as)	**huyamos**	**huyéramos** *or* **huyésemos**
(vosotros/as)	**huyáis**	**huyerais** *or* **huyeseis**
(ellos/ellas/ ustedes)	**huyan**	**huyeran** *or* **huyesen**

IMPERATIVE

huye / huid

Use the present subjunctive in all cases other than these tú and vosotros affirmative forms.

EXAMPLE PHRASES

No quiero que **huyas** como un cobarde. I don't want you to run away like a coward.

¡**Huye**! Si te atrapan, te matarán. Run! If they catch you, they'll kill you.

Remember that subject pronouns are not used very often in Spanish.

imponer (to impose)

	PRESENT	PRESENT PERFECT
(yo)	**impongo**	**he impuesto**
(tú)	**impones**	**has impuesto**
(él/ella/usted)	**impone**	**ha impuesto**
(nosotros/as)	**imponemos**	**hemos impuesto**
(vosotros/as)	**imponéis**	**habéis impuesto**
(ellos/ellas/ ustedes)	**imponen**	**han impuesto**

	PRETERITE	IMPERFECT
(yo)	**impuse**	**imponía**
(tú)	**impusiste**	**imponías**
(él/ella/usted)	**impuso**	**imponía**
(nosotros/as)	**impusimos**	**imponíamos**
(vosotros/as)	**impusisteis**	**imponíais**
(ellos/ellas/ ustedes)	**impusieron**	**imponían**

GERUND
imponiendo

PAST PARTICIPLE
impuesto

EXAMPLE PHRASES

La minifalda **se está imponiendo** de nuevo. The miniskirt is coming back into fashion.

Habían impuesto la enseñanza religiosa. They had made religious education compulsory.

El corredor nigeriano **se impuso** en la segunda carrera. The Nigerian runner triumphed in the second race.

Mi abuelo **imponía** mucho respeto. My grandfather commanded a lot of respect.

Remember that subject pronouns are not used very often in Spanish.

imponer

	FUTURE	CONDITIONAL
(yo)	**impondré**	**impondría**
(tú)	**impondrás**	**impondrías**
(él/ella/usted)	**impondrá**	**impondría**
(nosotros/as)	**impondremos**	**impondríamos**
(vosotros/as)	**impondréis**	**impondríais**
(ellos/ellas/ ustedes)	**impondrán**	**impondrían**

	PRESENT SUBJUNCTIVE	IMPERFECT SUBJUNCTIVE
(yo)	**imponga**	**impusiera** *or* **impusiese**
(tú)	**impongas**	**impusieras** *or* **impusieses**
(él/ella/usted)	**imponga**	**impusiera** *or* **impusiese**
(nosotros/as)	**impongamos**	**impusiéramos** *or* **impusiésemos**
(vosotros/as)	**impongáis**	**impusierais** *or* **impusieseis**
(ellos/ellas/ ustedes)	**impongan**	**impusieran** *or* **impusiesen**

IMPERATIVE

impón / imponed

Use the present subjunctive in all cases other than these tú and vosotros affirmative forms.

EXAMPLE PHRASES

Impondrán cuantiosas multas. They'll impose heavy fines.

Remember that subject pronouns are not used very often in Spanish.

imprimir (to print)

	PRESENT	PRESENT PERFECT
(yo)	**imprimo**	**he imprimido**
(tú)	**imprimes**	**has imprimido**
(él/ella/usted)	**imprime**	**ha imprimido**
(nosotros/as)	**imprimimos**	**hemos imprimido**
(vosotros/as)	**imprimís**	**habéis imprimido**
(ellos/ellas/ ustedes)	**imprimen**	**han imprimido**

	PRETERITE	IMPERFECT
(yo)	**imprimí**	**imprimía**
(tú)	**imprimiste**	**imprimías**
(él/ella/usted)	**imprimió**	**imprimía**
(nosotros/as)	**imprimimos**	**imprimíamos**
(vosotros/as)	**imprimisteis**	**imprimíais**
(ellos/ellas/ ustedes)	**imprimieron**	**imprimían**

GERUND
imprimiendo

PAST PARTICIPLE
imprimido, impreso

EXAMPLE PHRASES

¿Puedes **imprimir** el documento? Can you print the document?

Se imprimieron sólo doce copias del libro. Only twelve copies of the book were printed.

Una experiencia así **imprime** carácter. An experience like that is character-building.

Remember that subject pronouns are not used very often in Spanish.

imprimir

	FUTURE	CONDITIONAL
(yo)	imprimiré	imprimiría
(tú)	imprimirás	imprimirías
(él/ella/usted)	imprimirá	imprimiría
(nosotros/as)	imprimiremos	imprimiríamos
(vosotros/as)	imprimiréis	imprimiríais
(ellos/ellas/ ustedes)	imprimirán	imprimirían

	PRESENT SUBJUNCTIVE	IMPERFECT SUBJUNCTIVE
(yo)	imprima	imprimiera *or* imprimiese
(tú)	imprimas	imprimieras *or* imprimieses
(él/ella/usted)	imprima	imprimiera *or* imprimiese
(nosotros/as)	imprimamos	imprimiéramos *or* imprimiésemos
(vosotros/as)	imprimáis	imprimierais *or* imprimieseis
(ellos/ellas/ ustedes)	impriman	imprimieran *or* imprimiesen

IMPERATIVE

imprime / imprimid

Use the present subjunctive in all cases other than these tú and vosotros affirmative forms.

EXAMPLE PHRASE

Imprímelo en blanco y negro. Print it in black and white.

Remember that subject pronouns are not used very often in Spanish.

ir (to go)

	PRESENT	PRESENT PERFECT
(yo)	voy	he ido
(tú)	vas	has ido
(él/ella/usted)	va	ha ido
(nosotros/as)	vamos	hemos ido
(vosotros/as)	vais	habéis ido
(ellos/ellas/ ustedes)	van	han ido

	PRETERITE	IMPERFECT
(yo)	fui	iba
(tú)	fuiste	ibas
(él/ella/usted)	fue	iba
(nosotros/as)	fuimos	íbamos
(vosotros/as)	fuisteis	ibais
(ellos/ellas/ ustedes)	fueron	iban

GERUND
yendo

PAST PARTICIPLE
ido

EXAMPLE PHRASES

¿Puedo **ir** contigo? Can I come with you?

Estoy yendo a clases de natación. I'm taking swimming classes.

Había ido a comprar el pan. She'd gone to buy the bread.

Anoche **fuimos** al cine. We went to the movies last night.

Remember that subject pronouns are not used very often in Spanish.

ir

	FUTURE	CONDITIONAL
(yo)	**iré**	**iría**
(tú)	**irás**	**irías**
(él/ella/usted)	**irá**	**iría**
(nosotros/as)	**iremos**	**iríamos**
(vosotros/as)	**iréis**	**iríais**
(ellos/ellas/ ustedes)	**irán**	**irían**

	PRESENT SUBJUNCTIVE	IMPERFECT SUBJUNCTIVE
(yo)	**vaya**	**fuera** *or* **fuese**
(tú)	**vayas**	**fueras** *or* **fueses**
(él/ella/usted)	**vaya**	**fuera** *or* **fuese**
(nosotros/as)	**vayamos**	**fuéramos** *or* **fuésemos**
(vosotros/as)	**vayáis**	**fuerais** *or* **fueseis**
(ellos/ellas/ ustedes)	**vayan**	**fueran** *or* **fuesen**

IMPERATIVE

ve / id

Use the present subjunctive in most cases other than these tú and vosotros affirmative forms. However, in the 'let's' affirmative form, vamos is more common than vayamos.

EXAMPLE PHRASES

El domingo **iré** a verla. I'll go to see her on Sunday.

Dijeron que **irían** en tren. They said they'd go by train.

¡Que te **vaya** bien! Take care of yourself!

Quería pedirte que **fueras** en mi lugar. I wanted to ask you if you'd go instead of me.

No **te vayas** sin despedirte. Don't go without saying goodbye.

Remember that subject pronouns are not used very often in Spanish.

jugar (to play)

	PRESENT	PRESENT PERFECT
(yo)	**juego**	**he jugado**
(tú)	**juegas**	**has jugado**
(él/ella/usted)	**juega**	**ha jugado**
(nosotros/as)	**jugamos**	**hemos jugado**
(vosotros/as)	**jugáis**	**habéis jugado**
(ellos/ellas/ ustedes)	**juegan**	**han jugado**

	PRETERITE	IMPERFECT
(yo)	**jugué**	**jugaba**
(tú)	**jugaste**	**jugabas**
(él/ella/usted)	**jugó**	**jugaba**
(nosotros/as)	**jugamos**	**jugábamos**
(vosotros/as)	**jugasteis**	**jugabais**
(ellos/ellas/ ustedes)	**jugaron**	**jugaban**

GERUND
jugando

PAST PARTICIPLE
jugado

EXAMPLE PHRASES

Juego futbol todos los domingos. I play soccer every Sunday.
Están jugando en el jardín. They're playing in the yard.
Le **jugaron** una mala pasada. They played a dirty trick on him.
Se jugaba la vida continuamente. She was constantly risking her life.

Remember that subject pronouns are not used very often in Spanish.

jugar

	FUTURE	CONDITIONAL
(yo)	**jugaré**	**jugaría**
(tú)	**jugarás**	**jugarías**
(él/ella/usted)	**jugará**	**jugaría**
(nosotros/as)	**jugaremos**	**jugaríamos**
(vosotros/as)	**jugaréis**	**jugaríais**
(ellos/ellas/ ustedes)	**jugarán**	**jugarían**

	PRESENT SUBJUNCTIVE	IMPERFECT SUBJUNCTIVE
(yo)	**juegue**	**jugara** *or* **jugase**
(tú)	**juegues**	**jugaras** *or* **jugases**
(él/ella/usted)	**juegue**	**jugara** *or* **jugase**
(nosotros/as)	**juguemos**	**jugáramos** *or* **jugásemos**
(vosotros/as)	**juguéis**	**jugarais** *or* **jugaseis**
(ellos/ellas/ ustedes)	**jueguen**	**jugaran** *or* **jugasen**

IMPERATIVE

juega / jugad

Use the present subjunctive in all cases other than these tú and vosotros affirmative forms.

EXAMPLE PHRASES

Ambos partidos se **jugarán** el domingo. Both games will be played on Sunday.

Jugarías mejor si estuvieras más relajado. You'd play better if you were more relaxed.

No **juegues** con tu salud. Don't take risks with your health.

El médico le aconsejó que **jugara** más y leyera menos. The doctor advised him to play more and read less.

Remember that subject pronouns are not used very often in Spanish.

leer (to read)

	PRESENT	PRESENT PERFECT
(yo)	**leo**	**he leído**
(tú)	**lees**	**has leído**
(él/ella/usted)	**lee**	**ha leído**
(nosotros/as)	**leemos**	**hemos leído**
(vosotros/as)	**leéis**	**habéis leído**
(ellos/ellas/ ustedes)	**leen**	**han leído**

	PRETERITE	IMPERFECT
(yo)	**leí**	**leía**
(tú)	**leíste**	**leías**
(él/ella/usted)	**leyó**	**leía**
(nosotros/as)	**leímos**	**leíamos**
(vosotros/as)	**leísteis**	**leíais**
(ellos/ellas/ ustedes)	**leyeron**	**leían**

GERUND
leyendo

PAST PARTICIPLE
leído

EXAMPLE PHRASES

Hace mucho tiempo que no **leo** nada. I haven't read anything for ages.
Estoy leyendo un libro muy interesante. I'm reading a very interesting book.
No **había leído** nada suyo. I hadn't read anything by her.
Lo **leí** hace tiempo. I read it a while ago.
Antes **leía** mucho más. I used to read a lot more before.

Remember that subject pronouns are not used very often in Spanish.

leer

	FUTURE	CONDITIONAL
(yo)	leeré	leería
(tú)	leerás	leerías
(él/ella/usted)	leerá	leería
(nosotros/as)	leeremos	leeríamos
(vosotros/as)	leeréis	leeríais
(ellos/ellas/ ustedes)	leerán	leerían

	PRESENT SUBJUNCTIVE	IMPERFECT SUBJUNCTIVE
(yo)	lea	leyera *or* leyese
(tú)	leas	leyeras *or* leyeses
(él/ella/usted)	lea	leyera *or* leyese
(nosotros/as)	leamos	leyéramos *or* leyésemos
(vosotros/as)	leáis	leyerais *or* leyeseis
(ellos/ellas/ ustedes)	lean	leyeran *or* leyesen

IMPERATIVE

lee / leed

Use the present subjunctive in all cases other than these tú and vosotros affirmative forms.

EXAMPLE PHRASES

Si se portan bien, les **leeré** un cuento. If you behave yourselves, I'll read you a story.

Yo **leería** también la letra pequeña. I'd read the fine print as well.

Quiero que lo **leas** y me digas qué piensas. I want you to read it and tell me what you think.

No **leas** tan rápido. Don't read so fast.

Remember that subject pronouns are not used very often in Spanish.

levantar (to lift; to raise; to pick up)

	PRESENT	PRESENT PERFECT
(yo)	levanto	he levantado
(tú)	levantas	has levantado
(él/ella/usted)	levanta	ha levantado
(nosotros/as)	levantamos	hemos levantado
(vosotros/as)	levantáis	habéis levantado
(ellos/ellas/ ustedes)	levantan	han levantado

	PRETERITE	IMPERFECT
(yo)	levanté	levantaba
(tú)	levantaste	levantabas
(él/ella/usted)	levantó	levantaba
(nosotros/as)	levantamos	levantábamos
(vosotros/as)	levantasteis	levantabais
(ellos/ellas/ ustedes)	levantaron	levantaban

GERUND
levantando

PAST PARTICIPLE
levantado

EXAMPLE PHRASES

Fue la primera en **levantar** la mano. She was the first to raise her hand.

Siempre **se levanta** de mal humor. He's always in a bad mood when he gets up.

Hoy **me levanté** temprano. I got up early this morning.

Levantó la maleta como si no pesara nada. He lifted up the suitcase as if it weighed nothing.

Me levanté y seguí caminando. I got up and continued walking.

Remember that subject pronouns are not used very often in Spanish.

levantar

	FUTURE	CONDITIONAL
(yo)	**levantaré**	**levantaría**
(tú)	**levantarás**	**levantarías**
(él/ella/usted)	**levantará**	**levantaría**
(nosotros/as)	**levantaremos**	**levantaríamos**
(vosotros/as)	**levantaréis**	**levantaríais**
(ellos/ellas/ ustedes)	**levantarán**	**levantarían**

	PRESENT SUBJUNCTIVE	IMPERFECT SUBJUNCTIVE
(yo)	**levante**	**levantara** *or* **levantase**
(tú)	**levantes**	**levantaras** *or* **levantases**
(él/ella/usted)	**levante**	**levantara** *or* **levantase**
(nosotros/as)	**levantemos**	**levantáramos** *or* **levantásemos**
(vosotros/as)	**levantéis**	**levantarais** *or* **levantaseis**
(ellos/ellas/ ustedes)	**levanten**	**levantaran** *or* **levantasen**

IMPERATIVE

levanta / levantad

Use the present subjunctive in all cases other than these tú and vosotros affirmative forms.

EXAMPLE PHRASES

La noticia le **levantará** el ánimo. This news will raise her spirits.

Si pudiera **me levantaría** siempre tarde. I'd sleep in every day, if I could.

No me **levantes** la voz. Don't raise your voice to me.

Levanta la tapa. Lift the lid.

Levanten la mano si tienen alguna duda. Raise your hands if you are unclear about anything.

Remember that subject pronouns are not used very often in Spanish.

llover (to rain)

PRESENT
llueve

PRESENT PERFECT
ha llovido

PRETERITE
llovió

IMPERFECT
llovía

GERUND
lloviendo

PAST PARTICIPLE
llovido

EXAMPLE PHRASES

Hace semanas que no **llueve**. It hasn't rained in weeks.
Está lloviendo. It's raining.
Le **llovieron** las ofertas. He received a lot of offers.
Llovió sin parar. It rained nonstop.
Llovía a cántaros. It was pouring rain.

Remember that subject pronouns are not used very often in Spanish.

llover

FUTURE

llroverá

CONDITIONAL

llovería

PRESENT SUBJUNCTIVE

llueva

IMPERFECT SUBJUNCTIVE

lloviera *or* lloviese

IMPERATIVE

not used

EXAMPLE PHRASES

Sabía que le **lloverían** las críticas. She knew she would come in for a lot of criticism.

Espero que no **llueva** este fin de semana. I hope it won't rain this weekend.

Si no **lloviera**, podríamos salir a dar una vuelta. We could go for a walk if it didn't rain.

Remember that subject pronouns are not used very often in Spanish.

lucir (to look; to shine; to show off)

	PRESENT	PRESENT PERFECT
(yo)	**luzco**	**he lucido**
(tú)	**luces**	**has lucido**
(él/ella/usted)	**luce**	**ha lucido**
(nosotros/as)	**lucimos**	**hemos lucido**
(vosotros/as)	**lucís**	**habéis lucido**
(ellos/ellas/ ustedes)	**lucen**	**han lucido**

	PRETERITE	IMPERFECT
(yo)	**lucí**	**lucía**
(tú)	**luciste**	**lucías**
(él/ella/usted)	**lució**	**lucía**
(nosotros/as)	**lucimos**	**lucíamos**
(vosotros/as)	**lucisteis**	**lucíais**
(ellos/ellas/ ustedes)	**lucieron**	**lucían**

GERUND
luciendo

PAST PARTICIPLE
lucido

EXAMPLE PHRASES

Luces muy bien. You look very well.
Quería **lucir** sus conocimientos. He wanted to show off his knowledge.
Te luciste con la comida. You've outdone yourself with the meal.

Remember that subject pronouns are not used very often in Spanish.

lucir

	FUTURE	CONDITIONAL
(yo)	luciré	luciría
(tú)	lucirás	lucirías
(él/ella/usted)	lucirá	luciría
(nosotros/as)	luciremos	luciríamos
(vosotros/as)	luciréis	luciríais
(ellos/ellas/ ustedes)	lucirán	lucirían

	PRESENT SUBJUNCTIVE	IMPERFECT SUBJUNCTIVE
(yo)	luzca	luciera *or* luciese
(tú)	luzcas	lucieras *or* lucieses
(él/ella/usted)	luzca	luciera *or* luciese
(nosotros/as)	luzcamos	luciéramos *or* luciésemos
(vosotros/as)	luzcáis	lucierais *or* lucieseis
(ellos/ellas/ ustedes)	luzcan	lucieran *or* luciesen

IMPERATIVE

luce / lucid

Use the present subjunctive in all cases other than these tú and vosotros affirmative forms.

EXAMPLE PHRASES

Lucirá un traje muy elegante. She will be wearing a very elegant outfit.

Luciría más con otros zapatos. It would look better with a different pair of shoes.

Quiero que esta noche **luzcas** tú el collar. I want you to wear the necklace tonight.

Remember that subject pronouns are not used very often in Spanish.

morir (to die)

	PRESENT	PRESENT PERFECT
(yo)	muero	he muerto
(tú)	mueres	has muerto
(él/ella/usted)	muere	ha muerto
(nosotros/as)	morimos	hemos muerto
(vosotros/as)	morís	habéis muerto
(ellos/ellas/ ustedes)	mueren	han muerto

	PRETERITE	IMPERFECT
(yo)	morí	moría
(tú)	moriste	morías
(él/ella/usted)	murió	moría
(nosotros/as)	morimos	moríamos
(vosotros/as)	moristeis	moríais
(ellos/ellas/ ustedes)	murieron	morían

GERUND
muriendo

PAST PARTICIPLE
muerto

EXAMPLE PHRASES

¡**Me muero** de hambre! I'm starving!

Se está muriendo. She's dying.

Se le **había muerto** el gato. His cat had died.

Se murió el mes pasado. He died last month.

Me moría de ganas de contárselo. I was dying to tell her.

Remember that subject pronouns are not used very often in Spanish.

morir

	FUTURE	CONDITIONAL
(yo)	**moriré**	**moriría**
(tú)	**morirás**	**morirías**
(él/ella/usted)	**morirá**	**moriría**
(nosotros/as)	**moriremos**	**moriríamos**
(vosotros/as)	**moriréis**	**moriríais**
(ellos/ellas/ ustedes)	**morirán**	**morirían**

	PRESENT SUBJUNCTIVE	IMPERFECT SUBJUNCTIVE
(yo)	**muera**	**muriera** *or* **muriese**
(tú)	**mueras**	**murieras** *or* **murieses**
(él/ella/usted)	**muera**	**muriera** *or* **muriese**
(nosotros/as)	**muramos**	**muriéramos** *or* **muriésemos**
(vosotros/as)	**muráis**	**murierais** *or* **murieseis**
(ellos/ellas/ ustedes)	**mueran**	**murieran** *or* **muriesen**

IMPERATIVE

muere / morid

Use the present subjunctive in all cases other than these tú and vosotros affirmative forms.

EXAMPLE PHRASES

Cuando te lo cuente **te morirás** de risa. You'll die laughing when I tell you.

Yo **me moriría** de vergüenza. I'd die of shame.

Cuando **me muera**... When I die...

¡Por favor, no **te mueras**! Please don't die!

Remember that subject pronouns are not used very often in Spanish.

mover (to move)

	PRESENT	PRESENT PERFECT
(yo)	muevo	he movido
(tú)	mueves	has movido
(él/ella/usted)	mueve	ha movido
(nosotros/as)	movemos	hemos movido
(vosotros/as)	movéis	habéis movido
(ellos/ellas/ ustedes)	mueven	han movido

	PRETERITE	IMPERFECT
(yo)	moví	movía
(tú)	moviste	movías
(él/ella/usted)	movió	movía
(nosotros/as)	movimos	movíamos
(vosotros/as)	movisteis	movíais
(ellos/ellas/ ustedes)	movieron	movían

GERUND
moviendo

PAST PARTICIPLE
movido

EXAMPLE PHRASES

El perro no dejaba de **mover** la cola. The dog kept wagging its tail.

Se está moviendo. It's moving.

No **se movieron** de casa. They didn't leave the house.

Antes **se movía** en esos ambientes. He used to move in those circles.

Remember that subject pronouns are not used very often in Spanish.

mover

	FUTURE	CONDITIONAL
(yo)	**moveré**	**movería**
(tú)	**moverás**	**moverías**
(él/ella/usted)	**moverá**	**movería**
(nosotros/as)	**moveremos**	**moveríamos**
(vosotros/as)	**moveréis**	**moveríais**
(ellos/ellas/ ustedes)	**moverán**	**moverían**

	PRESENT SUBJUNCTIVE	IMPERFECT SUBJUNCTIVE
(yo)	**mueva**	**moviera** *or* **moviese**
(tú)	**muevas**	**movieras** *or* **movieses**
(él/ella/usted)	**mueva**	**moviera** *or* **moviese**
(nosotros/as)	**movamos**	**moviéramos** *or* **moviésemos**
(vosotros/as)	**mováis**	**movierais** *or* **movieseis**
(ellos/ellas/ ustedes)	**muevan**	**movieran** *or* **moviesen**

IMPERATIVE

mueve / moved

Use the present subjunctive in all cases other than these tú and vosotros affirmative forms.

EXAMPLE PHRASES

Prométeme que no **te moverás** de aquí. Promise me you won't move from here.

No **te muevas**. Don't move.

Mueve un poco las cajas para que podamos pasar. Move the boxes a bit so that we can get past.

Remember that subject pronouns are not used very often in Spanish.

nacer (to be born)

	PRESENT	PRESENT PERFECT
(yo)	**nazco**	**he nacido**
(tú)	**naces**	**has nacido**
(él/ella/usted)	**nace**	**ha nacido**
(nosotros/as)	**nacemos**	**hemos nacido**
(vosotros/as)	**nacéis**	**habéis nacido**
(ellos/ellas/ ustedes)	**nacen**	**han nacido**

	PRETERITE	IMPERFECT
(yo)	**nací**	**nacía**
(tú)	**naciste**	**nacías**
(él/ella/usted)	**nació**	**nacía**
(nosotros/as)	**nacimos**	**nacíamos**
(vosotros/as)	**nacisteis**	**nacíais**
(ellos/ellas/ ustedes)	**nacieron**	**nacían**

GERUND
naciendo

PAST PARTICIPLE
nacido

EXAMPLE PHRASES

Nacen cuatro niños por minuto. Four children are born every minute.

Nació en 1980. He was born in 1980.

¿Cuándo **naciste**? When were you born?

Tu todavía no **habías nacido**. You hadn't been born yet.

Remember that subject pronouns are not used very often in Spanish.

nacer

	FUTURE	CONDITIONAL
(yo)	**naceré**	**nacería**
(tú)	**nacerás**	**nacerías**
(él/ella/usted)	**nacerá**	**nacería**
(nosotros/as)	**naceremos**	**naceríamos**
(vosotros/as)	**naceréis**	**naceríais**
(ellos/ellas/ ustedes)	**nacerán**	**nacerían**

	PRESENT SUBJUNCTIVE	IMPERFECT SUBJUNCTIVE
(yo)	**nazca**	**naciera** *or* **naciese**
(tú)	**nazcas**	**nacieras** *or* **nacieses**
(él/ella/usted)	**nazca**	**naciera** *or* **naciese**
(nosotros/as)	**nazcamos**	**naciéramos** *or* **naciésemos**
(vosotros/as)	**nazcáis**	**nacierais** *or* **nacieseis**
(ellos/ellas/ ustedes)	**nazcan**	**nacieran** *or* **naciesen**

IMPERATIVE

nace / naced

Use the present subjunctive in all cases other than these tú and vosotros affirmative forms.

EXAMPLE PHRASES

Nacerá el año que viene. It will be born next year.

Queremos que **nazca** en México. We want it to be born in Mexico.

Si **naciera** hoy, sería tauro. He'd be a Taurus if he were born today.

Remember that subject pronouns are not used very often in Spanish.

negar (to deny; to refuse)

	PRESENT	PRESENT PERFECT
(yo)	**niego**	**he negado**
(tú)	**niegas**	**has negado**
(él/ella/usted)	**niega**	**ha negado**
(nosotros/as)	**negamos**	**hemos negado**
(vosotros/as)	**negáis**	**habéis negado**
(ellos/ellas/ ustedes)	**niegan**	**han negado**

	PRETERITE	IMPERFECT
(yo)	**negué**	**negaba**
(tú)	**negaste**	**negabas**
(él/ella/usted)	**negó**	**negaba**
(nosotros/as)	**negamos**	**negábamos**
(vosotros/as)	**negasteis**	**negabais**
(ellos/ellas/ ustedes)	**negaron**	**negaban**

GERUND
negando

PAST PARTICIPLE
negado

EXAMPLE PHRASES

No lo puedes **negar**. You can't deny it.

Me niego a creerlo. I refuse to believe it.

Se negó a venir con nosotros. She refused to come with us.

Decían que era el ladrón, pero él lo **negaba**. They said that he was the thief, but he denied it.

Remember that subject pronouns are not used very often in Spanish.

negar

	FUTURE	CONDITIONAL
(yo)	**negaré**	**negaría**
(tú)	**negarás**	**negarías**
(él/ella/usted)	**negará**	**negaría**
(nosotros/as)	**negaremos**	**negaríamos**
(vosotros/as)	**negaréis**	**negaríais**
(ellos/ellas/ ustedes)	**negarán**	**negarían**

	PRESENT SUBJUNCTIVE	IMPERFECT SUBJUNCTIVE
(yo)	**niegue**	**negara** *or* **negase**
(tú)	**niegues**	**negaras** *or* **negases**
(él/ella/usted)	**niegue**	**negara** *or* **negase**
(nosotros/as)	**neguemos**	**negáramos** *or* **negásemos**
(vosotros/as)	**neguéis**	**negarais** *or* **negaseis**
(ellos/ellas/ ustedes)	**nieguen**	**negaran** *or* **negasen**

IMPERATIVE

niega / negad

Use the present subjunctive in all cases other than these tú and vosotros affirmative forms.

EXAMPLE PHRASES

No me **negarás** que es barato. You can't say it's not cheap.

Si lo **negaras**, nadie te creería. If you denied it, nobody would believe you.

No lo **niegues**. Don't deny it.

Remember that subject pronouns are not used very often in Spanish.

oír (to hear; to listen)

	PRESENT	PRESENT PERFECT
(yo)	**oigo**	**he oído**
(tú)	**oyes**	**has oído**
(él/ella/usted)	**oye**	**ha oído**
(nosotros/as)	**oímos**	**hemos oído**
(vosotros/as)	**oís**	**habéis oído**
(ellos/ellas/ ustedes)	**oyen**	**han oído**

	PRETERITE	IMPERFECT
(yo)	**oí**	**oía**
(tú)	**oíste**	**oías**
(él/ella/usted)	**oyó**	**oía**
(nosotros/as)	**oímos**	**oíamos**
(vosotros/as)	**oísteis**	**oíais**
(ellos/ellas/ ustedes)	**oyeron**	**oían**

GERUND
oyendo

PAST PARTICIPLE
oído

EXAMPLE PHRASES

No **oigo** nada. I can't hear anything.

Estábamos oyendo las noticias. We were listening to the news.

¿**Oíste** eso? Did you hear that?

Lo **oí** por casualidad. I heard it by chance.

No **oía** muy bien. He couldn't hear very well.

Remember that subject pronouns are not used very often in Spanish.

oír

	FUTURE	CONDITIONAL
(yo)	**oiré**	**oiría**
(tú)	**oirás**	**oirías**
(él/ella/usted)	**oirá**	**oiría**
(nosotros/as)	**oiremos**	**oiríamos**
(vosotros/as)	**oiréis**	**oiríais**
(ellos/ellas/ ustedes)	**oirán**	**oirían**

	PRESENT SUBJUNCTIVE	IMPERFECT SUBJUNCTIVE
(yo)	**oiga**	**oyera** *or* **oyese**
(tú)	**oigas**	**oyeras** *or* **oyeses**
(él/ella/usted)	**oiga**	**oyera** *or* **oyese**
(nosotros/as)	**oigamos**	**oyéramos** *or* **oyésemos**
(vosotros/as)	**oigáis**	**oyerais** *or* **oyeseis**
(ellos/ellas/ ustedes)	**oigan**	**oyeran** *or* **oyesen**

IMPERATIVE

oye / oíd

Use the present subjunctive in all cases other than these tú and vosotros affirmative forms.

EXAMPLE PHRASES

Oye, ¿tú qué te crees? Listen, who do you think you are?

Oigan bien. Listen carefully.

Remember that subject pronouns are not used very often in Spanish.

oler (to smell)

	PRESENT	PRESENT PERFECT
(yo)	**huelo**	**he olido**
(tú)	**hueles**	**has olido**
(él/ella/usted)	**huele**	**ha olido**
(nosotros/as)	**olemos**	**hemos olido**
(vosotros/as)	**oléis**	**habéis olido**
(ellos/ellas/ ustedes)	**huelen**	**han olido**

	PRETERITE	IMPERFECT
(yo)	**olí**	**olía**
(tú)	**oliste**	**olías**
(él/ella/usted)	**olió**	**olía**
(nosotros/as)	**olimos**	**olíamos**
(vosotros/as)	**olisteis**	**olíais**
(ellos/ellas/ ustedes)	**olieron**	**olían**

GERUND
oliendo

PAST PARTICIPLE
olido

EXAMPLE PHRASES

Huele a pescado. It smells of fish.

El perro **estaba oliendo** la basura. The dog was sniffing the trash.

A mí el asunto me **olió** mal. I thought there was something fishy about it.

Olía muy bien. It smelled really nice.

Remember that subject pronouns are not used very often in Spanish.

oler

	FUTURE	CONDITIONAL
(yo)	**oleré**	**olería**
(tú)	**olerás**	**olerías**
(él/ella/usted)	**olerá**	**olería**
(nosotros/as)	**oleremos**	**oleríamos**
(vosotros/as)	**oleréis**	**oleríais**
(ellos/ellas/ ustedes)	**olerán**	**olerían**

	PRESENT SUBJUNCTIVE	IMPERFECT SUBJUNCTIVE
(yo)	**huela**	**oliera** *or* **oliese**
(tú)	**huelas**	**olieras** *or* **olieses**
(él/ella/usted)	**huela**	**oliera** *or* **oliese**
(nosotros/as)	**olamos**	**oliéramos** *or* **oliésemos**
(vosotros/as)	**oláis**	**olierais** *or* **olieseis**
(ellos/ellas/ ustedes)	**huelan**	**olieran** *or* **oliesen**

IMPERATIVE

huele / oled

Use the present subjunctive in all cases other than these tú and vosotros affirmative forms.

EXAMPLE PHRASES

Con esto ya no **olerá**. This will take the smell away.

Si estuviera fresco, no **olería** así. If it were fresh, it wouldn't smell like that.

Remember that subject pronouns are not used very often in Spanish.

pagar (to pay; to pay for)

	PRESENT	PRESENT PERFECT
(yo)	**pago**	he pagado
(tú)	**pagas**	has pagado
(él/ella/usted)	**paga**	ha pagado
(nosotros/as)	**pagamos**	hemos pagado
(vosotros/as)	**pagáis**	habéis pagado
(ellos/ellas/ ustedes)	**pagan**	han pagado

	PRETERITE	IMPERFECT
(yo)	**pagué**	pagaba
(tú)	**pagaste**	pagabas
(él/ella/usted)	**pagó**	pagaba
(nosotros/as)	**pagamos**	pagábamos
(vosotros/as)	**pagasteis**	pagabais
(ellos/ellas/ ustedes)	**pagaron**	pagaban

GERUND
pagando

PAST PARTICIPLE
pagado

EXAMPLE PHRASES

Se puede **pagar** con tarjeta de crédito. You can pay by credit card.
¿Cuánto te **pagan** al mes? How much do they pay you a month?
Lo **pagué** en efectivo. I paid for it in cash.
Me **pagaban** muy poco. I got paid very little.

Remember that subject pronouns are not used very often in Spanish.

pagar

	FUTURE	CONDITIONAL
(yo)	**pagaré**	**pagaría**
(tú)	**pagarás**	**pagarías**
(él/ella/usted)	**pagará**	**pagaría**
(nosotros/as)	**pagaremos**	**pagaríamos**
(vosotros/as)	**pagaréis**	**pagaríais**
(ellos/ellas/ ustedes)	**pagarán**	**pagarían**

	PRESENT SUBJUNCTIVE	IMPERFECT SUBJUNCTIVE
(yo)	**pague**	**pagara** *or* **pagase**
(tú)	**pagues**	**pagaras** *or* **pagases**
(él/ella/usted)	**pague**	**pagara** *or* **pagase**
(nosotros/as)	**paguemos**	**pagáramos** *or* **pagásemos**
(vosotros/as)	**paguéis**	**pagarais** *or* **pagaseis**
(ellos/ellas/ ustedes)	**paguen**	**pagaran** *or* **pagasen**

IMPERATIVE

paga / pagad

Use the present subjunctive in all cases other than these tú and vosotros affirmative forms.

EXAMPLE PHRASES

Yo te **pagaré** la entrada. I'll pay for your ticket.

¡Quiero que **pague** por lo que me ha hecho! I want him to pay for what he's done to me!

Si **pagara** sus deudas, se quedaría sin nada. He'd be left with nothing if he paid his debts.

No les **pagues** hasta que lo hayan hecho. Don't pay them until they've done it.

Págame lo que me debes. Pay me what you owe me.

Remember that subject pronouns are not used very often in Spanish.

partir (to cut; to leave)

	PRESENT	PRESENT PERFECT
(yo)	**parto**	**he partido**
(tú)	**partes**	**has partido**
(él/ella/usted)	**parte**	**ha partido**
(nosotros/as)	**partimos**	**hemos partido**
(vosotros/as)	**partís**	**habéis partido**
(ellos/ellas/ ustedes)	**parten**	**han partido**

	PRETERITE	IMPERFECT
(yo)	**partí**	**partía**
(tú)	**partiste**	**partías**
(él/ella/usted)	**partió**	**partía**
(nosotros/as)	**partimos**	**partíamos**
(vosotros/as)	**partisteis**	**partíais**
(ellos/ellas/ ustedes)	**partieron**	**partían**

GERUND
partiendo

PAST PARTICIPLE
partido

EXAMPLE PHRASES

¿Te **parto** un trozo de queso? Shall I cut you a piece of cheese?

Partiendo de la base de que... Assuming that...

El remo **se partió** en dos. The oar broke in two.

Remember that subject pronouns are not used very often in Spanish.

partir

	FUTURE	CONDITIONAL
(yo)	**partiré**	**partiría**
(tú)	**partirás**	**partirías**
(él/ella/usted)	**partirá**	**partiría**
(nosotros/as)	**partiremos**	**partiríamos**
(vosotros/as)	**partiréis**	**partiríais**
(ellos/ellas/ ustedes)	**partirán**	**partirían**

	PRESENT SUBJUNCTIVE	IMPERFECT SUBJUNCTIVE
(yo)	**parta**	**partiera** *or* **partiese**
(tú)	**partas**	**partieras** *or* **partieses**
(él/ella/usted)	**parta**	**partiera** *or* **partiese**
(nosotros/as)	**partamos**	**partiéramos** *or* **partiésemos**
(vosotros/as)	**partáis**	**partierais** *or* **partieseis**
(ellos/ellas/ ustedes)	**partan**	**partieran** *or* **partiesen**

IMPERATIVE

parte / partid

Use the present subjunctive in all cases other than these tú and vosotros affirmative forms.

EXAMPLE PHRASES

La expedición **partirá** mañana de París. The expedition will leave from Paris tomorrow.

Eso le **partiría** el corazón. That would break his heart.

Pártelo por la mitad. Cut it in half.

Remember that subject pronouns are not used very often in Spanish.

pedir (to ask for; to ask)

	PRESENT	PRESENT PERFECT
(yo)	pido	he pedido
(tú)	pides	has pedido
(él/ella/usted)	pide	ha pedido
(nosotros/as)	pedimos	hemos pedido
(vosotros/as)	pedís	habéis pedido
(ellos/ellas/ ustedes)	piden	han pedido

	PRETERITE	IMPERFECT
(yo)	pedí	pedía
(tú)	pediste	pedías
(él/ella/usted)	pidió	pedía
(nosotros/as)	pedimos	pedíamos
(vosotros/as)	pedisteis	pedíais
(ellos/ellas/ ustedes)	pidieron	pedían

GERUND
pidiendo

PAST PARTICIPLE
pedido

EXAMPLE PHRASES

¿Cuánto **pide** por el carro? How much is he asking for the car?

La casa **está pidiendo** a gritos una mano de pintura. The house is crying out to be painted.

Pedimos dos cervezas. We ordered two beers.

No nos **pidieron** el pasaporte. They didn't ask us for our passports.

Pedían dos millones de rescate. They were demanding two million in ransom.

Remember that subject pronouns are not used very often in Spanish.

pedir

	FUTURE	CONDITIONAL
(yo)	**pediré**	**pediría**
(tú)	**pedirás**	**pedirías**
(él/ella/usted)	**pedirá**	**pediría**
(nosotros/as)	**pediremos**	**pediríamos**
(vosotros/as)	**pediréis**	**pediríais**
(ellos/ellas/ ustedes)	**pedirán**	**pedirían**

	PRESENT SUBJUNCTIVE	IMPERFECT SUBJUNCTIVE
(yo)	**pida**	**pidiera** *or* **pidiese**
(tú)	**pidas**	**pidieras** *or* **pidieses**
(él/ella/usted)	**pida**	**pidiera** *or* **pidiese**
(nosotros/as)	**pidamos**	**pidiéramos** *or* **pidiésemos**
(vosotros/as)	**pidáis**	**pidierais** *or* **pidieseis**
(ellos/ellas/ ustedes)	**pidan**	**pidieran** *or* **pidiesen**

IMPERATIVE

pide / pedid

Use the present subjunctive in all cases other than these tú and vosotros affirmative forms.

EXAMPLE PHRASES

Si se entera, te **pedirá** explicaciones. If he finds out, he'll ask you for an explanation.

Nunca te **pediría** que hicieras una cosa así. I'd never ask you to do anything like that.

Y que sea lo último que me **pidas**. And don't ask me for anything else.

Pídele el teléfono. Ask her for her phone number.

Remember that subject pronouns are not used very often in Spanish.

pensar (to think)

	PRESENT	PRESENT PERFECT
(yo)	**pienso**	**he pensado**
(tú)	**piensas**	**has pensado**
(él/ella/usted)	**piensa**	**ha pensado**
(nosotros/as)	**pensamos**	**hemos pensado**
(vosotros/as)	**pensáis**	**habéis pensado**
(ellos/ellas/ ustedes)	**piensan**	**han pensado**

	PRETERITE	IMPERFECT
(yo)	**pensé**	**pensaba**
(tú)	**pensaste**	**pensabas**
(él/ella/usted)	**pensó**	**pensaba**
(nosotros/as)	**pensamos**	**pensábamos**
(vosotros/as)	**pensasteis**	**pensabais**
(ellos/ellas/ ustedes)	**pensaron**	**pensaban**

GERUND
pensando

PAST PARTICIPLE
pensado

EXAMPLE PHRASES

¿**Piensas** que vale la pena? Do you think it's worth it?
¿Qué **piensas** del aborto? What do you think about abortion?
Está pensando en comprarse una casa. He's thinking about buying a house.
¿Lo **pensaste** bien? Have you thought about it carefully?
Pensaba que vendrías. I thought you'd come.

Remember that subject pronouns are not used very often in Spanish.

pensar

	FUTURE	CONDITIONAL
(yo)	**pensaré**	**pensaría**
(tú)	**pensarás**	**pensarías**
(él/ella/usted)	**pensará**	**pensaría**
(nosotros/as)	**pensaremos**	**pensaríamos**
(vosotros/as)	**pensaréis**	**pensaríais**
(ellos/ellas/ ustedes)	**pensarán**	**pensarían**

	PRESENT SUBJUNCTIVE	IMPERFECT SUBJUNCTIVE
(yo)	**piense**	**pensara** *or* **pensase**
(tú)	**pienses**	**pensaras** *or* **pensases**
(él/ella/usted)	**piense**	**pensara** *or* **pensase**
(nosotros/as)	**pensemos**	**pensáramos** *or* **pensásemos**
(vosotros/as)	**penséis**	**pensarais** *or* **pensaseis**
(ellos/ellas/ ustedes)	**piensen**	**pensaran** *or* **pensasen**

IMPERATIVE

piensa / pensad

Use the present subjunctive in all cases other than these tú and vosotros affirmative forms.

EXAMPLE PHRASES

Yo no me lo **pensaría** dos veces. I wouldn't think twice.

Me da igual lo que **piensen**. I don't care what they think.

Si **pensara** eso, te lo diría. If I thought that, I'd tell you.

No **pienses** que no quiero ir. Don't think that I don't want to go.

No lo **pienses** más. Don't give it another thought.

Remember that subject pronouns are not used very often in Spanish.

perder (to lose)

	PRESENT	PRESENT PERFECT
(yo)	pierdo	he perdido
(tú)	pierdes	has perdido
(él/ella/usted)	pierde	ha perdido
(nosotros/as)	perdemos	hemos perdido
(vosotros/as)	perdéis	habéis perdido
(ellos/ellas/ ustedes)	pierden	han perdido

	PRETERITE	IMPERFECT
(yo)	perdí	perdía
(tú)	perdiste	perdías
(él/ella/usted)	perdió	perdía
(nosotros/as)	perdimos	perdíamos
(vosotros/as)	perdisteis	perdíais
(ellos/ellas/ ustedes)	perdieron	perdían

GERUND
perdiendo

PAST PARTICIPLE
perdido

EXAMPLE PHRASES

Siempre **pierde** las llaves. He's always losing his keys.

Ana es la que saldrá **perdiendo**. Ana is the one who will lose out.

Había perdido dos kilos. He'd lost two kilos.

Perdimos dos a cero. We lost two-nothing.

Perdían siempre. They always used to lose.

Remember that subject pronouns are not used very often in Spanish.

perder

	FUTURE	CONDITIONAL
(yo)	**perderé**	**perdería**
(tú)	**perderás**	**perderías**
(él/ella/usted)	**perderá**	**perdería**
(nosotros/as)	**perderemos**	**perderíamos**
(vosotros/as)	**perderéis**	**perderíais**
(ellos/ellas/ ustedes)	**perderán**	**perderían**

	PRESENT SUBJUNCTIVE	IMPERFECT SUBJUNCTIVE
(yo)	**pierda**	**perdiera** *or* **perdiese**
(tú)	**pierdas**	**perdieras** *or* **perdieses**
(él/ella/usted)	**pierda**	**perdiera** *or* **perdiese**
(nosotros/as)	**perdamos**	**perdiéramos** *or* **perdiésemos**
(vosotros/as)	**perdáis**	**perdierais** *or* **perdieseis**
(ellos/ellas/ ustedes)	**pierdan**	**perdieran** *or* **perdiesen**

IMPERATIVE

pierde / perded

Use the present subjunctive in all cases other than these tú and vosotros affirmative forms.

EXAMPLE PHRASES

Apúrate o **perderás** el tren. Hurry up or you'll miss the train.

¡No **te** lo **pierdas**! Don't miss it!

No **pierdas** esta oportunidad. Don't miss this opportunity.

Remember that subject pronouns are not used very often in Spanish.

poder (to be able to)

	PRESENT	PRESENT PERFECT
(yo)	**puedo**	**he podido**
(tú)	**puedes**	**has podido**
(él/ella/usted)	**puede**	**ha podido**
(nosotros/as)	**podemos**	**hemos podido**
(vosotros/as)	**podéis**	**habéis podido**
(ellos/ellas/ ustedes)	**pueden**	**han podido**

	PRETERITE	IMPERFECT
(yo)	**pude**	**podía**
(tú)	**pudiste**	**podías**
(él/ella/usted)	**pudo**	**podía**
(nosotros/as)	**pudimos**	**podíamos**
(vosotros/as)	**pudisteis**	**podíais**
(ellos/ellas/ ustedes)	**pudieron**	**podían**

GERUND
pudiendo

PAST PARTICIPLE
podido

EXAMPLE PHRASES

¿**Puedo** entrar? Can I come in?

Puede que llegue mañana. He may arrive tomorrow.

No **pude** venir antes. I couldn't come before.

Pudiste haberte lastimado. You could have hurt yourself.

¡Me lo **podías** haber dicho! You could have told me!

Remember that subject pronouns are not used very often in Spanish.

poder

	FUTURE	CONDITIONAL
(yo)	**podré**	**podría**
(tú)	**podrás**	**podrías**
(él/ella/usted)	**podrá**	**podría**
(nosotros/as)	**podremos**	**podríamos**
(vosotros/as)	**podréis**	**podríais**
(ellos/ellas/ ustedes)	**podrán**	**podrían**

	PRESENT SUBJUNCTIVE	IMPERFECT SUBJUNCTIVE
(yo)	**pueda**	**pudiera** *or* **pudiese**
(tú)	**puedas**	**pudieras** *or* **pudieses**
(él/ella/usted)	**pueda**	**pudiera** *or* **pudiese**
(nosotros/as)	**podamos**	**pudiéramos** *or* **pudiésemos**
(vosotros/as)	**podáis**	**pudierais** *or* **pudieseis**
(ellos/ellas/ ustedes)	**puedan**	**pudieran** *or* **pudiesen**

IMPERATIVE

puede / poded

Use the present subjunctive in all cases other than these tú and vosotros affirmative forms.

EXAMPLE PHRASES

Estoy segura de que **podrá** conseguirlo. I'm sure he'll succeed.

¿**Podrías** ayudarme? Could you help me?

Ven en cuanto **puedas**. Come as soon as you can.

Me fui para que **pudieran** hablar. I left so they could talk.

Remember that subject pronouns are not used very often in Spanish.

poner (to put)

	PRESENT	PRESENT PERFECT
(yo)	**pongo**	**he puesto**
(tú)	**pones**	**has puesto**
(él/ella/usted)	**pone**	**ha puesto**
(nosotros/as)	**ponemos**	**hemos puesto**
(vosotros/as)	**ponéis**	**habéis puesto**
(ellos/ellas/ ustedes)	**ponen**	**han puesto**

	PRETERITE	IMPERFECT
(yo)	**puse**	**ponía**
(tú)	**pusiste**	**ponías**
(él/ella/usted)	**puso**	**ponía**
(nosotros/as)	**pusimos**	**poníamos**
(vosotros/as)	**pusisteis**	**poníais**
(ellos/ellas/ ustedes)	**pusieron**	**ponían**

GERUND
poniendo

PAST PARTICIPLE
puesto

EXAMPLE PHRASES

¿Dónde **pongo** mis cosas? Where shall I put my things?
¿Le **pusiste** azúcar a mi café? Did you put sugar in my coffee?
Todos **nos pusimos** de acuerdo. We all agreed.

Remember that subject pronouns are not used very often in Spanish.

poner

	FUTURE	CONDITIONAL
(yo)	**pondré**	**pondría**
(tú)	**pondrás**	**pondrías**
(él/ella/usted)	**pondrá**	**pondría**
(nosotros/as)	**pondremos**	**pondríamos**
(vosotros/as)	**pondréis**	**pondríais**
(ellos/ellas/ ustedes)	**pondrán**	**pondrían**

	PRESENT SUBJUNCTIVE	IMPERFECT SUBJUNCTIVE
(yo)	**ponga**	**pusiera** *or* **pusiese**
(tú)	**pongas**	**pusieras** *or* **pusieses**
(él/ella/usted)	**ponga**	**pusiera** *or* **pusiese**
(nosotros/as)	**pongamos**	**pusiéramos** *or* **pusiésemos**
(vosotros/as)	**pongáis**	**pusierais** *or* **pusieseis**
(ellos/ellas/ ustedes)	**pongan**	**pusieran** *or* **pusiesen**

IMPERATIVE

pon / poned

Use the present subjunctive in all cases other than these tú and vosotros affirmative forms.

EXAMPLE PHRASES

Lo **pondré** aquí. I'll put it here.

¿Le **pondrías** más sal? Would you add more salt?

Ponlo ahí. Put it over there.

Remember that subject pronouns are not used very often in Spanish.

prohibir (to ban; to prohibit)

	PRESENT	PRESENT PERFECT
(yo)	**prohíbo**	**he prohibido**
(tú)	**prohíbes**	**has prohibido**
(él/ella/usted)	**prohíbe**	**ha prohibido**
(nosotros/as)	**prohibimos**	**hemos prohibido**
(vosotros/as)	**prohibís**	**habéis prohibido**
(ellos/ellas/ ustedes)	**prohíben**	**han prohibido**

	PRETERITE	IMPERFECT
(yo)	**prohibí**	**prohibía**
(tú)	**prohibiste**	**prohibías**
(él/ella/usted)	**prohibió**	**prohibía**
(nosotros/as)	**prohibimos**	**prohibíamos**
(vosotros/as)	**prohibisteis**	**prohibíais**
(ellos/ellas/ ustedes)	**prohibieron**	**prohibían**

GERUND
prohibiendo

PAST PARTICIPLE
prohibido

EXAMPLE PHRASES

Deberían **prohibirlo**. It should be banned.

Te **prohíbo** que me hables así. I won't have you talking to me like that!

Le **prohibieron** la entrada. She was not allowed in.

El tratado **prohibía** el uso de armas químicas. The treaty prohibited the use of chemical weapons.

Remember that subject pronouns are not used very often in Spanish.

prohibir

	FUTURE	CONDITIONAL
(yo)	**prohibiré**	**prohibiría**
(tú)	**prohibirás**	**prohibirías**
(él/ella/usted)	**prohibirá**	**prohibiría**
(nosotros/as)	**prohibiremos**	**prohibiríamos**
(vosotros/as)	**prohibiréis**	**prohibiríais**
(ellos/ellas/ ustedes)	**prohibirán**	**prohibirían**

	PRESENT SUBJUNCTIVE	IMPERFECT SUBJUNCTIVE
(yo)	**prohíba**	**prohibiera** *or* **prohibiese**
(tú)	**prohíbas**	**prohibieras** *or* **prohibieses**
(él/ella/usted)	**prohíba**	**prohibiera** *or* **prohibiese**
(nosotros/as)	**prohibamos**	**prohibiéramos** *or* **prohibiésemos**
(vosotros/as)	**prohibáis**	**prohibierais** *or* **prohibieseis**
(ellos/ellas/ ustedes)	**prohíban**	**prohibieran** *or* **prohibiesen**

IMPERATIVE

prohíbe / prohibid

Use the present subjunctive in all cases other than these tú and vosotros affirmative forms.

EXAMPLE PHRASES

Tarde o temprano lo **prohibirán**. Sooner or later they'll ban it.

Yo esa música la **prohibiría**. If it were up to me, that music would be banned.

"**prohibido** fumar" "no smoking"

Remember that subject pronouns are not used very often in Spanish.

querer (to want; to love)

	PRESENT	PRESENT PERFECT
(yo)	quiero	he querido
(tú)	quieres	has querido
(él/ella/usted)	quiere	ha querido
(nosotros/as)	queremos	hemos querido
(vosotros/as)	queréis	habéis querido
(ellos/ellas/ ustedes)	quieren	han querido

	PRETERITE	IMPERFECT
(yo)	quise	quería
(tú)	quisiste	querías
(él/ella/usted)	quiso	quería
(nosotros/as)	quisimos	queríamos
(vosotros/as)	quisisteis	queríais
(ellos/ellas/ ustedes)	quisieron	querían

GERUND
queriendo

PAST PARTICIPLE
querido

EXAMPLE PHRASES

Lo hice sin **querer.** I didn't mean to do it.
Te **quiero**. I love you.
Quiero que vayas. I want you to go.
No **quería** decírmelo. She didn't want to tell me.

Remember that subject pronouns are not used very often in Spanish.

querer

	FUTURE	CONDITIONAL
(yo)	**querré**	**querría**
(tú)	**querrás**	**querrías**
(él/ella/usted)	**querrá**	**querría**
(nosotros/as)	**querremos**	**querríamos**
(vosotros/as)	**querréis**	**querríais**
(ellos/ellas/ ustedes)	**querrán**	**querrían**

	PRESENT SUBJUNCTIVE	IMPERFECT SUBJUNCTIVE
(yo)	**quiera**	**quisiera** *or* **quisiese**
(tú)	**quieras**	**quisieras** *or* **quisieses**
(él/ella/usted)	**quiera**	**quisiera** *or* **quisiese**
(nosotros/as)	**queramos**	**quisiéramos** *or* **quisiésemos**
(vosotros/as)	**queráis**	**quisierais** *or* **quisieseis**
(ellos/ellas/ ustedes)	**quieran**	**quisieran** *or* **quisiesen**

IMPERATIVE

quiere / quered

Use the present subjunctive in all cases other than these tú and vosotros affirmative forms.

EXAMPLE PHRASES

Siempre la **querré**. I will always love her.

Querría que no hubiera pasado nunca. I wish it had never happened.

¡Por lo que más **quieras**, cállate! For goodness sake, shut up!

Quisiera preguntar una cosa. I'd like to ask something.

Remember that subject pronouns are not used very often in Spanish.

reducir (to reduce)

	PRESENT	PRESENT PERFECT
(yo)	**reduzco**	**he reducido**
(tú)	**reduces**	**has reducido**
(él/ella/usted)	**reduce**	**ha reducido**
(nosotros/as)	**reducimos**	**hemos reducido**
(vosotros/as)	**reducís**	**habéis reducido**
(ellos/ellas/ ustedes)	**reducen**	**han reducido**

	PRETERITE	IMPERFECT
(yo)	**reduje**	**reducía**
(tú)	**redujiste**	**reducías**
(él/ella/usted)	**redujo**	**reducía**
(nosotros/as)	**redujimos**	**reducíamos**
(vosotros/as)	**redujisteis**	**reducíais**
(ellos/ellas/ ustedes)	**redujeron**	**reducían**

GERUND
reduciendo

PAST PARTICIPLE
reducido

EXAMPLE PHRASES

Al final todo **se reduce** a eso. In the end it all comes down to that.

Se había reducido la tasa de natalidad. The birth rate had fallen.

Sus gastos **se redujeron** a la mitad. Their expenses were cut by half.

Remember that subject pronouns are not used very often in Spanish.

reducir

	FUTURE	CONDITIONAL
(yo)	**reduciré**	**reduciría**
(tú)	**reducirás**	**reducirías**
(él/ella/usted)	**reducirá**	**reduciría**
(nosotros/as)	**reduciremos**	**reduciríamos**
(vosotros/as)	**reduciréis**	**reduciríais**
(ellos/ellas/ ustedes)	**reducirán**	**reducirían**

	PRESENT SUBJUNCTIVE	IMPERFECT SUBJUNCTIVE
(yo)	**reduzca**	**redujera** *or* **redujese**
(tú)	**reduzcas**	**redujeras** *or* **redujeses**
(él/ella/usted)	**reduzca**	**redujera** *or* **redujese**
(nosotros/as)	**reduzcamos**	**redujéramos** *or* **redujésemos**
(vosotros/as)	**reduzcáis**	**redujerais** *or* **redujeseis**
(ellos/ellas/ ustedes)	**reduzcan**	**redujeran** *or* **redujesen**

IMPERATIVE

reduce / reducid

Use the present subjunctive in all cases other than these tú and vosotros affirmative forms.

EXAMPLE PHRASES

Reducirán la producción en un 20%. They'll cut production by 20%.

Reduzca la velocidad. Reduce speed.

Remember that subject pronouns are not used very often in Spanish.

rehusar (to refuse)

	PRESENT	PRESENT PERFECT
(yo)	rehúso	he rehusado
(tú)	rehúsas	has rehusado
(él/ella/usted)	rehúsa	ha rehusado
(nosotros/as)	rehusamos	hemos rehusado
(vosotros/as)	rehusáis	habéis rehusado
(ellos/ellas/ustedes)	rehúsan	han rehusado

	PRETERITE	IMPERFECT
(yo)	rehusé	rehusaba
(tú)	rehusaste	rehusabas
(él/ella/usted)	rehusó	rehusaba
(nosotros/as)	rehusamos	rehusábamos
(vosotros/as)	rehusasteis	rehusabais
(ellos/ellas/ustedes)	rehusaron	rehusaban

GERUND
rehusando

PAST PARTICIPLE
rehusado

EXAMPLE PHRASES

Rehúso tomar parte en esto. I refuse to take part in this.
Había rehusado varias ofertas de trabajo. He had declined several job offers.
Su familia **rehusó** hacer declaraciones. His family refused to comment.

Remember that subject pronouns are not used very often in Spanish.

rehusar

	FUTURE	CONDITIONAL
(yo)	rehusaré	rehusaría
(tú)	rehusarás	rehusarías
(él/ella/usted)	rehusará	rehusaría
(nosotros/as)	rehusaremos	rehusaríamos
(vosotros/as)	rehusaréis	rehusaríais
(ellos/ellas/ ustedes)	rehusarán	rehusarían

	PRESENT SUBJUNCTIVE	IMPERFECT SUBJUNCTIVE
(yo)	rehúse	rehusara *or* rehusase
(tú)	rehúses	rehusaras *or* rehusases
(él/ella/usted)	rehúse	rehusara *or* rehusase
(nosotros/as)	rehusemos	rehusáramos *or* rehusásemos
(vosotros/as)	rehuséis	rehusarais *or* rehusaseis
(ellos/ellas/ ustedes)	rehúsen	rehusaran *or* rehusasen

IMPERATIVE

rehúsa / rehusad

Use the present subjunctive in all cases other than these tú and vosotros affirmative forms.

Remember that subject pronouns are not used very often in Spanish.

reír (to laugh)

	PRESENT	PRESENT PERFECT
(yo)	**río**	**he reído**
(tú)	**ríes**	**has reído**
(él/ella/usted)	**ríe**	**ha reído**
(nosotros/as)	**reímos**	**hemos reído**
(vosotros/as)	**reís**	**habéis reído**
(ellos/ellas/ ustedes)	**ríen**	**han reído**

	PRETERITE	IMPERFECT
(yo)	**reí**	**reía**
(tú)	**reíste**	**reías**
(él/ella/usted)	**rio**	**reía**
(nosotros/as)	**reímos**	**reíamos**
(vosotros/as)	**reísteis**	**reíais**
(ellos/ellas/ ustedes)	**rieron**	**reían**

GERUND
riendo

PAST PARTICIPLE
reído

EXAMPLE PHRASES

Se echó a **reír**. She burst out laughing.

Se ríe de todo. She doesn't take anything seriously.

¿De qué **te ríes**? What are you laughing at?

Siempre **están riéndose** en clase. They're always laughing in class.

Me reía mucho con él. I always had a good laugh with him.

Remember that subject pronouns are not used very often in Spanish.

reír

	FUTURE	CONDITIONAL
(yo)	**reiré**	**reiría**
(tú)	**reirás**	**reirías**
(él/ella/usted)	**reirá**	**reiría**
(nosotros/as)	**reiremos**	**reiríamos**
(vosotros/as)	**reiréis**	**reiríais**
(ellos/ellas/ ustedes)	**reirán**	**reirían**

	PRESENT SUBJUNCTIVE	IMPERFECT SUBJUNCTIVE
(yo)	**ría**	**riera** *or* **riese**
(tú)	**rías**	**rieras** *or* **rieses**
(él/ella/usted)	**ría**	**riera** *or* **riese**
(nosotros/as)	**riamos**	**riéramos** *or* **riésemos**
(vosotros/as)	**riais**	**rierais** *or* **rieseis**
(ellos/ellas/ ustedes)	**rían**	**rieran** *or* **riesen**

IMPERATIVE

ríe / reíd

Use the present subjunctive in all cases other than these tú and vosotros affirmative forms.

EXAMPLE PHRASES

Te reirás cuando te lo cuente. You'll laugh when I tell you about it.

Que **se rían** lo que quieran. Let them laugh as much as they want.

No **te rías** de mí. Don't laugh at me.

¡Tú **ríete**, pero pasé muchísimo miedo! You may laugh, but I was really frightened.

Remember that subject pronouns are not used very often in Spanish.

reñir (to quarrel; to argue)

	PRESENT	PRESENT PERFECT
(yo)	riño	he reñido
(tú)	riñes	has reñido
(él/ella/usted)	riñe	ha reñido
(nosotros/as)	reñimos	hemos reñido
(vosotros/as)	reñís	habéis reñido
(ellos/ellas/ ustedes)	riñen	han reñido

	PRETERITE	IMPERFECT
(yo)	reñí	reñía
(tú)	reñiste	reñías
(él/ella/usted)	riñó	reñía
(nosotros/as)	reñimos	reñíamos
(vosotros/as)	reñisteis	reñíais
(ellos/ellas/ ustedes)	riñeron	reñían

GERUND
riñendo

PAST PARTICIPLE
reñido

EXAMPLE PHRASES

Se pasan el día entero **riñendo**. They spend the whole day quarreling.

Reñimos por una tontería. We argued over something stupid.

Remember that subject pronouns are not used very often in Spanish.

reñir

	FUTURE	CONDITIONAL
(yo)	reñiré	reñiría
(tú)	reñirás	reñirías
(él/ella/usted)	reñirá	reñiría
(nosotros/as)	reñiremos	reñiríamos
(vosotros/as)	reñiréis	reñiríais
(ellos/ellas/ ustedes)	reñirán	reñirían

	PRESENT SUBJUNCTIVE	IMPERFECT SUBJUNCTIVE
(yo)	riña	riñera *or* riñese
(tú)	riñas	riñeras *or* riñeses
(él/ella/usted)	riña	riñera *or* riñese
(nosotros/as)	riñamos	riñéramos *or* riñésemos
(vosotros/as)	riñáis	riñerais *or* riñeseis
(ellos/ellas/ ustedes)	riñan	riñeran *or* riñesen

IMPERATIVE

riñe / reñid

Use the present subjunctive in all cases other than these tú and vosotros affirmative forms.

EXAMPLE PHRASES

¡No **riñán** más! Stop fighting!

Remember that subject pronouns are not used very often in Spanish.

repetir (to repeat)

	PRESENT	PRESENT PERFECT
(yo)	**repito**	**he repetido**
(tú)	**repites**	**has repetido**
(él/ella/usted)	**repite**	**ha repetido**
(nosotros/as)	**repetimos**	**hemos repetido**
(vosotros/as)	**repetís**	**habéis repetido**
(ellos/ellas/ ustedes)	**repiten**	**han repetido**

	PRETERITE	IMPERFECT
(yo)	**repetí**	**repetía**
(tú)	**repetiste**	**repetías**
(él/ella/usted)	**repitió**	**repetía**
(nosotros/as)	**repetimos**	**repetíamos**
(vosotros/as)	**repetisteis**	**repetíais**
(ellos/ellas/ ustedes)	**repitieron**	**repetían**

GERUND
repitiendo

PAST PARTICIPLE
repetido

EXAMPLE PHRASES

¿Podría **repetir**lo, por favor? Could you repeat that, please?

Le **repito** que es imposible. I'm telling you again that it is impossible.

Se lo **he repetido** mil veces, pero no escucha. I've told him hundreds of times but he won't listen.

Repetía una y otra vez que era inocente. He kept repeating that he was innocent.

Remember that subject pronouns are not used very often in Spanish.

repetir

	FUTURE	CONDITIONAL
(yo)	repetiré	repetiría
(tú)	repetirás	repetirías
(él/ella/usted)	repetirá	repetiría
(nosotros/as)	repetiremos	repetiríamos
(vosotros/as)	repetiréis	repetiríais
(ellos/ellas/ ustedes)	repetirán	repetirían

	PRESENT SUBJUNCTIVE	IMPERFECT SUBJUNCTIVE
(yo)	repita	repitiera *or* repitiese
(tú)	repitas	repitieras *or* repitieses
(él/ella/usted)	repita	repitiera *or* repitiese
(nosotros/as)	repitamos	repitiéramos *or* repitiésemos
(vosotros/as)	repitáis	repitierais *or* repitieseis
(ellos/ellas/ ustedes)	repitan	repitieran *or* repitiesen

IMPERATIVE

repite / repetid

Use the present subjunctive in all cases other than these tú and vosotros affirmative forms.

EXAMPLE PHRASES

Espero que no se **repita**. I hope this won't happen again.

Repitan el ejercicio. Repeat the exercise.

Remember that subject pronouns are not used very often in Spanish.

resolver (to solve)

	PRESENT	PRESENT PERFECT
(yo)	**resuelvo**	**he resuelto**
(tú)	**resuelves**	**has resuelto**
(él/ella/usted)	**resuelve**	**ha resuelto**
(nosotros/as)	**resolvemos**	**hemos resuelto**
(vosotros/as)	**resolvéis**	**habéis resuelto**
(ellos/ellas/ ustedes)	**resuelven**	**han resuelto**

	PRETERITE	IMPERFECT
(yo)	**resolví**	**resolvía**
(tú)	**resolviste**	**resolvías**
(él/ella/usted)	**resolvió**	**resolvía**
(nosotros/as)	**resolvimos**	**resolvíamos**
(vosotros/as)	**resolvisteis**	**resolvíais**
(ellos/ellas/ ustedes)	**resolvieron**	**resolvían**

GERUND
resolviendo

PAST PARTICIPLE
resuelto

EXAMPLE PHRASES

Trataré de **resolver** tus dudas. I'll try to answer your questions.
Enojarse no **resuelve** nada. Getting angry doesn't help at all.
Resolvimos el problema entre todos. We solved the problem together.

Remember that subject pronouns are not used very often in Spanish.

resolver

	FUTURE	CONDITIONAL
(yo)	**resolveré**	**resolvería**
(tú)	**resolverás**	**resolverías**
(él/ella/usted)	**resolverá**	**resolvería**
(nosotros/as)	**resolveremos**	**resolveríamos**
(vosotros/as)	**resolveréis**	**resolveríais**
(ellos/ellas/ ustedes)	**resolverán**	**resolverían**

	PRESENT SUBJUNCTIVE	IMPERFECT SUBJUNCTIVE
(yo)	**resuelva**	**resolviera** *or* **resolviese**
(tú)	**resuelvas**	**resolvieras** *or* **resolvieses**
(él/ella/usted)	**resuelva**	**resolviera** *or* **resolviese**
(nosotros/as)	**resolvamos**	**resolviéramos** *or* **resolviésemos**
(vosotros/as)	**resolváis**	**resolvierais** *or* **resolvieseis**
(ellos/ellas/ ustedes)	**resuelvan**	**resolvieran** *or* **resolviesen**

IMPERATIVE

resuelve / resolved

Use the present subjunctive in all cases other than these tú and vosotros affirmative forms.

EXAMPLE PHRASES

No te preocupes, ya lo **resolveremos**. Don't worry, we'll sort it out.

Yo lo **resolvería** de otra forma. I'd sort it out another way.

Hasta que no lo **resuelva** no descansaré. I won't rest until I've sorted it out.

Remember that subject pronouns are not used very often in Spanish.

reunir (to put together; to gather)

	PRESENT	PRESENT PERFECT
(yo)	**reúno**	**he reunido**
(tú)	**reúnes**	**has reunido**
(él/ella/usted)	**reúne**	**ha reunido**
(nosotros/as)	**reunimos**	**hemos reunido**
(vosotros/as)	**reunís**	**habéis reunido**
(ellos/ellas/ustedes)	**reúnen**	**han reunido**

	PRETERITE	IMPERFECT
(yo)	**reuní**	**reunía**
(tú)	**reuniste**	**reunías**
(él/ella/usted)	**reunió**	**reunía**
(nosotros/as)	**reunimos**	**reuníamos**
(vosotros/as)	**reunisteis**	**reuníais**
(ellos/ellas/ustedes)	**reunieron**	**reunían**

GERUND
reuniendo

PAST PARTICIPLE
reunido

EXAMPLE PHRASES

Hemos conseguido **reunir** suficiente dinero. We've managed to raise enough money.

Hace tiempo que no **me reúno** con ellos. I haven't seen them in ages.

Reunió a todos para comunicarles la noticia. He called them all together to tell them the news.

No **reunía** los requisitos. She didn't satisfy the requirements.

Remember that subject pronouns are not used very often in Spanish.

reunir

	FUTURE	CONDITIONAL
(yo)	**reuniré**	**reuniría**
(tú)	**reunirás**	**reunirías**
(él/ella/usted)	**reunirá**	**reuniría**
(nosotros/as)	**reuniremos**	**reuniríamos**
(vosotros/as)	**reuniréis**	**reuniríais**
(ellos/ellas/ ustedes)	**reunirán**	**reunirían**

	PRESENT SUBJUNCTIVE	IMPERFECT SUBJUNCTIVE
(yo)	**reúna**	**reuniera** *or* **reuniese**
(tú)	**reúnas**	**reunieras** *or* **reunieses**
(él/ella/usted)	**reúna**	**reuniera** *or* **reuniese**
(nosotros/as)	**reunamos**	**reuniéramos** *or* **reuniésemos**
(vosotros/as)	**reunáis**	**reunierais** *or* **reunieseis**
(ellos/ellas/ ustedes)	**reúnan**	**reunieran** *or* **reuniesen**

IMPERATIVE

reúne / reunid

Use the present subjunctive in all cases other than these tú and vosotros affirmative forms.

EXAMPLE PHRASES

Se reunirán el viernes. They'll meet on Friday.

Necesito encontrar un local que **reúna** las condiciones. I need to find premises that will meet the requirements.

Consiguió que su familia **se reuniera** tras una larga separación. She managed to get her family back together again after a long separation.

Remember that subject pronouns are not used very often in Spanish.

rogar (to beg; to pray)

	PRESENT	PRESENT PERFECT
(yo)	**ruego**	**he rogado**
(tú)	**ruegas**	**has rogado**
(él/ella/usted)	**ruega**	**ha rogado**
(nosotros/as)	**rogamos**	**hemos rogado**
(vosotros/as)	**rogáis**	**habéis rogado**
(ellos/ellas/ ustedes)	**ruegan**	**han rogado**

	PRETERITE	IMPERFECT
(yo)	**rogué**	**rogaba**
(tú)	**rogaste**	**rogabas**
(él/ella/usted)	**rogó**	**rogaba**
(nosotros/as)	**rogamos**	**rogábamos**
(vosotros/as)	**rogasteis**	**rogabais**
(ellos/ellas/ ustedes)	**rogaron**	**rogaban**

GERUND
rogando

PAST PARTICIPLE
rogado

EXAMPLE PHRASES

Les **rogamos** acepten nuestras disculpas. Please accept our apologies.
Te **ruego** que me lo devuelvas. Please give it back to me.
"Se **ruega** no fumar" "Please do not smoke"
Me **rogó** que lo perdonara. He begged me to forgive him.
Le **rogaba** a Dios que se curara. I prayed to God to make him better.

Remember that subject pronouns are not used very often in Spanish.

rogar

	FUTURE	CONDITIONAL
(yo)	**rogaré**	**rogaría**
(tú)	**rogarás**	**rogarías**
(él/ella/usted)	**rogará**	**rogaría**
(nosotros/as)	**rogaremos**	**rogaríamos**
(vosotros/as)	**rogaréis**	**rogaríais**
(ellos/ellas/ ustedes)	**rogarán**	**rogarían**

	PRESENT SUBJUNCTIVE	IMPERFECT SUBJUNCTIVE
(yo)	**ruegue**	**rogara** *or* **rogase**
(tú)	**ruegues**	**rogaras** *or* **rogases**
(él/ella/usted)	**ruegue**	**rogara** *or* **rogase**
(nosotros/as)	**roguemos**	**rogáramos** *or* **rogásemos**
(vosotros/as)	**roguéis**	**rogarais** *or* **rogaseis**
(ellos/ellas/ ustedes)	**rueguen**	**rogaran** *or* **rogasen**

IMPERATIVE

ruega / rogad

Use the present subjunctive in all cases other than these tú and vosotros affirmative forms.

EXAMPLE PHRASES

Ruega por mí. Pray for me.

Remember that subject pronouns are not used very often in Spanish.

romper (to break)

	PRESENT	PRESENT PERFECT
(yo)	rompo	he roto
(tú)	rompes	has roto
(él/ella/usted)	rompe	ha roto
(nosotros/as)	rompemos	hemos roto
(vosotros/as)	rompéis	habéis roto
(ellos/ellas/ ustedes)	rompen	han roto

	PRETERITE	IMPERFECT
(yo)	rompí	rompía
(tú)	rompiste	rompías
(él/ella/usted)	rompió	rompía
(nosotros/as)	rompimos	rompíamos
(vosotros/as)	rompisteis	rompíais
(ellos/ellas/ ustedes)	rompieron	rompían

GERUND
rompiendo

PAST PARTICIPLE
roto

EXAMPLE PHRASES

La cuerda **se** va a **romper**. The rope is going to snap.

Siempre **están rompiendo** cosas. They're always breaking things.

Se había roto una taza. A cup had gotten broken.

Se rompió el jarrón. The vase broke.

Remember that subject pronouns are not used very often in Spanish.

romper

	FUTURE	CONDITIONAL
(yo)	rompere	rompería
(tú)	romperás	romperías
(él/ella/usted)	romperá	rompería
(nosotros/as)	romperemos	romperíamos
(vosotros/as)	romperéis	romperíais
(ellos/ellas/ ustedes)	romperán	romperían

	PRESENT SUBJUNCTIVE	IMPERFECT SUBJUNCTIVE
(yo)	rompa	rompiera *or* rompiese
(tú)	rompas	rompieras *or* rompieses
(él/ella/usted)	rompa	rompiera *or* rompiese
(nosotros/as)	rompamos	rompiéramos *or* rompiésemos
(vosotros/as)	rompáis	rompierais *or* rompieseis
(ellos/ellas/ ustedes)	rompan	rompieran *or* rompiesen

IMPERATIVE

rompe / romped

Use the present subjunctive in all cases other than these tú and vosotros affirmative forms.

EXAMPLE PHRASES

Yo nunca **rompería** una promesa. I'd never break a promise.

Si lo **rompiera**, tendría que pagarlo. If you broke it, you'd have to pay for it.

Cuidado, no lo **rompas**. Careful you don't break it.

Remember that subject pronouns are not used very often in Spanish.

saber (to know)

	PRESENT	PRESENT PERFECT
(yo)	sé	he sabido
(tú)	sabes	has sabido
(él/ella/usted)	sabe	ha sabido
(nosotros/as)	sabemos	hemos sabido
(vosotros/as)	sabéis	habéis sabido
(ellos/ellas/ ustedes)	saben	han sabido

	PRETERITE	IMPERFECT
(yo)	supe	sabía
(tú)	supiste	sabías
(él/ella/usted)	supo	sabía
(nosotros/as)	supimos	sabíamos
(vosotros/as)	supisteis	sabíais
(ellos/ellas/ ustedes)	supieron	sabían

GERUND
sabiendo

PAST PARTICIPLE
sabido

EXAMPLE PHRASES

No lo **sé**. I don't know.

¿**Sabes** una cosa? Do you know what?

¿Cuándo lo **supiste**? When did you find out?

No **supe** qué responder. I didn't know how to answer.

Pensaba que lo **sabías**. I thought you knew.

Remember that subject pronouns are not used very often in Spanish.

saber

	FUTURE	CONDITIONAL
(yo)	**sabré**	**sabría**
(tú)	**sabrás**	**sabrías**
(él/ella/usted)	**sabrá**	**sabría**
(nosotros/as)	**sabremos**	**sabríamos**
(vosotros/as)	**sabréis**	**sabríais**
(ellos/ellas/ ustedes)	**sabrán**	**sabrían**

	PRESENT SUBJUNCTIVE	IMPERFECT SUBJUNCTIVE
(yo)	**sepa**	**supiera** *or* **supiese**
(tú)	**sepas**	**supieras** *or* **supieses**
(él/ella/usted)	**sepa**	**supiera** *or* **supiese**
(nosotros/as)	**sepamos**	**supiéramos** *or* **supiésemos**
(vosotros/as)	**sepáis**	**supierais** *or* **supieseis**
(ellos/ellas/ ustedes)	**sepan**	**supieran** *or* **supiesen**

IMPERATIVE

sabe / sabed

Use the present subjunctive in all cases other than these tú and vosotros affirmative forms.

EXAMPLE PHRASES

Nunca se **sabrá** quién la mató. We'll never know who killed her.

Si no le tuvieras tanto miedo al agua, ya **sabrías** nadar. If you weren't so afraid of water, you'd already be able to swim.

Que yo **sepa**, vive en París. As far as I know, she lives in Paris.

¡Si **supiéramos** al menos dónde está! If only we knew where he was!

Remember that subject pronouns are not used very often in Spanish.

sacar (to take out; to get)

	PRESENT	PRESENT PERFECT
(yo)	**saco**	**he sacado**
(tú)	**sacas**	**has sacado**
(él/ella/usted)	**saca**	**ha sacado**
(nosotros/as)	**sacamos**	**hemos sacado**
(vosotros/as)	**sacáis**	**habéis sacado**
(ellos/ellas/ ustedes)	**sacan**	**han sacado**

	PRETERITE	IMPERFECT
(yo)	**saqué**	**sacaba**
(tú)	**sacaste**	**sacabas**
(él/ella/usted)	**sacó**	**sacaba**
(nosotros/as)	**sacamos**	**sacábamos**
(vosotros/as)	**sacasteis**	**sacabais**
(ellos/ellas/ ustedes)	**sacaron**	**sacaban**

GERUND
sacando

PAST PARTICIPLE
sacado

EXAMPLE PHRASES

Voy a **sacar** la basura. I'm going to take out the trash.
¿Me **sacas** una foto? Will you take a photo of me?
Estás sacando las cosas de quicio. You're blowing things out of all proportion.
Ya **saqué** los boletos. I already bought the tickets.
¿De dónde **sacaba** tanto dinero? Where did he get so much money from?

Remember that subject pronouns are not used very often in Spanish.

sacar

	FUTURE	CONDITIONAL
(yo)	sacaré	sacaría
(tú)	sacarás	sacarías
(él/ella/usted)	sacará	sacaría
(nosotros/as)	sacaremos	sacaríamos
(vosotros/as)	sacaréis	sacaríais
(ellos/ellas/ ustedes)	sacarán	sacarían

	PRESENT SUBJUNCTIVE	IMPERFECT SUBJUNCTIVE
(yo)	saque	sacara *or* sacase
(tú)	saques	sacaras *or* sacases
(él/ella/usted)	saque	sacara *or* sacase
(nosotros/as)	saquemos	sacáramos *or* sacásemos
(vosotros/as)	saquéis	sacarais *or* sacaseis
(ellos/ellas/ ustedes)	saquen	sacaran *or* sacasen

IMPERATIVE

saca / sacad

Use the present subjunctive in all cases other than these tú and vosotros affirmative forms.

EXAMPLE PHRASES

Quiero que **saques** esa bicicleta de casa inmediatamente. I want you to get that bike out of the house immediately.

No **saques** la cabeza por la ventanilla. Don't lean out of the window.

Remember that subject pronouns are not used very often in Spanish.

salir (to go out; to work out)

	PRESENT	PRESENT PERFECT
(yo)	salgo	he salido
(tú)	sales	has salido
(él/ella/usted)	sale	ha salido
(nosotros/as)	salimos	hemos salido
(vosotros/as)	salís	habéis salido
(ellos/ellas/ ustedes)	salen	han salido

	PRETERITE	IMPERFECT
(yo)	salí	salía
(tú)	saliste	salías
(él/ella/usted)	salió	salía
(nosotros/as)	salimos	salíamos
(vosotros/as)	salisteis	salíais
(ellos/ellas/ ustedes)	salieron	salían

GERUND
saliendo

PAST PARTICIPLE
salido

EXAMPLE PHRASES

Hace tiempo que no **salimos**. We haven't been out for a while.

Está saliendo con un compañero de trabajo. She's dating a work colleague.

Su foto **salió** en todos los periódicos. Her picture appeared in all the newspapers.

Salía muy tarde de trabajar. He used to finish work very late.

Remember that subject pronouns are not used very often in Spanish.

salir

	FUTURE	CONDITIONAL
(yo)	**saldré**	**saldría**
(tú)	**saldrás**	**saldrías**
(él/ella/usted)	**saldrá**	**saldría**
(nosotros/as)	**saldremos**	**saldríamos**
(vosotros/as)	**saldréis**	**saldríais**
(ellos/ellas/ ustedes)	**saldrán**	**saldrían**

	PRESENT SUBJUNCTIVE	IMPERFECT SUBJUNCTIVE
(yo)	**salga**	**saliera** *or* **saliese**
(tú)	**salgas**	**salieras** *or* **salieses**
(él/ella/usted)	**salga**	**saliera** *or* **saliese**
(nosotros/as)	**salgamos**	**saliéramos** *or* **saliésemos**
(vosotros/as)	**salgáis**	**salierais** *or* **salieseis**
(ellos/ellas/ ustedes)	**salgan**	**salieran** *or* **saliesen**

IMPERATIVE

sal / salid

Use the present subjunctive in all cases other than these tú and vosotros affirmative forms.

EXAMPLE PHRASES

Te dije que **saldría** muy caro. I told you it would wind up being very expensive.
Espero que todo **salga** bien. I hope everything works out all right.
Si **saliera** elegido... If I were elected...
Por favor, **salgan** por la puerta de atrás. Please leave through the back door.

Remember that subject pronouns are not used very often in Spanish.

satisfacer (to satisfy)

	PRESENT	PRESENT PERFECT
(yo)	**satisfago**	**he satisfecho**
(tú)	**satisfaces**	**has satisfecho**
(él/ella/usted)	**satisface**	**ha satisfecho**
(nosotros/as)	**satisfacemos**	**hemos satisfecho**
(vosotros/as)	**satisfacéis**	**habéis satisfecho**
(ellos/ellas/ustedes)	**satisfacen**	**han satisfecho**

	PRETERITE	IMPERFECT
(yo)	**satisfice**	**satisfacía**
(tú)	**satisficiste**	**satisfacías**
(él/ella/usted)	**satisfizo**	**satisfacía**
(nosotros/as)	**satisficimos**	**satisfacíamos**
(vosotros/as)	**satisficisteis**	**satisfacíais**
(ellos/ellas/ustedes)	**satisficieron**	**satisfacían**

GERUND
satisfaciendo

PAST PARTICIPLE
satisfecho

EXAMPLE PHRASES

No me **satisface** nada el resultado. I'm not at all satisfied with the result.
Eso **satisfizo** mi curiosidad. That satisfied my curiosity.
Aquella vida **satisfacía** todas mis necesidades. That lifestyle satisfied all my needs.

Remember that subject pronouns are not used very often in Spanish.

satisfacer

	FUTURE	CONDITIONAL
(yo)	**satisfaré**	**satisfaría**
(tú)	**satisfarás**	**satisfarías**
(él/ella/usted)	**satisfará**	**satisfaría**
(nosotros/as)	**satisfaremos**	**satisfaríamos**
(vosotros/as)	**satisfaréis**	**satisfaríais**
(ellos/ellas/ ustedes)	**satisfarán**	**satisfarían**

	PRESENT SUBJUNCTIVE	IMPERFECT SUBJUNCTIVE
(yo)	**satisfaga**	**satisficiera** *or* **satisficiese**
(tú)	**satisfagas**	**satisficieras** *or* **satisficieses**
(él/ella/usted)	**satisfaga**	**satisficiera** *or* **satisficiese**
(nosotros/as)	**satisfagamos**	**satisficiéramos** *or* **satisficiésemos**
(vosotros/as)	**satisfagáis**	**satisficierais** *or* **satisficieseis**
(ellos/ellas/ ustedes)	**satisfagan**	**satisficieran** *or* **satisficiesen**

IMPERATIVE

satisfaz *or* **satisface / satisfaced**

Use the present subjunctive in all cases other than these tú and vosotros affirmative forms.

EXAMPLE PHRASES

Le **satisfará** saber que hemos cumplido nuestros objetivos. You'll be happy to know that we have achieved our objectives.

Tengo que aceptarlo aunque no me **satisfaga**. I have to accept it even though I'm not happy about it.

Remember that subject pronouns are not used very often in Spanish.

seguir (to follow; to go on)

	PRESENT	PRESENT PERFECT
(yo)	**sigo**	he seguido
(tú)	**sigues**	has seguido
(él/ella/usted)	**sigue**	ha seguido
(nosotros/as)	**seguimos**	hemos seguido
(vosotros/as)	**seguís**	habéis seguido
(ellos/ellas/ ustedes)	**siguen**	han seguido

	PRETERITE	IMPERFECT
(yo)	**seguí**	seguía
(tú)	**seguiste**	seguías
(él/ella/usted)	**siguió**	seguía
(nosotros/as)	**seguimos**	seguíamos
(vosotros/as)	**seguisteis**	seguíais
(ellos/ellas/ ustedes)	**siguieron**	seguían

GERUND
siguiendo

PAST PARTICIPLE
seguido

EXAMPLE PHRASES

Si **sigues** así, acabarás mal. If you go on like this you'll come to a bad end.

Siguió cantando como si nada. He went on singing as if there was nothing wrong.

Los **seguimos** mucho rato. We followed them for a long time.

Nos **habían seguido**. They had followed us.

Remember that subject pronouns are not used very often in Spanish.

seguir

	FUTURE	CONDITIONAL
(yo)	**seguiré**	**seguiría**
(tú)	**seguirás**	**seguirías**
(él/ella/usted)	**seguirá**	**seguiría**
(nosotros/as)	**seguiremos**	**seguiríamos**
(vosotros/as)	**seguiréis**	**seguiríais**
(ellos/ellas/ ustedes)	**seguirán**	**seguirían**

	PRESENT SUBJUNCTIVE	IMPERFECT SUBJUNCTIVE
(yo)	**siga**	**siguiera** *or* **siguiese**
(tú)	**sigas**	**siguieras** *or* **siguieses**
(él/ella/usted)	**siga**	**siguiera** *or* **siguiese**
(nosotros/as)	**sigamos**	**siguiéramos** *or* **siguiésemos**
(vosotros/as)	**sigáis**	**siguierais** *or* **siguieseis**
(ellos/ellas/ ustedes)	**sigan**	**siguieran** *or* **siguiesen**

IMPERATIVE

sigue / seguid

Use the present subjunctive in all cases other than these tú and vosotros affirmative forms.

EXAMPLE PHRASES

Nos seguiremos viendo. We will go on seeing each other.

Quiero que **sigas** estudiando. I want you to go on with your studies.

Si **siguieras** mis consejos, te iría muchísimo mejor. You'd be much better off if you followed my advice.

Siga por esta calle hasta el final. Go straight till you get to the end of the street.

Remember that subject pronouns are not used very often in Spanish.

sentir (to feel; to be sorry)

	PRESENT	PRESENT PERFECT
(yo)	siento	he sentido
(tú)	sientes	has sentido
(él/ella/usted)	siente	ha sentido
(nosotros/as)	sentimos	hemos sentido
(vosotros/as)	sentís	habéis sentido
(ellos/ellas/ ustedes)	sienten	han sentido

	PRETERITE	IMPERFECT
(yo)	sentí	sentía
(tú)	sentiste	sentías
(él/ella/usted)	sintió	sentía
(nosotros/as)	sentimos	sentíamos
(vosotros/as)	sentisteis	sentíais
(ellos/ellas/ ustedes)	sintieron	sentían

GERUND
sintiendo

PAST PARTICIPLE
sentido

EXAMPLE PHRASES

Te vas a **sentir** sola. You'll feel lonely.

Siento mucho lo que pasó. I'm really sorry about what happened.

Sintió mucho la muerte de su padre. He was greatly affected by his father's death.

No **sentí** nada. I didn't feel a thing.

Me sentía muy mal. I didn't feel well at all.

Remember that subject pronouns are not used very often in Spanish.

sentir

	FUTURE	CONDITIONAL
(yo)	**sentiré**	**sentiría**
(tú)	**sentirás**	**sentirías**
(él/ella/usted)	**sentirá**	**sentiría**
(nosotros/as)	**sentiremos**	**sentiríamos**
(vosotros/as)	**sentiréis**	**sentiríais**
(ellos/ellas/ ustedes)	**sentirán**	**sentirían**

	PRESENT SUBJUNCTIVE	IMPERFECT SUBJUNCTIVE
(yo)	**sienta**	**sintiera** *or* **sintiese**
(tú)	**sientas**	**sintieras** *or* **sintieses**
(él/ella/usted)	**sienta**	**sintiera** *or* **sintiese**
(nosotros/as)	**sintamos**	**sintiéramos** *or* **sintiésemos**
(vosotros/as)	**sintáis**	**sintierais** *or* **sintieseis**
(ellos/ellas/ ustedes)	**sientan**	**sintieran** *or* **sintiesen**

IMPERATIVE

siente / sentid

Use the present subjunctive in all cases other than these tú and vosotros affirmative forms.

EXAMPLE PHRASES

Al principio **te sentirás** un poco raro. You'll feel a bit strange at first.

Yo **sentiría** mucho que se fuera de la empresa. I'd be really sorry if you left the firm.

No creo que lo **sienta**. I don't think she's sorry.

Sería mucho más preocupante si no **sintiera** la pierna. It would be much more worrying if he couldn't feel his leg.

Remember that subject pronouns are not used very often in Spanish.

ser (to be)

	PRESENT	PRESENT PERFECT
(yo)	**soy**	**he sido**
(tú)	**eres**	**has sido**
(él/ella/usted)	**es**	**ha sido**
(nosotros/as)	**somos**	**hemos sido**
(vosotros/as)	**sois**	**habéis sido**
(ellos/ellas/ ustedes)	**son**	**han sido**

	PRETERITE	IMPERFECT
(yo)	**fui**	**era**
(tú)	**fuiste**	**eras**
(él/ella/usted)	**fue**	**era**
(nosotros/as)	**fuimos**	**éramos**
(vosotros/as)	**fuisteis**	**erais**
(ellos/ellas/ ustedes)	**fueron**	**eran**

GERUND
siendo

PAST PARTICIPLE
sido

EXAMPLE PHRASES

Soy colombiano. I'm Colombian.

Fue un duro golpe. It was a major blow.

¿**Fuiste** tú el que llamó? Was it you who called?

Era de noche. It was dark.

Había sido sacerdote. He had been a priest.

Remember that subject pronouns are not used very often in Spanish.

ser

	FUTURE	CONDITIONAL
(yo)	**seré**	**sería**
(tú)	**serás**	**serías**
(él/ella/usted)	**será**	**sería**
(nosotros/as)	**seremos**	**seríamos**
(vosotros/as)	**seréis**	**seríais**
(ellos/ellas/ ustedes)	**serán**	**serían**

	PRESENT SUBJUNCTIVE	IMPERFECT SUBJUNCTIVE
(yo)	**sea**	**fuera** *or* **fuese**
(tú)	**seas**	**fueras** *or* **fueses**
(él/ella/usted)	**sea**	**fuera** *or* **fuese**
(nosotros/as)	**seamos**	**fuéramos** *or* **fuésemos**
(vosotros/as)	**seáis**	**fuerais** *or* **fueseis**
(ellos/ellas/ ustedes)	**sean**	**fueran** *or* **fuesen**

IMPERATIVE

sé / sed

Use the present subjunctive in all cases other than these tú and vosotros affirmative forms.

EXAMPLE PHRASES

Será de Joaquín. Maybe it's Joaquín's.

Eso **sería** maravilloso. That would be wonderful.

O **sea**, que no vienes. So you're not coming.

No **seas** tan perfeccionista. Don't be such a perfectionist.

¡**Sean** buenos! Behave yourselves!

Remember that subject pronouns are not used very often in Spanish.

soler (to be in the habit of; to be accustomed to)

	PRESENT	PRESENT PERFECT
(yo)	**suelo**	*not used*
(tú)	**sueles**	
(él/ella/usted)	**suele**	
(nosotros/as)	**solemos**	
(vosotros/as)	**soléis**	
(ellos/ellas/ ustedes)	**suelen**	

	PRETERITE	IMPERFECT
(yo)	*not used*	**solía**
(tú)		**solías**
(él/ella/usted)		**solía**
(nosotros/as)		**solíamos**
(vosotros/as)		**solíais**
(ellos/ellas/ ustedes)		**solían**

GERUND
soliendo

PAST PARTICIPLE
not used

EXAMPLE PHRASES

Suele salir a las ocho. He usually goes out at eight.

Solíamos ir todos los años a la playa. We used to go to the beach every year.

Remember that subject pronouns are not used very often in Spanish.

soler

	FUTURE	CONDITIONAL
(yo)	*not used*	*not used*
(tú)		
(él/ella/usted)		
(nosotros/as)		
(vosotros/as)		
(ellos/ellas/ ustedes)		

	PRESENT SUBJUNCTIVE	IMPERFECT SUBJUNCTIVE
(yo)	**suela**	**soliera** *or* **soliese**
(tú)	**suelas**	**solieras** *or* **solieses**
(él/ella/usted)	**suela**	**soliera** *or* **soliese**
(nosotros/as)	**solamos**	**soliéramos** *or* **soliésemos**
(vosotros/as)	**soláis**	**solierais** *or* **solieseis**
(ellos/ellas/ ustedes)	**suelan**	**solieran** *or* **soliesen**

IMPERATIVE

not used

Remember that subject pronouns are not used very often in Spanish.

soltar (to let go of; to release)

	PRESENT	PRESENT PERFECT
(yo)	suelto	he soltado
(tú)	sueltas	has soltado
(él/ella/usted)	suelta	ha soltado
(nosotros/as)	soltamos	hemos soltado
(vosotros/as)	soltáis	habéis soltado
(ellos/ellas/ustedes)	sueltan	han soltado

	PRETERITE	IMPERFECT
(yo)	solté	soltaba
(tú)	soltaste	soltabas
(él/ella/usted)	soltó	soltaba
(nosotros/as)	soltamos	soltábamos
(vosotros/as)	soltasteis	soltabais
(ellos/ellas/ustedes)	soltaron	soltaban

GERUND
soltando

PAST PARTICIPLE
soltado

EXAMPLE PHRASES

Al final logró **soltarse**. Eventually she managed to break free.
¿Por qué no **te sueltas** el pelo? Why don't you wear your hair down?
Habían soltado a los rehenes. They had released the hostages.
Soltó una carcajada. He burst out laughing.

Remember that subject pronouns are not used very often in Spanish.

soltar

	FUTURE	CONDITIONAL
(yo)	**soltaré**	**soltaría**
(tú)	**soltarás**	**soltarías**
(él/ella/usted)	**soltará**	**soltaría**
(nosotros/as)	**soltaremos**	**soltaríamos**
(vosotros/as)	**soltaréis**	**soltaríais**
(ellos/ellas/ ustedes)	**soltarán**	**soltarían**

	PRESENT SUBJUNCTIVE	IMPERFECT SUBJUNCTIVE
(yo)	**suelte**	**soltara** *or* **soltase**
(tú)	**sueltes**	**soltaras** *or* **soltases**
(él/ella/usted)	**suelte**	**soltara** *or* **soltase**
(nosotros/as)	**soltemos**	**soltáramos** *or* **soltásemos**
(vosotros/as)	**soltéis**	**soltarais** *or* **soltaseis**
(ellos/ellas/ ustedes)	**suelten**	**soltaran** *or* **soltasen**

IMPERATIVE

suelta / soltad

Use the present subjunctive in all cases other than these tú and vosotros affirmative forms.

EXAMPLE PHRASES

Te **soltaré** el brazo si me dices dónde está. I'll let go of your arm if you tell me where he is.

Te dije que lo **soltaras**. I told you to let it go.

No **sueltes** la cuerda. Don't let go of the rope.

¡**Suéltame**! Let me go!

Remember that subject pronouns are not used very often in Spanish.

sonar (to sound; to ring)

	PRESENT	PRESENT PERFECT
(yo)	**sueno**	**he sonado**
(tú)	**suenas**	**has sonado**
(él/ella/usted)	**suena**	**ha sonado**
(nosotros/as)	**sonamos**	**hemos sonado**
(vosotros/as)	**sonáis**	**habéis sonado**
(ellos/ellas/ ustedes)	**suenan**	**han sonado**

	PRETERITE	IMPERFECT
(yo)	**soné**	**sonaba**
(tú)	**sonaste**	**sonabas**
(él/ella/usted)	**sonó**	**sonaba**
(nosotros/as)	**sonamos**	**sonábamos**
(vosotros/as)	**sonasteis**	**sonabais**
(ellos/ellas/ ustedes)	**sonaron**	**sonaban**

GERUND
sonando

PAST PARTICIPLE
sonado

EXAMPLE PHRASES

¿Te **suena** su nombre? Does her name sound familiar?

Justo en ese momento **sonó** el timbre. Just then the bell rang.

Sonabas un poco triste por teléfono. You sounded a bit sad on the phone.

Estaba sonando el teléfono. The phone was ringing.

Remember that subject pronouns are not used very often in Spanish.

sonar

	FUTURE	CONDITIONAL
(yo)	**sonaré**	**sonaría**
(tú)	**sonarás**	**sonarías**
(él/ella/usted)	**sonará**	**sonaría**
(nosotros/as)	**sonaremos**	**sonaríamos**
(vosotros/as)	**sonaréis**	**sonaríais**
(ellos/ellas/ ustedes)	**sonarán**	**sonarían**

	PRESENT SUBJUNCTIVE	IMPERFECT SUBJUNCTIVE
(yo)	**suene**	**sonara** *or* **sonase**
(tú)	**suenes**	**sonaras** *or* **sonases**
(él/ella/usted)	**suene**	**sonara** *or* **sonase**
(nosotros/as)	**sonemos**	**sonáramos** *or* **sonásemos**
(vosotros/as)	**sonéis**	**sonarais** *or* **sonaseis**
(ellos/ellas/ ustedes)	**suenen**	**sonaran** *or* **sonasen**

IMPERATIVE

suena / sonad

Use the present subjunctive in all cases other than these tú and vosotros affirmative forms.

EXAMPLE PHRASES

Hay que esperar a que **suene** un pitido. We have to wait until we hear a beep.

¡**Suénate** la nariz! Blow your nose!

Remember that subject pronouns are not used very often in Spanish.

temer (to be afraid)

	PRESENT	PRESENT PERFECT
(yo)	temo	he temido
(tú)	temes	has temido
(él/ella/usted)	teme	ha temido
(nosotros/as)	tememos	hemos temido
(vosotros/as)	teméis	habéis temido
(ellos/ellas/ ustedes)	temen	han temido

	PRETERITE	IMPERFECT
(yo)	temí	temía
(tú)	temiste	temías
(él/ella/usted)	temío	temía
(nosotros/as)	temimos	temíamos
(vosotros/as)	temisteis	temíais
(ellos/ellas/ ustedes)	temieron	temían

GERUND
temiendo

PAST PARTICIPLE
temido

EXAMPLE PHRASES

No le **teme** a nadie. He's not afraid of anyone.

Me temo que no. I'm afraid not.

Se temen lo peor. They fear the worst.

Empezó a llover. –**Me** lo **temía**. "It's started raining." – "I was afraid it would."

Temían por su seguridad. They feared for their safety.

Remember that subject pronouns are not used very often in Spanish.

temer

	FUTURE	CONDITIONAL
(yo)	**temeré**	**temería**
(tú)	**temerás**	**temerías**
(él/ella/usted)	**temerá**	**temería**
(nosotros/as)	**temeremos**	**temeríamos**
(vosotros/as)	**temeréis**	**temeríais**
(ellos/ellas/ ustedes)	**temerán**	**temerían**

	PRESENT SUBJUNCTIVE	IMPERFECT SUBJUNCTIVE
(yo)	**tema**	**temiera** *or* **temiese**
(tú)	**temas**	**temieras** *or* **temieses**
(él/ella/usted)	**tema**	**temiera** *or* **temiese**
(nosotros/as)	**temamos**	**temiéramos** *or* **temiésemos**
(vosotros/as)	**temáis**	**temierais** *or* **temieseis**
(ellos/ellas/ ustedes)	**teman**	**temieran** *or* **temiesen**

IMPERATIVE

teme / temed

Use the present subjunctive in all cases other than these tú and vosotros affirmative forms.

EXAMPLE PHRASES

No **temas.** Don't be afraid.

Remember that subject pronouns are not used very often in Spanish.

tener (to have)

	PRESENT	PRESENT PERFECT
(yo)	**tengo**	**he tenido**
(tú)	**tienes**	**has tenido**
(él/ella/usted)	**tiene**	**ha tenido**
(nosotros/as)	**tenemos**	**hemos tenido**
(vosotros/as)	**tenéis**	**habéis tenido**
(ellos/ellas/ ustedes)	**tienen**	**ha tenido**

	PRETERITE	IMPERFECT
(yo)	**tuve**	**tenía**
(tú)	**tuviste**	**tenías**
(él/ella/usted)	**tuvo**	**tenía**
(nosotros/as)	**tuvimos**	**teníamos**
(vosotros/as)	**tuvisteis**	**teníais**
(ellos/ellas/ ustedes)	**tuvieron**	**tenían**

GERUND
teniendo

PAST PARTICIPLE
tenido

EXAMPLE PHRASES

Tengo dos hermanos. I have two brothers.
Había tenido una gripa muy fuerte. She'd had a very bad flu.
Tuvimos que irnos. We had to leave.
No **tenía** suficiente dinero. She didn't have enough money.
Estamos teniendo muchos problemas. We're having a lot of problems.

Remember that subject pronouns are not used very often in Spanish.

tener

	FUTURE	CONDITIONAL
(yo)	**tendré**	**tendría**
(tú)	**tendrás**	**tendrías**
(él/ella/usted)	**tendrá**	**tendría**
(nosotros/as)	**tendremos**	**tendríamos**
(vosotros/as)	**tendréis**	**tendríais**
(ellos/ellas/ ustedes)	**tendrán**	**tendrían**

	PRESENT SUBJUNCTIVE	IMPERFECT SUBJUNCTIVE
(yo)	**tenga**	**tuviera** *or* **tuviese**
(tú)	**tengas**	**tuvieras** *or* **tuvieses**
(él/ella/usted)	**tenga**	**tuviera** *or* **tuviese**
(nosotros/as)	**tengamos**	**tuviéramos** *or* **tuviésemos**
(vosotros/as)	**tengáis**	**tuvierais** *or* **tuvieseis**
(ellos/ellas/ ustedes)	**tengan**	**tuvieran** *or* **tuviesen**

IMPERATIVE

ten / tened

Use the present subjunctive in all cases other than these tú and vosotros affirmative forms.

EXAMPLE PHRASES

Tendrás que pagarlo tú. You'll have to pay for it yourself.

Tendrías que comer más. You should eat more.

No creo que **tenga** suficiente dinero. I don't think he has enough money.

Si **tuviera** tiempo, haría un curso de francés. If I had time, I'd take a French course.

Ten cuidado. Be careful.

No **tengas** miedo. Don't be afraid.

Remember that subject pronouns are not used very often in Spanish.

tocar (to touch; to play)

	PRESENT	PRESENT PERFECT
(yo)	**toco**	**he tocado**
(tú)	**tocas**	**has tocado**
(él/ella/usted)	**toca**	**ha tocado**
(nosotros/as)	**tocamos**	**hemos tocado**
(vosotros/as)	**tocáis**	**habéis tocado**
(ellos/ellas/ ustedes)	**tocan**	**han tocado**

	PRETERITE	IMPERFECT
(yo)	**toqué**	**tocaba**
(tú)	**tocaste**	**tocabas**
(él/ella/usted)	**tocó**	**tocaba**
(nosotros/as)	**tocamos**	**tocábamos**
(vosotros/as)	**tocasteis**	**tocabais**
(ellos/ellas/ ustedes)	**tocaron**	**tocaban**

GERUND
tocando

PAST PARTICIPLE
tocado

EXAMPLE PHRASES

Toca el violín. He plays the violin.

Te **toca** manejar. It's your turn to drive.

Me **tocó** el peor asiento. I ended up with the worst seat.

Me **tocaba** tirar a mí. It was my turn.

Tocaban muy bien. They played very well.

Remember that subject pronouns are not used very often in Spanish.

tocar

	FUTURE	CONDITIONAL
(yo)	**tocaré**	**tocaría**
(tú)	**tocarás**	**tocarías**
(él/ella/usted)	**tocará**	**tocaría**
(nosotros/as)	**tocaremos**	**tocaríamos**
(vosotros/as)	**tocaréis**	**tocaríais**
(ellos/ellas/ ustedes)	**tocarán**	**tocarían**

	PRESENT SUBJUNCTIVE	IMPERFECT SUBJUNCTIVE
(yo)	**toque**	**tocara** *or* **tocase**
(tú)	**toques**	**tocaras** *or* **tocases**
(él/ella/usted)	**toque**	**tocara** *or* **tocase**
(nosotros/as)	**toquemos**	**tocáramos** *or* **tocásemos**
(vosotros/as)	**toquéis**	**tocarais** *or* **tocaseis**
(ellos/ellas/ ustedes)	**toquen**	**tocaran** *or* **tocasen**

IMPERATIVE

toca / tocad

Use the present subjunctive in all cases other than these tú and vosotros affirmative forms.

EXAMPLE PHRASES

Sabía que me **tocaría** ir a mí. I knew I'd be the one to have to go.

No lo **toques**. Don't touch it.

Tócalo, otra vez. Play it again.

Remember that subject pronouns are not used very often in Spanish.

torcer (to twist)

	PRESENT	PRESENT PERFECT
(yo)	**tuerzo**	**he torcido**
(tú)	**tuerces**	**has torcido**
(él/ella/usted)	**tuerce**	**ha torcido**
(nosotros/as)	**torcemos**	**hemos torcido**
(vosotros/as)	**torcéis**	**habéis torcido**
(ellos/ellas/ ustedes)	**tuercen**	**han torcido**

	PRETERITE	IMPERFECT
(yo)	**torcí**	**torcía**
(tú)	**torciste**	**torcías**
(él/ella/usted)	**torció**	**torcía**
(nosotros/as)	**torcimos**	**torcíamos**
(vosotros/as)	**torcisteis**	**torcíais**
(ellos/ellas/ ustedes)	**torcieron**	**torcían**

GERUND
torciendo

PAST PARTICIPLE
torcido

EXAMPLE PHRASES

El sendero **tuerce** luego a la derecha. Later on the path curves around to the right.

Me **torció** la muñeca. He twisted my wrist.

Las cosas se empezaron a **torcer**. Things started to go wrong.

Remember that subject pronouns are not used very often in Spanish.

torcer

	FUTURE	CONDITIONAL
(yo)	**torceré**	**torcería**
(tú)	**torcerás**	**torcerías**
(él/ella/usted)	**torcerá**	**torcería**
(nosotros/as)	**torceremos**	**torceríamos**
(vosotros/as)	**torceréis**	**torceríais**
(ellos/ellas/ ustedes)	**torcerán**	**torcerían**

	PRESENT SUBJUNCTIVE	IMPERFECT SUBJUNCTIVE
(yo)	**tuerza**	**torciera** *or* **torciese**
(tú)	**tuerzas**	**torcieras** *or* **torcieses**
(él/ella/usted)	**tuerza**	**torciera** *or* **torciese**
(nosotros/as)	**torzamos**	**torciéramos** *or* **torciésemos**
(vosotros/as)	**torzáis**	**torcierais** *or* **torcieseis**
(ellos/ellas/ ustedes)	**tuerzan**	**torcieran** *or* **torciesen**

IMPERATIVE

tuerce / torced

Use the present subjunctive in all cases other than these tú and vosotros affirmative forms.

EXAMPLE PHRASES

Tuerza a la izquierda. Turn left.

Tuércelo un poco más. Twist it a little more.

Remember that subject pronouns are not used very often in Spanish.

traer (to bring)

	PRESENT	PRESENT PERFECT
(yo)	**traigo**	**he traído**
(tú)	**traes**	**has traído**
(él/ella/usted)	**trae**	**ha traído**
(nosotros/as)	**traemos**	**hemos traído**
(vosotros/as)	**traéis**	**habéis traído**
(ellos/ellas/ ustedes)	**traen**	**han traído**

	PRETERITE	IMPERFECT
(yo)	**traje**	**traía**
(tú)	**trajiste**	**traías**
(él/ella/usted)	**trajo**	**traía**
(nosotros/as)	**trajimos**	**traíamos**
(vosotros/as)	**trajisteis**	**traíais**
(ellos/ellas/ ustedes)	**trajeron**	**traían**

GERUND
trayendo

PAST PARTICIPLE
traído

EXAMPLE PHRASES

¿Me puedes **traer** una toalla? Can you bring me a towel?
Nos **está trayendo** muchos problemas. It's causing us a lot of trouble.
¿**Trajiste** lo que te pedí? Did you bring what I asked for?
Traía un vestido nuevo. She was wearing a new dress.
No **trajo** el dinero. He didn't bring the money.

Remember that subject pronouns are not used very often in Spanish.

traer

	FUTURE	CONDITIONAL
(yo)	**traeré**	**traería**
(tú)	**traerás**	**traerías**
(él/ella/usted)	**traerá**	**traería**
(nosotros/as)	**traeremos**	**traeríamos**
(vosotros/as)	**traeréis**	**traeríais**
(ellos/ellas/ ustedes)	**traerán**	**traerían**

	PRESENT SUBJUNCTIVE	IMPERFECT SUBJUNCTIVE
(yo)	**traiga**	**trajera** *or* **trajese**
(tú)	**traigas**	**trajeras** *or* **trajeses**
(él/ella/usted)	**traiga**	**trajera** *or* **trajese**
(nosotros/as)	**traigamos**	**trajéramos** *or* **trajésemos**
(vosotros/as)	**traigáis**	**trajerais** *or* **trajeseis**
(ellos/ellas/ ustedes)	**traigan**	**trajeran** *or* **trajesen**

IMPERATIVE

trae / traed

Use the present subjunctive in all cases other than these tú and vosotros affirmative forms.

EXAMPLE PHRASES

Me pregunto qué **se traerán** entre manos. I wonder what they're up to.

Dile que **traiga** a algún amigo. Tell him to bring a friend with him.

Le pedí que **trajera** las fotos. I asked her to bring the photos.

Remember that subject pronouns are not used very often in Spanish.

valer (to be worth)

	PRESENT	PRESENT PERFECT
(yo)	**valgo**	**he valido**
(tú)	**vales**	**has valido**
(él/ella/usted)	**vale**	**ha valido**
(nosotros/as)	**valemos**	**hemos valido**
(vosotros/as)	**valéis**	**habéis valido**
(ellos/ellas/ ustedes)	**valen**	**han valido**

	PRETERITE	IMPERFECT
(yo)	**valí**	**valía**
(tú)	**valiste**	**valías**
(él/ella/usted)	**valió**	**valía**
(nosotros/as)	**valimos**	**valíamos**
(vosotros/as)	**valisteis**	**valíais**
(ellos/ellas/ ustedes)	**valieron**	**valían**

GERUND
valiendo

PAST PARTICIPLE
valido

EXAMPLE PHRASES

¿Cuánto **vale** eso? How much is that?

No puede **valerse** por sí mismo. He can't look after himself.

No le **valió** de nada suplicar. Begging got her nowhere.

No **valía** la pena. It wasn't worth it.

Remember that subject pronouns are not used very often in Spanish.

valer

	FUTURE	CONDITIONAL
(yo)	**valdré**	**valdría**
(tú)	**valdrás**	**valdrías**
(él/ella/usted)	**valdrá**	**valdría**
(nosotros/as)	**valdremos**	**valdríamos**
(vosotros/as)	**valdréis**	**valdríais**
(ellos/ellas/ ustedes)	**valdrán**	**valdrían**

	PRESENT SUBJUNCTIVE	IMPERFECT SUBJUNCTIVE
(yo)	**valga**	**valiera** *or* **valiese**
(tú)	**valgas**	**valieras** *or* **valieses**
(él/ella/usted)	**valga**	**valiera** *or* **valiese**
(nosotros/as)	**valgamos**	**valiéramos** *or* **valiésemos**
(vosotros/as)	**valgáis**	**valierais** *or* **valieseis**
(ellos/ellas/ ustedes)	**valgan**	**valieran** *or* **valiesen**

IMPERATIVE

vale / valed

Use the present subjunctive in all cases other than these tú and vosotros affirmative forms.

EXAMPLE PHRASES

Valdrá unos 500 dólares. It must be worth around 500 dollars.

Valdría más si fuera antiguo. It would be worth more if it were an antique.

Remember that subject pronouns are not used very often in Spanish.

vencer (to win; to beat)

	PRESENT	PRESENT PERFECT
(yo)	venzo	he vencido
(tú)	vences	has vencido
(él/ella/usted)	vence	ha vencido
(nosotros/as)	vencemos	hemos vencido
(vosotros/as)	vencéis	habéis vencido
(ellos/ellas/ ustedes)	vencen	han vencido

	PRETERITE	IMPERFECT
(yo)	vencí	vencía
(tú)	venciste	vencías
(él/ella/usted)	venció	vencía
(nosotros/as)	vencimos	vencíamos
(vosotros/as)	vencisteis	vencíais
(ellos/ellas/ ustedes)	vencieron	vencían

GERUND
venciendo

PAST PARTICIPLE
vencido

EXAMPLE PHRASES

Tienes que **vencer** el miedo. You must overcome your fear.
Finalmente lo **venció** el sueño. He was finally overcome by sleep.
Lo **vencía** la curiosidad. His curiosity got the better of him.

Remember that subject pronouns are not used very often in Spanish.

vencer

	FUTURE	CONDITIONAL
(yo)	**venceré**	**vencería**
(tú)	**vencerás**	**vencerías**
(él/ella/usted)	**vencerá**	**vencería**
(nosotros/as)	**venceremos**	**venceríamos**
(vosotros/as)	**venceréis**	**venceríais**
(ellos/ellas/ ustedes)	**vencerán**	**vencerían**

	PRESENT SUBJUNCTIVE	IMPERFECT SUBJUNCTIVE
(yo)	**venza**	**venciera** *or* **venciese**
(tú)	**venzas**	**vencieras** *or* **vencieses**
(él/ella/usted)	**venza**	**venciera** *or* **venciese**
(nosotros/as)	**venzamos**	**venciéramos** *or* **venciésemos**
(vosotros/as)	**venzáis**	**vencierais** *or* **vencieseis**
(ellos/ellas/ ustedes)	**venzan**	**vencieran** *or* **venciesen**

IMPERATIVE

vence / venced

Use the present subjunctive in all cases other than these tú and vosotros affirmative forms.

EXAMPLE PHRASES

Nuestro ejército **vencerá**. Our army will be victorious.

No dejes que te **venza** la impaciencia. Don't let your impatience get the better of you.

Remember that subject pronouns are not used very often in Spanish.

venir (to come)

	PRESENT	PRESENT PERFECT
(yo)	vengo	he venido
(tú)	vienes	has venido
(él/ella/usted)	viene	ha venido
(nosotros/as)	venimos	hemos venido
(vosotros/as)	venís	habéis venido
(ellos/ellas/ ustedes)	vienen	han venido

	PRETERITE	IMPERFECT
(yo)	vine	venía
(tú)	viniste	venías
(él/ella/usted)	vino	venía
(nosotros/as)	vinimos	veníamos
(vosotros/as)	vinisteis	veníais
(ellos/ellas/ ustedes)	vinieron	venían

GERUND
viniendo

PAST PARTICIPLE
venido

EXAMPLE PHRASES

Vengo a menudo. I come here often.

La casa **se está viniendo** abajo. The house is falling apart.

Vino en taxi. He came by taxi.

Vinieron a verme al hospital. They came to see me in the hospital.

La noticia **venía** en el periódico. The news was in the paper.

Remember that subject pronouns are not used very often in Spanish.

venir

	FUTURE	CONDITIONAL
(yo)	**vendré**	**vendría**
(tú)	**vendrás**	**vendrías**
(él/ella/usted)	**vendrá**	**vendría**
(nosotros/as)	**vendremos**	**vendríamos**
(vosotros/as)	**vendréis**	**vendríais**
(ellos/ellas/ ustedes)	**vendrán**	**vendrían**

	PRESENT SUBJUNCTIVE	IMPERFECT SUBJUNCTIVE
(yo)	**venga**	**viniera** *or* **viniese**
(tú)	**vengas**	**vinieras** *or* **vinieses**
(él/ella/usted)	**venga**	**viniera** *or* **viniese**
(nosotros/as)	**vengamos**	**viniéramos** *or* **viniésemos**
(vosotros/as)	**vengáis**	**vinierais** *or* **vinieseis**
(ellos/ellas/ ustedes)	**vengan**	**vinieran** *or* **viniesen**

IMPERATIVE

ven / venid

Use the present subjunctive in all cases other than these tú and vosotros affirmative forms.

EXAMPLE PHRASES

¿Crees que **vendrá**? Do you think he'll come?

A mí me **vendría** mejor el sábado. Saturday would be better for me.

No **vengas** si no quieres. Don't come if you don't want to.

¡**Ven** aquí! Come here!

Remember that subject pronouns are not used very often in Spanish.

ver (to see)

	PRESENT	PRESENT PERFECT
(yo)	veo	he visto
(tú)	ves	has visto
(él/ella/usted)	ve	ha visto
(nosotros/as)	vemos	hemos visto
(vosotros/as)	veis	habéis visto
(ellos/ellas/ ustedes)	ven	han visto

	PRETERITE	IMPERFECT
(yo)	vi	veía
(tú)	viste	veías
(él/ella/usted)	vio	veía
(nosotros/as)	vimos	veíamos
(vosotros/as)	visteis	veíais
(ellos/ellas/ ustedes)	vieron	veían

GERUND
viendo

PAST PARTICIPLE
visto

EXAMPLE PHRASES

No **veo** muy bien. I can't see very well.

Están viendo la televisión. They're watching TV.

No la **había visto**. I hadn't seen her.

¿**Viste** lo que pasó? Did you see what happened?

Los **veía** a todos desde la ventana. I could see them all from the window.

Remember that subject pronouns are not used very often in Spanish.

ver

	FUTURE	CONDITIONAL
(yo)	**veré**	**vería**
(tú)	**verás**	**verías**
(él/ella/usted)	**verá**	**vería**
(nosotros/as)	**veremos**	**veríamos**
(vosotros/as)	**veréis**	**veríais**
(ellos/ellas/ ustedes)	**verán**	**verían**

	PRESENT SUBJUNCTIVE	IMPERFECT SUBJUNCTIVE
(yo)	**vea**	**viera** *or* **viese**
(tú)	**veas**	**vieras** *or* **vieses**
(él/ella/usted)	**vea**	**viera** *or* **viese**
(nosotros/as)	**veamos**	**viéramos** *or* **viésemos**
(vosotros/as)	**veáis**	**vierais** *or* **vieseis**
(ellos/ellas/ ustedes)	**vean**	**vieran** *or* **viesen**

IMPERATIVE

ve / ved

Use the present subjunctive in all cases other than these tú and vosotros affirmative forms.

EXAMPLE PHRASES

Eso ya se **verá**. We'll see.

¡Si **vieras** cómo ha cambiado todo aquello! If you could see how all that has changed!

Veamos, ¿qué le pasa? Let's see now, what's the matter?

Remember that subject pronouns are not used very often in Spanish.

verter (to pour)

	PRESENT	PRESENT PERFECT
(yo)	vierto	he vertido
(tú)	viertes	has vertido
(él/ella/usted)	vierte	ha vertido
(nosotros/as)	vertemos	hemos vertido
(vosotros/as)	vertéis	habéis vertido
(ellos/ellas/ ustedes)	vierten	han vertido

	PRETERITE	IMPERFECT
(yo)	vertí	vertía
(tú)	vertiste	vertías
(él/ella/usted)	vertió	vertía
(nosotros/as)	vertimos	vertíamos
(vosotros/as)	vertisteis	vertíais
(ellos/ellas/ ustedes)	vertieron	vertían

GERUND
vertiendo

PAST PARTICIPLE
vertido

EXAMPLE PHRASES

Primero **viertes** el contenido del sobre en un tazón. First you empty the contents of the package into a bowl.

Vertió un poco de leche en la cacerola. He poured some milk into the saucepan.

Se vertían muchos residuos radioactivos en el mar. A lot of nuclear waste was dumped in the sea.

Remember that subject pronouns are not used very often in Spanish.

verter

	FUTURE	CONDITIONAL
(yo)	**verteré**	**vertería**
(tú)	**verterás**	**verterías**
(él/ella/usted)	**verterá**	**vertería**
(nosotros/as)	**verteremos**	**verteríamos**
(vosotros/as)	**verteréis**	**verteríais**
(ellos/ellas/ ustedes)	**verterán**	**verterían**

	PRESENT SUBJUNCTIVE	IMPERFECT SUBJUNCTIVE
(yo)	**vierta**	**vertiera** *or* **vertiese**
(tú)	**viertas**	**vertieras** *or* **vertieses**
(él/ella/usted)	**vierta**	**vertiera** *or* **vertiese**
(nosotros/as)	**vertamos**	**vertiéramos** *or* **vertiésemos**
(vosotros/as)	**vertáis**	**vertierais** *or* **vertieseis**
(ellos/ellas/ ustedes)	**viertan**	**vertieran** *or* **vertiesen**

IMPERATIVE

vierte / verted

Use the present subjunctive in all cases other than these tú and **vosotros** *affirmative forms.*

EXAMPLE PHRASES

Se verterán muchas lágrimas por esto. A lot of tears will be shed over this.

Ten cuidado no **viertas** el café. Be careful you don't knock over the coffee.

Remember that subject pronouns are not used very often in Spanish.

vestir (to dress)

	PRESENT	PRESENT PERFECT
(yo)	**visto**	**he vestido**
(tú)	**vistes**	**has vestido**
(él/ella/usted)	**viste**	**ha vestido**
(nosotros/as)	**vestimos**	**hemos vestido**
(vosotros/as)	**vestís**	**habéis vestido**
(ellos/ellas/ustedes)	**visten**	**han vestido**

	PRETERITE	IMPERFECT
(yo)	**vestí**	**vestía**
(tú)	**vestiste**	**vestías**
(él/ella/usted)	**vistió**	**vestía**
(nosotros/as)	**vestimos**	**vestíamos**
(vosotros/as)	**vestisteis**	**vestíais**
(ellos/ellas/ustedes)	**vistieron**	**vestían**

GERUND
vistiendo

PAST PARTICIPLE
vestido

EXAMPLE PHRASES

Tengo una familia que **vestir** y alimentar. I have a family to feed and clothe.
Viste bien. She's a sharp dresser.
Estaba vistiendo a los niños. I was dressing the children.
Me vestí en cinco minutos. I got dressed in five minutes.

Remember that subject pronouns are not used very often in Spanish.

vestir

	FUTURE	CONDITIONAL
(yo)	**vestiré**	**vestiría**
(tú)	**vestirás**	**vestirías**
(él/ella/usted)	**vestirá**	**vestiría**
(nosotros/as)	**vestiremos**	**vestiríamos**
(vosotros/as)	**vestiréis**	**vestiríais**
(ellos/ellas/ ustedes)	**vestirán**	**vestirían**

	PRESENT SUBJUNCTIVE	IMPERFECT SUBJUNCTIVE
(yo)	**vista**	**vistiera** *or* **vistiese**
(tú)	**vistas**	**vistieras** *or* **vistieses**
(él/ella/usted)	**vista**	**vistiera** *or* **vistiese**
(nosotros/as)	**vistamos**	**vistiéramos** *or* **vistiésemos**
(vosotros/as)	**vistáis**	**vistierais** *or* **vistieseis**
(ellos/ellas/ ustedes)	**vistan**	**vistieran** *or* **vistiesen**

IMPERATIVE

viste / vestid

Use the present subjunctive in all cases other than these tú and vosotros affirmative forms.

EXAMPLE PHRASES

Se vistió de princesa. She dressed up as a princess.

Vestía jeans y una camiseta. He was wearing jeans and a shirt.

Su padre **vestirá** de uniforme. Her father will wear a uniform.

¡**Vístete** de una vez! For the last time, go and get dressed!

Remember that subject pronouns are not used very often in Spanish.

vivir (to live)

	PRESENT	PRESENT PERFECT
(yo)	vivo	he vivido
(tú)	vives	has vivido
(él/ella/usted)	vive	ha vivido
(nosotros/as)	vivimos	hemos vivido
(vosotros/as)	vivís	habéis vivido
(ellos/ellas/ ustedes)	viven	han vivido

	PRETERITE	IMPERFECT
(yo)	viví	vivía
(tú)	viviste	vivías
(él/ella/usted)	vivió	vivía
(nosotros/as)	vivimos	vivíamos
(vosotros/as)	vivisteis	vivíais
(ellos/ellas/ ustedes)	vivieron	vivían

GERUND
viviendo

PAST PARTICIPLE
vivido

EXAMPLE PHRASES

Me gusta **vivir** sola. I like living on my own.

¿Dónde **vives**? Where do you live?

Siempre **viveron** muy bien. They always had a very comfortable life.

Vivían de su pensión. They lived on his pension.

Remember that subject pronouns are not used very often in Spanish.

vivir

	FUTURE	CONDITIONAL
(yo)	**viviré**	**viviría**
(tú)	**vivirás**	**vivirías**
(él/ella/usted)	**vivirá**	**viviría**
(nosotros/as)	**viviremos**	**viviríamos**
(vosotros/as)	**viviréis**	**viviríais**
(ellos/ellas/ ustedes)	**vivirán**	**vivirían**

	PRESENT SUBJUNCTIVE	IMPERFECT SUBJUNCTIVE
(yo)	**viva**	**viviera** *or* **viviese**
(tú)	**vivas**	**vivieras** *or* **vivieses**
(él/ella/usted)	**viva**	**viviera** *or* **viviese**
(nosotros/as)	**vivamos**	**viviéramos** *or* **viviésemos**
(vosotros/as)	**viváis**	**vivierais** *or* **vivieseis**
(ellos/ellas/ ustedes)	**vivan**	**vivieran** *or* **viviesen**

IMPERATIVE

vive / vivid

Use the present subjunctive in all cases other than these tú and vosotros affirmative forms.

EXAMPLE PHRASES

Viviremos en el centro de la ciudad. We'll live downtown.

Si pudiéramos, **viviríamos** en el campo. We'd live in the country if we could.

Si **vivieran** más cerca, nos veríamos más a menudo. We'd see each other more often if you lived nearer.

¡**Viva**! Hurray!

Remember that subject pronouns are not used very often in Spanish.

volcar (to overturn)

	PRESENT	PRESENT PERFECT
(yo)	**vuelco**	**he volcado**
(tú)	**vuelcas**	**has volcado**
(él/ella/usted)	**vuelca**	**ha volcado**
(nosotros/as)	**volcamos**	**hemos volcado**
(vosotros/as)	**volcáis**	**habéis volcado**
(ellos/ellas/ ustedes)	**vuelcan**	**han volcado**

	PRETERITE	IMPERFECT
(yo)	**volqué**	**volcaba**
(tú)	**volcaste**	**volcabas**
(él/ella/usted)	**volcó**	**volcaba**
(nosotros/as)	**volcamos**	**volcábamos**
(vosotros/as)	**volcasteis**	**volcabais**
(ellos/ellas/ ustedes)	**volcaron**	**volcaban**

GERUND
volcando

PAST PARTICIPLE
volcado

EXAMPLE PHRASES

La camioneta **volcó**. The van rolled over.

Se vuelca en su trabajo. She throws herself into her work.

Remember that subject pronouns are not used very often in Spanish.

volcar

	FUTURE	CONDITIONAL
(yo)	**volcaré**	**volcaría**
(tú)	**volcarás**	**volcarías**
(él/ella/usted)	**volcará**	**volcaría**
(nosotros/as)	**volcaremos**	**volcaríamos**
(vosotros/as)	**volcaréis**	**volcaríais**
(ellos/ellas/ ustedes)	**volcarán**	**volcarían**

	PRESENT SUBJUNCTIVE	IMPERFECT SUBJUNCTIVE
(yo)	**vuelque**	**volcara** *or* **volcase**
(tú)	**vuelques**	**volcaras** *or* **volcases**
(él/ella/usted)	**vuelque**	**volcara** *or* **volcase**
(nosotros/as)	**volquemos**	**volcáramos** *or* **volcásemos**
(vosotros/as)	**volquéis**	**volcarais** *or* **volcaseis**
(ellos/ellas/ ustedes)	**vuelquen**	**volcaran** *or* **volcasen**

IMPERATIVE

vuelca / volcad

Use the present subjunctive in all cases other than these tú and vosotros affirmative forms.

EXAMPLE PHRASES

Si sigues moviéndote, harás que **vuelque** el bote. If you keep on moving like that, you'll make the boat capsize.

Ten cuidado, no **vuelques** el vaso. Be careful not to knock over the glass.

Vuelca el contenido sobre la cama. Empty the contents onto the bed.

Remember that subject pronouns are not used very often in Spanish.

volver (to return; to go/come back)

	PRESENT	PRESENT PERFECT
(yo)	**vuelvo**	**he vuelto**
(tú)	**vuelves**	**has vuelto**
(él/ella/usted)	**vuelve**	**ha vuelto**
(nosotros/as)	**volvemos**	**hemos vuelto**
(vosotros/as)	**volvéis**	**habéis vuelto**
(ellos/ellas/ ustedes)	**vuelven**	**han vuelto**

	PRETERITE	IMPERFECT
(yo)	**volví**	**volvía**
(tú)	**volviste**	**volvías**
(él/ella/usted)	**volvió**	**volvía**
(nosotros/as)	**volvimos**	**volvíamos**
(vosotros/as)	**volvisteis**	**volvíais**
(ellos/ellas/ ustedes)	**volvieron**	**volvían**

GERUND
volviendo

PAST PARTICIPLE
vuelto

EXAMPLE PHRASES

Mi padre **vuelve** mañana. My father's coming back tomorrow.

Volvió a casa. He went back home.

Volvía agotado de trabajar. I used to come back from work exhausted.

Remember that subject pronouns are not used very often in Spanish.

volver

	FUTURE	CONDITIONAL
(yo)	**volveré**	**volvería**
(tú)	**volverás**	**volverías**
(él/ella/usted)	**volverá**	**volvería**
(nosotros/as)	**volveremos**	**volveríamos**
(vosotros/as)	**volveréis**	**volveríais**
(ellos/ellas/ ustedes)	**volverán**	**volverían**

	PRESENT SUBJUNCTIVE	IMPERFECT SUBJUNCTIVE
(yo)	**vuelva**	**volviera** *or* **volviese**
(tú)	**vuelvas**	**volvieras** *or* **volvieses**
(él/ella/usted)	**vuelva**	**volviera** *or* **volviese**
(nosotros/as)	**volvamos**	**volviéramos** *or* **volviésemos**
(vosotros/as)	**volváis**	**volvierais** *or* **volvieseis**
(ellos/ellas/ ustedes)	**vuelvan**	**volvieran** *or* **volviesen**

IMPERATIVE

vuelve / volved

Use the present subjunctive in all cases other than these tú and vosotros affirmative forms.

EXAMPLE PHRASES

Todo **volverá** a la normalidad. Everything will return to normal.
Yo **volvería** a intentarlo. I'd try again.
No quiero que **vuelvas** allí. I don't want you to go back there.
No **vuelvas** por aquí. Don't come back here.
¡**Vuelve** a la cama! Go back to bed!

Remember that subject pronouns are not used very often in Spanish.

zurcir (to darn)

	PRESENT	PRESENT PERFECT
(yo)	**zurzo**	**he zurcido**
(tú)	**zurces**	**has zurcido**
(él/ella/usted)	**zurce**	**ha zurcido**
(nosotros/as)	**zurcimos**	**hemos zurcido**
(vosotros/as)	**zurcís**	**habéis zurcido**
(ellos/ellas/ ustedes)	**zurcen**	**han zurcido**

	PRETERITE	IMPERFECT
(yo)	**zurcí**	**zurcía**
(tú)	**zurciste**	**zurcías**
(él/ella/usted)	**zurció**	**zurcía**
(nosotros/as)	**zurcimos**	**zurcíamos**
(vosotros/as)	**zurcisteis**	**zurcíais**
(ellos/ellas/ ustedes)	**zurcieron**	**zurcían**

GERUND
zurciendo

PAST PARTICIPLE
zurcido

EXAMPLE PHRASES

¿Quién le **zurce** los calcetines? Who darns his socks?

Las sábanas estaban **zurcidas**. The sheets had been mended.

Remember that subject pronouns are not used very often in Spanish.

zurcir

	FUTURE	CONDITIONAL
(yo)	zurciré	zurciría
(tú)	zurcirás	zurcirías
(él/ella/usted)	zurcirá	zurciría
(nosotros/as)	zurciremos	zurciríamos
(vosotros/as)	zurciréis	zurciríais
(ellos/ellas/ ustedes)	zurcirán	zurcirían

	PRESENT SUBJUNCTIVE	IMPERFECT SUBJUNCTIVE
(yo)	zurza	zurciera *or* zurciese
(tú)	zurzas	zurcieras *or* zurcieses
(él/ella/usted)	zurza	zurciera *or* zurciese
(nosotros/as)	zurzamos	zurciéramos *or* zurciésemos
(vosotros/as)	zurzáis	zurcierais *or* zurcieseis
(ellos/ellas/ ustedes)	zurzan	zurcieran *or* zurciesen

IMPERATIVE

zurce / zurcid

Use the present subjunctive in all cases other than these tú and vosotros affirmative forms.

Remember that subject pronouns are not used very often in Spanish.

How to use the Verb Index

The verbs in bold are the model verbs which you will find in the Verb Tables. All the other verbs follow one of these patterns, so the number next to each verb indicates which pattern fits this particular verb. For example, **acampar** (*to camp*) follows the same pattern as **hablar** (number 340 in the Verb Tables).

All the verbs are in alphabetical order. Superior numbers ([1] etc) refer you to notes on page 468. These notes explain any differences between verbs and their model.

Notes

1 The verbs **anochecer**, **atardecer**, **granizar**, **helar**, **llover**, **nevar**, **nublarse** and **tronar** are used almost exclusively in the infinitive and third person singular forms.

2 The **past participle** of the verb **pudrir** is **podrido**.

Vocabulary

This section is divided into 50 topics, arranged in alphabetical order. This thematic approach enables you to learn related words and phrases together, so that you can become confident in using particular vocabulary in context.

Vocabulary within each topic is divided into nouns and useful phrases which are aimed at helping you to express yourself in idiomatic Spanish. Vocabulary within each topic is categorized to help you prioritize your learning. Essential words include the basic words you will need to be able to communicate effectively, important words help expand your knowledge, and useful words provide additional vocabulary which will enable you to express yourself more fully.

Nouns are grouped by gender: masculine ("el") nouns appear on the left-hand page, and feminine ("la") nouns on the right-hand page, enabling you to memorize words according to their gender. In addition, all feminine forms of adjectives are shown, as are irregular plurals.

At the end of the thematic section you will find a list of supplementary vocabulary, grouped according to parts of speech – adjective, verb, noun and so on. This is vocabulary which you will come across in many everyday situations.

ABBREVIATIONS

adj	adjective
adv	adverb
algn	alguien
conj	conjunction
f	feminine
inv	invariable
LAm	word used in Latin America
m	masculine
m+f	masculine and feminine form
Mex	word used in Mexico
n	noun
pl	plural
prep	preposition
sb	somebody
sing	singular
Sp	word used in Spain
sth	something

The swung dash ~ is used to indicate the basic elements of the compound and appropriate endings are then added.

PLURALS AND GENDER

In Spanish, if a noun ends in a vowel it generally takes –s in the plural (casa > casas). If it ends in a consonant (including y) it generally takes –es in the plural (reloj > relojes). If it doesn't follow these rules, then the plural will be shown in the text.

Although most masculine nouns use "el" and most feminine nouns use "la", you will find a few nouns grouped under feminine words which use "el" (el agua water; el arca chest; el aula classroom) because they are actually feminine. For more information, see Grammar section page 11.

ESSENTIAL WORDS *(masculine)*

el	**aduanero**	customs officer
el	**aeropuerto**	airport
el	**agente aduanal** (*Mex*)	customs officer
el	**agente de viajes**	travel agent
el	**alquiler de coches** (*Sp*)	car rental
el	**avión** (*pl* aviones)	plane
el	**boleto** (*LAm*), el **billete** (*Sp*)	ticket
el	**bolso**	bag
el	**carné de identidad** (*Sp*)	ID
el	**duty free**	duty-free (shop)
el	**equipaje**	luggage
el	**equipaje de mano**	carry-on luggage
el	**horario**	schedule, timetable
el	**número**	number
el	**pasajero**	passenger
el	**pasaporte**	passport
el	**pase de abordar** (*Mex*)	boarding pass
el	**(precio del) boleto** (*LAm*) *or* **billete** (*Sp*)	fare
el	**retraso**	delay
los	**sanitarios**	restrooms
el	**taxi**	taxi
el	**turista**	tourist
el	**viaje**	trip
el	**viajero**	traveler

USEFUL PHRASES

viajar en avión **to travel by plane**
un boleto (*LAm*) *or* billete (*Sp*) de ida **a one-way ticket**
un boleto (*LAm*) *or* billete (*Sp*) de ida y vuelta, un boleto redondo (*Mex*) **a round-trip ticket**
reservar un boleto (*LAm*) *or* un billete (*Sp*) de avión **to book a plane ticket**
"por avión" **"by airmail"**
facturar el equipaje, checar *or* documentar el equipaje (*Mex*) **to check in one's bags**
el avión despegó/aterrizó **the plane took off/landed**
el panel de llegadas/salidas **the arrivals/departures board**
el vuelo número 776 procedente de Buenos Aires/con destino a Buenos Aires **flight number 776 from Buenos Aires/to Buenos Aires**

ESSENTIAL WORDS *(feminine)*

la **aduana**	customs
la **aduanera**	customs officer
la **agente aduanal** (*Mex*)	customs officer
la **agente de viajes**	travel agent
la **cancelación** (*pl* cancelaciones)	cancelation
la **conexión** (*pl* conexiones)	connection
la **entrada**	entrance
la **identificación**	ID
la **información** (*pl* informaciones)	information desk; information
la **llegada**	arrival
la **maleta**	suitcase, bag
la **pasajera**	passenger
la **petaca** (*Mex*)	suitcase, bag
la **puerta de embarque**	departure gate
la **renta de autos** (*Mex*)	car rental
la **reservación** (*LAm*), **la reserva** (*Sp*)	reservation
la **salida**	departure; exit
la **salida de emergencia**	emergency exit
la **tarifa**	fare
la **tarjeta de embarque**	boarding pass
la **terminal**	terminal
la **turista**	tourist
la **viajera**	traveler

USEFUL PHRASES

recoger el equipaje **to pick up one's baggage**
"recogida de equipajes" **"baggage claim"**
perdí la conexión **I missed my connection**
pasar por la aduana **to go through customs**
tengo algo que declarar **I have something to declare**
no tengo nada que declarar **I have nothing to declare**
registrar el equipaje **to search the bags**

IMPORTANT WORDS *(masculine)*

el **accidente de avión**	plane crash
el **boleto** (*LAm*) *or* el **billete** (*Sp*) **electrónico**	e-ticket
el **carrito**	cart
el **cinturón de seguridad** (*pl* cinturones ~ ~)	seat belt
el **helicóptero**	helicopter
el **mapa**	map
el **mareo (en avión)**	airsickness
el **piloto**	pilot
el **reloj**	clock, watch
el **vuelo**	flight

USEFUL WORDS *(masculine)*

el **asiento**	seat
el **aterrizaje**	landing
el **auxiliar de vuelo**	flight attendant
el **control de seguridad**	security check
el **controlador aéreo**	air-traffic controller
los **derechos de aduana**	customs duty
el **despegue**	take-off
el **detector de metales**	metal detector
el **embarque**	boarding
el **espacio para aseo para bebés**	baby change facility
el **horario**	schedule, timetable
el **jumbo**	jumbo jet
los **mandos**	controls
el **paracaídas** (*pl inv*)	parachute
el **radar**	radar
el **reactor**	jet plane/engine
el **sobrecargo** (*Mex*)	flight attendant
el **vacacionista** (*LAm*)	vacationer

USEFUL PHRASES

a bordo **on board**; "prohibido fumar" **"no smoking"**
"abróchense el cinturón de seguridad" **"fasten your seat belts"**
estamos sobrevolando la ciudad de México **we are flying over Mexico City**
estoy mareado **I feel nauseous**; secuestrar un avión **to hijack a plane**

IMPORTANT WORDS *(feminine)*

la **duración** (*pl* duraciones)	length; duration
la **escalera eléctrica** *or* **mecánica**	escalator
la **piloto**	pilot
la **sala de embarque**	departure area
la **velocidad**	speed

USEFUL WORDS *(feminine)*

el **ala** (*f pl* las alas)	wing
la **altitud**	altitude
la **altura**	height
la **auxiliar de vuelo**	flight attendant
la **barrera del sonido**	sound barrier
la **bolsa de aire**	air pocket
la **caja negra**	black box
la **cinta transportadora**	carousel
la **controladora aérea**	air-traffic controller
la **escala**	stopover
la **etiqueta**	label
la **hélice**	propeller
la **línea aérea**	airline
la **pista (de aterrizaje)**	runway
la **sobrecargo** (*Mex*)	flight attendant
la **terminal**	terminal
la **tienda libre de impuestos**	duty-free shop
la **torre de control**	control tower
la **tripulación** (*pl* tripulaciones)	crew
la **turbulencia**	turbulence
la **vacacionista** (*LAm*)	vacationer
la **ventanilla**	window

USEFUL PHRASES

"pasajeros del vuelo AB251 con destino a Lima embarquen por la puerta 51"
"flight AB251 to Lima now boarding at gate 51"

hicimos escala en Nueva York **we stopped over in New York**

un aterrizaje forzoso *or* de emergencia **an emergency landing**

un aterrizaje violento **a crash landing**

cigarrillos libres de impuestos **duty-free cigarettes**

ESSENTIAL WORDS *(masculine)*

el **animal**	animal
el **buey** (*pl* ~es)	ox
el **caballo**	horse
el **cachorro**	puppy
el **cerdo**	pig
el **conejo**	rabbit
el **cordero**	lamb
el **elefante**	elephant
el **gato**	cat
el **gatito**	kitten
el **hámster** (*pl* ~s)	hamster
el **león** (*pl* leones)	lion
el **pájaro**	bird
el **pelaje**	fur, coat
el **pelo**	coat, hair
el **perro**	dog
el **perrito**	puppy
el **pescado**	fish
el **pez** (*pl* peces)	fish
el **potro**	foal
el **ratón** (*pl* ratones)	mouse
el **ternero**	calf
el **tigre**	tiger
el **zoo** (*pl* ~s)	zoo
el **zoológico**	zoo

USEFUL PHRASES

me gustan los gatos, odio las serpientes, prefiero los ratones I like cats, I hate snakes, I prefer mice

tenemos 2 mascotas we have 2 pets

no tenemos mascotas we have no pets

los animales salvajes wild animals

los animales domésticos *or* las mascotas pets

el ganado livestock

poner un animal en una jaula to put an animal in a cage

liberar un animal to set an animal free

ESSENTIAL WORDS *(feminine)*

el **ave** (*f pl* las aves)	bird
la **gata**	cat (female)
la **oveja**	ewe
la **perra**	dog (female)
la **tortuga**	turtle, tortoise
la **vaca**	cow

IMPORTANT WORDS *(feminine)*

la **cola**	tail
la **jaula**	cage

USEFUL PHRASES

el perro ladra/gruñe the dog barks/growls
el gato maúlla/ronronea the cat meows/purrs
me gusta la equitación *or* andar a caballo I like horseback riding
a caballo on horseback
"cuidado con el perro" "beware of the dog"
"no se admiten perros" "no dogs allowed"
"¡quieto!" (*to a dog*) "down, boy!"
los derechos de los animales animal rights

USEFUL WORDS *(masculine)*

el **asno**	donkey
el **burro**	donkey
el **camello**	camel
el **canguro**	kangaroo
el **caparazón** (*pl* caparazones)	shell (*of turtle*)
el **casco**	hoof
el **cerdo**	pig
el **ciervo**	deer
el **cocodrilo**	crocodile
el **colmillo (de elefante)**	(elephant) tusk
el **conejillo de Indias**	guinea pig
el **cuerno**	horn
el **erizo**	hedgehog
el **guajolote** (*Mex*)	turkey
el **hipopótamo**	hippopotamus
el **hocico**	snout
el **lobo**	wolf
el **macho cabrío**	goat (male)
el **mono**	monkey
el **murciélago**	bat
el **oso**	bear
el **oso polar**	polar bear
el **pavo**	turkey
el **pony** (*pl* ~s)	pony
el **rinoceronte**	rhinoceros
el **sapo**	toad
el **tiburón** (*pl* tiburones)	shark
el **topo**	mole
el **toro**	bull
el **zorro**	fox

USEFUL WORDS *(feminine)*

la **ardilla**	squirrel
el **asta** (*f pl* las astas)	antler
la **ballena**	whale
la **boca**	mouth
la **bolsa**	pouch (*of a kangaroo*)
la **cabra**	goat (female)
la **crin**	mane
la **culebra**	(grass) snake
la **foca**	seal
la **garra**	claw
la **jirafa**	giraffe
la **joroba**	hump (*of a camel*)
la **leona**	lioness
la **liebre**	hare
la **melena**	mane
la **mula**	mule
la **pata**	paw
la **pezuña**	hoof
la **piel**	fur; hide (*of a cow, elephant, etc*)
la **rana**	frog
las **rayas**	stripes (*of a zebra*)
la **serpiente**	snake
la **tienda de animales**	pet store
la **tigresa**	tigress
la **trampa**	trap
la **trompa**	trunk (*of an elephant*)
la **yegua**	mare
la **zebra**	zebra

ESSENTIAL WORDS *(masculine)*

el **casco**	helmet
el **ciclismo**	cycling
el **ciclista**	cyclist
el **faro**	light
el **freno**	brake
el **neumático** (*Sp*)	tire

IMPORTANT WORDS *(masculine)*

el **pinchazo**	flat tire

USEFUL WORDS *(masculine)*

el **ascenso**	climb
el **asiento** (*LAm*)	seat
el **candado**	padlock
el **carril para bicicletas**	bicycle lane
el **desviador** *or* **descarrilador**	derailleur
el **descenso**	descent
el **dínamo** (*LAm*)	generator
el **eje**	hub
el **guardabarros** (*pl inv*) (*Sp*)	fender
el **kit de reparación de pinchazos** (*pl* ~s ~ ~ ~ ~)	flat repair kit
el **kit de reparación de ponchaduras** (*pl* ~s ~ ~ ~ ~) (*Mex*)	flat repair kit
el **manillar** (*Sp*)	handlebars
el **manubrio** (*LAm*)	handlebars
el **pedal**	pedal
el **portaequipajes** (*pl inv*)	rack
el **radio**	spoke
el **reflector**	reflector
el **sillín** (*pl* sillines) (*Sp*)	seat
el **timbre**	bell

USEFUL PHRASES

ir en bici(cleta) to go by bike
andar en bici(cleta) to bike
vine en bici(cleta) I came by bike

ESSENTIAL WORDS *(feminine)*

la **bici**	bike
la **bicicleta**	bicycle
la **bicicleta de montaña**	mountain bike
la **llanta** (*LAm*)	tire
la **salpicadera** (*Mex*)	fender

IMPORTANT WORDS *(feminine)*

la **ponchadura** (*Mex*)	flat tire
la **rueda**	wheel
la **velocidad**	speed; gear

USEFUL WORDS *(feminine)*

la **alforja**	saddlebag
la **barra**	crossbar
la **bomba**	pump
la **cadena**	chain
la **cuesta**	slope
la **cumbre**	top (*of a hill*)
la **dínamo** (*Sp*)	generator
la **luz delantera** (*pl* luces ~s)	front light
la **pendiente**	slope
la **subida**	climb
la **válvula**	valve

USEFUL PHRASES

ir a dar una vuelta *or* a pasear en bici(cleta) to go for a bike ride
se me ponchó una llanta (*Mex*) I had a flat
arreglar una ponchadura (*Mex*) *or* un pinchazo to fix a flat
la rueda delantera/trasera the front/back wheel
inflar las llantas *(LAm)* to inflate the tires
brillante, reluciente shiny
oxidado(a) rusty
fluorescente fluorescent

ESSENTIAL WORDS *(masculine)*

el **cielo**	sky
el **gallo**	rooster
el **ganso**	goose
el **guajolote** (*Mex*)	turkey
el **loro**	parrot
el **pájaro**	bird
el **pato**	duck
el **pavo**	turkey
el **periquito**	parakeet
el **pollito**	chick

USEFUL WORDS *(masculine)*

el **avestruz** (*pl* avestruces)	ostrich
el **búho**	owl
el **buitre**	vulture
el **canario**	canary
el **cardenal**	cardinal
el **cisne**	swan
el **cuervo**	raven; crow
el **cuco**	cuckoo
el **estornino**	starling
el **faisán** (*pl* faisanes)	pheasant
el **gorrión** (*pl* gorriones)	sparrow
el **halcón** (*pl* halcones)	falcon
el **huevo**	egg
el **martín pescador** (*pl* martines ~es)	kingfisher
el **nido**	nest
el **pájaro carpintero**	woodpecker
el **pavo real**	peacock
el **petirrojo**	robin
el **pico**	beak
el **pingüino**	penguin
el **ruiseñor**	nightingale
el **zopilote**	black vulture

ESSENTIAL WORDS *(feminine)*

la **gallina**	hen

USEFUL WORDS *(feminine)*

el **águila** (*f pl* las águilas)	eagle
el **ala** (*f pl* las alas)	wing
la **alondra**	lark
el **ave** (*f pl* las aves)	bird
el **ave de rapiña** (*f pl* las ~s ~ ~)	bird of prey
el **ave rapaz** (*f pl* las ~s rapaces)	bird of prey
la **cigüeña**	stork
la **codorniz** (*pl* codornices)	quail
la **gaviota**	seagull
la **golondrina**	swallow
la **grulla**	crane
la **jaula**	cage
la **paloma**	pigeon; dove
la **perdiz** (*pl* perdices)	partridge
la **pluma**	feather
la **urraca**	magpie

USEFUL PHRASES

volar **to fly**
levantar el vuelo **to fly away**
construir un nido **to build a nest**
silbar **to whistle**
cantar **to sing**
la gente los pone en jaulas **people put them in cages**
hibernar **to hibernate**
poner un huevo **to lay an egg**
un ave migratoria **a migratory bird**

ESSENTIAL WORDS *(masculine)*

el **brazo**	arm
el **cabello**	hair
el **corazón** (*pl* corazones)	heart
el **cuerpo**	body
el **dedo**	finger
el **diente**	tooth
el **estómago**	stomach
el **ojo**	eye
el **pelo**	hair
el **pie**	foot
el **rostro**	face

IMPORTANT WORDS *(masculine)*

el **cuello**	neck
el **hombro**	shoulder
el **mentón**	chin
el **pecho**	chest; breast; bust
el **pulgar**	thumb
el **tobillo**	ankle

USEFUL PHRASES

parado(a) standing
sentado(a) sitting
acostado(a) lying

ESSENTIAL WORDS *(feminine)*

la **boca**	mouth
la **cabeza**	head
la **espalda**	back
la **garganta**	throat
la **mano**	hand
la **nariz** (*pl* narices)	nose
la **oreja**	ear
la **pierna**	leg
la **rodilla**	knee

IMPORTANT WORDS *(feminine)*

la **barbilla**	chin
la **cara**	face
la **ceja**	eyebrow
la **frente**	forehead
la **lengua**	tongue
la **mejilla**	cheek
la **piel**	skin
la **sangre**	blood
la **voz** (*pl* voces)	voice

USEFUL PHRASES

grande big
alto(a) tall
pequeño(a) small
bajo(a) short
gordo(a) fat
flaco(a) skinny
delgado(a) slim
bonito(a) pretty
feo(a) ugly

USEFUL WORDS *(masculine)*

el **cerebro**	brain
el **codo**	elbow
el **cutis** (*pl inv*)	skin, complexion
el **dedo del pie**	toe
el **dedo índice**	forefinger
el **dedo gordo**	the big toe
los **dedos de los pies**	toes
el **esqueleto**	skeleton
el **gesto**	gesture
el **hígado**	liver
el **hueso**	bone
el **labio**	lip
el **músculo**	muscle
el **muslo**	thigh
el **párpado**	eyelid
el **pulmón** (*pl* pulmones)	lung
el **puño**	fist
el **rasgo**	feature
el **riñón** (*pl* riñones)	kidney
el **seno**	breast
el **talle**	waist
el **talón** (*pl* talones)	heel
el **trasero**	bottom

USEFUL PHRASES

sonarse (la nariz) to blow one's nose
cortarse las uñas to cut one's nails
cortarse el pelo to have one's hair cut
encogerse de hombros to shrug one's shoulders
asentir/decir que sí con la cabeza to nod one's head
negar/decir que no con la cabeza to shake one's head
ver to see; oír to hear; sentir to feel
oler to smell; tocar to touch; probar to taste
estrecharle la mano a alguien to shake hands with somebody
saludar a alguien con la mano to wave to somebody
señalar algo to point at something

USEFUL WORDS *(feminine)*

la **arteria**	artery
la **cadera**	hip
la **carne**	flesh
la **columna (vertebral)**	spine
la **costilla**	rib
la **facción** (*pl* facciones)	feature
la **mandíbula**	jaw
la **muñeca**	wrist
la **nuca**	nape (*of the neck*)
la **pantorrilla**	calf (*of the leg*)
la **pestaña**	eyelash
la **planta del pie**	sole of the foot
la **pupila**	pupil (*of the eye*)
la **sien**	temple (*of the head*)
la **talla**	size
la **tez** (*pl* teces)	complexion
la **uña**	nail
la **vena**	vein

USEFUL PHRASES

contorno de caderas **hip measurement**
cintura **waist measurement**
contorno de pecho **chest measurement**
sordo(a) **deaf**
ciego(a) **blind**
mudo(a) **mute**
discapacitado(a) **disabled**
disminuido(a) psíquico(a) **person with learning disabilities**
es más alto que tú **he is taller than you**
ha crecido mucho **(s)he has grown a lot**
estoy demasiado gordo(a) *or* tengo sobrepeso **I am overweight**
está más gorda/delgada **she has put on/lost weight**
mide 1,47 metros **(s)he is 1.47 meters tall**
pesa 40 kilos **(s)he weighs 40 kilos**

SEASONS

la **primavera**	spring
el **verano**	summer
el **otoño**	fall, autumn
el **invierno**	winter

MONTHS

enero	January	**julio**	July
febrero	February	**agosto**	August
marzo	March	**septiembre**	September
abril	April	**octubre**	October
mayo	May	**noviembre**	November
junio	June	**diciembre**	December

DAYS OF THE WEEK

lunes	Monday
martes	Tuesday
miércoles	Wednesday
jueves	Thursday
viernes	Friday
sábado	Saturday
domingo	Sunday

USEFUL PHRASES

en primavera/verano/otoño/invierno in spring/summer/the fall/winter
en mayo in May
el 10 de julio de 2006 on July 10, 2006
es 3 de diciembre it's December 3rd
los sábados voy al club on Saturdays I go to the club
el sábado fui al club on Saturday I went to the club
el próximo sábado/el sábado pasado next/last Saturday
el sábado anterior/siguiente the previous/following Saturday

CALENDAR

el **calendario**	calendar
el **día**	day
los **días de la semana**	days of the week
el **día festivo**	national holiday
la **estación** (*pl* estaciones)	season
el **mes**	month
la **semana**	week

USEFUL PHRASES

el día de los Inocentes *celebrated on December 28 in the Spanish speaking world, similar to April Fools' Day*
la broma del día de los Inocentes *practical joke similar to an April fool*
el primero de mayo May Day
el día de la Hispanidad *or* de la raza Columbus Day (*October* 12)
el himno nacional national anthem
el día D D-Day
el día de los enamorados *or* de San Valentín Valentine's Day
el día de Todos los Santos All Saints' Day (*November* 1)
el día de muertos All Souls' Day (*November* 2)
la Semana Santa Easter
el Domingo de Resurrección *or* de Pascua Easter Sunday
el Miércoles de Ceniza Ash Wednesday
el Viernes Santo Good Friday
la Cuaresma Lent
la Pascua judía Passover
el Ramadán Ramadan
el Hanukkah Hanukkah *or* Chanukah
el Adviento Advent
la Nochebuena Christmas Eve
la Navidad Christmas
en Navidad during Christmas
el día de Navidad Christmas Day
la noche de Fin de Año New Year's Eve
el día de Año Nuevo New Year's Day
la cena *or* fiesta de Fin de Año New Year's Eve dinner *or* party

ESSENTIAL WORDS *(masculine)*

el **aniversario de boda**	wedding anniversary
el **cumpleaños** (*pl inv*)	birthday
el **(día del) santo**	saint's day
el **divorcio**	divorce
el **matrimonio**	marriage
el **regalo**	gift, present

IMPORTANT WORDS *(masculine)*

el **compromiso**	engagement
el **festival**	festival
los **fuegos artificiales**	fireworks; fireworks display
el **nacimiento**	birth
el **parque de diversiones**	amusement park

USEFUL WORDS *(masculine)*

el **bautismo**	baptism
el **cementerio**	cemetery
el **entierro**	burial
el **festival folclórico**	folk festival
el **funeral**	funeral
el **testigo**	witness
el **regalo de Navidad**	Christmas gift

USEFUL PHRASES

celebrar el cumpleaños **to celebrate one's birthday**
mi hermana nació en 1995 **my sister was born in 1995**
acaba de cumplir 17 años **she's/he's just turned 17**
me regaló esto **(s)he gave me this**
¡te lo regalo! **I'm giving it to you!**
gracias **thank you**
divorciarse **to get divorced**
casarse **to get married**
comprometerse (con algn) **to get engaged (to sb)**
mi padre murió hace dos años **my father died two years ago**
enterrar **to bury**

ESSENTIAL WORDS *(feminine)*

la **boda**	wedding
la **cita**	appointment; date
la **fecha**	date
la **fiesta**	festival, holiday; party

IMPORTANT WORDS *(feminine)*

las **fiestas**	festivities
la **feria**	fair
la **muerte**	death
la **hoguera**	bonfire

USEFUL WORDS *(feminine)*

la **ceremonia**	ceremony
la **dama de honor**	bridesmaid
la **invitación de boda** (*pl* invitaciones ~ ~)	wedding invitation
la **jubilación** (*pl* jubilaciones)	retirement
la **luna de miel**	honeymoon
la **procesión** (*pl* procesiones)	procession; march
la **tarjeta de felicitación**	greeting card
la **testigo**	witness

USEFUL PHRASES

bodas de plata/oro/diamante silver/golden/diamond wedding anniversary
desear a algn (un) Feliz Año to wish sb a Happy New Year
dar *or* hacer una fiesta to have a party
invitar a los amigos to invite one's friends
elegir un regalo to choose a gift
¡Feliz navidad! Merry Christmas!
¡Feliz cumpleaños! happy birthday!
(con) nuestros mejores deseos (with) best wishes
¡Felices Pascuas! Happy Easter!; Merry Christmas!

ESSENTIAL WORDS *(masculine)*

los	**aseos** (*Sp*)	restrooms
los	**baños** (*LAm*)	bathrooms; washrooms
el	**basurero** *or* el **bote de la basura** (*LAm*)	garbage can
el	**bote**	can
el	**camping** (*pl* ~s)	camping; campsite
el	**campista**	camper
el	**cerillo** (*LAm*)	match
el	**cubo de la basura** (*Sp*)	garbage can
el	**cuchillo**	knife
el	**emplazamiento**	site, location
el	**espejo**	mirror
el	**gas**	gas
el	**guarda**	warden
el	**lavabo**	sink
el	**plato**	plate
los	**servicios** (*Sp*)	restrooms
el	**suplemento**	extra charge
el	**tenedor**	fork
el	**trailer** (*pl* ~s) (*LAm*)	trailer
el	**vehículo**	vehicle

IMPORTANT WORDS *(masculine)*

el	**abrelatas** (*pl inv*)	can opener
el	**colchón inflable** (*pl* colchones ~s)	airbed
el	**detergente**	detergent
el	**enchufe**	plug
el	**hornillo**	stove
el	**sacacorchos** (*pl inv*)	corkscrew
el	**saco de dormir**	sleeping bag
el	**tomacorriente** (*LAm*)	socket

USEFUL PHRASES

ir de *or* hacer camping **to go camping**
acampar **to camp**
armar una tienda *or* carpa **to pitch a tent**
hacer una hoguera **to build a fire**

ESSENTIAL WORDS *(feminine)*

el	**agua (no) potable** (*f*)	(non-)drinking water
la	**alberca** (*Mex*)	swimming pool
la	**caja**	box
la	**cama plegable**	cot
la	**campista**	camper
la	**caravana** (*Sp*)	trailer
la	**carpa** (*LAm*)	tent
la	**cerilla** (*Sp*)	match
la	**cocina de camping-gas**	gas stove
la	**comida enlatada**	canned food
la	**cuchara**	spoon
la	**ducha**	shower
la	**estufa de camping-gas** (*Mex*)	gas stove
la	**lata**	can
la	**lavadora**	washing machine
la	**linterna**	flashlight
la	**mesa**	table
la	**navaja**	penknife
la	**noche**	night
la	**piscina** (*Sp*)	swimming pool
la	**sala**	room; hall
la	**silla reclinable**	deckchair
la	**tienda (de campaña)**	tent
la	**tumbona** (*Sp*)	deckchair

IMPORTANT WORDS *(feminine)*

la	**barbacoa**	barbecue
la	**bolsa de dormir**	sleeping bag
las	**instalaciones sanitarias**	washing facilities
la	**lavandería**	Laundromat®
la	**mochila**	backpack
las	**normas**	rules
la	**ropa lavada/para lavar**	laundry
la	**sala de juegos**	gameroom
la	**sombra**	shade; shadow
la	**toma de corriente**	socket

ESSENTIAL WORDS *(masculine)*

el **agricultor**	farmer
el **auxiliar de vuelo**	flight attendant
el **banco**	bank
el **bombero**	firefighter, fireman
el **cajero**	check-out clerk; cashier
el **cartero**	mailman, postal carrier
el **diseñador de páginas web**	web designer
el **electricista**	electrician
el **empleado**	employee
el **empresario**	businessman; employer
el **enfermero**	nurse
el **farmacéutico**	pharmacist
el **informático**	IT specialist
el **jefe**	boss, superior
el **maestro**	(elementary school) teacher
el **mecánico**	mechanic
el **médico**	doctor
el **minero**	miner
el **oficio**	trade
el **policía**	policeman, police officer
el **profesor**	teacher; professor
el **redactor**	editor
el **secretario**	secretary
el **sobrecargo** (*Mex*)	flight attendant
el **soldado**	soldier
el **sueldo**	salary; wages
el **taxista**	taxi driver
el **trabajo**	job; work
el **vendedor**	sales assistant

USEFUL PHRASES

interesante/poco interesante interesting/not very interesting
es cartero he is a mailman
trabajar to work
hacerse, volverse to become

ESSENTIAL WORDS *(feminine)*

la **agricultora**	farmer
la **ambición** (*pl* ambiciones)	ambition
la **auxiliar de vuelo**	flight attendant
la **cajera**	check-out clerk; cashier
la **cartera**	postal carrier
la **empleada**	employee
la **enfermera**	nurse
la **estrella** (*m+f*)	star
la **fábrica**	factory
la **informática**	IT specialist
la **jefa**	boss, superior
la **jubilación** (*pl* jubilaciones)	retirement
la **maestra**	(elementary school) teacher
la **mecanógrafa**	typist
la **médico** *or* la **médica**	doctor
la **oficina**	office
la **profesión** (*pl* profesiones)	profession
la **profesora**	teacher; professor
la **recepcionista**	receptionist
la **redactora**	editor
la **secretaria**	secretary
la **sobrecargo** (*Mex*)	flight attendant
la **vendedora**	sales assistant
la **vida**	life
la **vida laboral**	working life

USEFUL PHRASES

trabajar para ganarse la vida to work for one's living
mi ambición es ser juez(a) it is my ambition to be a judge
¿en qué trabajas? what do you do (for a living)?
solicitar un trabajo to apply for a job

IMPORTANT WORDS *(masculine)*

el **aprendizaje**	apprenticeship
el **asalariado**	wage earner
el **aumento**	raise
el **autor**	author
el **cocinero**	cook
el **colega**	colleague
el **comerciante**	shopkeeper
el **contrato**	contract
el **conserje**	caretaker
el **decorador**	interior designer
el **desempleado**	unemployed person
el **desempleo**	unemployment
el **empleo**	job, position
el **fontanero** (*Sp*)	plumber
el **futuro**	future
el **gerente**	manager
el **hombre de negocios**	businessman
el **mercado laboral**	job market
el **negocio** *or* los **negocios**	business
el **óptico**	optician
el **peluquero**	hairdresser
el **piloto**	pilot
el **pintor**	painter
el **plomero** (*LAm*)	plumber
el **presidente**	president; chairperson
el **sindicato**	trade union
el **trabajador**	worker
el **trabajo**	job

USEFUL PHRASES

estar desempleado(a) to be unemployed

contrato indefinido/temporal/a término fijo permanent/temporary/fixed-term contract

IMPORTANT WORDS *(feminine)*

la **agencia de trabajo temporal**	temp agency
la **asalariada**	wage earner
la **biblioteca**	library
la **carrera**	career
la **carta adjunta**	cover letter
la **cocinera**	cook
la **colega**	colleague
la **conserje**	caretaker
la **entrevista (de trabajo)**	(job) interview
la **gerente**	manager
la **huelga**	strike
la **mujer de negocios**	businessperson (female)
la **oficina de empleo**	employment office
la **peluquera**	hairdresser
la **pintora**	painter
la **política**	politics
la **presidenta**	president; chairperson
la **solicitud**	application
la **trabajadora**	worker

USEFUL PHRASES

"empleos" "seeking employment"
"vacantes" "help wanted"
estar en/pertenercer a un sindicato to be in a union
ganar 600 dólares a la semana to earn $600 a week
una subida *or* un aumento de sueldo a pay raise
declararse en huelga *or* ir a la huelga to go on strike
estar en huelga to be on strike
trabajar jornada completa/media jornada to work full-time/part-time
trabajar horas extra(s) to work overtime
reducción de la jornada laboral reduction in working hours

USEFUL WORDS *(masculine)*

el **abogado**	lawyer
el **albañil**	construction worker
el **arquitecto**	architect
el **artista**	artist
el **carpintero**	carpenter
el **cirujano**	surgeon
el **contador** (*LAm*), el **contable** (*Sp*)	accountant
el **cosmonauta**	cosmonaut
el **cura**	priest
el **curso de formación**	training course
el **diputado**	representative, congressman
el **diseñador**	designer
el **ejecutivo**	executive
el **escritor**	writer
el **fotógrafo**	photographer
el **funcionario público**	civil servant
el **horario**	schedule
el **ingeniero**	engineer
el **intérprete**	interpreter
el **investigador**	researcher
el **juez** (*pl* jueces)	judge
el **locutor**	announcer
el **marinero**	sailor
el **modelo**	model (*person*)
el **monje**	monk
el **notario**	notary public
el **paro** (*Sp*)	unemployment benefit
el **periodista**	journalist
el **(período de) trabajo en prácticas**	work placement
el **personal**	staff
el **político**	politician
el **procurador**	attorney
el **religioso**	monk
el **representante**	rep; sales rep
el **sacerdote**	priest
el **subsidio de desempleo**	unemployment benefit
el **traductor**	translator
el **veterinario**	veterinarian
el **viticultor**	vintner, wine grower

USEFUL WORDS *(feminine)*

la **abogada**	lawyer
la **administración** (*pl* administraciones)	administration
el **ama de casa** (*f pl* amas ~ ~)	housewife
la **artista**	artist
la **compañía**	company
la **contadora** (*LAm*), la **contable** (*Sp*)	accountant
la **empresa**	company
la **formación**	training
la **funcionaria pública**	civil servant
la **indemnización por desempleo**	severance pay
la **intérprete**	interpreter
la **jueza**	judge
la **locutora**	announcer
la **modelo**	model (*person*)
la **modista**	dressmaker
la **monja**	nun
la **orientación profesional**	career counseling
la **periodista**	journalist
la **policía**	police officer, policewoman
la **religiosa**	nun
la **representante**	rep; sales rep
la **taquimecanógrafa**	shorthand typist
la **traductora**	translator

USEFUL PHRASES

el trabajo temporal **seasonal work**
un empleo temporal/permanente **a temporary/permanent job**
un trabajo a tiempo parcial *or* a medio tiempo **a part-time job**
contratar a algn **to hire sb**
echar a algn **to fire sb**
despedir a algn **to dismiss sb**
buscar trabajo **to look for work**
hacer un curso de formación profesional **to attend a training course**
marcar *or* checar (*Mex*) tarjeta al entrar a/al salir de trabajar **to clock in/out**
fichar (*Sp*) al entrar a/al salir de trabajar **to clock in/out**
trabajar en horario flexible **to work flextime**

ESSENTIAL WORDS *(masculine)*

el **aceite**	oil
el **agente de policía**	police officer, policeman
el **aparcamiento** (*Sp*)	parking lot
el **atasco**	traffic jam
el **automóvil**	car
el **aventón** (*Mex*)	ride
el **camión** (*pl* camiones)	truck; (*Mex*) bus
el **carnet** *or* **carné de conducir** (*Sp*) (*pl* ~s *or* ~s ~ ~)	driver's license
el **carro** (*LAm*)	car
el **chofer** *or* el **chófer** (*Sp*)	driver; chauffeur
el **ciclista**	cyclist
el **coche**	car
el **conductor**	driver
el **cruce**	intersection
el **diesel**	diesel
el **embotellamiento**	traffic jam
el **estacionamiento** (*LAm*)	parking lot
los **faros**	headlights
el **freno**	brake
el **garage** (*LAm*), el **garaje** (*Sp*)	garage
el **kilómetro**	kilometer
el **litro**	liter
la **llanta** (*LAm*)	tire
el **mapa de carreteras**	road map
el **mecánico**	mechanic
el **neumático** (*Sp*)	tire
el **número**	number
el **parking** (*pl* ~s)	parking lot
el **peaje**	toll
el **peatón** (*pl* peatones)	pedestrian
el **radar**	speed radar
el **semáforo**	traffic light
el **trailer** (*pl* ~s) (*LAm*)	trailer
el **viaje**	journey

ESSENTIAL WORDS *(feminine)*

el **agua** (*f*)	water
la **autopista**	freeway, highway
la **autopista de peaje**	toll road, turnpike
la **caravana** (*Sp*)	trailer
la **carretera**	road
la **chofer** (*LAm*), la **chófer** (*Sp*)	driver; chauffeur
la **ciclista**	cyclist
la **cochera**	garage
la **conductora**	driver
la **desviación** (*pl* desviaciones)	detour
la **dirección** (*pl* direcciones)	direction; address
la **dirección asistida** (*pl* direcciones ~s)	power steering
la **distancia**	distance
la **estación de servicio** (*pl* estaciones ~ ~)	gas station
la **gasolina**	gasoline
la **gasolina sin plomo**	unleaded gasoline
la **licencia** *or* **libreta de manejar** (*LAm*)	driver's license
la **placa** (*LAm*), la **matrícula** (*Sp*)	license plate
la **policía**	police
la **póliza de seguros**	insurance policy
la **ventanilla**	(car) window

USEFUL PHRASES

pedir aventón (*Mex*) to hitch a ride
viajar de aventón (*Mex*) to hitchhike
frenar bruscamente to brake suddenly
100 kilómetros por hora 100 kilometers an hour
¿tienes licencia de manejar? do you have a driver's license?
vamos a dar una vuelta (en coche/carro) we're going for a drive/ride (in the car)
¡lleno, por favor!, ¡llénelo, por favor! fill 'er up please!
tomar la carretera a/hacia Morelia take the road to Morelia
es un viaje de tres horas it's a 3-hour drive
de camino vimos ... on the way we saw ...
adelantar a algn/un carro to pass sb/a car
rebasar a algn (*Mex*) to pass sb

IMPORTANT WORDS *(masculine)*

el	**accidente (de tráfico** *or* **de tránsito)**	(traffic) accident
el	**automovilista**	driver, motorist
el	**camionero**	truck driver; (*Mex*) bus driver
el	**choque**	collision
el	**cinturón de seguridad** (*pl* cinturones ~ ~)	seat belt
el	**claxon** (*pl* cláxones *or* ~s)	horn
el	**clutch** (*Mex*)	clutch
el	**daño**	damage
el	**embrague**	clutch
el	**maletero** (*Sp*)	trunk (*of a car*)
el	**motociclista**	motorcyclist
el	**motor**	engine
los	**papeles (del coche)**	license and registration
el	**pinchazo**	flat
el	**seguro**	insurance
el	**surtidor (de gasolina)**	gas pump
el	**tablero de mando**	dashboard
el	**tráfico** *or* **tránsito**	traffic
el	**túnel de lavado de coches**	car wash

USEFUL PHRASES

primero enciendes el motor *or* pones el motor en marcha **first you turn on the engine**
el motor arranca *or* se pone en marcha **the engine engages**
el coche se pone en marcha **the car moves off**
estamos circulando **we're driving along**
acelerar **to accelerate**; continuar **to continue**
reducir *or* aminorar la velocidad **to slow down**
detenerse **to stop**; estacionar (el coche) **to park (the car)**
apagar el motor **to turn off the engine**
parar con el semáforo en rojo **to stop at the red light**

IMPORTANT WORDS *(feminine)*

la **autoescuela** (*Sp*)	driving school
la **automovilista**	driver, motorist
la **avería**	breakdown
la **batería**	battery
la **cajuela** (*Mex*)	trunk (*of a car*)
la **calle de sentido único**	one-way street
la **carrocería**	body work
la **colisión** (*pl* colisiones)	collision
la **documentación (del coche)**	license and registration
la **escuela de conductores** *or* **de manejo** (*LAm*)	driving school
la **frontera**	border
la **glorieta**	traffic circle
la **grúa**	tow truck
la **marca**	make (*of car*)
la **motociclista**	motorcyclist
la **pieza de repuesto**	spare part
la **póliza de seguros**	insurance policy
la **ponchadura** (*Mex*)	flat
la **prioridad**	right of way
la **prueba del alcohol**	Breathalyzer® test
la **puerta**	(*car*) door
la **refacción** (*Mex*)	spare part
la **rotonda**	traffic circle
la **rueda**	tire; wheel
la **rueda de repuesto**	spare tire
la **velocidad**	speed; gear

USEFUL PHRASES

hubo un accidente **there was an accident**
hubo seis heridos en el accidente **six people were injured in the accident**
¿puedo ver la documentación *or* los papeles del coche, por favor? **may I see your license and registration, please?**
pinchar, tener un pinchazo **to have a flat**; arreglar **to repair** *or* **to fix**
se me ponchó una llanta (*Mex*) **I had a flat**
tener una avería **to break down**
me quedé sin gasolina **I ran out of gas**

USEFUL WORDS *(masculine)*

el **acelerador**	accelerator
el **acotamiento** (*Mex*)	shoulder
el **(anillo) periférico** (*LAm*)	beltway
el **arcén** (*pl* arcenes) (*Sp*)	shoulder
el **autolavado**	car wash
el **botón de arranque** (*pl* botones ~ ~)	starter
el **capó**	hood
el **carburador**	carburetor
el **camellón** (*Mex*)	median strip
el **carril**	lane
el **catalizador**	catalytic converter
el **cofre** (*Mex*)	hood
el **consumo de gasolina**	gas consumption
el **cuentakilómetros** (*pl inv*)	speedometer
el **desvío**	detour
el **herido**	casualty
el **intermitente** (*Sp*)	indicator
el **lavacoches** (*pl inv*)	car wash
el **límite de velocidad**	speed limit
el **limpiador** (*Mex*)	windshield wiper
el **limpiaparabrisas** (*pl inv*)	windshield wiper
el **parabrisas** (*pl inv*)	windshield
el **paragolpes** (*pl inv*) (*LAm*)	bumper
el **parquímetro**	parking meter
el **pedal**	pedal
el **portaequipajes**	roof rack
el **profesor de manejo** (*LAm*)	driving instructor
el **remolque**	trailer
el **retrovisor**	rear-view mirror
el **(sistema de navegación) GPS**	satellite navigation system
el **volante**	steering wheel

USEFUL PHRASES

en la hora pico (*LAm*) *or* punta (*Sp*) **during rush hour**

le pusieron una multa de 100 dólares **he got a 100 dollar fine**

¿está asegurado? **are you insured?**

está aprendiendo a manejar **(s)he is learning to drive**

ponerse el cinturón de seguridad **to put on one's seat belt**

USEFUL WORDS *(feminine)*

el **área de servicio** (*f pl* las áreas ~ ~)	service area
la **caja de cambios**	transmission
la **carretera de circunvalación** (*Sp*)	beltway
la **clase de manejo** (*LAm*)	driving lesson
la **curva**	bend
la **defensa** (*Mex*)	bumper
la **direccional** (*LAm*)	indicator
la **estación de servicio** (*pl* estaciones ~ ~)	gas station
la **gasolinera**	gas station
la **infracción de tráfico** *or* **tránsito** (*pl* infracciones ~ ~)	traffic offense
la **matrícula**	license plate number
la **mediana** (*Sp*)	median strip
la **multa**	fine
la **parada de emergencia**	emergency stop
la **presión**	pressure
la **profesora de manejo** (*LAm*)	driving instructor
la **señal de tráfico** *or* **tránsito**	road sign
la **vía de acceso**	access road
la **víctima** (*m+f*)	casualty
la **zona urbanizada**	developed area

USEFUL PHRASES

la rueda delantera/trasera the front/back wheel
tenemos que desviarnos we have to take a detour
una multa por exceso de velocidad a fine for speeding
contratar a un chofer (*LAm*) *or* a un chófer (*Sp*) to hire a driver
"ceda el paso" "yield"
"prohibido el paso" "no entry"
"prohibido estacionar" "no parking"
"obras" "road work" *or* "highway repairs"

ESSENTIAL WORDS *(masculine)*

el **abrigo**	overcoat; coat
el **bañador** (*Sp*)	swimsuit
el **bolsillo**	pocket
el **bolso** (*Sp*)	bag, purse
el **botón** (*pl* botones)	button
el **calcetín** (*pl* calcetines)	sock
los **calzoncillos**	underpants; boxer shorts
el **calzón** *or* los **calzones** (*LAm*)	panties
el **camisón** (*pl* camisones)	nightgown
el **cuello**	collar
el **impermeable**	raincoat
los **jeans** (*LAm*)	jeans
el **jersey** (*pl* ~s) (*Sp*)	sweater
el **número (de zapato)**	(shoe) size
el **pantalón** (*pl* pantalones)	pants, trousers
los **pantalones de mezclilla** (*Mex*)	jeans
los **(pantalones) vaqueros**	jeans
el **pañuelo**	handkerchief
el **paraguas** (*pl inv*)	umbrella
el **pijama** (*Sp*)	pajamas
el **sombrero**	hat
el **suéter** (*LAm*)	sweater
el **talle**	waist
el **traje**	suit (*for man*); costume
el **traje de baño**	swimsuit
el **traje de chaqueta**	suit (*for woman*)
el **vestido**	dress
el **zapato**	shoe

IMPORTANT WORDS *(masculine)*

el **cinturón** (*pl* cinturones)	belt
el **guante**	glove
los **shorts**	shorts
el **uniforme**	uniform

ESSENTIAL WORDS *(feminine)*

la	**bolsa**	bag; (*Mex*) purse; pocket
las	**bragas** (*Sp*)	panties
la	**camisa**	shirt
la	**camiseta**	t-shirt
la	**capucha**	hood
la	**chamarra** (*Mex*)	jacket
la	**chaqueta**	jacket
la	**corbata**	tie
la	**falda**	skirt
las	**medias**	pantyhose, stockings
la	**moda**	fashion
las	**pantaletas** (*Mex*)	panties
las	**pantimedias** (*Mex*)	pantyhose
la	**pijama** (*LAm*)	pajamas
la	**playera** (*Mex*)	t-shirt
la	**ropa**	clothes
la	**ropa interior**	underwear
la	**sandalia**	sandal
la	**talla**	size

IMPORTANT WORDS *(feminine)*

la	**americana** (*Sp*)	jacket (*for man*)
la	**blusa**	blouse
la	**bota**	boot
la	**pantufla** (*LAm*)	slipper
las	**prendas de vestir**	clothes, garments
la	**zapatilla** (*Sp*)	slipper
la	**zapatilla** (*Mex*)	shoe (*for woman*)

USEFUL PHRASES

en la mañana me visto in the morning I get dressed
en la noche me desvisto in the evening I get undressed
cuando llego a casa me cambio when I get home, I get changed
llevar, llevar puesto to wear
ponerse to put on
(eso) te queda bien that suits you
¿qué talla tienes (*or* tiene)? what size do you wear?

USEFUL WORDS *(masculine)*

los	**accesorios**	accessories
el	**bastón** (*pl* bastones)	walking stick
el	**brasier** (*LAm*)	bra
el	**cárdigan** (*pl* ~s)	cardigan
el	**chaleco**	vest
el	**chándal** (*pl* ~s) (*Sp*)	sweatsuit
los	**cordones**	(shoe)laces
el	**delantal**	apron
el	**desfile de modas**	fashion show
el	**foulard** (*pl* ~s)	scarf
el	**lazo**	bow
el	**mono** (*Sp*)	overalls
el	**ojal**	buttonhole
los	**pantis** (*Sp*)	tights
los	**pants** (*pl inv*) (*Mex*)	sweatsuit; sweatpants
el	**pañuelo**	scarf
el	**overol** (*LAm*)	overalls
el	**polar**	fleece jacket
el	**polo**	polo shirt
el	**probador**	fitting room
el	**sujetador** (*Sp*)	bra
los	**tenis** (*LAm*)	sneakers, running shoes
los	**tirantes**	suspenders
el	**traje de etiqueta**	dress suit
el	**traje de noche**	evening gown
el	**traje pantalón** (*pl* ~s ~)	pants suit
el	**vestido** *or* **traje de novia**	wedding gown
los	**zapatos de tacón**	high heels
los	**zapatos de tacón de aguja**	stiletto heels

USEFUL WORDS *(feminine)*

las	**agujetas** (*Mex*)	(shoe) laces
la	**alpargata**	espadrille
la	**alta costura**	high fashion, haute couture
la	**bata**	dressing gown
las	**bermudas**	Bermuda shorts
la	**boina**	beret
la	**bufanda**	scarf
las	**chanclas**	thongs (*sandals*)
la	**corbata de moño** (*LAm*)	bow tie
la	**cinta**	ribbon
la	**cremallera** (*Sp*)	zipper
la(s)	**enagua(s)**	slip, petticoat
la	**falda pantalón** (*pl* ~s ~)	culottes
la	**gorra**	cap
la	**limpieza en seco**	dry cleaning
la	**manga**	sleeve
la	**pajarita** (*Sp*)	bow tie
la	**rebeca** (*Sp*)	cardigan
la	**ropa lavada/para lavar**	laundry
la	**sudadera**	sweatshirt
la	**sudadera con capucha**	hooded top
la	**tintorería**	dry cleaner's
las	**zapatillas de deporte** (*Sp*)	sneakers, running shoes

USEFUL PHRASES

largo(a) **long**; corto(a) **short**
un vestido de manga corta/larga **a short-sleeved/long-sleeved dress**
estrecho(a), ajustado(a) **tight**
amplio(a), suelto(a) **loose**
una falda ajustada *or* ceñida **a tight skirt**
a rayas, de rayas **striped**; a cuadros, de cuadros **checkered**; de lunares **polka-dotted**
ropa de sport, ropa informal **casual clothes**
a la moda, de moda **fashionable**; moderno(a) **trendy**
pasado(a) de moda, anticuado(a) **old-fashioned**

amarillo(a)	yellow
azul	blue
azul celeste	sky blue
azul claro	pale blue
azul marino	navy blue
azul oscuro	dark blue
beige	beige
beis (*Sp*)	beige
blanco(a)	white
el **color**	color
crudo(a)	natural
dorado(a)	golden
granate	maroon
gris	gray
malva	mauve
marrón (*pl* marrones)	brown
naranja	orange
negro(a)	black
rojo(a)	red
rojo fuerte *or* **intenso**	bright red
rosa	pink
turquesa	turquoise
verde	green
violeta	purple

USEFUL PHRASES

¿de qué color tienes (*or* tiene) los ojos/el pelo? what color are your eyes/ is your hair?
el azul te sienta bien blue looks good on you; the blue one looks good on you
pintar algo de azul to paint sth blue
los zapatos azules blue shoes
los zapatos azul claro light blue shoes
tiene los ojos verdes (s)he has green eyes
cambiar de color to change color
la Casa Blanca the White House
un (hombre) blanco a white man
una (mujer) blanca a white woman
un (hombre) negro a black man
una (mujer) negra a black woman
blanco como la nieve as white as snow
Blancanieves Snow White
Caperucita Roja Little Red Riding Hood
ponerse colorado(a) *or* rojo(a) to turn red
sonrojarse de vergüenza to blush with shame
blanco(a) como el papel as white as a sheet
un ojo morado a black eye
un filete rojo *or* a la inglesa (*Mex*) a rare steak
un filete muy poco hecho (*Sp*) a rare steak

ESSENTIAL WORDS *(masculine)*

el **monitor**	monitor
el **mouse** (*LAm*)	mouse
el **ordenador (personal)** (*Sp*)	(personal) computer
el **programa**	program
el **programador**	programmer
el **teclado**	keyboard
el **ratón** (*pl* ratones) (*Sp*)	mouse

USEFUL WORDS *(masculine)*

el **archivo**	file
el **cartucho de tinta**	ink cartridge
el **CD-ROM** (*pl inv*)	CD-ROM
el **corrector ortográfico**	spellchecker
el **correo electrónico**	email
el **cursor**	cursor
los **datos**	data
el **disco duro**	hard disk
el **documento**	document
el **email**	email
el **fichero** (*Sp*)	file
el **fólder** (*LAm*)	folder
el **icono**	icon
el **internauta**	internet user
el **juego de ordenador** (*Sp*)	computer game
el **mail** (*pl* ~s)	email (message)
el **menú**	menu
el **módem** (*pl* ~s)	modem
el **navegador**	browser
el **paquete de programas**	software package
el **pirata informático**	hacker
el **portátil**	laptop
el **procesador de textos**	word processor
el **servidor**	server
el **sitio web**	website
el **software** (*pl inv*)	software
el **soporte (físico)**	hardware
el **virus** (*pl inv*)	virus
el **wifi**	Wi-Fi®

ESSENTIAL WORDS *(feminine)*

la **computadora** (*LAm*)	computer
la **impresora**	printer
la **informática**	IT, computer science

USEFUL WORDS *(feminine)*

la **aplicación** (*pl* aplicaciones)	program
la **banda ancha**	broadband
la **base de datos**	database
la **carpeta** (*Sp*)	folder
la **computadora portátil** (*LAm*)	laptop
la **copia de seguridad**	back-up
la **copia impresa**	print out
la **dirección de correo (electrónico)** (*pl* direcciones ~ ~ (~))	email address
la **función** (*pl* funciones)	function
la **grabadora de DVD**	DVD burner
la **hoja de cálculo**	spreadsheet
la **interfaz** (*pl* interfaces)	interface
la **internauta**	internet user
(la) **Internet**	Internet
la **llave USB**	USB key
la **memoria**	memory
la **memoria RAM**	RAM, random access memory
la **memoria ROM**	ROM, read-only Memory
la **página de inicio**	homepage
la **pantalla**	screen
la **papelera de reciclaje**	recycle bin, trash
la **red**	network
la **unidad de disco**	disk drive
la **ventana**	window
la **Web** (*pl* ~s)	Web
la **webcam** (*pl* ~s)	webcam

USEFUL PHRASES

copiar to copy; eliminar, suprimir to delete; formatear to format
bajar *or* descargar un archivo to download a file
guardar to save; imprimir to print; teclear to key, to type
navegar por Internet to surf the internet

COUNTRIES (*masculine*)

	Brasil	Brazil
	Canadá	Canada
	Chile	Chile
	Ecuador	Ecuador
	EE.UU.	USA
	El Salvador	El Salvador
	Estados Unidos	United States
	Japón	Japan
	México	Mexico
el	**país**	country
	Panamá	Panama
	Paraguay	Paraguay
	Perú	Peru
	Puerto Rico	Puerto Rico
el	**Tercer Mundo**	the Third World
	Uruguay	Uruguay

USEFUL PHRASES

mi país de origen my native country
la capital de Argentina the capital of Argentina
¿de qué país eres (*or* es)? what country do you come from?
soy de (los) Estados Unidos/de Canadá I come from the United States/ from Canada
nací en Ecuador I was born in Ecuador
me voy a Chile I'm going to Chile
acabo de regresar de (los) Estados Unidos I have just come back from the United States
los países en (vías de) desarrollo the developing countries
los países de habla hispana Spanish-speaking countries

COUNTRIES (*feminine*)

	África	Africa
	Alemania	Germany
	América	America
	América del Sur	South America
	Argentina	Argentina
	Asia	Asia
	Bolivia	Bolivia
	Centroamérica	Central America
(la)	**China**	China
	Colombia	Colombia
	Costa Rica	Costa Rica
	Cuba	Cuba
	España	Spain
	Europa	Europe
	Francia	France
	Gran Bretaña	Great Britain
	Guatemala	Guatemala
	Honduras	Honduras
(la)	**India**	India
	Inglaterra	England
	Irlanda	Ireland
	Italia	Italy
	Nicaragua	Nicaragua
la	**República Dominicana**	the Dominican Republic
	Sudamérica	South America
la	**Unión Europea,** la **UE**	the European Union, the EU
	Venezuela	Venezuela

NATIONALITIES

ESSENTIAL WORDS *(masculine)*

un **americano**	an American
un **argentino**	an Argentinian
un **boliviano**	a Bolivian
un **chileno**	a Chilean
un **colombiano**	a Colombian
un **costarricense**	a Costa Rican
un **cubano**	a Cuban
un **dominicano**	a Dominican
un **ecuatoriano**	an Ecuadorean
un **español**	a Spaniard
un **guatemalteco**	a Guatemalan
un **hondureño**	a Honduran
un **mexicano**	a Mexican
un **nicaragüense**	a Nicaraguan
un **panameño**	a Panamanian
un **paraguayo**	a Paraguayan
un **peruano**	a Peruvian
un **puertorriqueño**	a Puerto Rican
un **salvadoreño**	a Salvadorian
un **uruguayo**	a Uruguayan
un **venezolano**	a Venezuelan

USEFUL PHRASES

es italiano **he is Italian**
es italiana **she is Italian**
la campiña italiana **the Italian countryside**
una ciudad italiana **an Italian town**

ESSENTIAL WORDS *(feminine)*

una **americana**	an American
una **argentina**	an Argentinian
una **boliviana**	a Bolivian
una **chilena**	a Chilean
una **colombiana**	a Colombian
una **costarricense**	a Costa Rican
una **cubana**	a Cuban
una **dominicana**	a Dominican
una **ecuatoriana**	an Ecuadorean
una **española**	a Spaniard
una **guatemalteca**	a Guatemalan
una **hondureña**	a Honduran
una **mexicana**	a Mexican
una **nicaragüense**	a Nicaraguan
una **panameña**	a Panamanian
una **paraguaya**	a Paraguayan
una **peruana**	a Peruvian
una **puertorriqueña**	a Puerto Rican
una **salvadoreña**	a Salvadorian
una **uruguaya**	a Uruguayan
una **venezolana**	a Venezuelan

USEFUL PHRASES

soy americano – hablo inglés I am American – I speak English
soy americana I am American
un(a) extranjero(a) a foreigner
en el extranjero abroad
la nacionalidad nationality

USEFUL WORDS *(masculine)*

un **africano**	an African
un **alemán** (*pl* alemanes)	a German
un **árabe**	an Arab
un **brasileño**	a Brazilian
un **canadiense**	a Canadian
un **chino**	a Chinese
un **europeo**	a European
un **francés** (*pl* franceses)	a Frenchman
un **indio**	an Indian
un **inglés** (*pl* ingleses)	an Englishman
un **irlandés** (*pl* irlandeses)	an Irishman
un **italiano**	an Italian
un **japonés** (*pl* japoneses)	a Japanese

USEFUL WORDS *(feminine)*

una **africana**	an African
una **alemana**	a German
una **árabe**	an Arab
una **brasileña**	a Brazilian
una **canadiense**	a Canadian
una **china**	a Chinese
una **europea**	a European
una **francesa**	a Frenchwoman
una **india**	an Indian
una **inglésa**	an Englishwoman
una **irlandesa**	an Irishwoman
una **italiana**	an Italian
una **japonesa**	a Japanese

ESSENTIAL WORDS *(masculine)*

el **aire**	air
el **albergue juvenil**	youth hostel
el **árbol**	tree
el **arroyo**	stream
el **bastón** (*pl* bastones)	walking stick
el **bosque**	wood; forest
el **camino**	way
el **campesino**	farmer; peasant
el **campo**	country, countryside; field
el **cazador**	hunter
el **granjero**	farmer
el **mercado**	market
el **paisaje**	scenery
el **paseo**	walk
el **picnic** (*pl* ~s)	picnic
el **pueblo**	village
el **puente**	bridge
el **río**	river
el **ruido**	noise
el **sendero**	path; track
el **terreno**	soil; ground
el **turista**	tourist
el **valle**	valley

USEFUL PHRASES

al aire libre in the open air
sé el camino al pueblo I know the way to the village
(ir a) andar en bicicleta to go cycling
los vecinos *or* los habitantes de la zona the locals
fuimos de picnic we had a picnic

ESSENTIAL WORDS *(feminine)*

la **camioneta**	van; station wagon
la **campesina**	farmer; peasant
la **carretera**	road
la **cazadora**	hunter
la **cerca**	fence
la **excursión** (*pl* excursiones)	hike; excursion
la **granja**	farm, farmhouse
la **granjera**	farmer
la **montaña**	mountain
la **piedra**	stone; rock
la **región** (*pl* regiones)	area; district
la **tierra**	land; earth; soil; ground
la **torre**	tower
la **turista**	tourist
la **vagoneta** (*Mex*)	van
la **valla** (*Sp*)	fence

USEFUL PHRASES

en el campo **in the country**
ir (de excursión) al campo **to go to the country**
vivir en el campo/en la ciudad **to live in the country/in town**
cultivar la tierra **to cultivate the land**

IMPORTANT WORDS *(masculine)*

el **agricultor**	farmer
el **lago**	lake
el **mesón** (*pl* mesones)	inn
el **polvo**	dust
el **ranchero** (*Mex*)	rancher
el **rancho** (*Mex*)	ranch

USEFUL WORDS *(masculine)*

el **arbusto**	bush
el **barro** *or* el **lodo**	mud
los **binoculares**	binoculars
el **charco**	puddle
el **estanque**	pond
el **guijarro**	pebble
el **heno**	hay
el **matorral**	bushes
el **maíz**	maize; corn
el **molino (de viento)**	(wind)mill
el **palo**	stick
el **pantano**	marsh
el **poste telegráfico**	telephone pole
los **prismáticos**	binoculars
el **seto**	hedge
el **trigo**	wheat

USEFUL PHRASES

agrícola **agricultural**
apacible, tranquilo(a) **peaceful, tranquil**
en la cima de la colina **at the top of the hill**
caer en una trampa **to fall into a trap**

IMPORTANT WORDS *(feminine)*

la **agricultora**	farmer
la **agricultura**	agriculture
la **calzada**	road surface
la **cima**	top (*of a hill*)
la **colina**	hill
la **gente del campo**	country people
la **hoja**	leaf
la **posada**	inn
la **propiedad**	property; estate
la **ranchera** (*Mex*)	rancher
la **tranquilidad**	peace, tranquility

USEFUL WORDS *(feminine)*

la **aldea**	village
la **bota de goma**	rubber boot
la **bota de hule** (*Mex*)	rubber boot
la **cantera**	quarry
la **cascada**	waterfall
la **caza**	hunting; shooting
la **cosecha**	crop; harvest
la **fuente**	spring; source
la **llanura**	plain
la **orilla**	bank (*of a river*)
las **ruinas**	ruins
la **señal**	signpost
la **trampa**	trap
la **vendimia**	grape harvest
la **zanja**	ditch

USEFUL PHRASES

perderse to lose one's way; to get lost
recoger la cosecha to bring in the harvest
vendimiar, hacer la vendimia to harvest the grapes

ESSENTIAL WORDS *(masculine)*

el **aspecto**	appearance
el **bigote**	moustache
el **cabello**	hair
el **color**	color
los **ojos**	eyes
el **pelo**	hair
el **talle**	waist

USEFUL PHRASES

alegre cheerful
alto(a) tall
amable kind; nice
antiguo(a) old
bajo(a) short
barbudo(a), de barba bearded, with a beard
bonito(a) pretty
bueno(a) kind
calvo(a) bald
canoso(a) gray-haired
culto(a) well-educated, cultured
delgado(a) thin, slim
desagradable unpleasant
divertido(a), entretenido(a) amusing, entertaining
educado(a) polite
esbelto(a) slender, slim
feliz (*pl* felices) happy
feo(a) ugly
flaco(a) skinny
gordo(a) fat
gracioso(a) funny
grosero(a) rude
guapo handsome; guapa beautiful
güero(a) (*Mex*) blond(e)
horrible hideous
infeliz (*pl* infelices), desgraciado(a) unhappy, unfortunate
inteligente intelligent
lindo(a) (*LAm*) pretty, nice
joven (*pl* jóvenes) young

ESSENTIAL WORDS *(feminine)*

la **barba**	beard
la **edad**	age
la **estatura**	height; size
las **gafas**	glasses
la **identidad**	ID
la **lágrima**	tear
la **persona**	person
la **talla**	size; height

USEFUL PHRASES

largo(a) long
malo(a) naughty
moreno(a) dark-haired; dark-skinned
mono(a) cute
nervioso(a), tenso(a) nervous, tense
optimista/pesimista optimistic/pessimistic
pequeño(a) small, little
rubio(a) blond(e)
serio(a) serious
tímido(a) shy
tonto(a) stupid
tranquilo(a) calm
viejo(a) old
parece triste (s)he looks sad
estaba llorando (s)he was crying
sonreía (s)he was smiling
la muchacha tenía lágrimas en los ojos the girl had tears in her eyes
un hombre de estatura mediana a man of average height
mido 1 metro 70 *or* uno setenta I am 1 meter 70 tall
¿de qué color son tus (*or* sus) ojos/es tu (*or* su) pelo? what color are your eyes/ is your hair?
soy rubia *or* (*Mex*) güera I am blonde
me/le están saliendo canas I'm/(s)he's going gray
tengo los ojos azules/verdes I have blue/green eyes
pelo moreno *or* castaño dark *or* brown hair
pelo castaño light brown hair; pelo rizado curly hair
pelirrojo(a) red-haired
pelo negro/canoso black/gray hair
pelo teñido dyed hair

IMPORTANT WORDS *(masculine)*

el **carácter** (*pl* caracteres)	character; nature
el **grano**	pimple
el **humor**	mood

USEFUL WORDS *(masculine)*

el **chino** (*Mex*)	curl
el **defecto**	fault
el **fleco** (*Mex*)	bangs
el **flequillo** (*Sp*)	bangs
el **gesto**	gesture
el **gigante**	giant
los **hoyuelos**	dimples
los **lentes** *or* **anteojos**	glasses
los **lentes de contacto**	contact lenses
el **lunar**	mole, beauty mark
el **parecido**	resemblance
el **permanente** (*Mex*)	perm
el **peso**	weight
el **rizo**	curl

USEFUL PHRASES

tiene buen carácter (s)he is good-tempered
tiene mal genio *or* carácter (s)he is bad-tempered
tener la tez pálida *or* muy blanca to have a pale complexion
tener el pelo lacio to have straight hair
tener el pelo rizado *or* (*Mex*) chino to have curly hair
usar lentes *or* anteojos (*LAm*) to wear glasses
llevar gafas (*Sp*) to wear glasses
usar lentes de contacto to wear contact lenses

IMPORTANT WORDS *(feminine)*

la **belleza**	beauty
la **calidad**	(good) quality
la **costumbre**	habit
la **curiosidad**	curiosity
la **expresión** (*pl* expresiones)	expression
la **fealdad**	ugliness
la **mirada**	look
la **sonrisa**	smile
la **tez** (*pl* teces)	complexion
la **voz** (*pl* voces)	voice

USEFUL WORDS *(feminine)*

las **arrugas**	wrinkles
la **cicatriz** (*pl* cicatrices)	scar
la **dentadura**	teeth
la **dentadura postiza**	dentures, false teeth
las **pecas**	freckles
la **permanente**	perm
la **timidez**	shyness

USEFUL PHRASES

siempre estoy de buen humor I am always in a good mood
está de mal humor (s)he is in a bad mood
se enojó (s)he got angry
Marita se parece a su madre Marita looks like her mother
mi hermano se come *or* se muerde las uñas my brother bites his nails

ESSENTIAL WORDS *(masculine)*

el **alemán**	German
el **alfabeto**	alphabet
el **alumno**	pupil; schoolboy
el **amigo**	friend
el **aprendizaje**	learning
el **club** (*pl* ~s *or* ~es)	club
el **colegio**	school
el **colegio de secundaria**	secondary school
el **comienzo del curso**	beginning of the semester
el **compañero de clase**	school friend
el **concierto**	concert
el **cuaderno**	notebook
los **deberes**	homework
el **día**	day
el **dibujo**	drawing
el **director**	principal
el **dormitorio**	dormitory
el **error**	mistake
el **escolar**	schoolboy
el **español**	Spanish
el **estudiante**	student
el **estudio (de)**	study (of)
los **estudios**	studies
el **examen** (*pl* exámenes)	exam, test
el **experimento**	experiment
el **francés**	French
el **gimnasio**	gym
el **grupo**	group
el **horario**	schedule, timetable
el **idioma**	language
el **inglés**	English
el **intercambio**	exchange
el **italiano**	Italian
el **laboratorio**	laboratory
el **lápiz** (*pl* lápices)	pencil
el **libro**	book
el **maestro**	elementary school teacher
el **mapa**	map
el **ordenador** (*Sp*)	computer

ESSENTIAL WORDS *(feminine)*

la	**alberca** (*Mex*)	swimming pool
la	**alumna**	pupil; schoolgirl
la	**amiga**	friend
el	**aula** (*f pl* las aulas)	classroom
la	**biología**	biology
la	**cafetería**	cafeteria
la	**calificación**	grade
las	**ciencias**	science
la	**clase**	class; year; classroom
las	**clases**	lessons
las	**clases prácticas**	lab
la	**compañera de clase**	school friend
la	**computadora** (*LAm*)	computer
la	**directora**	principal
la	**educación física**	PE
la	**electrónica**	electronics
la	**enseñanza**	education; teaching
la	**escolar**	schoolgirl
la	**escuela**	school
la	**escuela primaria**	elementary school
la	**estudiante**	student
la	**excursión** (*pl* excursiones)	trip; hike; outing
la	**física**	physics
la	**frase**	sentence
la	**geografía**	geography
la	**gimnasia**	gym
la	**goma (de borrar)**	eraser
la	**grabadora**	tape recorder
la	**guardería**	day care center
la	**historia**	history; story
la	**informática**	computer studies
la	**lección** (*pl* lecciones)	lesson
la	**lectura**	reading
las	**lenguas extranjeras**	foreign languages
la	**maestra**	elementary school teacher
las	**matemáticas**	mathematics
la	**materia (escolar)**	(school) subject
la	**música**	music
la	**natación**	swimming

ESSENTIAL WORDS (*masculine continued*)

el **premio**	prize
el **profesor**	teacher; professor
el **progreso**	progress
el **recreo**	recess
el **resultado**	result
el **semestre**	semester
el **trabajo**	work
los **trabajos manuales**	handicrafts, shop

USEFUL PHRASES

trabajar **to work**
aprender **to learn**
estudiar **to study**
¿cuánto tiempo hace que aprendes (*or* aprende) español? **how long have you been studying Spanish?**
aprenderse algo de memoria **to learn sth by heart**
hago la tarea todos los días **I do my homework every day**
mi hermana menor va a la escuela, yo voy a secundaria **my kid sister goes to elementary school – I go to junior high**
enseñar español **to teach Spanish**
el/la profesor(a) de alemán **the German teacher**
mejoré en matemáticas **I've made progress in math**
hacer *or* presentar un examen **to take an exam *or* a test**
aprobar un examen **to pass an exam *or* a test**
reprobar un examen (*LAm*) **to fail an exam *or* a test**
suspender un examen (*Sp*) **to fail an exam *or* a test**
sacar un aprobado **to get a passing grade**

ESSENTIAL WORDS *(feminine continued)*

la **piscina**	swimming pool
la **pizarra**	blackboard
la **pregunta**	question
la **prepa** *or* **preparatoria** (*Mex*)	high school; prep school
la **preprimaria** (*Mex*)	kindergarten
la **profesora**	teacher; professor
la **química**	chemistry
la **respuesta**	answer
la **sala de profesores**	faculty room
la **secundaria**	secondary education; junior high-school
la **tarea** (*LAm*)	homework
la **universidad**	college; university
las **vacaciones**	vacation
las **vacaciones de verano**	summer vacation

USEFUL PHRASES

fácil **easy**; difícil **difficult**
interesante **interesting**
aburrido(a) **boring**
leer **to read**; escribir **to write**
escuchar **to listen (to)**
mirar **to look at, watch**
repetir **to repeat**
contestar, responder **to answer, to reply**
hablar **to speak**
es la primera *or* la mejor de la clase **she is top of the class**
es la última *or* la peor de la clase **she is bottom of the class**
entrar a la clase **to go into the classroom**
cometer un error **to make a mistake**
corregir **to correct**
cometí un error gramatical **I made a grammatical error**
cometí una falta de ortografía **I made a spelling mistake**
me equivoqué **I made a mistake**
siempre saca buenas calificaciones **(s)he always gets good grades**
contesta (*or* contesten) la pregunta **answer the question**
¡levanten la mano! **raise your hand!**

IMPORTANT WORDS *(masculine)*

el **bachillerato**	GED course/certificate
el **certificado**	certificate
el **colegio privado** *or* **particular**	private school
el **colegio público** *or* **oficial**	public school
el **corredor**	hall, corridor
el **despacho**	office
el **día libre**	day off
el **diploma**	diploma
el **estuche para lápices**	pencil case
el **examen escrito** (*pl* exámenes ~s)	written exam
el **examen oral** (*pl* exámenes ~es)	oral exam
el **expediente**	file
el **papel**	paper
el **pasillo**	hall, corridor
el **patio (de recreo)**	playground, schoolyard

USEFUL PHRASES

repasar to revise
repasaré otra vez la lección mañana I'll go over the lesson again tomorrow
hacer una composición to write a composition
hacer un trabajo sobre los mayas to do an assignment on the Mayas

IMPORTANT WORDS *(feminine)*

la **carpeta**	file folder
la **conferencia**	lecture
el **fólder** (*LAm*)	folder
las **normas**	rules
la **regla**	rule; ruler
la **selectividad** (*Sp*)	college entrance examination
la **traducción** (*pl* traducciones)	translation
la **versión** (*pl* versiones)	translation (*into a foreign language*)

USEFUL PHRASES

presente **present**
ausente **absent**
castigar a un(a) alumno(a) **to punish a student**
¡silencio! **be quiet!**
la maestra me puso falta **the teacher marked me as absent**
nunca falta a clase **he never misses school**
faltó a clase ayer **(s)he didn't come/go to school yesterday**
la Facultad de arquitectura **the School of Architecture**
un compañero de facultad **a friend from college**

USEFUL WORDS *(masculine)*

el **block** (*pl* ~s)	notepad
el **bolígrafo**	ballpoint pen
el **borrador**	rough draft
el **cálculo**	calculation
el **castigo**	detention; punishment
el **comportamiento**	behavior
el **conserje**	janitor
el **corrector (líquido)**	Wite-Out®, correction fluid
el **diccionario**	dictionary
el **ejercicio**	exercise
el **examinador**	examiner
el **gis** (*Mex*)	chalk, piece of chalk
el **griego**	Greek
el **inspector**	school inspector
el **internado**	boarding school
el **interno**	boarder
el **latín**	Latin
el **libro de texto**	textbook
el **maletín** (*pl* maletines)	briefcase
el **marcador** (*Mex*)	marker, magic marker
el **plumón** (*Mex*)	felt-tip pen
el **portafolios** (*pl inv*)	briefcase
el **pupitre**	desk
el **rotulador** (*Sp*)	felt-tip pen
el **sacapuntas** (*pl inv*)	pencil sharpener
el **test** (*pl* ~s)	test
el **trabajo**	essay
el **trimestre**	term
el **vestuario**	changing room
el **vocabulario**	vocabulary

USEFUL WORDS *(feminine)*

el	**álgebra** (*f*)	algebra
la	**aritmética**	arithmetic
la	**calculadora**	calculator
la	**caligrafía**	handwriting
la	**carpintería**	woodwork
las	**ciencias del medio ambiente**	natural science
las	**ciencias naturales**	natural history
la	**conserje**	janitor
la	**enseñanza religiosa**	religious instruction
la	**entrega de premios**	awards ceremony
la	**fila**	row (*of seats etc*)
la	**geometría**	geometry
la	**gramática**	grammar
la	**inspectora**	school inspector
la	**interna**	boarder
la	**mancha**	stain
la	**ortografía**	spelling
la	**pizarra (electrónica) interactiva**	interactive whiteboard
la	**poesía**	poetry; poem
la	**prueba**	test
la	**tinta**	ink
la	**tiza**	chalk
la	**traducción directa/inversa** (*pl* traducciones ~s)	translation into one's own language/a foreign language

ESSENTIAL WORDS *(masculine)*

el	**aerogenerador**	windmill, wind turbine
el	**aire**	air
los	**animales**	animals
los	**árboles**	trees
el	**bosque**	wood
el	**calentamiento global**	global warming
el	**carro** (*LAm*)	car
el	**coche**	car
el	**diesel**	diesel
el	**ecologista**	environmentalist
el	**gas**	gas
los	**gases de escape**	exhaust fumes
el	**gasoil**	diesel
el	**generador eólico**	windmill, wind turbine
el	**mapa**	map
el	**mar**	sea
el	**medio ambiente**	environment
el	**mundo**	world
el	**país**	country
el	**parque eólico**	wind farm
el	**pescado**	fish
el	**tiempo**	weather; time
los	**Verdes**	the Greens
el	**vidrio**	glass

IMPORTANT WORDS *(masculine)*

el	**acontecimiento**	event
el	**aluminio**	aluminum
el	**calor**	heat
el	**clima**	climate
el	**contaminante**	pollutant
el	**daño**	damage
el	**detergente**	detergent
el	**futuro**	future
el	**gobierno**	government
el	**impuesto**	tax
el	**lago**	lake
el	**planeta**	planet
el	**río**	river

ESSENTIAL WORDS *(feminine)*

el	**agua** (*f*)	water
las	**botellas**	bottles
la	**contaminación**	pollution
la	**costa**	coast
la	**cuestión** (*pl* cuestiones)	question
la	**ecología**	ecology
la	**energía eólica**	wind energy
la	**energía nuclear**	nuclear power
la	**energía renovable**	renewable energy
la	**especie**	species
la	**fábrica**	factory
la	**flor**	flower
la	**fruta**	fruit
la	**gasolina**	gasoline
la	**isla**	island
la	**lluvia**	rain
la	**montaña**	mountain
la	**planta**	plant
la	**playa**	beach
la	**región** (*pl* regiones)	region; area
la	**temperatura**	temperature
la	**tierra**	earth
la(s)	**verdura(s)**	vegetables

IMPORTANT WORDS *(feminine)*

la	**central nuclear**	nuclear power plant
la	**crisis** (*pl inv*)	crisis
las	**legumbres**	pulses; vegetables
la	**selva**	forest; jungle
la	**solución** (*pl* soluciones)	solution
las	**verduras**	vegetables
la	**zona**	zone

USEFUL WORDS *(masculine)*

el **aerosol**	aerosol
los **alimentos orgánicos**	organic food
el **canal**	canal
el **catalizador**	catalytic converter
el **CFC (clorofluorocarbono)**	CFC
los **científicos**	scientists
el **combustible**	fuel
el **continente**	continent
el **desarrollo sustentable** *or* **sostenible**	sustainable development
el **desierto**	desert
el **ecosistema**	ecosystem
el **fertilizante**	(artificial) fertilizer
el **investigador**	researcher
el **océano**	ocean
el **OGM (organismo genéticamente modificado)**	GMO
el **producto**	product
los **productos químicos**	chemicals
el **reciclado**, el **reciclaje**	recycling
los **residuos nucleares/industriales**	nuclear/industrial waste
el **universo**	universe
el **vertedero**	dumping ground

USEFUL PHRASES

es muy respetuoso con el medio ambiente he's very environmentally-minded
un producto ecológico an eco-friendly product; an organic product
un producto orgánico *or* biológico an organic product
en el futuro in the future
destruir to destroy
contaminar to contaminate; to pollute
prohibir to ban
salvar to save
reciclar to recycle
verde green

USEFUL WORDS *(feminine)*

las	**aguas negras** (*LAm*)	sewage
las	**aguas residuales**	sewage
la	**capa de ozono**	ozone layer
la	**catástrofe**	disaster
la	**contaminación acústica**	noise pollution
la	**lluvia ácida**	acid rain
la	**luna**	moon
la	**marea negra** *or* **la mancha de petróleo**	oil spill
la	**población** (*pl* poblaciones)	population
la	**selva tropical**	tropical rainforest

USEFUL PHRASES

biodegradable **biodegradable**
nocivo(a) ***or*** dañino(a) para el medio ambiente **harmful to the environment**
gasolina sin plomo **unleaded gasoline**
(las) especies en peligro de extinción **endangered species**

ESSENTIAL WORDS *(masculine)*

el **abuelo**	grandfather
los **abuelos**	grandparents
los **adultos**	adults
el **apellido**	surname
el **apellido de soltera**	maiden name
el **bebé**	baby
el **hermano**	brother
el **hijo**	son
el **hombre**	man
el **joven** (*pl* jóvenes)	young man
los **jóvenes**	young people
el **marido**	husband
los **mayores**	grown-ups
el **muchacho**	boy, young man
el **niño**	child, boy
el **nombre**	name
el **nombre (de pila)**	first *or* Christian name
el **novio**	boyfriend; bridegroom
el **padre**	father
los **padres**	parents
el **papá**	dad, daddy
el **pariente**	relative
el **primo**	cousin
el **prometido**	fiancé
el **señor**	gentleman, man
el **tío**	uncle

USEFUL PHRASES

¿qué edad tiene (*or* tienes)?, ¿cuántos años tiene (*or* tienes)? how old are you?
tengo 15 años – él tiene 40 años I'm 15 – he is 40
¿cómo se llama (*or* te llamas)? what is your name?
me llamo Daniela my name is Daniela
se llama Paco his name is Paco
prometido(a) engaged; casado(a) married
divorciado(a) divorced; separado(a) separated
casarse con algn to marry sb
casarse to get married; divorciarse to get divorced

ESSENTIAL WORDS *(feminine)*

la **abuela**	grandmother
la **edad**	age
la **esposa**	wife
la **familia**	family
la **gente**	people
la **hermana**	sister
la **hija**	daughter
la **joven** (*pl* jóvenes)	young girl
la **madre**	mother
la **mamá**	mom, mommy
la **muchacha**	girl, young woman
la **mujer**	woman; wife
la **niña**	child, girl
la **novia**	girlfriend; bride
la **persona**	person
la **prima**	cousin
la **prometida**	fiancée
la **señora**	lady, woman
la **tía**	aunt

USEFUL PHRASES

más joven/mayor que yo younger/older than me
¿tiene (*or* tienes) hermanos? do you have any brothers *or* sisters?
tengo un hermano y una hermana I have one brother and one sister
no tengo hermanos I don't have any brothers *or* sisters
soy hijo(a) único(a) I am an only child
toda la familia the whole family
crecer to grow
envejecer to get old, to age
me llevo bien con mis padres I get along with my parents
mi madre trabaja my mother works

IMPORTANT WORDS *(masculine)*

el	**adolescente**	teenager
el	**esposo**	husband
el	**nieto**	grandson
los	**nietos**	grandchildren
el	**padrastro**	stepfather
el	**sobrino**	nephew
el	**soltero**	bachelor
el	**suegro**	father-in-law
el	**vecino**	neighbor
el	**viudo**	widower

USEFUL WORDS *(masculine)*

el	**ahijado**	godson
el	**anciano**	elderly man
el	**apodo**	nickname
el	**chaval** (*Sp*)	kid
el	**chavo** (*Mex*)	kid
los	**cuates** (*Mex*)	twins; pals, buddies
el	**cuñado**	brother-in-law
los	**gemelos (idénticos)**	(identical) twins
el	**hermanastro**	stepbrother
el	**hijastro**	stepson
el	**huérfano**	orphan
el	**jubilado**	retired person, retiree
los	**mellizos**	twins
el	**mote**	nickname
el	**padrino**	godfather
los	**recién casados**	newlyweds
los	**trillizos**	triplets
el	**viejo**	old man
el	**yerno**	son-in-law

USEFUL PHRASES

nacer **to be born**; vivir **to live**; morir **to die**; nací en 1990 **I was born in 1990**
mi abuela murió **my grandmother is dead**
murió en 1995 **(s)he died in 1995**

IMPORTANT WORDS *(feminine)*

la **adolescente**	teenager
la **madrastra**	stepmother
la **nieta**	granddaughter
la **sobrina**	niece
la **soltera**	single woman
la **suegra**	mother-in-law
la **vecina**	neighbor
la **viuda**	widow

USEFUL WORDS *(feminine)*

la **ahijada**	goddaughter
el **ama de casa** (*f pl* las amas ~ ~)	housewife
la **anciana**	elderly woman
la **chavala** (*Sp*)	kid
la **chava** (*Mex*)	kid
las **cuatas** (*Mex*)	twins
la **cuñada**	sister-in-law
las **gemelas (idénticas)**	(identical) twins
la **hermanastra**	stepsister
la **hijastra**	stepdaughter
la **huérfana**	orphan
la **jubilada**	pensioner
la **madrina**	godmother
las **mellizas**	twins, twin sisters
la **niñera**	nanny
la **nuera**	daughter-in-law
la **pareja**	couple
la **vejez**	old age
la **vieja**	old woman

USEFUL PHRASES

es soltero(a) he/she is single
es viudo he is a widower; es viuda she is a widow
soy el/la menor I am the youngest; soy el/la mayor I am the eldest
mi hermana mayor my eldest sister

ESSENTIAL WORDS *(masculine)*

el **agricultor**	farmer
el **animal**	animal
el **bosque**	forest
el **buey**	ox
el **caballo**	horse
el **cabrito**	kid
el **campo**	country, countryside; field
el **cerdo**	pig
el **chivo**	kid
el **gato**	cat
el **granjero**	farmer
el **guajolote** (*Mex*)	turkey
el **invernadero**	greenhouse
el **pato**	duck
el **pavo**	turkey
el **perro**	dog
el **perro pastor** (*pl* ~s ~)	sheepdog
el **pollo**	chicken
el **pueblo**	village
el **rancho** (*Mex*)	ranch
el **ranchero** (*Mex*)	rancher
el **ternero**	calf

IMPORTANT WORDS *(masculine)*

el **campesino**	farmer; peasant
el **cordero**	lamb
el **gallo**	rooster
el **tractor**	tractor

USEFUL PHRASES

un maizal **a cornfield**; un trigal **a wheat field**
la agricultura ecológica *or* biológica *or* orgánica **organic farming**
los pollos ecológicos *or* criados en libertad **free range chickens**
los huevos ecológicos **free range eggs**
cuidar los animales **to take care of the animals**
recolectar **to harvest**
recoger la cosecha **to harvest the crops**

ESSENTIAL WORDS *(feminine)*

la **agricultora**	farmer
la **camioneta**	van; station wagon
la **cerca**	fence
la **cerda**	sow
la **finca**	farm
la **gallina**	hen
la **granja**	farm; farmhouse
la **granjera**	farmer; farmer's wife
la **oveja**	sheep; ewe
la **puerta**	gate
la **ranchera** (*Mex*)	farmer
la **tierra**	earth; ground
la **vaca**	cow
la **vagoneta** (*Mex*)	van
la **valla** (*Sp*)	fence
la **yegua**	mare

IMPORTANT WORDS *(feminine)*

la **campesina**	farmer; peasant
la **colina**	hill

USEFUL PHRASES

vivir en el campo to live in the country
trabajar en una granja to work on a farm
recolectar el heno to make hay

USEFUL WORDS *(masculine)*

el **abono**	manure; fertilizer
el **arado**	plow
el **barro** *or* el **lodo**	mud
el **burro**	donkey
el **carnero**	ram
el **centeno**	rye
el **cerdo**	pig
el **cereal**	cereal
el **chiquero** (*LAm*)	pigsty
el **cobertizo**	shed
el **corral**	farmyard
el **elote** (*Mex*)	corncob; corn
el **espantapájaros** (*pl inv*)	scarecrow
el **establo**	barn
el **estanque**	pond
el **estiércol**	manure
el **gallinero**	henhouse
el **ganado**	cattle
el **ganso**	goose
el **granero**	granary
el **grano**	grain, seed
el **heno**	hay
el **maíz**	maize; corn
el **molino (de viento)**	(wind)mill
el **paisaje**	landscape
el **pajar**	loft
el **páramo**	moor, heath
el **pastor**	shepherd
el **pollito**	chick
el **potro**	foal
el **pozo**	well
el **rebaño**	(*sheep*) flock; (*cattle*) herd
el **suelo**	ground, earth
el **surco**	furrow
el **toro**	bull
el **trigo**	wheat

USEFUL WORDS *(feminine)*

la **avena**	oats
la **cabra**	goat
la **carretilla**	wheelbarrow
la **cebada**	barley
la **cosecha**	crop; harvest
la **cosechadora**	combine harvester
la **escalera**	ladder
la **ganadería**	cattle farming
la **lana**	wool
la **paja**	straw
la **pocilga** (*Sp*)	pigsty
la **recolección** (*pl* recolecciones)	harvest
la **uva**	grapes
la **vendimia**	grape harvest, grape picking
la **viña**	vine
la **zanja**	ditch

ESSENTIAL WORDS *(masculine)*

el **marisco** (*Sp*)	seafood
los **mariscos** (*LAm*)	seafood
el **pescado**	fish (*as food*)
el **pez** (*pl* peces)	fish
el **pez de colores** (*pl* peces ~ ~)	goldfish

IMPORTANT WORDS *(masculine)*

el **cangrejo**	crab
el **insecto**	insect

USEFUL WORDS *(masculine)*

el **acuario**	aquarium
el **arenque**	herring
el **atún** (*pl* atunes)	tuna fish
el **avispón** (*pl* avispones)	hornet
el **bacalao**	cod
el **calamar**	squid
el **camarón** (*pl* camarones)	shrimp
el **cangrejo de río**	crayfish
el **grillo**	cricket
el **gusano**	worm
el **gusano de seda**	silkworm
el **langostino**	jumbo shrimp
el **lenguado**	sole
el **mejillón** (*pl* mejillones)	mussel
el **mosquito**	mosquito
el **pulpo**	octopus
el **renacuajo**	tadpole
el **salmón** (*pl* salmones)	salmon
el **saltamontes** (*pl inv*)	grasshopper
el **tiburón** (*pl* tiburones)	shark
el **zancudo** (*LAm*)	mosquito

USEFUL PHRASES

nadar to swim
volar to fly
vamos a ir a pescar we're going fishing

ESSENTIAL WORDS *(feminine)*

el **agua** (*f*)	water

IMPORTANT WORDS *(feminine)*

la **mosca**	fly
la **sardina**	sardine

USEFUL WORDS *(feminine)*

la **abeja**	bee
el **aguamala** (*f pl* las aguamalas) (*Mex*)	jellyfish
el **ala** (*f pl* las alas)	wing
la **anguila**	eel
la **araña**	spider
la **avispa**	wasp
la **catarina** (*Mex*)	ladybug
la **cigarra**	cicada
la **cucaracha**	cockroach
la **hormiga**	ant
la **langosta**	lobster
la **libélula**	dragonfly
la **mariposa**	butterfly
la **mariquita** (*Sp*)	ladybug
la **medusa**	jellyfish
la **merluza**	hake
la **mosca**	fly
la **oruga**	caterpillar
la **ostra**	oyster
la **polilla**	moth
la **pulga**	flea
la **rana**	frog
la **telaraña**	spider's web
la **trucha**	trout

USEFUL PHRASES

una picadura de abeja/avispa a bee/wasp sting

ESSENTIAL WORDS *(masculine)*

los	**abarrotes** (*Mex*)	groceries; grocery store
el	**aceite**	oil
el	**alcohol**	alcohol
el	**almuerzo**	lunch; (*Mex*) mid-morning snack
el	**aperitivo**	appetizer; aperitif
el	**arroz**	rice
el	**azúcar**	sugar
el	**bar**	bar
el	**bistec** (*pl* ~es *or* ~s)	steak
el	**bote**	can
el	**café**	coffee; café, coffee shop
el	**café con leche**	coffee with milk, light coffee
el	**camarero** (*Sp*)	waiter
el	**caramelo**	candy
los	**cereales**	cereals
el	**chocolate (caliente)**	(hot) chocolate
el	**cocinero**	cook
el	**croissant** (*Sp*)	croissant
el	**cuarto**	quarter (*bottle/liter etc*)
el	**cuernito** (*Mex*)	croissant
el	**cuchillo**	knife
el	**desayuno**	breakfast
el	**dueño**	owner
el	**entrecot** (*pl inv or* ~s)	sirloin steak
el	**filete**	tenderloin
el	**helado**	ice cream
el	**huevo**	egg
el	**huevo duro** *or* **cocido**	hard-boiled egg
el	**huevo frito** *or* (*Mex*) **estrellado**	fried egg
el	**huevo pasado por agua** *or* **tibio**	soft-boiled egg
los	**huevos revueltos**	scrambled eggs
el	**jamón** (*pl* jamones)	ham
el	**jugo de fruta** (*LAm*)	fruit juice
el	**marisco** (*Sp*)	seafood
los	**mariscos** (*LAm*)	seafood
el	**menú del día**	fixed-price menu
el	**mesero** (*LAm*)	waiter
el	**pan**	bread
el	**pastel**	cake; pie

ESSENTIAL WORDS *(feminine)*

la **aceituna**	olive
el **agua (mineral)** (*f*)	(mineral) water
la **bandeja**	tray
la **bebida**	drink
la **botella**	bottle
la **caja**	box
la **carne**	meat
la **carne de puerco** (*Mex*)	pork
la **carne de res** (*Mex*)	beef
la **carne de vaca**	beef
la **carnicería**	butcher's
la **carta**	menu
la **cena**	dinner
la **cerveza**	beer
la **charola** (*LAm*)	tray
la **Coca-Cola®** (*pl* ~s)	Coke®
la **comida**	lunch; meal; food
la **comida precocinada** *or* **preparada**	TV dinner
la **copa**	glass (stemmed)
la **cuchara**	spoon
la **cuenta**	check, bill
la **ensalada**	salad
la **ensalada mixta**	mixed salad
la **fruta**	fruit
el **hambre** (*f*)	hunger
la **hamburguesa**	hamburger
la **lata**	can
la **leche**	milk
las **legumbres**	vegetables
la **limonada**	lemonade
la **mantequilla**	butter
la **mermelada**	jam
la **mermelada (de cítricos)**	marmalade
la **mesa**	table
la **mesera** (*LAm*)	waitress
la **panadería**	baker's
las **papas fritas** (*LAm*)	French fries; potato chips

ESSENTIAL WORDS (*masculine continued*)

el **paté**	pâté
el **pay** (*Mex*)	pie
el **pescado**	fish
el **picnic** (*pl* ~s)	picnic
el **platillo**	saucer; (*Mex*) dish
el **plato**	plate; dish; course
el **plato del día**	today's special
el **pollo (asado)**	(roast) chicken
el **postre**	dessert
el **primer plato**	first course, appetizer
el **puerco** (*Mex*)	pork
el **queso**	cheese
el **restaurante**	restaurant
el **salami**, el **salchichón** (*pl* salchichones)	salami
el **sándwich** (*pl* ~es)	sandwich
el **servicio**	service
el **supermercado**	supermarket
el **tazón**	bowl
el **té**	tea
el **tenedor**	fork
el **vaso**	glass
el **vinagre**	vinegar
el **vino**	wine
el **yogur(t)**	yogurt
el **zumo de fruta** (*Sp*)	fruit juice

USEFUL PHRASES

cocinar **to cook**; comer **to eat**
beber **to drink**; tragar **to swallow**
mi plato favorito **my favorite dish**
¿qué vas (*or* va) a beber? **what are you having to drink?**
está bueno *or* rico **it's nice**
tener hambre **to be hungry**
tener sed **to be thirsty**

ESSENTIAL WORDS (*feminine continued*)

la	**pastelería**	pastries
las	**patatas fritas** (*Sp*)	French fries; potato chips
la	**pescadería**	fish shop
la	**repostería**	desserts
la	**sal**	salt
la	**salchicha**	sausage
la	**sed** (*pl inv*)	thirst
la	**sidra**	cider
la	**sopa**	soup
la	**tarta**	tart
la	**taza**	cup
la	**ternera**	veal
la	**tienda de abarrotes** (*Mex*)	grocery store
la	**tortilla** (*Mex*)	tortilla
la	**tortilla de papas** (*LAm*)	Spanish omelette
la	**tortilla española**	Spanish omelette
la	**tostada**	toast
las	**verduras**	vegetables

IMPORTANT WORDS (*feminine*)

la	**barbacoa**	(*Mex*) meat cooked in a hole in the ground; (*Sp*) barbecue
la	**cafetería**	cafeteria
la	**camarera** (*Sp*)	waitress
la	**carne a la parrilla**	grilled meat
la	**cerveza de barril**	draft beer
la	**chef** (*pl* ~s)	chef
la	**chuleta de cerdo** (*Sp*)	pork chop
la	**chuleta de puerco** (*Mex*)	pork chop
la	**crema**	cream
la	**cucharita**	teaspoon
la	**cuchara (de postre)**	dessert spoon
la	**cuchara de servir**	tablespoon
la	**garrafa**	carafe
la	**harina**	flour
la	**jarra**	pitcher

IMPORTANT WORDS *(masculine)*

el **ajo**	garlic
el **almíbar**	syrup
el **asado**	roast meat; (*LAm*) barbecue
el **bolillo** (*Mex*)	bread roll
los **caracoles**	snails
el **carrito**	cart
el **chef** (*pl* ~s)	chef
el **cocinero jefe**	chef
el **conejo**	rabbit
el **cordero**	lamb
el **cubierto**	cover charge; place setting; piece of silverware
los **cubiertos**	silverware
el **gusto**	taste
el **olor**	smell
el **precio con todo incluido**	all-inclusive price
el **precio fijo**	set price
el **sabor**	flavor
el **suplemento**	extra charge
el **tentempié**	snack
el **tocino** (*LAm*)	bacon

USEFUL WORDS *(masculine)*

el **abrelatas** (*pl inv*)	can opener
el **beicon** (*Sp*)	bacon
el **bollo**	roll, sweet bun
el **cacao**	cocoa
el **catsup** (*LAm*)	ketchup
el **champán** (*pl* champanes)	champagne
el **coñac** (*pl* ~s)	brandy
el **corcho**	cork
el **cubito (de hielo)**	ice cube
el **estofado**	stew
el **hígado**	liver
el **ketchup**	ketchup
el **mantel**	tablecloth
los **mejillones**	mussels
el **panecillo** (*Sp*)	roll

IMPORTANT WORDS *(feminine continued)*

la **mayonesa**	mayonnaise
la **mostaza**	mustard
la **nata** (*Sp*)	cream
la **parrillada** (*LAm*)	barbecue
la **pimienta**	pepper
la **pizza**	pizza
la **propina**	tip
la **receta**	recipe
la **selección** (*pl* selecciones)	choice
la **telera** (*Mex*)	bread roll
la **tetera**	teapot
la **torta** (*Mex*)	sandwich (in a bread roll)
la **vainilla**	vanilla
la **vajilla**	dishes; dinner service

USEFUL WORDS *(feminine)*

las **aves**	poultry
la **botana** (*Mex*)	hors d'oeuvre, appetizer
la **carta de vinos**	wine list
la **caza**	game
la **champaña** (*LAm*)	champagne
la **chuleta**	chop
la **crema batida** (*LAm*)	whipped cream
la **gelatina**	Jell-O®

USEFUL PHRASES

lavar los platos **to do the dishes**
desayunar, tomar el desayuno **to have breakfast**
delicioso(a) **delicious**; repugnante **disgusting**
¡buen provecho! **enjoy your meal!**; ¡salud! **cheers!**
¡la cuenta, por favor! **the check please!**
"servicio (no) incluido" **"service (not) included"**
comer fuera **to eat out**
invitar a algn a comer **to invite sb to lunch**
tomar una copa **to have a drink**

USEFUL WORDS (*masculine continued*)

el **paté de hígado**	liver pâté
el **popote** (*Mex*)	(drinking) straw
el **puré de papas** (*LAm*)	mashed potatoes
el **puré de patatas** (*Sp*)	mashed potatoes
los **riñones**	kidneys
el **rosbif** (*pl inv or* ~s)	roast beef
el **sacacorchos** (*pl inv*)	corkscrew
el **tapón** (*pl* tapones)	cork
el **termo**	flask
el **whisky, whiskey** (*pl* ~s)	whisky

USEFUL PHRASES

poner la mesa to set the table; recoger la mesa to clear the table
probar algo to taste sth
¡eso huele bien! that smells good!
vino blanco/rosado/tinto white/rosé/red wine
un filete poco hecho/en su punto/bien hecho (*Sp*) a rare/medium/well-done steak
un filete a la inglesa/a punto/bien cocido (*Mex*) a rare/medium/well-done steak

USEFUL WORDS *(feminine continued)*

la **infusión** (*pl* infusiones)	herbal tea
la **jalea**	jelly
la **margarina**	margarine
la **miel**	honey
la **nata montada** (*Sp*)	whipped cream
las **natillas**	custard
la **pajita** (*Sp*)	(drinking) straw
la **pasta**	pasta
la **rebanada de pan**	slice of bread
la **salsa**	sauce
la **servilleta**	napkin
la **tisana**	herbal tea
las **tripas**	tripe
la **vinagreta**	vinaigrette dressing

SMOKING

el **cenicero**	ashtray
la **cerilla** (*Sp*)	match
el **cerillo** (*LAm*)	match
el **cigarrillo**	cigarette
el **cigarro**	cigar
el **encendedor**	lighter
la **pipa**	pipe
el **tabaco**	tobacco

USEFUL PHRASES

una caja de cerillos a box of matches
¿tienes (*or* tiene) fuego? do you have a light?
encender un cigarrillo to light up
"prohibido fumar" "no smoking"
no fumo I don't smoke
tienes que dejar de fumar you have to quit smoking
fumar es perjudicial para la salud smoking damages your health

ESSENTIAL WORDS *(masculine)*

el **ajedrez**	chess
el **amigo por correspondencia**	penpal
el **baile**	dance
el **billete** (*Sp*)	ticket
el **boleto** (*LAm*)	ticket
el **cantante**	singer
el **canto**	singing
el **canal de televisión**	TV channel
el **CD** (*pl inv or* ~s)	CD
el **celular** (*LAm*)	cell phone
el **cine**	movie theater, cinema
el **club** (*pl* ~s *or* ~es)	club
el **concierto**	concert
los **deportes**	sports
el **disco**	record (*LP, 45, etc*)
el **domingo** (*Mex*)	allowance
el **DVD** (*pl inv or* ~s)	DVD
el **espectáculo**	show
el **fin de semana**	weekend
el **folleto**	leaflet
el **futbolín** (*pl* futbolines)	foosball
el **hobby** (*pl* hobbies)	hobby
el **juego**	game
el **móvil** (*Sp*)	cell phone
el **museo**	museum; art gallery
los **naipes**	cards
el **paseo**	walk
el **periódico**	newspaper
el **programa**	program
el **radio** (*LAm*)	radio (set)
el **recital**	concert
el **reproductor** *or* **lector de CD/DVD/MP3**	CD/DVD/MP3 player
el **socio**	member (*of a club, etc*)
el **teatro**	theater
el **televisor**	TV (set)
el **tiempo libre**	free time
el **videojuego**	video game

ESSENTIAL WORDS *(feminine)*

la **afición** (*pl* aficiones)	hobby
la **amiga por correspondencia**	penpal
la **cámara (de fotos)**	camera
la **canción** (*pl* canciones)	song
la **cantante**	singer
las **cartas**	cards
la **discoteca**	disco
la **diversión** (*pl* diversiones)	entertainment
la **estrella (de cine)** (*m+f*)	(movie) star
la **excursión** (*pl* excursiones)	trip; outing; hike
la **fiesta**	party
la **foto**	photo
la **historieta**	comic strip
Internet	Internet
la **lectura**	reading
la **mesada** (*LAm*)	allowance
la **música (pop/clásica)**	(pop/classical) music
las **noticias**	news
la **novela**	novel
la **novela policíaca**	detective novel
la **película**	movie; roll of film (*for a camera*)
la **pista de patinaje**	skating rink
la **prensa**	the press
la **publicidad**	publicity
la **radio**	radio
la **revista**	magazine
la **televisión**	television
la **videoconsola**	video game console

USEFUL PHRASES

salgo con mis amigos **I go out with my friends**
leo el periódico **I read the newspaper**
veo la televisión **I watch television**
juego a las cartas *or* los naipes **I play cards**
juego al fútbol/al tenis **I play soccer/tennis**
juego fútbol/tenis (*LAm*) **I play soccer/tennis**
hacer bricolaje **to do-it-yourself**
hacer zapping **to channel surf**

IMPORTANT WORDS *(masculine)*

el **anuncio**	notice; poster
los **anuncios por palabras**	advertisements; small ads
el **concurso**	competition
los **dibujos animados**	cartoons
el **juguete**	toy
el **mensaje de texto**	text message
el **noticiero** (*LAm*)	news
el **novio**	boyfriend
el **ordenador (personal)** (*Sp*)	(personal) computer
los **pasatiempos**	leisure activities
el **PC** (*pl* ~s)	PC
el **programa**	program
el **SMS** (*pl inv*)	text message
el **telediario** (*Sp*)	news
el **video** (*LAm*), el **vídeo** (*Sp*)	video
el **website**	website

USEFUL WORDS *(masculine)*

el **aficionado**	fan
el **blog**	blog
el **campamento de verano**	summer camp
el **chat**	chat; chatroom
el **club nocturno** (*pl* ~s *or* ~es ~s)	night club
el **coro**	choir
el **crucigrama**	crossword puzzle(s)
el **juego de mesa**	board game
el **monopatín** (*pl* monopatines) (*Sp*)	skateboard
el **patín**	skate
el **videoclub** (*pl* ~s *or* ~es)	video store

USEFUL PHRASES

emocionante exciting
aburrido(a) boring
divertido(a) funny

IMPORTANT WORDS *(feminine)*

la **cámara digital**	digital camera
la **colección** (*pl* colecciones)	collection
la **computadora (personal)** (*LAm*)	(personal) computer
la **exposición** (*pl* exposiciones)	exhibition
la **filmadora** (*LAm*)	camcorder
la **grabadora de CD/DVD**	CD/DVD burner
la **noche**	evening
la **novia**	girlfriend
la **pintura**	painting
la **reunión** (*pl* reuniones)	meeting
la **serie**	serial
la **tarde**	afternoon, evening
la **telenovela**	soap (opera)
la **videocámara**	camcorder

USEFUL WORDS *(feminine)*

la **aficionada**	fan
la **diapositiva**	slide
la **fotografía**	photograph; photography
la **lista de éxitos**	charts
la **patineta** (*LAm*)	skateboard

USEFUL PHRASES

no está mal it's not bad
bastante bien quite good
bailar to dance
sacar *or* tomar fotos to take photos
estoy aburrido(a) I'm bored
nos reunimos los viernes we meet on Fridays
estoy ahorrando para comprarme una impresora I'm saving up to buy a printer
me gustaría dar la vuelta al mundo I'd like to go around the world

ESSENTIAL WORDS *(masculine)*

el **albaricoque** (*Sp*)	apricot
el **árbol frutal**	fruit tree
el **chabacano** (*Mex*)	apricot
el **durazno** (*LAm*)	peach
el **jitomate** (*Mex*)	tomato
el **limón** (*pl* limones)	lemon
el **limón amarillo** (*pl* limones ~s) (*Mex*)	lemon
el **limón verde** (*pl* limones ~s) (*Mex*)	lime
el **melocotón** (*pl* melocotones) (*Sp*)	peach
el **melón** (*pl* melones)	melon
el **plátano**	banana
el **pomelo**	grapefruit
el **tomate**	tomato

USEFUL WORDS *(masculine)*

el **aguacate**	avocado
el **anacardo** (*Sp*)	cashew nut
el **arándano**	blueberry
el **cacahuate** (*Mex*)	peanut
el **cacahuete** (*Sp*)	peanut
el **coco**	coconut
el **dátil**	date
los **frutos secos**	nuts
el **higo**	fig
el **kiwi**	kiwi fruit
el **mango**	mango
el **maní** (*pl* ~es) (*LAm*)	peanut

USEFUL PHRASES

un jugo de naranja/piña (*LAm*) an orange/a pineapple juice
un zumo de naranja/piña (*Sp*) an orange/a pineapple juice
un racimo de uvas a bunch of grapes
maduro(a) ripe
verde unripe
pelar una fruta to peel a fruit
resbalar al pisar una cáscara de plátano to slip on a banana peel

ESSENTIAL WORDS *(feminine)*

la **castaña (asada)**	(roasted) chestnut
la **cereza**	cherry
la **frambuesa**	raspberry
la **fresa**	strawberry
la **fruta**	fruit
la **lima**	lime
la **manzana**	apple
la **naranja**	orange
la **pasa**	raisin
la **pera**	pear
la **piel**	skin
la **piña**	pineapple
la **toronja** (*Mex*)	grapefruit
la **uva**	grape(s)

USEFUL WORDS *(feminine)*

la **almendra**	almond
la **avellana**	hazelnut
la **baya**	berry
la **ciruela**	plum
la **ciruela pasa**	prune
la **granada**	pomegranate
la **grosella negra**	blackcurrant
la **grosella (roja)**	redcurrant
la **mandarina**	tangerine
la **mora**	blackberry
la **nuez** (*pl* nueces)	walnut; (*Mex*) pecan nut
la **nuez de Castilla** (*pl* nueces ~~) (*Mex*)	walnut
la **papaya**	papaya
la **sandía**	watermelon
la **vid**	vine

ESSENTIAL WORDS *(masculine)*

el **armario**	cupboard
el **calefactor**	heater
el **clóset** (*LAm*)	closet
el **congelador** *or* el **freezer**	freezer
el **equipo (de música)**	stereo
el **espejo**	mirror
el **estante**	shelf
el **frigorífico** (*Sp*)	fridge, refrigerator
el **mueble**	piece of furniture
los **muebles**	furniture
el **refrigerador** (*LAm*)	fridge
el **reloj**	clock; watch
el **sillón** (*pl* sillones)	armchair
el **teléfono**	telephone

IMPORTANT WORDS *(masculine)*

el **aparador**	sideboard; (*Mex*) store window
el **aparato**	appliance
el **celular** (*LAm*)	cell phone
el **cuadro**	picture
el **escritorio**	(writing) desk
el **fregadero**	sink
el **(horno) microondas**	microwave oven
el **inalámbrico**	cordless phone
el **lavavajillas** (*pl inv*)	dishwasher
el **móvil** (*Sp*)	cell phone
el **piano**	piano
el **portátil**	laptop
el **reproductor** *or* **lector de CD/DVD**	CD/DVD player
el **sofá**	sofa
el **trinchador** (*Mex*)	sideboard

ESSENTIAL WORDS *(feminine)*

la **balda** *(Sp)*	shelf
la **cama**	bed
la **cocina (eléctrica/de gas)**	(electric/gas) stove
la **estufa**	heater; *(Mex)* stove
la **habitación** *(pl* habitaciones)	room
la **lámpara**	lamp
la **lavadora**	washing machine, washer
la **mesa**	table
la **nevera** *(Sp)*	fridge, refrigerator
la **pantalla (de lámpara)**	lampshade
la **radio**	radio
la **silla**	chair
la **televisión** *(pl* televisiones)	television

IMPORTANT WORDS *(feminine)*

la **aspiradora**	vacuum cleaner
la **biblioteca** *(LAm)*	bookcase
la **librería** *(Sp)*	bookcase
la **mesa de café**	coffee table
la **pintura**	painting
la **plancha**	iron
la **secadora**	dryer; *(Mex)* hair dryer

USEFUL WORDS *(masculine)*

el **asiento**	seat
el **bafle**	speaker
el **burro de planchar** (*Mex*)	ironing board
el **cajón** (*pl* cajones)	drawer
el **camión de mudanzas** (*pl* camiones ~ ~)	moving van
el **colchón** (*pl* colchones)	mattress
el **contestador**	answering machine
el **control remoto** (*LAm*)	remote control
el **horno**	oven
el **mando a distancia** (*Sp*)	remote control
el **marco**	frame
el **mobiliario**	furniture
el **paragüero**	umbrella stand
los **postigos**	shutters
el **robot de cocina** (*pl* ~ s ~ ~)	food processor
el **secador (de pelo)**	hairdryer
el **teléfono inalámbrico**	cordless telephone
el **tocador**	dressing table

USEFUL PHRASES

un departamento (*LAm*) *or* piso (*Sp*) amueblado a furnished apartment
encender/apagar la luz to turn the light on/off
haz tu cama make your bed
sentarse to sit down
poner *or* meter algo en el horno to put sth in the oven
correr las cortinas to draw the curtains
cerrar los postigos to close the shutters

USEFUL WORDS *(feminine)*

la **alfombra**	rug
la **antena**	antenna
la **antena parabólica**	satellite dish
la **balanza**	scale
la **báscula**	(bathroom) scale
la **bocina** (*Mex*)	speaker
la **cómoda**	chest of drawers
la **contestadora** (*Mex*)	answering machine
la **cuna**	crib
la **estantería**	shelves
la **lámpara de pie**	floor lamp
la **lámpara halógena**	halogen lamp
las **literas**	bunk beds
la **máquina de coser**	sewing machine
la **máquina de escribir**	typewriter
la **mesilla de noche**	nightstand
la **moqueta** (*Sp*)	wall-to-wall carpet
la **mudanza**	move
la **persiana**	blind
la **tabla de planchar**	ironing board
la **videocámara**	video camera, camcorder

USEFUL PHRASES

un departamento de 4 habitaciones a 4-room apartment

¡ya está el desayuno/la comida/la cena! breakfast/lunch/dinner is ready!

ESSENTIAL WORDS

el **Atlántico**	the Atlantic
el **Distrito Federal (DF)**	Mexico City
el **este**	the east
el **norte**	the north
el **oeste**	the west
el **Pacífico**	the Pacific
el **sur**	the south

USEFUL WORDS

Atenas	Athens
Berlín	Berlin
la **capital**	capital
el **Extremo Oriente**	the Far East
Londres	London
Moscú	Moscow
Nueva York	New York
el **Oriente Medio**	the Middle East
París	Paris
Pekín	Beijing
el **Polo Norte/Sur**	the North/South Pole
Roma	Rome

USEFUL PHRASES

ir a Londres/Nueva York to go to London/New York
soy de Oaxaca I come from Oaxaca
en el *or* al norte in *or* to the north
en el *or* al sur in *or* to the south
en el *or* al este in *or* to the east
en el *or* al oeste in *or* to the west

GREETINGS

hola hello
¿cómo está usted? *or* **¿cómo estás?** how are you?
¿qué tal? how are you?
bien fine (*in reply*)
encantado(a) pleased to meet you
hola hello (*on the telephone*)
bueno (*Mex*) hello (*on the telephone*)
buenas tardes good afternoon; good evening
buenas noches good evening; good night
adiós goodbye
hasta mañana see you tomorrow
hasta luego see you later

BEST WISHES

feliz cumpleaños happy birthday
feliz Navidad merry Christmas
feliz Año Nuevo happy New Year
felices Pascuas happy Easter; happy Christmas
recuerdos best wishes
saludos best wishes
bienvenido(a) welcome
enhorabuena congratulations
buen provecho enjoy your meal
que le (*or* **te) bien** all the best
que te diviertas (*or* **se divierta)** enjoy yourself
buena suerte good luck
buen viaje safe trip
¡salud! bless you (*after a sneeze*); cheers (*when drinking*)
a tu (*or* **su**, *etc*) **salud** to your good health

SURPRISE

Dios mío my goodness
¿qué?, ¿cómo? what?
entiendo oh, I see
vaya well, well
pues... well...
(¿)de verdad(?), (¿)sí(?) really(?)
(¿)estás (*or* está) de broma(?) you're kidding; are you kidding?
¡qué suerte! how lucky!

POLITENESS

perdone I'm sorry; excuse me
por favor please
gracias thank you
no, gracias no, thank you
sí, gracias yes, please
de nada you're welcome, not at all, don't mention it
con mucho gusto la llevo I'd be delighted to take you there

AGREEMENT

sí yes
por supuesto of course
de acuerdo OK
okey (*LAm*) OK
vale (*Sp*) OK
bueno fine

DISAGREEMENT

no no
claro que no of course not
ni hablar no way
no estoy de acuerdo I don't agree
creo *or* **pienso que no** I don't think so; I think not
estoy en contra de la pena de muerte I am against the death penalty
en absoluto not at all
al contrario on the contrary
no te metas en lo que no te importa mind your own business

DIFFICULTIES

socorro help
fuego fire
ay ouch
perdón (I'm) sorry; excuse me; I beg your pardon
lo siento I'm sorry
qué pena what a pity
qué lata (*LAm*) what a nuisance; how boring
estoy harto(a) I'm fed up
no aguanto más I can't stand it any more
qué horror how awful

ORDERS

cuidado be careful
para (*or* **pare**) stop
oiga, usted hey, you there
fuera de aquí get lost
silencio shh
basta ya that's enough
prohibido fumar no smoking
vamos come on, let's go
sigue *or* **siga** go ahead, go on
vámonos let's go

OTHERS

no tengo (ni) idea I have no idea
quizá, quizás perhaps, maybe
no (lo) sé I don't know
¿qué desea? can I help you?
aquí tienes there; there you are
ya voy I'm coming
no te preocupes don't worry
no merece la pena it's not worth it
a propósito by the way
cariño, querido(a) darling, honey
el (*or* **la**) **pobre** poor thing
tanto mejor so much the better
no me importa I don't mind
a mí me da igual it's all the same to me
mala suerte too bad
depende it depends
¿qué voy a hacer? what shall I do?
¿qué sentido tiene? what's the point?
me molesta it annoys me
me saca de quicio it gets on my nerves

ESSENTIAL WORDS *(masculine)*

el **accidente**	accident
el **dentista**	dentist
el **doctor**	doctor
el **enfermero**	nurse
el **enfermo**	patient
el **estómago**	stomach
el **hospital**	hospital
el **médico**	doctor

IMPORTANT WORDS *(masculine)*

el **algodón (hidrófilo)**	cotton wool
el **antiséptico**	antiseptic
el **comprimido**	pill, capsule
el **dolor**	pain
el **farmacéutico**	pharmacist
el **jarabe**	syrup
el **medicamento**	medicine, drug
el **paciente**	patient
el **resfriado**	cold
el **seguro**	insurance
el **yeso** (*LAm*)	plaster cast; plaster

USEFUL PHRASES

hubo un accidente there's been/there was an accident
la internaron (*LAm*) *or* ingresaron (*Sp*) en el hospital she was admitted to the hospital
debe permanecer en cama you/(s)he must stay in bed
estar enfermo(a) to be ill; sentirse mejor to feel better
cuidar to look after
me lastimé (*LAm*), me he hecho daño (*Sp*) I have hurt myself
me enyesaron el brazo (*LAm*) they put my arm in a cast
me corté el dedo I cut my finger
me torcí el tobillo I sprained my ankle
se rompió el brazo (s)he broke his/her arm
me quemé I burnt myself
me duele la garganta/la cabeza/el estómago I have a sore throat/a headache/a stomach ache
tener fiebre to have a temperature

ESSENTIAL WORDS *(feminine)*

la **aspirina**	aspirin
la **cama**	bed
la **cita**	appointment
la **curita** (*LAm*)	Band Aid®
la **dentista**	dentist
la **doctora**	doctor
la **enferma**	patient
la **enfermera**	nurse
la **farmacia**	pharmacy, drug store
la **médico/a**	doctor
la **pastilla**	pill, capsule
la **salud**	health
la **temperatura**	temperature
la **tirita** (*Sp*)	Band Aid®

IMPORTANT WORDS *(feminine)*

la **ambulancia**	ambulance
la **camilla**	stretcher
la **clínica**	clinic, hospital
la **consulta**	consultation
la **crema**	cream, ointment
la **cucharada**	spoonful
la **diarrea**	diarrhea
la **enfermedad**	illness
la **escayola** (*Sp*)	plaster cast
la **farmacéutica**	pharmacist
la **gripa** (*Mex*)	flu
la **gripe**	flu
la **herida**	wound, injury
la **insolación** (*pl* insolaciones)	sunstroke
la **inyección** (*pl* inyecciones)	injection, shot
la **medicina**	medicine
la **operación** (*pl* operaciones)	operation
la **paciente**	patient
la **píldora**	pill; the Pill (*birth control*)
las **quemaduras de sol**	sunburn
la **receta**	prescription
la **sangre**	blood
la **tableta**	tablet
urgencias	ER
la **venda**	bandage

USEFUL WORDS *(masculine)*

el **absceso**	abscess
el **acné**	acne
el **arañazo**	scratch
el **ataque**	fit
el **ataque al corazón**	heart attack
el **cáncer**	cancer
el **cardenal** (*Sp*)	bruise
el **embarazo**	pregnancy
el **estrés**	stress
el **mareo**	dizzy spell; sickness
el **microbio**	germ
el **moretón**	bruise
el **nervio**	nerve
el **preservativo**	condom
los **primeros auxilios**	first aid
el **pulso**	pulse
el **régimen**	diet
el **reposo**	rest
el **sarampión**	measles
el **shock**	shock
el **sida**	AIDS
el **tónico**	tonic
el **vendaje**	dressing
el **veneno**	poison

USEFUL PHRASES

tengo sueño I'm sleepy
tengo naúseas I feel nauseous
adelgazar to lose weight
engordar to put on weight
tragar to swallow
sangrar to bleed
vomitar to vomit
estar en forma to be in good shape
reposar, descansar to rest

USEFUL WORDS *(feminine)*

la **amigdalitis**	tonsillitis
anginas	sore throat; tonsillitis
la **apendicitis**	appendicitis
la **astilla**	splinter
la **cicatriz** (*pl* cicatrices)	scar
la **dentadura postiza**	dentures, false teeth
la **dieta**	diet
la **epidemia**	epidemic
la **fiebre del heno**	hay fever
la **migraña**	migraine
la **muleta**	crutch
la **náusea**	nausea
las **paperas**	mumps
la **pomada**	ointment
la **radiografía**	X-ray
la **recuperación**	recovery
la **rubeola**	German measles
la **silla de ruedas**	wheelchair
la **tos**	cough
la **tos ferina**	whooping cough
la **transfusión (de sangre)** (*pl* transfusiones (~ ~))	blood transfusion
la **varicela**	chickenpox
la **viruela**	smallpox

USEFUL PHRASES

curar to cure; curarse to get better
gravemente herido(a) seriously injured
¿tiene seguro? are you insured?
estoy resfriado(a) I have a cold
¡eso duele! that hurts!; me duele it hurts!
respirar to breathe
desmayarse to faint
toser to cough
morir to die
perder el conocimiento to lose consciousness
llevar el brazo en cabestrillo to have one's arm in a sling

ESSENTIAL WORDS *(masculine)*

el **almuerzo**	lunch; (*Mex*) mid-morning snack
el **ascensor**	elevator
el **balcón** (*pl* balcones)	balcony
los **baños públicos** (*LAm*)	restrooms
el **bar**	bar
el **camarero**	waiter
el **cambio**	change
el **cheque**	check
el **cuarto de baño**	bathroom
el **depósito**	deposit
el **desayuno**	breakfast
el **elevador** (*Mex*)	elevator
el **equipaje**	luggage
el **gerente**	manager
el **hotel**	hotel
el **huésped**	guest
el **número**	number
el **pasaporte**	passport
el **piso**	floor, story
el **precio**	price
el **recepcionista**	receptionist
el **restaurante**	restaurant
el **ruido**	noise
los **servicios**	services
el **teléfono**	telephone

USEFUL PHRASES

quisiera reservar una habitación **I would like to reserve a room**
una habitación con ducha/con regadera (*Mex*) **a room with a shower**
una habitación con baño **a room with a bath**
una habitación individual **a single room**
una habitación doble **a double room**

ESSENTIAL WORDS *(feminine)*

la **alberca** (*Mex*)	swimming pool
la **cama de matrimonio**	double bed
la **camarera** (*Sp*)	waitress
las **camas separadas**	twin beds
la **comida**	lunch; meal
la **comodidad**	comfort
la **cuenta**	bill
la **ducha**	shower
la **entrada**	entrance
la **escalera**	stairs
la **estancia**	stay
la **fecha**	date
la **ficha**	form
la **gerente/a**	manager
la **habitación** (*pl* habitaciones)	room
la **huésped**	guest
la **llave**	key
la **maleta**	suitcase
la **media pensión**	Modified American Plan
la **noche**	night
la **pensión** (*pl* pensiones)	guest house
la **pensión completa**	American Plan
la **petaca** (*Mex*)	suitcase
la **piscina**	swimming pool
la **recepción**	reception
la **recepcionista**	receptionist
la **salida de incendios**	fire escape
la **tarifa**	rate, rates
la **televisión** (*pl* televisiones)	television
la **vista**	view

USEFUL PHRASES

¿lleva algún documento de identidad? do you have any ID?
¿a qué hora se sirve el desayuno? what time is breakfast served?
limpiar la habitación to clean the room
"se ruega no molestar" "do not disturb"

IMPORTANT WORDS *(masculine)*

el **albergue** hostel
el **apagador** (*Mex*) light switch
el **baño** bathroom
el **interruptor** switch
el **lavabo** sink (bathroom)
el **precio total** all-inclusive price
el **recibo** receipt
el **switch** (*LAm*) light switch

USEFUL WORDS *(masculine)*

el **cocinero** cook
el **lobby** lobby
el **maître** head waiter
el **sommelier** wine waiter

USEFUL PHRASES

ocupado(a) occupied
libre vacant
limpio(a) clean
sucio(a) dirty
dormir to sleep
despertarse to wake up
"con todas las comodidades" "with all amenities"
¿me pueden llamar mañana a las siete? I'd like a wake-up call at 7 o'clock
una habitación con vista al mar a room overlooking the sea

IMPORTANT WORDS *(feminine)*

la **bañera**	bathtub
la **bienvenida**	welcome
la **camarera** *or* **mucama (de hotel)**	maid
la **casa de huéspedes**	guest house
la **factura**	bill
la **guía turística**	guidebook
la **propina**	tip
la **reclamación** (*pl* reclamaciones)	complaint
la **regadera** (*Mex*)	shower
la **tina** (*Mex*)	bathtub

USEFUL WORDS *(feminine)*

la **cocinera**	cook

USEFUL PHRASES

el desayuno se sirve en el comedor breakfast is served in the dining room
una habitación con media pensión Modified American Plan
un hotel de tres/cinco estrellas a three-/five-star hotel

ESSENTIAL WORDS *(masculine)*

el **aparcamiento** (*Sp*)	parking lot; parking space
el **ascensor**	elevator
el **balcón** (*pl* balcones)	balcony
el **bloque de departamentos** (*LAm*)	apartment building
el **bloque de pisos** (*Sp*)	apartment building
el **comedor**	dining room
el **cuarto de baño**	bathroom
el **departamento** (*LAm*)	apartment
el **dormitorio**	bedroom
el **edificio**	building
el **elevador** (*Mex*)	elevator
el **estacionamiento** (*LAm*)	parking lot; parking space
el **excusado** (*Mex*)	toilet
el **exterior**	exterior
el **garage** (*LAm*) *or* el **garaje** (*Sp*)	garage
el **interior**	interior
el **jardín** (*pl* jardines)	yard; garden
el **mueble**	piece of furniture
los **muebles**	furniture
el **numéro de teléfono**	phone number
el **patio**	yard
el **piso**	floor, story; (*Sp*) apartment
el **pueblo**	village
el **sótano**	basement
el **terreno**	plot of land

USEFUL PHRASES

estar en casa to be at home
ir a casa to go home
mirar por la ventana to look out of the window
en mi/tu/nuestra casa at my/your/our house
mudarse de casa to move (*to a new house or apartment*)
alquilar un departamento to rent an apartment

ESSENTIAL WORDS *(feminine)*

la **avenida**	avenue
la **calefacción (central)** (*pl* calefacciones (~es))	(central) heating
la **calle**	street
la **casa**	house
la **ciudad**	town; city
la **cocina**	kitchen
la **colonia (residencial)** (*Mex*)	suburb
la **comodidad**	amenity
la **dirección** (*pl* direcciones)	address
la **ducha**	shower
la **entrada**	entrance
la **entrada para coches**	driveway
la **escalera**	stairs
la **habitación** (*pl* habitaciones)	room
la **llave**	key
la **parcela**	plot of land
la **pared**	wall
la **planta**	floor, story
la **puerta**	door
la **puerta principal** *or* **de calle**	front door
la **recámara** (*Mex*)	bedroom
la **regadera** (*Mex*)	shower
la **sala**	living room
la **urbanización** (*pl* urbanizaciones)	housing development
la **ventana**	window
la **vista**	view

USEFUL PHRASES

vivo en una casa/en un departamento I live in a house/an apartment
(en el piso de) arriba upstairs
(en el piso de) abajo downstairs
en el primer piso on the first floor

IMPORTANT WORDS *(masculine)*

el **alojamiento**	accommodations
el **alquiler** (*Sp*)	rent
el **baño**	bathroom
el **césped**	lawn
el **corredor**	hall, corridor
el **departamento amueblado**	furnished apartment
el **dueño**	landlord; owner
el **humo**	smoke
el **interfón** (*Mex*)	intercom
el **lavabo**	sink; toilet
el **mantenimiento**	maintenance
el **mobiliario**	furniture
el **pasillo**	hall, corridor
el **portero**	superintendent
el **portero automático**	electronic doorkeeper
el **propietario**	owner; landlord
el **rellano**	landing
el **techo** (*LAm*)	roof; ceiling
el **tejado** (*Sp*)	roof
el **vecino**	neighbor

USEFUL WORDS *(masculine)*

el **ático**	attic
el **cuarto de huéspedes**	guest room
el **despacho**	study
el **desván**	attic
el **escalón** (*pl* escalones)	step
el **estudio**	studio apartment
el **inquilino**	tenant; lodger
el **muro**	wall
el **parquet** (*pl* ~s)	parquet floor
el **seto**	hedge
el **suelo**	floor
el **timbre**	door bell
el **tragaluz** (*pl* tragaluces)	skylight
el **umbral**	doorstep
el **vestíbulo**	foyer
el **vidrio**	window pane

IMPORTANT WORDS *(feminine)*

la **cerca**	fence
la **chimenea**	chimney; fireplace
la **dueña**	landlady; owner
la **mudanza**	move
la **portera**	superintendent
la **propietaria**	owner; landlady
la **renta** (*LAm*)	rent
la **señora de la limpieza**	janitor
la **vecina**	neighbor
la **vivienda**	housing; dwelling; house

USEFUL WORDS *(feminine)*

el **ama de casa** (*f pl* amas ~ ~)	housewife
la **antena**	antenna
el **azulejo**	(wall) tile
la **baldosa**	(floor) tile
la **buhardilla**	attic
la **caldera**	boiler
la **contraventana**	shutter
la **decoración** (*pl* decoraciones)	decoration
la **fachada**	front (*of a house*)
la **inquilina**	tenant; lodger
la **persiana**	blind
la **portería**	doorkeeper's area
la **puerta ventana**	French window
la **teja**	roof shingle; slate

USEFUL PHRASES

llamar a la puerta to knock on the door
tocar el timbre to ring the bell
renovar/decorar una casa to refurbish/to decorate a house
llamar por el interfón (*Mex*) *or* el portero automático (*Sp*) to call on the intercom

ESSENTIAL WORDS *(masculine)*

el	**apagador** (*Mex*)	switch
el	**armario**	cupboard
el	**basurero** *or* el **bote de la basura** (*LAm*)	garbage can
el	**buzón** (*pl* buzones)	letterbox
el	**cenicero**	ashtray
el	**cepillo**	brush
el	**clóset** (*LAm*)	closet
el	**cuadro**	picture
el	**cubo de la basura** (*Sp*)	trash can
el	**despertador**	alarm clock
el	**espejo**	mirror
el	**fregadero**	sink
el	**frigorífico** (*Sp*)	fridge
el	**gas**	gas
el	**grifo** (*Sp*)	faucet
el	**interruptor**	switch
el	**jabón** (*pl* jabones)	soap
el	**lavabo**	(bathroom) sink; toilet
la	**pasta de dientes**	toothpaste
el	**póster** (*pl* ~es *or* ~s)	poster
los	**quehaceres domésticos** *or* **de la casa**	housework
el	**radiador**	radiator
el	**radio** (*LAm*)	radio (set)
el	**refrigerador** (*LAm*)	fridge
el	**reproductor** *or* **lector de CD/DVD/MP3**	CD/DVD/MP3 player
el	**switch** (*LAm*)	switch
el	**televisor**	television set

USEFUL PHRASES

darse un baño, bañarse to take a bath; to take a shower
darse una ducha, ducharse to take a shower
darse un regaderazo (*Mex*) to take a shower
hacer los quehaceres *or* las tareas de la casa to do the housework
me gusta cocinar I like cooking

ESSENTIAL WORDS *(feminine)*

el	**agua** (*f*)	water
la	**alfombra**	carpet, rug
la	**almohada**	pillow
la	**balanza**	scale
la	**báscula**	(bathroom) scale
la	**bandeja**	tray
la	**bañera**	bathtub
la	**cacerola**	saucepan
la	**cafetera**	coffee pot; coffee maker
la	**cobija** (*LAm*)	blanket
la	**cocina**	stove
las	**cortinas**	curtains, drapes
la	**ducha**	shower
la	**electricidad**	electricity
la	**estufa**	heater; (*Mex*) stove
la	**foto**	photo
la	**lámpara**	lamp
la	**lavadora**	washing machine, washer
la	**llave** (*LAm*)	faucet
la	**luz** (*pl* luces)	light
la	**manta**	blanket
la	**nevera** (*Sp*)	fridge, refrigerator
la	**radio**	radio
la	**regadera** (*Mex*)	shower
la	**sábana**	sheet
la	**servilleta**	napkin
las	**tareas domésticas** *or* **de la casa**	housework
la	**televisión** (*pl* televisiones)	television
la	**tina** (*Mex*)	bathtub
la	**toalla**	towel
la	**vajilla**	dishes

USEFUL PHRASES

ver la televisión to watch television
en televisión on television
prender *or* encender/apagar la tele to turn on/off the TV
tirar algo a la basura to throw sth away
lavar *or* fregar los platos to do the dishes

IMPORTANT WORDS *(masculine)*

el **bidé**	bidet
los **cubiertos**	silverware
el **cuchillo**	knife
el **detergente**	detergent
el **enchufe**	plug; socket
el **foco** (*LAm*)	light bulb
el **horno**	oven
el **lavavajillas** (*pl inv*)	dishwasher
el **polvo**	dust
el **sartén** (*pl* sartenes)	frying pan
el **tenedor**	fork

USEFUL WORDS *(masculine)*

el **adorno**	ornament
el **almohadón** (*pl* almohadones)	cushion
el **balde**	pail
el **burro de planchar** (*Mex*)	ironing board
el **cesto de la basura**	wastebasket
el **cojín** (*pl* cojines)	cushion
el **cubo** (*Sp*)	pail
el **edredón** (*pl* edredones ~s)	quilt, duvet
el **gancho (para colgar ropa)** (*LAm*)	coat hanger
el **(horno) microondas**	microwave oven
el **jarrón** (*pl* jarrones)	vase
el **molinillo de café**	coffee grinder
el **paño de cocina**	dishtowel
el **papel tapiz**	wallpaper
el **picaporte**	door handle
el **sacudidor** (*Mex*)	dust cloth
el **secador (para trastes)** (*Mex*)	dishtowel
el **trapo (del polvo)**	dust cloth

USEFUL PHRASES

enchufar/desenchufar **to plug (in)/to unplug**
pasar la aspiradora **to vacuum**
lavar la ropa **to do the laundry**

IMPORTANT WORDS *(feminine)*

la **aspiradora**	vacuum cleaner
la **bombilla** (*Sp*)	light bulb
la **cerradura**	lock
la **cubeta** (*Mex*)	pail
la **cuchara**	spoon
la **estufa**	heater; (*Mex*) stove
la **pintura**	paint; painting
la **receta**	recipe
la **ropa de cama**	sheets and pillowcases
la **ropa para lavar**	laundry
la **ropa sucia**	(dirty) laundry
la **sartén** (*pl* sartenes)	frying pan
la **señora de la limpieza**	cleaner

USEFUL WORDS *(feminine)*

la **basura**	garbage, trash
la **batidora**	mixer
la **batería de cocina**	set of pots and pans
la **escalera (de mano)**	ladder
la **escoba**	broom
la **esponja**	sponge
la **licuadora**	blender
la **manta eléctrica**	electric blanket
la **moqueta** (*Sp*)	wall-to-wall carpet
la **olla exprés** *or* **de presión**	pressure cooker
la **percha** (*Sp*)	coat hanger
la **plancha**	iron
la **tabla de planchar**	ironing board
la **tapa**	lid
la **tapicería**	upholstery
la **tostadora**	toaster

USEFUL PHRASES

barrer to sweep (up)
limpiar to clean

ESSENTIAL WORDS *(masculine)*

el **banco**	bank
el **billete (de banco)**	bank note
el **bolígrafo**	ballpoint pen
el **buzón** (*pl* buzones)	mailbox
el **cambio**	change
el **carné de identidad** (*Sp*)	ID card
el **cartero**	postal carrier, mailman
el **celular** (*LAm*)	cell phone
el **centavo**	cent
el **cheque**	check
el **código postal**	zip code
el **contrato telefónico**	phone contract
el **correo** (*LAm*)	post office
el **correo eletrónico**	email
el **documento de identidad**	ID card
el **depósito** (*LAm*)	deposit
el **dólar**	dollar
el **empleado**	clerk, teller
el **error**	mistake
el **fax**	fax
el **formulario**	form
el **impreso** (*Sp*)	form
el **indicativo (telefónico)**	area code
el **ingreso** (*Sp*)	deposit
el **justificante**	written proof
el **mensaje de texto**	text message
el **mostrador**	counter
el **móvil** (*Sp*)	cell phone
el **número**	number
el **paquete**	package
el **pasaporte**	passport
el **precio**	price
el **prefijo (telefónico)**	area code
el **sello**	postage stamp
el **sobre**	envelope
el **teléfono**	telephone
el **tono de marcado**	dial tone

USEFUL PHRASES

cobrar un cheque to cash a check
cambiar dinero to change money

ESSENTIAL WORDS *(feminine)*

la **bolsa**	bag, purse
la **caja**	checkout
la **carta**	letter
la **cartera**	postal carrier; wallet, billfold
la **clave LADA** (*Mex*)	area code
la **compañía telefónica** *or* **de teléfonos**	phone company
la **contestación**	reply
la **dirección** (*pl* **direcciones**)	address
la **empleada**	clerk, teller
la **estampilla**	postage stamp; rubber stamp
la **firma**	signature
la **forma** (*Mex*)	form
la **identificación**	ID
la **información**	information; directory assistance
la **llamada**	call
la **oficina de correo** (*LAm*) *or* **de correos** (*Sp*)	post office
la **oficina de turismo**	tourist information office
la **pluma**	pen
la **respuesta**	reply
la **tarjeta de crédito**	credit card
la **tarjeta de débito**	debit card
la **(tarjeta) postal**	postcard

USEFUL PHRASES

una llamada telefónica a phone call
llamar a algn por teléfono, telefonear a algn to call sb *or* make a call to sb
descolgar el teléfono to pick up the phone *or* to take the phone off the hook
marcar (el número) to dial (the number)
hola – soy el Dr Pérez hello, this is Dr. Pérez
está ocupado *or* la linea está ocupada the line is busy
no cuelgue hold the line
me equivoqué de número I got the wrong number
colgar to hang up
quisiera hacer una llamada internacional I'd like to make an international call

IMPORTANT WORDS *(masculine)*

el **ADSL**	broadband
el **archivo adjunto**	attachment
el **cheque de viajero** *or* (*Sp*) **de viaje**	traveler's check
el **cibercafé**	cybercafé
el **contestador (automático)**	answering machine
el **correo**	mail
el **correo de voz**	voicemail
el **crédito**	credit, loan
el **directorio (telefónico)** (*LAm*)	telephone book
el **domicílio**	home address
el **gasto**	expense
el **impuesto**	tax
el **mail** (*pl* ~s)	email
el **monedero**	change purse
el **pago**	payment
el **papel de carta**	writing paper
el **recargo**	extra charge
el **SMS** (*pl inv*)	text message
el **talonario de cheques** (*Sp*)	checkbook
el **telefonista**	operator
el **(teléfono) fijo**	landline
el **telegrama**	telegram
el **tipo de cambio**	exchange rate

USEFUL WORDS *(masculine)*

el **acceso al sistema**	login
el **apartado postal**	P.O. box
el **auricular**	receiver
el **destinatario**	addressee
el **documento adjunto**	attachment
el **giro postal**	postal money order
el **papel de envolver**	wrapping paper
el **remitente**	sender
el **tono de llamada**	ringtone

IMPORTANT WORDS *(feminine)*

la **banda ancha**	broadband
la **cabina telefónica**	phone booth
la **chequera** (*LAm*)	checkbook
la **contestadora (de teléfono)** (*Mex*)	answering machine
la **contraseña**	password
la **cuenta (bancaria)**	(bank) account
la **guía telefónica**	phone book
la **llamada telefónica**	phone call
la **oficina de objetos perdidos**	lost-and-found
la **ranura**	slot
la **recogida**	collection
la **recompensa**	reward
la **tarjeta de recarga (del celular)**	prepaid calling card
la **tarjeta telefónica**	(prepaid) phone card
la **tasa de cambio**	exchange rate
la **telefonista**	operator

USEFUL WORDS *(feminine)*

la **bocina** (*Mex*)	receiver
la **carta certificada**	certified letter
la **casa de cambio**	currency exchange office
la **destinataria**	addressee
la **llamada de larga distancia**	long-distance call
la **llamada internacional**	international call
la **llamada local**	local call
la **oficina de cambio**	currency exchange office
la **remitente**	sender
la **tarjeta SIM**	SIM card

USEFUL PHRASES

perdí la cartera I lost my wallet
llenar un formulario to fill out a form
en mayúsculas in block letters
hacer una llamada a cobro revertido to make a collect call
llamar por cobrar (*Mex*) to call collect

GENERAL SITUATIONS

¿cuál es su dirección? what is your address?
¿cómo se escribe? how do you spell that?
¿tiene cambio de 100 dólares? do you have change for a hundred-dollar bill?
escribir to write
responder *or* **contestar** to reply
firmar to sign
¿me puede ayudar por favor? can you help me, please?
¿cómo se va a la estación? how do I get to the station?
todo derecho *or* **todo recto** straight ahead
a la derecha to *or* on the right; **a la izquierda** to *or* on the left

LETTERS

Querido Carlos Dear Carlos
Querida Ana Dear Ana
Estimado Señor Dear Sir
Estimada Señora Dear Madam
recuerdos, saludos best wishes
un abrazo de, un beso de, besos de love from
lo/la saluda atentamente *or* **cordialmente** sincerely yours
besos y abrazos love and kisses
atentamente sincerely
reciba un atento saludo, le saluda atentamente sincerely yours
sigue (al dorso) over (see the reverse side)

E-MAILS

mandarle un mail *or* **un correo electrónico a algn** to email sb

CELL PHONES

mandarle un mensaje de texto *or* **un SMS a algn** to text sb

PRONUNCIATION GUIDE

Pronounced approximately as:

A	ah
B	bay
C	thay, say
D	day
E	ay
F	efay
G	khay
H	atchay
I	ee
J	khota
K	kah
L	elay
LL	elyay
M	emay
N	enay
Ñ	enyay
O	oh
P	pay
Q	koo
R	eray
S	essay
T	tay
U	oo
V	bay korta (*LAm*), oobay (*Sp*)
W	doblay bay (*LAm*), oobay doblay (*Sp*)
X	ekees
Y	ee griayga
Z	seta (*LAm*), theta (*Sp*)

ESSENTIAL WORDS *(masculine)*

el **abogado**	lawyer
el **accidente**	accident
el **carné de identidad** (*Sp*)	ID card
el **documento de identidad**	ID card
el **incendio**	fire
el **policía**	police officer, policeman
el **problema**	problem
el **robo**	burglary; theft

IMPORTANT WORDS *(masculine)*

el **atracador**	armed robber; mugger
el **atraco**	hold-up; mugging
el **consulado**	consulate
el **control policial**	checkpoint; roadblock
el **culpable**	culprit
el **daño** *or* **los daños**	damage
el **ejército**	army
el **espía**	spy
el **gobierno**	government
el **impuesto a la renta**	income tax
los **impuestos**	taxes
el **ladrón** (*pl* ladrones)	burglar; thief; robber
el **monedero**	change purse
el **muerto**	dead man
el **permiso**	permission
el **propietario**	owner; landlord
el **robo de identidad**	identity theft
el **testigo**	witness

USEFUL PHRASES

llamar a la policía **to call the police**
robar **to burglarize; to steal; to rob**
¡me robaron la cartera! **someone has stolen my wallet!**
¡socorro! **help!**; ¡al ladrón! **stop, thief!**
encarcelar **to imprison**; fugarse, escapar **to escape**

ESSENTIAL WORDS *(feminine)*

la **abogada**	lawyer
la **culpa**	fault
la **documentación**	papers
la **identidad**	identity
la **multa**	fine
la **policía**	police; police officer, policewoman
la **verdad**	truth

IMPORTANT WORDS *(feminine)*

la **atracadora**	armed robber; mugger
la **balacera**	shoot-out
la **banda**	gang
la **cartera**	wallet
la **comisaría**	police station
la **culpable**	culprit
la **denuncia**	report
la **espía**	spy
la **ladrona**	burglar; thief; robber
la **manifestación** (*pl* manifestaciones)	demonstration
la **muerta**	dead woman
la **muerte**	death
la **pena de muerte**	death penalty
la **póliza de seguros**	insurance policy
la **propietaria**	owner; landlady
la **recompensa**	reward
la **testigo**	witness

USEFUL PHRASES

un atraco a mano armada a hold-up
raptar *or* secuestrar a un niño to abduct a child
en la cárcel in prison
pelearse to fight; detener *or* arrestar to arrest
acusar a algn de algo to accuse sb of sth; to charge sb with sth
estar fichado -a to have a police record
balacear a algn (*Mex*) to shoot sb

USEFUL WORDS *(masculine)*

el **arresto**	arrest
el **asesinato**	murder
el **asesino**	murderer
el **botín** (*pl* botines)	loot
el **cadáver**	corpse
el **crimen** (*pl* crímenes)	murder; crime
el **criminal**	murderer; criminal
el **delincuente**	criminal
el **detective privado**	private detective
el **drogadicto**	drug addict
el **encarcelamiento**	imprisonment
el **estafador**	crook
el **gamberro** (*Sp*)	thug, hooligan
el **gángster** (*pl* ~s)	gangster
el **guarda**	guard; warden
el **guardia**	guard; police officer
el **inmigrante ilegal**	illegal immigrant
el **intento**	attempt
el **juez** (*pl* jueces)	judge
el **juicio**	trial
el **jurado**	jury
el **narcotraficante**	drug trafficker
el **narcotráfico**	drug trafficking
el **pandillero** (*Mex*)	thug, hooligan
el **pirómano**	arsonist
el **poli**	cop
el **preso**	prisoner
el **rehén** (*pl* rehenes)	hostage
el **rescate**	ransom; rescue
el **revólver**	revolver
el **secuestrador**	kidnapper; hijacker
el **secuestro**	kidnapping
el **secuestro aéreo**	hijacking
el **terrorismo**	terrorism
el **terrorista**	terrorist
el **traficante de drogas**	drug dealer
el **tribunal**	court

USEFUL WORDS *(feminine)*

la	**acusación** (*pl* acusaciones)	the prosecution; charge
el	**arma** (*f pl* las armas)	weapon
la	**asesina**	murderer
la	**bomba**	bomb
la	**cárcel**	prison
la	**celda**	cell
la	**criminal**	murderer; criminal
la	**declaración** (*pl* declaraciones)	statement
la	**defensa**	defence
la	**delincuencia**	crime
la	**delincuente**	criminal
la	**detective privada**	private detective
la	**detención** (*pl* detenciones)	arrest
la	**droga**	drug
la	**drogadicta**	drug addict
la	**estafadora**	crook
la	**fuga**	escape
la	**gamberra** (*Sp*)	thug, hooligan
la	**guarda**	guard; warden
la	**inmigrante ilegal**	illegal immigrant
la	**investigación** (*pl* investigaciones)	inquiry
la	**ley**	law
la	**narcotraficante**	drug trafficker
la	**pandillera** (*Mex*)	thug, hooligan
la	**pelea**	fight
la	**pirómana**	arsonist
la	**pistola**	gun
la	**poli**	the cops; cop
la	**prisión** (*pl* prisiones)	prison
la	**presa**	prisoner
la	**prueba**	proof
las	**pruebas**	evidence
la	**redada**	raid
la	**rehén** (*pl* rehenes)	hostage
la	**riña**	argument
la	**secuestradora**	kidnapper; hijacker
la	**terrorista**	terrorist
la	**traficante de drogas**	drug dealer

ESSENTIAL WORDS *(masculine)*

el **acero**	steel
el **algodón**	cotton
el **caucho**	rubber
el **cristal**	crystal; (*Sp*) glass
el **cuero**	leather
el **gas**	gas
el **gasoil**	diesel
el **hierro**	iron
el **metal**	metal
el **oro**	gold
el **plástico**	plastic
el **vidrio**	glass

IMPORTANT WORDS *(masculine)*

el **acero inoxidable**	stainless steel
el **aluminio**	aluminum
el **cartón**	cardboard
el **estado**	condition
el **hierro forjado**	wrought iron
el **ladrillo**	brick
el **papel**	paper
el **tejido**	fabric

USEFUL PHRASES

una silla de madera **a wooden chair**
una caja de plástico **a plastic box**
un anillo de oro **a gold ring**
en buen estado, en buenas condiciones **in good condition**
en mal estado, en malas condiciones **in bad condition**

ESSENTIAL WORDS *(feminine)*

la **lana**	wool
la **madera**	wood
la **piedra**	stone
la **piel**	fur; leather
la **plata**	silver
la **tela**	fabric

IMPORTANT WORDS *(feminine)*

la **fibra sintética**	synthetic fiber
la **seda**	silk

USEFUL PHRASES

un abrigo de piel **a fur coat**
un suéter de lana **a woolen jumper**
oxidado(a) **rusty**

USEFUL WORDS *(masculine)*

el **acrílico**	acrylic
el **alambre**	wire
el **ante**	suede
el **bronce**	bronze
el **carbón**	coal
el **cemento**	cement
el **cobre**	copper
el **concreto** (*LAm*)	concrete
el **encaje**	lace
el **estaño**	tin
el **hilo**	thread
el **hormigón**	concrete
el **latón**	brass
el **lino**	linen
el **líquido**	liquid
el **mármol**	marble
el **material**	material
el **mimbre**	wicker
el **pegamento**	glue
el **plomo**	lead
el **satín**	satin
el **terciopelo**	velvet
el **tweed**	tweed
el **yeso**	plaster

USEFUL WORDS *(feminine)*

la **arcilla**	clay
la **cera**	wax
la **cerámica**	ceramic
la **cola**	glue
la **cuerda**	string
la **escayola** (*Sp*)	plaster
la **gomaespuma**	foam rubber
la **hojalata**	tin, tinplate
la **lona**	canvas
la **loza**	pottery
la **mezclilla** (*Mex*)	denim
la **paja**	straw
la **pana**	corduroy
la **porcelana**	porcelain

ESSENTIAL WORDS *(masculine)*

el	**director de orquesta**	conductor
el	**grupo**	band
el	**instrumento musical**	musical instrument
el	**músico**	musician
el	**piano**	piano
el	**violín** (*pl* violines)	violin

USEFUL WORDS *(masculine)*

el	**acorde**	chord
el	**acordeón** (*pl* acordeones)	accordion
el	**arco**	bow
el	**atril**	music stand
el	**bajo**	bass
el	**bombo**	bass drum
el	**chelo**	cello
el	**clarinete**	clarinet
el	**contrabajo**	double bass
el	**estuche**	case
el	**estudio de grabación**	recording studio
el	**fagot**	bassoon
los	**instrumentos de cuerda**	string instruments
los	**instrumentos de percusión**	percussion instruments
los	**instrumentos de viento**	wind instruments
el	**jazz**	jazz
los	**metales**	brass
el	**micrófono**	microphone
el	**minidisco**	minidisc
el	**oboe**	oboe
el	**órgano**	organ
los	**platillos**	cymbals
el	**saxofón** (*pl* saxofones)	saxophone
el	**solfeo**	music theory
el	**solista**	soloist
el	**tambor**	drum
el	**triángulo**	triangle
el	**trombón** (*pl* trombones)	trombone
el	**violonchelo**	cello

ESSENTIAL WORDS *(feminine)*

la **banda**	band
la **batería**	drums, drum kit
la **directora de orquesta**	conductor
la **flauta**	flute
la **flauta dulce**	recorder
la **guitarra**	guitar
la **música**	music; musician
la **orquesta**	orchestra

USEFUL WORDS *(feminine)*

la **armónica**	harmonica
el **arpa** (*f pl* las arpas)	harp
la **batuta**	conductor's baton
la **composición** (*pl* composiciones)	composition
la **corneta**	bugle
la **cuerda**	string
la **gaita**	bagpipes
la **grabación digital** (*pl* grabaciones ~es)	digital recording
la **megafonía**	PA system
la **mesa de mezclas**	mixing deck
la **nota**	note
la **pandereta**	tambourine
la **solista**	soloist
la **tecla (de piano)**	(piano) key
la **trompeta**	trumpet
la **viola**	viola

USEFUL PHRASES

tocar *or* interpretar una pieza **to play a piece**
desafinar **to sing *or* play out of tune**
tocar el piano/la guitarra **to play the piano/the guitar**
tocar la batería **to play drums**
con Pedro en batería **with Pedro on drums**
practicar el piano **to practice the piano**
¿tocas en una banda? **do you play in a band?**

CARDINAL NUMBERS

cero	0	zero
uno (*m*), una (*f*)	1	one
dos	2	two
tres	3	three
cuatro	4	four
cinco	5	five
seis	6	six
siete	7	seven
ocho	8	eight
nueve	9	nine
diez	10	ten
once	11	eleven
doce	12	twelve
trece	13	thirteen
catorce	14	fourteen
quince	15	fifteen
dieciséis	16	sixteen
diecisiete	17	seventeen
dieciocho	18	eighteen
diecinueve	19	nineteen
veinte	20	twenty
veintiuno(a)	21	twenty-one
veintidós	22	twenty-two
veintitrés	23	twenty-three
treinta	30	thirty
treinta y uno(a)	31	thirty-one
treinta y dos	32	thirty-two
cuarenta	40	forty
cincuenta	50	fifty
sesenta	60	sixty
setenta	70	seventy
ochenta	80	eighty
noventa	90	ninety
cien	100	one hundred

CARDINAL NUMBERS (*continued*)

ciento uno(a)	101	a hundred and one
ciento dos	102	a hundred and two
ciento diez	110	a hundred and ten
ciento ochenta y dos	182	a hundred and eighty-two
doscientos(as)	200	two hundred
doscientos(as) uno(a)	201	two hundred and one
doscientos(as) dos	202	two hundred and two
trescientos(as)	300	three hundred
cuatrocientos(as)	400	four hundred
quinientos(as)	500	five hundred
seiscientos(as)	600	six hundred
setecientos(as)	700	seven hundred
ochocientos(as)	800	eight hundred
novecientos(as)	900	nine hundred
mil	1000	one thousand
mil uno(a)	1001	a thousand and one
mil dos	1002	a thousand and two
dos mil	2000	two thousand
dos mil seis	2006	two thousand and six
diez mil	10000	ten thousand
cien mil	100000	one hundred thousand
un millón	1000000	one million
dos millones	2000000	two million

USEFUL PHRASES

mil pesos **a thousand pesos**
un millón de dólares **one million dollars**
veintiún años **twenty-one years**
veintiuna páginas **twenty-one pages**
quinientos pesos **five hundred pesos**
quinientas veces **five hundred times**
el diez por ciento **ten per cent**

ORDINAL NUMBERS

primero(a)	1º, 1ª	first
segundo(a)	2º, 2ª	second
tercero(a)	3º, 3ª	third
cuarto(a)	4º, 4ª	fourth
quinto(a)	5º, 5ª	fifth
sexto(a)	6º, 6ª	sixth
séptimo(a)	7º, 7ª	seventh
octavo(a)	8º, 8ª	eighth
noveno(a)	9º, 9ª	ninth
décimo(a)	10º, 10ª	tenth
undécimo(a)	11º, 11ª	eleventh
duodécimo(a)	12º, 12ª	twelfth
decimotercero(a)	13º, 13ª	thirteenth
decimocuarto(a)	14º, 14ª	fourteenth
decimoquinto(a)	15º, 15ª	fifteenth
decimosexto(a)	16º, 16ª	sixteenth
decimoséptimo(a)	17º, 17ª	seventeenth
decimoctavo(a)	18º, 18ª	eighteenth
decimonoveno(a), decimonono(a)	19º, 19ª	nineteenth
vigésimo(a)	20º, 20ª	twentieth

Note:

Ordinal numbers are hardly ever used above 10th in spoken Spanish, and rarely at all above 20th. It's normal to use the cardinal numbers instead, except for **milésimo(a)**.

milésimo(a)	1000º, 1000ª	thousandth
dos milésimo(a)	2000º, 2000ª	two thousandth
millonésimo(a)	1000000º, 1000000ª	millionth
dos millonésimo(a)	2000000º, 2000000ª	two millionth

FRACTIONS

un medio	$\frac{1}{2}$	a half
uno(a) y medio(a)	$1\frac{1}{2}$	one and a half
dos y medio(a)	$2\frac{1}{2}$	two and a half
un tercio, la tercera parte	$\frac{1}{3}$	a third
dos tercios, las dos terceras partes	$\frac{2}{3}$	two thirds
un cuarto, la cuarta parte	$\frac{1}{4}$	a quarter
tres cuartos, las tres cuartas partes	$\frac{3}{4}$	three quarters
un sexto, la sexta parte	$\frac{1}{6}$	a sixth
tres y cinco sextos	$3\frac{5}{6}$	three and five sixths
un séptimo, la séptima parte	$\frac{1}{7}$	a seventh
un octavo, la octava parte	$\frac{1}{8}$	an eighth
un noveno, la novena parte	$\frac{1}{9}$	a ninth
un décimo, la décima parte	$\frac{1}{10}$	a tenth
un onceavo, la onceava parte	$\frac{1}{11}$	an eleventh
un doceavo, la doceava parte	$\frac{1}{12}$	a twelfth
siete doceavos, las siete doceavas partes	$\frac{7}{12}$	seven twelfths
un centésimo, la centésima parte	$\frac{1}{100}$	a hundredth
un milésimo, la milésima parte	$\frac{1}{1000}$	a thousandth

USEFUL PHRASES

ambos (*f* ambas), los dos (*f* las dos) **both of them**
un bote *or* una lata de tomates **a can of tomatoes**
una botella de cerveza **a bottle of beer**
una caja de chocolates **a box of chocolates**
(gran) cantidad de gente **lots of people**
un grupo de muchachas **a group of girls**
un centenar de personas **(about) a hundred people**
miles de turistas **thousands of tourists**
la mayoría *or* la mayor parte de la población **most of the population**
una cucharada de azúcar **a spoonful of sugar**
media taza de harina **half a cup of flour**
cien gramos de jamón **a hundred grammes of ham**
un kilo de manzanas **a kilo of apples**
medio kilo de manzanas **half a kilo of apples**
una docena de huevos **a dozen eggs**
media docena de huevos **half a dozen eggs**
un litro de leche **a liter of milk**
medio litro de leche **half a liter of milk**

USEFUL PHRASES

un metro de tela a meter of fabric
medio metro de tela half a meter of fabric
la mitad del pastel half of the cake
un montón de ropa a pile of clothes
mucho ruido a lot of noise
mucha agua a lot of water
muchos/muchas estudiantes a lot of students
un paquete de galletas a packet of cookies
un par de zapatos a pair of shoes
un plato de arroz a plate of rice
un poco de crema a little cream; some cream
una porción de pollo a portion of chicken
una rebanada de pan a slice of bread
un rebaño de ovejas a flock of sheep
un sobre de sopa a packet of soup
n terrón de azúcar a lump of sugar
un trozo de papel/pastel a piece of paper/cake
un vaso de jugo a glass of juice

ESSENTIAL WORDS *(masculine)*

el **anillo**	ring
el **cepillo**	brush
el **cepillo de dientes**	toothbrush
el **champú**	shampoo
el **desodorante**	deodorant
el **espejo**	mirror
el **maquillaje**	make-up
el **peine**	comb
el **perfume**	perfume
el **reloj**	watch

USEFUL WORDS *(masculine)*

el **aftershave**	aftershave
el **arete** (*LAm*)	earring
el **bilet** (*Mex*)	lipstick
el **broche**	brooch
el **colgante**	pendant
el **collar**	necklace
el **diamante**	diamond
los **efectos personales**	personal effects
el **esmalte (de uñas)**	nail polish
el **gemelo**	cufflink
el **kleenex**® (*pl inv*)	tissue
el **lápiz de labios** (*pl* lápices ~ ~)	lipstick
el **llavero**	keychain
el **maquillaje**	make-up
el **neceser**	toilet kit
el **papel higiénico**	toilet paper
el **peinado**	hairstyle
el **pendiente** (*Sp*)	earring
los **polvos compactos**	face powder
los **polvos para la cara**	face powder
el **quitaesmalte**	nail polish remover
el **rastrillo** (*Mex*)	(safety) razor
el **rímel**	mascara
el **rulo** (*Sp*)	roller
el **secador**	hairdryer
el **tubo** (*LAm*)	roller

ESSENTIAL WORDS *(feminine)*

el **agua de colonia** (*f*)	toilet water, eau de toilette
la **cadena**	chain
la **crema para la cara**	face cream
la **cuchilla de afeitar**	razor
la **joya**	jewel
la **máquina de afeitar** *or* **rasurar**	electric shaver
la **maquinilla de afeitar** (*Sp*)	(safety) razor
la **navaja**	razor
la **pasta de dientes**	toothpaste
la **pulsera**	bracelet
la **rasuradora** (*LAm*)	electric razor

USEFUL WORDS *(feminine)*

la **alianza**	wedding ring
la **base de maquillaje**	foundation
la **brocha de afeitar** *or* **rasurar**	shaving brush
la **crema de afeitar** *or* **rasurar**	shaving cream
la **esponja**	sponge
la **espuma de afeitar** *or* **rasurar**	shaving foam
la **mancuerna** *or* **mancuernilla** (*Mex*)	cufflink
la **manicura**	manicure
la **perla**	pearl
la **secadora** (*Mex*)	hair dryer
la **sombra de ojos**	eye shadow

USEFUL PHRASES

maquillarse to put on one's make-up
desmaquillarse to take off one's make-up
hacerse un peinado to do one's hair
peinarse to comb one's hair
cepillarse el pelo to brush one's hair
rasurarse (*LAm*) to shave
afeitarse to shave
lavarse/cepillarse los dientes to brush one's teeth

ESSENTIAL WORDS *(masculine)*

el **árbol**	tree
el **césped**	lawn
el **jardín** (*pl* jardines)	garden
el **jardinero**	gardener
el **pasto** (*LAm*)	grass; lawn
el **sol**	sun

IMPORTANT WORDS *(masculine)*

el **arbusto**	bush; shrub
el **banco**	bench
el **camino**	path
el **cultivo**	cultivation; growing
el **ramo de flores**	bunch of flowers
el **seto**	hedge

USEFUL PHRASES

plantar **to plant**
quitar las hierbas malas, deshierbar **to weed**
regalarle a algn un ramo de flores **to give sb a bunch of flowers**
cortar *or* podar el pasto *or* el césped **to mow the lawn**
"no pisar el césped" **"keep off the grass"**
a mi padre le gusta la jardinería **my father likes gardening**

ESSENTIAL WORDS *(feminine)*

la **flor**	flower
la **hierba**	grass; herb
la **hoja**	leaf
la **jardinera**	gardener; flower bed
la **jardinería**	gardening
la **lluvia**	rain
la **planta**	plant
la **rama**	branch
la **rosa**	rose
la **tierra**	land; soil; ground
las **verduras**	vegetables

IMPORTANT WORDS *(feminine)*

la **abeja**	bee
la **avispa**	wasp
la **cerca**	fence
las **hierbas malas**	weeds
la **raíz** (*pl* raíces)	root
la **sombra**	shade; shadow

USEFUL PHRASES

las flores están creciendo the flowers are growing
en el suelo on the ground
regar las plantas to water the flowers
recoger flores to pick flowers
irse a la sombra to go into the shade
quedarse en la sombra to remain in the shade
a la sombra de un árbol in the shade of a tree

USEFUL WORDS *(masculine)*

el **azafrán** (*pl* azafranes)	crocus
el **brote**	bud
el **clavel**	carnation
el **cortacésped**	lawnmower
el **crisantemo**	chrysanthemum
el **diente de león**	dandelion
el **estanque**	pond
el **follaje**	leaves
el **girasol**	sunflower
el **gusano**	worm
el **huerto**	vegetable garden
el **invernadero**	greenhouse
el **invierno**	winter
el **jacinto**	hyacinth
el **lirio**	lily; iris
el **macizo de flores**	flower bed
el **narciso**	daffodil
el **otoño**	autumn, fall
el **pensamiento**	pansy
el **ranúnculo**	buttercup
el **rocío**	dew
el **rosal**	rose bush
el **sendero**	path
el **suelo**	ground; soil
el **tallo**	stalk
el **tronco**	trunk (*of tree*)
el **tulipán** (*pl* tulipanes)	tulip
el **verano**	summer

USEFUL WORDS *(feminine)*

la **amapola**	poppy
la **baya**	berry
la **campanilla**	campanula, bellflower
la **carretilla**	wheelbarrow
la **cosecha**	crop
la **espina**	thorn
la **herramienta**	tool
la **hiedra**	ivy
la **hortensia**	hydrangea
las **lilas**	lilac
la **madreselva**	honeysuckle
la **manguera**	hose
la **margarita**	daisy
la **mariposa**	butterfly
la **orquídea**	orchid
la **peonía**	peony
la **podadora de pasto** (*Mex*)	lawn mower
la **primavera**	spring; primrose
la **regadera**	watering can
la **semilla**	seed
la **violeta**	violet

ESSENTIAL WORDS *(masculine)*

los	**anteojos** *or* **lentes de sol** (*LAm*)	sunglasses
el	**bañador** (*Sp*)	swimsuit, trunks
el	**bañista**	swimmer
el	**barco**	boat; ship
el	**barco de pesca**	fishing boat
el	**bikini** *or* **biquini**	bikini
el	**bote**	boat
el	**mar**	sea
el	**muelle**	pier, wharf, jetty
el	**paseo**	walk
el	**pescador**	fisherman
el	**pesquero**	fishing boat
el	**picnic** (*pl* ~s)	picnic
el	**puerto**	port, harbor
el	**puerto deportivo**	marina
el	**remo**	rowing; oar
el	**traje de baño**	swimsuit

IMPORTANT WORDS *(masculine)*

el	**cangrejo**	crab
el	**castillo de arena**	sandcastle
el	**fondo**	bottom
el	**horizonte**	horizon
el	**mareo**	seasickness
el	**vacacionista** (*LAm*)	vacationer

USEFUL PHRASES

en la playa at the seaside; at *or* on the beach
en el horizonte on the horizon
está mareado he is seasick
nadar to swim
ahogarse to drown
me voy a dar un baño I'm going for a swim
tirarse al agua, zambullirse to dive into the water
flotar to float

ESSENTIAL WORDS *(feminine)*

el **agua** (*f*)	water
la **arena**	sand
la **bañista**	swimmer
la **barca**	boat
la **costa**	coast
las **gafas de sol** (*Sp*)	sunglasses
la **isla**	island
la **natación**	swimming
la **pescadora**	fisherwoman
la **piedra**	stone
la **playa**	beach; seaside
las **quemaduras de sol**	sunburn
la **toalla**	towel

IMPORTANT WORDS *(feminine)*

la **colchoneta inflable**	air mattress
la **crema (de protección) solar**	sunscreen
la **silla reclinable**	deckchair
la **tabla de windsurf**	windsurfing board
la **travesía**	crossing
la **tumbona** (*Sp*)	deckchair
la **vacacionista**	vacationer

USEFUL PHRASES

en el fondo del mar at the bottom of the sea
hacer la travesía en barco to go across by boat
broncearse to get a tan
tomar el sol to sunbathe
estar bronceado(a) to be tanned
sabe nadar he can swim

USEFUL WORDS *(masculine)*

el	**acantilado**	cliff
el	**aire de mar**	sea air
el	**balde**	bucket
el	**(barco de) vapor**	steamer
los	**binoculares**	binoculars
el	**cabo**	cape
el	**crucero**	cruise
el	**cubo** (*Sp*)	bucket
el	**embarcadero**	pier
el	**estuario**	estuary
el	**faro**	lighthouse
el	**guijarro**	pebble
el	**marinero**	sailor
el	**marino**	sailor; naval officer
el	**mástil**	mast
el	**naufragio**	shipwreck
los	**náufragos**	shipwrecked people, castaways
el	**océano**	ocean
el	**oleaje**	swell
los	**prismáticos**	binoculars
el	**puente (de mando)**	bridge (*of a ship*)
los	**restos de un naufragio**	wreckage
el	**salvavidas** (*pl inv*)	lifeguard; life jacket
el	**socorrista**	lifeguard
el	**timón** (*pl* timones)	rudder
el	**transbordador**	ferry

USEFUL WORDS *(feminine)*

las **algas**	seaweed
el **ancla** (*f pl* las anclas)	anchor
la **bahía**	bay
la **balsa**	raft
la **bandera**	flag
la **barca**	small boat
la **boya**	buoy
la **brisa marina**	sea breeze
la **carga**	cargo
la **concha**	shell
la **corriente**	current
la **desembocadura**	mouth (*of a river*)
la **espuma**	foam
la **gaviota**	seagull
la **insolación** (*pl* insolaciones)	sunstroke
la **marea**	tide
la **marina**	navy; sailor; naval officer
la **marinera**	sailor
la **nave**	vessel
la **ola**	wave
la **orilla**	shore
la **pala**	shovel
la **pasarela**	gangway
la **roca**	rock
la **salvavidas** (*pl inv*) *or* **socorrista**	lifeguard
la **sombrilla**	beach umbrella, parasol
la **tripulación** (*pl* tripulaciones)	crew
la **vela**	sail; sailing

USEFUL PHRASES

tuve una insolación **I had sunstroke**
con la marea baja/alta **at low/high tide**
ir a navegar/remar **to go sailing/rowing**

ESSENTIAL WORDS *(masculine)*

los	**abarrotes** (*Mex*)	grocery store
los	**almacenes** (*LAm*)	department store
el	**banco**	bank
el	**billete (de banco)**	banknote
el	**cambio**	change
el	**centro comercial**	mall, shopping center
el	**cheque**	check
el	**cliente**	customer
el	**correo** (*LAm*)	post office
el	**departamento**	department
el	**dependiente**	sales assistant
el	**descuento**	discount
el	**dinero**	money
el	**dólar**	dollar
el	**estanco** (*Sp*)	tobacconist's
el	**euro**	euro
los	**grandes almacenes** (*Sp*)	department store
el	**hipermercado**	superstore
el	**mercado**	market
el	**número (de zapato)**	(shoe) size
el	**precio**	price
el	**regalo**	present
el	**souvenir** (*pl* ~s)	souvenir
el	**supermercado**	supermarket
el	**talonario de cheques** (*Sp*)	checkbook
el	**vendedor**	salesman

USEFUL PHRASES

comprar/vender to buy/sell
¿cuánto cuesta? how much does it cost?; how much is it?
¿cuánto es? how much is it?
pagué veinte dólares por esto, esto me costó veinte dólares I paid 20 dollars for this
en la carnicería/la panadería at the butcher's/bakery

ESSENTIAL WORDS *(feminine)*

la **agencia de viajes**	travel agent's
la **alimentación**	food
la **barata** (*Mex*)	sale, promotion
la **caja**	checkout
la **carnicería**	butcher's
la **clienta**	customer
la **compra**	purchase
la **dependienta**	sales assistant
la **farmacia**	pharmacy
la **florería** (*LAm*)	florist
la **floristería** (*Sp*)	florist
la **frutería**	fruit vendor's
la **lista**	list
la **oficina de correo** (*LAm*) *or* **de correos** (*Sp*)	post office
la **panadería**	bakery
la **pastelería**	cake shop
la **perfumería**	perfume shop/department
la **pescadería**	fish shop
la **rebaja**	price reduction
las **rebajas**	sale, promotion
la **sección** (*pl* secciones)	department
la **talla**	size
la **tarjeta de crédito**	credit card
la **tarjeta de débito**	debit card
la **tienda**	shop
la **tienda de abarrotes** (*Mex*)	grocery store
la **tienda de alimentación**	grocery store
la **tienda de departamentos** (*Mex*)	department store
la **vendedora**	saleswoman
la **verdulería**	fruit and vegetable store
la **zapatería**	shoe store

IMPORTANT WORDS *(masculine)*

el **aparador** (*Mex*)	store window
el **artículo**	article
el **carnicero**	butcher
el **comerciante**	shopkeeper
el **comercio**	trade; store
el **comercio justo**	fair trade
el **encargado**	manager
el **escaparate** (*Sp*)	store window
el **frutero**	fruit vendor
el **mercado**	market
el **monedero**	change purse
el **mostrador**	sales counter
el **panadero**	baker
el **pastelero**	confectioner, pastry chef
el **peluquero**	hairdresser
el **pescadero**	fish dealer
el **recibo**	receipt
el **tícket** (*pl* ~s)	receipt; ticket
el **verdulero**	fruit and vegetable vendor
el **zapatero**	shoemaker

USEFUL PHRASES

sólo estoy mirando I'm just looking
es demasiado caro it's too expensive
algo más barato something cheaper
es barato it's cheap
"pague en caja" "pay at the checkout"
¿lo quiere envuelto para regalo? would you like it gift wrapped?
debe de haber un error there must be some mistake

IMPORTANT WORDS *(feminine)*

la **biblioteca**	library
la **boutique**	boutique
la **calculadora**	calculator
la **carnicera**	butcher
la **cartera**	wallet
la **comerciante**	shopkeeper
la **encargada**	manager
la **escalera eléctrica** *or* **mecánica**	escalator
la **frutera**	fruit vendor
la **librería**	bookstore
la **marca**	brand
la **panadera**	baker
la **pastelera**	confectioner, pastry chef
la **peluquera**	hairdresser
la **pescadera**	fish dealer
la **promoción** (*pl* promociones)	special offer
la **reclamación** (*pl* reclamaciones)	complaint
la **tintorería**	dry cleaner's
la **verdulera**	fruit and vegetable vendor
la **vitrina** (*LAm*)	store window

USEFUL PHRASES

¿algo más? anything else?
S.A. (= *Sociedad Anónima*) Inc.
S.L. (= *Sociedad Limitada*) limited liability company
y Cía & Co
"en venta aquí" "on sale here"
en oferta, de oferta on sale
el café de comercio justo fair-trade coffee
de segunda mano second hand

USEFUL WORDS *(masculine)*

el **agente inmobiliario**	real estate agent
el **color**	color
el **gerente**	manager
el **joyero**	jeweler; jewelry case
el **librero**	bookseller
el **mandado** (*LAm*)	errand
el **óptico**	optician
el **producto**	product
los **productos**	produce
el **recado** (*Sp*)	errand
el **relojero**	watchmaker; clockmaker
el **trato**	deal
el **videoclub** (*pl* ~s)	video rental store

USEFUL PHRASES

horario **opening hours**
pagar en efectivo **to pay cash**
pagar con un cheque **to pay by check**
pagar con tarjeta de crédito **to pay by credit card**

USEFUL WORDS *(feminine)*

la	**agencia de viajes**	travel agent
la	**agencia inmobiliaria**	real estate agency
la	**agente inmobiliaria**	real estate agent
la	**cola**	line, queue
la	**compra**	purchase
las	**compras**	shopping
la	**ferretería**	hardware store
la	**gerente**	manager
la	**joyera**	jeweler
la	**joyería**	jewelry store
la	**lavandería**	laundry
la	**librera**	bookseller
la	**mercancía**	goods
la	**óptica**	optician; optician's
la	**papelería**	stationer's
la	**rebaja**	discount
la	**relojera**	watchmaker; clockmaker
la	**relojería**	watchmaker's; clockmaker's
la	**sucursal**	branch
la	**talla de cuello**	collar size
la	**venta**	sale

USEFUL PHRASES

ir de compras to go shopping
gastar to spend
ir a ver aparadores (*Mex*) to go window shopping
ir a ver escaparates, ir de escaparates (*Sp*) to go window shopping

ESSENTIAL WORDS *(masculine)*

el **aerobics**	aerobics
el **balón** (*pl* balones)	ball (*large*)
el **baloncesto** (*Sp*)	basketball
el **balonvolea** (*Sp*)	volleyball
el **básquetbol** (*LAm*), el **basquetbol** (*Mex*)	basketball
el **béisbol** (*LAm*), el **beisbol** (*Mex*)	baseball
el **billar**	billiards
el **campeón** (*pl* campeones)	champion
el **campeonato**	championship
el **campo**	field; (*golf*) course
el **ciclismo**	cycling
el **deporte**	sport
el **equipo**	team
el **esquí**	skiing; ski
el **esquí acuático**	water skiing
el **estadio**	stadium
el **fútbol**, el **futbol** (*Mex*)	soccer
el **fútbol** *or* **futbol** (*Mex*) **americano**	football
el **gimnasta**	gymnast
el **gol**	goal
el **golf**	golf
el **hockey**	hockey
el **juego**	game; play
el **jugador**	player
el **partido**	game
el **(método) Pilates**	Pilates
el **portero**	goalkeeper, goalie
el **puntaje** (*LAm*)	score
el **resultado**	result
el **rugby**	rugby
el **tenis**	tennis
el **vóleibol** (*LAm*), el **voleibol** (*Mex*)	volleyball

USEFUL PHRASES

jugar al tenis/al béisbol **to play tennis/baseball**
jugar tenis/beisbol (*Mex*) **to play tennis/baseball**
anotar un gol/un punto **to score a goal/a point**
¿cómo van? **what's the score?**
ganar/perder un partido **to win/lose a match**

ESSENTIAL WORDS *(feminine)*

la **alberca** (*Mex*)	swimming pool
la **campeona**	champion
la **cancha**	(*basketball/tennis*) court; (*LAm*) field
la **equitación**	horseback riding
la **gimnasia**	gymnastics
la **gimnasta**	gymnast
la **jugadora**	player
la **natación**	swimming
la **pelota**	ball
la **pesca**	fishing
la **piscina**	swimming pool
la **pista**	track
la **portera**	goal keeper, goalie
la **portería**	goal
la **tabla de windsurf**	windsurfing board
la **vela**	sailing; sail

USEFUL PHRASES

hacer deporte to play sports
empatar to equalize; to tie
correr to run; saltar to jump; lanzar to throw
derrotar *or* vencer a algn to beat sb
ganarle a algn to beat sb
nos ganaron cinco a dos they beat us five-two
van ganando cinco a dos they are leading five-two
un partido de tenis a tennis match
es socio de un club he belongs to a club
es socio del club de tenis he's a member of the tennis club
ir de pesca to go fishing
¿sabes nadar? can you swim?
ir a andar (*LAm*) *or* montar (*Sp*) en bicicleta to go cycling
ir a navegar *or* a hacer vela to go sailing
ir a correr *or* a hacer jogging to go jogging
patín de cuchilla/de ruedas/en línea (ice)skate/rollerskate/Rollerblade®
tiro al arco/al blanco archery/target practice
entrenar(se) to train

IMPORTANT WORDS *(masculine)*

los **bolos**	skittles (*a type of bowling*)
el **encuentro**	game, match

USEFUL WORDS *(masculine)*

el **adversario**	opponent
el **alpinismo**	mountaineering
el **árbitro**	referee; umpire
el **atletismo**	athletics
el **bádminton**	badminton
el **box** *or* el **boxeo**	boxing
el **buceo**	diving
el **chándal** (*Sp*)	sweatsuit; sweatpants
el **cronómetro**	stopwatch
el **descanso**	half-time
el **entrenador**	trainer; coach
el **espectador**	spectator
el **ganador**	winner
el **hipódromo**	racetrack
los **Juegos Olímpicos**	Olympic Games
el **Mundial de Fútbol**	Soccer World Cup
los **pants** (*pl inv*) (*Mex*)	sweatsuit; sweatpants
el **parapente**	paragliding
el **patinaje sobre hielo**	(ice) skating
el **perdedor**	loser
el **principiante**	beginner
el **remo**	rowing; oar
el **salto con garrocha** (*LAm*) *or* **con pértiga** (*Sp*)	pole vault
el **salto de altura**	high jump
el **salto de longitud**	long jump
el **squash**	squash
el **tanto**	goal; point
los **tenis** (*LAm*)	sneakers, running shoes
el **tiro**	shooting
el **torneo**	tournament
el **trineo**	sledge

IMPORTANT WORDS *(feminine)*

la	**bola**	ball (*small*)
la	**carrera**	race
las	**carreras (de caballos)**	horse racing
la	**defensa**	defense
la	**pista de esquí**	ski slope

USEFUL WORDS *(feminine)*

la	**adversaria**	opponent
la	**árbitra**	referee; umpire
la	**camiseta (de deporte)**	jersey, shirt
la	**caña de pescar**	fishing rod
la	**caza**	hunting
la	**copa**	cup
la	**Copa del Mundo**	World Cup
la	**eliminatoria**	heat
la	**entrenadora**	trainer, coach
la	**esgrima**	fencing
la	**espectadora**	spectator
la	**estación de esquí** (*pl* estaciones de ~)	ski resort
la	**etapa**	stage
la	**final**	final
la	**ganadora**	winner
la	**jabalina**	javelin
la	**lucha libre**	wrestling
la	**perdedora**	loser
la	**pesca**	fishing
la	**pista de hielo**	ice skating rink
la	**pista de patinaje**	skating rink
la	**principiante**	beginner
la	**prórroga**	extra time
la	**raqueta**	racket
la	**red**	net
la	**tribuna**	stand
las	**zapatillas de deporte** (*Sp*)	sneakers, running shoes

ESSENTIAL WORDS *(masculine)*

el **actor**	actor
el **ambiente**	atmosphere
el **asiento**	seat
el **auditorio**	auditorium; audience
el **boleto** (*LAm*)	ticket
el **cine**	movie theater
el **circo**	circus
el **cómico**	comedian
el **espectáculo**	show
el **payaso**	clown
el **programa**	program
el **público**	audience
el **show**	show
el **teatro**	theater
el **vestuario**	costumes
el **videoclip** (*pl* ~s)	music video
el **western** (*pl* ~s)	western

IMPORTANT WORDS *(masculine)*

el **acomodador**	usher
el **actor principal**	leading man
el **ballet** (*pl* ~s)	ballet
el **cartel**	notice; poster
el **director**	director
el **entreacto**	intermission
el **intermedio**	intermission
el **maquillaje**	make-up

USEFUL PHRASES

ir al teatro/al cine **to go to the theater/to the movies**
reservar un asiento **to reserve a seat**
mi actor preferido/actriz preferida **my favorite actor/actress**
durante el intermedio **during the intermission**
salir a escena **to come on stage**
interpretar el papel de **to play the part of**

ESSENTIAL WORDS *(feminine)*

la **actriz** (*pl* actrices)	actress
la **banda sonora**	soundtrack
la **boletería** (*LAm*)	box office
la **cómica**	comedian
la **cortina**	curtain
la **entrada**	ticket
la **estrella de cine**	film star
la **música**	music
la **obra (de teatro)**	play
la **ópera**	opera
la **orquesta**	orchestra
la **payasa**	clown
la **película**	film
la **sala**	auditorium; theater; screen (*at a multiplex*)
la **salida**	exit
la **sesión** (*pl* sesiones)	performance; showing, screening
la **taquilla**	box office

USEFUL PHRASES

bailar **to dance**
cantar **to sing**
filmar una película **to shoot a movie**
"próxima sesión: 21 horas" **"next showing: 9 p.m."**
"versión original" **"original version"**
"subtitulada" **"subtitled"**
"localidades agotadas" **"full house"**
aplaudir **to clap**
¡otra! **encore!**
¡bravo! **bravo!**
una película de ciencia ficción/de amor **a science fiction movie/a romance**
una película de aventuras/de terror **an adventure/a horror movie**

IMPORTANT WORDS (*masculine continued*)

el **primer actor**	leading man
el **protagonista**	star; leading man; main character
el **subtítulo**	subtitle
el **título**	title

USEFUL WORDS (*masculine*)

los **aplausos**	applause
el **apuntador**	prompter
el **argumento**	plot
los **bastidores**	wings
el **crítico**	critic
el **decorado**	scenery
el **director de escena**	producer; stage manager
el **dramaturgo**	playwright
el **ensayo (general)**	(dress) rehearsal
el **escenario**	stage; scene
el **espectador**	member of the audience
el **estrado**	platform
el **estreno**	opening night, premiere
el **foco**	spotlight
el **foso de la orquesta**	orchestra pit
el **guardarropa**	checkroom
el **guión** (*pl* guiones)	script
el **guionista**	scriptwriter
el **musical**	musical
el **palco**	box
el **papel**	part
el **personaje**	character
el **productor**	producer
el **realizador**	director (*cinema*); producer (*TV*)
el **reparto**	cast
el **vestíbulo**	foyer

IMPORTANT WORDS *(feminine)*

la **acomodadora**	usher
la **actriz principal** (*pl* actrices ~es)	leading lady
la **butaca**	seat
la **cartelera**	billboard; listings
la **comedia**	comedy
la **directora**	director
la **primera actriz** (*pl* ~s actrices)	leading lady
la **propina**	tip
la **protagonista**	star; leading lady; main character
la **reservación** (*LAm*), la **reserva** (*Sp*)	reservation

USEFUL WORDS *(feminine)*

la **actuación** (*pl* actuaciones)	acting, performance
la **apuntadora**	prompter
las **candilejas**	footlights
la **crítica**	review; critics; critic
la **directora de escena**	producer; stage manager
la **dramaturga**	playwright
la **escena**	scene
la **escenografía**	scenery
la **espectadora**	member of the audience
la **farsa**	farce
la **función** (*pl* funciones)	performance
la **guionista**	scriptwriter
la **pantalla**	screen
la **productora**	producer
la **puesta en escena**	production
la **realizadora**	director (*movie*); producer (*TV*)
la **representación** (*pl* representaciones)	performance
la **serie**	series; serial
la **tragedia**	tragedy

ESSENTIAL WORDS *(masculine)*

el **año**	year
el **cuarto de hora**	quarter of an hour
el **despertador**	alarm clock
el **día**	day
el **fin de semana**	weekend
el **instante**	moment
el **mes**	month
el **minuto**	minute
el **momento**	moment
el **reloj**	watch; clock
el **segundo**	second
el **siglo**	century
el **tiempo**	time

USEFUL PHRASES

a mediodía **at midday *or* noon**
a medianoche **at midnight**
pasado mañana **the day after tomorrow**
hoy **today**
hoy en día **nowadays**
anteayer, antes de ayer **the day before yesterday**
antier (*LAm*) **the day before yesterday**
mañana **tomorrow**
ayer **yesterday**
hace dos días **2 days ago**
dentro de dos días **in 2 days**
una semana **a week**
una quincena **two weeks**
todos los días **every day**
¿qué día es hoy? **what day is it?**
¿qué fecha es hoy? **what's the date?**
en este momento **at the moment**
en el siglo XXI **in the 21st century**
ayer por *or* en la noche **last night, yesterday evening**

ESSENTIAL WORDS *(feminine)*

la **hora**	hour; time (*in general*)
la **mañana**	morning
la **media hora**	half an hour
la **noche**	night; evening
la **quincena**	two weeks
la **semana**	week
la **tarde**	afternoon; evening

USEFUL PHRASES

es la una it's one o'clock
son las dos it's two o'clock
son las dos en punto it is 2 o'clock sharp
son las dos y cuarto/y media it's a quarter after two/two thirty
son veinticinco para las tres (*LAm*)/las tres menos veinticinco (*Sp*) it's twenty-five to three
son cuarto para las tres (*LAm*)/las tres menos cuarto (*Sp*) it's a quarter to three
el año pasado/próximo last/next year
la semana/el año que viene next week/year
dentro de media hora in half an hour
una vez once
dos/tres veces two/three times
varias veces several times
tres veces al año three times a year
érase una vez once upon a time there was
diez a la vez ten at a time
¿qué hora es? what time is it?
¿tiene hora? have you got the time?
hace un rato a while ago
dentro de un rato in a while
temprano early
tarde late
esta noche tonight

IMPORTANT WORDS *(masculine)*

el **día siguiente**	next day
el **futuro**	future; future tense
el **pasado**	past; past tense
el **presente**	present (*time*); present tense
el **retraso**	delay

USEFUL WORDS *(masculine)*

el **año bisiesto**	leap year
el **calendario**	calendar
el **cronómetro**	stopwatch
el **reloj de pie**	grandfather clock
el **reloj de pulsera**	wristwatch
el **reloj despertador**	alarm clock

USEFUL PHRASES

pasado mañana the day after tomorrow
dos días después two days later
el día antes *or* el día anterior the day before
un día sí y otro no every other day
en el futuro in the future
un día libre a day off
un día festivo *or* feriado a national holiday
un día laborable *or* de entre semana a weekday
(en) un día de lluvia, (en) un día lluvioso on a rainy day
al amanecer, al alba at dawn
(a) la mañana/tarde siguiente the following morning/evening
ahora now

USEFUL WORDS *(feminine)*

las **agujas**	hands (*of a clock*)
la **década**	decade
la **Edad Media**	Middle Ages
la **época**	time; era
la **esfera**	face (*of a clock*)

USEFUL PHRASES

llegas tarde **you are late**
llegas temprano **you are early**
este reloj adelanta/atrasa **this watch is fast/slow**
llegar a tiempo, llegar a la hora **to arrive on time**
¿cuánto tiempo? **how long?**
el tercer milenio **the third millennium**
no levantarse hasta tarde **to sleep in**
de un momento a otro **any minute now**
dentro de una semana **in a week's time**
el lunes que viene no, el otro **a week from Monday**
la noche antes, la noche anterior **the night before**
en esa época **at that time**

ESSENTIAL WORDS *(masculine)*

el **bricolaje**	do-it-yourself
el **taller**	workshop

USEFUL WORDS *(masculine)*

el **alambre (de púas)**	(barbed) wire
el **alfiler**	pin
el **alicate** *or* los **alicates**	pliers
el **andamio**	scaffolding
el **candado**	padlock
el **celo** (*Sp*)	Scotch® tape
el **cincel**	chisel
el **clavo**	nail
el **desarmador** (*Mex*)	screwdriver
el **destornillador**	screwdriver
el **durex®** *or* **diurex®** (*LAm*)	Scotch® tape
el **martillo**	hammer
el **muelle**	spring
el **pico**	pickax
el **pincel**	paintbrush
el **resorte**	spring
el **taladro**	drill
el **tornillo**	screw

USEFUL PHRASES

clavar un clavo con el martillo **to hammer in a nail**
"recién pintado(a)" **"wet paint"**
pintar **to paint**
empapelar **to wallpaper**

ESSENTIAL WORDS *(feminine)*

la **chinche** (*LAm*)	thumbtack
la **cuerda**	rope
la **herramienta**	tool
la **llave**	key; (*LAm*) faucet
la **llave inglesa**	wrench
la **máquina**	machine
la **reata** (*Mex*)	rope

USEFUL WORDS *(feminine)*

la **aguja**	needle
la **batería**	battery (*in car*)
la **caja de herramientas**	toolbox
la **cerradura**	lock
la **chincheta** (*Sp*)	thumbtack
la **cola**	glue
la **escalera (de mano)**	ladder
la **goma (elástica)**	rubber band
la **horca**	pitchfork
la **lima**	file
la **obra**	construction site
la **pala**	shovel, spade; dustpan
la **pila**	battery (*in a radio, etc*)
la **sierra**	saw
la **tabla**	plank
la **taladradora (neumática)**	(pneumatic) drill
las **tijeras**	scissors

USEFUL PHRASES

"prohibido el paso a la obra" "construction site: keep out"
práctico(a) handy
cortar to cut
reparar to repair
atornillar to screw (in)
desatornillar to unscrew

ESSENTIAL WORDS *(masculine)*

los **alrededores**	surroundings
el **aparcamiento** (*Sp*)	parking lot; parking space
el **autobús** (*pl* autobuses)	bus
el **ayuntamiento**	town hall; town council
el **banco**	bank; bench
el **barrio**	district
el **bloque de departamentos** (*LAm*)	apartment building
el **bloque de pisos** (*Sp*)	apartment building
el **café**	café, coffee shop; coffee
el **camión** (*Mex*)	bus; truck
el **carro** (*LAm*)	car
el **centro de la ciudad**	downtown
el **cine**	movie theater; cinema
el **coche**	car
el **correo** (*LAm*)	post office
el **edificio**	building
el **estacionamiento** (*LAm*)	parking lot; parking space
el **habitante**	inhabitant
el **hotel**	hotel
el **mercado**	market
el **metro**	subway
el **museo**	museum; art gallery
el **parking** (*pl* ~s)	parking lot
el **parque**	park
el **peatón** (*pl* peatones)	pedestrian
el **policía**	police officer, policeman
el **puente**	bridge
el **restaurante**	restaurant
el **suburbio**	suburb; slum area
el **taxi**	taxi
el **teatro**	theater
el **tour** (*pl* ~s)	tour
el **turista**	tourist

ESSENTIAL WORDS *(feminine)*

la **alberca** (*Mex*)	swimming pool
la **calle**	street
la **carretera**	road
la **catedral**	cathedral
la **ciudad**	town, city
la **colonia (residencial)** (*Mex*)	suburb
la **comisaría**	police station
la **contaminación**	air pollution
la **esquina**	corner
la **estación (de trenes)** (*pl* estaciones (~ ~))	(train) station
la **fábrica**	factory
la **gasolinera**	gas station
la **habitante**	inhabitant
la **lavandería automática**	Laundromat®
la **oficina**	office
la **oficina de correo**	post office
la **parada (del autobús)**	bus stop
la **parada (del camión)** (*Mex*)	bus stop
la **parada de taxis**	taxi stand
la **piscina**	swimming pool
la **plaza**	square
la **policía**	police officer, policewoman; police
la **terminal de camiones** (*Mex*) *or* **de autobuses** (*Sp*)	bus station
la **tienda**	shop
la **torre**	tower
la **turista**	tourist
la **vista**	view

USEFUL PHRASES

voy a la ciudad *or* al centro **I'm going into town**
en el centro (de la ciudad) **downtown**
en la plaza **in the square**
una calle de un solo sentido **a one-way street**
"dirección prohibida" **"no entry"**
cruzar la calle **to cross the road**
tomar un taxi/el metro **to take a taxi/the subway**

IMPORTANT WORDS *(masculine)*

el **abono**	season ticket
el **agente (de policía)**	police officer
el **alcalde**	mayor
el **atasco**	traffic jam
el **cartel**	notice; poster
el **castillo**	castle
el **cibercafé**	internet café
el **cruce**	intersection
el **embotellamiento**	traffic jam
el **lugar**	place
el **monumento**	monument
el **parquímetro**	parking meter
el **quiosco de periódicos**	newsstand
el **semáforo**	traffic light
el **sitio**	place
el **tráfico**	traffic
el **transeúnte**	passerby
el **tránsito**	traffic
el **zoológico**	zoo

USEFUL PHRASES

en la esquina de la calle on the corner of the street
vivir en las afueras to live on the outskirts
caminar to walk

IMPORTANT WORDS *(feminine)*

la	**acera** (*Sp*)	sidewalk
la	**agente (de policía)**	police officer
la	**alcaldesa**	mayor
la	**banqueta** (*Mex*)	sidewalk
la	**biblioteca**	library
la	**calle principal**	main street
la	**calzada**	road
la	**circulación**	traffic
la	**desviación** (*pl* desviaciones)	detour
la	**estación de servicio** (*pl* estaciones ~ ~)	gas station
la	**iglesia**	church
la	**máquina expendedora de boletos** (*LAm*) *or* **de billetes** (*Sp*)	ticket vending machine
la	**mezquita**	mosque
la	**parte antigua**	old town
la	**polución**	pollution
la	**sinagoga**	synagogue
la	**transeúnte**	passerby
la	**zona azul**	restricted parking zone
la	**zona industrial**	industrial park

USEFUL PHRASES

industrial industrial
histórico(a) historic
moderno(a) modern
bonito(a) pretty
feo(a) ugly
limpio(a) clean
sucio(a) dirty

USEFUL WORDS *(masculine)*

el **adoquín** (*pl* adoquines)	cobblestone
el **barrio residencial**	residential area
el **callejón sin salida** (*pl* callejones ~ ~)	cul-de-sac, dead end
el **camellón** (*Mex*)	median strip
el **cementerio**	cemetery
el **ciudadano**	citizen
el **cochecito**	baby carriage; stroller
el **concejo municipal**	town council
el **cruce peatonal** *or* **de peatones**	crosswalk
el **desfile**	parade
el **distrito**	district
el **edificio**	building
el **folleto**	leaflet
los **lugares de interés**	sights, places of interest
el **parque de bomberos** (*Sp*)	firehouse
el **paso peatonal** *or* **de peatones**	crosswalk
el **pavimento**	road surface, pavement
el **rascacielos** (*pl inv*)	skyscraper
el **sondeo de opinión**	opinion poll

USEFUL WORDS *(feminine)*

las	**afueras**	outskirts
la	**alcantarilla**	sewer
la	**cafetería**	coffee shop, café; cafeteria
la	**calle sin salida**	cul-de-sac, dead end
la	**cárcel**	prison
la	**carreola** (*Mex*)	stroller
la	**ciclovía**	bicycle lane
la	**ciudadana**	citizen
la	**cola**	line, queue
la	**curva**	bend, curve
la	**estación de bomberos** (*pl* estaciones ~ ~) (*LAm*)	firehouse
la	**estatua**	statue
la	**flecha**	arrow
la	**galería de arte**	art gallery
la	**glorieta**	traffic circle
la	**mediana** (*Sp*)	median strip
la	**muchedumbre**	crowd
la	**multitud**	crowd
la	**población** (*pl* poblaciones)	town; village; population
la	**señal de tráfico** *or* **tránsito**	road sign

ESSENTIAL WORDS *(masculine)*

el **aduanero**	customs officer
el **agente aduanal** (*Mex*)	customs officer
el **andén** (*pl* andenes)	platform
el **asiento**	seat
el **billete** (*Sp*)	ticket
el **billete de ida** (*Sp*)	one-way ticket
el **billete de ida y vuelta** (*Sp*)	round-trip ticket
el **billete sencillo** (*Sp*)	one-way ticket
el **boleto** (*LAm*)	ticket
el **boleto de ida** (*LAm*)	one-way ticket
el **boleto de ida y vuelta** (*LAm*) *or* **boleto redondo** (*Mex*)	round-trip ticket
el **compartimento**	compartment
el **descuento**	discount, price reduction
el **equipaje**	luggage
el **expreso**	express train
el **freno**	brake
el **horario**	timetable
el **maletero**	porter
el **metro**	subway
el **número**	number
el **pasaporte**	passport
el **plano**	map
el **precio del billete** (*Sp*) *or* **del boleto** (*LAm*)	fare
el **puente**	bridge
el **recargo**	surcharge
el **retraso**	delay
el **taxi**	taxi
el **tícket** (*pl* ~s)	ticket; receipt
el **tren**	train
el **vagón** (*pl* vagones)	coach, car
el **viaje**	journey
el **viajero**	traveler

ESSENTIAL WORDS *(feminine)*

la **aduana**	customs
la **aduanera**	customs officer
la **agente aduanal** (*Mex*)	customs officer
la **bici**	bike
la **bicicleta**	bicycle
la **boletería** (*LAm*)	ticket office
la **bolsa**	bag; (*Mex*) purse
la **cartera**	wallet
la **clase**	class
la **conexión** (*pl* conexiones)	connection
la **consigna**	baggage room
la **consigna automática**	baggage locker
la **dirección** (*pl* direcciones)	direction
la **entrada**	entrance
la **estación** (*pl* estaciones)	station
la **estación de metro** (*pl* estaciones ~ ~)	subway station
la **información**	information
la **línea**	line
la **llegada**	arrival
la **maleta**	suitcase
la **oficial de aduanas**	customs officer
la **oficina de objetos perdidos**	lost and found office
la **parada de taxis**	taxi stand
la **petaca** (*Mex*)	suitcase
la **reservación** (*LAm*), **la reserva** (*Sp*)	reservation
la **sala de espera**	waiting room
la **salida**	departure; exit
la **taquilla**	ticket office
la **vía**	track, line
la **viajera**	traveler

USEFUL PHRASES

reservar un asiento to reserve a seat
pagar un recargo, pagar un suplemento to pay an extra charge, to pay a surcharge
hacer/deshacer el equipaje to pack/unpack

IMPORTANT WORDS *(masculine)*

el **coche-cama** (*pl* ~s~)	sleeping car
el **coche-comedor** (*pl* ~s~)	dining car
el **conductor**	driver
el **destino**	destination
el **ferrocarril**	railroad

USEFUL WORDS *(masculine)*

el **abono**	season ticket
el **baúl**	trunk
el **descarrilamiento**	derailment
el **jefe de estación**	station master
el **maquinista**	engineer
el **paso a nivel**	grade crossing
el **silbato**	whistle
el **suplemento**	extra charge, surcharge
el **trayecto**	journey
el **(tren de) mercancías** (*pl* (~es ~) ~)	freight train

USEFUL PHRASES

tomar el tren **to take the train**
perder el tren **to miss the train**
subir al tren **to get on the train**
bajar del tren **to get off the train**
¿está libre este asiento? **is this seat taken?**
el tren lleva retraso **the train is late**
un vagón de fumadores/no fumadores **a smoking/non-smoking car**
"prohibido asomarse por la ventanilla" **"do not lean out of the window"**

IMPORTANT WORDS *(feminine)*

la **barrera**	barrier
la **conductora**	driver
la **duración** (*pl* duraciones)	length (of time)
la **escalera eléctrica** *or* **mecánica**	escalator
la **frontera**	border
la **litera**	couchette (*basic sleeping accommodations on a train*)
la **propina**	tip
la **tarifa**	fare

USEFUL WORDS *(feminine)*

la **alarma**	alarm
la **etiqueta**	label
la **jefa de estación**	station master
la **locomotora**	locomotive
la **maquinista**	engineer
la **vía férrea**	(railroad) line *or* track
las **vías**	rails

USEFUL PHRASES

te acompañaré a la estación I'll go to the station with you
iré a buscarte a la estación I'll pick you up at the station
el tren de las diez con destino a/procedente de Oaxaca the 10 o'clock train to/from Oaxaca

ESSENTIAL WORDS *(masculine)*

el **árbol**	tree
el **bosque**	wood

USEFUL WORDS *(masculine)*

el **abedul**	birch
el **abeto**	fir tree
el **acebo**	holly
el **albaricoque** (*Sp*)	apricot tree
el **árbol frutal**	fruit tree
el **arbusto**	bush
el **arce**	maple
el **brote**	bud
el **castaño**	chestnut tree
el **cerezo**	cherry tree
el **chabacano** (*Mex*)	apricot tree
el **chopo**	poplar
el **duraznero** (*LAm*)	peach tree
el **follaje**	foliage
el **fresno**	ash
el **huerto**	orchard
el **limonero**	lemon tree
el **manzano**	apple tree
el **melocotonero** (*Sp*)	peach tree
el **naranjo**	orange tree
el **nogal**	walnut tree
el **olmo**	elm
el **peral**	pear tree
el **pino**	pine
el **platanero**	banana tree
el **plátano**	plane tree
el **roble**	oak
el **sauce llorón** (*pl* ~s llorones)	weeping willow
el **tejo**	yew
el **tilo**	lime tree
el **tronco**	trunk
el **viñedo**	vineyard

ESSENTIAL WORDS *(feminine)*

la **hoja**	leaf
la **rama**	branch
la **selva (tropical)**	rainforest

USEFUL WORDS *(feminine)*

la **baya**	berry
la **corteza**	bark
la **encina**	evergreen tree
el **haya** (*f pl* las hayas)	beech
la **higuera**	fig tree
la **raíz** (*pl* raíces)	root
la **viña**	vineyard

ESSENTIAL WORDS *(masculine)*

el	**ajo**	garlic
los	**champiñones**	mushrooms
los	**chícharos** (*Mex*)	peas
los	**ejotes** (*Mex*)	string beans
los	**frijoles** (*LAm*)	beans
los	**guisantes** (*Sp*)	peas
los	**hongos** (*LAm*)	mushrooms
el	**jitomate** (*Mex*)	tomato
el	**pimiento**	pepper
el	**tomate**	tomato

USEFUL WORDS *(masculine)*

el	**apio**	celery
el	**berro**	watercress
el	**brócoli**	broccoli
el	**calabacín** (*pl* calabacines) (*Sp*)	zucchini
el	**col**	cabbage
el	**col de Bruselas**	Brussels sprout
el	**elote** (*Mex*)	sweet corn
los	**espárragos**	asparagus
los	**garbanzos**	chickpeas
el	**maíz (dulce** *or* **tierno)** (*Sp*)	sweet corn
el	**nabo**	turnip
el	**pepino**	cucumber
el	**perejil**	parsley
el	**poro** (*Mex*)	leek
el	**puerro**	leek
el	**rábano**	radish
el	**repollo**	cabbage

USEFUL PHRASES

cultivar verduras to grow vegetables
un elote (*Mex*), una mazorca de maíz (*Sp*) corncob

ESSENTIAL WORDS *(feminine)*

las **arvejas** (*LAm*)	peas
la **calabacita** (*Mex*)	zucchini
la **cebolla**	onion
la **coliflor**	cauliflower
la **ensalada**	salad
las **habichuelas** (*LAm*)	string beans
las **judías verdes** (*Sp*)	string beans
la **papa** (*LAm*), la **patata** (*Sp*)	potato
las **verduras**	vegetables
la **zanahoria**	carrot

USESFUL WORDS *(feminine)*

la **acelga** *or* las **acelgas**	Swiss chard
la **alcachofa**	artichoke
las **alubias**	navy beans
la **berenjena**	eggplant
la **calabaza**	pumpkin
la **cebolleta**	scallion
la **cebollita de Cambray** (*Mex*)	scallion
la **endibia**	endive
la **escarola**	escarole
la **espinaca** *or* las **espinacas**	spinach
las **judías** (*Sp*)	beans
la **lechuga**	lettuce
las **legumbres**	vegetables
las **lentejas**	lentils
la **remolacha**	beet

USEFUL PHRASES

zanahoria rallada **grated carrot**
orgánico(a), biológico(a), ecológico(a) **organic**
vegetariano(a) **vegetarian**

ESSENTIAL WORDS *(masculine)*

el **autobús** (*pl* autobuses)	bus
el **autocar** (*Sp*)	(long distance) bus
el **avión** (*pl* aviones)	airplane
el **barco de vela**	sailing ship; sailboat
el **bote**	boat
el **bote de remos**	rowboat
el **camión** (*pl* camiones)	truck; (*Mex*) bus
el **carro**	cart; (*LAm*) car
el **casco**	helmet
el **ciclomotor**	moped
el **coche**	car
el **helicóptero**	helicopter
el **medio de transporte**	means of transportation
el **metro**	subway
el **precio del boleto** (*LAm*) *or* **del billete** (*Sp*)	fare
el **taxi**	taxi
el **tráiler**	trailer
el **transbordador**	ferry
el **transporte público**	public transportation
el **tren**	train
el **vehículo**	vehicle
el **vehículo pesado**	heavy-duty vehicle

IMPORTANT WORDS *(masculine)*

el **camión de bomberos**	fire truck

USEFUL PHRASES

viajar to travel
fue a Dallas en avión he flew to Dallas
tomar el autobús/el metro/el tren to take the bus/the subway/the train
andar en bicicleta to go cycling
se puede ir en coche you can get there by car

ESSENTIAL WORDS *(feminine)*

la **bici**	bike
la **bicicleta**	bicycle
la **camioneta**	van; station wagon
la **distancia**	distance
la **moto**	motorbike
la **motocicleta**	motorcycle, motorbike
la **parte de atrás/de adelante**	back/front
la **parte delantera**	front
la **parte trasera**	back
la **vespa®**	scooter

IMPORTANT WORDS *(feminine)*

la **ambulancia**	ambulance
la **grúa**	tow truck

USEFUL PHRASES

reparar *or* arreglar el coche de algn to repair sb's car
un coche de alquiler a rental car
un coche *or* un carro de renta (*Mex*) a rental car
un coche deportivo a sports car
un coche de carreras a race car
arrancar to start, to move off

USEFUL WORDS *(masculine)*

el **aerodeslizador**	hovercraft
el **(barco de) vapor**	steamer
el **bulldozer** (*pl* ~s)	bulldozer
el **buque**	ship
el **camión articulado** (*pl* camiones ~s)	tractor-trailer, semi
el **camión cisterna** (*pl* camiones ~)	tanker
el **cohete**	rocket
el **hidroavión** (*pl* hidroaviones)	seaplane
el **jeep** (*pl* ~s)	jeep
el **navío**	ship
el **ovni (objeto volador no identificado)**	UFO (*unidentified flying object*)
el **petrolero**	oil tanker (*ship*)
el **planeador**	glider
el **platillo volador** (*LAm*) *or* **volante** (*Sp*)	flying saucer
el **portaaviones** (*pl inv*)	aircraft carrier
el **remolcador**	tug
el **remolque**	trailer
el **submarino**	submarine
el **tanque**	tank
el **teleférico**	cable car
el **telesilla**	chairlift
el **tranvía**	streetcar, tram
el **velero**	sailing ship; sailboat
el **yate**	yacht; pleasure cruiser

USEFUL WORDS *(feminine)*

la **barcaza**	barge
la **canoa**	canoe
la **carreta**	wagon; cart
la **lancha**	boat (*small*); launch
la **lancha de motor**	motorboat
la **lancha de salvamento**	lifeboat
la **lancha de socorro**	lifeboat
la **lancha neumática**	inflatable boat
la **lancha rápida**	speedboat
la **locomotora**	locomotive

ESSENTIAL WORDS *(masculine)*

el **aire**	air
el **boletín meteorológico** (*pl* boletines ~s)	weather report
el **calor**	heat
el **cielo**	sky
el **clima**	climate
el **este**	east
el **frío**	cold
el **grado**	degree
el **hielo**	ice
el **invierno**	winter
el **norte**	north
el **oeste**	west
el **otoño**	fall; autumn
el **paraguas** (*pl inv*)	umbrella
el **parte meteorológico**	weather report
el **pronóstico del tiempo**	(weather) forecast
el **sol**	sun; sunshine
el **sur**	south
el **tiempo**	weather
el **verano**	summer
el **viento**	wind

USEFUL PHRASES

¿qué tiempo hace? **what's the weather like?**
hace calor/frío **it's hot/cold**
hace un día precioso **it's a lovely day**
hace un día horrible **it's a horrible day**
al aire libre **in the open air**
hay niebla **it's foggy**
30° a la sombra **30° in the shade**
escuchar el pronóstico del tiempo **to listen to the weather forecast**
llover **to rain**
nevar **to snow**
llueve *or* está lloviendo **it's raining**
nieva *or* está nevando **it's snowing**

ESSENTIAL WORDS *(feminine)*

la **estación** (*pl* estaciones)	season
la **lluvia**	rain
la **niebla**	fog
la **nieve**	snow
la **nube**	cloud
la **primavera**	spring
la **región** (*pl* regiones)	region, area
la **temperatura**	temperature

USEFUL PHRASES

brilla el sol the sun is shining
sopla el viento the wind is blowing
hace un frío glacial it's freezing
tengo las manos heladas my hands are freezing
helarse to freeze
derretirse to melt
soleado(a) sunny
tormentoso(a) stormy
lluvioso(a) rainy
fresco(a) cool
variable changeable
húmedo(a) humid; damp
nublado(a) cloudy

IMPORTANT WORDS *(masculine)*

el **chubasco**	downpour, shower
el **humo**	smoke
el **polvo**	dust

USEFUL WORDS *(masculine)*

el **aguacero**	downpour
el **amanecer**	dawn, daybreak
el **anochecer**	nightfall, dusk
el **arco iris** (*pl inv*)	rainbow
el **barómetro**	barometer
el **cambio**	change
el **charco**	puddle
el **copo de nieve**	snowflake
el **crepúsculo**	twilight
el **deshielo**	thaw
el **granizo**	hail
el **huracán** (*pl* huracanes)	hurricane
el **pararrayos** (*pl inv*)	lightning rod
el **quitanieves** (*pl inv*)	snowplow
el **rayo**	bolt of lightning
el **rayo de sol**	ray of sunshine
el **relámpago**	flash of lightning
(los) **relámpagos**	lightning
el **rocío**	dew
el **trueno**	thunderclap
(los) **truenos**	thunder

IMPORTANT WORDS *(feminine)*

las	**precipitaciones**	rainfall
la	**sombrilla**	parasol
la	**tormenta**	storm
la	**visibilidad**	visibility

USEFUL WORDS *(feminine)*

el	**alba** (*f pl* las albas)	dawn
la	**atmósfera**	atmosphere
la	**brisa**	breeze
la	**bruma**	mist
la	**corriente (de aire)**	draught
la	**escarcha**	frost (*on the ground*)
la	**gota de lluvia**	raindrop
la	**helada**	frost (*weather*)
la	**inundación** (*pl* inundaciones)	flood
la	**luz de la luna**	moonlight
la	**mejora**	improvement
la	**nevada**	snowfall
la	**ola de calor**	heatwave
la	**oscuridad**	darkness
la	**puesta de sol**	sunset
la	**ráfaga de viento**	gust of wind
la	**sequía**	drought
la	**tormenta eléctrica**	thunderstorm

ESSENTIAL WORDS *(masculine)*

el	**albergue juvenil**	youth hostel
los	**baños públicos** (*LAm*)	public restrooms
el	**bote de la basura** (*LAm*)	garbage can
el	**comedor**	dining room
el	**cuarto de baño**	bathroom
el	**cubo de la basura** (*Sp*)	garbage can
el	**desayuno**	breakfast
el	**dormitorio**	dormitory
los	**lavabos**	washrooms
el	**mapa**	map
los	**servicios** (*Sp*)	restrooms
el	**silencio**	silence
el	**visitante**	visitor

IMPORTANT WORDS *(masculine)*

el	**carnet de socio** (*pl* ~s ~ ~)	membership card
el	**lavabo**	washroom; lavatory
el	**saco de dormir**	sleeping bag

ESSENTIAL WORDS *(feminine)*

la	**bolsa de dormir**	sleeping bag
la	**cama**	bed
la	**litera**	bunk bed
la	**cocina**	kitchen; cooking
la	**comida**	meal
la	**ducha**	shower
la	**estancia**	stay
la	**lista de precios**	price list
la	**noche**	night
la	**oficina**	office
la	**regadera** (*Mex*)	shower
la	**sábana**	sheet
la	**sala de juegos**	gameroom
la	**tarifa**	rate(s)
la	**toalla**	towel
las	**vacaciones**	holidays
la	**visitante**	visitor

IMPORTANT WORDS *(feminine)*

la	**caminata**	hike
la	**excursión** (*pl* excursiones)	trip
la	**guía**	guidebook
la	**mochila**	backpack
las	**normas**	rules
la	**ropa de cama**	bed linens

USEFUL PHRASES

pasar una noche en el albergue juvenil to spend a night at the youth hostel

quisiera alquilar una bolsa de dormir *or* un saco de dormir I would like to rent a sleeping bag

está todo ocupado there's no more room

The vocabulary items on pages 670 to 707 have been grouped under parts of speech rather than topics because they can apply in a wide range of circumstances. Use them just as freely as the vocabulary already given.

ARTICLES AND PRONOUNS

What is an article?
In English, an **article** is one of the words *the*, *a* and *an* which is given in front of a noun.

What is a pronoun?
A **pronoun** is a word you use instead of a noun, when you do not need or want to name someone or something directly, for example, *it*, *you*, *none*.

algo something; anything
alguien somebody, someone; anybody, anyone
alguno/alguna one; someone, somebody
algunos/algunas some, some of them; some of us, some of you, some of them
ambos/ambas both
aquel/aquella that
aquellos/aquellas those
cada each; every
cual which; who; whom
  lo cual which
cuál what, which one
cualquiera any one; anybody, anyone
  cualquiera de los dos/las dos either (*see also* Adjectives)
cualesquiera (*pl*) any (*see also* Adjectives)
cuanto/cuanta as much as
cuánto/cuánta how much
cuantos/cuantas as many as
cuántos/cuántas how many
cuyo/cuya/cuyos/cuyas whose
  en cuyo caso in which case
demasiado/demasiada too much
demasiados/demasiadas too many
dos: los/las dos both
el/la the
él he; him; it
  de él his
ella she; her; it
  de ella hers
ello it
ellos/ellas they; them
  de ellos/ellas theirs
ese/esa that
esos/esas those
este/esta this
estos/estas these
la her; it; you
las them; you
le him; her; it; you
les them; you
lo him; it; you
los/las the
los them; you
me me; myself
mi/mis my
(el)mío/(la) mía/(los) míos/(las) mías mine

mismo/misma/mismos/mismas same
mí mismo/misma; yo mismo/misma myself; **nosotros mismos/nosotras mismas** ourselves; **sí misma; ella misma** herself; **sí mismo; él mismo** himself; **sí mismos/sí mismas; ellos mismos/ellas mismas** themselves; **ti mismo/ti misma; tú mismo/tú misma; usted mismo/usted misma** yourself; **vosotros mismos/vosotras mismas; ustedes mismos/ustedes mismas** yourselves; **uno mismo/una misma** oneself
mucho/mucha a lot, lots; much (*see also* Adjectives; Adverbs)
muchos/muchas a lot, lots; many (*see also* Adjectives)
nada nothing
nada más nothing else
nadie nobody, no one; anybody, anyone
nadie más nobody else
ninguno/ninguna any; neither; either; none; no one, nobody
ninguno de los dos/ninguna de las dos neither (*see also* Adjectives)
ningunos/ningunas any; none (*see also* Adjectives)
nos us; ourselves; each other
nosotros/nosotras we; us
nuestro/nuestra/nuestros/nuestras our; ours
el nuestro/la nuestra/los nuestros/las nuestras ours
os you; yourselves; each other
otro/otra another, another one (*see also* Adjectives)
otros/otras others (*see also* Adjectives)
poco/poca not much, little **un poco** a bit, a little
dentro de poco shortly
pocos/pocas not many, few
que who; that
qué what; what a
quien/quienes who; whoever
quién/quiénes who
se him; her; them; you; himself; herself; itself; themselves; yourself; yourselves; oneself; each other
su/sus his; her; its; their; your; one's
(el) suyo/(la) suya/(los) suyos/(las) suyas his; her; its; their; your; hers; theirs; yours; one's own
tal/tales such
tampoco not...either, neither
te you; yourself
ti you
todo/toda (it) all
todo el mundo everybody, everyone (*see also* Adjectives)
todos/todas all; every; everybody; everyone (*see also* Adjectives)
tu/tus your
tú you
usted you
ustedes you
(el) tuyo/(la) tuya/(los) tuyos/(las) tuyas yours
un/una a; an; one
unos/unas some; a few; about, around
varios/varias several
vosotros/vosotras (*Sp*) you
vuestro/vuestra/vuestros/vuestras (*Sp*) your; yours
los vuestros/las vuestras (*Sp*) yours
yo I; me

CONJUNCTIONS

What is a conjunction?
A **conjunction** is a word such as *and*, *but*, *or*, *so*, *if* and *because*, that links two words or phrases of a similar type, or two parts of a sentence, for example, *Diane and I have been friends for years; I left because I was bored*.

ahora: ahora bien however;
ahora que now that
antes: antes de que before
así: así (es) que so
aunque although, though
como as
conque so, so then
consiguiente: por consiguiente so, therefore
cuando when; whenever; if
cuanto: en cuanto as soon as; as
dar: dado que since
decir: es decir that is to say
desde: desde que since
después: después de que after
e and
embargo: sin embargo still, however
entonces then
fin: a fin de que so that, in order that
forma: de forma que so that
hasta: hasta que until, till
luego therefore
manera: de manera que so that
mas but
más: más que more than
menos: menos que less than
mientras while; as long as
mientras que whereas;
mientras (tanto) meanwhile
modo: de modo que so that
momento: en el momento en que just as
ni or; nor; even
ni ... ni neither ... nor
o or
o ... o ... either ... or ...
para: para que so that
pero but
porque because
pronto: tan pronto como as soon as
pues then; well; since
puesto: puesto que since
que that
ser: o sea that is
a no ser que unless
si if; whether
si no otherwise
siempre: siempre que whenever; as long as, provided that
sino but; except; only
tal: con tal (de) que as long as, provided that
tanto: por (lo) tanto so, therefore
u or
vez: una vez que once
vista: en vista de que seeing that
y and
ya: ya que as, since

ADJECTIVES

What is an adjective?
An **adjective** is a 'describing' word that tells you more about a person or thing, such as their appearance, colour, size or other qualities, for example, *pretty, blue, big*.

abierto(a) open
absoluto(a) absolute
absurdo(a) absurd
académico(a) academic
accesible accessible; approachable
aceptable acceptable
acondicionado(a) equipped
con aire acondicionado air-conditioned
acostumbrado(a) accustomed; usual
activo(a) active
acusado(a) accused; marked
adecuado(a) appropriate
admirable admirable
aéreo(a) aerial
aficionado(a) enthusiastic
afilado(a) sharp
afortunado(a) fortunate, lucky
agitado(a) rough; upset; agitated; hectic
agotado(a) exhausted
agradable pleasant, agreeable
agresivo(a) aggressive
agrícola agricultural
agudo(a) sharp; acute
aislado(a) isolated
alegre happy; bright; lively; merry
alguno/alguna (*before masc sing* **algún)** some; any (*see also* Articles and Pronouns)
algunos/algunas some; several (*see also* Articles and Pronouns)
alternativo(a) alternating; alternative
alto(a) high; tall
amargo(a) bitter
ancho(a) broad; wide
anciano(a) elderly
animado(a) lively; cheerful
anónimo(a) anonymous
anormal abnormal
anterior former
antiguo(a) old; vintage; antique
anual annual
apagado(a) out; off; muffled; dull
aparente apparent
apasionado(a) passionate
apropiado(a) appropriate, suitable
aproximado(a) approximate, rough
arriba: de arriba top
asequible affordable
asombrado(a) amazed, astonished
asombroso(a) amazing, astonishing
áspero(a) rough, harsh
atestado(a) crowded; popular
atento(a) attentive; watchful
atractivo(a) attractive
automático(a) automatic
avanzado(a) advanced
bajo(a) low; short
barba: con *or* **de barba** bearded
barbudo(a) bearded
básico(a) basic

bastante enough; quite a lot of (*see also* Adverbs)
bien right; correct; fine
bienvenido(a) welcome
blando(a) soft
breve brief
brillante shining; bright
brutal brutal
bruto(a) rough; stupid; uncouth; gross
bueno(a) good
cada each; every
caliente hot; warm
callado(a) quiet
cansado(a) tired
capaz capable
cariñoso(a) affectionate
caro(a) expensive
cauteloso(a) cautious
central central
ceñido(a) tight
cercano(a) close; nearby
cerrado(a) closed; off
científico(a) scientific
cierto(a) true; certain
civil civil; civilian
claro(a) clear; light; bright
clásico(a) classical; classic
climatizado(a) air-conditioned
cobarde cowardly
comercial commercial
cómodo(a) comfortable
complejo(a) complex
completo(a) complete
complicado(a) complicated; complex
comprensivo(a) understanding
común common; mutual
concreto(a) specific; concrete
concurrido(a) crowded; popular
conmovedor(a) moving, touching
consciente conscious; aware
conservador(a) conservative
considerable considerable
constante constant
contemporáneo(a) contemporary
contento(a) happy; pleased
continuo(a) continuous
convencional conventional
correcto(a) correct, right
corriente ordinary; common
cortado(a) cut; closed; off; shy
creativo(a) creative
cristiano(a) Christian
crítico(a) critical
crudo(a) raw
cuadrado(a) square
cualquiera (*before masc and fem sing* **cualquier**) any (*see also* Articles and Pronouns)
cualesquiera any (*see also* Articles and Pronouns)
cuanto/cuanta as much as
cuánto/cuánta how much
cuantos/cuantas as many as
cuántos/cuántas how many
cultural cultural
curioso(a) curious
debido(a) due, proper
decepcionante disappointing
decidido(a) determined; decisive
delicado(a) delicate
delicioso(a) delicious
demasiado/demasiada too much
demasiados/demasiadas too many
democrático(a) democratic
derecho(a) right; straight
desafortunado(a) unfortunate
desagradable unpleasant
desconocido(a) unknown
desesperado(a) desperate

desierto(a) deserted
desnudo(a) naked; bare
despejado(a) clear
despierto(a) awake; sharp; alert
despreocupado(a) carefree; careless
destruido(a) destroyed
detallado(a) detailed
diestro(a) skilful; right-handed
difícil difficult
digno(a) dignified; **digno de** worthy of
diminuto(a) tiny
directo(a) direct
disgustado(a) upset; annoyed
disponible available
dispuesto(a) arranged; willing
distinguido(a) distinguished
distinto(a) different; various
divertido(a) funny, amusing; fun; entertaining
dividido(a) divided
divino(a) divine
doble double
domesticado(a) tame
doméstico(a) domestic
dos: los/las dos both
dulce sweet
duro(a) hard
económico(a) economic; economical
efectivo(a) effective
eficaz effective; efficient
eficiente efficient
eléctrico(a) electric
electrónico(a) electronic
elemental elementary
emocionante exciting
emotivo(a) emotional; moving
encantador(a) charming; lovely
enmascarado(a) masked
enorme enormous, huge
enterado(a) knowledgeable; well-informed; aware
entero(a) whole
equivalente equivalent
equivocado(a) wrong
escandaloso(a) shocking
esencial essential
especial special
específico(a) specific
espectacular spectacular
espeso(a) thick
espiritual spiritual
estrecho(a) narrow
estricto(a) strict
estropeado(a) broken (off); off
estupendo(a) marvellous, great
estúpido(a) stupid
étnico(a) ethnic
evidente obvious, evident
exacto(a) exact; accurate
excelente excellent
excepcional outstanding
exclusivo(a) exclusive
exigente demanding, exacting
experto(a) experienced
éxito: de éxito successful
exitoso(a) successful
exquisito(a) delicious; exquisite
extra extra; top-quality; bonus
extranjero(a) foreign
extraño(a) strange; foreign
extraordinario(a) extraordinary; outstanding; special
extremo(a) extreme
fácil easy
falso(a) false
familiar family; familiar
famoso(a) famous
federal federal
feroz fierce, ferocious

fijo(a) fixed; permanent
final final
financiero(a) financial
fino(a) fine; smooth; refined
firme firm; steady
físico(a) physical
flexible flexible
fluido(a) fluid; fluent
formal reliable; formal; official
frágil fragile; frail
frecuente frequent
fresco(a) fresh; cool; bold
fuerte strong; loud
futuro(a) future
general general
generoso(a) generous
genial brilliant; wonderful, great
gentil kind
genuino(a) genuine
global global
gordo(a) fat; big
grande (*before masc sing* **gran**) big; great
grandioso(a) grand; grandiose
habitual usual
herido(a) injured; wounded; hurt
hermoso(a) beautiful
histórico(a) historic; historical
holgado(a) loose
honrado(a) honest; respectable
horrible horrific; hideous; terrible
horroroso(a) dreadful; hideous; terrible
humano(a) human; humane
ideal ideal
idéntico(a) identical
igual equal
ilegal illegal
iluminado(a) illuminated, lit; enlightened
ilustrado(a) illustrated
imaginario(a) imaginary
impar odd
importante important
imposible impossible
imprescindible indispensable
impresionante impressive; moving; shocking
inaguantable unbearable
incapaz (de) incapable (of)
increíble incredible; unbelievable
inculto(a) uncultured
indefenso(a) defenseless
independiente independent
indiferente indifferent; unconcerned
individual individual; single
industrial industrial
inesperado(a) unexpected
inevitable inevitable
infantil childlike; childish
inflable inflatable
injusto(a) unfair
inmediato(a) immediate
inmenso(a) immense
inmune immune
inquieto(a) anxious; restless
intacto(a) intact
intencionado(a) deliberate
intenso(a) intense; intensive
interior interior; inside; inner; domestic
interminable endless
internacional international
interno(a) internal
interrumpido(a) interrupted
inútil useless
invisible invisible
izquierdo(a) left
junto(a) together

justo(a) just, fair; exact; tight
largo(a) long
legal legal
lento(a) slow
libre free
ligero(a) light; slight
limpio(a) clean
liso(a) smooth; straight; plain
listo(a) ready; bright
llamativo(a) bright; striking
llano(a) flat; straightforward
lleno(a) (de) full (of)
lluvioso(a) rainy, wet
loco(a) crazy, insane
lujo: de lujo luxurious
lujoso(a) luxurious
magnífico(a) magnificent; wonderful, superb
mal wrong; ill
maligno(a) malignant; evil, malicious
malo(a) bad
malvado(a) wicked
manso(a) meek; tame
maravilloso(a) marvelous, wonderful
marcado(a) marked
máximo(a) maximum
mayor bigger; elder, older
el/la...mayor the biggest...; the eldest...; the oldest...
mecánico(a) mechanical
médico(a) medical
medio(a) half; average
medioambiental environmental
mejor better
el/la mejor the best
menor smaller; younger
el/la...menor the smallest; the youngest
mental mental
militar military
minucioso(a) thorough; very detailed
mismo(a) same
misterioso(a) mysterious
moderado(a) moderate
moderno(a) modern
mojado(a) wet; soaked
molesto(a) annoying; annoyed; awkward; uncomfortable
montañoso(a) mountainous
mucho/mucha a lot of, lots of; much (*see also* Pronouns; Adverbs)
muchos/muchas a lot of, lots of; many (*see also* Pronouns)
muerto(a) dead
mundial worldwide, global
mutuo(a) mutual
nacido(a) born
nacional national; domestic
nativo(a) native
natural natural
necesario(a) necessary
negativo(a) negative
ninguno/ninguna (*before masc sing* **ningún**) no; none, any (*see also* Pronouns)
ningunos/ningunas no; none, any (*see also* Pronouns)
normal normal; standard
nuclear nuclear
nuevo(a) new
numeroso(a) numerous
obediente obedient
objetivo(a) objective
obligatorio(a) compulsory, obligatory
obvio(a) obvious
ocupado(a) busy; taken; engaged; occupied

oficial official
oportuno(a) opportune; appropriate
original original
oscuro(a) dark; obscure
otro/otra another
a/en otro lugar somewhere else; **otra cosa** something else; **otra persona** somebody else; **otra vez** again (*see also* Pronouns); **otros/otras** other (*see also* Pronouns)
pacífico(a) peaceful; peaceable
pálido(a) pale
par even
parado standing up
particular special; particular; private
patético(a) pathetic
peligroso(a) dangerous
peor worse
el peor the worst
perdido(a) lost; stray; remote
perfecto(a) perfect
personal personal
pesado(a) heavy; tedious; boring
picante hot (spicy)
pie: de pie standing (up)
poco/poca not much, little
pocos/pocas not many, few
poderoso(a) powerful
polémico(a) controversial
polvoriento(a) dusty; powdery
popular popular
portátil portable
posible possible; potential
positivo(a) positive
práctico(a) practical
precioso(a) lovely, beautiful; precious
preciso(a) precise; **ser preciso** to be necessary
preferido(a) favorite
preliminar preliminary
presentable presentable
presunto(a) alleged
previo(a) previous
primario(a) primary
principal main
privado(a) private
privilegiado(a) privileged
profundo(a) deep
prometido(a) promised; engaged
propio(a) own
próximo(a) near, close; next
psicológico(a) psychological
público(a) public
pueril childish
pulcro(a) neat
puntiagudo(a) pointed; sharp
puntual punctual
puro(a) pure
qué what; which; what a
querido(a) dear
químico(a) chemical
racial racial
radical radical
rápido(a) fast, quick
raro(a) strange, odd; rare
razonable reasonable
reacio(a) reluctant
real actual; royal
reciente recent
recto(a) straight; honest
redondo(a) round
refrescante refreshing
regional regional
regular regular
religioso(a) religious
repentino(a) sudden

repuesto: de repuesto spare
reservado(a) reserved
resistente resistant; tough
responsable (de) responsible (for)
revolucionario(a) revolutionary
ridículo(a) ridiculous
rival rival
romántico(a) romantic
rubio(a) fair, blond
ruidoso(a) noisy
rural rural
sabio(a) wise
sagrado(a) sacred
salvaje wild
salvo: a salvo safe
sanitario(a) sanitary; health
sano(a) healthy
  sano(a) y salvo(a) safe and sound
santo(a) holy
satisfecho(a) (de) satisfied (with)
seco(a) dry
secreto(a) secret
secundario(a) secondary
seguro(a) safe; secure; certain; sure
semejante similar
sencillo(a) simple; natural; single
sensacional sensational
sentado(a) sitting, seated
señalado(a) special
separado(a) separate
servicial helpful
severo(a) severe
sexual sexual
significativo(a) significant; meaningful
siguiente next, following
silencioso(a) silent; quiet
sincero(a) sincere
singular singular; outstanding
siniestro(a) sinister
situado(a) situated
sobra: de sobra spare
sobrante spare
social social
solemne solemn
sólido(a) solid
solo(a) alone; lonely; black; straight, neat
soltero(a) single
sombrío(a) sombre; dim
sonriente smiling
soportable bearable
sorprendente surprising
sospechoso(a) suspicious
suave smooth; gentle; mild; slight
sucio(a) dirty
superior top; upper; superior
supremo(a) supreme
supuesto(a) assumed; supposed
tal/tales such
tanto/tanta so much
tantos/tantas so many
técnico(a) technical
terrible terrible
típico(a) typical
tirante tight; tense
todo/toda all (*see also* Pronouns)
todos/todas all; every (*see also* Pronouns)
tolerante broad-minded
total total
tradicional traditional
tremendo(a) tremendous
triste sad
último(a) last
  el último the latest
ultrajante offensive; outrageous
único(a) only; unique
urgente urgent

útil useful, helpful
vacante vacant
vacío(a) empty
valiente brave, courageous
valioso(a) valuable
valor: de valor valuable
variado(a) varied
varios/varias several
vecino(a) neighboring
verdad: de verdad real
verdadero(a) real; true
viejo(a) old
vil villainous; vile
violento(a) violent; awkward
visible visible
vital vital
vivo(a) living; alive; lively
voluntario(a) voluntary

ADVERBS AND PREPOSITIONS

What is an adverb?
An **adverb** is a word usually used with verbs, adjectives or other adverbs that gives more Information about when, how, where, or in what circumstances something happens, or to what degree something is true, for example, *quickly*, *happily*, *now*, *extremely*, *very*.

What is a preposition?
A **preposition** is a word such as *at*, *for*, *with*, *into* or *from*, which is usually followed by a noun, pronoun, or, in English, a word ending in -ing. Prepositions show how people or things relate to the rest of the sentence, for example, *She's at home*; *a tool for cutting grass*; *It's from David*.

a to; at; into: onto
abajo down; downstairs; below
allá abajo down there;
abajo de (*LAm*) under
absolutamente absolutely
acá here, over here; now
acerca: acerca de about
actualmente at present
acuerdo: de acuerdo OK, okay
adelante forward; in front; at the front; opposite
en adelante from now on
hacia adelante forward;
adelante de (*LAm*) in front of ; opposite
además also; furthermore, moreover, in addition
además de as well as; besides
adentro inside; **adentro de** (*LAm*) inside; in; within
admirablemente admirably
afortunadamente fortunately
afuera outside; out **afuera de** (*LAm*) outside, out of
agradablemente nicely
ahora now; in a minute
hasta ahora so far
alcance: al alcance within reach
allá there, over there
allí there
alrededor de around
ansiosamente anxiously
ante before; in the face of; faced with
ante todo above all
antemano: de antemano beforehand, in advance
anteriormente previously, before
antes before **antes de** before
cuanto antes as soon as possible
lo antes posible as soon as possible
apartado: apartado de away from
aparte: aparte de apart from
apenas hardly, scarcely; only
aproximadamente approximately
aquí here; now
arriba up; upstairs; above
allá arriba up there; **arriba de** (*LAm*) on (top of)
así like that; like this
así como as well as

atentamente attentively, carefully; kindly; yours sincerely (*in letters*)
atrás behind; at the back; backwards; ago
hacia atrás backwards; **atrás de** (*LAm*) behind
aun even
aun así even so
aun cuando even if
aún still, yet; even
azar: al azar at random
bajo low; quietly; under
básicamente basically
bastante enough; quite a lot; quite (*see also* Adjectives)
bien well; carefully; very; easily
brevemente briefly
bruscamente abruptly
cambio: a cambio de in exchange for; in return for
en cambio instead
camino: de camino on the way
casi almost, nearly
caso: en el caso de (que) in the case of
en todo caso in any case
casualidad: por casualidad by chance
causa: a causa de because of
cerca (de) close (to); near (to)
claramente clearly
cómo how
como like; such as; as; about
completamente completely
con with
concreto: en concreto specifically, in particular
continuamente constantly
contra against
correctamente correctly
cortésmente politely
cuando when
cuándo when
cuanto: en cuanto a as regards, as for
cuánto how much; how far; how
cuenta: a fin de cuentas ultimately
teniendo en cuenta considering
cuidado: con cuidado carefully
cuidadosamente carefully
curiosamente curiously
curso: en el curso de in the course of
de of; from; about; by; than; in; if
debajo underneath
debajo de under; **por debajo** underneath; **por debajo de** under; below
débilmente faintly; weakly
delante in front; at the front; opposite
delante de in front of; opposite
hacia delante forward
por delante ahead; at the front
demasiado too; too much
dentro inside
dentro de inside; in; within
derecha: a la derecha on the right
desde from; since
desgraciadamente unfortunately
despacio slowly
después later; after(wards); then
después de after
detrás behind; at the back; on the back; after
detrás de behind; **por detrás** from behind; on the back
día: al día per day; up to date
diariamente on a daily basis
diario: a diario daily
donde where; wherever
dónde where
dondequiera anywhere

duda: sin duda definitely, undoubtedly
dulcemente sweetly; gently
durante during; for
durante todo/toda throughout
efecto: en efecto in fact
ejemplo: por ejemplo for example
en in; on; at; into; by
encima on top
encima de above; on top of;
por encima over; **por encima de** over; above
enfrente (de) opposite
enseguida right away; immediately
entonces then
desde entonces since then;
hasta entonces until then
entre among(st); between
especialmente especially, particularly; specially
evidentemente obviously, evidently
exactamente exactly
excepción: con la excepción de with the exception of
excepto except (for)
extranjero: en el extranjero overseas; abroad
extremadamente extremely
fácilmente easily
fielmente faithfully
fin: por fin finally; at last
finalmente eventually
forma: de alguna forma somehow
de esta forma like that; like this;
de ninguna forma in no way;
de otra forma otherwise;
de todas formas anyway
francamente frankly; really
frecuentemente frequently
frente: frente a opposite, facing; against
fuera outside; out
fuera de outside; out of
gana: de buena gana willingly, happily
de mala gana reluctantly
general: por lo general as a rule
generalmente generally
gracias: gracias a thanks to
gradualmente gradually
hacia towards
hasta to, as far as; up to; down to; until
honradamente honestly
igualmente equally; likewise
incluido including
inmediatamente immediately
intensamente intensely
izquierda: a la izquierda on the left
jamás never; ever
junto: junto a close to, near; next to; together with
junto con together with
justamente just; exactly; justly
lado: al lado (de) next door (to); near
al lado de alongside; **al otro lado de** across; **de un lado a otro** to and fro; **por este lado (de)** on this side (of)
largo: a lo largo de along
lejos (de) far (from)
ligeramente lightly; slightly
luego then; later, afterwards
desde luego certainly
mal badly; poorly
manera: de alguna manera somehow
de esta manera like that; like this;
de ninguna manera in no way;
de otra manera otherwise;
de todas maneras anyway

más more; plus
el/la más the most; **más allá de** beyond; **más bien** rather; **más cerca** closer; **más lejos** further; **más o menos** about; **más...que** more...than; **no más** no more
medio: en medio de in the middle of
por medio de by means of
mejor better
el/la mejor the best
menos less; minus **el/la menos** the least; **menos...que** less than; **por lo menos** at least
mentalmente mentally
menudo: a menudo often
misteriosamente mysteriously
modo: de algún modo somehow
de este modo like that; like this; **de ningún modo** in no way; **de otro modo** otherwise; **de todos modos** anyway
momento: en este momento at the moment
en ese mismo momento at that very moment
mucho a lot
no mucho not much (*see also* Pronouns; Adjectives)
muy very; too
naturalmente naturally
nerviosamente nervously
no no; not
nombre: en nombre de on behalf of
normalmente normally; usually
novedad: sin novedad safely
nunca never; ever
paciencia: con paciencia patiently
para for; to
para atrás backwards; **para la derecha** towards the right; **para siempre** forever
parte: de mi parte on my behalf; from me
en cualquier parte anywhere; **en gran parte** largely; **en otra parte** elsewhere; **en parte** partly, in part; **en todas partes** everywhere; **por otra parte** on the other hand
peligrosamente dangerously
peor worse
el/la peor the worst
perfectamente perfectly
persona: por persona per person
personalmente personally
pesadamente heavily
pesar: a pesar de in spite of; despite
a pesar de que even though
pie: a pie on foot
poco not very; not a lot; not much
poco a poco little by little, bit by bit
por because of; for; by; through
por qué why
precisamente precisely, exactly
primero first
principalmente mainly
principio: al principio at first
probable likely
probablemente probably
profundamente deeply
pronto soon; (*Sp*) early
propósito: a propósito deliberately; on purpose
qué how
querer: sin querer accidentally; unintentionally
quién: de quién/de quiénes whose
rápidamente fast, quickly
rápido quickly
realidad: en realidad in fact, actually
realmente really

recientemente recently, lately
regularmente regularly, on a regular basis
relativamente relatively
repente: de repente suddenly
seguida: en seguida right away
seguido (*LAm*) often
 todo seguido straight ahead
según according to; depending on
seguramente probably; surely
sencillamente simply
sentido: en este sentido in this respect
separado: por separado separately
ser: a no ser que unless
serio: en serio seriously; really
sí yes
siempre always
 como siempre as usual
siguiente: al/el día siguiente the next day
silencio: en silencio quietly; in silence
silenciosamente quietly, silently
sin without **sin embargo** still, however, nonetheless
siquiera: ni siquiera not even
sitio: en algún sitio somewhere
 en ningún sitio nowhere
sobre on; over; about
solamente only; solely
 solo only; solely
 tan solo only, just
suavemente gently; softly; smoothly
sumamente highly, extremely
supuesto: por supuesto of course
tal: tal como just as
 tal y como están las cosas under the circumstances;
 tal vez perhaps, maybe
también also, too
tampoco not ... either, neither
tan so; such
 tan ... como as ... as
tanto so much; so often
 tanto más all the more
tarde late
 más tarde later; afterwards
temprano early
 más temprano earlier
tiempo: a tiempo in time; on time
 al mismo tiempo at the same time; **mucho tiempo** long
todavía still; yet; even
todo: en todo/toda throughout
 todo lo más at (the) most
total in short; at the end of the day
 en total altogether, in all
totalmente totally, completely
través: a través de through; across
vano: en vano in vain
velocidad: a toda velocidad at full speed, at top speed
ver: por lo visto apparently
vez: algunas veces sometimes
 cada vez más more and more;
 cada vez menos less and less;
 de vez en cuando from time to time, now and then; **en vez de** instead of; **rara vez** rarely, seldom; **una vez** once; **una vez más** once more
vía: en vías de on its way to
 en vías de desarrollo developing;
 en vías de extinción endangered
vista: de vista by sight
 en vista de in view of
voz: en voz alta aloud; loudly
 en voz baja in a low voice
ya already
 ya mismo at once; **ya no** not any more, no longer

SOME EXTRA NOUNS

What is a noun?
A **noun** is a 'naming' word for a living being, thing or idea, for example, *woman*, *desk*, *happiness*, *Andrew*.

la abertura opening
el abismo gulf
el aburrimiento boredom
el abuso abuse
el acceso access
la acción (*pl* acciones) action
el acento accent
el ácido acid
el acontecimiento event
la actitud attitude
la actividad activity
el acuerdo agreement; settlement
la advertencia warning
la afirmación (*pl* afirmaciones) claim
la agencia agency
la agenda diary
el/la agente agent
la agitación (*pl* agitaciones) stir
el agujero hole
la alcantarilla drain
la alegría joy
el alfabeto alphabet
el alfiler pin
el/la aliado/a ally
el aliento breath
el alivio relief
el alma (*f*) soul
el almacén (*pl* almacenes) department store; warehouse
el/la amante lover
la ambición (*pl* ambiciones) ambition
la amenaza threat
el/la amigo(a) friend
la amistad friendship
el amor love
el análisis (*pl inv*) analysis
la anchura breadth; width
el/la anfitrión(ona) host/hostess
el ángel angel
el ángulo angle
la angustia anguish
el animal doméstico pet
la antigüedad antique; ancient times; length of service
el anuncio announcement
el anzuelo hook
la apertura opening
el apoyo support
la aprobación (*pl* aprobaciones) approval
la apuesta bet; stake
la armada navy
el arreglo compromise
la artesanía craft
el artículo article; item
la asociación (*pl* asociaciones) association
el asombro astonishment
el aspecto aspect
la astilla splinter
el asunto matter; issue; affair
el atajo shortcut
el ataúd coffin
la atención (*pl* atenciones) attention
el atentado attempt

la atracción; el atractivo attraction
la ausencia absence
la autoridad authority
la aventura adventure; affair
el aviso notice
la ayuda assistance, help
el/la ayudante assistant
el ayuntamiento council
el azar chance
la bala bullet
la barandilla rail
la barrera barrier
el barril barrel
la base base
la batalla battle
la batería battery
la beca grant; scholarship
el beso kiss
la Biblia Bible
la bomba bomb
la bondad kindness
el borde edge
la broma joke
el brote outbreak; bud
el bullicio bustle
la burbuja bubble
el cable cable
la caja box
la calcomanía transfer
el cálculo calculation
el caldo stock
la calidad quality
la calma calm
el camino path; way
el campamento camp
la campaña campaign
el camping (*pl* ~s) site
el canal channel
la canasta basket
la cantidad amount
el caos chaos
la capa layer
la capacidad ability; capacity
el capítulo chapter
la característica characteristic; feature
la caridad charity
el/la catedrático(a) professor
los celos jealousy (*sing*)
el centro center; focus; middle
el centro turístico resort
el cesto basket
el chiste joke
el cielo heaven; sky
el cierre closure
la cima top
el círculo circle
las circunstancias circumstances
la cita quote; extract; appointment
el/la civil civilian
la civilización (*pl* civilizaciones) civilization
la clase sort; class, classroom
la clasificación (*pl* clasificaciones) classification
la clave code
la codicia greed
la colegiatura (*Mex*) school fees
la columna column
el columpio swing
la combinación (*pl* combinaciones) combination
el combustible fuel
el comentario comment, remark
el/la comentarista commentator
las comillas: entre comillas inverted commas: in quotes
la comisión (*pl* comisiones) commission
el comité (*pl* comités) committee

el/la compañero(a) classmate; partner
la comparación (*pl* comparaciones) comparison
la compasión (*pl* compasiones) sympathy
la competencia (*LAm*) contest; competition
la competición (*pl* competiciones) (*Sp*) contest; competition
el/la competidor(a) rival
la comprensión (*pl* comprensiones) sympathy
el compromiso commitment
la comunicación (*pl* comunicaciones) communication
la comunidad community
la concentración (*pl* concentraciones) concentration
la conciencia conscience
la condecoración (*pl* condecoraciones) honor
la condición (*pl* condiciones) condition; status
la conducta conduct
la conexión (*pl* conexiones) connection
la conferencia lecture; conference
la confianza confidence
el conflicto conflict
el confort comfort
el congreso conference
la conmoción (*pl* conmociones) shock; disturbance
el conocimiento knowledge; consciousness
la consecuencia consequence
el consejo (piece of) advice
la construcción (*pl* construcciones) construction; structure
el/la consumidor(a) consumer
el contacto contact
el contenido content
el contexto context
el contorno outline
el contraste contrast
la contribución (*pl* contribución) contribution
la conversación (*pl* conversaciones) conversation
la copia copy
el corazón (*pl* corazones) heart; core
la corona crown
el/la corresponsal correspondent
la corrupción (*pl* corrupciones) corruption
la cortesía politeness
la cosa thing
las cosas stuff (*sing*); things
la costumbre custom
el crecimiento growth
el/la criado(a) servant
la crisis (*pl inv*) crisis
la crítica criticism
el cuadro picture
el cubierto place (setting); piece of silverware
el cuchicheo whispering
la cuenta count
por su cuenta of his own accord
el cuento tale
la cuestión (*pl* cuestiones) question
la cueva cave
el cuidado care
la culpa blame
la cultura culture
la cuota fee; (*LAm*) toll
la curiosidad curiosity
los datos data (*pl*)

el debate debate
el deber duty
la decepción (*pl* decepciones) disappointment
la decisión (*pl* decisiones) decision
el defecto fault
la definición (*pl* definiciones) definition
el/la dependiente(a) assistant
la depresión (*pl* depresiones) depression
el/la derecho(a) right
los derechos fee
el desagüe drain
el desarrollo development
el desastre disaster
el descanso break
el/la desconocido(a) stranger
la desdicha unhappiness
el deseo desire; wish; urge
el desgarrón (*pl* desgarrones) tear
la desgracia misfortune
el desorden disorder; mess
el destino destiny; fate
la destreza skill
la destrucción (*pl* destrucciones) destruction
la desventaja disadvantage
el detalle detail
la devolución (*pl* devoluciones) refund; return
el diagrama diagram
el diálogo dialogue
la diana target
el diario diary; journal
la diferencia difference
la dificultad difficulty
la dimensión (*pl* dimensiones) dimension
el/la dios(a) god/goddess
el/la diplomático(a) diplomat
el/la diputado(a) deputy
la dirección (*pl* direcciones) direction; address
la disciplina discipline
el discurso speech
la discusión (*pl* discusiones) argument; discussion
el diseño design
el dispositivo device
la disputa dispute
la distancia distance
la división (*pl* divisiones) division
el drama drama
la duda doubt
el eco echo
la economía economics (*sing*); economy
la edición (*pl* ediciones) edition
el efecto effect
el ejemplar copy
el ejemplo example
por ejemplo for instance
el/la elector(a) elector
la elegancia elegance
el elemento element
la encuesta survey
el/la enemigo(a) enemy
la energía energy
el entusiasmo enthusiasm; excitement
la envidia envy
la época period
el equilibrio balance
el equipo equipment
el error mistake
el escándalo scandal
el escape leak
la escasez shortage
la escritura writing

el esfuerzo effort
el espacio space
la espalda back
la especie species (*sing*)
el espectáculo show; sight
la esperanza hope
el espesor; la espesura thickness
el esquema outline; diagram
la estaca stake
la estancia stay
la estatua statue
el estilo style
la estrategia strategy
el estrés stress
la estructura structure
el estudio studio
la estupidez (*pl* estupideces) stupidity
la etapa stage
la excepción (*pl* excepciones) exception
el exceso excess
la excusa excuse
el/la exiliado(a) exile
el exilio exile
las existencias stock
el éxito success
la experiencia experience
el/la experto(a) expert
la explicación (*pl* explicaciones) explanation
la explosión (*pl* explosiones) explosion
  una explosión a bomb blast
las exportaciones exports
la exposición (*pl* exposiciones) exhibition
la expresión (*pl* expresiones) expression
la extensión (*pl* extensiones) extent
el extracto extract
el/la extranjero(a) foreigner
la fabricación (*pl* fabricaciones) manufacture
la facilidad facility
el factor factor
la falla flaw; defect; fault
la falta: absence
  falta (de) lack (of)
la fama reputation
el favor favor
la fe faith
la felicidad happiness
la fila row, line, rank
la filosofía philosophy
el fin end
la flecha arrow
el fondo background; bottom; fund
el/la forastero(a) stranger
la forma form; shape
la fortuna fortune
el fracaso failure
la frase sentence; phrase
la frente front
el frescor, la frescura freshness
la fuente source
la fuerza force; strength
la función (*pl* funciones) function
la ganancia gain
el gancho hook
los gastos expenses
la generación (*pl* generaciones) generation
el gol goal
el golfo gulf
el golpe bang; blow, punch; coup
la gotera leak
el grado degree
la gráfica, el gráfico chart
la grieta crack

el grito cry; scream
el grupo group
la guía guide
el hambre (*f*) hunger
el hecho fact
la higiene hygiene
la hilera row
el honor honor
los honorarios fees, honoraria
la honra honor
el hueco gap
la huella trace
el humo fumes (*pl*); smoke
el humor humor
la idea idea
  no tengo ni idea I haven't a clue
el idioma language
el/la idiota fool; idiot
la imagen (*pl* imágenes) image
la imaginación (*pl* imaginaciones) imagination
el impacto impact
el imperio empire
las importaciones imports
la importancia importance
la impresión (*pl* impresiones) impression
el impuesto tax; duty
el impulso urge
la inauguración (*pl* inauguraciones) opening
el incidente incident
la independencia independence
el índice index
la indirecta hint
la infancia childhood
el infierno hell
la influencia influence
los ingresos earnings
el/la inspector(a) inspector
el instante instant
la institución (*pl* instituciones) institution
el instituto institute
las instrucciones instructions
el instrumento instrument
la intención (*pl* intenciones) intention; aim
el interés (*pl* intereses) interest
la interrupción (*pl* interrupciones) interruption
el intervalo interval; gap
la investigación (*pl* investigaciones) research
la invitación (*pl* invitaciones) invitation
la ira anger
el/la jefe(a) boss; chief
el juego game; gambling
el juguete toy
la lágrima tear
la lata can
el/la lector(a) reader
la leyenda legend; caption
la libertad freedom
la licenciatura degree
el/la líder leader
la liga league
el límite boundary; limit
la limpieza cleanliness
la línea line
la liquidación (*pl* liquidaciones) sale; severance pay
la lista list
la literatura literature
el local premises (*pl*)
la locura madness, insanity
el logro achievement
la longitud length
el lugar place

el lujo luxury
la luz (*pl* luces) light
luz de la luna moonlight
el/la maestro(a) (elementary school) teacher; master
la magia magic
la manera manner
la máquina machine
la marca brand; mark
el marco frame
el margen (*pl* márgenes) margin
la máscara mask
la matrícula registration; enrollment; license plate (number)
el máximo maximum
la mayoría majority
el medio (de) means (of)
la mejora, la mejoría improvement
la memoria memory
la mente mind
el método method
la mezcla mixture
el miedo fear
el milagro miracle
la mina mine
el mínimo minimum
la minoría minority
la mirada glance
la misa mass
la misión (*pl* misiones) mission
el misterio mystery
el mito myth
la moda fashion; trend
la molestia annoyance
el molino mill
el montón (*pl* montones) mass; pile
la moral morals (*pl*)
el mordisco bite
el motivo pattern
el motor motor
el muchacho boy; lad
la muchedumbre crowd
la muestra sample
la muñeca doll
la naturaleza nature
el naufragio wreckage
la(s) náusea(s) nausea
la negociación (*pl* negociaciones) negotiation
el nervio nerve
la niñez childhood
el nivel level
el nombramiento appointment
la nota note
el número number; issue
la objeción (*pl* objeciones) objection
el objetivo objective; purpose; target
el objeto object; goal
las obras works
el odio hate
el/la oficial officer
la olla pot
el olor smell
la opción (*pl* opciones) option
la opinión (*pl* opiniones) opinion
la oportunidad chance; opportunity
la oposición (*pl* oposiciones) opposition
la orden (*pl* órdenes) order
la organización (*pl* organizaciones) organization
organización benéfica charity
el orgullo pride
el origen (*pl* orígenes) origin
la oscuridad darkness
la paciencia patience
la página page
la paja straw

la palabra word
el palacio palace
el palo stick
el pánico panic
el paquete pack; packet
la pareja couple
la parte part
  parte de arriba top; **parte delantera** front; **parte trasera** rear; **de parte de algn** on behalf of sb
el parto labor
  estar de parto to be in labor
el pasaje; el pasillo passage
la pasión (*pl* pasiones) passion
el paso (foot)step
el patrón (*pl* patrones) pattern
la pausa pause
el payaso clown
el pedazo piece
el pedido order; request
la pelea row
el peligro danger
la pena distress; penalty
el penal (*LAm*) penalty
el penalty (*pl* penalties) penalty
el pensamiento thought
el periódico newspaper; journal
el periodo, el período period
el/la perito(a) expert
el permiso permission
la persona person
el personal personnel
la perspectiva prospect
la pesadilla nightmare
la picadura bite; sting
la pieza piece; item; (*LAm*) room
la pila battery; pile
la pista clue
el placer delight; pleasure
el plan plan; scheme
el platillo (*Mex*) dish
el plato dish; plate
la plaza square
el poder power
el poema poem
la política politics (*sing*); policy
la póliza policy
el polvo dust
la pompa bubble
el porcentaje percentage
la porción (*pl* porciones) portion
el portavoz (*pl* portavoces) spokesman
la posibilidad possibility
la posición (*pl* posiciones) position
la práctica practice
la preferencia choice
la pregunta question
el premio award
la preparación (*pl* preparaciones) preparation
los preparativos arrangements; preparations
la presencia presence
la presión (*pl* presiones) pressure
el presupuesto budget; quote
la princesa princess
el príncipe prince
el principio beginning; principle
la prioridad priority
el problema problem; trouble
el proceso process
el/la profesor(a) teacher; professor
la profundidad depth
el programa schedule
la prohibición (*pl* prohibiciones) ban; prohibition
el propósito purpose
  a propósito on purpose
la propuesta proposal

la prosperidad prosperity
la protección (*pl* protecciones) protection
la protesta protest
las provisiones provisions
el proyecto plan; project
la publicidad publicity
la punta point
la puntería aim
el punto item; point
punto de partida starting point; **punto de vista** point of view
el/la querido(a) darling
la rabia rage
la raja crack
el rato while
la razón (*pl* razones) reason
la reacción (*pl* reacciones) reaction; response
la realidad reality
la rebanada slice
el/la rebelde rebel
el recado message
la recepción (*pl* recepciones) reception
la recesión (*pl* recesiones) recession
la reclamación (*pl* reclamaciones) claim
el recuerdo memory; souvenir; keepsake
el recurso resource
como último recurso as a last resort
la red network
la reducción (*pl* reducciones) reduction
la reforma reform
la regla ruler; period
la reina queen
la relación (*pl* relaciones) relationship
la religión (*pl* religiones) religion
el remate (*LAm*) auction
la reputación (*pl* reputaciones) status
el requisito requirement
la reserva fund; stock; reservation; booking
la resistencia resistance
la resolución (*pl* resoluciones) resolution
el respecto: con respecto a with regard to
el respeto respect
la respiración (*pl* respiraciones) breath
la responsabilidad responsibility
la respuesta reply; response
los restos remains; wreckage (*sing*)
el resultado outcome
el reto challenge
el retrato portrait; portrayal
la reunión (*pl* reuniones) meeting
la revista magazine; journal
el rey (*pl* ~es) king
el riel rail
el ritmo pace, rhythm
el/la rival rival
la rodaja slice
el ruido noise
la ruina ruin
el rumor rumor
la ruptura break
la rutina routine
el sacrificio sacrifice
el/la santo(a) saint
la sección (*pl* secciones) section
el secreto secret
el sector sector
la sed thirst
la seguridad security; safety

la selección (*pl* selecciones) selection; choice
el sentido sense; way; direction
el sentimiento feeling
la señal sign; mark
el señor man; gentleman; **el Señor** the Lord
el servicio service
la sesión (*pl* sesiones) session
el significado meaning
el silbato whistle
el silencio silence
el símbolo symbol
el sindicato trade union
el sistema system
el sitio place
la situación (*pl* situaciones) situation
el/la sobreviviente survivor
el/la socio(a) member
la soledad loneliness
el sollozo sob
la solución (*pl* soluciones) solution
la sombra shadow
el sondeo (de opinión) poll
el sonido sound
la sorpresa surprise
la sospecha suspicion
la subasta auction
el subtítulo caption
la subvención (*pl* subvenciones) grant
la suciedad dirtiness
el sueño sleep
la suerte luck
buena/mala suerte good/bad luck
la sugerencia suggestion
el suicidio suicide
la suma sum
la superficie surface
la supervisión (*pl* supervisiones) supervision
el/la superviviente survivor
el/la suplente substitute
el surtido choice
la sustancia substance
el/la sustituto(a) substitute
la táctica tactics (*pl*)
el talento talent
la tapa lid; top
la tapicería upholstery
el tapiz (*pl* tapices) tapestry
el tapón (*pl* tapones) top
la tarea task
la tarifa; la tasa rate
el teatro theater; drama
la técnica technique
la tecnología technology
el tema theme; issue
la tendencia trend
la tensión (*pl* tensiones) tension; strain
la tentativa attempt; bid
la teoría theory
el territorio territory
el terrón (*pl* terrones) lump
el texto text
la tienda store
la timidez shyness
el tipo type; kind; fellow, guy
la tirada, el tiraje edition
el título title
el tomo volume
la tortura torture
el total total
la tradición (*pl* tradiciones) tradition
la trampa trap
la tranquilidad calmness
la transferencia transfer

el tratamiento treatment
el trato deal; treatment
la tristeza sadness
el trozo bit; piece; slice
el truco trick
el tubo tube
la tumba grave
el tumor tumor
el turno turn
la unidad unit
la valentía bravery, courage
el valor value
el vapor steam
la variedad variety; range
la vela candle
el veneno poison
la ventaja advantage; asset
la verdad truth
la vergüenza shame; embarrassment
la versión (*pl* versiones) version
la victoria victory
la vida life
el vínculo bond; link
la violencia violence
la visita; visit; visitor
el/la visitante visitor
la vista sight
el volumen (*pl* volúmenes) volume
el/la voluntario(a) volunteer
el/la votante voter
la vuelta turn; return
  dar una vuelta to go for a stroll; **dar una vuelta en bicicleta** to go for a bike ride

VERBS

What is a verb?
A **verb** is a 'doing' word which describes what someone or something does, what someone or something is, or what happens to them, for example, *be*, *sing*, *live*.

abandonar to abandon
abrigar(se) to shelter; to wrap up (in warm clothes)
abrir to turn on
  abrir(se) to open
abrochar to fasten
aburrir to bore
  aburrirse to get bored
acabar de hacer algo to have just done sth
acampar to camp
aceptar to accept
acercarse (a) to approach
  acercarse a to go towards
aclarar(se) to clear
acompañar to accompany; to go with
aconsejar to advise; to suggest
acordarse de to remember
acostarse to lie down
acostumbrarse a algo/algn to get used to sth/sb
actuar to act; to operate
acusar to accuse
adaptar to adapt
adelantar to go forward; to overtake
adivinar to guess
admirar to admire
admitir to admit
adoptar to adopt
adorar to adore
adquirir to acquire; to purchase
afectar to affect
afirmar to assert; to state
agarrar to catch; to grab; to grasp
agradecer to thank (for)
aguantar to bear
ahorrar to save
ahuyentar to chase (off)
alcanzar to reach
  alcanzar a algn to catch up with sb;
  alcanzar a ver to catch sight of
alimentar to feed; to nourish
aliviar to relieve
almacenar to store
alojarse to stay
alquilar to hire; to rent: to let
amar to love
amenazar to threaten
amontonar to stack
andar to walk
anhelar to long for
animar to encourage
  animar a algn a hacer algo to urge sb to do sth
anunciar to advertise; to announce
añadir to add
apagar to switch off; to turn off; to put out
apagar to turn off
  apagarse to fade
aparecer to appear

apetecer to feel like, to want
me apetece un helado I would like an ice cream
aplastar to crush
aplaudir to applaud; to cheer; to clap
aplazar to postpone; to put back
aplicar a to apply to
apostar (a) to bet (on)
apoyar to support; to endorse
apoyar(se) to lean
apreciar to appreciate
aprender to learn
apretar to press; to squeeze
aprobar to approve of; to endorse
aprovechar to take advantage (of)
apuntar to take down
arañar to scratch
arrancar to pull out
arrastrar to drag
arrastrarse to crawl
arreglar to fix (up); to arrange; to settle
arreglárselas to cope; to manage
arrepentirse de to regret
arriesgar to risk
arrojar to hurl, to throw
arruinar to ruin
asar to bake
ascender to promote
asegurar to assure; to ensure; to secure
asentir con la cabeza to nod
asfixiar(se) to suffocate
asistir (a) to attend
asombrar to amaze; to astonish
asustar to alarm; to frighten; to startle
atacar to attack
atar to attach; to tie
atender to treat
atender a to attend to
atraer to attract
atrasar to hold up
atreverse (a hacer algo) to dare (to do sth)
aumentar to increase; to raise
avanzar to advance
averiarse to break down
averiguar to check
avisar to warn
ayudar to help
azotar to whip
bailar to dance
bajar: to come down; to go down; to lower
bajar (de): to get off; **bajar de** to get out of
balbucir to stammer
barrer to sweep
basar algo en to base sth on
batir to whip; to beat
besar to kiss
bombardear to bomb
brillar to shine; to sparkle
bromear to joke
burlarse de to make fun of
buscar to look for; to search; to seek
caerse to fall (down)
se me cayó I dropped it
calcular to estimate
calentar(se) to heat (up)
callarse to be quiet
cambiar to alter; to exchange
cambiar(se) to change
cancelar to cancel
cantar to sing
capturar to capture
carecer de to lack
cargar (de) to load (with)

causar to cause
cavar to dig
celebrar to celebrate
centellear to sparkle
cerrar: to turn off: to close; to fasten
cerrar(se): to shut; **cerrar con llave** to lock
charlar to chat
chillar to scream
chismear to gossip
chocar con to bump into
chupar to suck
citar to quote
clasificarse to qualify
cobrar to claim; to get
coger to catch; to grab; to seize
colaborar to collaborate
coleccionar to collect
colgar to hang (up)
colocar to place
combinar to combine
comenzar (a) to start (to)
cometer to commit
compaginar to combine
comparar to compare
compartir to share
compensar to compensate (for)
compensar por to make up for
competir en to compete in
complacer to please
completar to complete; to make up
comprar (a) to buy (from)
comprender to comprise
comunicar to communicate
conceder to grant
concentrarse to concentrate
concertar to arrange
concluir to conclude; to accomplish
condenar to condemn; to sentence
conducir to lead
conectar to connect
confesar to confess
confiar to trust
confiar en to rely on
confirmar to confirm
confundir (con) to confuse (with)
confundir a algn con to mistake sb for
congelar to freeze
conocer to know
conseguir to achieve; to get; to secure
conseguir (hacer) to succeed (in doing)
considerar to consider; to rate
constar de to consist of
hacer constar to record
constituir to constitute; to make up
construir to build; to put up
consultar to consult
consumir to consume
contar to count; to tell
contar con to depend on
contemplar to contemplate
contener to contain; to hold
contestar to answer
continuar to continue; to keep; to resume
contribuir to contribute
controlar to control
convencer to convince
convenir to suit
convertir to convert
copiar to copy
correr to run
cortar to cut (off); to mow
costar to cost
crear to create
crecer to grow
creer to believe; to reckon

criar to bring up
criticar to criticize
cruzar to cross
cubrir (de) to cover (with)
cuchichear to whisper
cuidar to look after; to take care of; to mind
  cuidar de to take care of
cultivar to cultivate
cumplir to accomplish; to carry out
curar to heal
dañar to harm
dar to give:
  dar a to overlook; **dar asco a** to disgust; **dar de comer a** to feed; **dar la bienvenida** to welcome; **dar marcha atrás** to reverse; **dar saltitos** to hop; **dar un paseo** to go for a stroll; **dar un puñetazo a** to punch; **dar una bofetada a** to slap; **dar vergüenza a** to embarrass; **dar vuelta a** to turn; **darse cuenta de algo** to become aware of sth; **darse por vencido** to give up; **darse prisa** to hurry
deber must; to owe
  deber hacer algo to be supposed to do sth; **debo hacerlo** I must do it
decepcionar to disappoint
decidir(se) (a) to decide (to)
decidirse (a) to make up one's mind (to)
decir to say; to tell
declarar to declare
  declarar culpable to convict; **declararse en huelga** to (go on) strike
decorar to decorate
dedicar to devote
defender to defend
definir to define
dejar to leave
  dejar caer to drop
deletrear to spell
demorar(se) to delay
demostrar to demonstrate
depender de to depend on
derribar to demolish
desanimar to discourage
desaparecer to disappear
desarrollar(se) to develop
descansar to rest
descargar to unload
describir to describe
descubrir to discover; to find out
desear to desire; to wish
deshacerse de to get rid of
deslizar(se) to slip
desnudarse to strip
despedir to dismiss
despegar to take off
despejar(se) to clear
despertar(se) to wake up
desprenderse to come off
desteñirse to fade
destruir to smash; to destroy
desviar to divert
detener to arrest
determinar to determine
detestar to detest
devolver to bring back; to give back; to send back
  devolver a su sitio to put back
dibujar to draw
diferenciarse (de) to differ (from)
dimitir to resign
dirigir to conduct; to direct; to manage
disculparse (de) to apologize (for)
discutir to argue; to debate; to discuss

diseñar to design
disfrazar to disguise
disfrutar to enjoy
disminuir to decline; to decrease; to diminish
distinguir to distinguish
distribuir to distribute
divertir to divert
  divertirse to enjoy oneself
dividir to divide; to split
doblar to fold
  doblar(se) to double
dominar to dominate; to master
ducharse to shower
dudar to doubt
durar to last
echar to pour:
  echar a algn to throw sb out; **echar a algn la culpa de algo** to blame sb for sth; **echar al correo** to post; **echar de menos** to miss; **echar una mirada a algo** to glance at sth; **echarse** to lie; **echarse a llorar** to burst into tears; **echarse a reír** to burst out laughing
educar to bring up; to educate
ejecutar to execute
elegir to choose; to select; to elect
elogiar to praise
emocionar to excite
empatar to draw, to tie
empezar(a) to begin (to)
emplear to employ
empujar to push
encarcelar to imprison
encender to switch on; to turn on; to light
encerrar to shut in
encontrar to find; to meet
enfocar to focus
enjugar to wipe
enseñar to teach; to show
entender to understand
enterarse de to hear about
enterrar to bury
entrar (en) to enter
entregarse to give oneself up; to surrender
entrevistar to interview
enviar to send
envolver to wrap up
equivocarse to make a mistake; to be mistaken
erigir to erect
escapar (de) to escape (from)
escarbar to dig
escoger to choose; to pick
esconderse to hide
escuchar to listen (to)
especializarse en to specialize in
especular to gamble
esperar to wait (for); to expect; to hope
establecer to establish; to set up
  establecerse to settle
estallar to blow up
estar to be
  estar acostumbrado a algo/algn to be used to sth/sb; **estar de acuerdo** to agree; **estar de pie** to be standing; **estar dispuesto a hacer algo** to be prepared to do sth; to be willing to do sth; **estar equivocado** to be wrong; **estar involucrado en algo** to be involved in sth
estirar(se) to stretch (out)
estrecharse la mano to shake hands
estrellar(se) to crash

estropear to ruin
estropear(se) to spoil
estudiar to study; to investigate
evitar (hacer) to avoid (doing)
exagerar to exaggerate
examinar to examine
examinarse to take an exam
excitar to excite
exclamar to exclaim
excluir to exclude; to suspend
existir to exist
experimentar to experience
explicar to explain
explorar to explore
explotar to explode
exponer to display
exportar to export
expresar to express
exprimir to squeeze
expulsar temporalmente to suspend
extender to spread: to extend
extender(se) to spread out
extrañar (*LAm*) to miss
fabricar to manufacture
faltar to be lacking; to fail
felicitar to congratulate
fiarse de to trust
financiar to finance
fingir to pretend (to)
firmar to sign
flotar to float
fluir to flow
formar(se) to form
forzar a algn a hacer (algo) to force sb to do (sth)
fotografiar to photograph
frecuentar to frequent
freír to fry
funcionar to work
(hacer) funcionar to operate
fustigar to whip
ganar to earn; to gain
garantizar to guarantee
gastar to spend: to waste
gastar(se) to wear (out)
gemir to groan
golpear to knock, to hit; to beat
grabar to record
gritar to shout; to scream; to cry
guardar to keep; to store
guiar to guide
gustar to like
haber to have
hablar to speak; to talk
hacer to do; to make; to bake
hacer añicos to shatter; **hacer campaña** to campaign; **hacer comentarios** to comment; **hacer daño a** to hurt; **hacer las maletas** to pack; **hacer preguntas** to ask questions; **hacer público** to issue; **hacer señas** *or* **una señal** to signal; **hacer una lista de** to list; **hacer una oferta** to bid; **hacer una pausa** to pause; **hacer una señal con la mano** to wave; **hacerse** to become; to get; **hacerse adulto** to grow up; **hacer(se) pedazos** to smash
helarse to freeze
herir to injure
hervir to boil
huir to flee; to run away *or* off
identificar to identify
iluminar(se) to light
imaginar to imagine
impedir to prevent (from)
implicar to imply; to involve
imponer to impose
importar to matter; to mind;

to care
¡no me importa! I don't care!;
¿y a quién le importa? who cares?
impresionar to impress
imprimir to print
inclinar to bend
inclinarse to bend down
incluir to include
indicar to point out; to indicate
influir to influence
informar to inform
inscribirse to register
insinuar to hint
insinuar to imply
insistir en to insist on
instruir to educate
insultar to insult
intentar to attempt to
interesar to interest
interesarse por to be interested in
interrogar to question
interrumpir to interrupt
introducir to introduce
invadir to invade
investigar to investigate
invitar to invite
invitar a algn a algo to treat sb to sth
ir to go
ir a buscar a algn to fetch sb;
ir bien a to suit; **ir deprisa** to dash;
ir en bicicleta to ride a bike
irse to go away
irritar to irritate; to aggravate
jugar to play; to gamble
juntarse con to join
jurar to swear
justificar to justify
juzgar to judge
lamentarse to moan
lamer to lick
lanzar to throw; to launch
lanzarse a to rush into
leer to read
levantar to raise; to put up; to lift
levantarse to get up; to rise
limpiar to clean
llamar to call
llamar por teléfono to ring;
llamarse to be called
llegar to arrive
llenar (de) to fill (with)
llevar to carry; to bear; to wear
llevar a cabo to carry out
llevarse to take
llorar to cry, weep
llover to rain
llover a cántaros to pour
luchar to fight; to struggle
maltratar to abuse
manchar to dirty
mandar to command, to order
manifestarse to demonstrate
mantener to maintain; to support
mantener el equilibrio to balance
marcharse to depart; to leave
medir to measure
mejorar(se) to improve
mencionar to mention
mentir to lie
merecer to deserve, to merit
meterse en to get into
mezclar to mix
mimar to spoil
mirar to look (at); to watch
mirar fijamente to stare at
modificar to adjust
molestar to annoy; to disturb;
to trouble
montar a caballo to ride
morder to bite

morir to die
mostrar to display; to point out
mostrar(se) to show
mover to move
multiplicar to multiply
nacer to be born
necesitar to need
negar to deny
negarse (a) to refuse (to)
negociar to negotiate
notar to note
obedecer to obey
obligar a algn a to oblige sb to
observar to notice; to observe
obstruir to block
obtener to obtain
ocasionar to bring about
ocultar to hide
ocupar to occupy
ocuparse de to deal with
ocurrir to occur
odiar to hate
ofender to offend
ofrecer to offer
ofrecerse a hacer algo to volunteer to do sth
oír to hear
oler to smell
olvidar to forget
operar a algn to operate on sb
oponerse a to oppose; to object to
organizar(se) to organize
otorgar to award
pagar to pay
pararse to come to a halt, to stop
parecer to seem (to); to look
parecerse a to look like, to resemble
participar en to take part in
partir to share
partir(se) to split
pasar to pass; to overtake; to spend
pedir to request; to order
pedir a algn que haga algo to ask sb to do sth; **pedir algo a algn** to ask sb for sth; **pedir algo prestado a algn** to borrow sth from sb
pegar to hit; to stick; to strike
pensar to think
pensar en to think about; **pensar hacer** to intend to do
perder to miss
perder a algn de vista to lose sight of sb
perdonar a to forgive
perdurar to survive
permitir to allow, to permit, to let
permitirse to afford
perseguir to pursue
persuadir to persuade
pertenecer a to belong to
pesar to weigh
picar to bite
pinchar(se) to burst
planchar to iron
plegar to fold
poder to be able to; can; might
¿puedo llamar por teléfono?: may I use your phone?; **el profesor podría venir ahora:** the teacher might come now; **puede que venga más tarde** he might come later
poner to put; to lay
poner de relieve to highlight; **poner en duda** to question; **poner en el suelo** to put down; **poner en orden** to tidy; **ponerse** to put on; **ponerse de pie** to stand up; **ponerse en contacto con** to contact

portarse to behave
poseer to own, to possess
practicar to practice
precipitarse to rush
predecir to predict
preferir to prefer
preguntar (por) to inquire (about)
 preguntarse to wonder
prender fuego to catch fire
preocupar to trouble; to bother
 preocuparse (por) to worry (about)
preparar(se) to prepare
prescindir de to do without
presentar to present; to introduce
prestar to lend
prevenir to warn
prever to foresee
privar to deprive
probar to prove
producir to produce
prohibir to ban, to prohibit; to forbid
prometer to promise
pronosticar to predict
pronunciar to pronounce
propagarse to spread
proponer to propose
proteger to protect
protestar to protest
proveer to provide
publicar to publish
quedar to remain
 quedarse to stay
quejarse (de) to complain (about)
quemar to burn
querer to want (to); to love; to like
quitar to remove
 quitar algo a algn to take sth from sb; **quitarse** to take off
reaccionar to react; to respond
realizar to fulfil; to realize
reanudar to resume
recalcar to emphasize; to stress
rechazar to reject
recibir to receive
 recibirse (*LAm*) to qualify
reclamar to demand; to claim
recoger to pick (up); to collect; to gather
recomendar to recommend
reconocer to recognize
recordar to remember; to recall
 recordarle a algn to remind sb of
recuperarse to recover
reducir(se) to reduce
reembolsar to refund
referirse a to refer (to)
 en lo que se refiere a ... as regards ...
reflejar, reflexionar to reflect
reformar to reform
regañar to tell off
regar to water
registrar to register; to examine
regresar to return; to come back; to go back; (*LAm*) to give back; to send back
regresarse (*LAm*) to return; to come back; to go back
reír to laugh
 reírse de to laugh at
relajarse to relax
relatar to report
renovar to renew
rentar (*LAm*) to rent; to hire; to let
reñir to quarrel; to argue
reparar to repair, to mend
repartir to deal; to deliver
repetir(se) to repeat
reponer to replace
reponerse to recover

representar to perform; to represent
requerir to require
resbalar to slide
reservar to book; to reserve
resistir to hold out
  resistir(se) to resist
resolver to solve
respetar to respect
respirar to breathe
responder to reply, to answer; to respond
restaurar to restore
resultar to prove
retar to challenge
retirar(se) to withdraw
reunir(se) to collect
  reunirse to get together; to meet
revelar to reveal
rodear (de) to surround (with)
romper(se) to break; to tear; to burst
ruborizarse to blush
saber a to taste of
saber to know
  sé nadar I can swim
sacar to bring out; to take out
  sacar brillo to polish
sacudir to shake
salir to emerge
saltar to leap
saludar to greet
  saludar con la cabeza to nod
salvar to rescue; to save
secar(se) to dry
seguir to follow
  seguir haciendo algo to go on doing sth
sentarse to sit (down)
sentir to feel; to be sorry
  sentir(se) to feel
señalizar to indicate
ser to be
servir to serve
significar to mean
sobrevivir to survive
solicitar to apply to; to seek
soltar to release
sonar to sound; to ring
  (hacer) sonar to ring
sonreír to smile
sorprender to surprise
sospechar to suspect
subir to climb; to come up; to go up
  subir a to get on; to board
suceder to happen
sufrir (de) to suffer (from)
  sufrir un colapso to collapse
sugerir to suggest
sujetar to fix
suministrar to supply
suponer to assume; to suppose; to involve
surgir to emerge
suspender to suspend; to fail
suspirar to sigh
sustituir to replace
telefonear to telephone
temblar to shake
temer to fear
tener to have; to hold
  tener antipatía a to dislike; **tener cuidado** to be careful; **tener éxito** to be successful; **tener frío** to be cold; **tener hambre** to be hungry; **tener lugar** to take place; **tener mala suerte** to be unlucky; **tener miedo** to be afraid; **tener que** to have to; **tener que ver con** to concern; **tener razón** to be right; **tener sed** to be thirsty; **tener suerte** to be

lucky; **tener tendencia a hacer algo** to tend to do sth **tener trece/veinte años** to be thirteen/twenty years old
terminar to end; to finish
tirar to throw away
tirar de to pull
tocar to touch; to play; to ring
tomar to take
torcer to twist
trabajar to work
traducir to translate
traer to bring
traicionar to betray
tranquilizar(se) to calm down
trasladar to transfer
tratar to treat
tratar (de) to try (to);
tratar con to deal with
unir to join
unir(se) to unite
untar to spread
usar to use
vaciar(se) to empty
vacilar to hesitate
valer to be worth
variar to vary
vencer to conquer, to defeat, to overcome
vender to sell; to stock
venir to come
venirse abajo to collapse
ver to see
visitar to visit
vislumbrar to catch sight of
vivir to live
volar to fly
volcar to overturn
volver to come back; to go back; to return
volver(se) to turn round; to become; (*LAm*) to come back; to go back
volverse hacia to turn towards
votar to vote